CRITICAL SURVEY
OF
POETRY

CRITICAL SURVEY
OF
POETRY

English Language Series

REVISED EDITION

Pop-Sou

6

Edited by
FRANK N. MAGILL

SALEM PRESS
Pasadena, California   Englewood Cliffs, New Jersey

Library of Congress Cataloging-in-Publication Data
Critical survey of poetry. English language series/edited
    by Frank N. Magill. — Rev. ed.
        p.   cm.
    Includes bibliographical references and index.
    1. English poetry—Dictionaries. 2. American
poetry—Dictionaries. 3. English poetry—
Bio-bibliography. 4. American poetry—Bio-
bibliography. 5. Poets, English—Biography—
Dictionaries. 6. Poets, American—Biography—
Dictionaries.
I. Magill, Frank Northen, 1907-
PR502.C85   1992   92-3727
821.009′03—dc20   CIP
ISBN 0-89356-834-1 (set)
ISBN 0-89356-840-6 (volume 6)

LIST OF AUTHORS IN VOLUME 6

CRITICAL SURVEY OF POETRY

1

ALEXANDER POPE

Born: London, England; May 21, 1688
Died: Twickenham, England; May 30, 1744

Principal poetry

Pastorals, 1709; *An Essay on Criticism*, 1711; *The Rape of the Lock*, 1712, 1714; *Windsor Forest*, 1713; *The Iliad of Homer*, 1715-1720, (translation); *The Works of Mr. Alexander Pope*, 1717 (first collected edition including "Elegy to the Memory of an Unfortunate Lady" and *Epistle from Eloisa to Abelard*); *Cytherea*, 1723; *The Odyssey of Homer*, 1725-1726 (translation); *The Dunciad*, 1728-1743; *Moral Essays*, 1731-1735; *Imitations of Horace*, 1733-1737; *An Essay on Man*, 1733-1734; *Epistle to Dr. Arbuthnot*, 1735; *One Thousand Seven Hundred and Thirty-Eight*, 1738; *Epilogue to the Satires*, 1738; *The Twickenham Edition of the Poems of Alexander Pope*, 1939-1967 (John Butt, general editor, 11 volumes).

Other literary forms

Apart from original poetry, Alexander Pope's works include an edition of William Shakespeare, translations of the *Iliad* (1715-1720) and the *Odyssey* (1725-1726), an edition of his personal correspondence, and a prose satire entitled *Peri Bathos: Or, The Art of Sinking in Poetry* (1727). Pope's edition of Shakespeare is chiefly of interest for the response which it brought from Lewis Theobald, a rival editor of Shakespeare's plays. Although not always unjust in his criticisms, Theobald did overlook some of the genuine excellences of Pope's edition, especially Pope's penetrating introduction. (It must be admitted, however, that even this is vitiated at times by Pope's inability to appreciate Shakespeare's so-called deviations from the eighteenth century notion of "correctness.") The translations from Homer are not strictly literal, but are rather adaptations of Homer's genius to the conventions and expectations of Augustan sensibility. Still, they are regarded as the most readable and eloquent versions of Homer to come out of the eighteenth century, notwithstanding the numerous instances of periphrasis (the substitution of a phrase such as "finny prey" for "fish") which belie the vigor of the original.

Pope's edition of his own letters is among the most notorious of his publications. By allowing several of his letters to be published without his apparent permission, Pope was able to bring out an ostensibly "correct" version of his private correspondence, the chief purpose of which was to present him in a favorable light to posterity. Understandably, the letters are rather too self-conscious and artificial for modern tastes.

Peri Bathos is a hilarious instructional booklet detailing all the elements that are necessary to produce poetry which is vulgar, tautological, florid, and inane. One other composition of Pope surely deserves mention: an essay contributed to *The Guardian* on the aesthetics of gardening. Pope had a decisive influence on the development of eighteenth century taste in gardens. In opposition to the rigid formalities which characterized the landscaping of the period, Pope held that gardens should be arranged in a more natural manner.

Achievements

Pope's position in the history of English poetry has been, at times, a subject of acrimonious debate. In his own day, Pope's achievement was frequently obfuscated by the numerous political controversies which surrounded his name. Although he finally emerged, in the estimation of the eighteenth century, as the greatest English poet since John Milton, his reputation soon reached its lowest ebb during the Romantic and Victorian periods; he was derided by Thomas De Quincey as an author of "moldy commonplaces" and demoted by Matthew Arnold to the position of being a "classic of [English] prose." Even in Edith Sitwell's generally favorable study (1930), Pope is appreciated for achieving, in certain poems, a richness of imagery "almost" as lush as that of John Keats. In short, it was not until recently that the balance was redressed. Pope is now recognized as one of the consummate craftsmen of the English language.

Responding to and expressing the fundamental aesthetic tenets of the Augustan age, Pope cannot be fully appreciated or understood without some awareness of the neoclassical assumptions which undergird his compositions. Pope's audience was more homogeneous than Shakespeare's and less enthusiastic (in Samuel Johnson's meaning of that term) than Milton's. As a result, he eschews the dramatic intensity and colloquial richness of the former and bypasses the mythopoeic passion and religious afflatus of the latter. (It must be remembered, however, that the Miltonic allusions in, say, *The Rape of the Lock* are not intended to derogate Milton, but to expose, by sheer force of contrast, the small-mindedness of eighteenth century society.)

Sophisticated allusion, verbal brilliance, the promulgation of moral and aesthetic standards—these are the components of Pope's poetic art. The audience for which Pope wrote was small, urban, and keenly intelligent, capable of appreciating a high degree of technical virtuosity in its poets. These poets were not expected to indulge in lyrical effusions on the subject of their private griefs or to thrust forward their own personal speculations on the end and aim of human existence. On the contrary, their purpose was to crystallize in language conspicuous for its clarity, balance, and poise, the cultural standards, aesthetic ideals, and moral certitudes which they could presume to hold in common with a sensitive and educated audience. As Pope's career progressed, these ideals seemed increasingly remote from the political and literary arenas where he was forced to contend; hence, his later poetry— especially *The Dunciad*—reveals a growing rift between Pope and his public.

On the whole, however, Pope's is a public voice which distills in witty and unforgettable couplets the values of self-control, civic virtue, uncorrupted taste, critical intelligence, and spiritual humility.

As a youth, Pope was exhorted by William Walsh, a former member of John Dryden's literary circle, to pursue "correctness" in his compositions. Pope's career as a poet witnesses to the assiduity with which he acted on Walsh's advice. No poet has brought to the rhyming couplet an equivalent degree of perfection or given to the form, distinguished by its technical difficulty, a greater suppleness and elasticity in the expression of various moods and situations. From the farcical brilliance of *The Rape of the Lock* and the passionate intensities of *Epistle from Eloisa to Abelard* to the dignified discursiveness of *An Essay on Man* and the nervous energy of *The Dunciad*, Pope attains a perfect balance between thought and expression, between verbal wit and the felt rendering of experience.

Biography

The two most important elements in Alexander Pope's life were his being born a Catholic and his contracting, during his twelfth year, a severe tubercular infection from which he never fully recovered. Because of his Catholicism, Pope was compelled to live outside of London and was not allowed to enroll in a formal university program. Because of his illness, Pope attained a height of only four and a half feet, suffered from migraine headaches, was obliged to wear several pairs of hose and an elaborate harness to compensate for the slightness of his legs and the curvature of his spine, and was subject to frequent and caustic ridicule by critics, such as John Dennis, who directed their rancor at his physical deformities as much as at his poetic efforts. Pope's physical ailments and the acrimony with which political and literary pundits attacked both his person and his work should never be forgotten in evaluating, say, the optimistic faith of *An Essay on Man* or the acidulous satire of *The Dunciad*. The affirmations of the former poem were not written out of ignorance of human suffering, and the vituperations of the latter poem cannot be understood apart from the contumely which Pope suffered at the hands of his adversaries—Lady Mary Wortley Montague, Lord Hervey, John Dennis, Joseph Addison, and Lewis Theobald, to name a few. Pope's reference in *Epistle to Dr. Arbuthnot* to "this long disease, my life," is no literary confabulation but an accurate description of his sufferings.

There were, however, compensations. In the library of his father, a wealthy linen merchant who retired to a vast estate at Binfield in 1700, Pope acquired a profound, if desultory, knowledge of English history and letters. In his youth he was, moreover, the special favorite of William Wycherley, who encouraged the publication of Pope's *Pastorals* in Jacob Tonson's *Miscellany* (1709). In 1713, Pope was to find companionship and support in "The Scriblerus Club," a Tory brotherhood which included among its principal members

Jonathan Swift, John Gay, and John Arbuthnot. Together, they inveighed against the scientific rationalism and aggressive commercialism which, they believed, threatened the survival of humanistic values in the first half of the eighteenth century. It is important to remember that the political climate of Pope's day was such that poetic compositions were less frequently evaluated on their intrinsic merits than on the sponsorship which they were accorded by either Tory or Whig. Thus Pope's literary career was plagued at its inception by mean-spirited attacks from henchmen of the political and literary establishment.

Pope's masterful translation of the *Iliad*, from which he earned £9,000, enabled him to retire in 1719 with his mother (for whom he scrupulously cared until the end of her life) to Twickenham: a neoclassical villa designed in part by Pope himself, where he was able to indulge his love of gardening and to escape from the contumacious atmosphere of literary London. Here, in the companionship of Swift, Gay, Bolingbroke, and Arbuthnot, Pope was granted some respite from the venomous attacks upon his person and character, the history of which virtually makes up the rest of his recorded biography. Apart from a deep attachment to Martha Blount, a Catholic neighbor sympathetic to Pope's aspirations and literary ideals, his life was a constant endeavor to stem the materialistic current of his times by iterating in polished and penetrating couplets a theocentric humanism which espoused the virtues of self-discipline, the recognition of metaphysical values, and the need for standards of measure and restraint.

Analysis

Alexander Pope's poetry is an unmistakable challenge to the post-Romantic sensibilities of the twentieth century reader. John Stuart Mill's dictum that "eloquence is *heard*, poetry is overheard," seems entirely contradicted by the public and topical voice which characterizes the epistles, satires, and philosophic exordiums of Pope. The language of introspective reverie which poets, from the nineteenth century on, cultivate in lonely self-communion among the bowers of a refined aestheticism could not be further removed from the racy, tough, and contentious idiom of Pope. That is not to say that Pope's language is devoid of sculptured phrases or chiseled locutions; on the contrary, his compositions are exquisitely wrought and develop with an inevitability that makes Pope, after William Shakespeare, the most quoted poet in the English language. Following the translation of the *Iliad*, however, Pope's works became increasingly didactic and satirical in nature and engaged in topical assaults on the foibles, idiosyncrasies, and shortcomings that characterized the literary and political arena during the reigns of Anne and George II. The astonishing thing is that these topical satires of literary hacks long since forgotten and social customs consigned to oblivion, touch, time and again, upon that which is enduring and universal in the moral being of humanity. The literary battles and political machinations which gave occasion to Pope's vitriolic utterances may be forgotten, but the integrity with which Pope affirmed the centrality of letters, the tempering spirit of humanism, the need for standards, and the cultivation of reverence as indispensable ingredients of a just and balanced society, retains its relevance in the broken world of the twentieth century.

Like Vergil, Pope began as a writer of pastorals; his first poems, composed when he was sixteen, are delicate evocations of an idyllic world of shepherds and shepherdesses poised among settings reminiscent of François Boucher and Jean Fragonard. These highly stylized exercises won for him the accolades of contemporary critics and gave him the confidence to essay the next task which tradition prescribed for the developing poet: the epic. Pope's translation of the *Iliad*, the first books of which appeared in 1715, was a watershed in his poetic career. Though Pope had already written poems which prefigure his later orientation as a satirist, it was the publication of the *Iliad* that triggered the wholly irrational and unexpected assault upon Pope's life, family, writings, and physiognomy by his political enemies and rivals to poetic fame. These attacks diverted Pope from the musings of *Windsor Forest*, the perorations of *An Essay on Criticism*, and the witticisms of *The Rape of the Lock*, and obliged him, to paraphrase a Nobel laureate, "to grab his century by the throat." After 1719, Pope's career is notable for the increasing venom of his pen and the sustained brilliance of his polemic.

Pope's first important utterance gives us direct access to the critical values of the Augustans and remains the best and most compendious statement of a poetic tradition which extends from Horace to Nicolas Boileau. Indeed, as a distillation of neoclassical attitudes, Pope's *An Essay on Criticism* is without a peer. The critical assumptions on which the poem is based could not be further removed from the splintered aesthetics and boneless relativism of the present: as a statement of poetic intention and practice, it provides a necessary corrective to the farrago of contradictions which characterize the contemporary critical scene. Pope vigorously attacks the notion that taste is a purely subjective matter, arguing that a deterioration in aesthetic values is both a symptom and a portent of a general disequilibrium in the moral being of the individual and the political fabric of society. The poem's controlling symbol is the sun—an emblem of universal reason and light whose rays are an expression of the original creative word, or *logos*. Individual taste is evaluated from the perspective of this light-giving word, which is identified in the poem as "Unerring Nature, still divinely bright,/ One clear, unchanged, and universal light." Though individual judgments may differ, they may and should be regulated—as watches by the sun—in accordance with objective standards of value and taste. Thus, the rules which govern the composition of poetry are not arbitrary inventions, but expressions of the natural law of measure and restraint: "Those Rules of old discovered, not devised/ Are nature still, but Nature methodized;/ Nature, like Liberty, is but restrained/ By the same laws which first herself ordained."

The first duty of a poet and a critic, then, is to recognize the law of human limit, and to balance individual judgments by constant and circumspect reference to a hierarchy of inherited values. Pope does not recommend the self-abnegation of the poet in the face of his predecessors, but rather his need to adapt to his own time those values which inform ancients and moderns alike and which are of continued relevance because their source is eternal and their origin beyond the vagaries of individual taste. Still, Pope maintains that the success of a composition must be estimated by the value and significance of the poet's purpose and the artistic integrity with which that purpose is fulfilled, rather than by arbitrary and invidious comparisons between works of antithetical spirit and intention. In this regard, "Pegasus, a near way to take,/ May boldly deviate from the common track;/ From vulgar bounds with brave disorder part,/ And snatch a grace beyond the reach of art."

There is, however, one important qualification to this expansionist poetics: namely, that although the poet's deviations may elude the letter of aesthetic law, they must not violate the spirit of that law: "Moderns, beware! or if you must offend/ Against the precept ne'er transgress its end." As Pope argues at the opening of Part II of *An Essay on Criticism*, the poet and the critic must never allow themselves to become victims of pride or to equate the spark of their peculiar talents or insights with the all-embracing splendors of the eternal *logos*. Poets and critics of lesser rank, according to Pope, allow their obsession with the parts of a composition to take precedence over their comprehension of its total design. An efflorescence of decorative detail in a poet and a pedantic and small-minded preoccupation with minutiae in a critic are unmistakable indications of debilitated sensibility and false judgment: "But true Expression, like th' unchanging Sun,/ Clears and improves whate'er it shines upon." To value sound over sense, expression over content, nuance over theme, is to sacrifice instruction to delight and to worship the dead letter at the expense of the living spirit.

Furthermore, the prosody of a poetic composition should be judged by the following criteria: "'Tis not enough no harshness gives offence,/ The sound must seem an echo to the sense." Pope crystallizes this point in a series of couplets rich in verbal pyrotechnics. The lines sing, strain, limp, or lilt in accordance with the action described:

> Soft is the strain when Zephyr gently blows,
> And the smooth stream in smoother numbers flows:
> But when loud surges lash the sounding shore,
> The hoarse, rough verse should like the torrent roar:
> When Ajax strives some rock's vast weight to throw,
> The line too labours, and the words move slow;
> Not so, when swift Camilla scours the plain,

Flies o'er th' unbending corn, and skims along the main.

Here, as so often, the restraint of the couplet inspires Pope to rhythmic feats which make a game of art and bear witness to his own adage: "The winged courser, like the generous horse/ Shows most true mettle when you check his force."

After attacking the patronage system and the proclivity of critics to celebrate poets of superior social rank while denigrating those genuine talents who arouse jealousy and spite, Pope goes on to affirm that, in their ultimate issues, literary, social, and moral values are mutually interdependent. A vacillating and fickle critic inconstant in his service to the muse is thus compared to a degenerate amorist who abandons the lawful embraces of his wife for the specious thrills of a strumpet. Constipated scribblers who "Strain out the last droppings of their sense/ And rhyme with all the rage of Impotence," and Restoration rakes who combine "Dulness with Obscenity . . ./ As shameful sure as Impotence in love," underscore Pope's sense that larger issues of decorum, decency, and health are involved in questions of literary tact. For Pope, the authentic poet and critic is honest and circumspect, capable of elasticity in his judgment but constrained by nature and common sense. He does not neglect the rigors of composition in a false straining for effect nor abandon moral and metaphysical principles in order to flatter public taste. Pope never deserted the values adduced in *An Essay on Criticism* and the poem may be profitably used as a yardstick to measure the underlying integrity of Pope's poetic vision and the vigilance with which he applied it to the literary and cultural aberrations of his age.

An Essay on Criticism was followed by *Windsor Forest* and *The Rape of the Lock*; the former poem is an expression of unity in diversity in which the ecological balance of Windsor Forest is perceived as analogous to the balanced and harmonious development of the British realm following the Peace of Utrecht. Pope's perception of a concordant cosmic design maintained by the mutual subservience of antagonistic forces adumbrates the more compelling philosophic arguments of *An Essay on Man*.

Pope's most brilliant achievement in his early work is, of course, *The Rape of the Lock*. Its sophisticated humor and virtuoso technique are unsurpassed. In this genial spoof of a society abandoned to the pursuit of spurious values, Pope avoids the extreme indignation of his later satires. Instead, he takes an impish delight in the conventions and rituals which are the object of his gentle mockery. Though Belinda and the Baron may be self-regarding fools, the poet obviously relishes their behavior.

The poem itself derives from an actual quarrel between Arabella Fermour and her suitor, Lord Petre. At the request of his friend, John Caryll, Pope undertook the poem, hoping, through his raillery, to laugh the young beau and belle into common sense. Not surprisingly, the tempers of Miss Fermour and Lord Petre were not mollified when, in consequence of Pope's poem, their misadventures became the talk of the town.

Pope's principal strategy in this mock-epic is to stand the conventions of epic poetry on their heads. By counterpointing the dramatic situations and epic conventions of Homer, Vergil, and Milton with the fatuities of a vain coquette and a foppish Lord, Pope exposes the pretensions and trivialities of the eighteenth century upper class. Hence, the battle for Troy, Latium, or Heaven becomes a bathetic war between the sexes; the celestial powers of the *Iliad* or *Paradise Lost* (1667) are reduced to diminutive sylphs; and the ferocious appetites of the Homeric warrior are replaced by the pampered palates of a degenerate aristocracy. As in *An Essay on Criticism*, the controlling metaphor is the sun. Belinda's propensity to arrogate to herself the divine attributes of that celestial orb reflects the expansive self-conceit permeating her entire culture. As they are over and over in Belinda's world, the finite preoccupations of pleasure, seduction, flirtation, and gossip are accorded an infinite status. The worship of these things becomes, in consequence, obsessional and demonic. Thus the sylphs who whisper in Belinda's ear on the eve of her molestation by the Baron recall the seductive whispers of Milton's Satan in the ear of the sleeping Eve. Moreover, as Belinda sits before her boudoir mirror and allows herself to be transformed by the ministrations of her attendant sylphs, the religious connotations of Pope's imagery underscore the debasement of true worship into self-worship through "the sacred rites of Pride." Still, Pope's condemnation of Belinda's world is not unequivocal: the radiance, iridescence, and bejeweled splendor of this perfumed society retain a vestige of that divine light which the society caricatures or distorts.

In the last analysis, however, Belinda's chastity is not a positive virtue but an expression of vanity. Her aloofness is a deliberate and insulting challenge to her suitors, whose numbers swell as she remains unfixed and flirtatious. Nowhere is this more apparent than in Belinda's outcry in Canto IV, after the Baron has successfully clipped and stolen a lock of her hair: "Oh hadst thou, cruel! been content to seize/ Hairs less in sight, or any hairs but these!" Belinda is not consciously aware of the comic and lewd implications of her statement, but Pope's cruel joke is definitely intended at her expense. Belinda's unconscious preference for a private seduction over a public insult— that the Baron should have seized "hairs less in sight"—reveals how virtue and chastity remain for her largely a matter of appearance. With the exception of Clarissa, who councils Belinda to exercise restraint, humility, and humor, the moral spinelessness of this society—its appalling indifference to standards and its inability to discriminate between the trivial and the tragic—is epitomized in Pope's use of the couplet and in his juxtaposition of incongruous images. For example, Belinda's cries at the Baron's violation of her lock are described as follows: "Not louder shrieks to pitying heaven are cast,/ When husbands, or when lap dogs breathe their last;/ Or when rich China vessels fallen from high/ In glittering dust, and painted fragments lie!" The deaths of husbands and of lap dogs, the breaking of china and the loss of virginity are reduced to the same level.

The poem ends in a mock apotheosis. In the midst of the fracas between Belinda and the Baron, the pilfered lock ascends comet-like to the starry heavens to assume its place among the other constellations. Pope concludes with a poignant reminder of mortality and an implicit plea for Belinda to attain fulfillment in marriage and love: "For, after all the murders of your eye,/ When after millions slain, yourself shall die;/ When those fair suns shall set, as set they must,/ And all those tresses shall be laid in dust,/ This Lock, the Muse shall consecrate to fame,/ And midst the stars inscribe Belinda's name."

Following *The Rape of the Lock*, Pope's efforts were directed toward a mode of composition with which he is not usually identified: the elegiac verses "Elegy to the Memory of an Unfortunate Lady" and the romantic psycho-drama, *Epistle from Eloisa to Abelard*. The "Elegy" is, perhaps, only partially successful; its chief interest lies in the poet's vacillation between a Christian and a stoic understanding of the lady's death. *Epistle from Eloisa to Abelard* is another matter altogether. G. Wilson Knight claims that it "is certainly Pope's greatest human poem and probably the greatest short love poem in our language"—a judgment from which few critics are likely to dissociate themselves.

In the form of an epistle to her beloved and banished Abelard, Pope's Eloisa dramatically expresses the psychological tensions which threaten her reason and divide her soul. Confined to a monastery (ironically founded by Abelard), she receives, at length, a letter from her former lover that reawakens her suppressed passion. The recrudescence of these feelings not only threatens her stability, but also, in her own estimation, endangers her soul; and her situation is rendered even more poignant by the fact that Abelard, having been castrated by henchmen in the employ of her outraged uncle, can neither respond to nor share in her struggles against the flesh. Here the couplet is used not only ironically to counterpose discordant images, as in *The Rape of the Lock*, but also to reflect, in balanced antitheses, the very struggles of Eloisa's soul. In the extravagance of her affliction, Eloisa takes on the attributes of a Shelleyan heroine, preferring damnation with Abelard to redemption without him: "In seas of flame my plunging soul is drowned,/ While altars blaze, and angels tremble round." Even as she submits to the decrees of Heaven and composes herself to meet her maker, she erotically mingles her love for Abelard with her struggle for salvation: "Thou Abelard! the last sad office pay,/ And smooth my passage to the realms of day,/ See my lips tremble, and my eyeballs roll,/ Suck my last breath, and catch my flying soul!" *Epistle from Eloisa to Abelard* belies the notion that Pope was incapable of composing in the pathetic mode. As Lord Byron observed, "If you search for passion, where is it to be found stronger than in the *Epistle from Eloisa to Abelard.*"

Between *Epistle from Eloisa to Abelard* and *An Essay on Man*, Pope composed a preliminary version of *The Dunciad* (1728); but it was not until 1742 that the poem appeared in its final form. Pope's principal achievements from 1731 to 1737 were *An Essay on Man* and associated ethical epistles. These moral essays encompass a variety of subjects: two addresses, to the Earl of Burlington and Lord Bathurst, respectively, on the uses of riches; a study of the Ruling Passion in the development of individual character, addressed to Lord Cobham; and an epistle to Martha Blount on the hypocrisy of women in sophisticated society. The key to each of these studies of the foibles and idiosyncrasies of human character is provided by *An Essay on Man*—Pope's most celebrated poem during his own lifetime and the chief source of his international fame. The poem deserves close study. As a synthesis of eighteenth century apologetic thought on the nature of man, the existence of evil, and the harmony of the creation, it is unsurpassed. Apart from its creedal assertions—which are considerable and not to be dismissed as glib rationalizations or "moldy commonplaces," as Thomas De Quincey would have it— the poem's chief merit lies in Pope's ability to express in taut and pellucid couplets the fundamentals of a religion derived from natural law. In a word, it exemplifies Pope's dictum that "True Wit is Nature to advantage dress'd/ What oft was thought but ne'er so well expressed."

Although Pope's ontology is based on reason and observation as opposed to dogma or revelation, the poem does not deny metaphysical axioms. On the contrary, it continually approximates to "some sphere unknown." The recognition of this metaphysical "sphere" is elaborated in language which is purged of sectarian or denominational accretions, reflecting Pope's belief in a natural illumination or "way" vouchsafed to all men irrespective of particular creeds, forms of worship, or varieties of belief. In short, it is an eighteenth century *tao* which reflects and transcends the thought and expression of the period. Pope's poem is intended to develop in the reader a capacity to recognize the interdependencies of all things; to attune himself, in thought and action, to the whole of creation; and to accept, in humility and reverence, his appointed place in the cosmic design.

The first epistle is chiefly concerned with demonstrating that man's place in the scheme of creation is providentially ordained. Pope claims that man's apparent limitations are blessings in disguise: if man were possessed of a prescience greater than that with which divine wisdom has endowed him, he would pose a threat to cosmic order—that "great chain, that draws all to agree"—and attempt to make himself the center of the universe. This would be in direct opposition to ". . . the first Almighty Cause," that "Acts not by partial, but by general laws." Although man's limitations tax him sorely and the apparent indifference of the universe offends his sense of justice, it is precisely those limitations which allow for his being in existence at all and permit him to develop, through interaction with others, a conscious sense of identity. If natural laws were suspended every time a person is threatened by their operation, the world would turn topsy-turvy and the order of both the universe and human society would fall into chaos. Hence, "The general Order, since the whole began,/ Is kept in Nature, and is kept in Man." Furthermore, if man were granted access to the divine plan and made privy to the Creator's will, his stature as a being midway between the Infinite and nothing would be destroyed. Pope reasons: "If nature thundered in his opening ears,/ And stunned him with the music of the spheres,/ How would he wish that Heaven had left him still/ The whispering Zephyr and the purling rill?" To be sure, man, through an act of faith, must develop the capacity to perceive the infinite in and through the finite, but to cherish the illusion that, in his present state, he is or should be equal to the "Mind of All" is to "invert the laws/ Of Order" and to sin "against th' Eternal Cause."

Pope cautions that man should not expect more from life than it is capable of providing and that he should look to death for the fulfillment of that hope which has been implanted in him as a sign of his transcendent destiny. This is to comport oneself authentically to the divine will: "Hope humbly then, with trembling pinions soar,/ Wait the greater teacher Death, and God adore./ What future bliss, he gives not thee to know/ But gives that Hope to be thy blessing now." In the last analysis, true happiness is a consequence of one's adjustment to that "stupendous whole,/ Whose body Nature is, and God the soul." From this proceeds the recognition that "All nature is but art, unknown to thee,/ All Chance, Direction, which thou canst not see,/ All Discord, Harmony, not understood;/ All partial Evil, universal Good."

For Pope, as it is in great things so it is in small. As a microcosm of the Universe, man's internal being reflects those same polarities and tensions which, held in harmonious balance, sustain and animate the cosmic scheme. Just as nature may deviate from that balance in eruptions, earthquakes, and cosmic catastrophes, so man's equilibrium may itself be usurped by the dominance of a particular passion or impulse. Pope argues, however, that man's mental constitution, despite its precarious balance, witnesses to the ingenuity of his Maker. Reason, by itself, is not enough to activate, kindle, and inspire our existence. Without the promptings of passion, humanity would sink into a contemplative torpor. Thus, "Two Principles in human nature reign;/ Self-love, to urge, and Reason, to restrain." In the elaboration of these mental categories, Pope strikingly anticipates Sigmund Freud. Pope's "self-love" and "Reason" are roughly equivalent to Freud's "Id" and "Super-Ego."

Like Freud, Pope recognizes that "Self-Love"—the id, or pleasure-principle—is the source of those instinctual urges which give vitality and movement to our lives. He also affirms that "Reason"—the Superego, or reality-principle—is necessary to direct those urges into socially acceptable channels and to keep them from becoming self-destructive. To expunge these passions altogether would destroy the human organism and rob life of its daring and splendor. Thus, "Love, Hope, and Joy, fair pleasure's smiling train,/ Hate, Fear, and Grief, the family of pain,/ These mixed with art, and to due bounds confined,/ Make and maintain the balance of the mind:/ The lights and shades, whose well-accorded strife/ Gives all the strength and color of our life." Moreover, each person possesses "One Master Passion" which gives his life impetus and direction. Without that passion his life would proceed without tremor, but his potential for virtue and creation would be severely diminished.

Like Freud, Pope here posits a theory of sublimation which recognizes that all virtues and achievements are transformations of subliminal and potentially destructive energies: "Nor Virtue, male or female, can we name,/ But what will grow on Pride, or grow on shame./ Thus Nature gives us (let it check our pride)/ The virtue nearest to our vice allied." Hence, lust, restrained and harmonized by Reason, becomes love: spleen becomes honesty; envy, emulation; avarice, prudence; and idleness or sloth—as Friedrich Nietzsche himself observed—philosophy. Finally, "Even mean Self-love becomes, by force divine,/ The scale to measure others' wants by thine./ See, and confess, one comfort still must rise,/ 'Tis this, Though Man's a fool, yet God is wise."

After examining, in Epistle II, the internal economy of human nature, Pope next scrutinizes the relationship between the individual and society. Not surprisingly, Pope's perception of society as an association of countervailing forces parallels his remarks on human psychology and cosmic order. Just as virtue is a product of sublimated vice, so human institutions—families, religious organizations, political bodies—are a product of human weakness. If man is born needy and deficient, that is not an argument against divine dispensation; on the contrary, it is precisely those deficiencies that necessitate the formation of a society based on mutual solicitude and love. In this way, self-love imperceptibly yields to social love—a love which is directly inspired by our need for and reliance on one another. The image that Pope uses to characterize this movement from self-love to social love and, finally, to cosmic love, is that of a pebble dropped in a peaceful lake: "Self-love but serves the virtuous mind to wake,/ As the small pebble stirs the peaceful lake;/ The center moved, a circle straight succeeds,/ Another still, and still another spreads;/ Friend, parent, neighbor, first it will embrace;/ His country next; and next all human race." At length, these spreading circles, and widening arcs of worship encompass the whole of Being and reflect, in miniature, the love of God for his creation. As Maynard Mack observes: "The controlling theme of *An Essay on Man* is the theme of constructive renunciation. By renouncing the exterior false paradises, man finds the true one within. By acknowledging his weakness, he learns his strengths. By subordinating himself to the whole, he finds his real importance in it."

Although it is important to estimate Pope's achievement in *An Essay on Man* in terms of his stated purpose, there is perhaps one legitimate criticism to which the poem gives rise: Pope's failure to recognize and express the intense spiritual struggle involved in accepting one's place in the divine plan. To be sure, Pope's response to those who would question God's justice is not dissimilar from the response accorded Job: "Where was thou when the foundations of the world were laid?" Unlike the Hebrew poet, however, Pope fails to dramatize the efforts of the individual to adhere to the divine will. Pope seems to regard all questionings of or disputations with providence as manifestations of human pride. In this way Pope vitiates the existential validity of his doctrines and devalues man's struggle to bring his will and intelligence into conformity with the Creator. As one critic remarks: "The wisdom that teaches us not to weep cannot dry our tears, still less can it draw them forth." In the final analysis, however, *An Essay on Man* is a compelling and thoughtful theodicy. As a poetry of statement it comes as close as any statement or assertion can to justifying and explaining the cosmic order. If it leaves the existential dimension of that order out of account, it must be remembered that Pope's intention is to "vindicate the ways of God to Man" through argument and persuasion rather than to *justify* those ways through drama or personal testimony.

The next phase of Pope's career is characterized by rage and indignation at a literary and social milieu in which intellectual blankness and moral bankruptcy are the accepted standard. Pope's voice becomes increasingly apocalyptic as he contemplates, with derision and dismay, the opportunistic secularism of the Augustan age. In the Horatian satires and epistles Pope expresses his outrage at the moral breakdown in the court of George II and the brutalizing cynicism in the administration of Robert Walpole, where "Not to be corrupted is the shame."

From an aesthetic point of view, the most interesting of these Horatian diatribes is *Epistle to Dr. Arbuthnot*. Again Pope astonishes us with the expressive capabilities of the rhyming couplet. By using enjambment and an almost syncopated rhythm to resist the couplet's natural tendency to fall into balanced antitheses with neatly placed caesuras in the middle of a line, Pope is able to capture the idiomatic flavor of a living conversation. One can hear Pope's labored breathing as he slams the door on those flatterers and careerists who have pursued him to the very threshold of Twickenham: "Shut, shut the door, good John!, fatigued I said,/ Tie up the Knocker, say I'm sick, I'm dead./ The Dog Star rages! nay 'tis past a doubt,/ All Bedlam, or Parnassus, is let out." The poem is not merely an attack on Pope's detractors—Atticus (Addison), Bufo (The Earl of Halifax), and Sporus (Lord Hervey)—but a withering indictment of a literary establishment which pursues reputation, influence, fashion, and power to the neglect of truth.

The ultimate expression of Pope's outrage at a world which ravages the principles of order adduced in *An Essay on Man* and subverts the disciplined training of the moral sensibility and character to curry favor is, of course, *The Dunciad*. Like *The Rape of the Lock*, *The Dunciad* is a mock-epic; but unlike its predecessor the satire here is scathing to the last degree. In its first version, Pope's principal antagonist was Lewis Theobald, a humorless and dry-as-dust pedant who is chiefly remembered for having pilloried Pope's edition of Shakespeare. In the final version, Theobald is replaced by Colly Cibber, a negligible drudge who, according to Pope, achieved the position of poet laureate through flattery and the propitiation of Dullness. As the King of Dunces, Cibber presides over a factious following of dilettantes and poetasters. In Book IV, the reign of Dullness shakes the very foundations of civilization as chaos supplants cosmos and moral order is overthrown. Educators, scientists, lawyers, politicians, pedants, and versifiers are all subjected to the withering scorn of Pope's pen. Each has allowed the allures of self-advertisement to compromise the disinterested search for value and truth. In short, *The Dunciad* is a vision of cultural fragmentation and breakdown in which the holistic vision of *An Essay on Man* deteriorates into the deconstructionism, the intellectual madness and lawlessness of those who only "See Nature in some partial narrow shape,/ And let the Author of the whole escape." The arts and sciences, perverted from their true function, become soulless self-reflections of man's skill: "Art after art goes out and All is Night,/ Lo! thy dread empire, CHAOS! is restored,/ Light dies before thy uncreating word./ Thy hand, great Anarch! lets the curtain fall;/ And universal Darkness buries All."

The Dunciad is a trenchant and corrosive probing of the moral, political, and cultural decay of a society controlled by self-important publicists, crass careerists, and opportunistic power-brokers. It is perhaps regrettable that Pope felt the need to encrust this poem with tedious and obscure references to the intellectual disloyalists of his day. Even so, the cumbersome and tortuous inventory of malodorous statesmen and maleficent critics is arguably at one with the poem's substance; the burden which they impose on the reader is a verbal equivalent to their stifling effect on a society from which every vestige of the spirit has been systematically expunged. Moreover, it is important to remember that these references are themselves a parody of "bookful blockheads ignorantly read/ With loads of learned lumber in their head." As Austin Warren observes apropos of Pope's dunces: "The context provides the categories which are permanent, while the proper names are annually replaceable."

Viewed as a whole, Pope's achievement is astonishing in its range and diversity. As the guardian and interpreter of a spiritual tradition distilled from the collective wisdom of Western culture, Pope articulates a "coherent romanticism," as it has been termed by G. Wilson Knight, which has as immediate a bearing on the fractured world of the twentieth century as it had on the refractory world of the Augustans. For those who believe that the preservation of humanistic letters and the survival of spiritual values are inextricably intertwined, Pope's poetry will continue to carry urgency and command attention.

Stephen I. Gurney

Other major works

NONFICTION: *An Essay on Criticism*, 1711; *Peri Bathos: Or, The Art of Sinking in Poetry*, 1727; *Mr. Pope's Literary Correspondence*, 1735-1737; *The Correspondence of Alexander Pope*, 1956 (G. Sherburn, editor, 5 volumes); *The Literary Criticism of Alexander Pope*, 1965.

MISCELLANEOUS: *The Works of Mr. Alexander Pope*, 1717-1741; *Works of Shakespear*, 1723-1725 (edited, 6 volumes).

Bibliography

Damrosch, Leopold, Jr. *The Imaginative World of Alexander Pope*. Berkeley: University of California Press, 1987. Damrosch's book is highly recommended for its success in the "imaginative recovery" of Pope, his work, and his world. This is a full and rich treatment, covering a wide range of topics and providing social, political, scientific, and religious contexts within which to read Pope's work.

Hammond, Brean S. *Pope*. Atlantic Highlands, N.J.: Humanities Press, 1986. This is an excellent entry in the Harvester New Readings series, and is particularly recommended for its willingness to bring the most recent critical approaches to bear on Pope. Hammond's five chapters are thematically organized, dealing in turn with Pope's life, his politics, his "ideology," his writing career, and his attitudes toward women. A bibliography follows the text.

Mack, Maynard. *Alexander Pope*. New York: W. W. Norton, 1985. Mack's grand and elegant work immediately—and rightfully—took its place as the "definitive" biography of Pope. Bringing to his task a lifetime of distinguished scholarship, Mack paints a complex, fully dimensioned portrait of Pope while managing at the same time an especially rich re-creation of English society during the period known as the "Age of Pope."

Pollak, Ellen. *The Poetics of Sexual Myth: Gender and Ideology in the Verse of Swift and Pope*. Chicago: University of Chicago Press, 1985. An important "revisionist" reading of Pope's views of women. Difficult, but highly rewarding.

Rogers, Pat. *An Introduction to Pope*. London: Methuen, 1975. This excellent introduction to Pope and his work is accessible, stylish, and full of textual and contextual insights. A scholar of great erudition, Rogers is particularly adept at providing readings of individual poems against a bright background of Pope's career and age. A useful reading list follows the text.

Rumbold, Valerie. *Women's Place in Pope's World*. Cambridge, England: Cambridge University Press, 1989. Although Pope has long been celebrated for his sympathetic portraits of women, critics like Rumbold have taken long and close looks at Pope's highly complex attitudes toward the "opposite sex." Rumbold's work is very successful at examining the social roles open to women in the generally oppressive, restricted world of eighteenth century England.

Weinbrot, Howard. *Alexander Pope and the Traditions of Formal Verse Satire*. Princeton, N.J.: Princeton University Press, 1982. Pope's greatest achievements as a poet were in the genre of satire, and he and his contemporaries were very aware of the rich satiric traditions bequeathed them by such classical predecessors as Horace, Juvenal, and Persius. Weinbrot thoroughly examines these traditions and considers their influence on Pope and the satiric enterprise in general in early eighteenth century England.

EZRA POUND

Born: Hailey, Idaho; October 30, 1885
Died: Venice, Italy; November 1, 1972

Principal poetry
   A Lume Spento, 1908; *A Quinzaine for This Yule*, 1908; *Personae*, 1909; *Exultations*, 1909; *Provença*, 1910; *Canzoni*, 1911; *Ripostes*, 1912; *Cathay*, 1915 (translation); *Lustra*, 1916; *Quia Pauper Amavi*, 1919; *Hugh Selwyn Mauberley*, 1920; *Umbra*, 1920; *Poems 1918 1921*, 1921; *Indiscretions*, 1923; *A Draft of XVI Cantos*, 1925; *Personae: The Collected Poems of Ezra Pound*, 1926; *A Draft of the Cantos 17-27*, 1928; *Selected Poems*, 1928; *A Draft of XXX Cantos*, 1930; *Eleven New Cantos XXXI-XLI*, 1934; *Homage to Sextus Propertius*, 1934 (translation); *Alfred Venison's Poems: Social Credit Themes*, 1935; *The Fifth Decad of Cantos*, 1937; *Cantos LII-LXXI*, 1940; *A Selection of Poems*, 1940; *The Pisan Cantos*, 1948; *The Cantos of Ezra Pound*, 1948; *Selected Poems*, 1949; *The Translations of Ezra Pound*, 1953; *Section: Rock-Drill 85-95 de los cantares*, 1955; *Thrones: 96-109 de los cantares*, 1959; *Drafts and Fragments of Cantos CX-CXVII*, 1968; *Selected Cantos*, 1970; *The Cantos of Ezra Pound I-CXVII*, 1970; *Selected Poems: 1908-1959*, 1975; *Collected Early Poems*, 1976 (Michael J. King, editor).

Other literary forms
   Ezra Pound was the most influential translator of poetry in the twentieth century. He translated, sometimes with assistance, from Greek, Latin, Provençal, Italian, French, German, Old English, Chinese, and Japanese. The *Translations of Ezra Pound* (1953) contains most of his poetic translations; there are also two separate books of Chinese translations, *The Classic Anthology Defined by Confucius* (or *The Confucian Odes*, 1954) and *Confucius* (1969), which gathers together in one volume Pound's translations of *The Analects*, the *Chung Yung* (*The Unwobbling Pivot*), and the *Ta Hio* (*The Great Digest*).
   Pound wrote a great deal of criticism. His music criticism has been collected in *Ezra Pound and Music* (1977); the best of his art criticism is found in *Gaudier-Brzeska: A Memoir* (1916) and his miscellaneous pieces have been brought together in *Ezra Pound and the Visual Arts* (1980). More important than either of these was his literary criticism, which, though more the notes of a working poet than a systematic body of doctrine, influenced many of the important poets of the century. *Literary Essays* (1954) and *ABC of Reading* (1934) contain the best of Pound's formal criticism, though the informal criticism found in *The Letters of Ezra Pound, 1907-1941* (1950) is at least as interesting.
   Pound's translations and criticism have aroused controversy, but nothing in

comparison with that aroused by his writings on social, political, and economic questions. These include *ABC of Economics* (1933), *Jefferson and/or Mussolini* (1935), *Guide to Kulchur* (1938), and *Impact: Essays on Ignorance and the Decline of American Civilization* (1960); Pound's *Selected Prose, 1909-1965* (1973) includes a generous sampling of his writing in this area.

It testifies to the diversity of Pound's interests that even this account far from exhausts Pound's work in other forms. He composed an opera, *The Testament of François Villon* (1926); one of his first books, *The Spirit of Romance* (1910), was an extended discussion of medieval literature; he translated Confucius into Italian as well as English; and his contributions to periodicals number in the thousands.

Achievements

There is more disagreement over Pound's achievements than over those of any other modern poet. There can be no disagreement, however, over Pound's extraordinary importance in the literary history of the twentieth century. Such importance derives in large measure from the close relationship that he enjoyed with so many of the twentieth century's leading writers. While serving as W. B. Yeats's secretary (from 1913 to 1915), he introduced Yeats to Japanese Nō drama, which served as a model for Yeats's subsequent plays for dancers. In the same period, he discovered, promoted, and found publishers for James Joyce and T. S. Eliot. Later, in 1922, he edited Eliot's masterpiece, *The Waste Land*, into final form. In 1914, he and Wyndham Lewis founded the Vorticist movement and the short-lived but seminal magazine *Blast*. During these years, he was actively involved with some of the most exciting literary journals of the period, including *Poetry*, *The Egoist*, *The Little Review*, and *The Dial*.

In the 1920's, as he began to write the long poem that would occupy him for fifty years, the *Cantos*, his pace of activity as a promoter of other writers declined. Nevertheless, he was an important influence on several generations of American poets, from his contemporaries William Carlos Williams and Marianne Moore to E. E. Cummings, Louis Zukofsky, Charles Olson, and others. It is no exaggeration to say that the literary history of the twentieth century is unthinkable without Pound.

Pound's work as a translator was as multifarious and stimulating as his activities on behalf of other writers. With Pound's Chinese translations in mind, Eliot in his introduction to Pound's *Selected Poems* called Pound "the inventor of Chinese poetry for our time." His versions of Sextus Propertius, Arnaut Daniel, and Guido Cavalcanti have done a great deal to increase interest in these poets. More important, Pound's example has redefined the art of translation and has influenced several generations of poets. The enormous importance of translation in contemorary poetry can largely be traced to Pound's groundbreaking work. Nevertheless, his translations have also been attacked as hopelessly inaccurate; his scholarship has been said to be nonexistent; and it must be granted that Pound's translations, in attempting to catch the spirit of the original, often do great violence to the letter.

The achievement of Pound's early verse (that written between 1908 and 1920) is, to put it simply, that he created, with Eliot, the modern poetic idiom in English and American poetry. Breaking free from the Victorian style in which he had begun, he began to write concise, laconic, austere poems in free verse, in which the line was the chief unit of composition. This style is usually called Imagism, a useful term as long as one remembers that Pound was the instigator of the style and movement, not simply one among equals. The best-known Imagist poem is Pound's famous two-line poem, "In a Station of the Metro" (1913), but Pound quickly outgrew the tight, haikulike style of his Imagist period (1912-1914), applying its concision and characteristically elliptical juxtapositions in longer, more complex, and more substantial poems.

This change quickly bore fruit in *Homage to Sextus Propertius* (first published in *Quia Pauper Amavi*, 1919), a kind of translation whose problematic status as a translation has diverted critical attention from its substance, and *Hugh Selwyn Mauberley*, one of the classics of modernism. Even before completing the dense, witty *Hugh Selwyn Mauberley*, Pound had begun what was to be the work of a lifetime, the *Cantos*. He first published sections from the *Cantos* in 1917; the poem was left unfinished at his death in 1972. The *Cantos* has been praised as the greatest long poem of the twentieth century, but it has also been vigorously attacked or simply dismissed without comment. For a number of reasons, the achievement of the *Cantos* remains a matter of great controversy and may not be settled soon.

Biography

It seems appropriate that Ezra Loomis Pound should have been born on the frontier (in Hailey, Idaho, in 1885) and then moved to Philadelphia at the age of two, to be reared in the suburb of Wyncote until his education at the University of Pennsylvania Hamilton College (Ph.B. 1905, and M.A. 1906). Pound, though always presenting himself as the ultimate American, kept moving east, in search of culture, in a voyage that would lead him to England, then to France, finally to Italy, and in spirit all the way to China.

Wrong turnings in Pound's career always took the form of moving west. After his education in romance languages and philology—what today would be called comparative literature—he took a teaching position at Wabash College in Crawfordsville, Indiana. Given his scholarly bent, he might easily have become a teacher and a scholar, but a scandal involving Pound's offering a night's hospitality to a destitute woman ended his career at Wabash and, as it was to turn out, his academic career as well.

He left for Venice in 1908, published his first book of poems there, *A*

Lume Spento, and then went to London, where he was to spend the next twelve years remaking literature. Tiring of London after World War I, he moved to Paris in 1921; in 1924 he moved again, to the lovely Italian seaside town of Rapallo. In his twenty years of residence there, he became increasingly enamored of the policies of Italy's Fascist ruler, Benito Mussolini. When war broke out between Italy and the United States in 1941, Pound stayed in Italy, either unable or unwilling to return home (the record is not entirely clear), and broadcast on Rome Radio throughout the war. In July, 1943, he was indicted for treason for his talks; in 1945 he was taken into custody by the American Army. Though returned to Washington for trial and in some danger of being executed for treason, Pound was never tried. He pleaded unfitness to stand trial by reason of insanity—he had suffered a complete breakdown from his harsh treatment after his capture in Italy—and was sent to Saint Elizabeths Hospital, where he was to remain until 1958. Finally, after a worldwide campaign on Pound's behalf, the indictment against him was dismissed. He immediately left for Italy and spent the remaining years of his life there, mostly in Venice. Deeply scarred by his experiences, convinced that his political activities had been a mistake, and unable to finish the *Cantos*, Pound refused to speak throughout most of the last ten years of his life.

Analysis

In 1926, Ezra Pound took the title of his third collection of verse, *Personae*, as the title for his collected shorter poems, which complicated his bibliography but afforded his readers a valuable cue. *Persona* in Latin means "mask," and in the 1909 volume *Personae*, there are a number of poems in which Pound takes on the persona, the mask, of an earlier poet and speaks in his voice. By calling his collected shorter poems *Personae*, Pound indicates that this device of the persona, far from being confined to a single volume, is central to his poetry.

Thus Pound's personality is not directly expressed in his poetry; it is found almost nowhere in his work. This clashes strongly with the Romantic notion that poetry is the expression of a poet's personality. One could say that, for Pound, poetry is the expression of someone else's personality. Pound's choice of personae, however, is never haphazard and his own sensibility and voice come through in the choice of the persona. In Pound's best works, the mask that the poet assumes is a perfect fit: the original speaker is rendered so expertly that readers can take the poem as their own and see Pound as merely a poetic midwife; yet the reader can also view the poem as Pound's through and through and see the original speaker as a mask that Pound has donned for the occasion.

It should be easy to see how this poetic of the persona is also a poetic of translation, and much of the fascination to be found in Pound's early work lies in watching him attempt to bring "translation" and "original composition" together. Poets from the time of Ovid to that of Samuel Johnson would not have seen these as distinct categories, but Romanticism, in its insistence that poetry was what could not be translated, separated what Johnson would have seen as one activity into two very different ones. Pound's early work preserves this Romantic dichotomy even though attempting to transcend it: he translated Cavalcanti and Arnaut Daniel, and wrote poems using Cino da Pistoia and Bertran de Born as personae.

Pound's choice of these Provençal and early Italian poets indicates the indebtedness of his early work to the Victorian poets Robert Browning and Dante Gabriel Rossetti. Pound's notion of the persona owes much to Browning's choice of Cino and Bertran as personae. Rossetti's translations of the early Italian poets helped to direct Pound's interest in these poets and, though Pound wanted to translate Cavalcanti employing a modern idiom, a look at his Cavalcanti translations reveals how much he was still caught in Rossetti's idiom as late as 1912. Nevertheless, though his early work did derive from Browning and Rossetti, his aim was always to go beyond them. He was not a dramatic poet, having none of Browning's interest in rendering a dramatic situation; nor was he, really, a translator, with the translator's self-effacement. He wanted to write translations which were original compositions; he wanted to put Browning and Rossetti together.

He succeeded in such a project only when he moved away from the Provençal and early Italian material with which he had worked from 1909 to 1912. In 1913, he reworked a group of poems from H. A. Giles's *History of Chinese Literature*, "After Ch'u Yuan," "Liu Ch'e," "Fan-piece, for her Imperial Lord," and "Ts'ai Chi'h." Impressed by the quality of these translations (or rather re-translations), Mary Fenollosa got in touch with Pound and asked him if he would be interested in editing her husband's manuscripts. Ernest Fenollosa, an important Orientalist and long-time resident of Japan, had left rough manuscript translations of Chinese poetry and Japanese drama. Pound agreed, and in 1915 the first fruits of Pound's work appeared: *Cathay*, a book of translations from the Chinese.

It was with the publication of *Cathay* that Pound became a major poet and began to write the kind of poetry he had long wanted to write. The poems in *Cathay* are far more than beautiful translations, though they are that. Pound selected, translated, and published these poems—in 1915—as an indirect way of writing about Europe in the midst of World War I. In other words, Pound *translated* poems about war, exile, parting, and loss as a way of writing "war poetry." This was not, however, immediately recognized; the poems were regarded simply as translations and readers missed or ignored the implicit relation between the world of the poems and the world of the translator.

Pound's first extended poem, *Homage to Sextus Propertius*, was called an homage in order to make Pound's presence in the poem clear. It works in the same way that *Cathay* does: it is a translation of Propertius, a very lively if not overly accurate one; but here too translation and original composition fuse. Pound is interested in Propertius because he sees an extraordinary parallel between Propertius' times and his own and between their respective situations. Both, according to Pound, are ironic sensualists surrounded by an imbecilic Empire, and the thrust of Pound's poem is to assert a parallel between Propertius' Rome and Pound's London. Despite the title, Pound's intention of using Propertius to make his own statement was not grasped and the *Homage to Sextus Propertius* has never received its due as Pound's most important poem before the *Cantos.* It was attacked by classicists as a horrible mistranslation, and in places it is. Perhaps the most notorious phrase in the poem is Pound's reference to "a frigidaire patent." Pound put in such phrases deliberately to signal to the reader that this poem is about the London of frigidaire patents, not simply about Rome. Instead, these phrases were seen as Pound's crude attempt to modernize his idiom, and so what should have provided valuable clues to Pound's intention were rejected as tasteless excrescences.

Cathay and the *Homage to Sextus Propertius* thus represent the main line of Pound's development toward the *Cantos* because they combine his poetic of the persona with an indirect way of commenting on the present by means of implicit parallels with the past. Pound's reconciliation of the split between translation and original composition in these poems, however, was beyond his audience. Even the most sophisticated of his readers did not get the point, and it is only with the perspective offered by the *Cantos,* which work in the mode of *Cathay* and the *Homage to Sextus Propertius,* that one can see the return to the present implicit in these works. In the wake of the stormy reception of the *Homage to Sextus Propertius,* Pound wrote *Hugh Selwyn Mauberley,* which presents virtually the same perceptions about London as the *Homage to Sextus Propertius,* but with the subtle temporal loop between Rome and London replaced by an ironic persona, Hugh Selwyn Mauberley. Mauberley's relation to Pound is problematic: he shares certain traits with him, yet the poem is only tangentially autobiographical. It is perhaps most accurate to say that Mauberley is a self that Pound sloughed off, or the kind of figure that Pound might have become had he stayed in England. Mauberley, though fighting the stupidity and crassness he finds in English literary life, will not win that fight, and, the reader feels, he knows it. The dominant mood of *Hugh Selwyn Mauberley* is a resigned acceptance of lesser hopes and aspirations. Written just after World War I, it clearly expresses Pound's disillusionment with the course of history and with the state of English civilization. For these reasons, it is often referred to as Pound's farewell to London. It is also Pound's farewell to poems using a persona alone, without the more complicated temporal loops of *Cathay* and *Homage to Sextus Propertius,* and his farewell to the short, independent poem. After 1920, aside from a few stray political poems written in the 1930's, Pound's work in poetry was confined to the *Cantos*, a massive, sprawling eight-hundred-page poem that dwarfs the early poetry discussed so far.

Pound had always wanted to write a long poem, in this, as in other ways, remaining faithful to the traditional model of the poetic career. According to this model, he actually began his "epic" very early, for sections of the *Cantos* began to appear as early as 1917, though the first section to be published in book form, *A Draft of XVI Cantos*, did not appear until 1925. The last section of the *Cantos* to be published, *Drafts and Fragments of Cantos CX-CXVII*, came out in 1968, fully fifty-one years after the first, and it marked not the completion of the poem but its abandonment, as Pound at the age of eighty-two realized that he could not finish it.

This circumstance makes discussion of the *Cantos* extraordinarily difficult. Perhaps the difficulty is best expressed by asking a simple question: Does one refer to the poem in the singular or the plural? That in turn leads to another question, involving one's critical approach to the work: Is it one long, unified poem, or is it a collection of separate parts? It is not easy to describe what unifies the poem, aside from Pound's claim that it is one poem. The first canto begins with a translation of Homer, the second with a few lines about Robert Browning's *Sordello*, and the third with an autobiographical reminiscence of being a young and poor traveler in Venice. The poem freely moves across all times and all places and all languages as well, as phrases in most of the major European languages and hundreds of Chinese ideograms dot the text. A majority of the cantos have explicit sources outside the poem, and clues to such source material are to be found within the poem. Cantos VIII-XI, for example, constitute a detailed portrait of Sigismundo Malatesta, the fifteenth century ruler of the Italian city of Rimini; Cantos LIII-LXI summarize twenty-five hundred years of Chinese history. Nevertheless, the kind of material included changes considerably in the course of the poem, so this does not really tie it together either. The *Cantos*, in short, are probably more complicated than any other poem written since the Renaissance.

The reader's difficulty in subsuming all these materials under one unifying scheme should not, however, blind one to the fact that Pound hoped that the reader would be able to discover such a design. He did set out to write a unified poem, even if he took unprecedented risks in doing so. What complicates the issue is that his ideas about the structure of the poem changed, which should come as no great surprise, given the fifty-odd years that the poem occupied him. To make sense of the *Cantos*, therefore, one must approach them historically, precisely as a poem written across fifty years. The *Cantos* do not have the unified structure of, say, *The Divine Comedy* (c. 1320); there is no shortcut through them, no helpful map or schema. Nevertheless, they are hardly 117 different poems, for the various cantos are integrated by a web of interconnections and they must be read with an attentive eye for what brings them together.

This summary may make one wonder, why bother? Certainly, though the *Cantos* are Pound's most important work, no reader should begin with them. Only a reader convinced of the value of the earlier work ventures into the *Cantos*; but many of those who do, find the work totally compelling. Such readers fall into a number of (not necessarily distinct) categories. First, there are those who are held by the beauty and majesty of Pound's language. Even those who consider the *Cantos* a jumble in formal terms concede that certain passages are among the most impressive poetry of the twentieth century. Consequently, Pound has been the poet's poet; his has been the greatest single poetic influence on his own contemporaries and on the poetry of today. The second group of "Poundians" are those who find Pound's ideas compelling. They are the readers that Pound hoped to have, for the *Cantos* constitute perhaps the most ambitious didactic poem of the twentieth century. Although this group forms a distinct minority, many who cannot accept Pound's ideas still feel that his very attempt to write such an intellectually ambitious poem is worthy of praise. Pound single-handedly made it again possible to include serious intellectual and political matters in poetry. Moreover, the *Cantos* is a fascinating intellectual argosy, no matter what one's opinions of Pound's ideas may be. Readers who fall under his spell learn about Chinese history and the Chinese language, early Italian poetry, and hundreds of other things. Thus, the *Cantos*, whatever their difficulties, have their rewards.

What follows cannot under the circumstances be a deep reading, but a brief overview of the *Cantos* may prove helpful to the reader curious about this strange but fascinating work. The 115 cantos available in the collected edition are customarily divided into four sections: Cantos I-XXX are known as the Early Cantos; Cantos XXXI-LXXI are the Middle Cantos; Cantos LXXIV-LXXXIV are *The Pisan Cantos*; and Cantos LXXXV-CXVII are the Later Cantos. These sections are further subdivided. Certain sections have been titled by Pound himself: Cantos LXXXV-XCV are known as *Rock-Drill* and Cantos XCVI-CIX are known as *Thrones*, the titles under which these sections were originally published. Other sections have acquired titles by convention: Cantos VIII-XI are the Malatesta Cantos; Cantos LII-LXI the Chinese History Cantos; Cantos LXII-LXXI the Adams Cantos. Although material in every section escapes any ready classification, the *Cantos* in any given section tend to gather around one common theme.

The theme of the Early Cantos is the Renaissance, as the two longest sequences in this section are about Sigismundo Malatesta and sixteenth century Venice. The one feature of the *Cantos* that never changes is that they are always, no matter how indirectly or obliquely, really about the present. The implicit return to the present in the Early Cantos is that Pound is wondering whether his own era can fulfill its potential to be a new Renaissance. It has the turbulence of Malatesta's time; has it the brilliance? Toward the end of the 1920's and the Early Cantos, Pound grows less optimistic about contemporary culture and more interested in the economic and political conditions that allow art to flourish. In an implicit contrast with Malatesta's support for the arts treated in the Malatesta Cantos, the Venetian Cantos relate how Titian failed to paint works the government had commissioned, in effect defrauding the state.

This change in Pound's focus and vision prepares the reader for the new direction taken by the Middle Cantos. The cultural and artistic material of the Early Cantos is replaced by political and economic material. Cantos XXXI-LXXI present a series of images of good and bad rulers and good and bad banks: mostly good rulers—Thomas Jefferson, John Adams, Martin Van Buren, Duke Pietro Leopoldo of Tuscany—and bad banks. For Pound there has been only one good bank in history, the Monte dei Paschi Bank in Siena, and modern banking practices are responsible for the growing disorder of the modern world. History for Pound at this point is a Manichaean struggle between the forces of order and disorder, and Cantos LII-LXI summarize twenty-five hundred years of Chinese history because this struggle between order and disorder can be seen most clearly there. According to Pound, the forces of order are the Confucians, and the ideas of Confucius are the most reliable guide to the creation of political order.

None of this would have excited much interest or controversy in itself, but Pound, as always, applies his vision to the present. The implicit thrust of the Middle Cantos is that Benito Mussolini, the Fascist ruler of Italy, is the modern embodiment of the Confucian will to order; the forces of disorder are modern banks and speculative capitalists. This preception led Pound toward anti-Semitism, as he identified the Jews with the usurious banking practices he deplored. Pound, as has already been discussed, attempted to put these political ideas into action as well as putting them in his poem. The resulting personal consequences and the collapse of Mussolini's regime in 1945 were obviously catastrophic for Pound, as his thirteen years in an insane asylum attest. The artistic consequences were disastrous as well, for the contemporary political implications of the *Cantos* were rendered hopelessly out of date and exposed as absurd. Mussolini had obviously not proved to be the twentieth century's Great Emperor; Pound's poem was in praise of a murderous buffoon.

This turn of events doomed Pound's poem to be unfinished and unfinishable, at least in the sense of having a single, articulated direction and structure. What resulted, however, was paradoxically the most brilliant section of the poem. Pound, writing in a prison camp, with all action blocked, no prospect beyond incarceration or execution, his beloved Italy and much of the rest of Europe in ruins, his political vision and his poem in a similar state of ruin, could not continue to write the Confucian epic of the Middle Cantos. Forced into a fresh start, he wrote *The Pisan Cantos*, Cantos LXXIV-LXXXIV, which are in sharp contrast to what has come before in a number of respects.

First of all, *The Pisan Cantos* mark at least a temporary abandonment of the ordering and definition of universals so prominent in the Middle Cantos. This modification has broad implications, as Pound's formal imperative to order particulars had been linked to his Confucian politics of order. No longer is he exclusively concerned with defining what constitutes a good or a bad bank, or a good or a bad ruler. There is a new willingness on Pound's part to stay with the fragment or detail, to respect its concreteness, rather than to align it with other details for the purpose of defining a generality.

In *The Pisan Cantos*, consequently, Pound comes to accept a new measure of disorder, and this allows him to open the poem to new kinds of material. He includes elements that resist generalization, such as details from nature, snippets of conversation he overhears in the detention camp, personal memories, particularly of his first years in London, and selected images and passages of poetry. These details are set out page after page, in a bewildering if dazzling array, in many languages and on every conceivable subject, without any apparent plan or order. In the earlier cantos, one canto might be set in Homeric Greece and the next in Renaissance Greece, but in *The Pisan Cantos* this kind of juxtaposition occurs on the level of the line: a quotation from Mencius will follow a detail about how olive trees look in the wind, details about economics will follow a line of conversation overheard by Pound in the camp. In these cantos, Pound feels free to include whatever he wants, and he freely moves from particular to particular by means of haikulike juxtapositions.

This change ought to make *The Pisan Cantos* the most baffling and unrewarding section of the *Cantos* but, mysteriously, precisely the opposite is true. When, earlier in the *Cantos*, Pound puts a canto about the Renaissance next to one about Confucius, the reader feels that the juxtaposition must be significant and he is likely to feel at a loss if—as is often the case—no apparent reason for such a juxtaposition emerges. In *The Pisan Cantos*, however, there are so many such juxtapositions for the reader to grasp that he should not be expected—at a first reading, at any rate—to puzzle over every one. In other words, both poet and reader adopt (or need to adopt) a more relaxed attitude about both content and sequence in *The Pisan Cantos*. Pound no longer attempts to order his materials; instead, he proceeds confident that it is ordered. That confidence is justified by the entirety of *The Pisan Cantos* as, despite the open, fluid style, these cantos do organize themselves around certain themes. To put it more precisely, the reader, attentive to certain repetitions, discovers the organizing themes of the sequence. The reader does in a sense have to put the poem together, but the elements are there to work with. At the end of the first Pisan canto, Canto LXXIV, Pound turns to the reader and asks whether he has seen that the fragments are parts of a whole. Alluding to the rose pattern formed when a field of iron filings is touched by a magnet's field of force, he asks, "Hast'ou seen the rose in the steel dust?"

It is natural that different readers will have different answers to this question. Pound's analogy is inexact because he has not transformed the shape of the fragments already included in the pages of his poem. He can at most transform the way they are seen. *The Pisan Cantos* are nevertheless universally considered to be the best section of the *Cantos*, so one may conclude that Pound is not alone in seeing a rose in their steel dust.

Critics divide much more sharply on the Later Cantos. In *Rock-Drill* and *Thrones*, though continuing in the more open style achieved in *The Pisan Cantos*, Pound returns to promoting his views on order, and anyone is likely to protest who regards with pleasure the personal turn taken in *The Pisan Cantos*. Nevertheless, although these cantos do not maintain the high level of achievement of *The Pisan Cantos*, *Rock-Drill* in particular is much more interesting than the Middle Cantos. Pound maintains much the same views on society, but he recognizes that he will not see his ideals realized in his lifetime and this lessens his messianic intensity. It also leads him into extended lyric passages that move away from his social and political concerns. At times in these Late Cantos, therefore, Pound is a prophet who will, he hopes, be justified by history, and at other times, like Stephen Dedalus in *Ulysses* (1922), history for him is a nightmare from which he is trying to awake.

By the wonderful yet terrible *Drafts and Fragments of Cantos CX–CXVII*, the mood of nightmare dominates. By this time, the history from which he wishes to awake is in large part the history of his own poem. The publication of *Drafts and Fragments of Cantos CX–CXVII* in 1968 marked Pound's formal abandonment of the poem four years before his death. This abandonment seems to have been an act very close to despair. Cantos CXVI and CXVII contain confessions of failure similar to those found in a number of Pound's late statements and interviews. He not only felt that his political activities and his anti-Semitism had been stupid and shallow, but he also felt that the *Cantos* were a failure. In formal terms, he was certainly right. As he says in Canto CXVI, he could not make it cohere. Yet he does not stop there. He continues, "it coheres all right/ even if my notes do not cohere." Just as *The Pisan Cantos* began in tragedy but ended in triumph, here Pound abandons the poem in an act of humility that somehow goes a long way toward redeeming what has come before. These notes, these CXVII cantos, may not be the coherent structure Pound had hoped for, but Pound is confident that the order he sought to express is out there. He invites the reader to go beyond him to grasp it, to find that it does cohere.

Whether or not to do this is, of course, up to the reader, and different readers, as has been emphasized here, respond and will continue to respond to this invitation in radically different ways. For some, it does cohere, and Pound is the greatest English-language poet of the twentieth century. For others, it simply fails to cohere, and Pound is not worth the bother. For still others, the patterns of coherence are so overwhelmingly totalitarian that Pound should be condemned—not even discussed lest his ideas infect others. The truth, as always, lies somewhere in between, but much of the interest of Pound is that it does not lie comfortably in between.

Reed Way Dasenbrock

Other major works

PLAY: *The Testament of François Villon*, 1926 (translation into opera).

NONFICTION: *The Spirit of Romance*, 1910; *Gaudier-Brzeska: A Memoir*, 1916; *The Chinese Written Character as a Medium for Poetry*, 1920 (editor); *Instigations of Ezra Pound, Together with an Essay on the Chinese Written Character by Ernest Fenollosa*, 1920; *Antheil and the Treatise on Harmony*, 1924; *Imaginary Letters*, 1930; *How to Read*, 1931; *ABC of Economics*, 1933; *ABC of Reading*, 1934; *Make It New*, 1934; *Social Credit: An Impact*, 1935; *Jefferson and/or Mussolini*, 1935; *Polite Essays*, 1937; *Guide to Kulchur*, 1938; *Orientamenti*, 1938; *What Is Money For?*, 1939; *Carta da Visita*, 1942 (*A Visiting Card*, 1952); *Introduzione alla natura economica degli S.U.A.*, 1944 (*An Introduction to the Economic Nature of the United States*, 1950); *L'America, Roosevelt, e le cause della guerra presente*, 1944 (*America, Roosevelt, and the Causes of the Present War*, 1951); *Orro e lavoro*, 1944 (*Gold and Work*, 1952); "*If This Be Treason . . .*," 1948; *The Letters of Ezra Pound, 1907-1941*, 1950; *Lavoro ed usura*, 1954; *Literary Essays*, 1954; *Impact: Essays on Ignorance and the Decline of American Civilization*, 1960; *Nuova economia editoriale*, 1962; *Patria Mia and the Treatise on Harmony*, 1962; *Pound/Joyce: The Letters of Ezra Pound to James Joyce*, 1967; *Selected Prose, 1909-1965*, 1973; *Ezra Pound and Music: The Complete Criticism*, 1977; "*Ezra Pound Speaking*": *Radio Speeches of World War II*, 1978; *Letters to Ibbotson, 1935-1952*, 1979; *Ezra Pound and the Visual Arts*, 1980; *From Syria: The Worksheets, Proofs, and Text*, 1981; *Pound/Ford: The Story of a Literary Friendship*, 1982; *Ezra Pound and Dorothy Shakespear: Their Letters, 1909-1914*, 1984; *The Letters of Ezra Pound and Wyndham Lewis*, 1985.

TRANSLATIONS: *The Sonnets and Ballate of Guido Cavalcanti*, 1912; *Cathay: Translations by Ezra Pound for the Most Part from the Chinese of Rihaku, from the Notes of the Late Ernest Fenollosa and the Decipherings of the Professors Mori and Ariga*, 1915; '*Noh' or Accomplishment*, 1916 (with Ernest Fenollosa); *The Natural Philosophy of Love*, 1922 (of Remy de Gourmont's work); *The Testament of François Villon*, 1926 (translation into opera); *Rime*, 1932 (of Guido Cavalcanti's poetry); *Homage to Sextus Propertius*, 1934; *Digest of the Analects*, 1937 (of Confucius' work); *Italy's Policy of Social Economics, 1930-1940*, 1941 (of Odon Por's work); *Confucius: The Unwobbling Pivot and the Great Digest*, 1947; *The Translations of Ezra Pound*, 1953; *The Classic Anthology Defined by Confucius*, 1954 (*The Confucian Odes*); *Women of Trachis*, 1956 (of Sophocles' play); *Love Poems of Ancient*

Egypt, 1964; *Confucius,* 1969.

ANTHOLOGIES: *Des Imagistes: An Anthology,* 1914; *Catholic Anthology 1914-1915,* 1915; *Active Anthology,* 1933; *Confucius to Cummings: An Anthology of Poetry,* 1964 (with Marcella Spann).

Bibliography

Froula, Christine. *A Guide to Ezra Pound's Selected Poems.* New York: New Directions, 1983. This competent and useful companion to the poems is an aid to the reader's understanding of Pound's experimental style and serves as a good accompaniment to his early work. Includes a select bibliography and an index.

Heymann, David. *Ezra Pound: The Last Rower.* New York: Viking Press, 1976. This work offers a detailed look at the case for treason which the United States brought against Pound at the end of World War II. By presenting a careful examination of Pound's political and economic beliefs, Heymann attempts to reconcile the poet's life and work. Supplemented by letters, photographs, and an index.

Kenner, Hugh. *The Poetry of Ezra Pound.* London: Faber & Faber, 1951. Rev. ed. Lincoln: University of Nebraska Press, 1985. This classic examination and exposition of Pound's poetry addresses and clarifies most of the obvious misunderstandings that have occurred to those not familiar with his work. This volume does not attempt to be a critical study. Originally published by Faber & Faber in 1951, this edition includes a new preface by the author and a foreword by James Laughlin. Complemented by a select bibliography and an index.

Knapp, James F. *Ezra Pound.* Boston: Twayne, 1979. One of the Twayne United States Author series, this volume offers a good, basic introduction to, and an overview of, Pound's work. Augmented by a select bibliography and an index.

Laughlin, James. *Pound as Wuz: Essays and Lectures on Ezra Pound.* Saint Paul, Minn.: Graywolf Press, 1987. A substantial biographical portrait of Pound composed of a collection of recent biographical and critical pieces written by Laughlin. This useful volume is written by one of Pound's closest friends and literary associates. Supplemented by a select bibliography and an index.

Stock, Noel, ed. *Ezra Pound Perspectives: Essays in Honor of His Eightieth Birthday.* Chicago: H. Regnery, 1965. This volume contains essays and tributes from a wide range of Pound's contemporaries including Ernest Hemingway, Conrad Aiken, Allen Tate, and Wyndham Lewis. Edited and includes an introduction by Stock. Complemented by illustrations.

_____. *The Life of Ezra Pound.* 1970. Rev. ed. San Francisco: North Point Press, 1982. This biography follows Pound from his birth in Idaho through his years abroad in England and Italy, to his arrest for treason, his return to the United States, his incarceration in Saint Elizabeths Hospital, and finally, to his return to Italy. This expanded edition, first published in 1970, includes bibliographical references, photographs, and an index.

E. J. PRATT

Born: Western Bay, Newfoundland; February 4, 1882
Died: Toronto, Ontario; April 26, 1964

Principal poetry

Rachel: A Sea Story of Newfoundland in Verse, 1917; *Newfoundland Verse*, 1923; *The Witches' Brew*, 1925; *Titans*, 1926; *The Iron Door: An Ode*, 1927; *The Roosevelt and the Antinoe*, 1930; *Many Moods*, 1932; *The Titanic*, 1935; *The Fable of the Goats and Other Poems*, 1937; *Brébeuf and His Brethren*, 1940; *Dunkirk*, 1941; *Still Life and Other Verse*, 1943; *Collected Poems*, 1944; *They Are Returning*, 1945; *Behind the Log*, 1947; *Ten Selected Poems*, 1947; *Towards the Last Spike*, 1952; *Magic in Everything*, 1955; *The Collected Poems of E. J. Pratt*, 1958; *Here the Tides Flow*, 1962.

Other literary forms

E. J. Pratt's career as a poet began with an unpublished verse drama, *Clay*. The play is weak in many ways, but as a whole it shows Pratt's early interest in dramatic intensity, a characteristic of his later poetry. *Clay* reveals the poet's increasing ability to control monologue and dialogue within a larger literary structure. Other literary efforts include two short stories ("'Hooked': A Rocky Mountain Experience," 1914, and "Golfomania," 1924), critical articles, reviews, and introductions to books (most notably, Herman Melville's 1929 edition of *Moby Dick*, and Thomas Hardy's 1937 edition of *Under the Greenwood Tree*). Two other works of significance are his published thesis, *Pauline Eschatology* (1917) and his religious verses and hymns, included in Denzil D. Ridout's *United to Serve* (1927).

Achievements

To define Pratt's accomplishment is problematic: he is the best-known and most respected of all Canadian poets, yet he is an isolated and a solitary figure. His achievement is based on compelling and moving lyric and narrative verse, but his poetic masters cannot be easily traced and his poetic disciples cannot be found. Pratt avoided formulating a strict poetic creed, and he refused to follow the rules of any poetic school; thus he cannot be conveniently categorized or explained. Pratt's artistic vision is indisputably broad, warm, humanistic, and universal. Courage in the face of a hostile natural environment, fidelity to the values that cultivate and civilize, compassion for those not always able to endure the trials of simple existence—these compose the core of Pratt's preoccupation as a poet. His success in making these concerns concrete, particular, and forceful twice won him the Governor General's Award, Canada's most coveted prize for literature.

Part of Pratt's success rests in his conviction that poetry is public writing, not private exposé or confession. By using plain language and traditional end-rhyme, as well as disarmingly simple plots or events (subtly enhancing all of these through wit, irony, and contemporary themes), Pratt created a poetry that caught the attention and earned the admiration of both the general reader and the scholar. If anything, his career marks the culmination of the poetry and poetic craft which preceded him—that of Bliss Carman, Charles G. D. Roberts, F. R. Scott, and Archibald Lampman; it also led the way to the acceptance of modernism, though Pratt stops just short of being Canada's first indisputable modernist.

Pratt's most significant contributions to Canadian literature lie in the concreteness and precision of his "impersonal" lyrics and his fast-paced, economical, direct narratives. His lyrics resemble small sculptures; the visual and emotional impact of feeling arrested in words durable as stone attracts the reader's eye. The representative images of love or hope or loss or fear captured in these poems are never clever, abstruse, academic, or strained. Pratt was the first Canadian poet to present an image and then refrain from commenting, explaining, moralizing, or philosophizing for the reader—tendencies which often characterized the poets who preceded him.

In the narratives, Pratt's contribution is even more significant. In poems such as *The Titanic* and *Brébeuf and His Brethren*, he gave shape to and refined the "documentary" narrative in verse, a form no longer popular. Pratt can be viewed as the last practitioner of direct narratives in Canadian writing. Second, Pratt was the last Canadian who did not fall under the spell of modernism *à la* T. S. Eliot or Ezra Pound. Pratt wrestled with a poetic form which he himself termed *extravaganza*. The form is based on wit, comedy, hyperbole, and discontinuity, and the narratives of this type may represent the first literary form of significance created by a Canadian.

Biography

Edwin John Pratt was born in Newfoundland, the son of John Pratt, a Methodist missionary from Yorkshire, and of Fanny Knight, a sea-captain's daughter. Pratt spent his first twenty-three years in Newfoundland, and his early life in the outport villages marked him: the sea can be felt in his rhythms and the coastal shore perceived in his imagery. In 1901, he was graduated from the Methodist College in St. John's. For nearly six years, Pratt was a probationer in the Methodist ministry who taught and preached in various villages. In 1907, he elected to go to Toronto to study philosophy at Victoria College. He soon earned his M.A. degree, then decided to complete a B.A. in divinity. In 1917, having again changed his field of study, he received his Ph.D. in psychology. Pratt married Viola Whitney in 1918; two years later she gave birth to their only child, Mildred Claire. Also in 1920, Pratt shifted careers again: this time he became a professor of English at Victoria College, a position he retained until his retirement in 1954, when the title Professor

Emeritus was conferred upon him. Pratt died ten years later. In academic terms, then, this poet's training was unusually long and varied; its effects can be seen in his poetry. Pratt's early life in Newfoundland taught him to love poetry that was as direct and immediate as a ballad of the sea, and his later years of education in philosophy, divinity, psychology, and literature supplied his characteristic themes. Pratt's language is clear and plain, not regional; his themes are universal, not private.

Analysis

The poetry of E. J. Pratt falls into three categories: the shorter lyrics, the documentarylike narratives, and the *extravaganzas*. The division in form, however, does not suggest a division in outlook. Pratt is almost always concerned with the clash between the human, as individual or group, and the amoral strength and power of the natural world. As a man, Pratt admired courage, civilization, and compassion; as a poet, he celebrated their purpose, function, and value. He saw man inhabiting a world where there are no answers about the rightness of values, but he also perceived that no man can live without them. Pratt did not preach or lecture his readers, nor did he argue with them; rather, he showed his readers the paradoxes and ironies which result when a morally sensitive being inhabits an essentially amoral world.

The theme is examined most easily in Pratt's lyrics. The short poems are often elusive and complex, rich in meaning and powerful in impact. Many of the poems, moreover, begin in Pratt's own experience, but by the time he has finished with them, they are purified of the narrowly private and personal. Once Pratt has finished with a lyric, it stands open for all readers of all ages.

A poem such as "Erosion" is typical of Pratt's artistry and technical mastery. When Pratt was a young boy in a Newfoundland fishing village, his father, a minister, would often, as the most trying of his duties, have to announce to a woman the death at sea of her husband or son. The shock recorded in the woman's face etched itself on the poet's mind immediately, but it took him nearly thirty years to record the experience properly in verse.

The final version of the poem is only eight lines long, and Pratt omits everything that would detract from his central idea—the impact of the sea's force upon the woman's life. Pratt dismisses his father's presence, his own presence, and the announcement of death. In their place, the poet stresses the passage of time. The first stanza of the poem portrays the sea's unending effort to "trace" features into a cliff. The features in the stone, as all those who have walked along a shoreline know, have a disconcertingly "human" look. In Pratt's poem, then, the sea has, for more than a thousand years, attempted to humanize nature (the cliff) by giving it a face.

The second stanza of the poem stresses that the woman looking at the sea-carving changes dramatically in the mere hour of watching the power and strength of a storm at sea. Possibly her son or husband is in a ship caught in that storm, but the poet deliberately avoids commenting on that point. It is enough to know that the sea has failed to complete the face in the cliff, and that the woman's face, in an hour, has turned to granite. The result, the poem suggests, is that the face of the cliff and the face of the woman resemble each other. The complex response that the short poem elicits, then, is that the sea may be humanizing the cliff, but that it is dehumanizing the woman, for she takes on a more elemental, stonelike appearance.

The poem, then, records the irony of an amoral world that appears to humanize, but, in fact, dehumanizes. The poem, however, is multileveled. Throughout the eight lines, the sea is compared to an artist who traces and sculpts his forms with diligence and care. To attribute artistic qualities to the sea outlines its creative, rather than its destructive, power. The reader who puzzles over this positive feature is on the way to an understanding of Pratt's complexity, despite the seeming simplicity. A second reading of this elusive poem suggests that the woman may be merely overawed by the sea's power, magnificence, and force. Recalcitrant nature, insensitive to the movements and powers surrounding it, requires centuries to change; the woman is transformed in her moment of insight. The rock passively undergoes its metamorphosis as the sea carves its pattern upon it. The permanence, durability, and strength of the cliff rest upon its impassive and insensible state.

The woman, in sharp contrast, observes the storm at sea and undergoes a metamorphosis springing from the inner source of being, the emotions. Unlike the cliff, which is acted upon by an outside force, the woman actively responds to what she sees. Her sensibility, in other words, sets her apart from nature. Furthermore, her ability to feel is similar to that of the sea, yet stronger; what the sea can do in a thousand years, her emotions can do in an hour. At the same time, the sculpture of the cliff resembles the sculpture on her face, a parallelism that suggests the truly complex, ambiguous, and ironic tone of the poem. The essential quality which distinguishes a human being from nature (the ability to feel) is precisely the characteristic that underscores the resemblance to it, since both must suffer physical "erosion." Ironically, the inner ability to respond affirms that human sensitivity, perception, and insight are both magnificent and frightening—in a word, awesome. Loneliness, fear, isolation, and loss are felt by all humans, and Pratt points out the irony of all human experience—the very ability to *feel* emotions can both ennoble and destroy.

In numerous other poems, Pratt constantly reinvigorates his theme by illustrating how man can be both elevated and demeaned by the qualities he cherishes most. In "The Shark," a speaker sees this "tubular" creature as the symbol of man's need to inhabit a world filled by creatures wholly other than man, for they are "cold-blooded." The very ability to perceive differences isolates man and adds to his fear and loneliness. In "From Stone to Steel," Pratt sees man's inherent urge to offer sacrifices as the supreme example both of man's noblest virtue and of his most ignominious vice. On the one hand, the sacrifice indicates a belief in something or someone higher than man, thereby leading humans to the grace of the temple. On the other hand, the urge to sacrifice may be abused, leading man to tyranny and barbarism, for man can also force others to *become* sacrificed.

In the lyrics, no emotion presented by Pratt is simple or clear-cut. In fact, he delights in tracing the complexities of emotions that all humans feel and experience, but can never explain or understand. When a reader turns to the longer narratives, he is again astounded by Pratt's mastery of a direct, clear story which, on careful reading, demands all of a reader's intelligence, sensibility, and emotion. The most notable of these narratives are "The Ice-Floes," *The Titanic*, *The Roosevelt and the Antinoe*, and *Brébeuf and His Brethren*. All of the narratives listed here share the quality of "documentary" realism. Pratt carefully researched and studied the materials for these poems, and one of their features is historical accuracy. The poems are, however, profound studies of human emotion. In each work, furthermore, Pratt concentrates on the interest of a community in crisis.

"The Ice-Floes" centers upon the Newfoundland seal-hunt. A group of hunters form the focus, although the events are recorded through one spokesman. The narrative concentrates on the dangers undertaken by the men in order that they may survive in a hostile environment. The very courage, determination, and relentlessness that they display, however, makes them the victims of the elements they are attempting to overcome. Staying too late and too long on the ice floes, wholly immersed in the challenge of their hunt, they become trapped by a sudden, violent storm. Like the seals they hunt, the men have become the victims of a force they cannot master. Their dogged endurance and determination has betrayed them.

In *The Titanic* and *The Roosevelt and the Antinoe*, Pratt again explores the need for courage, fidelity, and compassion. In *The Titanic*, he ruthlessly documents the sleep of human reason. The ship's machinery is believed to be infallible. The illusion that man can rival God by creating an unsinkable ship leads to *hubris*. The intelligence which can design the ocean liner fails to recognize that no human creation is perfect. The delusion holds to the end; man has created the very force that takes him to death at sea. In *The Roosevelt and the Antinoe*, the form of presentation is reversed. The captain of the ship perceives that success is based on the unpredictable toss of a wave and that no resource known to man can foretell the result. Without the courage to try, without the conviction that nature is fundamentally indifferent, Pratt's captain learns to understand, no human achievement is possible.

The final poem of interest in Pratt's series of documentary narratives is *Brébeuf and His Brethren*. The poem is acknowledged as his masterpiece in this vein. It presents the lives of the martyrs who brought the Christian faith to Canada and who eventually died at the hands of the Indians. The climax of the poem is crucial to an understanding of the whole. Brébeuf is violently tortured by the Indians, who celebrate his murder with a mock baptism and communion. Dying, Brébeuf must endure the abuse of the very religious rites that he has taught the Indians. The rituals which are to cleanse, ennoble, and enlighten the spirit merely allow the Indians to indulge in barbarism and brutality, culminating in cannibalism. The poem, then, echoes the ambiguous sacrifices of "From Stone to Steel" and indicates Pratt's ever-increasing sense of irony in human experience and action.

In the atomic age, far removed from the pioneers and early settlers, an age wherein the products of intelligence have given man reason to fear even the best in himself, Pratt is not foreign or incomprehensible or old-fashioned. The documentary narratives may appear traditional, but their philosophical outlook is extremely modern.

One further strand of Pratt's development should be discussed here, his *extravaganzas*: *The Witches' Brew*, *Titans* ("The Cachalot" and "The Great Feud"), *The Fable of the Goats*, and *Towards the Last Spike*. All of these works are characterized by wit, irony, and humor. Each is based on some kind of trial, and, by the end of every one of them, the reader's ability to master ambiguities, inconsistencies, and paradoxes is fully tested as well. In the *extravaganzas*, Pratt vigorously displays that no intuition or perception or theory about reality is adequate to explain the world that man inhabits. In *The Witches' Brew*, a tour de force about an alcoholic orgy among sea-creatures who are visited by an incongruous assemblage of theorizers about reality—from John Calvin to Immanuel Kant—no one, including the narrator, can explain the behavior of Tom, the rakish cat from Zanzibar. The cat is partly a creature of evolution and partly a creature derived from some magic spark, but once drunk he is brutal, callous, and dangerous. *The Witches' Brew* is a black comedy centering upon man's inexplicable beginnings and his intrinsic irrationality. No one in the poem, least of all Tom, can understand why he does the things he does, and not one of the wise shades can provide an answer.

In many ways the narrative is amusing, but it is equally terrifying, for Tom murders all of his kin in the course of the poem. At each turn of events, moreover, the reader questions why the cat should be compelled to destroy every warm-blooded creature in sight. Pratt seems to be drawing upon his eclectic education to dismiss theories of Christianity, science, philosophy, and evolution. The world, Pratt's *extravaganzas* insist, will not conform to the expectations, wishes, theories, or desires of man or creature.

Such a vision, however, should not be read as pessimism. For Pratt, the acknowledgement of human reason, is central because the admission compels men to rely on compassion, understanding, and mercy, rather than on theory or abstraction. Alexander Pope once expressed this notion by declaring that "a little knowledge is a dangerous thing"; Pratt would modify the line this way: the illusion that the quantity of knowledge can replace its quality is even more dangerous than the knowing of nothing at all.

In *Towards the Last Spike*, Pratt's last major narrative, he redevelops his *extravaganza* by muting its outrageousness. He now blends *extravaganza* and narrative to examine the history of the Canadian transcontinental railway. The final product is Pratt's most daring experiment, and, if it fails, it fails only in the sense that Pound's *Cantos* (1925-1972) dealing with John Adams may be said to have failed. The deliberate fragmentation, the mixture of history and invention, and the blend of the actual and the literary often tax the reader beyond endurance.

The poem is necessary, however, for a complete understanding of Pratt's aims as a poet. In *Towards the Last Spike*, Pratt wished to unify the various strands of his writing. The poem dramatizes what man can achieve with courage, compassion, and fidelity to the values that advance the ambitions of a culture. Pratt chooses for subject matter the forging of a railway line which, both metaphorically and literally, made a physical reality of a nation previously only dreamed of and talked about. It is, above all, a positive vision, although the poem is neither naïvely optimistic nor overly idealistic about human success in a world that is fundamentally *other* than sentient man. The universe cannot be conquered, controlled, or explained in Pratt's poetic vision, but man can be dignified by his actions. *Towards the Last Spike*, in a huge "Panorama," records Pratt's belief that man does not simply exist in a monstrous world, but that he is a being burdened with the awesome task of using his vision, courage, and endurance to accomplish the dreams with which he is, for some inexplicable reason, born. This constant determination to face the test is, for E. J. Pratt, man's central claim to dignity.

Ed Jewinsky

Other major works

SHORT FICTION: " 'Hooked': A Rocky Mountain Experience," 1914; "Golfomania," 1924.

NONFICTION: *Pauline Eschatology*, 1917; "Introduction," in *Moby Dick*, 1929; "Introduction," in *Under the Greenwood Tree*, 1937.

Bibliography

Bold, Alan, ed. *Longman Dictionary of Poets*. Harlow, England: Longman, 1985. A brief entry on Pratt mentions his work as an editor of *Canadian Poetry Magazine* from 1936 to 1943. Acknowledges Pratt as a major figure in poetry and praises his poem *The Titanic* for Pratt's ability to "combine narration with commentary."

Djwa, Sandra. *E. J. Pratt: The Evolutionary Vision*. Vancouver: Copp Clark, 1974. An authoritative and insightful study of Pratt and a must for scholars of his work. Particularly noteworthy is how Djwa delineates Pratt's views on the roles of fate and free will in determining human action. Especially informative is the section on how Pratt adapts his many sources for *The Titanic.*

Gingell, Susan. *E. J. Pratt on His Life and Poetry.* Toronto: University of Toronto Press, 1983. A valuable resource of Pratt's evaluation of his life and work from the mid-1920's to the 1950's. This volume provides much understanding about Pratt and his creative process. Included are two interviews Pratt gave on Canadian television in the 1950's. Gingell's introduction explores the nature of Pratt's commentaries on his work and appraises their value in terms of their literary and social context.

Pitt, David G. *E. J. Pratt: The Truant Years, 1882-1927.* Toronto: University of Toronto Press, 1984. A full-length biography of Pratt, highly recommended for Pratt's scholars. It is meticulously researched and contains plenty of biographical details to enhance understanding of Pratt's poems.

Vinson, James. *Great Writers of the English Language: Poets.* New York: St. Martin's Press, 1979. The entry on Pratt acknowledges that he is regarded as Canada's "pre-eminent narrative poet." Cites *Brébeuf and His Brethren* as his finest long narrative, an example of his ability to establish dramatic coherency in his verse. Notes also Pratt's preoccupation with primeval themes of conflict in his poems.

Wilson, Milton. *E. J. Pratt.* Canadian Writers. 2. Toronto: McClelland and Stewart, 1969. A concise but comprehensive literary criticism of Pratt's works, emphasizing his strength as a narrative poet. Discusses his shorter, more lyrical poems, his longer narratives, as well as the sea poems and *Brébeuf and His Brethren.*

F. T. PRINCE

Born: Kimberley, South Africa; September 13, 1912

Principal poetry

Poems, 1938; *Soldiers Bathing and Other Poems*, 1954; *The Stolen Heart*, 1957; *The Doors of Stone: Poems, 1938-1962*, 1963; *Memoirs in Oxford*, 1970; *Drypoints of the Hasidim*, 1975; *Afterword on Rupert Brooke*, 1976; *Collected Poems*, 1979 (includes *A Last Attachment*); *The Yüan Chên Variations*, 1981; *Later On*, 1983; *Walks in Rome*, 1987.

Other literary forms

F. T. Prince has written widely in addition to his poetry. Among his more important publications are *The Italian Element in Milton's Verse* (1954), *William Shakespeare: The Poems* (1963), and *The Study of Form and the Renewal of Poetry* (1964).

Achievements

Equally distinguished as poet and scholar, Prince brings to all of his work a formidable and wide-ranging intellect, an informed compassion, and a remarkable eloquence. In addition, his poetry demonstrates that he has a perfect ear. Never involved in "movements" in the politics of literature, he has sometimes seemed a lonely figure, yet other poets have always been aware of his quality and importance, and his dedication to his craft has been a signal influence on younger writers at times when contemporary work has seemed to have lost its way. A consummate craftsman, at home in free or fixed forms, he is almost unique in being able to place all of his learning at the service of his poetry.

His work has been recognized by the award of honorary doctorates in literature from both the University of Southampton and New York University, and he has been invited to visit many overseas universities.

Biography

Frank Templeton Prince was born in Kimberley, Cape Province, South Africa, where his father, Henry Prince, was a prosperous businessman in the diamond trade. His mother, Margaret Hetherington Prince, had been a teacher. Both parents were English. Prince was a sensitive and studious child. He already possessed keen powers of observation and an eye for detail which led to an early interest in painting. His mother's influence and the stories and poems she read to Prince and his sister encouraged the boy to write, and he was a poet from the age of fifteen.

After a short period in which he trained as an architect, Prince went to

England in 1931 and entered Balliol College, Oxford. He took a first-class honors degree in English in 1934. It is apparent that the move to Oxford was both important and inevitable, since the poet's sensibility and culture were, almost from the start, strongly European. He went up to Oxford already fluent in French and deeply read in French poetry. He supported this by reading Dante in Italian and by making several visits to Italy. He found the whole period of the Renaissance, and in particular its art, highly congenial.

A meeting with T. S. Eliot in 1934 probably led to the later inclusion of Prince's first collection, *Poems*, in the Faber and Faber poetry list in 1938. Eliot recognized Prince's ability as well by printing the younger poet's "An Epistle to a Patron" in the *Criterion*, which Eliot edited.

During 1934-1935, Prince was a Visiting Fellow at Princeton University, but he returned to London to work at the Royal Institute of International Affairs, an unlikely office for so apolitical a man. He was, however, writing, and a meeting with William Butler Yeats in 1937, when Prince traveled to Dublin to meet the great man, suggests that poetry held pride of place in his mind.

There is no acknowledgement in Prince's work at this point that Europe was on the point of war, but the poet was soon to be personally involved. He was commissioned into the Intelligence Corps of the British army in 1940, and sent to Bletchley Park. This was the Government Communications Centre, hardly a typical army environment. Men were allowed to wear civilian clothes, discipline was relaxed, and among the creative people involved there, many were not of the type to worry unduly about military correctness. The poet Vernon Watkins served there, as did the composer Daniel Jones, a friend of Dylan Thomas. Prince was at Bletchley Park until March, 1943, when he was posted to Cairo. Before leaving, he married Elizabeth Bush. There are two daughters of the marriage.

His time in Egypt, which lasted until 1944, gave Prince the experience which resulted in the writing of his best-known poem, "Soldiers Bathing." On his return, Prince spent several months as an interpreter in Italian prisoner-of-war camps in England before his demobilization.

In 1946, Prince began his academic career, being appointed lecturer in English at the University of Southampton, at that time a small university in an interesting city, which must have been a pleasant appointment for Prince. In any event, he stayed there for nearly thirty years, becoming eventually professor of English and, between 1962 and 1965, dean of the faculty of arts. It was there, moreover, that he wrote the great bulk of his postwar poetry. He was a Visiting Fellow of All Souls College, Oxford, in 1968, and Clark Lecturer at Cambridge in 1972.

His retirement from Southampton was unexpectedly early, but he continued to teach at universities abroad, among them Brandeis University in Boston and Washington University in St. Louis. This period allowed his American admirers, among them John Ashbery, to show their respect for his work and to assist in its dissemination.

Prince continues to have a permanent home in Southampton and, if he travels less frequently, continues to write.

Analysis

The *Collected Poems* of 1979 brought together all the early work from *Poems* and *Soldiers Bathing and Other Poems* which F. T. Prince wanted to retain. He also included the whole of *The Doors of Stone* and four long, late poems, *Memoirs in Oxford, Drypoints of the Hasidim, Afterword on Rupert Brooke,* and *A Last Attachment.* These poems may be safely considered the work by which Prince would wish to be judged.

The first poem is "An Epistle to a Patron," so admired by Eliot. When one recalls that the great young poet of the day was W. H. Auden and that the most admired poetry then was political and very aware of the contemporary world, Prince's lines are startling.

> My lord, hearing lately of your opulence in promises and your house
> Busy with parasites, of your hands full of favours, your statutes
> Admirable as music, and no fear of your arms not prospering, I have
> Considered how to serve you . . .

The reader is at once in Renaissance Italy, a period much favored by Prince and one in which he is at home. Yet, although the poem is written in the first person, it must not be assumed that the voice is Prince's voice. Rather, the poem is a dramatic monologue. It is not in the manner of Robert Browning either, although it moves in an area Browning sometimes occupied. Its splendid opulence, its sonorous and bewitching periods, are not like Browning. Nor do they hide the slyness, the mockery behind the flattery with which this postulant addresses his hoped-for patron. Ben Jonson could have written it, but it is a strange invention for the late 1930's. And if Prince uses the first person voice, as he does often throughout his career, rarely does he speak as himself—then he is a more everyday speaker altogether—but rather as a real resident of those times and places into which his learning and his curiosity have led him. His manner is courtly and aristocratic. If he uses, as he does in the opening lines of "To a Man on His Horse," a poetic inversion, it is for the dance of the statement, because he wants the movement:

> Only the Arab stallion will I
> Envy you. Along the water
> You dance him with the morning on his flanks . . .

The early work is full of such lines, stately, strangely out of time, full, too, of references to painters such as Paolo Veronese or statesmen such as Edmund Burke. It is a paradox when one realizes that Prince's most famous poem, "Soldiers Bathing," is not at all like the rest of the early work, that it is written about ordinary men, poor, bare, forked animals of the twentieth century. It gave Prince an immediate fame and is known to many readers who know nothing else the poet has written.

"Soldiers Bathing" is a poem of sixty-six lines, organized in six irregular verse paragraphs. The lines are not of regular length, and they rhyme in couplets. In it, the poet, an army officer, watches his men as, forgetting momentarily the stress and mire of war, they swim and play in the sea. It is often a clumsy poem, the longer second line of some of the couplets occasionally dragging along without grace, the structure and movement absurdly prosaic for a poet of Prince's skill. Yet it is intensely moving. The extraordinary syntax of the last line of the first stanza, so written, surely, to accommodate the rhyme, has been noted by many critics, particularly by Vernon Scannell in *Not Without Glory.* "Their flesh worn by the trade of war, revives/ And my mind towards the meaning of it strives." It is also, however, full of marvelous compassion, as Prince, recalling Michelangelo's cartoon of soldiers bathing, is able to unite friend and foe, dead and living soldiers, through his insight into the continuing folly of wars. He does this through his knowledge of art, but his own comfort comes from his religion. Prince is a Catholic, and the reader's understanding of his poetry is incomplete without this knowledge. He arrives at a sad conclusion: "Because to love is frightening we prefer/ The freedom of our crimes." He began the poem under "a reddening sky"; he ends it "while in the west/ I watch a streak of blood that might have issued from Christ's breast." This is a typical movement in a poem by Prince, one in which the plain and dissimilar elements are united in an understanding brought about by the poet's belief.

The great popularity of that fine poem tended to overshadow a number of poems which might more surely have suggested the nature and direction of Prince's gift. There were, for example, some love poems of great beauty and passion. He was to develop this ability until, in July, 1963, an anonymous reviewer in *The Times Literary Supplement* could write of Prince that he is "one of the best love poets of the age, a lyricist of great charm and tenderness and emotion, counter-balanced by a subtlety of thought and metaphor which often reminds one of Donne. . . . " The reference to John Donne is felicitous, since there is an affinity in the work of these men, brought into even clearer focus by Prince's liking for and familiarity with the seventeenth century.

The Doors of Stone, then, contains poems of all the categories noted so far: monologues such as "Campanella" and "Strafford," love poems such as the eighteen sections of "Strombotti," poems suggested, like "Coeur de Lion," by history. They demonstrate once again the curious, elusive quality of Prince's poetry; it possesses dignity, honesty, even directness, yet the poet himself remains aloof, often behind masks.

Almost as a rebuff to that opinion, Prince's next book was a long auto-biographical poem, *Memoirs in Oxford*. Written in a verse form suggested by the one Percy Bysshe Shelley used in *Peter Bell the Third* (1839), it is at once chatty, clever, and revealing. It is particularly helpful about the poet's early life. It is also a delightful and accomplished poem—and a very brave one. To write a long poem in these days is unusual; to abandon what seems to be one's natural gift for eloquence and adopt a different tone altogether in which to write a long poem might seem foolhardy. Yet it is a very successful poem, having the virtues of clarity, wit, and style as well as some of the attraction of a good novel.

Prince's father was of partly Jewish extraction, which might account for his interest in those "Dark hollow faces under caps/ In days and lands of exile . . . and among unlettered tribes" which figured so strongly in his next long poem, *Drypoints of the Hasidim*. Hasidism was a popular Jewish religious movement of the eighteenth and nineteenth centuries, and Prince's poem is a long meditation on the beliefs of this movement. Despite its learning, it is extremely clear, like all of Prince's poetry. Rarely can there have been a poet so scholarly and knowledgeable whose verse is so accessible.

As if to emphasize his virtuosity, Prince's next work is a verse reconstruction of the life and times of Rupert Brooke, the young and handsome poet whose early death in World War I assured him of fame. Using the information provided by Christopher Hassall in his biography of Brooke, Prince wrote from his own standpoint of "the damned successful poet" and also added, years after his own war, a commentary on youth and love and the ironies of war. The texture of these lines is far removed from the great splendors of the young Frank Prince:

> But Bryn quite blatantly prefers
> Walking alone on Exmoor to the drawing-room
> With the Ranee, and she finds all the girls so odd . . .

It does, however, contain a real feeling of the times, despite occasional prosiness.

Prince has never been afraid of the long poem; even as a young man, he wrote pieces of unusual length for modern times. *A Last Attachment* is based on Laurence Sterne's *Journal to Eliza* (1904). Shorter than the two poems previously noted, it once again considers the recurring problems which are central to Prince's preoccupations: love, the onset of age, an inability to settle and be content, jealousy, the triumphs and failures of the creative and artistic life—all great problems, glanced at, too, in *The Yüan Chên Variations*. They are problems that no doubt beset Prince himself, but he has chosen with dignity and objectivity to consider them most often through a series of characters taken from literature or history or art, rather than use direct personal experience. He has written of them all with elegance and seriousness and with great skill and honesty. His poetry is sometimes said to be unfashionable, and so it is if the word means that he belongs to no group, is determined to be his own man. He has always commanded the respect of his fellow poets, and that, very probably, is a guarantee of his importance and his growing stature.

Leslie Norris

Other major works

NONFICTION: *The Italian Element in Milton's Verse*, 1954; *William Shakespeare: The Poems*, 1963; *The Study of Form and the Renewal of Poetry*, 1964.

TRANSLATION: *Sir Thomas Wyatt*, 1961 (of Sergio Baldi's biography).

Bibliography

Davie, Donald. "Beyond the Here and Now." *The New York Times Book Review*, April 8, 1979, 13, 43. In reviewing *Collected Poems*, Davie notes that Prince has done nothing as fine as "Soldiers Bathing," considered one of the best poems to come out of World War II. He criticizes Prince for not "giving us what we ask for," although he concedes that *Collected Poems* will be well liked.

Levi, Peter. "F. T. Prince." *Agenda* 15 (Summer/Autumn, 1977): 147-149. An appreciative review of Prince, commending him for his craftsmanship. Levi calls him a distinguished poet and scholar, one who is both intelligent and curious. Reviews *Drypoints of the Hasidim* and discusses the iambic pentameter verse and the allusive stories that form a complete sequence of the history of Hasidism.

Nigam, Alka. *F. T. Prince: A Study of His Poetry.* Salzburg, Austria: Institut fur Anglistik and Amerikanstik, 1983. In the foreword, Prince himself praises Nigam for her "careful and sensitive" study of his poetry. In this full-length study, Nigam analyzes Prince's art and vision, including a historical background of his poetry and its place in twentieth century verse. Contains solid literary criticism. A must for Prince scholars.

Stanford, Donald E., ed. *Dictionary of Literary Biography.* Vol. 20 in *British Poets, 1914-1945.* Detroit: Gale Research, 1983. Stanford acknowledges the praise for Prince by other poets and cites Prince's lyrical talent as being as fine as the most accomplished of modern poets. Discusses Prince's excursions to Italy, his association with T. S. Eliot, and his meeting with William Butler Yeats, who influenced his work. In evaluating Prince's work since 1970, Stanford notes that he is the finest living poet writing in metric forms.

Vinson, James, and D. L. Kirkpatrick, eds. *Contemporary Poets.* 4th ed. New York: St. Martin's Press, 1985. Lists his academic accomplishments and publications, as well as selected secondary sources. Mentions the Leonardo and Michelangelo poems as well as the classic "Soldiers Bathing," commenting on its effect on the reader that is both "urgent and poignant." Notes that it is the specialist who will go on to read Prince's works other than "Soldiers Bathing."

MATTHEW PRIOR

Born: Wimborne, England; July 21, 1664
Died: Wimpole, England; September 18, 1721

Principal poetry

A Satyr on the Modern Translators, 1685; *Satyr on the Poets: In Imitation of the Seventh Satyr of Juvenal*, 1687; *An English Ballad*, 1695; *Carmen Saeculare, For the Year 1700. To the King*, 1700; *Poems on Several Occasions*, 1707, 1709; *Solomon on the Vanity of the World*, 1718; *Lyric Poems*, 1741.

Other literary forms

Matthew Prior is primarily known for his poetry.

Achievements

Matthew Prior does not have the literary stature of his contemporaries Alexander Pope or John Dryden, but he is probably the foremost "Augustan" poet after them. Augustan poetry takes its name from the Rome of Caesar Augustus, patron of the arts, with whose values many English poets of the late seventeenth and eighteenth centuries felt a special kinship. One way for a poet to establish his ties with ancient Rome was to write the kinds of poetry that the Romans wrote; a hierarchy of such kinds or genres in art had existed since the Renaissance. Prior wrote in all of them except epic poetry, which stood at the pinnacle of the hierarchy and was the form which Dryden and Pope so brilliantly exploited satirically. Prior's strength was in some of the lesser genres, including odes, pastorals, verse narratives, epigrams, satires, verse essays, elegies, and epitaphs. According to the British *Dictionary of National Biography*, Prior "is one of the neatest of English epigrammatists, and in occasional pieces and familiar verses has no rival in English." Samuel Johnson, the dominant literary figure of the later eighteenth century, wrote that Prior's "diligence has placed him amongst the most correct of the English poets; and he was one of the first that resolutely endeavored at correctness." Prior may not have possessed the force of Dryden or the penetrating vision of Pope, but he achieved an elegance seldom matched by poets of any age.

Biography

Matthew Prior, born July 21, 1664, was himself aware of his limitations as a poet. In his "Essay on Learning," he observes: "I had two Accidents in Youth which hindred me from being quite possest with the Muse." One was the accident of his education. He had been singularly fortunate, as the son of a laborer, to have been assisting in his uncle's tavern one day when Lord Dorset found him reading Horace and asked him to turn an ode into English. Impressed with the result, Dorset undertook to provide for Prior's subsequent education. Advantageous as this sponsorship proved, Prior lamented that he was "bred in a Colledge where prose was more in fashion than Verse . . . so that Poetry which by the bent of my Mind might have become the business of my Life, was by the Happyness of my Education only the Amusement of it." The other accident of youth was, likewise, a form of success in activities other than writing poetry. As secretary to the newly appointed ambassador to The Hague for King William in 1691, Prior showed such political and business aptitude that he found himself serving in various diplomatic roles over the next twenty-two years, including negotiator for the Treaty of Utrecht in 1711-1712, a treaty that would become popularly known—especially among Queen Anne's Whig opposition—as "Matt's Peace."

When the Queen died in 1714 and the Whigs assumed power, Prior found himself under house arrest. His friends came to his financial rescue after his release in 1716, and Lord Harley helped Prior purchase Down Hall, whose condition he joked about in one of his last poems: "Oh! now a low, ruined white shed I descern/ Until'd, and unglaz'd, I believe 'tis a barn." After some rebuilding under the direction of the architect James Gibbs, however, Prior was able to spend his last years, like Horace on his Sabine Farm, in rural retirement. Prior died while visiting Lord Harley in 1721, equally famous for his political career as for his poetic one. Even if he was not the foremost poet of his age, Prior is to be admired as a late Renaissance embodiment of the "universal man," a statesman and a poet.

Analysis

Prior's political and poetical interests served each other well when special events called for panegyrical poems. Much of Prior's early poetry is of this kind. His first published poem was an ode, "On the Coronation of the Most August Monarch K. James II, and Queen Mary. The 23rd. of April, 1685." Prior writes that he cannot prevent his fancy from imagining the king, rowing up the Thames with his company, to be crowned. Prior compares the impending arrival with Jason's when he bore the golden fleece back to Greece, with the rising of the sun, with a Roman triumph, and with the first coming of Christ. The urge to draw such analogies was typical of Augustan poets, but to do so in praise of the king was to risk seeming self-serving, if not obsequious. Indeed, many writers of birthday odes to the king or queen were exactly that. Prior avoids the trap by framing his praise as a flight of fancy, as a prompting of his soul which he cannot restrain as he anticipates the event.

Prior's poems of praise do not always take the stricter poetic forms that the term "ode" may imply. His 565-line poem to the king, *Carmen Saeculare, For the Year 1700. To the King*, is in rhymed quatrains, or linked pairs of couplets. In 1695, he wrote a ballad to celebrate the English recapture of Namur from France, a poem that mocks a French "victory" poem of 1692, stanza by stanza.

Perhaps the best example of Prior's ability to carry off a difficult task with elegance is his poem "To a Child of Quality of Five Years Old: The Author suppos'd Forty." To write a poem praising the child of a nobleman (the Earl of Jersey) is to risk sentimentality, if not fulsomeness. Prior amuses his readers by amusing himself with the idea that an age difference will always separate this girl from him. He can lament her indifference now, as if he were a Petrarchan lover, and at the same time describe the reality of seeing his verses used to curl her doll's hair. His regrets are not wholly contrived since, trapped by old age, Prior will indeed "be past making love,/ When she begins to comprehend it." Unlike the occasional poems, of little interest today, this lyrical ode reveals Prior's ability to bring freshness to a potentially tedious subject and to execute a difficult task with grace.

Prior wrote numerous love poems which in their use of artificial diction, their shepherds and shepherdesses, and their imaginary, timeless, deity-inhabited landscape of Arcadia, are pastoral. In the last of a sequence of poems about Cloe, his mistress in these poems, he calls their dispute a "Pastoral War"; she is no milkmaid, however, and Prior's pastorals are personal lyrics as well as exercises within this conventional genre. Prior implies his regard for his mistress, Cloe, in traditional ways: Cupid mistakes Venus for Cloe and shoots his mother, or Venus mistakes a picture of Cloe for one of herself. In "Cloe Hunting," Apollo mistakes her for his sister Cynthia, only to be chided by Cupid.

In later poems to Cloe, however, the pastoral setting becomes less important, while the relation between Prior and Cloe becomes less convention-bound and more psychologically interesting. In "A Lover's Anger," Prior begins peevishly to chide Cloe for being two hours late. Cloe protests that a rosebud has fallen into her dress and invites him to look at the mark it has made on her breast. Prior looks and immediately forgets what he had been about to say, having been drawn from the world of watches and missed appointments into her innocent paradise, where one need worry only about love and, occasionally, a falling rosebud. Clearly, however, the pastoral condition is a temporary and imaginary refuge from the real world, which also exists in the poem. In "Cloe Jealous," Prior's beloved is no longer content to believe in the "pastoral" world that idealized their relationship. Although at first Cloe pretends to weep for "Two poor stragling Sheep," she quickly reveals that she really worries that she is losing her beauty. Prior's "Answer to Cloe Jealous, in the same Stile. The Author sick" avoids her concerns as he describes himself as a dying shepherd, never more to torment her with jealousy. "A Better Answer," he decides, is to treat her as an equal, to flatter her into accepting his infidelities as mere "Art," whereas his "Nature" is to love Cloe best. "I court others in Verse; but I love Thee in Prose," he adds, neglecting to point out that this very answer is another set of verse fabrications. This is one of Prior's most delightful poems, and one that pushes the Cloe series of love lyrics beyond the ordinary limits of its convention; "A Better

Answer" both assumes and undercuts the pastoral tradition, while, at the same time, the poem reasserts it.

Prior is perhaps less successful as a storyteller than he is as a lyricist. The best-told of his ribald tales is "Hans Carvel," the Rabelaisian story of a man who, "Impotent and Old,/ Married a Lass of LONDON Mould." Hans contracts with Satan (in the shape of a lawyer) to restrain his wife's social activities. In solving his problem, Hans finds that the devilish joke is on him, in an ending that Samuel Johnson accurately describes as "not over-decent." By contrast, "Henry and Emma: A Poem, Upon the Model of the Nut-brown Maid," is a moral tale. Most readers agree that the testing of Emma by Henry, who pretends to be leaving for a life of exile to see whether she will accompany him, makes both characters unsympathetic. The possibility exists that Prior meant the poem to be an ironic adaptation, a mocking of the fidelity endorsed in the original, but the evidence for this reading is thin. In either case, Johnson's charge that the dialogue is "dull and tedious" cannot be refuted.

There can be little disputing Prior's excellence as a writer of epigrams, or short verses with a surprising turn or insight. His best known epigram he calls "A True Maid": "No, no; for my Virginity,/ When I lose that, says ROSE, I'll dye:/ Behind the Elmes, last night, cry'd DICK/ Rose, were You not extreamly Sick?" An epigram of unknown date pushes a philosophical commonplace to a very unphilosophical conclusion: "RISE not till Noon, if Life be but a Dream,/ As Greek and Roman Poets have Exprest:/ Add good Example to so grave a Theme,/ For he who Sleeps the longest lives the best." Epigrams have been described as having a sting in the tail, and Prior's sting is sharp enough to lead one to wonder whether he had a natural bent for satire that his political interests led him to restrict.

Prior did write some satires on nonpolitical subjects. One of his earliest poems is *A Satyr on the Modern Translators*, on John Dryden in particular for his translation of Ovid's *Epistles* (1681-1683). In a letter, Prior objects: "Our Laureate might in good manners have left the version of Latin authors to those who had the happiness to understand them." Imitations of the Roman literati, on the other hand, were not an abuse of their work but rather an almost obligatory exercise. For example, Prior wrote *Satyr on the Poets: In Imitation of the Seventh Satyr of Juvenal*. Perhaps Prior's most original piece is "Alma: Or, The Progress of the Mind," which he wrote while under arrest in 1715-1716. Johnson found the poem in need of a design, while others have argued that Pyrrhonism unifies it. Satire, however, is traditionally loose in its structure, and "Alma" is surely a satire on intellectual systems. The poem's main speaker is Matt, a system-builder. The poem was inspired by *Hudibras* (Part I, 1663; Part II, 1664; Part III, 1678) Prior says, and Matt's less learned companion, Dick, like Ralpho or Don Quixote's Sancho Panza, is not readily impressed by Matt's ethereal notions. The soul or mind, poetically termed "Alma," Matt explains, sits in judgment over the testimony of the senses. He goes on to develop a theory that the mind enters the toes at birth, makes its way to the midsection by adulthood, and causes the enmity and senility of later age when it rises from the seat of action to the head, from which it escapes—ever upward—at death. Dick questions Matt, usually to be put in his place, but Dick does have the last say in the last stanza, where he rejects this sort of wisdom in favor of folly—and calls for a bottle of wine. When one considers the satire of Prior's friend Jonathan Swift in *The Mechanical Operation of the Spirit* (1710), one senses the limits of Prior's explorations as a satirist. Nevertheless, "Alma" is original enough to be of considerable historical interest.

The poem that Prior believed he would be remembered for is *Solomon on the Vanity of the World*, his longest poem, in which Solomon examines knowledge, pleasure, and power, in turn, as sources of human happiness. Not surprisingly, since texts from Ecclesiastes precede each section, Solomon concludes that all human endeavor is vain. Before he submits to the will of his Creator, however, Solomon reflects at length, and even at their best the reflections are disappointing. Book II, for example, opens with the building of a palace and garden, as grand as wealth can provide. There is no ironic edge to the description, which might have made Solomon's folly more evident; instead, the expensive undertaking sounds very magnificent and Solomon's sudden change of attitude—"I came, beheld, admir'd, reflected, griev'd"— seems unmotivated. Everyone has experienced a sense of "the Work perfected, the Joy was past," but one hopes for more than commonplaces, or at least for more pleasure in the weaving of a fabric on which the commonplaces can be stitched, in a poem of 2,652 lines.

Epitaphs are meant for tombstones, and Prior composed them throughout his career, from his "An Epitaph on True, her Majesty's Dog," in 1693, to a surprisingly long one for his own tomb in the Poets' Corner of Westminster Abbey. Elegies are about loss, and when they are about a specific death they become occasional poems. One of Prior's best poems is his verse portrait "Jinny the Just," about a recently deceased serving woman whom he describes as "the best Wench in the Nation." She is "just" in that she is naturally moderate, "between the Coquette, and the Prude." In one stanza (of thirty-five), Prior seems to capture the essence of a lifetime: "While she read and accounted and pay'd and abated/ Eat and Drank, play'd and work't, laught and cry'd, lov'd and hated/ As answer'd the End of her being created." Jinny actually existed, though her identity has never been discovered. She is assumed to have been Prior's mistress for a time, and Prior's lifelong preference for women of the lower classes seemed evidence, to his friends, of Prior's own humble origins. Prior never married.

Prior wrote in other genres as well, from verse epistles and songs to prologues and epilogues for plays. Indeed, there is virtually no kind of poem that he did not attempt, with the exception of the epic. His age expected such versatility from a serious poet, and it regarded him as one of its best. Even if today's readers have relegated him to the second rank, they must acknowledge his virtuosity.

James R. Aubrey

Other major works

SHORT FICTION: *Dialogues of the Dead*, 1721.

MISCELLANEOUS: *The Literary Works of Matthew Prior*, 1959 (H. Bunker Wright and Monroe K. Spears, editors).

Bibliography

Eves, Charles K. *Matthew Prior: Poet and Diplomatist*. New York: Columbia University Press, 1939. Prior's uncommonly rich life will probably always be more interesting than his poetry, and Eves's biography remains the best modern treatment of that life. Well written and still useful, especially when combined with Frances Mayhew Rippy's Twayne entry.

Kline, Richard B. "Tory Prior and Whig Steele: A Measure of Success?" *Studies in English Literature* 9 (Summer, 1969): 427-437. Any evaluation of Prior's poetry must recognize the intensely active role that politics played in his life and work. By pairing Prior with the redoubtable Whig Sir Richard Steele, Kline provides a nice sense of the complex political climate of the late seventeenth and early eighteenth centuries.

Rippy, Frances Mayhew. *Matthew Prior*. New York: Twayne, 1986. This is the single best assessment of Prior's life and work, and, given the paucity of critical materials, an invaluable source book. Follows the Twayne format in providing a biography, critical evaluations of the major works, and an attempt to "contextulize" Prior. Includes a chronology and a bibliography.

Sitter, John. "About Wit: Locke, Addison, Prior, and the Order of Things." *Rhetorics of Order/Ordering of Rhetorics in English Neoclassical Literature*, edited by J. Douglas Canfield and J. Paul Hunter. Newark: University of Delaware Press, 1989. A very nice attempt to place Prior within the early neoclassical tradition—a tradition influenced as much by the empiricist philosophy of Locke as by the "classics."

Spears, Monroe K. "Some Ethical Aspects of Matthew Prior's Poetry." *Studies in Philology* 45 (October, 1948): 606-629. This is one of three essays on Prior published by Spears in 1948. ("Matthew Prior's Attitude Toward Natural Science" appeared in *Publications of the Modern Language Society* 63, June: 485-507, and "Matthew Prior's Religion" in *Philological Quarterly* 27, April: 159-180). Taken together, these provide an excellent context within which to read Prior's work.

FRANCIS QUARLES

Born: Romford, England; 1592
Died: London, England; September 8, 1644

Principal poetry

A Feast for Wormes Set Forth in a Poeme of the History of Jonah, 1620; *Pentelogia: Or, The Quintessence of Meditation,* 1620 (appended to *A Feast for Wormes*), 1626 (published as a separate chapbook); *Hadassa: Or, The History of Queene Ester,* 1621; *Job Militant, with Meditations Divine and Morall,* 1624; *Sions Elegies, Wept by Jeremie the Prophet,* 1624; *An Alphabet of Elegies Upon the Much and Truly Lamented Death of . . . Doctor Ailmer,* 1625; *Sions Sonets Sung by Solomon the King,* 1624; *Argalus and Parthenia,* 1629; *The Historie of Samson,* 1631; *Divine Fancies: Digested into Epigrammes, Meditations, and Observations,* 1632 (in four books); *Divine Poems,* 1633; *Emblemes: Divine and Moral,* 1635 (in five books); *Hieroglyphikes of the Life of Man,* 1638; *Solomons Recantation, Entituled Ecclesiastes Paraphrased,* 1645; *The Shepheards Oracles: Delivered in Certain Eglogues,* 1646; *Hosanna: Or, Divine Poems on the Passion of Christ,* 1647.

Other literary forms

In later life Francis Quarles published a pious work in prose called *Enchiridion, Containing Institutions Divine and Moral* (1640). This very popular collection of aphorisms on religious and ethical subjects was reissued in an expanded edition the year after its original publication. It is notable for its stylish phrasing and wordplay.

Always strongly royalist in his sympathies, Quarles produced several prose works of a political nature toward the end of his life, as the struggle between king and Commons became more pronounced. *Observations Concerning Princes and States Upon Peace and Warre* (1642) may perhaps be grouped with such works; although it is essentially another collection of pious meditations, it had obvious political implications in such volatile times, similar to those of the poetry in *The Shepheards Oracles.* More explicitly polemical is *The Loyal Convert* (1644), a defense of the king's political and religious position. Of a like nature are *The Whipper Whipt* (1644) and *The New Distemper* (c. 1644). The three royalist polemics were republished under the collective title *The Profest Royalist in His Quarrell with the Times* (1645) shortly after the author's death.

Among Quarles' other posthumous publications are *Judgement and Mercy for Afflicted Soules: Or, Meditations, Soliloquies, and Prayers* (1646; an unauthorized and inaccurate edition of Part II of this work had been published in 1644 under the title *Barnabas and Boanerges: Or, Wine and Oyl for Afflicted Soules*). *Judgement and Mercy for Afflicted Soules* is a book of prose meditations which would today probably be classified as prose poems. Also among the posthumous works, and somewhat surprisingly, is a play—or rather an interlude or masque—called *The Virgin Widow: A Comedie* (1649, written in 1641 or 1642). This comedy in mixed prose and verse is less amusing than it might have been, overwhelmed as it is by its strong didactic purpose and allegorical framework.

Achievements

Nowhere in literary history is the fickleness of fashion more clearly illustrated than in the case of Quarles. As Horace Walpole, looking back on the earlier period from the vantage point of 1757, aptly observed in a letter to George Montagu, "Milton was forced to wait till the world had done admiring Quarles." In the century of William Shakespeare, John Donne, Ben Jonson, Robert Herrick, George Herbert, John Milton, Richard Crashaw, Andrew Marvell, Henry Vaughan, and John Dryden, Quarles was by far the most popular poet.

The success of Quarles in his own day can be explained in relation to those very weaknesses which deny him an audience today and mark his productions as mere historical curiosities, for Quarles had a special genius for popularization. His objective throughout his career was to reach a wide audience with an uplifting message. In this objective—so unlike Milton's appeal to a "fit audience though few"—he succeeded as few authors have; yet his success is exactly analogous to the success of a contemporary poet such as Rod McKuen. The difference is only that the seventeenth century was profoundly moved by religious and political emotions, whereas in contemporary society it is romantic love alone that can fire the imagination of the general public.

Biography

Francis Quarles was a younger son of an old gentry family settled in Essex. He was born in 1592 at his father's manor of Stewards at Romford and baptized on May 8 of the same year. One of his sisters became by marriage an aunt of the poet Dryden. Quarles attended Christ's College, Cambridge, receiving the degree of B.A. in 1608 while still in his teens. Afterwards he spent some time at Lincoln's Inn studying law, although there is no indication that he ever pursued the law as a profession. In 1613 he embarked on what promised to be a career as a courtier with an appointment as Cup-Bearer to Princess Elizabeth on her marriage to Frederick V, Elector of the Palatinate. Quarles accompanied the couple to Germany, but he had returned to England before the terrible reversal of their fortunes in 1620, when the armies of the Emperor expelled them from Bohemia, where Frederick had served briefly as elective king.

Back in England, Quarles married Ursula Woodgate on May 28, 1618. He and his wife had eighteen children. The eldest son, John, grew up to become a minor poet in his own right. It was shortly after his marriage that Quarles began publishing poetry, and numerous volumes of his biblical paraphrases and other religious poems issued from the press in rapid succession.

As a result of a reputation for piety that grew as each new volume was published, Quarles was offered the post of private secretary to James Ussher, then Bishop of Meath, later Anglican Archbishop of Armagh and Primate of Ireland. Quarles and his whole family lived in Ussher's episcopal palace in Dublin. Ussher is remembered as the author of a biblical chronology cited by fundamentalists in their rejection of the theory of evolution, and he was helped in his historical researches by Quarles. Yet curiously it was during this period that Quarles published his first secular work, *Argalus and Parthenia*.

Retiring to Essex, Quarles spent several years preparing his next work for publication. This was *Emblemes*, the volume which brought him his greatest fame. It was an immediate and enormous success, which Quarles followed up a few years later by issuing another volume in a similar vein, *Hieroglyphikes of the Life of Man*. This was the last book of his poetry published during his lifetime; during the remaining years of his life, however, he did publish occasional elegies as chapbooks.

In 1639 Quarles was appointed to succeed the playwright Thomas Middleton in the largely ceremonial office of Chronologer to the City of London. Taking up his residence in London, he thereafter devoted himself to prose composition. In addition to an extremely popular manual of piety, as the political situation worsened he also began writing polemical tracts in defense of the king's policies. With these he became politically suspect to the Parliamentarians despite the continued attraction his poetry had for the whole Puritan party. The Parliamentary army searched his library, and manuscripts are said to have been burned. If any of his manuscripts were destroyed at the time, they must have been of a political nature, since after his death in 1644 his widow published a number of works of various other sorts, including a play and religious works in both prose and verse.

Analysis

Francis Quarles was not an innovator. Most of his works are in genres which were already riding a wave of popularity when he wrote—in fact, genres that had just become popular. He had a special knack for seeing the basic principles governing such genres and for creating works that adhered to these aesthetic principles with stark simplicity and without deep-felt personal involvement of the sort that is now regarded as the hallmark of, for example, the Metaphysical poets, the poets among Quarles' fellows who have enjoyed the highest critical prestige in the twentieth century. Of course, it is not to be doubted that Quarles had deeply felt religious and political beliefs, but the popular success he enjoyed in his own day was a direct consequence of his inability to express more than surface impressions and clichés—or, to

put the most positive face on his achievement—of his willingness to circum-
scribe his literary compositions by those surface impressions and clichés that
express the popular imagination. It was with considerable truth that in the
second half of the seventeenth century an antiquary described Quarles as
"the sometime darling of our plebeian judgment."

Quarles' popularization of the emblem is of great historical interest. The
enormous sales of emblem books in the seventeenth century are at first hard
to understand. Certainly the special attraction of such works for the Puritans
was as an alternative to the images that their religious beliefs proscribed inside
churches, and Quarles was phenomenally popular with this group despite his
avowed royalism and his support of episcopacy. For other readers, emblems
were expressions of the fashionable baroque sensibility.

Emblems are, indeed, more important to the history of poetry than the
fleeting popularity of emblem books during the seventeenth century would
suggest. The emblematic frame of mind was fundamental to the age, informing
many of the works of its major poets, and especially those of such Meta-
physicals as Herbert. In fact, to understand Metaphysical imagery it is necessary to know something of the emblem tradition. Quarles' abiding historical
significance is as the exemplary writer of emblem books. It is, however,
important to remember that the works of Quarles always illustrate and synthesize trends; they capitalize on rather than inaugurate fashions. Herbert
wrote emblematically but not because he had read Quarles. It was Quarles
who read—and in his way popularized—Herbert. Although Herbert was certainly influenced by emblem books, Quarles' own emblem books were not
published until after Herbert's death.

The art of the emblem consists of the successful marshaling of three things:
a motto or scriptural text, a picture, and a poem or epigram. Emblem books
had been published in English before Quarles, but his were the first English
emblem books to be based exclusively on biblical texts, even though similar
Continental works had been circulating and their popularity with English
audiences had, in fact, inspired Quarles to produce his works. The shift in
popularity from secular to religious emblems at the end of the sixteenth
century has been chronicled by Mario Praz.

The emblem poet chooses a motto; he commissions an engraving to provide
a literalist illustration of the motto; but from the modern point of view he
creates only the epigram commenting on the significance of the motto and
making use of the imagery of the picture. In the case of *Emblemes* and
Hieroglyphikes of the Life of Man, Quarles' contribution was, in fact, somewhat less. According to Gordon S. Haight, all but ten of the mottoes and
illustrations in *Emblemes*, for example, were derived from two Continental
emblem books, although the illustrations were redrawn and newly engraved—
in somewhat less than inspired fashion. Quarles' poems in *Emblemes* are not,
however, mere translations of the anonymous *Typus Mundi* (1629, *Image of*

the World) and of Herman Hugo's *Pia Desideria* (1624, *Holy Cravings*). As Rosemary Freeman points out, the similarities between Quarles' emblem poems and those of his sources are for the most part only such as inevitably occur when two authors treat the same subject.

In fact, Quarles' poems tend to overwhelm his illustrations and take on a life beyond the scope of true emblems. The poor quality of the engravings aside, Pope's jibe in *The Dunciad* (1728-1743) that "the pictures for the page atone," that "Quarles is sav'd by beauties not his own," is thus somewhat wide of the mark. Poetry so interrelated with illustration could not, of course, retain its popularity when fashions in the visual arts changed.

Quarles nevertheless achieved some critical respectability in the nineteenth century as a result of his skillful metrics. Since then, fashions in content have changed. Indeed, the bizarre imagery of Quarles' emblem illustrations is probably more in tune with contemporary taste than are his religious values. The chief recommendation of Quarles' emblem poetry today is its metrical control and variety. Although the diction is sometimes questionable and the subject matter is usually conventional, at least in these emblem poems Quarles did not hobble himself even further by restricting his verse to the couplet.

The poems of *Emblemes* chronicle the troubled relationship of Anima, the soul, and Divine Love, pictured throughout as the Infant Jesus. The poems of *Hieroglyphikes of the Life of Man*, a shorter volume utilizing a somewhat wider range of verse forms, belabor the image of a candle to illustrate the workings of God's grace.

The systematic practice of meditation was a popular pursuit in the seventeenth century, and works of devotion based on principles of meditation, as Helen C. White has shown, were popular reading matter in a way that transcended sectarian interests. In fact, the two standard guidebooks of meditative technique in Protestant England were by Roman Catholics. Quarles' works in the meditation genre are in the tradition of *The Spiritual Exercises* (1548) of St. Ignatius Loyola, which emphasize an initial composition of place (a descriptive setting of the scene), rather than in the tradition of St. Francis de Sales, whose recommendation of sensuous immediacy was so influential with the Metaphysical poets.

Often described by Quarles simply as biblical paraphrases, his meditations typically deal with material from the historical books of the Old Testament. As a result, while the meditations of Donne and Thomas Traherne can still be appreciated for their powerful personal involvement with salvation and while the meditative poems of Richard Crashaw can still overwhelm modern readers with their sensuousness, the meditations of Quarles now seem to be simply quaint—to be merely decorative distortions of the compelling simplicities of biblical chronicle. *A Feast for Wormes, Hadassa, Job Militant,* and *The Historie of Samson* are works in this vein. In *The Historie of Samson,* in particular, Quarles seems to miss the spiritual and even the dramatic point of the story (so effectively retold by Milton) when he devotes seven times as much space to the woman of Timnath as to the final destruction of the Philistines.

Leaving Old Testament material and turning to the Passion and Death of Christ for material in *Pentelogia* and *Hosanna*, Quarles is no more successful. He tends to moralize a scene rather than to evoke it, and his work is at best uneven, showing lapses of taste and diction as, indeed, Grosart—Quarles' warmest appreciator—admits. The purely analytic and contemplative sections that follow the explicit paraphrases in all the works of this group, however, contribute to meditative objectives in a more consistent way. Quarles usually writes in couplets, and the analytic sections in particular occasionally achieve some of the grace and lucidity of Alexander Pope.

In fact, the best of Quarles' work ostensibly in the meditative genre is in the *Divine Fancies*, a book which uses meditative technique very impressionistically. In the *Divine Fancies* Quarles moves into explicit epigram, a more congenial format for couplets since it is the nature of epigram to be pointed, biting, limited. The epigrams of *Divine Fancies* are also essentially argumentative rather than devotional and thus really not meditative in tone. They frequently summarize in a few terse lines some point of catechism, but they have no poetic resonance. In fact, despite W. K. Jordan's description of Quarles as an early advocate of a kind of religious toleration, these epigrams reveal a considerable narrowness of spirit on points of sectarian dispute, especially those concerning church discipline.

Another popular form which Quarles adapted was the pastoral. Pastoral works are descriptions of the lives of shepherds by people who know a great deal about poetic technique but very little about sheep. The object is to create an idealized world beyond the distractions of this world. Secular pastoral does so chiefly to provide enjoyment; works in this genre are romances. Religious pastoral does so to promote understanding of spiritual realities. Quarles works in both genres.

Argalus and Parthenia, his secular pastoral, is a versification of Sir Philip Sidney's *Arcadia* (1590). While usefully circumscribing the wild richness of Sidney's interminable prose romance, Quarles unwisely chooses his favorite verse form, the couplet, for this work. Couplets easily become tedious in a long narrative work unless the constant rhymes can be given a satirical point, as in *The Rape of the Lock* (1712, 1714) by Alexander Pope or *Hudibras* (1663, 1664, 1678) by Samuel Butler, but, even though Quarles substitutes for Sidney's engaging gaiety a tone of cool detachment, he fails to take the further step into satire.

Quarles' chief religious pastoral is in *The Shepheards Oracles*. The eclogues—or dialogues—in this work are textbook illustrations of how religious pastoral works. The pastoral poet begins by taking literally Christ's image of Himself as the Good Shepherd. Indeed, it is from this image that the conventional term *pastor* for priest is derived. The dialogues of *The Shep-heards Oracles* concern a wide variety of subjects from the Nativity to the wars of religion. Roman Catholics and Dissenters come in for considerable abuse.

Two works very hard to classify are *Sions Elegies, Wept by Jeremie the Prophet* and *Sions Sonets Sung by Solomon the King.* Each is in form no more than a free translation of a book of the bible. The lament of the Prophet Jeremiah for the lost Jerusalem that Quarles presents in *Sions Elegies, Wept by Jeremie the Prophet* has more in common with traditional works of re-ligious pastoral than with the elegiac poems that Quarles wrote about his contemporaries. Through Jeremiah, Quarles is asking his readers to contem-plate religious truths. *Sions Sonets Sung by Solomon the King* is a free ren-dering of The Song of Solomon. Quarles carefully includes marginal glosses so that the reader will not lose sight of the religious allegory and think he is reading love poems.

Quarles also wrote a number of elegies; his most famous work in the genre is his epitaph for the poet Michael Drayton (1631), which appears on Dray-ton's memorial in Westminster Abbey. Quarles' only substantial book of ele-giac poetry is *An Alphabet of Elegies.* These twenty-two short poems and an epitaph commemorate Dr. Aylmer, Archdeacon of London. The twelve-line verse form is a kind of truncated sonnet with a sprightliness at odds with— or perhaps redeeming—the lugubrious content.

Archbishop Ussher is commemorated in one of the poems in *Divine Fan-cies,* and included in *The Shepheards Oracles* is an elegy for the great Prot-estant hero Gustavus II Adolphus, King of Sweden. Published as individual chapbooks in Quarles' later years were elegies commemorating Sir Julius Caesar (1636); Jonathan Wheeler (1637); Dr. Wilson of the Rolles (1638); Mildred, Lady Luckyn (1638); Sir Robert Quarles, the poet's brother (1639); Sir John Wostenholme (1640); and the Countess of Cleveland and her sister Cicily Killigrew (1640). Interesting for its verse forms but not included in Grosart's standard edition is a chapbook called *Threnodes on the Lady Mar-shall . . . and . . . William Cheyne* (c. 1641); and recently Karl Joseph Höltgen has identified both an epitaph for Sir Charles Caesar and the in-scription on the D'Oyley monument at Hambleden as being by Quarles.

Edmund Miller

Other major works

PLAY: *The Virgin Widow: A Comedie,* 1649 (masque).

NONFICTION: *Enchiridion, Containing Institutions Divine and Moral,* 1640; *Observations Concerning Princes and States Upon Peace and Warre,* 1642; *The Loyal Convert,* 1644; *The Whipper Whipt,* 1644; *The New Distemper,* c. 1644; *The Protest Royalist in His Quarrell with the Times,* 1645; *Judgement and Mercy for Afflicted Soules: Or, Meditations, Soliloquies, and Prayers,* 1646.

Bibliography

Diehl, Houston. "Into the Maze of Self: The Protestant Transformation of the Image of the Labarynth." *Journal of Medieval and Renaissance Studies* 16 (Fall, 1986): 281-301. Quarles' poetry was a major factor in the change of meaning of the maze in literature. Quarles used the emblem of the maze to mean the soul, or the interior life of the individual.

Gillmeister, Heiner. "Early English Games in the Poetry of Francis Quarles." In *Proceedings of the XI HISPA International Congress*, edited by J. A. Mangan. Glasgow: Jordanhill College of Education, 1986. Gillmeister explores Quarles' use of British games played in the Middle Ages. He uses them both to add metaphorical meaning and structure to his poetry.

Gosse, Edmund. *The Jacobean Poets.* New York: Charles Scribner's Sons, 1894. This is an old book that nevertheless gives good comprehensive coverage of twelve poets from the late sixteenth and early seventeenth century. The chapter on Quarles provides a short biography and discusses his major works. Suitable for all students.

Hassan, Masoodul. *Francis Quarles: A Study of His Life and Poetry.* Aligarh, India: Aligarh Muslim University, 1966. This volume is one of the few modern books on Quarles, and so is valuable to any student of his work. As the title suggests, Hassan provides a comprehensive biography interwoven with an analysis of Quarles' major works. Includes a bibliography.

Leach, Elsie. "The Popularity of Quarles' Emblems: Images of Misogyny." *Studies in Iconography* 9 (1983): 83-97. Feminist critic Leach describes the moral and divine imagery used by Quarles in his poetry in terms of how it supported the status quo of men's domination over women. An interesting and unusual study of the Jacobean era poet. Valuable for serious Quarles scholars.

CARL RAKOSI

Born: Berlin, Germany; November 6, 1903

Principal poetry

Selected Poems, 1941; *Amulet*, 1967; *Ere-VOICE*, 1971; *Ex Cranium, Night*, 1975; *My Experiences in Parnassus*, 1977; *The Collected Poems of Carl Rakosi*, 1986.

Other literary forms

Although Carl Rakosi is known principally for his poetry, he has published a collection of nonfiction writings, *The Collected Prose of Carl Rakosi* (1983).

Achievements

Carl Rakosi came to public attention fairly late. Between 1939 and 1965, he wrote no poetry. A young English poet who was doing research at the State University of New York at Buffalo contacted him and asked about his post-1941 work; it was this query that spurred him to begin writing once more. His *Selected Poems*, published by New Directions in 1941, had received little notice, but the growing audience for poetry in the 1960's welcomed *Amulet*, his second New Directions book. Since that time, New Directions, Black Sparrow Press, and the National Poetry Foundation at the University of Maine have kept his writing in print, and it has continued to spark the interest of critics and a new generation of poets and readers.

Rakosi is a master of kindly sarcasm. As an immigrant to the United States, he has the remove necessary to view—and reveal—the flaws and foibles of American culture. Yet his poems often move beyond national boundaries, revealing the essential human being beneath the timeless weave of self-deception. These unveilings often focus on Rakosi himself.

Biography

Carl Rakosi was born on November 6, 1903, to Hungarian nationals, Leopold Rakosi and Flora Steiner, who were at that time living in Berlin. The young Rakosi was brought to the United States in 1910; his father and stepmother reared him and his brother in various Midwestern cities—Chicago; Gary, Indiana; and Kenosha, Wisconsin.

Rakosi made many attempts to begin a career. After earning his B.A. in literature at the University of Wisconsin at Madison, he tried social work in Cleveland and New York City. He returned to Madison for an M.A. in educational psychology and then worked as the staff psychologist in the personnel department at Bloomingdale's for a time. He taught English at the University of Texas at Austin and made forays into law school (in Austin) and medical school (in Galveston). Having found neither law nor medicine congenial, he taught high school in Houston for two years. At the outset of the Depression, he tried social work again, returning to Chicago to work at the Cook County Bureau of Public Welfare. By now he had changed his name, to Callman Rawley. He served a two-year stint as a supervisor at the Federal Transit Bureau in New Orleans; then, following a period of working as a field supervisor for Tulane University, he started to work—in a pioneering role—as a family therapist at the Jewish Family Welfare Society in New York. At the same time, he pursued graduate studies at the University of Pennsylvania; in 1940 he received an M.A. in social work.

His professional course was now clear. After three years as a case supervisor at the Jewish Social Service Bureau in St. Louis, and two years as assistant director of the Jewish Children's Bureau in Cleveland, in 1945 he became executive director of the Jewish Family and Children's Service in Minneapolis. He continued in this post until 1968; between 1958 and 1968 he also had a private practice.

One notes in this chronology the marked absence of any job directly connected to writing. Rakosi's first spell as a poet had resulted in publication in the prestigious *Little Review*, alongside James Joyce's *Ulysses* (1922) in serial form; he had also been included in *An "Objectivists" Anthology* (1932), edited by Louis Zukofsky, which many years later came to be seen as a landmark event. The long hiatus that followed has been described thus by Rakosi himself:

> By 1939 writing was coming harder and slower to me as more of me became involved in social work and in reading and writing professional articles. . . . I wrote some sixty . . . and my evenings were swallowed up by the things that a man who is not a writer normally spends his time on in a big city: the theater, concerts, professional meetings, friends, girlfriends. . . . In addition, my Marxist thinking had made me lose respect for poetry itself. So there was nothing to hold me back from ending the problem by stopping to write. I did that. I also stopped reading poetry. I couldn't run the risk of being tempted.

In December, 1965, he received a letter from British poet Andrew Crozier asking what had become of his poetry since 1941. This letter prompted him to take up his pen once again.

The results were soon made available to the poetry-reading public in a series of books; the work was much anthologized, and Rakosi was asked to give readings at a number of distinguished venues. This Rip Van Winkle of poetry had reawakened to a different decade—one for which his gifts appeared to have been waiting.

In 1939, Rakosi was married to Leah Jaffe. Their daughter, Barbara, was born in St. Louis in 1940, and a son, George, was born in Cleveland in 1943.

The couple stayed together for half a century; Leah Jaffe Rakosi died in San Francisco in 1988.

Analysis

Because of his early connection with Louis Zukofsky, Carl Rakosi is often spoken of as an Objectivist poet. When both poets were young, Zukofsky had been advised by Ezra Pound to start a literary movement, the better to draw attention to his own poetry. Pound told him that he need not look for complete agreement among the members of his movement, as long as certain views were held in common. Zukofsky took his mentor at his word. He contacted several poets of his generation (along with William Carlos Williams, who was some twenty years their senior) and published their work as the *Objectivists Anthology*, with an introduction by himself. This essay has long been puzzled over by students of American poetry.

Rakosi himself found Zukofsky's definition of Objectivism baffling. "It was so at odds," he says, "with any association I could make with the word *Objectivist*, which has *object* in its belly." Rakosi has characterized Zukofsky's tone in the essay as "aloof" and "rebuffing," as if he were simultaneously presenting the poetry for inspection and arrogantly dismissing his readership. Zukofsky's explanation, according to Rakosi, fit only his own poetry. There was a fundamental gulf between Zukofsky and the three other poets most often named as Zukofsky's fellow Objectivists: Charles Reznikoff, George Oppen, and Rakosi. These three "were credited with a place in literary history for the wrong reason, because of a name."

Nevertheless, Rakosi came to like the label "Objectivist." Although Zukofsky's tortuous definition left him cold, the name "conveyed a meaning which was, in fact, my objective: to present objects in their most essential reality and to make of each poem an object, meaning by this the opposite of vagueness, loose bowels and streaming, sometimes screaming, consciousness." Even as Zukofsky spurned the term, Rakosi welded it to his own practice. He aimed to convert the subjective experience into an object "by feeling the experience sincerely; by setting boundaries to it and incorporating only those parts which belong together." The poem, he has said, should be like a sculpture; the reader should be able to come at it from any angle and find it "solid and coherent." Honesty and craftsmanship are the qualities needed for constructing such poems.

As is often the case when a poet supplies a definition of poetry, there is a certain amount of question-begging here. What guarantee can the poet give (even to himself) of his own sincerity and honesty? By what criteria does one decide which parts belong together? Will everyone who "views" (reads) the poem find it solid and coherent? If so, how does one account for readers' variation in taste? Yet Rakosi's aims become clearer when they are viewed in historical context and in the light of his actual practice.

Zukofsky launched his movement in 1930, some two decades after Ezra Pound and H. D. (Hilda Doolittle) had declared themselves Imagists in the process of renovating poetry by throwing out "bad habits dear to the poets of the Victorian age." Zukofsky was heavily influenced by Pound and by another inductee in the Imagist movement, William Carlos Williams. Given that Rakosi, Reznikoff, Oppen, and others anthologized under Zukofsky's editorship were also mindful of and to some extent sympathetic with the principles of Imagism, it is small wonder that there are several points of resemblance between Imagism and the Objectivists.

The theoretical writing of Ezra Pound, however, had a lucidity of expression that frequently eluded Zukofsky. In "A Retrospect" Pound articulated the following principles for Imagism:

1. Direct treatment of the "thing" whether subject or objective
2. To use absolutely no word that does not contribute to the presentation.
3. As regarding rhythm: to compose in the sequence of the musical phrase, not in sequence of a metronome.

The result is well known: a radical reappraisal of poetic terms and practice; the birth within English-language poetry of "the modern"; "free" verse; a cessation of "moral tagging" or other explicit aid to the reader as to the poem's meaning; an endeavor to rescue the art from the muddyings to which it had been subjected when its practitioners sought to truck and higgle with the increasingly wide—and not necessarily deep—audience brought by universal education.

Rakosi's brief lyrics are rightfully classified as modernist for their terse, stripped-down qualities, which give the *impression* (and that is what counts) of sincerity and honesty. Yet they could hardly be called straightforward—and that is fortunate. They have far too much art to them. In fact, it is hard to take at face value Rakosi's oft-repeated assurances of his ingenuous nature, for his poems strike one as weapons of supreme irony. Ingenuousness is simply one of the more empowering poses available to such an artist, although on any given occasion he may be actually ingenuous. Reading Rakosi, it is hard to forget that for many years he worked as a psychotherapist, picking with care the words needed to lead his clients toward self-discovery. Not that he lied to them—quite the contrary: he had to stay with what was true. His role was to select, from all there was to talk about, that which he perceived as being of most use in the present. At any given moment much had to be suppressed; otherwise there would have been a blurring of outline, a loss of necessary definition and discovery.

These are the considerations and requisite skills of the psychotherapist—and in Rakosi's poetry they are also the chief characteristics. Here is "The Experiment with a Rat":

Every time I nudge that spring
                                    a bell rings
and a man walks out of a cage
assiduous and sharp
                            like one of us
and brings me cheese.

How did he fall
                            into my power?

One notes the absence of a rhyme scheme and regular rhythm, but one also notices subtle juxtapositions of sound, rhythms that are less obvious than the iambic but distinct nevertheless, Pound's "cadence of the musical phrase." The vocabulary is spare, and there are only two adjectives, segregated on their own line, as though to prevent their contaminating the rest of the poem. Most of the words are of Anglo-Saxon provenance, giving the Latinate "assiduous" a certain shock value. The tone is quiet, casual, even offhand. The reader may not at first grasp the radical nature of the point of view, for the casual air disarms attention. Suddenly one realizes how the tables have been turned—almost. While it is true that the laboratory assistant endures a trapped existence akin to that of the laboratory rat—a fact it could be salutary for the assistant to acknowledge—the slight exaggeration involved in equating rat and human being implies another truth. When one is actually trapped like the rat, one is quite capable of denying it by the kind of presumption evidenced in the final question.

"Family Portrait, Three Generations" is similarly thought-provoking:

all looking
                        into the lens,
eyes wide,
                        straight ahead:
holding:

"We're plain,
                        we're church goers,
Who dares
            say anything
against that?"

As if he were a combination of camera and tape recorder, the poet refrains from any direct comment upon the phenomena he presents "objectively." Because of this approach, the poem has the ring of truth. It is not easy to see how the poet has in fact rigged things—he has put words in the mouths of his subjects. Yet, after all, are these not exactly the right words? Surely this is what these good folk "say"—not in words, but in their demeanor, their bearing, their lives. Every reader has known someone like the family in the poem. Perhaps the reader has a bit of it in himself. Do not most human beings lead their lives principally in the eyes of others, afraid of censure, terrified of scandal?

Many of Rakosi's poems are equally disarming, apparently simple, certainly economical studies of American life. He sees Americans with remarkable clarity—piercing through democrat's clothing to reveal the would-be emperor underneath. No doubt the dislocations of his own life—being virtually abandoned by his parents for most of his infancy, and coming to the United States at the age of seven and having to replace German and Hungarian with English—helped shape Rakosi into the careful observer who wrote these poems. Perhaps one should in fact identify a third dislocation and view his twenty-five-year poetic hiatus as a further estrangement that came to enhance his later work. He is certainly not one of the herd.

Rakosi had even held himself apart from the movement with which he has been so often associated, Objectivism. His eye is always cool; his poetry is elegant even when he chooses to write in the vernacular; in his poems great and trivial become the same (since nothing can manifest itself except in the everyday); the surfaces of his work never ruffle.

In reading Rakosi one is reminded at times of that other master of elegance in American poetry, Wallace Stevens. In 1925, in fact, Rakosi wrote a six-part poem called "Domination of Wallace Stevens." It is a remarkable pastiche, and all the more noteworthy when one realizes that it was written by a young man of twenty-two. It begins, "Clear me with this master music/ when the coryphee skips on the oak floor/ and the clouds depress me like the lower keys." The reader soon encounters "Miss Ordway in a plush repose,/ counting the curves pitched in her portly mirrors/ by seven bored and pygmy globes." This is excellent fun, and by the poem's end the reader may well judge that Stevens had been dominated by young Carl Rakosi, and that the domination of the man twice his age had been shaken off. Yet like Jacob, who wrestled with the angel and limped thereafter, throughout his career Rakosi recurs to certain tones—one might call them "dictive gestures"—that set an echo of the other poet resonating between text and reader, as in "The Transmutation into English":

> And let them watch their examples,
> for in England the example of quintessence
> is *The Law Of England*
> *is the quintessence of reason.*
>
> They will try to sneak into heaven on that word.

Rakosi's sparer idiom, however, always reasserts itself quickly and most effectively. The Protestant Stevens and the Jewish Rakosi, the classic American and the recent immigrant, do make a strange couple, as Rakosi no doubt knows. It is a knowledge that he probably savors—for, after all, he can "do"

Stevens, while Stevens never "did" Rakosi.

Rakosi has said that of the four principal Objectivists, it was Reznikoff for whom he felt the greatest affinity. At times he has taken a leaf from the older poet's book and let document testify with no more interference than arrangement. Reznikoff's *Testimony* (1934) made use of court transcripts in this way; for Rakosi, notes to the welfare department at times said all there was to be said. "VI Dirge," for example, comes from the gathering called "American Nymphs":

> This is
>   to let
> you know
>   that my husband
> got his
>   project cut off
> two weeks ago
>   and I
> have not
>   had any
> relief since.

Rakosi's work can be hilarious, kindly, and sarcastic all at once—and the masterful self-restraint the reader is induced to picture him exercising makes his terseness all the more amusing. The moment of deflation proves to be worth the wait, as in "The Review," which quotes a journalistic piece that pictures a famous American poet on a stage, gazing at an audience with "Olympian disdain." The quote is followed by Rakosi's eloquently brief comment: "Aw sheeit!" This final exclamation might only be an echo of what the Olympian figure himself muttered, looking out at an audience that was projecting—as the reviewer did—tragic and heroic qualities onto him. This kind of sympathy always hovers about Rakosi's satire, a constant possibility. When Faust puts a word wrong, Rakosi will hear him, but that angel will always save the poem from utter condemnation.

David Bromige

Other major work
NONFICTION: *Collected Prose*, 1984.

Bibliography
Bromige, David, et al. "The Royaumont Conference." *Poetry Flash* (November, 1989-June, 1990). Full account of the September, 1989, conference on the Objectivists held at the Abbeye Royaumont near Paris, with American and French poets as panelists and Carl Rakosi, the only surviving Objectivist poet, as featured speaker. Bromige's article, in the November, 1989,

issue, discusses some of the conference's salient issues; one such issue, the matter of opacity in the poem, stirred up a controversy that was carried on in letters and articles from January through June, 1990. Rakosi contributed a revealing letter.

Heller, Michael. "The Objectivists: Some Discreet Observations." *The Ohio Review* 26 (1981): 85-95. Discusses each of the principal Objectivists— Oppen, Reznikoff, and Zukofsky as well as Rakosi—and gives illuminating commentary on the work of each.

Rakosi, Carl. "Carl Rakosi." In *Contemporary Authors, Autobiography Series*, edited by Adele Sarkissian, vol. 5. Detroit: Gale Research, 1987. Rakosi's autobiographical entry runs for seventeen large pages, which are amply illustrated with photographs of the poet at various times of his life. This is an invaluable document, revealing the man behind the poems and also showing connections between the life and the art. Oddly, however, this extremely full accounting stops in 1965 with the resumption of Rakosi's writing career.

_____. *The Collected Prose of Carl Rakosi.* Edited by Burton Hatlen. Orono, Maine: National Poetry Foundation, 1984. These pieces shed much light on the poetry. "Poetry, like metaphysics, craves to find something permanent behind changing appearances, some yet unknown form of a transcendent nature," Rakosi says in "Day Book." Hatlen, editor of the volume, supplies an afterword, "Carl Rakosi and the Re-invention of the Epigram." This essay touches also on other aspects of Rakosi's writing, beginning with a general survey of the work in its historical setting. His inevitable mention of Reznikoff, Zukofsky, and Oppen is thought-provoking: Hatlen postulates that these three poets share "a distinctively (but not exclusively) Jewish sense of speech as sacred event, of language as, not 'about' the world, but constitutive of it."

_____. Interview by L. S. Dembo. In *The Contemporary Writer*, by L. S. Dembo. Madison: University of Wisconsin Press, 1972. Rakosi and Dembo engage in an interesting, revealing discussion of such matters as Rakosi's Marxism, the influence of Wallace Stevens on his poetry, his views of Zukofsky and other of his contemporaries, and his compositional process. (He says that his first draft is generally "raw data" that has been somehow changed by "a mystery.")

SIR WALTER RALEIGH

Born: Hayes Barton, England; c. 1552
Died: London, England; October 29, 1618

Principal poetry

Selections of Raleigh's poetry were published in various anthologies during his lifetime but not collected until later: *Poems of Sir Walter Raleigh, with a Biographical and Critical Introduction*, 1813; *The Poems of Sir Walter Raleigh*, 1962 (Agnes Latham, editor).

Other literary forms

Almost immediately after his execution in 1618, Sir Walter Raleigh's reputation as a patriotic and courageous opponent to James I developed, and as opposition to James and Charles I increased, many prose works were attributed to Raleigh from about 1625 through the end of the seventeenth century. Of those certainly written by Raleigh, there are two pamphlets, *A Report of the Fight About the Iles of Açores* (1591) and *The Discoverie of the Large, Rich and Bewtiful Empyre of Guiana* (1596), which express the aggressive buoyancy of Elizabethan imperialist designs on South America and of the control of trade to the New World. Raleigh's major work outside his poetry is the monumental, unfinished *The History of the World* (1614), dedicated to and yet containing scarcely disguised criticism of King James, who had him imprisoned between 1603 and 1616, and who (after Raleigh's hopeless expedition to Guiana to find El Dorado) had him executed. *The History of the World* was part therapy, part histrionic pique and, like most of Raleigh's career, significant far beyond its surface ambiguities and chronological contradictions. Torn between being an account of the "unjointed and scattered frame of our English affairs" and a universal history, it is a tribute as well to the dead Queen Elizabeth, "Her whom I must still honour in the dust," and an indictment of what Raleigh perceived as the corruption of the Jacobean court. For Raleigh, in *The History of the World* as much as in his poetry, the court was his stage, a place of "parts to play," in which survival depended on "fashioning of our selves according to the nature of the time wherein we live," and the power of which dominated his language and, in the most absolute sense, his life. Like his poems, *The History of the World* is a moving and (far beyond his knowledge) revealing document of the power of the court over the men and women who struggled within it.

Achievements

Raleigh's importance belies the slimness of his poetic output. The author of perhaps two dozen extant poems and a number of brief verse translations, the latter appearing in his *The History of the World*, Raleigh is nevertheless one of the most important of the Elizabethan courtly makers, articulating with

fearful clarity not merely the gaudy surface and fashions of the late Elizabethan age, but also much of the felt pressure of the court, his society's
dominant social power, upon the lives and sensibilities of those caught in it.
Raleigh described himself toward the end of his life as "a seafaring man, a
Souldior and a Courtier," and his poetry articulates much of what drove him to
those vocations. He knew, deeply and bitterly, that, as he puts it in *The History of the World*, there is nothing more to "becoming a wise man" than "to
retire himself from Court." Yet the court was his stage and it was, he wrote,
the "token of a worldly wise man, not to warre or contend in vaine against
the nature of the times wherein he lived." The achievement of his poetry is
that it gives reverberating expression to the struggles of those who lived in
and were controlled by the Elizabethan court. Most of his poems look, on
the surface, like delicate, even trivial, songs, complaints, and compliments
typical of Petrarchanism; but they are rich, if often confused, responses to
the complex and powerful set of discourses, symbolic formations, and systems
of representation that constituted the Elizabethan court. They offer a unique
insight into the interplay between the social text of Elizabethan society (the
events that made Raleigh's history) and the literary text (the poems that he
made of those events). He is, in many ways, the quintessential court poet of
the Elizabethan period inasmuch as his poems are haunted by, determined
by, and finally silenced by, the power of the court.

Biography

(Sir) Walter Raleigh (or Ralegh) was the quintessential *arriviste*: born in
Devon, educated at Oxford, he rapidly became a court favorite, was knighted
in 1584, but fell into disgrace when, after a bitter rivalry with the up-and-
coming younger Earl of Essex, he was imprisoned for seducing one of the
Queen's Maids-of-Honor, Elizabeth Throckmorton, whom he later married.
He was increasingly unpopular for, among other things, his flamboyant life-
style. When James came to the throne, Raleigh was sentenced to death for
treason, although the sentence was reduced to imprisonment in the Tower
of London. During his imprisonment, between 1603 and 1616, Raleigh became
a close friend of the Prince of Wales, wrote extensively, and became a center
of influence and even of counterestablishment power. He was released by
James in 1616 and sent on an ill-fated expedition to Guiana, and on his return,
executed—his death bewailed by as many people in 1617 as it had been desired
fourteen years earlier.

Analysis

If readers take him at his face value (or at the value of one of his many
faces) Sir Walter Raleigh epitomized, accepted, and chose to live out the
daring expansiveness and buoyancy of the Elizabethan court. He conceived
of his own life as a poem, as a flamboyant epic gesture, and his poems were

the manifestations of his public role and his political ambitions. However disguised in the garment of Petrarchan plaint, mournful song, lament for lost love, *carpe diem* or *ubi sunt* motif, Raleigh's poems are the articulation of the ruthless and sometimes blatant struggle for power that created and held together the court of Elizabeth. "Then must I needes advaunce my self by skyll,/ And lyve to serve, in hope of your goodwyll" he (possibly) wrote— and advancing himself with skill meant using the court as an arena of self-assertion, or (in another of the metaphors which disseminate contradictions throughout his work) as a new world to be conquered.

Raleigh's career as a poet and a courtier (the two are almost inseparable, literary and social text repeatedly writing and rewriting each other throughout his life) should not be simply seen as the daring, willful assertion of the gentleman adventurer who strode into the Queen's favor with a graceful and opportune sweep of his cloak. That would be to take too much for granted at least some of his poems and the power in which, through them, Raleigh hoped to participate. Raleigh's poetry is put into play both by and in power; it demonstrates, probably more clearly than that of any other Elizabethan poet, the unconscious workings of power upon discourse, specifically upon the language which it controlled, selected, organized, and distributed through approved and determined procedures, delimiting as far as possible the emergence of oppositional forces and experiences. The Elizabethan court used poetry and poets alike as the means of stabilizing and controlling its members. To confirm its residual values, it tried to restrict poet and poem as far as possible to the dominant discourses of a colorful, adventurous world, but only at the cost of a frustrating, and, in Raleigh's case, despairing powerlessness.

Much of Raleigh's poetry looks like typical Petrarchan love poetry—it can be, and no doubt was, to many members of its original audience, read as such. The surface of his verse presents the typical paraphernalia of the Petrarchan lyric—hope and despair, pleasure and fortune, fake love, frail beauty, fond shepherds, coy mistresses, deceitful time. The magnificent "As you came from the holy land," which is possibly by Raleigh, can be read as a superbly melancholy affirmation of love, one of the most moving love lyrics of the language. "Nature that washt her hands in milke" takes the reader through a witty blazon of the perfect mistress' charms, her outside made of "snow and silke," her "inside . . . only of wantonesse and witt." Like all Petrarchan mistresses, she has "a heart of stone" and so the lover is poised, in frustration, before his ideal. Then in the second half of the poem, Raleigh ruthlessly tears down all of the ideals he has built. What gives the poem its power is the unusually savage use of the Elizabethan commonplace of Time the destroyer, the thief—ravaging, lying, rusting, and annihilating. Time "turnes snow, and silke, and milke, to dust." What was to the lover the "food of joyes" is ceaselessly fed into the maw of death by time and remorsely turned into excreta; the moistness of the mistress' wantonness rendered dry and repulsive.

Likewise, the reply to Christopher Marlowe's "The Passionate Shepherd" is an impressively terse expression of the *carpe diem* principle, creating an impassioned stoical voice through the stylistic conventions of the plain Elizabethan voice. Typically, Raleigh has superb control of mood, movement, voice modulation, and an appropriately direct rhetoric.

Raleigh's poems are those of the gifted amateur—seemingly casual compliment, occasional verse typically dropped, as the manuscript title of another poem has it, "into my Lady Laiton's pocket." Such a poem looks like one of the many erotic lyrics of the Renaissance which, as Michel Foucault has written, allowed men to overhear and will another to "speak the truth of" their sexuality. Raleigh's poetry, however, does more than introduce sexuality into discourse: inevitably the language of erotic compliment and complaint is inseparable from the language of power. Despite their seemingly trivial, light, or occasional nature—epitaphs on Sir Philip Sidney's death, "A farewell to false love," dedicatory poems to works by George Gascoigne or Edmund Spenser, or poems directly or indirectly written to the Queen—their significance reverberates far beyond their apparently replete surface configuration of stock metaphor and gracefully logical structure.

Raleigh's predominant public roles were those of a man who consciously identified entirely with what he perceived as the dominant forces of his society—and, like his poetry, Raleigh's life is like a palimpsest, requiring not only reading but also interpretation and demystification in depth. As Stephen Greenblatt has suggestively argued, "Ralegh" is in a way a curiously hollow creation, the production of many roles in the theater of the court. Greenblatt has argued that Raleigh saw his life as a work of art, and the court as a "great theater" in which the boldest author would be the most successful. His career from the late 1570's might suggest that his multiplicity reflects an inner hollowness as he shifts back and forth among the roles of courtier, politician, explorer, freethinker, poet, philosopher, lover, and husband. In Raleigh's public career, two dominant discourses clash and contradict—one seeing all human activity as an assertion of the adaptability of the actor, the other a pessimistic view of life as an empty, futile, and unreal theater. While Raleigh adapted to different roles as his ambitions shifted, his very restlessness bespeaks the power of the court. Unlike Sir Philip Sidney, who was a courtier by birth and privilege, Raleigh became one because his identity and survival depended on it. His place in a world that was dangerous and unpredictable was never stable, and even its apparently fixed center, the Queen, was unpredictable and arbitrary.

Introducing Raleigh's role as a poet, it must be noted how the term "possibly" must be continually used to qualify assertions about the authorship of many of the poems attributed to him. Despite the confident assertions of some modern editors, Michael Rudick has shown that scholars do not in fact know whether many of the poems attributed to Raleigh in the manuscripts and miscellanies in which Elizabethan court poetry habitually circulated are in fact his; despite possessing more holograph material for Raleigh than for any other Elizabethan poets except Sir Thomas Wyatt and Robert Sidney, scholars can only speculate about the authorship of many of the best poems attributed to him. Even modern editors and biographers attribute poems to him on primarily sentimental grounds, but in one important sense, the lack of definitive attribution does not matter: Elizabethan court poetry often speaks with the voice of a collectivity, its authors *scriptors* or spokesmen for the values of a dominant class and its ideology. In short, the author's relationship to the languages that traverse him is much more complex than is allowed for by the sentimental nineteenth century biographical criticism which has held sway in Raleigh scholarship until very recently. In any court lyric, there is an illimitable series of pre-texts, subtexts, and post-texts which call into question any concept of its "author" as a free, autonomous person. Raleigh's poems, like those of Sidney or Spenser, are sites of struggle, attempts by Raleigh (or whatever court poet may have "written" them) to write himself into the world. Hence there is a sense in which we should speak of "Raleigh" as the symptomatic court poet, rather than Raleigh the poet—or, perhaps, of "Raleigh" and "his" poems alike as texts, requiring always to be read against what they seem to articulate, often speaking out in their silences, in what they cannot or dare not say but nevertheless manage to express.

Some of the poems are, however, very explicit about their ideological source, even verging on propagandist art. "Praisd be Dianas faire and harmles light" is a poem (again possibly by Raleigh) which reifies the ideals of the court in a hymn of celebration, demanding in ways that other Elizabethan lyrics rarely do, allegiance to the magical, timeless world of the Elizabethan court, in which no challenge to the replete atmosphere can be admitted and in which the readers are permitted to share only so long as they acknowledge the beauty of the goddess whom the poem celebrates. The poem's atmosphere is incantatory, its movement designed like court music to inculcate unquestioning reverence and subordination. Only the subhuman (presumably any reader foolish, or treasonous, enough to dissent from its vision) are excluded from the charm and power that it celebrates: "A knowledge pure it is hir worth to kno,/ With Circes let them dwell that thinke not so."

George Puttenham mentions Raleigh's poetry approvingly as "most lofty, insolent and passionate," and by the mid-1580's, when he expressed his view, Raleigh already had the reputation of being a fine craftsman among the "crew of courtly makers, noblemen and gentlemen" of Elizabeth's court. In what another of Raleigh's contemporaries called the "*Terra infirma* of the Court," Raleigh used his verse as one of the many means of scrambling for position. His verse, in C. S. Lewis' words, is that of the quintessential adaptable courtly amateur, "blown this way and that (and sometimes lifted into real poetry)." He is the lover, poor in words but rich in affection; passions are likened to "floudes and streames"; the lover prays "in vayne" to "blinde fortune" but nevertheless resolves: "But love, farewell, thoughe fortune conquer thee,/ No fortune base nor frayle shall alter mee" ("In vayne my Eyes, in vayne yee waste your tears"). However apparently depoliticized these poems are, they are the product of the allurement and dominance of the court, their confidence less that of the poet himself than of the power of the structures in which he struggles to locate himself. His characteristic pose is that of the worshiper, devoted to the unapproachable mistress or, as the idealizing devotee with the Queen as the unwavering star, the chaste goddess, the imperial embodiment of justice, the timeless principle around which the universe turns. In the way that Ben Jonson's masques were later to embody the ideology of the Jacobean court, so Raleigh's poems evoke the collective fantasy of the Elizabethan— a world that is harmonious and static, from which all change has been exorcized.

Aside from this miscellany (sometimes startlingly evocative, invariably competent and provoking), there are four closely connected and important poems, all undoubtedly Raleigh's, which were found in his own handwriting among the Cecil Papers in Hatfield House, north of London, the family home of Raleigh's great enemy Robert Cecil. They are: "If Synthia be a Queene, a princes, and supreame," "My boddy in the walls captivated," "Sufficeth it to yow, my joyes interred"—the second of which is headed "The 11th: and last booke of the Ocean to Scinthia," and the fourth "The end of the bookes, of the Oceans love to Scinthia, and the beginninge of the 12 Boock, entreatinge of Sorrow." The existence of a poem, or poems, directly written to the Queen and entitled *Cynthia* seems to be mentioned by Spenser in *The Faerie Queene* (1590) and it is usually characterized as being parts of or related to the Hatfield poems. It is probably, however, that the third and fourth poems were written, or at least revised, during Raleigh's imprisonment in 1592.

"The 11th: and last booke of the Ocean to Scinthia," the most important of the group, appears to be a scarcely revised draft of an appeal, if not to the Queen herself, at least to that part of Raleigh's mind occupied by her power. It lacks narrative links; its four-line stanzas are often imperfect, with repetitions and gaps which presumably would have been revised later. Its unfinished state, however, makes it not only a fascinating revelation of Raleigh's personal and poetic anguish, but in its very fragmentariness it is perhaps the clearest example in Elizabethan court poetry of the way the dynamics and contradictions of power speak through a text. "The 11th: and last booke of the Ocean to Scinthia" repeatedly deconstructs the philosophy to which it gives allegiance: its incoherences, gaps, uncertainties, and repetitions both affirm and negate Elizabethan mythology. What in Raleigh's other poems is expressed as complete ideological closure is undermined by the fractures and symptomatic maladjustments of the text. Nowhere in Elizabethan poetry is a poem as obviously constitutive of ideological struggle.

The poem is addressed to a patently transparent "Cynthia" who has withdrawn her favor from the faithful lover. Raleigh projects himself as a despairing lover fearfully aware that his service has been swept into oblivion, simultaneously acknowledging that honors inevitably corrupt and that he cannot keep from pursuing them. The "love" that he has seemingly won includes favors that open doors not only to glory but also to ruin and death. Yet even knowing this, it is as if he cannot help himself "seeke new worlds, for golde, for prayse, for glory," with the tragic result that "Twelve yeares intire I wasted in this warr." The result of his "twelve yeares" dedication has been imprisonment and disgrace. Yet he is helpless before his own inability to abandon the glories of office. "Trew reason" shows power to be worthless, yet even while he knows that "all droopes, all dyes, all troden under dust" he knows also that the only stability in the world of power is the necessity of instability and emulation.

The Petrarchan motifs with which the successful courtier has played so effectively, almost on demand—the helpless lover wooing the unapproachable mistress who is the unattainable goal of desire—have suddenly and savagely been literalized. The role that Raleigh has played has exploded his habitual adaptability. He cannot protest that the game of the despairing lover is only a game; it has now become real. In 1592 he wrote to Cecil: "My heart was never broken till this day, that I hear the queen goes away so far off—whom I have followed so many years with so great love and desire, in so many journeys, and am now left behind her in a great prison alone." The letter is an obvious echo of the lines from Raleigh's adaption of the Walsingham ballad, "As you came from the holy land." The contradictions of Raleigh's life which the poem now voices had been repressed and silenced during his imprisonment, but now they are revealed as terrifyingly real. By marrying, Raleigh himself has ceased to play Elizabeth's game; he has thus found that the role of masochistic victim in which he cast himself for political advantage has been taken literally and he has become an outcast. "The 11th: and last booke of the Ocean to Scinthia" expresses the agony of a man whose choices and commitments have been built on the myth of a changeless past in an ever-moving power struggle. The very unfinished quality of Raleigh's fragment is the perfect formal expression of the disruptiveness that has overwhelmed him.

It is fortunate that another key poem in this period is among the Hatfield manuscripts. "The Lie" is a release of explicit rage, a struggle to find form for deep frustration and venom, finding no alternative to renunciation and repulsion. It is a statement of deeply felt impotence, probably written after Raleigh's release from prison in 1592, but before he was restored to favor. Raleigh's poem is seemingly total in its rejection of the ideology by which he has lived: natural law, universal harmony, love, and court artifice are all rejected in a mood of total condemnation. Yet Raleigh's poem is neither philosophically nihilistic nor politically radical: the force of his revulsion from the court does not allow for any alternative to it. What dies is the "I" of the poem, as he gives the lie to the world, and takes refuge in a savage *contemptus mundi*. "The Lie" is at once an explosion of frustration and beneath ideological confidence. In such poems the ideology is betrayed by writing itself; the poem constantly releases an anxiety for realities which challenge the surface harmonies and struggle unsuccessfully to be heard against the dominant language of the court poetic mode. What readers start to recognize as Raleigh's characteristic melancholic formulation of the persistence of "woe" or pain as the very mark of human self-consciousness is the special telltale sign of his texts as sites of struggle and repression. "The life expires, the woe remaines" is a refrain echoed by "Of all which past, the sorrow, only stays" ("Like truthless dreams") and by phrases in *The History of the World* such as "Of all our vain passions and affections past, the sorrow only abideth." Such recurring motifs impart more than a characteristic tone to Raleigh's verse. They point to the frustrated insurrection of subjugated experience struggling to find expression, knowing that there are no words permitted for it.

Raleigh's poems, then, are haunted by what they try to exorcise: a fragility which arises from the repressed political uncertainties of court life in the 1580's and 1590's and which undermines his chosen role as the spokesman of a replete court ideology. Despite its confident surface, all of his verse is less a celebration of the Queen's power than a conspiracy to remain within its protection. The Petrarchan clichés of "Like truthless dreams, so are my joys expired" and the Neoplatonic commonplaces of the "Walsingham" ballad become desperate pleas for favor, projections into lyric poems of political machinations. "Concept begotten by the eyes" also starts out as a stereotypical contrast between "desire" and "woe" and emerges as a poignant cry of radical insecurity and a powerless acknowledgment that the personality of the court poet and of Raleigh himself is a creation of the discourses he has uneasily inhabited and from which he now feels expelled. The Hatfield poems illustrate with wonderful clarity what all Elizabethan court poetry tries to repress: that however the poet asserts his autonomy, he is constituted through ideology, having no existence outside the social formation and the signifying practice legitimized by the power of the court. Raleigh, like every other poet who wrestled within the court, does not speak so much as he is spoken.

More than twenty years later, after a revival of fortunes under Elizabeth, arrest, imprisonment, release, and rearrest under James, Raleigh prematurely brought his history to an end. The work, written to justify God's providential control of time, articulates a view of history that radically undercuts its author's intentions. For Raleigh, history has no final eschatological goal, no ultimate consummation. It consists only of the continual vengeance of an angry God until "the long day of mankinde is drawing fast towards an evening, and the world's Tragedie and time neare at an end." A few years later, on the eve of his execution, Raleigh took up the last lines of the lyric written twenty-five years before on the ravages of time which he had felt all his life—

> Even such is tyme which takes in trust
> Our yowth, our Joyes, and all we have,
> And payes us butt with age and dust:
> When we have wandred all our wayes,
> Shutts up the storye of our dayes.

—and appends to it in two new lines the only hope of which he could conceive, a *deus ex machina* to rescue him, in a way that neither Queen nor King had, from the grip of time's power: "And from which earth and grave and dust/ The Lord shall raise me up I trust." It is a cry of desperation, not a transformation of "the consuming disease of time" as he puts it in *The History of the World*. What is finally triumphant over Raleigh is the power of the world in which he courageously yet blindly struggled and of which his handful of poems are an extraordinarily moving acknowledgment and testament.

Gary F. Waller

Other major works

NONFICTION: *A Report of the Fight About the Iles of Açores*, 1591; *The Discoverie of the Large, Rich and Bewtiful Empyre of Guiana*, 1596; *The History of the World*, 1614.

MISCELLANEOUS: *Works of Sir Walter Ralegh*, 1829 (Thomas Birch and William Oldys, editors, 8 volumes); *Selected Prose and Poetry*, 1965 (Agnes Latham, editor).

Bibliography

Greenblatt, Stephen J. *Sir Walter Ralegh: The Renaissance Man and His Roles*. New Haven, Conn.: Yale University Press, 1973. Greenblatt discusses Raleigh's role-playing and theatrical nature as demonstrated in his court poetry and in *The History of the World*, both of which receive chapter-length treatments. He also provides the context for *The Discoverie of the Large, Rich and Bewtiful Empyre of Guiana*, which he regards as reflecting Raleigh's personal sorrow and the national myths of his age.

Oakeshott, Walter. *The Queen and the Poet*. New York: Barnes & Noble Books, 1961. The first book to analyze in depth Raleigh's poetry, Oakeshott's study concerns his subject's relationship to Queen Elizabeth, the person his "occasional" poetry was designed to please or placate. Using passages from Edmund Spenser and William Shakespeare's *Love's Labour's Lost*, Oakeshott places the poems in their context. The second half of the book contains an edition of the poems associated with the Queen, with the Cynthia poems receiving extensive explication.

Rowse, A. L. *Sir Walter Ralegh: His Family and Private Life*. New York: Harper and Brothers, 1962. The first truly significant biography of Raleigh, Rowse's book offers a new perspective, one gained from the recently discovered diary of Sir Arthur Throckmorton, Raleigh's brother-in-law, on Raleigh's life and writing. Rowse, an expert biographer knowledgeable about Renaissance England, has supplemented his text with many illustrations.

Stein, Arnold. *The House of Death: Messages from the English Renaissance.* Baltimore: The Johns Hopkins University Press, 1986. In a chapter entitled "Dying in Jest and Earnest: Ralegh," Stein discusses three Raleigh poems about death, "The Life of Man," a jest at the theatrical nature of life; "The Lie," a defiant defense against persecution; and "The Passionate Man's Pilgrimage," a comparison of Christian and secular justice.

Tennenhouse, Leonard. "Sir Walter Ralegh and the Literature of Clientage." In *Patronage in the Renaissance*, edited by Guy Fitch Lytle and Stephen Orgel. Princeton, N.J.: Princeton University Press, 1981. Tennenhouse examines Raleigh's lyric poetry, with its Petrarchan themes, in the light of their political significance: Political service becomes love, and reward becomes favor for the courtier/lover. Raleigh's *The History of the World* is likewise read in terms of the poet's own position at court, for Tennenhouse believes the history operates analogically, using the past to criticize the present.

Waller, Gary. *English Poetry of the Sixteenth Century.* London: Longman, 1986. Waller deconstructs Raleigh's poetry, which he claims demonstrates how power works on language. For Waller, Raleigh's poetry simultaneously pays homage to and criticizes the courtly arena where he must play different roles. "As You Come from the Holy Land" and one of the "Scinthia" poems, thus, become poems of tension and value.

DUDLEY RANDALL

Born: Washington, D. C.; January 14, 1914

Principal poetry

Poem Counterpoem, 1966 (with Margaret Danner); *Cities Burning*, 1968; *Love You*, 1970; *More to Remember: Poems of Four Decades*, 1971; *After the Killing*, 1973; *A Litany of Friends: Poems Selected and New*, 1981, 1983.

Other literary forms

Although Dudley Randall did not widely publish his poetry until the early 1960's, he has been writing throughout much of his life. Despite his primary interest in poetry, Randall has published a number of short stories, articles, and reviews (many in the 1960's as well) in such journals as *Negro Digest*, *Black World*, *Umbra*, *Free Lance*, and *The Black Academy Review*. In the mid-1960's, however, Randall's founding of the Broadside Press consumed much of his energy, and he began to direct most of his writing toward poetry and critical articles. Although much of his time continues to be devoted to his publishing ventures, Randall has also been at work for many years on a novel, which remains in progress.

Beyond his own poetry, it is as an editor and publisher that Randall's literary talents have been most significant. His establishment of the Broadside Press in Detroit enabled him to edit *For Malcolm: Poems on the Life and the Death of Malcolm X* (1967) as the second publication of the press. His introductory essay succinctly foreshadows the influence that Malcolm X was to have on many of the newly emerging black poets of the 1960's; it also helped to introduce many of the contributors to readers of black literature. In 1969, aware that many current anthologies excluded or gave only limited representation to black poets, Randall edited and published *Black Poetry: A Supplement to Anthologies Which Exclude Black Poets*, which brought such omissions to the attention of larger publishing houses in the country. By 1971, a number of black poetry anthologies were in circulation, but many of them were seriously flawed by too-narrow criteria for selection. Randall's *The Black Poets* (1971) from Bantam Books enjoyed wide distribution in an inexpensive paperback format and corrected many of the deficiencies of previous black poetry anthologies. Presenting a full range of black poetry from folklore and spirituals to the Black Nationalist poets of the late 1960's, the anthology offered a substantial selection from each of its contributors and stressed the continuity of a rich oral tradition while delineating various periods in the history of black American poetry. It quickly became one of the most widely read and influential anthologies of its kind.

In his critical writings Randall has been a moderating voice, maintaining respect for poets of earlier periods while accepting the new directions of black poetry since the 1960's. One important article, "The Black Aesthetic in the Thirties, Forties, and Fifties" (*The Black Aesthetic*, 1971, Addison Gayle, Jr., editor), clearly establishes the vital role of such poets as Sterling Brown, Margaret Walker, Melvin Tolson, Robert Hayden, and Gwendolyn Brooks, among others who wrote in the wake of the Harlem Renaissance. In providing an essential chapter in black literary history, Randall, here and in other essays, countered eloquently the tendency for young black poets in the 1960's to dismiss gifted, significant writers because they seemed too accommodationist. On the other hand, Randall's productive generosity in publishing and reviewing introduced a great variety of young black poets to literary America and provided an unparalleled availability of black poetry, in general, not only to the black community, but also to the mainstream reading public.

Two additional literary forms must be mentioned in assessing Randall's career: interviews and translations. Because his work for Broadside Press has demanded so much of his time, Randall's critical writing has suffered in quantity; many insights into literary history, political developments and Randall's own methods of composition, however, can be found in several published interviews. While such interviews are frequently useful in understanding his own work, they are also immensely instructional in the field of black poetry. Randall's translations from Russian, Latin, and French are also worthy of note. While he has not translated extensively from the works of any single writer, he has published translations from major figures influential on his own poetic sensibilities. From an interest in the Russian Alexander Pushkin's heritage as a black man (in the lineage of Hannibal), Randall has translated several of his love poems. He has also translated the war poems of K. M. Simonov. Translating from the Latin, he has mastered the classical lyricism of Catullus. From Paul Verlaine, Randall has assimilated much of the early French symbolism.

While he is well practiced in classical and European forms and techniques, Randall has studied equally thoroughly the folk forms of the black heritage. In these forms, he has absorbed the patterns of dialect and commonsensible observation that informed much of the black poetry in the 1960's. Much of this "new" poetry—including some of Randall's own—is available on tape recordings, through Broadside Press. These tape recordings highlight the performance qualities of the black oral tradition. Randall himself is a gifted and effective reader of his own works.

Achievements

Randall's principal literary accomplishment is the founding of Broadside Press in September, 1965. With an initial investment of twelve dollars, he began by issuing a run of one broadside (a poem printed on a single sheet). These inexpensive broadsides could be folded and carried to be read on lunch breaks, on buses, or virtually anytime, anywhere. They could also be posted just about anywhere as well; thus, Randall's idea succeeded in bringing poetry to the ordinary citizens of the community: the venture was more educational than commercial. (This idea has since been imitated by small presses all over the country.) Within a few years, Broadside was publishing anthologies, volumes by new poets, criticism, and recordings. By example, other black writers also began to establish independent presses that specialized in reaching the black community with inexpensive editions of poetry, most notably Haki R. Madhubuti's Third World Press. One can fairly credit Randall, then, as one of the most influential black publishers of his time: his refusal to place commercial interests ahead of literary education has helped to inform a whole generation of the richness and diversity of black poetic traditions. In doing so, he has introduced new African-American writers, and he has fostered an awareness of the reciprocity between black writers in the United States and Africa.

Randall's own poetry, however, has not been without acclaim in its own right. While the critical reception in reviews has been laudatory, however, thorough critical appraisal has been oddly sparse, at best. Despite the lack of proper critical assessment, Randall remains a significant member of the "post-renaissance" generation that followed the Harlem Renaissance. Along with Hayden and Brooks, he has assimilated into his poetry the variety of techniques and experimentation offered by modernism without extensive imitation of any of the modernists. Despite his lack of wide publication until the early 1960's, Randall has pursued poetry consistently with an openness to sources the world over as well as with a persistent study of the literary heritage of blacks. Fusing the eloquence and power of the classical lyric with the terseness and common sense of the oral tradition, yet remaining in the context of modernism, Randall's voice concentrates on the integrity of craft, music, and delight in his poetry. His rhythm is graceful without becoming strained; his tone is compassionate without becoming sentimental; his images are precise without becoming obscure; his diction is relevant without becoming contrived; his themes are universal without becoming clichéd. Even without widespread critical evaluation, Randall's work has not gone unnoticed. In 1962, he received the Tompkins Award from Wayne State University for both poetry and fiction, and in 1966, he received the same award for poetry. In recognition of his contributions to black literature, he received the Kuumba Liberation Award in 1973.

Biography
Born in 1914 to Arthur and Ada Randall, Dudley Felker Randall spent his childhood in Washington, D.C., his birthplace, and East St. Louis. His father was responsible for the young Randall's awareness of political commitment; he frequently campaigned for blacks seeking political office, and he took

Randall with him to hear such speakers as James Weldon Johnson and W. E. B. DuBois (although Randall reports that at the time he "preferred playing baseball"). Randall's public education continued when his family moved to Detroit. By this time, he was conscious not only of the political process, but also of black literature. Having first begun to write poetry at the early age of thirteen, Randall purchased a copy of Jean Toomer's *Cane* (1923) when he was sixteen; he was so impressed by Toomer's precise images and powerful symbolism that Toomer became—and remains—his favorite black poet. By 1930, the time of his graduation from the public school system, also at sixteen, Randall was well read in the major writers of the Harlem Renaissance.

After graduation in the midst of the Great Depression, Randall eventually found work as a foundry worker for the Ford Motor Company from 1932 to 1937. Sometime in 1933, he met the poet Robert Hayden, also living in Detroit, with whom he shared his poetry and discussed the major poets of the time. Their exchange of poems and ideas was to help him sharpen his skills and was to remain a mutually enriching friendship for many years. By 1938, Randall had taken a job with the U.S. Post Office as a letter carrier, work he was to continue until 1951, except for his service in the United States Army during World War II as a member of the signal corps in the South Pacific (1942-1946). After returning from military duty, Randall attended Wayne State University and was graduated in 1949. While still working for the Post Office, Randall also managed to complete work for a master's degree in library science from the University of Michigan in 1951.

Degree in hand, Randall began his career as a librarian by accepting an appointment with Lincoln University in Jefferson City, Missouri, where he remained until 1954. He was promoted to associate librarian when he moved to Baltimore to work for Morgan State College for the next two years. In 1956, he returned to Detroit, where he was to work for the Wayne County Federated Library System until 1969, first as a branch librarian and then as head of the reference and interloan department (1963-1969). Randall's introduction to several relatively unknown black poets from Detroit at a planning meeting for a special issue of *Negro History Bulletin* in 1962 led to his determination to see more work by new black poets become available; thus, he became the founding editor of the Broadside Press in 1965. His collaboration with Margaret Danner, who had founded Boone House, a Detroit cultural center, produced his first published book of poems, *Poem Counterpoem* from Broadside Press (its first publication as well).

With the publication of Randall's second book, *Cities Burning*, his reputation as a poet and publisher grew, and he doubled as poet-in-residence and reference librarian for the University of Detroit from 1969 to 1975. During this time, he also taught courses in black literature at the university, gave a number of readings, and was involved in conferences and seminars throughout the country. In 1966, Randall, with a delegation of black artists, visited Paris, Prague, and the Soviet Union, where he read his translations and his own poems to Russian audiences. In 1970, he visited West Africa, touring Ghana, Togo, and Dahomey, and meeting with African writers. Since his retirement in 1975, Randall has continued his involvement in writing conferences and readings, but he devotes the majority of his time to the Broadside Press and his own writing.

Analysis

Like fellow black writers of the "post-renaissance" school that followed the Harlem Renaissance, Dudley Randall embraces not only the concerns of modernism in discovering new modes of expression and technique, but also the increasing awareness of a black literary heritage that begins in slave songs and spirituals. While much of his earlier work experiments with classical forms, primarily the rhymed lyric and the sonnet, Randall also works in free verse and with the terseness of folk expression. He cherishes the freedom of the individual poet to explore ideas and forms central in his poetry. Although he is primarily lyrical in his tone, his work demonstrates sensitivity to the ordinary experiences of the working man, the political struggles of black Americans, and the sanctity of personal relationships. Cognizant of new developments and "trendy" fashions in poetry, Randall never allows himself the comforting isolation of an art-for-art's-sake poetics; instead, he insists on the integrity of the fundamental values of joy, music, and craft in his poetry while lyrically rendering common experiences in the form of new insights which are comprehensible for the majority of readers. He embodies, in short, that sometimes too-often-neglected maxim of Sir Philip Sidney's in *Defence of Poesie* (1595) that poetry ought "to teach and delight." That Randall achieves both while using an essentially modern black idiom ensures him of a significant place among his generation of poets.

The polarities of tension in Randall's poetry seem to be the necessity of personal love and social change. These themes underlie most of his poems, which sometimes focus on the one value while faintly suggesting the other but more often than not are characteristic of a tension between the two. In one early poem from his first book, *Poem Counterpoem*, Randall reflects on his youthful experience as a foundry worker while he visits an ailing coworker many years later in a hospital. In "George," the speaker recalls "the monstrous, lumpish cylinder blocks" that too often "clotted the line and plunged to the floor/ With force enough to tear your foot in two." George's response to the industrial hazards of the assembly line was to step calmly aside; working side by side with the older man in his younger days, the speaker looked to George as an example of quiet endurance, even though George, "goggled, with mask on [his] mouth and shoulders bright with sweat," was not particularly articulate in his guidance of the young Randall. George's "highest accolade," in fact, following the clean-up of "blocks clogged up" which came "thundering down like an avalanche," was the gnomic folk expression: "'You're not afraid of sweat. You're strong as a mule.'" As the speaker visits George in a "ward where old men wait to die," he realizes that George "cannot read the books" brought to him while he sits "among the senile wrecks,/ The psychopaths, the incontinent." In the transition from the first stanza (set in the past) to the second (set in the present), the long lines of the first (which suggest the rhythm of the assembly line) give way to a shorter line that underscores George's confinement. When George falls from his chair in the course of the visit, his visitor lifts him back into it "like a cylinder block" and assures him: "'You'll be here/ A long time yet, because you're strong as a mule.'"

While the poem relates little more than the memory of assembly line comradeship and the subsequent visit many years later, it suggests a great deal more than that. The sheer physical drudgery of the foundry site is apparent in both imagery and rhythm; George's quiet but resolute determination to survive the toll of accidents is also implicit, but he survives only to find himself relegated to little more than a warehouse for the aged. Juxtaposed, however, with the dismal irony of George's fate is Randall's emphasis on the personal bond of mutual respect between the two men. Just as George encouraged him, the younger man now offers the aging George the same encouragement that he once offered the young worker. George's persistence in overcoming his fear of death, however, is not enough to restore his dignity. The social conditions must change as well, and that will necessitate formal education; this, too, as Randall's own biography might suggest, has been an inadvertent gift from the older man. In stressing the personal bond between them and yet not losing sight of their common experience in the workplace, Randall celebrates the endurance of friendship while condemning the dehumanizing factors of the assembly line and the hospital. That all of this is expressed in one brief mirrored, metaphorical aphorism suggests that the simple eloquence of the poem itself is, like George, rich beneath its surface.

Randall's second book, *Cities Burning*, focuses on the disintegrating cities during the urban riots and civil struggles of the 1960's. His observations on social change are not, however, solely the result of the 1960's, for several of these poems were written much earlier. "Roses and Revolution," for example, was written in 1948 and attests to Randall's exploration of the dual themes of personal love and social change long before that tumultuous decade. Hauntingly prophetic, Randall's apocalyptic poem speaks of "the lighted cities" that "were like tapers in the night." He sees "the Negro lying in the swamp with his face blown off" and "in northern cities with his manhood maligned." Men work but take "no joy in their work." As a result of the inner turmoil caused by prejudice and oppression, love becomes severely distorted; they greet "the hard-eyed whore with joyless excitement" and sleep "with wives and virgins in impotence." While the poem's speaker searches for meaningful value "in darkness/ and felt the pain of millions," he sees "dawn upon them like the sun," a vision of peace and beauty in which weapons are buried "at the bottom of the ocean/ like the bones of dinosaurs buried under the shale of eras." Here people "create for others the house, the poem, the game of athletic beauty." Having described the misery in the first stanza and the vision of deliverance in the second stanza, Randall proceeds to analyze its meaning in the third: "Its radiance would grow and be nourished suddenly/ burst into terrible and splendid bloom/ the blood-red flower of revolution."

As it is for many of the poems in this volume, the title of the collection is somewhat misleading with respect to "Roses and Revolution," for the city in *Cities Burning* is mankind and the fires are transforming agents. While acknowledging the violence and destruction as literal events, Randall also sees revolution occurring within the heart of man as well. The real revolution is "not for power or the accumulation of paper," greed for money, but for a blossoming of love that can occur when the black American no longer feels "the writhing/ of his viscera like that of the hare hunted down or the bear at bay." The symbolic rose no longer holds its power for transformation unless it is "blood-red" in its "terrible and splendid bloom," for Randall does not sentimentalize love at the expense of the political process.

In "Ballad of Birmingham," for example, Randall dramatically presents a dialogue between a black mother, who fears for her daughter's safety and forbids her to "march the streets of Birmingham/ to make our country free," and the girl herself, who is willing to risk the "clubs and hoses, guns and jails" in order to assert her rights. Obeying her mother, the daughter goes "to church instead" to "sing in the children's choir" rather than join the other children in the freedom march. The historical event on which the ballad is based was the bombing of a black church in Birmingham on September 15, 1963, when four teenage girls were murdered in a dynamite explosion while they were attending a Bible class. When the mother hears the explosion, she rushes to the scene of the violence; although she claws "through bits of glass and brick," she finds only a shoe: "O, here's the shoe my baby wore,/ but, baby, where are you?" Her protective reluctance to become involved in the civil rights struggle, although understandable, has failed to preserve her loving security for her daughter or even her daughter herself. Despite the elegiac ballad form, Randall's dramatic irony here is politically and personally potent: love cannot hide from death in the pursuit of freedom; it must risk it.

Randall, however, is unwilling to endorse violence for its own sake—in revolution or in literature. In "The Rite" and in "Black Poet, White Critic," he addresses, respectively, both the young militant black poet who would annihilate the pioneers of the black literary tradition and the white critic who would deny that such a tradition even existed. The young poet in "The Rite" murders an older poet, whom he views as reactionary, but in sacrificing him to the new revolutionary program, the young poet ritually "drank his blood and ate his heart," thus drawing his revolutionary sustenance from his forebears without conscious knowledge of doing so. That the older writer provides continuing life for the younger one—and is conscious of that fact—not only endorses the persistence of the political struggle, but also establishes a political context for black literature that reaches back to protest elements in the slave songs. The struggle is nothing new to Randall's generation, or to those generations before him; yet the older poet is quite willing to offer his life in order to broaden the continuity of that protest. On the other hand, Randall challenges—in "Black Poet, White Critic"—the establishment critic who "advises/ not to write on controversial subjects/ like freedom or murder" to reexamine his own critical premises. The critic suggests "universal themes/ and timeless symbols/ like the white unicorn," to which Randall responds: "A *white* unicorn?" Refusing to deny his own heritage and experience as a black man, he realizes that the argument is bogus in any context: the timeless drama of Sophocles or William Shakespeare can hardly be said to ignore freedom and murder. Randall, then, implies that the critic who so blatantly misreads his own literary tradition fears not so much a lack of quality on the part of black poets as the fulfillment of that advice on "universal themes" and "timeless symbols" that would indict the critic's own racism and shoddy intellect as a result of that racism. Black poets might, indeed, write *too well*.

Randall's third volume of poems, *Love You*, consists entirely of lyric love poems, but unlike those in *Cities Burning*, these poems more frequently use open forms and free verse. While the previous volume is more likely to explore ideas, the poems in this one concentrate on feelings (although the poems in both volumes, of course, embrace both ideas and feelings). The emphasis in *Love You* shifts from the complexity of the political struggle to the complexity of interpersonal conflicts and seems to suggest that social change requires the resolution of such conflicts before its advances can be permanent. These poems, like those in *More to Remember: Poems of Four Decades*, are drawn from several decades, and they offer the intimate but not confessional experience of the classical lyricist. Along with his selected poems, those in *Love You* offer a full range of poetic device and subject matter, although the themes generally oscillate between the polarities of personal love and social change. In his 1973 volume, *After the Killing*, Randall moves to a lyrical form that is closer to free-verse folk expression than the lyric poems of his earlier work. The themes, however, remain generally the same, although he introduces an emphasis on Pan-African concerns, particularly in the section "African Suite," which is based in part on his travels to West Africa.

Randall may be remembered as an outstanding publisher and editor who was also a poet, but he has written a sufficient number of moving poems to keep him in anthologies for many years to come. Some of his ballads, such as "Ballad of Birmingham," have been set to music and popularized in that fashion. His terse expression and probing voice in poems such as "Black Poet, White Critic" will remind readers that poetry can indeed teach much about what it means to be human without compromising the inherent delight in reading—and living.

Michael Loudon

Other major works

ANTHOLOGIES: *For Malcolm: Poems on the Life and the Death of Malcolm X*, 1967; *Black Poetry: A Supplement to Anthologies Which Exclude Black Poets*, 1969; *The Black Poets*, 1971.

Bibliography

Melhem, D. H. "Dudley Randall: A Humanist View." *Black American Literature Forum* 17 (1983): 157-167. This excellent article surveys Randall's poetry and includes a biographical overview of his life and career and brief analyses of significant poems. Melhem stresses that Randall is a humanist, a label the poet himself accepts. Includes notes that are somewhat useful in finding other sources on Randall, especially general surveys and interviews.

Miller, R. Baxter. "Dudley Randall." In *Afro-American Poets Since 1955*, edited by Trudier Harris and Thadious M. Davis. Vol. 41 in *Dictionary of Literary Biography*. Detroit: Gale Research, 1985. In this excellent scholarly essay, Miller gives a general introduction to the life and career of Randall. Emphasis is placed not only on the founding of Broadside Press but also on the poetic career of Randall. While mostly a general survey, it contains some useful, though brief, analyses of individual poems. Includes a short bibliography.

Randall, Dudley. "Black Publisher, Black Writer: An Answer." *Black World* 24 (March, 1975): 32-37. This article records Randall's own reflections about the world of black publishing houses and the pros and cons concerning a black writer's use of a black or white publisher. Although interesting, the article does not address Randall's profession as a poet. He does, however, make several general remarks concerning other black poets, and he does comment on the role of oral tradition in poetry.

_____. "Interviews: Dudley Randall." *Black Books Bulletin* 1 (Winter, 1972): 23-26. An informative but short article dealing mostly with Randall's involvement with Broadside Press. Includes some discussion of Randall's poetry and the earlier African-American poets who have influenced him. Randall makes general comments about African-American poetry which may shed some light on his own poems.

Redding, Saunders. "The Black Arts Movement in Negro Poetry." *The Amer-*

ican Scholar 42 (1973): 330-336. This article attempts to criticize the "increasing rigidity" of the black arts movement, with particular regard to the "new concept of the black and blackness." In contrast to those within this movement, Randall, though a publisher of many poets in the movement, exhibits an earlier, more humanistic tradition in touch with the American past. While of interest, this article would be of minimal use in doing research on specific Randall poems.

Rowell, Charles H. "In Conversation with Dudley Randall." *Obsidian* 2, no. 1 (1976): 32-44. In this important interview focusing primarily on Randall's poetic career rather than his role as a publisher, the poet discusses his background and the influences on his life and work. Includes some useful discussion of Randall's indebtedness to the Harlem Renaissance, his views of poetry, and his process of composition. Randall also comments on his poems collected in *Cities Burning* and *After the Killing*, among others. Notes leading to other sources are included.

JOHN CROWE RANSOM

Born: Pulaski, Tennessee; April 30, 1888
Died: Gambier, Ohio; July 3, 1974

Principal poetry

Poems About God, 1919; *Armageddon*, 1923; *Chills and Fever*, 1924; *Grace After Meat*, 1924; *Two Gentlemen in Bonds*; 1927; *Selected Poems*, 1945, 1963, 1969; *Poems and Essays*, 1955.

Other literary forms

John Crowe Ransom published a substantial body of prose devoted to social and literary criticism. Mildred Brooks Peters, in the bibliography in her book, *John Crowe Ransom* (1968), lists 124 of his essays and articles and more than seventy signed book reviews. The essays and articles appeared in many journals, notably *The Kenyon Review*, the *Fugitive*, and *The Sewanee Review*. The social criticism is concentrated in a ten-year period from the late 1920's through the mid-1930's. Of particular interest in this category are his contributions to the agrarian manifesto *I'll Take My Stand* (1930) for which he wrote the Introduction and the leading essay, "Reconstructed but Unregenerate." He was to write more than two dozen essays of social criticism in this period, including "The South Defends Its Heritage" (1929), "Modern with a Southern Accent" (1935), "The South Is a Bulwark" (1936), and "What Does the South Want," which was included in *Who Owns America? A Declaration of Independence* (1936).

The greater bulk of Ransom's prose is devoted to literary criticism, dating from his essays in the *Fugitive* and the *Literary Review* in the early 1920's. His three principal book-length collections are *God Without Thunder* (1930), *The World's Body* (1938), and *The New Criticism* (1941). In the first, he established the terms for one of his most fundamental philosophical and critical concerns, the dangers inherent in the abstractions of scientific thought. Recapturing the "completeness of actual experience," in contrast to such abstractions, is possible, he held, only through art and religious myth. That line of thought was to be pursued through *The World's Body* in "Poetry: A Note in Ontology," and in *The New Criticism*, with its final essay, "Wanted: An Ontological Critic." The thesis central to Ransom's thought is that poetry constitutes a kind of knowledge, and that it is at least as valid as science as one index to the nature of reality.

Achievements

Ransom's distinguished career as man of letters has three clearly definable categories. He was a poet, a literary and social critic, and a teacher and editor. While it is in terms of the first two categories that he is principally known to the world, the third might be seen as all-encompassing and thus as the major achievement. His roles as teacher and editor made him a central figure in the development of Fugitive poetry and the New Criticism, as well as, though to a somewhat lesser degree, agrarianism.

Central to that all-encompassing achievement as teacher and editor was a philosophical quest that sent him in search of a cognitive process to counter the overwhelmingly pervasive abstractions of modern science. That quest, with its roots in nineteenth century Romanticism, was central to the Modernist period and to the development of the New Criticism. Ransom and his peers were trying to solve the century-old problem of the nature of the relationship between the imaginative re-creation of experience and the empirical and rational analysis of it. Thus for Ransom, as for Allen Tate, Cleanth Brooks, and Robert Penn Warren, poetry must be defined as a kind of knowledge, deserving a place in serious epistemological and ontological considerations at least equal to that afforded scientific knowledge. The development and application of that definition as a major premise of the New Criticism is one of Ransom's two historic achievements. The second is his poetry.

The 1969 *Selected Poems* contains eighty poems, counting separately the originals and the revisions of the final "Sixteen Poems in Eight Pairings." It is a slim harvest, however one counts, almost entirely written between 1919 and 1927. Its most distinctive characteristics are its mannered style, depending particularly on quaint and archaic diction and a carefully modulated cadence, and its ironic tone and perspective. The consensus is that the best of his poetry will constitute Ransom's most enduring achievement.

Biography

John Crowe Ransom was born in Pulaski, Tennessee, in 1888. His father was a Methodist minister and the family moved with such frequency that the children were taught at home, Ransom not entering public school until he was ten years old. The relationship thus established with his father in the role of teacher-critic became an enduring one, Ransom valuing critical exchanges over his work with his father throughout his lifetime. That early and enduring relationship can be seen as a kind of paradigm of the series of similar relationships that were to be central to Ransom's development well into his mature years. He thrived on discussion groups or circles, characterized by critical exchanges, such as those in which he participated as an undergraduate at Vanderbilt and Oxford, and especially, with his fellow Fugitives, Agrarians, and New Critics. The exchanges with his father when he was a boy foreshadow his exchanges in his maturity with Allen Tate.

Ransom's career was divided almost equally between his tenures at Vanderbilt and Kenyon College. After receiving his B.A. from Vanderbilt in 1909, he went as a Rhodes Scholar to Oxford, where he took a second B.A. in 1913. In 1914, he began his teaching career at Vanderbilt as an instructor. Except for his two years in the armed forces during World War I, and a leave

of absence on a Guggenheim Fellowship in 1931, that tenure went uninterrupted until 1937, when he resigned to take a position at Kenyon College.
While at Vanderbilt he, Donald Davidson, Allen Tate, and Robert Penn
Warren, among others, participated in a discussion group which led between
1922 and 1925 to the publication of the poetry magazine the *Fugitive*. His
association with that group continued into the 1930's, when their interests
and writing shifted from poetry to social and then to literary criticism. Known
as Fugitives in the 1920's, the group became known as the Agrarians around
1930, with their publication of *I'll Take My Stand*, and later, with considerably less cohesiveness, as the New Critics. Ransom left Vanderbilt to go to
Kenyon College, where he founded both the *Kenyon Review*, which he edited until his retirement in 1958, and the Kenyon School of English.

    After his retirement, Ransom taught on short-term appointments at North-
western, Ohio State, and Vanderbilt. He continued to give public readings
and to lecture occasionally until 1968, after which he accepted no invitations
to do either outside Gambier. In addition to his early scholarships, he received
numerous awards and prizes, attesting the national recognition of his stature
as perhaps the most influential scholar-critic of his generation. In 1947, he
was awarded a life membership in the National Institute of Arts and Letters.
In 1951, he received the Institute's Russell Loines Award for Poetry and the
Bollingen Prize. He became an honorary consultant in American Literature
for the Library of Congress in 1957, and *Selected Poems* (1963), won the 1964
National Book Award. He was elected to membership in the American Academy of Arts and Letters in 1966 and received the Academy's Emerson-
Thoreau medal in 1968.

    Ransom and his wife Robb Reavill had three children. He died quietly in
his sleep at home in Gambier, Ohio, in the early morning hours of July 3,
1974.

Analysis

    Three salient features of John Crowe Ransom's poetry are his irony, the
distinctive, highly mannered texture of his verse, and the relationship between
the two. Ransom admired Robert Frost as poet, but his reservations about
Frost derived from what he considered the relative thinness of Frost's poetic
texture. Frost's colloquial style, Ransom objected, reduces the textural richness of the verse to the barest minimum. What it actually does is to lower
the sensitivity to its textural character by making the verse look and sound
like more or less ordinary speech. Frost's style is calculated to create the
effect that there is no style at all. Ransom's style, in contrast, is highly mannered, calculated to call attention to itself through its texture. His use of the
texture of that mannered style to mask the terrible ironies of existence is his
principal achievement as a modern poet.

    A particularly good example of one of Ransom's exercises in ironic masking is "Bells for John Whiteside's Daughter." The paraphrasable content of the poem, Ransom's "structure," is easily accounted for. Adults, presumably the family, are awaiting the beginning of the funeral of a very young girl who has died unexpectedly. As they wait, they remember how active the child was, with dramatic recollections of her playing at war and of her chasing geese across the lawn into the pond. The slightness of the subject in summary, though universal and poignant, provides a dramatic illustration of how much the structure of the poem depends for its transformation into art upon texture, that is, upon diction, imagery, metaphor, and meter.

One of Ransom's most distinctive touches throughout his poetry is his use of archaic diction. In "Bells for John Whiteside's Daughter" the word "bruited" is the only technically archaic word, but as such it stands at the center of a nexus filled out by "harried" and "brown study," and by the allusion to William Shakespeare's *Hamlet, Prince of Denmark* (c. 1600-1601) in line 7. What all four have in common is their Renaissance currency. In the *Oxford English Dictionary*, one finds the conjecture that "brown study" derives "originally from brown in sense of 'gloomy,'" and an example attributed to "Dice-Play 6" of 1532. The first example from the same source for "bruit" is from John Skelton for 1528, and the second example for "harry" is from John Palsgrave for 1530. Additional coherence for the nexus comes from the tonal appropriateness of both "bruit" and "harry" to the playing at war, and from the Shakespearean allusion to taking up arms, which comes out of the context not only of Hamlet's personal anguish, but also of a state troubled by rumors of war. Knowing this significantly deepens one's appreciation of the poem. It also contributes a great deal to one's understanding of what Ransom means by texture.

Other examples of noteworthy diction in the poem are "astonished," "tireless," "vexed," and "primly." "Tireless," the most explicitly ironic of the four, is at the center of the disparity between what should be—a young, vibrant body full of vitality and energy—and what is—a dead child. The ironic treatment of that disparity, a kind of masking which obscures the awful reality, comes into focus when the stilled heart is described as "tireless." Further, the word catches up in summation the flow of energy that begins with the first line of the poem and continues down through the fourth stanza. The adults in attendance are so accustomed to that energy that they are first, in stanza 1, "astonished" at the child's "brown study," and finally, in stanza 5, "vexed" at it. That is, they never really credit it for what it is. Startled at first, they continue to mask the untimely death with their vexation, a defense against grief. It is as if the child is to be blamed for dying, as if she is guilty of wanton misbehavior, and that, first having defied her elders, she now adds insult to injury by lying there before them "so primly propped." The apparent tonal and thematic rightness of that final phrase is such as to invite questions about the causes of its effectiveness, one of which is clearly the emphasis given by alliteration. There is, however, just as clearly, more to it than that, the more having to do in part with versification and meter.

The alliterative emphasis to the final descriptive passage is reinforced by its place at the very end of the poem, and by the accentual pattern of the whole of the line, which throws two of its three stresses onto the key syllables "prim" and "propped." The words "lying" and "primly," natural trochees, pick up the principal rhythmical character of the poem which derives from the recurrence throughout of alternate feminine endings. The falling rhythm of "body" and "study," and of the alternate lines of each of the verses, except the third, is concentrated in the last line, which ends with the counterpoint of a stressed masculine ending. Such intricate precision of phrasing and meter reinforces the impression that the concept of "primness" embodies the poem's tonal and thematic essence. Further, each of the stanzas is characterized by a similar though not identical precision. The first and last stanzas are most alike in that each is end-stopped. In contrast, the three central stanzas are open, running on from the second line of stanza two to the exclamation point at the end of stanza four. The middle, or third, stanza is unique metrically, being the only one of the five not characterized by alternate feminine endings. This uniqueness underscores its centrality and the three-part structure of the poem.

The beginning of the poem is clearly contained in the first stanza, as the end is in the last. The body of the poem is made up of the three middle stanzas, with its metrically unique center and its fairy-tale ascription of human language to geese who cry "Alas." The beginning and the end contain the adult responses to the child's behavior and death—astonishment, vexation, and an all-encompassing primness. Though the point of view is technically consistent throughout the poem—the editorial "we" of the adult audience— a transformation takes place in the body of the poem where the reader enters the child's world vicariously. It is a world of imaginary wars played out under orchard trees. The stick that is part of the regal image of the "Lady with rod," has probably been in hand all along as sword, as she did battle with her shadow, and as stick-horse to carry her on her harrying raids against the geese. At the very center of this truly remarkable poem, the adults' world and the child's world come together momentarily in the word "Alas." Talking geese scuttling before the queen of the realm are the essential stuff of fairy-land. The one word they utter, however, unites them in their annoyance with the sternly vexed adults who, poignantly in retrospect, always have wanted before all else that the child be still and quiet. The child's perverse response to that most familiar of adult admonitions provides the savage irony of the poem which is masked by the intricate texture and thus contained, as if in a crucible at white-hot intensity, for all who would read.

As one of Ransom's very best poems, "Bells for John Whiteside's Daughter" is also representative of his most distinctive verse and of his ironic treatment of the ordinary but universal human dilemma: death or dying, or moral choices that hinge upon the relationship between body and soul, constitute his principal subject matter. Other useful examples of both his themes and his considerable talents for the felicitous blending of the parts into the whole poem are "Janet Waking," "Piazza Piece," and "The Equilibrists."

"Janet Waking" tells, not of a child's death, but of her painful first confrontation with it. Instead of geese, the poem has a pet chicken, "Old Chucky," who has died unexpectedly in the night, presumably from a bee sting. Janet, waking, finds the hen dead and will not be consoled or "instructed" in how "deep" is the "kingdom of death." As with "Bells for John Whiteside's Daughter," it is diction and phrasing which most clearly mark the poem with Ransom's distinctive touch. The "deeply morning" of stanza 1 parallels the "how . . . purply did the knot swell" of stanza 5. The colloquial use of "kept" at the end of the first stanza is balanced by the "crying her brown hen . . . to rise" of stanza 6. The one word which does most, however, to establish the poem's characteristic mannered quaintness is "transmogrifying." This strikingly unusual word, whose origins are unknown, comes at the very middle of the poem and carries, with its two meanings, the theme and counter-theme of the poem. One of the meanings of "transmogrify" is "to astonish utterly." That definition, the very word itself, and its adjectival modification of the bee in its act of stinging Chucky's "poor old bald head," all taken together are humorous in effect. Ransom treads a dangerously thin line in this poem with his nearly comic presentation of this most mundane of subjects—a pet chicken stung by a transmogrifying bee. This seems to have none of the sobering substance of his account of the death of a child, and the risk that Ransom takes is that the reader may be at best simply amused by the tale. The second meaning of "transmogrify," however, is "to transform," and it is with Chucky's "transformation" and its effect on Janet that Ransom is most concerned.

The impact of this transformation from life to death is the subject of the final two stanzas. The shift in tone from the nearly comic presentation of the pet hen's death of the first five stanzas is effected in part simply by the shift in focus from Chucky to Janet. The name "Chucky," so important in itself in establishing the earlier tone, is absent from the closing stanzas. Rather, readers focus on Janet in her grief, "kneeling" and "weeping fast." The textural contribution to that tonal shift, however, is so characteristically significant as to provide another very illustrative example of Ransom's distinctive style. The paraphrasable substance of the final stanzas, that Janet is heartbroken over the death of her hen, simply fails to account for the emotional intensity of the verse itself. A mature, rational judgment of that bare substance would put it into perspective as one of those childhood experiences that, sad enough for the moment, will very quickly be forgotten, or if remembered at all, fondly so. It is "texture," of course, that makes the difference between that rational perspective and the deeper impact which the poem makes upon the sensibility. Central to that texture, with its accompanying tonal shift, is Janet's admonition, "kneeling on the wet grass," to her hen (significantly not "chicken" nor "Chucky" here) to "rise and walk upon it." The immediate and compelling association is with Christ's walking on the water. The secondary, though equally compelling association, is with Christ's raising of Lazarus from the dead and of his own resurrection. In the middle of that allusion, offering substantial tonal support, is the biblical phrase "the daughters of men," from the sixth chapter of Genesis. In that textural context, the mature, rational perspective on the child's experience is replaced by the deeply sobering realization that her anguish and her plea are the universal, timeless manifestations of mortal man's basic dilemma.

The irony of "Janet Waking" depends upon the juxtaposition of the nearly comic account of bald old Chucky's demise with the sudden confrontation with the mystery of death. The "waking" of the title, like the word "transmogrify," carries the essential irony. Janet wakens literally at first to her breakfast with her family and to her concern for her pet. At the end of the poem there is a second wakening, this time to the beginning of the understanding of mortality. There is less masking here than in "Bells for John Whiteside's Daughter," where the adults hold vexation like a shield between themselves and the girl's death. Janet, in contrast, has nothing between her and raw grief save the ineffectual efforts at "instructing" her in "how deep/ Was the forgetful kingdom of death." That instruction comes from the "us" of line two, from the world of adults who are again attempting, as in "Bells for John Whiteside's Daughter," to soften the impact of the grimmest of realities. These adults, however, are closer to the fire, closer to the truth as Ransom himself perceived it about the "kingdom of death."

There is what might be considered a kind of realistic core to "Bells for John Whiteside's Daughter," and to an even greater degree to "Janet Waking." The occasion and circumstances of each are credible and filled out with particular and concrete details. In other poems, such as "Piazza Piece," and, more particularly, "The Equilibrists," Ransom moves in the direction of pure allegory. Although there are two "real" figures, a man and a woman, in "Piazza Piece," one of Ransom's finely turned sonnets, it is clear that they are not to be seen with the literal individuality of John Whiteside's daughter or of Janet. They represent types, *the* beautiful young woman and *the* old man, and ultimately symbols rather than individuals. For if the gentleman in the dustcoat, a "grey man," is to have the "lovely lady soon," as he says he must, he is not to be taken literally as a suitor, but rather as the personification of death. His words come to her "dry and faint as in a dream," suggesting that her awareness of him is filtered up from the subconscious, an awareness that she resists and from which she turns away, waiting for her true love. In her choice, she represents all women and, indeed, all men. She has none of the individualized particularity of the children of the other two poems, and little, if any, of their poignance. This is not to suggest that "Piazza Piece" is not a very successful poem. It is. Rather, it is to illustrate the difference between Ransom's treatment of his central theme in it and in poems like "Bells for John Whiteside's Daughter" and "Janet Waking." In his notes to his revision of "Here Lies a Lady," a poem more like these two than the allegorical mode of the sonnet, Ransom describes the third stanza, which tells of the lady's death, as 'almost unutterably painful." That intensity is muted in "Piazza Piece," where Ransom steps back from the experiential fire of his theme to assume a more philosophical posture.

The irony of "Piazza Piece" is dramatic irony, which depends upon a relatively high degree of aesthetic distance between reader and character. The reader is invited to consider the human dilemma rather than to feel the experience with the participants. In "The Equilibrists" Ransom moves even further away from the immediacy of Janet's awakening in one of his most allegorical poems. The lovers here have no individuality: no names, no physical characteristics at all save physical beauty, no distinguishing marks of character except for the universal counter-forces of desire and honor. They are, then, not a particular pair of lovers but all lovers, and they are ultimately to be seen, in the terms of the Epitaph, as even more abstract than that. Although there are two lovers throughout the poem, there is also the early implication that the two forces keeping them in that tortured equilibrium might be equated with a basic conflict in either one of them as human beings. That is, in stanza 2, the conflict is seen in terms of *one* head, presumably the woman's, a conflict between the tower, the skull where the gray doves are housed, and the lips, the "quaint orifice" which breathes heat upon the kiss. In the Epitaph, strangers are admonished to "tread light" out of respect for the grave of the equilibrists. Then comes the line, "Mouldered the lips and ashy *the* tall skull," (emphasis added). The conflict is "really" between any two lovers, but it is also really to be found in any one human being. The forces keeping the lovers in orbit are contained in each of them. The tortured equilibrium is between the conceptual reality of the head and the physical reality of the flesh, symbolized by the lips, synecdoche for the body's beauty, for passion and desire. Ransom has here reduced his most fundamental theme, the psychic tensions arising out of the dualism of body and soul, to its barest terms. The remarkable thing about the achievement is that he succeeded so well in fleshing out this allegorical skeleton with the substance of concrete and even sensual imagery; that, to use his terms for it, he found the appropriate and dramatic texture for one of his most abstract structures.

The concreteness of the texture of "The Equilibrists" is achieved primarily by means of allusion. The first three stanzas, with their jacinth, myrrh, and ivory, their "body's field, with the gaunt tower above," and their invitation to "bruise and break" the lilies, echo that most sensual of poems, *The Song of Solomon*. The sword imagery of the fourth and sixth stanzas call up one famous pair of tortured lovers, Tristan and Isolde, as the torments of Hell of stanza 12 call up that other, Dante's Paolo and Francesca. Thus, although the lovers of the poem have no individuality of their own, the particularity of their passion and their anguish is made vivid and dramatic by allusion to their famous predecessors. The overwhelming sweetness of the flesh that they know is chronicled by the singer of *The Song of Solomon*. Their anguished efforts to resolve the conflict beween passion and desire is the substance of the romance of Tristan and Isolde. The tortured equilibrium, which is the best resolution they can achieve, is the resolution of the damned, of the great lovers who "lie in hell."

The allusive texture of the poem is complemented by distinctive metrics and characteristic diction. As he often does, Ransom establishes a counterpoint in his meter by varying line length and juxtaposing masculine and feminine endings within his otherwise quite regular verse. His cadence is thus characterized by a tension between a very modern improvisational movement and the formal restraints of seemingly very conventional quatrains. The striking diction is largely concentrated in stanza 9, with its "puddled," "devising," "gibbeted," and "descanting." "Saeculum," of stanza 10, "stuprate," of stanza 12, and the nice play on "tinder" of stanza 11, are all noteworthy. Yet the readers' attention must be focused on stanza 9 with its quantitative density of quaint diction, that most distinctive of Ransom's touches, and to the question to which it points: "Man, what would you have?" Substance and style come together here to bare the very heart of the poet by bringing into sharp focus his most fundamental concern and his most characteristic aesthetic mode; the intensity of the question is moderated, at least partially masked, by the quaintness of the diction.

Ransom's most pervasive thematic concern is given philosophical and explicit expression in "The Equilibrists." In the body of his most intensely effective lyrical poetry, that concern is the underlying premise, implicit in the concretely experiential terms of death and dying. Resolve the question "Man, what would you have?" and there is no ironic tension in "Bells for John Whiteside's Daughter." Accept the resolution and there is no anguish in "Janet Waking"—nor in "Blue Girls," "Vision by Sweetwater," "Emily Hardcastle, Spinster," "Necrological," "Dead Boy," or "Here Lies a Lady," among others. The tensions and the anguish at the heart of Ransom's poetry derive from his preoccupation with mortality. That preoccupation gives rise to various dualistic patterns, body and soul, feeling and reason, youth and age, passion and honor, that must all be held, like the bridal couple in Keats's ode, in a state of suspended animation in the imagination. Grief for the death of a child *in time* passes. That same grief *in the imagination* is by definition beyond the ameliorative effects of time. Where Keats gives us the essence of poignance, Ransom gives us the fundamental anguish of mortal beings aware of their mortality. To contain the fierce heat of that essence, he devised the well-wrought urn of his highly mannered texture and style.

Lloyd N. Dendinger

Other major works

NONFICTION: *I'll Take My Stand: The South and the Agrarian Tradition, by Twelve Southerners*, 1930; *God Without Thunder: An Unorthodox Defense of Orthodoxy*, 1930; *Topics for Freshman Writing*, 1935; *The World's Body*, 1938; *The New Criticism*, 1941; *A College Primer of Writing*, 1943; *Studies in Modern Criticism from the "Kenyon Review,"* 1951 (editor); *American Poetry at Mid-century*, 1958 (with Delmore Schwartz and John Hall Wheelock); *Symposium on Formalist Criticism*, 1967 (with others); *The Kenyon Critics*, 1967 (editor); *Beating the Bushes: Selected Essays, 1941-1970*, 1972; *Selected Letters of John Crowe Ransom*, 1985 (Thomas Daniel Young and George Core, editors).

Bibliography

Gelpi, Albert. "Robert Frost and John Crowe Ransom." In *A Coherent Splendor: The American Poetic Renaissance, 1916-1950*. Cambridge, England: Cambridge University Press, 1987. Gelpi stresses Ransom's connection with Robert Frost; the two poets admired each other and Frost helped to promote Ransom's work. Ransom viewed his main task as restoring poetic diction. He sharply opposed idealism, stressed irony and paradox, and aimed at presenting a world stripped of illusion. Gelpi provides a very useful metrical analysis of "Janet Waking" enabling the reader to see how Ransom achieves his ironic mood. Gelpi also includes a discussion of Ransom's ideological views, as expressed in the *Fugitive*, the journal of the Southern Agrarians.

Pearce, Roy Harvey. *The Continuity of American Poetry*. Middletown, Conn.: Wesleyan University Press, 1987. In an earlier edition (1961), this work became a standard survey of American poetry. Ransom was a pedagogical poet, using his verse to teach lessons about life. He thought that human sensibility operated within strict limits and attempted to inculcate this view through the irony of his poetic diction. Death is a frequent theme in Ransom's work. Pearce brings out very well the conflict in Ransom between insistence on realism and devotion to a particular vision of history and tradition.

Suchard, Alan, et al. "Crosscurrents of Modernism." In *Modern American Poetry, 1865-1950*. Amherst: University of Massachusetts Press, 1989. Suchard, although aware of Ransom's merits, is restrained in his enthusiasm. He sees Ransom as a poet of death. Although devoted to tradition, his poems in fact convey the breakdown of faith and the enigmatic nature of existence. His irony is often presented by the use of charming and old-

fashioned forms, such as ballads, to express dark thoughts. Suchard claims
that Ransom's devotion to New Criticism helped discourage innovation in
American poetry.

Turco, Lewis P. *Visions and Revisions of American Poetry*. Fayetteville: University of Alabama Press, 1986. Turco sees Ransom as an agonist: a poet
who spends most of his time elaborating a theory of poetry. Much of Ransom's work is thus embodied in essays as he wrote few poems. Of these,
the best are "Bells for John Whiteside's Daughter" and "Blue Girls." These
poems date from the 1920's, and Ransom's return to poetry in the 1960's
was unsuccessful. Turco calls Ransom an academic poet, a term he does
not intend as praise.

Waggoner, Hyatt H. "Irony and Orthodoxy." In *American Poets: From the
Puritans to the Present*. Baton Rouge: Louisiana State University Press,
1984. Waggoner notes Ransom's witty, elegant language but claims that
this serves mainly to cover up the precarious balance of his poetry. He
was torn between devotion to tradition and realism. A detailed analysis of
"Antique Haunts" is given in order to illustrate Ransom's ambiguity. The
poem is a defense of the Southern way of life, but Ransom's own perspective is deliberately elusive.

Wellek, René. "John Crowe Ransom." In *A History of Modern Criticism:
American Criticism, 1900-1950*. Vol. 6. New Haven, Conn.: Yale University Press, 1986. The best analysis of Ransom's philosophy. Wellek claims
that Ransom's key thought is the contingency of the world. Objects do not
form a unified system but are separate. Pluralism thus becomes a key artistic value. The aim of poetry is mimesis: the particularity of things must
be described. Wellek also clarifies Ransom's dichotomy between structure
and texture.

HENRY REED

Born: Birmingham, England; February 22, 1914

Principal poetry
A Map of Verona: Poems, 1946.

Other literary forms
Most of Henry Reed's work has been in genres other than poetry. His first publication was a critical study, *The Novel Since 1939* (1946), and he has also translated Paride Rombi's *Perdu and His Father* (1954) and Dino Buzzati's *Larger than Life* (1962). Mainly, however, Reed has been a prolific creator of drama, especially radio plays. In particular, he has enjoyed a fruitful literary relationship with the Italian language and the Italian playwright Ugo Betti, a number of whose works Reed has translated and adapted for radio broadcast in London and for stage production in London and New York. His adaptations of Betti include *The Queen and the Rebels*, *The Burnt Flower-Bed*, and *Summertime*, all produced in London in 1955 and published as *Three Plays* (1956); later adaptations of Betti were *Island of Goats*, produced in New York in 1955 and published as *Crime on Goat Island* (1955), and *Corruption in the Palace of Justice*, produced in New York in 1958. He also adapted Natalia Ginzburg's play *The Advertisement* (1968) for production in London in 1968 and in New York in 1974. Reed's most fruitful relationship, however, has been with the British Broadcasting Corporation, for which he has written or adapted some forty to fifty radio plays, including the previously mentioned works by Betti. Reed's writing for radio began with *Moby Dick: A Play for Radio from Herman Melville's Novel* (1947), brief lyric sections of which form the last part of Reed's collection *A Map of Verona: Poems*.

Achievements
In Britain, Reed has perhaps been better known for his radio plays and his adaptations of Ugo Betti than for his poetry, whereas in the United States he has been known almost exclusively for his poetry—or, more specifically, for "Naming of Parts" and "Judging Distances," which originally appeared with a third poem ("Unarmed Combat") under the general title "Lessons of the War." Much anthologized for introductory literature courses, these two humorous lyrics emphasizing the futility of war have been read by possibly half the undergraduate population of the United States during the past two decades. During the period of the Vietnam War especially, the two poems struck a responsive chord in the hearts of American college students. These two fine poems deserve the circulation they have achieved, but unfortunately the rest of Reed's poetry is little known in this country. His other work is

even less known, except possibly among scholars of drama and Italian.

For a first collection of poetry, *A Map of Verona: Poems* maintains a remarkably high quality throughout, though it does not entirely escape the unevenness typical of first collections. For the sake of completeness, and perhaps for its greater explicitness, the less-inspired third poem of the "Lessons of the War" group should be read. Among other poems which stand out, and which illustrate other aspects of Reed's poetic talent, are "A Map of Verona," "The Door and the Window," "The Builders," a group entitled "Tintagel" ("Tristram," "Iseult Blaunchesmains," "King Mark," and "Iseult la Belle"), and a group entitled "Triptych" ("Chrysothemis," "Antigone," and "Philoctetes"). Finally, admirers of T. S. Eliot, as well as other readers, should not miss Reed's wicked little parody, "Chard Whitlow/(Mr. Eliot's Sunday Evening Postscript)."

Perhaps time will smooth out some of the imbalances in Reed's reputation, but as a poet he will likely remain known as someone who strangely produced only one early collection and who is best known for his gently humorous antiwar sentiments. No doubt Reed himself can well appreciate the irony of this situation, since one of his favorite poetic subjects is the person transfixed in time by a single defining (and somewhat immobilizing) act. Reed's act of poetic self-definition, however, is certainly not the whole story of his writing career. He will probably also be known as something of a media pioneer, a writer who could switch smoothly from print to performance to electronic medium. These smooth transitions were forecast in the nature of his poetry.

Biography

Henry Reed was born and educated in Birmingham, a sprawling manufacturing center in the English Midlands. There is no evidence that this setting had much influence on his poetry, unless it encouraged a desire to travel to and write about sunnier climes. He attended the King Edward VI School in Birmingham and took an M.A. degree at the University of Birmingham.

The influence of his education is evident throughout Reed's poetry, which, like the poetry of so many young Britons from the universities, smacks somewhat of Survey of British Literature. For example, one can detect echoes of Andrew Marvell, Alfred, Lord Tennyson, Matthew Arnold, Joseph Conrad, and Eliot. In addition, many of Reed's subjects are literary in inspiration. Seemingly, the weight of the great tradition bore down heavily on Reed, and reaction to this weight could have contributed to his move from poetry to radio plays.

Certainly another influence on Reed's writing career was his experience of World War II, when he served in the Royal Army and with the Foreign Office. His military training provided inspiration for the poems in the "Lessons of the War" series. In addition, the war brought him to London, where he subsequently formed the association with the BBC which has since defined his career.

Analysis

In "A Map of Verona," Henry Reed states that "maps are of place, not time," while in "Judging Distances" one reads that "maps are of time, not place." These two versions of reality are not as contradictory as they might appear, if one considers the source of each. The first version comes from Reed himself, while the second is the official army doctrine mechanically voiced by a training officer to a group of recruits. The first version acknowledges the inability of man's puny symbols to represent reality, while the second asserts the military's wishful thinking, its need to be in control, to pour reality into a uniform and make it stand up and salute. One cannot blame the military for trying, as indeed it must, but the futility of its efforts is laughable: in "Judging Distances" the military theory is demolished, appropriately enough, by a pair of lovers in the distance, who finish making love even as the training officer and woebegone recruits watch.

Like the military, though with somewhat more success, Reed in his poems is intent on creating maps of reality. In his poems, both place and time have important roles, as they intersect with human actions. Reed is interested in place for its own sake, but he is also interested in its effects on human actions. Even more, he is interested in how human actions reverberate in time—the anticipation of actions, how actions fade from memory, how the meaning of actions changes with time, how, on the other hand, actions define and transfix personalities. For Reed, reality is as fluid as the stream in his poem "Lives" that cannot be caged. To try as best he can to catch and bottle this reality, Reed concentrates on dramatic moments or their consequences, particularly their moral consequences. Supporting Reed's penchant for the dramatic is his gift of mimicry, for capturing the sound of the human voice, as amply demonstrated in his parodies of T. S. Eliot and of the training officer in the "Lessons of the War" poems. Thus, it should come as no surprise that, although Reed writes in a variety of forms, some of his best poems are dramatic monologues. It should also come as no surprise that he eventually changed to writing drama.

Perhaps the most important poem for understanding Reed's ontology, and a good poem in its own right, is "A Map of Verona." At first, it seems no more than a pleasant travel advertisement: for "a whole long winter season" Reed's thoughts have dwelt on an open map of Verona. His intention to visit Verona reminds him of a stay in another Italian city, "My youthful Naples." Naples is associated in his mind with "a practice in sorrow," with "a sketch in tenderness, lust, and sudden parting." No doubt at the time this experience, despite its air of youthful experimentation, was deeply moving; now, however, he can barely recall its "underground whispers of music." Reed does recall, though, that he once studied an open map of Naples with the same expectation with which he now studies the map of Verona, and his map-studies then were totally "useless," since "maps are of place, not time." Still, studying the map of Verona and hearing other travelers relate their tourist impressions of the city help to "calm" Reed's "winter of expectations." The city of Verona does indeed exist, and "one day" Reed will go there: "in tomorrow's cave the music/ Trembles and forms inside the musician's mind." Meanwhile, echoing the poem's epigraph from Arthur Rimbaud, Reed can only wonder "in what hour of beauty" and "in what good arms" he will attain "those regions and that city." Finally, he wonders "what good Arms shall take them away again."

On both a literal and a symbolic level, "A Map of Verona" suggests the nature of experience. Among other things, Reed seems to say that, for the most part, people's lives are suspended between remembrance and expectation. Then, when a big moment comes, people are often too youthful to appreciate it or too experienced to believe that it will last. Still, even though remembrance fades and expectation is uncertain, both enrich one's life. Indeed, their enriching context makes it possible for a person to know a big moment when it arrives. Then there is always the potential for the big, fulfilling moment to come, in whatever "hour of beauty" or in whatever "good arms." In "A Map of Verona," the city of Verona, a jewel of Western civilization and the home of Romeo and Juliet, symbolizes this fulfillment.

Reading "A Map of Verona" is good preparation for reading the "Lessons of the War" poems. Though vastly different in subject, the two poems are not as different in theme as might appear; they merely approach much the same theme from different directions. Despite the tenuous nature of experience and the way so much of life hangs between memory and expectations, "A Map of Verona" asserts the potential for human fulfillment. If there is one sure way of cutting off that potential, and typically at an early age, it is war. The incongruity—indeed, insanity—of war is suggested in the "Lessons of the War" poems by the way time and place conspire against the military training going on. While a training officer tries to hammer home his dull lessons, springtime is bursting out all over: flowers are blooming, bees are "assaulting and fumbling the flowers," and lovers are making love. While nature moves full speed ahead toward the fulfillment of life, the soldiers train to eliminate life and in so doing put their own lives on the line. How such lessons go against the grain is also rendered dramatically in the person of Reed's recruit, who has trouble paying attention and through whose mind the reader hears the training officer's words and the recruit's spoken and unspoken responses. His rather obsessional notions demonstrate the difficulty, in springtime, of turning a young man's fancy to thoughts of war.

Although the theme of these poems is sober, their predominant tone is not. Their tone is established by the humorous dramatic situation, especially as this situation is reflected in the diction. Each of the poems begins with a parody of the training officer that reveals his routine mentality, his jargonistic but otherwise limited vocabulary, and his limited knowledge. All of these provide marvelous openings for the clever young recruit, who responds to the officer's military litany by twisting it into poetic or profound—but always humorous—meanings. In "Naming of Parts," for example, the officer's break-down on a rifle's parts gives the recruit a fertile field for sexual puns. This particular instance of contrasting diction, like the general contrast between the voice of the training officer and the voice of the recruit, reinforces the theme of the military's sterile, deadening influence.

The "Lessons of the War" poems well illustrate Reed's talent for humor, but most of his poems are somber both in theme and tone. What does not change is Reed's eye for the dramatic situation. His sense of drama can be felt strongly in two groups of poems that consist mostly of dramatic mono-logues and that might be considered the peak of Reed's poetic achievement. These are the two groups entitled "Tintagel" and "Triptych." "Tintagel" consists of four poems named after the principals in the Tristram story: "Tris-tram," "Iseult Blaunchesmains," "King Mark," and "Iseult la Belle." In a note, Reed indicates that these four characters "represent four aspects of a problem known (in one or more of these aspects) to most men and women." He depends on the reader's knowledge of the Tristram legend to fill in the details—that these characters represent four corners of a love quadrangle with one side missing: Iseult Blaunchesmains loves Tristram who loves Iseult la Belle who returns his love but is married to King Mark. Already the poems sound like the scenario of an Italian drama or opera, and as the four characters speak their loves and sorrows, either through their own voices or the voice of a sympathetic narrator, they sound more and more like Luigi Pirandello's six characters, doomed to repeat their roles to eternity. They have, in effect, become archetypal characters transfixed in time by their self-defining actions. They are like some traumatized people in real life, locked into one searing emotional experience that repeats itself endlessly in their consciousness.

The three characters in "Triptych," all from Greek drama, have likewise defined their personalities for all time through their actions. Here, however, the characters are not equally condemned; indeed, Reed notes that the speak-ers in the three poems "represent a moral progression, culminating in a decision." The three poems are "Chrysothemis," "Antigone," and "Philoc-tetes." Chrysothemis and Philoctetes speak for themselves in dramatic mono-logues, but in the second poem two witnesses to Antigone's death react to it in a dialogue. Chrysothemis, the sister of Electra and Orestes, represents the onlooker who will not get involved no matter how many atrocities she witnesses; after the house of Atreus has decimated itself, she stays behind to care for the remaining children and the decaying house. The house symbolizes her moral state, though she tries to believe she is playing a useful role. The main speaker in "Antigone" is a chance onlooker who, though not involved in the action, is sensitive to its moral consequences, in particular to the way

Antigone acts unhesitatingly on what she knows is right. Finally, the ostracized Philoctetes represents the person who wants to get involved and is rejected, but who overcomes his bitter suffering and sense of personal wrong to act decisively when the time comes: even after years of intense frustration, he goes as straight to his mark as do his blessed arrows. The traumatized person is not necessarily transfixed in time; rebirth is possible.

These two groups of poems involving serious drama verge closer and closer to drama itself. The last group of five poems in *A Map of Verona: Poems* comes from an actual drama, Reed's radio version of *Moby Dick* for the BBC. In a note, Reed refers to these poems as "lyric interludes." The transition from poet to dramatist is complete. Very likely Reed's friends mourned the transition, but very likely William Shakespeare's friends did the same.

Harold Branam

Other major works

LONG FICTION: *Perdu and His Father*, 1954 (translation); *Larger Than Life*, 1962 (translation).

PLAYS: *Moby Dick: A Play for Radio from Herman Melville's Novel*, 1947 (radio play); *Island of Goats*, 1955 (also known as *Crime on Goat Island*); *Three Plays*, 1956 (translation); *Corruption in the Palace of Justice*, 1958 (translation); *The Advertisement*, 1968 (adaptation); *The Streets of Pompeii and Other Plays for Radio*, 1971; *Hilda Tablet and Others: Four Pieces for Radio*, 1971.

NONFICTION: *The Novel Since 1939*, 1946.

Bibliography

Drakakis, John, ed. *British Radio Drama*. Cambridge, England: Cambridge University Press, 1981. Contains an excellent chapter by Roger Savage which, although ultimately concerned with Reed's radio plays, gives exceptional biographical information and makes numerous references to the poetry. It embraces Reed's career and acknowledges his work as a poet, critic, translator, and dramatist. This introductory essay includes notes with references that are reviews of Reed's work and some articles not necessarily concerning him directly.

Gunter, Liz, and Jim Linebarger. "Tone and Voice in Henry Reed's 'Judging Distances.'" *Notes on Contemporary Literature* 18 (March, 1988): 9-10. Provides an informative analysis of the structure and theme of Reed's poetry. Useful information on Reed's poetic and technical devices.

O'Toole, Michael. "Henry Reed, and What Follows the 'Naming of Parts.'" In *Functions of Style*, edited by David Birch and Michael O'Toole. London: Pinter, 1988. Examines the stylistics of modern English. Central to an appreciation and understanding of Reed's poetic works. Includes a foreword by M. A. K. Halliday.

LIZETTE WOODWORTH REESE

Born: Waverly, Maryland; January 9, 1856
Died: Baltimore, Maryland; December 17, 1935

Principal poetry
A Branch of May, 1887; *A Handful of Lavender*, 1891; *A Quiet Road*, 1896; *A Wayside Lute*, 1909; *Spicewood*, 1920; *Wild Cherry*, 1923; *The Selected Poems of Lizette Woodworth Reese*, 1926; *Little Henrietta*, 1927; *White April, and Other Poems*, 1930; *Pastures and Other Poems*, 1933; *The Old House in the Country*, 1936.

Other literary forms
Although primarily a poet, Lizette Woodworth Reese published at least fourteen short stories, which appeared in various literary magazines, including *Harper's Magazine*, *Lippincott's*, and *Outlook*. Five of these fictional pieces are reprinted in her semiautobiographical work *The York Road* (1931). In *A Victorian Village* (1929), Reese reminisces about her girlhood in and around Waverly, a hamlet on the outskirts of Baltimore. Reese's only other major work is the unfinished *Worleys* (1936), a fictional piece published after her death. She also wrote a few essays on teaching and published several magazine poems which were not included in any of her books.

Achievements
By the time Reese retired at the age of sixty-five from her position as a public school English teacher, she had published only about half of her poems. Yet to come were the poems in *Wild Cherry*, the new work contained in *The Selected Poems of Lizette Woodworth Reese*, and the long elegy *Little Henrietta*. Also still to come was the somewhat belated recognition as a significant contributor to the mainstream of American lyricism. By 1924, Reese began receiving the awards and honors that she deserved. The College of William and Mary initiated Reese as an honorary member of Phi Beta Kappa. In 1925, the Tudor and Stuart Club at The Johns Hopkins University selected Reese for honorary membership. The most public expression of recognition occurred on December 15, 1926, when the George H. Doran Company, publisher of *The Selected Poems of Lizette Woodworth Reese*, hosted a testimonial dinner for Reese at the Brevoort Hotel in New York. Many prominent literary figures of the day attended, including DuBose Heyward, Edwin Markham, Carl Van Doren, Elinor Wylie, William Rose Benét, and Robert Frost. Other honors followed: in 1931, Reese received the Percy Bysshe Shelley Memorial Award for achievement in poetry; in the same year, an honorary Doctor of Letters degree from Goucher College; and, in 1934, designation as National Honor Poet of Poetry Week.

Ultimately, Reese's place in American literary history may depend on the impetus that she gave to a modern, native lyricism. This impetus dates from the publication of her first book in 1887, more than twenty years before the flowering of the Imagist movement. Reese, who styled herself a "conventional traditionist" and spoke unflatteringly of the "precious imagists," was, nevertheless, a poet whose work is characterized by many of the qualities that the imagists praised: simplicity, concentration, sharp sensory appeal, and, as Ezra Pound demanded, "direct treatment of the thing." David Perkins says in *A History of Modern Poetry* (1976) that Reese handled images "in a way that anticipates Imagist poetry," and other critics have noted the modern texture of her verse, lying under the traditional structure of rhymed quatrains and sonnets. Forgiving her lapses into "poetic" diction and inversions ("hath," "grasses green") and stock rhymes ("fall/all," "spring/thing"), one still detects a genuine voice, a voice that breaks with the genteel tradition to which Reese has been unfairly assigned.

Ironically, Reese has been to some extent the victim of the success of her famous sonnet "Tears." First published by *Scribner's Magazine* in 1899, and later included in *A Wayside Lute*, "Tears" has been anthologized so frequently that even a serious student of American poetry might conclude that Reese wrote one brilliant sonnet and little else of merit. H. L. Mencken said that "we have here a sonnet that no other American has ever approached." Such singular praise for "Tears" from Mencken and others (Padraic Colum said that he knew it by heart) tended to distinguish it as *the* Reese poem, identifying it in the public's mind in much the same way that William Ernest Henley and "Invictus" are inevitably linked.

Finally, Reese's achievement should be gauged in terms of her influence. In *American Poetry Since 1900* (1923), Louis Untermeyer considers Reese the "forerunner of Sara Teasdale, Edna St. Vincent Millay and the new generation to whom simplicity in song is a first essential." Influence is difficult to assess in precise terms, but one often hears echoes of Reese in the poetry of the younger lyricists. Teasdale and Wylie particularly admired Reese's work, and Wylie was a featured speaker at the Brevoort Testimonial.

Biography

Lizette Woodworth Reese and her twin sister, Sophia Louisa, were born, according to their mother, "in the worst storm of the winter" of 1856 at their maternal grandparents' house in Waverly, Maryland. Of Welsh descent on her father's side and German on her mother's, she early learned to love, as she recalls in one poem, the "Saxon tang" which "clung to our elders' speech." Her preference then for the Anglo-Saxon monosyllable came naturally to her reticent, yet vivid, lyrics which seem to blend what she called the "silent" tendency of her father's Welsh ancestry, while retaining the vivacity of her talkative, musically inclined mother, Louisa Gabler Reese.

Mrs. Reese and the young twins moved in with her parents during the Civil

War while her husband, David Reese, served with the Confederate forces and her brother with the Union. In *A Victorian Village*, Reese recalls the Civil War days in the border state of Maryland: "Between the blue forces and the gray we were ground between two millstones of terror." Against this terror stood her sprightly, devoutly religious mother from whom the girl acquired a love of gardening and growing things—the lilac bushes, hawthorn trees, daffodils, and succory blossoms which the visual and olfactory imagery of her poetry constantly evokes.

As a well-read girl of seventeen with what she called the "gift of authority," Reese began teaching English at St. John's Parish School in Waverly. After two years, she transferred to the Baltimore district where she taught in three different high schools, eventually retiring in 1921 from Western High after a forty-five-year career. To honor her on the occasion of her retirement, Western High erected a bronze tablet inscribed with her celebrated sonnet "Tears."

Although she never married, lived all her life near or in Baltimore, and taught English for more than four decades, Reese was not a sheltered "school-marm." She was a founding member of "The Women's Literary Club of Baltimore" and enjoyed an active public life which included readings and lectures for civic and literary groups. She knew and corresponded with many members of literary society, especially Louise Imogen Guiney, Edmund Clarence Stedman, John Hall Wheelock, Untermeyer, and Mencken. Although Reese was a woman of literary affairs, the world of her poetry is the Maryland world of trees, flowers, and country lanes where she first learned, through her own sensory perception, the metaphorical equivalence between a mood and the natural stimuli which engender it.

Analysis

Several critics have identified Reese's major thematic concern, which she herself specifies in the imperative opening of her poem "To a Town Poet": "Snatch the departing mood;/ Make yours its emptying reed, and pipe us still/ Faith in the time. . . ." Reese follows her own advice as she explores in poem after poem the "departing mood," ranging from bittersweet recollections to the intense memory that redeems some part of an otherwise irrecoverable past. "To a Town Poet," Reese's manifesto for a native lyricism proclaims "faith in our common blood" and directs the poet's attention *toward* the "huddled trees," the "smoky ways," the "vendor, swart but free" and *away* from the period's sentimental, genteel verse with its stilted diction, classical allusions, and didactic guidance. Reese did not, however, mean a lyricism like Walt Whitman's free verse; she meant a lyricism in the traditional forms from which she herself rarely departed and to which some poets, such as Millay and Frost, turned during the modern lyric renaissance.

A fascination with mood—with the fine gradations of multiple sensations—certainly goes back to Reese's girlhood. Growing up with the terror of war,

the young Lizette enjoyed the contentment that she found in the natural setting of her grandfather's farm, stories which she delightfully retells in *A Victorian Village*. She took additional comfort in the Victorian literature which
she eagerly read—particularly Charles Dickens and Alfred, Lord Tennyson,
her masters in the school of literary mood.

Considering her work in its historical and social milieu, one finds a poetry
oblivious to the "gilded age" and its associated social problems. Reese was
not indifferent to the issues of her time, but she did not consider her lyrics
as a forum for any causes except those of emotion and beauty. Her subjects
may vary from love to death to nature, but the theme almost always comes
back to the belief that an appreciation of experience depends on isolating the
"mood" associated with it and then crystallizing it through sensory appeals,
especially the tactile, auditory, and olfactory imagery which further distinguishes her poetic voice.

The key to a formal appreciation of Reese's work lies in the recognition
of her poetic voice. This voice, heard throughout her eleven books of poetry,
makes a unique contribution to the American impulse toward a modern lyric
verse. Examining her prosody, diction, rhythms, and syntax, one soon discovers a repetitively expressive pattern, with artistic variations, that constitutes a talented poetic voice. An outstanding feature of this voice is her
penchant for the Anglo-Saxon monosyllable. She wanted to write a lyric that
was native both in locale and tongue, and, accordingly, she wanted to avoid
the Latinate, polysyllabic words of which her genteel contemporaries were
much too fond. In "Betrayed," the first poem in her first book, the word
"perfect" is the only polysyllabic word, and she continued to favor spare and
economical diction. This preference for the simple, native words permitted
her to achieve a "classical" American idiom, an idiom less showy than Whitman's, less intense than Emily Dickinson's, yet vivid and evocative in its own
quiet manner.

One metrical trait of Reese's voice is the substitution of a trochaic foot in
the prevailing iambic meter, especially in the initial position where the trochee
and the following iamb actually constitute a choriambus. The choriambus,
such as "Blówn líke ă fláme" and "Heáped iñ thĕ róads," then becomes a
"long foot" that frames or freezes an image, particularly with an active verb
in the dynamic stress position where it militates against the rhythmical stasis
of imagery locked into what Paul Fussell, in *Poetic Meter and Poetic Form*
(1965), calls "the pleasantly predictable, manageable world of the iambic."

In the first stage of Reese's long literary career are exemplified all the
characteristic traits and tricks of her poetic voice. Her thematic concern with
the "departing mood"—to an extent that theme and tone become one—
consistently typifies the poems of the early period. Reese is not, however,
merely a poet of mood like the poetasters who contributed sentimental verse
to the ladies' magazines. She is, rather, a poet who locates the gentle irony

where the woof of a pleasant image interlaces, and thus partly obscures and softens, the warp of hard reality. The bittersweet, the wistful, the poignant are the emotional province of Reese's voice, but these emotions come from an artistic distance, from an awareness by the lyric persona that mood is not only crystallized feeling but also recaptured thought. Mood is then, for Reese's lyric speaker, a complex response to the sensory appeal of imagery, and the mood itself becomes the healthy equilibrium between the venting of emotion on the one hand and the containing of emotion on the other.

"In Time of Grief," from *A Quiet Road*, illustrates the essential method of Reese's early lyricism. The poem combines an array of images within its tight structure of three ballad-stanza quatrains. Noteworthy is the emphasis on olfactory imagery, for Reese knows that the sense of smell, as effectively as sight or sound, evokes memories and their associated feelings. The lyric speaker, referring to the box shrub along the "wall of stone," says that "Its odor through my house was blown/ Into the chamber there." Compatibly mixing her sensory impressions, she defines this "scent" in auditory and tactile terms: "As though one spoke a word half meant/ That left a sting behind." The brief resolution of the poem leaves the speaker uncertain about the abstract quality of "grief" but comforted in the knowledge of "how keen the box can be/ After a fall of rain." Thus Reese's lyric persona encounters an ironic variation: the "reality" of abstractions (grief, love, beauty, truth) is hardly separable from the masking, imagistic "appearance," because, unexpected and unsummoned, the departing mood may instantly return when the sensory conditions are right.

Published in 1909 on the threshold of the New Poetry, *A Wayside Lute* represents an advance in stylistic variations and dramatic vigor, even though Reese's standard themes of mood and memory, along with her poetic staples— the poplar trees, the color white, the month of April—remain the same. Unexpectedly, it is the Petrarchan sonnet "Tears"—a poem neither concerned with the departing mood nor informed by her usual images—which distinguishes this collection. In "Tears," Reese still relies on the heavy monosyllabic diction, the trochaic inversions, and the auditory imagery ("A call to battle," "The last echo," "The burst of music"), but she widens her poetic scope to ponder the brevity of life and, in the apostrophe that comprises the sestet, to ask the "Chieftains, and bards, and keepers of the sheep" to release her from a mood she can no longer tolerate: "Loose me from tears, and make me see aright/ How each hath back what once he stayed to weep." The understated effect of "stayed," suggesting only a pause, exercises the ironic control which prevents the poem from stumbling into sentimentality. In the climactic last line, the lyric speaker who wants an "intimation of immortality" cites two—one a bard and one a keeper of the sheep—who stayed to weep: "Homer his sight, David his little lad!" Here, in one memorable line, Reese sweeps up, and juxtaposes, two representatives from the great shaping forces of Western civilization: the Hellenic tradition of humanistic culture and the Judeo-Christian tradition of religious hope. The optimistic thread in each branch justifies the enlightening exclamation which closes the sestet—a lyric shout back to the "old, old dead" that the promise of immortality is implicit in the ironic brevity of life.

In the third stage of her career, Reese reaches the height of her lyric voice, achieving her finest sustained yet tightly controlled lyricism. This control is evident in *Spicewood*, where half the poems are Petrarchan sonnets, each one containing six, rather than the prescribed five, rhymes in one of two patterns: either abba, cddc, efg, efg, or abab, cdcd, efg, efg. In poetic voice and imagery, these sonnets are typically Reese's, but they are plaintive notes of a speaker who is more introspective and less exuberant, and fully prone to sound the characteristically modern theme of alienation still comprehended in the resonance of mood and memory.

In this period, Reese elevates some of her favorite images to the eminence of symbol. The color white, for example, makes the transition from a descriptive to a symbolic term, becoming what Robert D. Rhode calls "a manifold symbol. . . . It is a spiritual force that inspires, tortures, and subdues." "In Vain," one of the finest lyrics in *Wild Cherry*, illustrates the new symbolic aura for the word "white." In the first three quatrains, the lyric speaker, remembering a lost lover, cries "for a world empty of you" but realizes that "Some small thing thereabout/ Would bring the same hurt back again." As usual, the speaker emphasizes the aching, inescapable mood which sensory impressions will inevitably provoke. In the climactic quatrain, struggling against the lovesick mood, the lyric "I" yearns for "the smell of yarrow flowers . . . set/ In a lost field." Then, reinforcing the olfactory imagery, the forsaken lover simply repeats the desire with the modifying color and conditions: "White yarrow flowers,/ Out in the August wet." There is no complete subject/verb relationship in the quatrain; it works its culminating effect strictly through the exposition of imagery. One should not incorrectly conclude that the flowers have an antecedent in "some small thing" that would remind the lyric "I" of the lost lover or that, in the opposite direction, they represent a remedy for heartache. The speaker simply ponders submission to the sensory assault of the strongly scented yarrow and its eye-catching whiteness—a whiteness meaning, on the sensory level, more than brilliance or color, and meaning, on the metaphorical level, more than "pristine" or "virginal," and pointing, ironically, toward the muted eroticism of a "lost field . . ./ Out in the August wet." Here, as in other notable lyrics from this period ("A Puritan Lady," "Fog," "Alien"), Reese invests the color white with a private symbolism that defines a complex mood and finally rounds, in "Reparation," to the philosophy that "what is fair is permanent." For Reese, the single word which best renders the essence of "fair"—not merely as synonym but as the natural stimulant of, and symbolic correlative for, mood and memory—is "white."

Readers of *The Selected Poems of Lizette Woodworth Reese* should be aware that the George H. Doran Company could not get permission from the Norman, Remington Company, the publishers of *Spicewood* and *Wild Cherry*, to reprint poems from these two volumes, thus precluding a proper estimation of Reese's talent by anyone who mistakenly believes that the book contains a representative "selection" of her best work.

Little Henrietta, written in thirty-nine ten-line stanzas, excluding a three-couplet poem entitled "Shelter" and "An Epitaph," is actually an elegy for a child whom the young Reese knew in Waverly. Uncharacteristically Reese does not employ regular rhyme, although there are occasional true and slant rhymes. With a sure sense of her own talent, Reese knew that the traditional elegiac mode offered her poetic voice a perfect medium with its flower symbolism, meditative mood, and expression of grief which submits to Christian consolation. A significant part of her achievement is in the poem's structural design: the first fifteen stanzas serve as an introductory narrative which details Henrietta's childhood and the impression which she made on her friends and elders, leading up to her death in stanza fifteen. The last twenty-four stanzas follow the general pattern of the pastoral elegy with a questioning invocation in stanza 16: "Have we not waked at time," the narrator asks, "And thought our eyes amiss?" The digression on the church, in stanzas 22-25, is not condemnatory, as in John Milton's "Lycidas," but the narrator feels the irony of the funeral that "left us naked by a churchyard wall." A neglected contribution to the elegiac genre in American literature, *Little Henrietta* ranks with "Tears" as Reese's major achievement.

The poems from Reese's last period, written after she had turned seventy, betray a weakening of her poetic voice. Although *White April* and *Pastures* contain poems which recapture the old lyric energy—"White April" and "Women" in the former volume, "A Country Doctor" and "Cynical Advice" in the latter—there is a tendency, avoided in her early work, toward didactic conclusions and moral sentiment.

Published posthumously in 1936, *The Old House in the Country* is a curious addition to the Reese canon. It is a rhymed, autobiographical poem in fifty-two ten-line stanzas, the structure used so successfully in *Little Henrietta*; yet, without the internal conventions of the elegy, this poem lacks unity, causing single stanzas to fragment into separate poems.

Reading Reese's work from this distance, one necessarily considers it on two levels: first, on the basic plane of its lyrical beauty—developed and extended by a poetic voice that maintains its typifying notes and themes throughout her work—and, second, on the plane of its influence, where Reese promoted by example a trend that hastened American lyricism away from a pseudoclassical gentility toward an image-conscious modernity.

Ronald K. Giles

Other major works

FICTION: *Worleys*, 1936.
SHORT FICTION: *The York Road*, 1931.
NONFICTION: *A Victorian Village*, 1929.

Bibliography

Harris, R. P. "April Weather: The Poetry of Lizette Woodworth Reese." *The South Atlantic Quarterly* 29 (April, 1930): 200-207. This essay, appearing before Reese died in 1935, is an early and valuable recognition of her place in American lyric poetry. Surveying her career, Harris shows that, even during the period that Edmund Clarence Stedman called "a twilight interval" (1890-1910), Reese was publishing the "clear, natural lyrics" that anticipated the later works of Edna St. Vincent Millay and Sara Teasdale.

Hill, Phyllis. *Who Will Sing My Songs?* Hagerstown, Md.: Freline, 1988. As a "dialogue" between the author of the book and Reese, the text will appeal primarily to young readers who seek an introduction to her philosophy of life and her poetry. Contains some photographs of Reese, a brief bibliography, and a selection of her poems.

Kindilien, Carlin T. "The Village World of Lizette Woodworth Reese." *The South Atlantic Quarterly* 56 (January, 1957): 91-104. This essay begins with a biographical sketch of Reese, but then quite perceptively analyzes the distinguishing characteristics of her poetry: its simplicity of diction and imagery, its embrace of the natural world, and its spiritual aesthetic. Concludes with a pertinent comparison of Reese and Emily Dickinson.

Morris, Lawrence S. "Some Flowers Down a Lane." *The New Republic* 48 (August 25, 1926): 23-24. A brief but sensitive review of *The Selected Poems of Lizette Woodworth Reese*, this essay touches on the characteristic themes and beauties of Reese's verse, particularly her fascination with mood, memory, and grief.

Rhode, Robert D. "Lizette W. Reese: 'Fair White Gospeler.'" *The Personalist* 31 (1950): 390-398. Using Reese as an example of the teacher-poet, Rhode illustrates how she writes within, but ultimately transcends, the didactic nature of the genteel tradition. Rhode acutely analyzes Reese's choice of "white" and "April" as symbolically important words that help her escape "the excesses of narcissistic romanticism on the one hand, and of ethical nihilism on the other."

KENNETH REXROTH

Born: South Bend, Indiana; December 22, 1905
Died: Montecito, California; June 6, 1982

Principal poetry

A Prolegomenon to a Theodicy, 1932; *In What Hour*, 1940; *The Phoenix and the Tortoise*, 1944; *The Signature of All Things*, 1949; *The Dragon and the Unicorn*, 1952; *Fourteen Poems by O. V. de L. Milosz*, 1952, 1982 (translation); *The Art of Worldly Wisdom*, 1953; *Thou Shalt Not Kill*, 1955; *A Bestiary*, 1955; *Poems from the Japanese*, 1955, 1957, 1964 (translation); *One Hundred Poems from the French*, 1955, 1972 (translation); *One Hundred Poems from the Chinese*, 1956, 1965 (translation); *Thirty Spanish Poems of Love and Exile*, 1956 (translation); *In Defense of the Earth*, 1956; *Poems from the Greek Anthology*, 1962 (translation); *Natural Numbers*, 1963; *The Homestead Called Damascus*, 1963; *The Collected Shorter Poems*, 1966; *The Collected Longer Poems*, 1967; *The Heart's Garden, The Garden's Heart*, 1967; *The Spark in the Tinder of Knowing*, 1968; *Pierre Reverdy Selected Poems*, 1969 (translation); *Love in the Turning Year: One Hundred More Poems from the Chinese*, 1970 (translation); *Sky Sea Birds Trees Earth House Beasts Flowers*, 1971; *The Orchid Boat: Women Poets of China*, 1972 (translation with Ling Chung); *New Poems*, 1974; *One Hundred More Poems from the Japanese*, 1974 (translation); *The Silver Swan*, 1976; *On Flower Wreath Hill*, 1976; *The Burning Heart: Women Poets of Japan*, 1977 (translation with Atsumi Ikuko); *Seasons of Sacred Lust: Selected Poems of Kazuko Shiraishi*, 1978 (translation with Carol Tinker, Atsumi Ikuko, John Solt, and Morita Yasuyo); *The Love Poems of Marichiko*, 1978; *Li Ch'ing Chao: Complete Poems*, 1979 (translation with Ling Chung); *The Morning Star*, 1979.

Other literary forms

In addition to thirty-two books of poetry, of which thirteen are translations from six languages, Kenneth Rexroth philosophically developed his erotic mysticism in verse drama, autobiographies, and critical essays. His four ritual plays of ecstatic transcendence in the midst of collapsing Classical Greek civilization, influenced by Japanese Nō and Greek tragedy, were collected in 1951 as *Beyond the Mountains*, premiered by the Living Theater in New York. Praised as one of his most enduring achievements by William Carlos Williams, the classical scholar George Woodcock, and the Japanese scholars Kodama Sanehide and Sakurai Emiko, *Beyond the Mountains* is distinguished by its faithfulness both to the Eastern and to the Western traditions that fed its subtle form, by its passionate characters who dramatize modern as well as ancient spiritual crises, and by its sensuously intellectual style. In *An Autobiographical Novel* (1966, 1978) and *Excerpts from a Life* (1981), Rexroth's adventures are boldly narrated just as he spoke—with the uncanny power of epigrammatically characterizing everyone he met. Moreover, his religious, philosophical, and literary ideas are amplified in his wide-ranging essays, which have served to expand the audience for modern poetry. Most of his essays have been collected in *Bird in the Bush: Obvious Essays* (1959); *Assays* (1961); Classics Revisited (1968); *The Alternative Society: Essays from the Other World* (1970); *With Eye and Ear* (1970); *American Poetry in the Twentieth Century* (1971); *The Elastic Retort* (1973); and *Communalism, from the Neolithic to 1900* (1975). There are also important introductory essays in his editions of *Selected Poems of D. H. Lawrence* (1947, 1961); *The New British Poets* (1949); and *The Buddhist Writings of Lafcadio Hearn* (1977). In Great Britain a selection of Rexroth's prose and poetry has been edited by Eric Mottram as *The Kenneth Rexroth Reader* (1972).

Achievements

Rexroth wrote in the tradition of contemplative, mystical, visionary, philosophical, and prophetic poets such as William Butler Yeats, D. H. Lawrence, Walt Whitman, William Blake, Dante, Tu Fu, Seami, and Sappho, all of whom influenced him. Rextroth was an eclectic student of many traditions from many cultures: Judeo-Christian, Classical Greek and Roman, Chinese, and Japanese. He was a modernist poet with a passionate commitment to tradition—to that which has lasted for centuries and is worth saving. His work as a whole, expository and autobiographical prose as well as passionate love lyrics, heartrending elegies, ferocious satires, and richly intellectual epic-reveries and dramas, must be read in the context of these diverse traditions. His style ranges from cubist innovations that ally him with Ezra Pound, Gertrude Stein, T. S. Eliot, and other revolutionists of the word, to the limpid simplicity he learned from Chinese and Japanese masters. This stylistic variety, however, is informed by an unwavering central vision—a vision of mystical love, universal responsibility, and spiritual realization.

Rexroth's contributions to diverse literary and intellectual movements are suggested by Louis Zukofsky's inclusion of "Prolegomenon to a Theodicy," a long, cubist, philosophical revery, in *An "Objectivists Anthology"* of 1932, and by Rexroth's membership in the Industrial Workers of the World, the John Reed Clubs, and the San Francisco "Libertarian Circle," among other revolutionary organizations, in which nonviolent, communitarian anarchism set an independent line in opposition to totalitarian communism and fascism as well as to the injustices of capitalistic democracy. His leadership in the "Libertarian Circle" was indispensable to the San Francisco Poetry Renaissance years before the Beats emerged in 1956, when Rexroth introduced Allen Ginsberg and others at the famous debut of *Howl*. He helped to advance the work of such poets as Denise Levertov, Gary Snyder, Jerome Rothenberg, Shiraishi Kazuko, and many others, and his translations of women poets of

China and Japan were deliberately feminist contributions.

Rexroth's work is read widely in Asia and Europe as well as in the United States. His international reputation has been aided by the popularity of his translations, his extensive travels and publication abroad, his collaboration with many writers in Europe and Asia, and the steady support of James Laughlin, whose New Directions has published twenty of Rexroth's books to date. Rexroth's anthology, *The New British Poets*, his edition of D. H. Lawrence's poetry, and Eric Mottram's *Kenneth Rexroth Reader* extended his influence in England; and his reputation in Europe is suggested by the *Akademische Austauschdienst* Award from West Berlin which, with a Rockefeller grant, allowed him to travel around the world in 1967 on a poetry tour. Several tours of Asia, some of them sponsored by the United States Agency of International Communication, indicate the esteem with which he is held in that part of the world.

Other honors received by Rexroth include two California Silver Medal Awards (1941), two Guggenheim Fellowships (1948-1949), a Chapelbrook Award and a Eunice Teitjens Award from *Poetry* magazine (1957), a Longview Award (1963), a Shelley Award from the Poetry Society of America and an Amy Lowell Fellowship (1958), a grant from the National Institute of Arts and Letters (1964), and a W. C. Williams Award from *Contact* magazine (1965). He contributed to many prestigious magazines and newspapers, conducted a program of poetry and comment on KPFA in San Francisco, and, despite his aversion to academic restrictions and his lack of any degrees, taught at San Francisco State College, the University of Wisconsin at Milwaukee, and the University of California at Santa Barbara, besides giving lectures and readings at many other universities around the world.

Biography

Born in South Bend in 1905, Kenneth Rexroth grew up in Indiana, Michigan, Ohio, and Illinois. His ancestors were scholars, peasants, and religious and political dissenters from Germany and Ireland, along with native and black Americans, and pioneers, all of whom enriched his unique personality. His parents were sophisticated travelers who took him on his first European tour when he was seven. After they died a few years later, he became independently active in Chicago as a precocious and revolutionary painter, poet, actor, and journalist—appearing as a character in James T. Farrell's *Studs Lonigan* (1934). After exploring Europe, Mexico, and the West Coast, he moved to San Francisco in 1927, where he made his home until moving to Santa Barbara in the late 1960's. Eastern and Western contemplative practices affected the visionary orientation of his poetry, painting, and philosophy. During World War II, he was a conscientious objector, working in a psychiatric hospital where he was severely injured by a patient. He also assisted interned and otherwise harassed Japanese-Americans, and his friendships with Orientals deepened his lifelong interest in Asian culture, especially Buddhism, which harmonizes in his work with an ecologically based sense of universal community.

He was married to Andrée Dutcher, an anarchist painter, from 1927 until her death in 1940; to Marie Kass, a nurse, from 1940 until their divorce in 1948; and to Marthe Larsen, a member of the "Libertarian Circle," from 1949 until their divorce in 1961. Two daughters, Mary and Katherine, were born to them in 1950 and 1954 respectively. In 1974, he married the poet Carol Tinker, and they spent a year in Kyoto before returning to their home in Montecito. Rexroth also toured Asia in 1967, 1972, 1978, and 1980. He died on June 6, 1982.

Analysis

The Collected Shorter Poems offers a brilliant diversity of styles and forms drawn from Kenneth Rexroth's work over four decades. "Andromeda Chained to the Rock the Great Nebula in Her Heart" and other cubist poems share affinities with Gertrude Stein and Louis Zukofsky, as well as with African and native American song. In a more direct style are exquisite lyrics of love and nature, such as "We Come Back"; fierce intellectual satires such as "Last Visit to the Swimming Pool Soviets" (with aspersions on the so-called chic Hollywood leftists); prophetic poems of revolutionary heroism and defeat, such as "From the Paris Commune to the Kronstadt Rebellion"; and Chinese translations.

"Yin and Yang," Rexroth's most liturgical poem of natural cycles, is an Easter vision of resurrecting birds, flowers, and constellations in which imagery and rhythms are perfectly balanced. In it, the moon, moving through constellations from Leo to Virgo, fertilizes the Virgin, and the ear of wheat symbolizes the creative process of nature as it did in the Eleusinian mysteries. As moonlight proclaims the climactic coming of spring, under the world the sun swims in Pisces, the double fish and the Chinese symbol of Yin and Yang, the harmonious interactions of darkness and light, coldness and heat, female and male. The regular prosody, supporting the orderly revelation of mythology, is a combination of accentual and syllabic patterns. All but three lines have nine syllables each, and most lines have three accents each, with a fundamentally dactyllic movement supporting the prophetic tone of this memorable poem.

"When We with Sappho," perhaps Rexroth's greatest love poem, begins with his first translation, done as a teenager and convincing him that he was a creative artist; there follows his sacramental lyric of erotic bliss, in which he and the woman he loves—also his Muse—merge in a summer meadow into the immortal world of Sappho. As he speaks intimately, hypnotically repeating "summer," each body becomes a "nimbus" over the world, as they unite in thunder, before separating toward death.

"A Letter to William Carlos Williams" centers on the sacramental value of poetry as living speech, person to person (rather than as a text analyzed as an object). The style echoes the intimate ebb and flow of conversation with an old friend, whom he compares with St. Francis (whose flesh united with all lovers, including birds and animals) and Brother Juniper (a wise fool who laughed at indignities). Citing the quiet imagery of daily life in Williams' poetry, Rexroth praises Williams' stillness (like that of the Quaker George Fox and the peace of Jesus), and the poem concludes with a utopian vision of a beautiful Williams River, as a young woman of the future tells her children how it used to be the filthy Passaic, and how the poet Williams had embodied in his poetry a creative community of sacramental relationships.

Rexroth's most famous protest poem, "Thou Shalt Not Kill," has been recorded with jazz accompaniment. An elegy for Dylan Thomas, it mourns the destruction of many poets in this depersonalizing, violent century. Young men, Rexroth proclaims, are being murdered all over the world—such as Saints Stephen, Lawrence, and Sebastian—by the Superego in uniform. The second section is reminiscent of "Lament for the Makaris," the elegy by the sixteenth century Scottish poet William Dunbar; in it Rexroth laments the impoverishment and deaths of many poets from Edward Arlington Robinson through Elinor Wylie and Countée Cullen to Ezra Pound. The third section, in a deepening tone, tells of many others struck down by the Moloch of the modern world. Accusations become lyrical in the last section, as nearly everyone is blamed for having a hand in the destruction of poetic vision—even writers such as T. S. Eliot and Ernest Hemingway who have enjoyed fame and power. The poem has been condemned by some critics but praised by others as a passionate call for prophetic vision.

The Collected Longer Poems, which should be read as a whole work, reveals Rexroth's spiritual and artistic development as summarized in the introduction to the original publication of *The Phoenix and the Tortoise* in 1944—from despair and abandon in the face of the violent collapse of civilization, through erotic mysticism and sacramental marriage, to a sense of universal responsibility. *The Homestead Called Damascus*, the first of five long philosophical reveries in the collection, is a richly allusive work reminiscent of Marcel Proust and Wallace Stevens. The loose syllabic verse—generally nine syllables per line—allows Rexroth considerable freedom for discursive, philosophical reflections. In Part I, the Damascan brothers, Thomas and Sebastian, whose names suggest the themes of skepticism and martyrdom that are interwoven throughout the poem, seek some kind of erotic-mystical escape from the decaying civilization symbolized by the mansion, the landscape, and the dreamy Renaissance girl, Leslie. In Part II, Sebastian yearns for an earth goddess envisioned as a black stripper named Maxine, whereas Thomas seeks faith in the black wounds of Jesus. Part III elaborates the dilemma between erotic-heroic mysteries and the decadence of domestic bliss. Both alternatives paralyze the brothers, although they speculate about the "ambivalent vicarity" of each person symbolizing others. In the final part, Thomas settles for this philosophical notion, while Sebastian sinks into sterility. Although the poem suffers from some obscurity of characterization and theme, it is a work of serious speculation, resplendent with hallucinatory images, mythological puns, and metaphysical questioning.

A Prolegomenon to a Theodicy, Rexroth's second long poem, is a search for transcendent perfection within the flux of experience, a search conducted by means of a cubist aesthetic in which he analyzes and recombines the elements of experience and language. He passes through a Dantean Hell before envisioning the Apocalypse in the most explicitly Christian imagery to be found in any of his poems. In his third long poem, *The Phoenix and the Tortoise*, whose title and theme of mystical love are derived from William Shakespeare's *The Phoenix and the Turtle*, Rexroth develops a religious, ecological viewpoint in which World War II and the injustices of all governments are anarchistically denounced, while value painfully emerges out of personal love. The style is clear, direct, often epigrammatically conveying a deeper faith in life than the previous two long poems. The fourth long poem, *The Dragon and the Unicorn*, is a postwar travel narrative in which Rexroth searches for the meaning of responsibility and its source in love as he proceeds across the United States and Europe. Witnessing the physical and spiritual effects of war and historical depersonalization, he condemns the collectivities of church, state, political parties, armies, and corporations for suppressing and destroying personality, and he celebrates the community of lovers that actually, miraculously, continues to exist.

The last long poem in the collection, *The Heart's Garden, The Garden's Heart*, extends this celebration of actuality. It is a masterpiece of poetic communion with the *tao* in Japan, rich in allusions to Asian poetry and Buddhist wisdom, and culminating, in a musical style that shines with the sensuous imagery of rural and urban Japan, in the most fully realized passages of illumination in all of his poetry. Hearing the music of waterfalls, he listens deep in his mind to transcendent music, overcoming the gap between actuality and Otherness. He does not seek visions, but rests in the innocent vision of actuality, which is also ultimate. Professor Kodama Sanehide of Doshisha Women's College in Kyoto has traced intricate allusions to Japanese poetry in this poem and others, leading him to conclude that of all American poets, Rexroth best understands Japanese culture. Certainly *The Heart's Garden, The Garden's Heart* is the most delightfully and wisely realized of his long poems.

Asian influences, apparent from the beginning of Rexroth's career, intensify in his later work, which includes several volumes of Chinese and Japanese translations, with women poets being singled out in three of them. Buddhist allusions radiate from *New Poems, On Flower Wreath Hill* (his sixth long reverie), *The Silver Swan*, and, most of all, *The Love Poems of Marichiko* (a long sequence of Tantric ecstasy).

Rexroth has sometimes been criticized for being more concerned with philosophical speculation than with the subtleties of language, but these charges seem as superficial as the categorization of his work, by some early reviewers, as merely West Coast nature poetry; there is a vast range of linguistic and prosodic technique in his work. At one extreme is the cubist free verse of *A Prolegomenon to a Theodicy*, at the other extreme is the syllabic versification of much of his poetry of direct statement, influenced by Greek, Chinese, and Japanese traditions. Often nine syllables are a norm around which lines ranging from seven to ten syllables are skillfully arranged, the sounds falling into remarkable melodic patterns rare in modern poetry. Rexroth's vowel-patterns are especially distinctive, a technique absorbed from Japanese poetry. Sometimes jazz rhythms ("Travelers in Ere whom," for example), and ballad stanzas ("Songs for Marie's Lute-Book"), as well as a host of other styles, forms, and techniques are employed.

Finally, the many translations are of enormous value. They have not only introduced many readers to poetry in Chinese, Japanese, and European languages, but they also deserve to be read as enduring works of art in their own right. The translations are organically inseparable from Rexroth's other work, bringing to life voices that harmonize with his own, in a complex but coherent vision of worldwide community.

Morgan Gibson

Other major works

PLAY: *Beyond the Mountains*, 1951.

NONFICTION: *Bird in the Bush: Obvious Essays*, 1959; *Assays*, 1961; *An Autobiographical Novel*, 1966, 1978; *Classics Revisited*, 1968; *The Alternative Society: Essays from the Other World*, 1970; *With Eye and Ear*, 1970; *American Poetry in the Twentieth Century*, 1971; *The Elastic Retort*, 1973; *Communalism, from the Neolithic to 1900*, 1975; *Excerpts from a Life*, 1981.

Bibliography

The Ark 14 (1980). This Festschrift honors Rexroth with entries by more than one hundred writers, critics, and friends. Includes brief tributes to the poet, essays (some especially helpful on the Japanese influences), drawings by Morris Graves, an introduction by the editor, and notes on the contributors.

Gibson, Morgan. *Kenneth Rexroth*. New York: Twayne, 1972. The first book-length study of Rexroth, this volume is a good introduction to his life and work. Chronological in approach, the book traces the step-by-step progression of Rexroth's career. Supplemented by a chronology, notes, a good select bibliography (including an annotated list of secondary sources), and an index.

_____. *Revolutionary Rexroth: Poet of East-West Wisdom*. Hamden, Conn.: Archon Books, 1986. This book expands *Kenneth Rexroth* (1972) in order to assess the poet's entire career. Benefiting from the close friendship with Rexroth, Gibson traces the evolution of themes and styles, and in separate chapters, analyzes the poems, plays, translations, and essays. Contains notes, a comprehensive bibliography (including an unannotated list of secondary sources), and an index.

Grisby, Gordon K. "The Presence of Reality: The Poetry of Kenneth Rexroth." *The Antioch Review* 31 (Fall, 1971): 405-422. Grisby links the directness and clarity of Rexroth's style to the nature of his vision. Influenced by Chinese poetry and the ideas of Martin Buber, Rexroth achieves a kind of wisdom. Many well-chosen examples from the poems illustrate the main themes of Rexroth's poetry.

Hamalian, Linda. *A Life of Kenneth Rexroth*. New York: W. W. Norton, 1991. The first book-length biography of Rexroth, this volume should be definitive for years to come. Relying on extensive interviews with Rexroth and other key individuals, Hamalian covers in detail his entire life. Illustrating both positive and negative qualities, this book corrects Rexroth's account in *An Autobiographical Novel* (Garden City, N.Y.: Doubleday, 1966).

Hartzell, James, and Richard Zumwinkle. *Kenneth Rexroth: A Checklist of His Published Writings*. Los Angeles: Friends of the University of California in Los Angeles Library, 1967. This bibliography, covering 1929 to 1965, illustrates the quantity and variety of Rexroth's writing. Most entries include brief descriptive but not evaluative annotations. The poems in Rexroth's collections are listed individually and in sequence. Ten illustrations give a good sense of the poet's personality. Contains a foreword by Lawrence Clark Powell.

Rexroth, Kenneth. "An Interview with Kenneth Rexroth." Interview by Cyrena N. Pondrom. *Contemporary Literature* 10 (Summer, 1969): 313-331. Reprinted in *The Contemporary Writer: Interviews with Sixteen Writers and Poets*, edited by L. S. Dembo and Cyrena N. Pondrom. Madison: University of Wisconsin Press, 1972. This thorough, excellent interview focuses on the mystical and philosophical ideas underlying Rexroth's poetry. Rexroth explains in detail the effects he tries to achieve in a poem. The influence of Oriental culture, especially that of Buddhism, is abundantly illustrated.

CHARLES REZNIKOFF

Born: Brooklyn, New York; August 31, 1894
Died: New York, New York; January 22, 1976

Principal poetry

Rhythms, 1918; *Rhythms II*, 1919; *Poems*, 1920; *Uriel Accosta: A Play and a Fourth Group of Verse*, 1921; *Jerusalem the Golden*, 1934; *Separate Ways*, 1936; *Going To and Fro and Walking Up and Down*, 1941; *By the Waters of Manhattan: Selected Verse*, 1962; *Testimony: The United States 1885-1890 Recitative*, 1965; *By the Well of Living and Seeing: New and Selected Poems 1918-1973*, 1974; *Holocaust*, 1975; *Poems 1918-1936: Volume I of the Complete Poems of Charles Reznikoff*, 1976; *Poems 1937-1975: Volume II of the Complete Poems of Charles Reznikoff*, 1977; *Poems 1918-1975: The Complete Poems of Charles Reznikoff*, 1989.

Other literary forms

In addition to poetry, Charles Reznikoff wrote fiction and verse drama and was active as a translator, historian, and editor. His novels include *By the Waters of Manhattan* (1930, a title Reznikoff also used for a later collection of his poetry) and *The Manner "Music"* (1977). The novels, as well as his historical work such as *Early History of a Sewing Machine Operator* (1936), are, like his poetry, sharply observed but detached, nearly autobiographical accounts and impressions of family and working life. Although thematically much of his fiction and history may be compared with the "proletarian" literature of the 1930's. Its spareness and restraint give it a highly individual stamp. Reznikoff also wrote a historical novel, *The Lionhearted* (1944), which portrays the fate of English Jewry during the reign of Richard the Lionhearted.

Reznikoff's verse plays, such as *Uriel Accosta* and *Meriwether Lewis* (1922), extend his interest in the individual in history along dramatic lines. The plays make use of choruslike recitations both to convey offstage occurrence and to develop character much in the manner of the classical theater.

Reznikoff was the editor of the collected papers of Louis Marshall and a translator of two volumes of Yiddish stories and history. Much of his work in law was in writing and editing for the legal encyclopedia *Corpus Juris*. His few prose comments on the art of writing poetry are contained in a slim volume of prose entitled *First, There Is the Need* (1977).

Achievements

A rubric for Reznikoff's career might well read: early, nearly precocious development; late recognition. Reznikoff, without ever seeking to be unique, was one of the twentieth century's most original writers virtually with the publication of his first work. His abandonment, as early as 1918, of the verse conventions of late nineteenth century poetry, and his utilization of proselike rhythms anticipates a kind of American plain song which is to be found in the work of the most diverse poets writing today. Reznikoff, in reinventing the image as an element of realist rather than symbolic notation, has also made a significant contribution to the notion of imagery as the cornerstone of the modern poem.

His highly unconventional and imaginative use of historical materials sets him off from the vogues of confessional and psychological poetry, but only in recent years have literary critics begun to appreciate the unprecedented and original manner in which Reznikoff brought history, both contemporary and biblical, alive.

Understanding and appreciation of Reznikoff's work began to increase in his late years. In 1971, he was the recipient of the Morton Dauwen Zabel Award for Poetry from the National Institute of Arts and Letters.

Biography

Born in a Jewish ghetto in Brooklyn and ultimately to live most of his life in New York City, Charles Reznikoff drew, for all his writing, on the very circumstances and surroundings of his life. Like his near-contemporary, William Carlos Williams, the "local" was to be the source of all that was universal in his work. Reznikoff sought out his poems not only in the lives of those around him, in the newly immigrant populations seething in the New York streets, but also in the European and biblical histories, and even customs, which these immigrant groups had brought with them to the New World.

Graduating from a high school in Brooklyn, Reznikoff spent a year at the new School of Journalism of the University of Missouri but returned to New York to enter the New York University Law School, a decisive move for both his livelihood and his poetry. The influence of his legal training and his work in law were to affect his notions of poetry profoundly; his love of "the daylight meaning of words," as he put it in one of his autobiographical poems, stemmed from this education, and it was this sense of language that from the beginning Reznikoff developed into one of the most unique and moving bodies of contemporary poetry. Reznikoff actually practiced law only briefly; he worked a number of years for *Corpus Juris*, the legal encyclopedia, however, and maintained his interest in the law throughout his entire career.

Except for short sojourns elsewhere, Reznikoff lived and worked in New York City. One three-year period, however, was spent in Hollywood working for a film producer; this visit was the source of some of Reznikoff's wittiest verse and furnished the background for his novel *The Manner "Music."* On his return to New York from Hollywood, Reznikoff took up freelance writing, editing, and translating.

Reznikoff was one of the city's great walkers; late in his life, he would still stroll for miles on foot through the city's parks and streets. In this regard, he was close to the boulevardiers and *flâneurs* of nineteenth century Paris so aptly described by Walter Benjamin. Like them, he was attracted to the anonymity of the solitary walker, to the possibility of a simultaneous distance and engagement. Out of such walks, Reznikoff fashioned an extraordinary body of poetry, one which only now after his death is receiving adequate critical attention. From younger poets and from those poets around him, George Oppen, Louis Zukofsky, and William Carlos Williams, attention had been there from the beginning. Reznikoff had early discovered something new and of major importance in the writing of poetry and stayed with it, despite neglect, throughout his long and fruitful life.

Analysis

Of all the poets loosely gathered under the "Objectivist" label coined by Zukofsky for Harriet Monroe's *Poetry* magazine in 1931, none seems to have been quite as "objective" as Charles Reznikoff. In him, legal training and the moral imperative of the Jew as a historical witness combine with the objectivist and imagist principles, which guided such writers as William Carlos Williams and Louis Zukofsky, to produce a body of poetry distinguished by its clarity, judgment, and tact. This notion of witness or bystander, of someone who is at the scene of events but not of the events themselves, is implicit in all Reznikoff's work. Such titles as *By the Waters of Manhattan*, *Testimony*, *Separate Ways*, *Going To and Fro and Walking Up and Down*, and *By the Well of Living and Seeing* are indicative of a poetic stance that was to be, as Reznikoff once put it, "content at the periphery of such wonder." This "wonder" was to embrace both the urban experience, in particular its relation to the life of newly immigrant Jews, but also to range across such topics as early Jewish history, legal proceedings in nineteenth and twentieth century America, and the Holocaust of European Jewry.

Reznikoff's stance is not so much concerned with a conventional sense of poetic distance or with irony per se as with precision of realization. The modern city, the source of much of Reznikoff's most memorable work, is for him a place one continually passes through, a locus of large anonymous forces encountered tangentially yet which overshadow and overwhelm the experience of the city inhabitant. The truths of the city are multiple, highly individualized, and—in Reznikoff—caught not as part of some grand design but as minor resistances to its forces. Victories and defeats occur not in the towers and offices of government but in street corner and kitchen tableaux in which individual fate is registered. Thus, in his work, the urban environment and the lives caught up in the vast workings of the city and of history tend to remain resolutely what they are, to resist being read analogically or symbolically. The poems hover on the edge of factual materiality with few gestures toward the literary. Yet their construction has a cleanliness and freshness found in few other contemporaries. One goes to Reznikoff's work not only for its poetic beauty and its surety of language but also for its historical testimony.

Reznikoff began to publish his work in 1918, when the traditionalist devices of fixed meter and rhyme were already under attack from Ezra Pound's and T. S. Eliot's modernism. Yet Reznikoff was not to traffic in the obviously unconventional or extreme writing of the early twentieth century avant-garde. Even the Imagist movement, which certainly influenced Reznikoff and to which he pays homage, was refined and transmuted by him into something that would not be particularly recognizable to the founders of the movement. The "image" of the Imagists was something decidedly literary, something used for its allusive or symbolic effect, whereas in Reznikoff it becomes a construction, made out of observation and precise detail, concerned primarily to render a datum.

This "nonliterary" use of the image characterizes all Reznikoff's work. His poems strike the reader almost as a kind of low-key reportage, making use of proselike speech rhythms and barely discernible shifts in discourse from statement to simile or metaphor, as in this early example: "Suddenly we noticed we were in darkness/ So we went into the house and lit the lamp/ And sat around, dark spaces about a sun." This shorn-down language inhabits a number of linguistic realms at once; the datum and its meaning for the poet are so inextricably linked that the usual suspension of belief or accounting for poetic license no longer applies. The poetry has about it a "documentary" effect, one that is both tactful and powerful by virtue of its being stripped, it would seem, of any attempt by the poet to persuade.

Reznikoff's poetry can be likened to the photograph, something profoundly and intimately linked to the visible world, and yet, by virtue of the camera angle or constraint of the frame, necessarily and profoundly something selected. As with the photograph, where what is beyond the frame may be hinted at by that which is included, Reznikoff's poems, while framing actual particularities and occasions, resonate with a life of associations far beyond the frame of the image which the language constructs. This image, less metaphoric than informative, becomes a possibility for emotional response but not an occasion for dictating it. If through Reznikoff one sees or knows a certain life intimately, a history, custom or usage, it is because in his work the lyricist and the chronicler are joined with minimal rhetorical flourish.

This poetic technique, which Reznikoff called "recitative," stresses the evidential or communicative aspect of language over the figurative; it unites all Reznikoff's work, from the early *Rhythms* published in 1918 up to and through the late volumes *Testimony* and *Holocaust*. This minimal use of poetic devices such as rhyme, metaphor, or exaggerated imagery results in a restrained tone that balances irony, sarcasm, and humor with emotional distance. It is particularly apt for the short two- or three-line poem (one of Reznikoff's trademarks) that combines a wise knowingness and bleak hilarity, as in: "Permit me to warn you/ against this automobile rushing to embrace you/ with outstretched fender." It also attains a meditative strength, as in: "Among the heaps of brick and plaster lies/ a girder, still itself among the rubbish." Here, the double reading of "still itself" transforms the poem from mere description to enigmatic philosophy.

Such surety of technique makes Reznikoff's poems radiate with both completeness of finish *and* mystery, as though their author, while knowing much, says little. Indeed, they sustain an aphoristic or epigrammatic tone, even in poems of great length and over a wide variety of subject matter.

In Reznikoff, this reticence has little to do with modesty. Rather, understatement becomes a device for achieving accurate registration, for giving subjects their due in the reader's mind by not imposing attitudes or judgments on experience. It is, in its way, a form of humility, a desire, as Reznikoff noted, that "we, whose lives are only a few words" meet in the thing seen and not in the personality of the see-er.

At the very center of Reznikoff's writing, concomitant with the objectivity of his technique, is the aloneness of the moral witness, of a deep and abiding solitude that moved C. P. Snow, in commenting on Reznikoff's work, to regard him as a lonely writer. In Reznikoff, this isolation is less a product of experience than of fundamental choice. As he says of his life in the poem "Autobiography: New York": "I am alone—and glad to be alone . . . I like the sound of the street—but I, apart and alone,/ beside an open window/ and behind a closed door." This desire for isolation, for witnessing as from a distance, can be traced back to the traditions embedded in Jewish religious and philosophical works which influenced him. In the Cabalistic tradition which informs Reznikoff's work, language, as Gershom Scholem notes, "reflects the fundamental spiritual nature of the world." The Cabalists, Scholem points out, "revel in objective description." This sacred attitude toward language is manifest in Reznikoff. As he says in one of his poems, "I have learned the Hebrew blessing before eating bread./ Is there no blessing before reading Hebrew?"

Coupled with this respect for language is the influence of Reznikoff's early legal training on his poetic style. As he relates of his law school days: "I found it delightful . . ./ to use words for their daylight meaning/ and not as prisms/ playing with the rainbows of connotation." Like Williams, Reznikoff seems to have thoroughly refused the artifice of high style in favor of the "daylight meaning" of words, to produce a style which is at once humane and communicative.

As Reznikoff's few prose comments on his poetry make clear, craft and technique stem for him from communicative and ethical concerns as opposed to literary ones, and it is this urge to communicate which is his primary motive. One finds in his work that nearly lost sense of the poet as reteller of tales, as tribal historian. The poet, according to Reznikoff (perhaps in particular the Jewish poet of the People of the Book) stands always with history at his back. For such a poet, the work is not one of self-expression but of a desire to be an agency for those voices lost or denied in time, for individuals caught up in historical forces beyond their control.

This urge to reclaim in Reznikoff has deeper implications, however, as demonstrated in one of Reznikoff's longer historical poems, *Jews in Babylonia*, where a collagist technique initially yokes natural phenomena—the passing of seasons, growth of plants, and the behavior of animals—with simple actions of the biblical tradesmen: "Plane the wood into boards; chisel the stone." The rhythms here are stately and the imagery peaceful. As the poem continues, however, the harmony begins to come apart. Now there is "A beast with its load/ and a bit in its mouth" and "the horn gores/ the hoof kicks/ the teeth bite." The shift in tone becomes even more "unnatural": "The bread has become moldy/ and the dates blown down by the wind . . . the dead woman has forgotten her comb." The lines become a litany of ruin and decay which has both historical and metaphysical implications: "But where are the dead of the Flood . . . the dead of Nebuchadnezzar?" until finally the images express a kind of visionary chaos where "the hyena will turn into a bat/ and a bat will turn into a thorn," where what is seen is "the blood of his wounds/ and the tears of her eyes" and "the Angel of Death in time of war/ does not distinguish/ between the righteous and the wicked."

The effect of this technique is to create something that seems at once cinematic and apocalyptic, forcefully in keeping with the historical situation itself while at the same time suggesting both foreboding and prophecy. In this regard, Reznikoff's work is no simple addition or nostalgic reminder of the past but, like the songs and poems of the biblical prophets, a potential guide to personal and social action. As he says of his grandfather's lost poetry in "By the Well of Living and Seeing": "All the verse he wrote was lost—except for what/ still speaks through me/ as mine."

It is in Reznikoff's most difficult and controversial works, *Testimony* and *Holocaust*, that his sense of historical urgency and the need to testify culminate. In these works, Reznikoff may be said to have created a new poetic form (or as some critics have claimed, absence of form) which is meant to do justice to the full weight of man's inhumanity to man. In these two works, legal records—American courtroom proceedings in *Testimony* and the Nuremberg war crimes trials and the accounts of victims and witnesses in the case of *Holocaust*—are unsparingly worked into verse form, shorn of poetic devices. The author's hand appears solely in the austere editing and lineation of the historical record. Here, the "poetic" by its very absence in the poetry seems to be both witness and prosecutor, a reminder to the reader not only of the events that have occurred but also the life, grace, and possibility denied by the events. The works curiously penetrate the reader's consciousness since, by leaving all the individual interpretation, they undermine, in their account of devastating cruelty and horror, the reader's conventional notions of civilization and culture.

Such penetration, accomplished in such a "hands off" manner, has the further effect of evoking and calling to account the reader's humanity. It is this effect which gives Reznikoff's "objectivity" such moral power. This wedding of artistic means and the procedures of the law courts gives to Reznikoff's work a unique contemporaneity, one which honors and respects the individual while in no way striving for egocentric novelty. This is a *communitas* at its most moving and profound. It can be said of Reznikoff that he is one of the few contemporary poets to have transformed literary artistry into a major historical vision.

Michael Heller

Other major works

LONG FICTION: *By the Waters of Manhattan*, 1930; *The Lionhearted*, 1944; *The Manner "Music,"* 1977

PLAYS: *Uriel Accosta: A Play and a Fourth Group of Verse*, 1921; *Chatterton, The Black Death, and Meriwether Lewis: Three Plays*, 1922; *Coral and Captive Israel: Two Plays*, 1923.

NONFICTION: *Early History of a Sewing Machine Operator*, 1936; *First, There Is the Need*, 1977.

Bibliography

Gefin, Laszlo K. *Ideogram: History of a Poetic Method*. Austin: University of Texas Press, 1982. Gefin cites Reznikoff as one of the poets who use the synthetical or ideogramic method in their poetry. He sees this composition as an "aesthetic form extending from a postlogical and even posthumanist consciousness." In the chapter entitled "Sincerity and Objectification," Gefin remarks on the influence of Chinese poetry on Reznikoff and, at the same time, calls him the "Giacometti of poetry," because he pares down his words to bare essentials.

Heller, Michael. "Reznikoff's Modernity." *The American Book Review* 2 (July/August, 1980): 3. Reviews a number of Reznikoff's works in the light of modernism. States that this poet stands out in the continuity of his work rather than the more usual modernist discontinuity. Admires Reznikoff's restraint and his ability to allow readers to come to their own conclusions.

Hindus, Milton. *Charles Reznikoff: Man and Poet*. Orono, Maine: The National Poetry Foundation, 1984. A full-length study, initially conceived to correct the relative obscurity and neglect dealt to Reznikoff. Half the volume is devoted to the author's personal accounts of Reznikoff's life; the latter half is a compilation of important critical essays on his poetry. Includes a section on his prose and concludes with a useful and thorough annotated bibliography of his works. Highly recommended for Reznikoff's scholars.

Lehman, David. *"Holocaust." Poetry* 128 (April, 1976): 37-45. In reviewing *Holocaust*, Lehman does not really classify Reznikoff as an Objectivist because of his "authentic and original voice." He cites his capacity for irony along with human sympathy, considered a rarity in American poets and praises Reznikoff for opening the "mouth of suffering" and making it "quiver with the voice of survival."

Reznikoff, Charles. *Family Chronicle.* New York: Markus Wiener, 1988. A fascinating background account of the Reznikoff family, from their origins in Russia to their immigration to America and establishment in New York. Contains three accounts of family members, including "Needle Trade," an autobiographical piece by Charles Reznikoff, and much useful information that illuminates the themes in his poetry.

ADRIENNE RICH

Born: Baltimore, Maryland; May 16, 1929

Principal poetry

A Change of World, 1951; *The Diamond Cutters and Other Poems*, 1955; *Snapshots of a Daughter-in-Law*, 1963; *Necessities of Life*, 1966; *Selected Poems*, 1967; *Leaflets*, 1969; *The Will to Change*, 1971; *Diving into the Wreck*, 1973; *Poems: Selected and New, 1950-1974*, 1975; *Twenty-one Love Poems*, 1975; *The Dream of a Common Language*, 1978; *A Wild Patience Has Taken Me This Far*, 1981; *Sources*, 1983; *The Fact of a Doorframe: Poems Selected and New, 1950-1984*, 1984; *Your Native Land, Your Life*, 1986; *Time's Power*, 1989.

Other literary forms

Of Woman Born: Motherhood as Experience and Institution (1976) is an analysis of the changing meanings of childbirth and motherhood in Anglo-American culture. Adrienne Rich draws upon personal experience as well as sources in mythology, sociology, economics, the history of medicine, and literature to develop her analysis. *On Lies, Secrets, and Silences: Selected Prose 1966-1978* (1979) is a collection of essays on women writers (including Anne Bradstreet, Anne Sexton, Charlotte Brontë, and Emily Dickinson) and feminism. *Blood, Bread, and Poetry: Selected Prose 1979-1985* (1986) followed with further essays on women writers and feminist criticism.

Achievements

Rich's work has been at the vanguard of the women's movement in America. Her poems and essays explore her own experience and seek to develop a "common language" for women to communicate their values and perceptions. She has received numerous awards, including two Guggenheim fellowships, the National Institute of Arts and Letters award for poetry (1960), several prizes from *Poetry* magazine, the first annual Ruth Lilly Poetry Prize, the Shelley Memorial Award of the Poetry Society of America (1971), and the National Book Award for *Diving into the Wreck* in 1974. For several years she coedited (with Michelle Cliff) the lesbian feminist journal *Sinister Wisdom*.

Biography

Adrienne Cecil Rich was born in 1929, into a white, middle-class Southern family. Her father, Arnold Rice Rich, taught medicine at The Johns Hopkins University. Her mother, Helen Jones Rich, was trained as a composer and concert pianist but gave up her career to devote herself to her husband and two daughters. She carried out their early education at home, until the girls began to attend school in fourth grade. Arnold Rich encouraged his daughter to read and to write poetry. From his library, she read the work of such writers as Matthew Arnold, William Blake, Thomas Carlyle, John Keats, Dante Gabriel Rossetti, and Alfred, Lord Tennyson. Rich was graduated from Radcliffe College in 1951, the year her first volume of poetry was published. She traveled in Europe and England on a Guggenheim Fellowship in 1952-1953.

Rich married Alfred H. Conrad in 1953 and in the next few years gave birth to three sons, David (1955), Paul (1957), and Jacob (1959). She lived with her family in Cambridge, Massachusetts, from 1953 to 1966, but spent 1961-1962 in the Netherlands on another Guggenheim Fellowship. In 1964, Rich began her involvement in the New Left, initiating a period of personal and political growth and crisis. In 1966, the family moved to New York, where Conrad taught at City College of New York. Rich also began to teach at City College, where she worked for the first time with disadvantaged students. Conrad died tragically in 1970. Rich continued teaching at City College and then Rutgers University until 1979, when she moved to western Massachusetts.

Rich eventually moved to California and has continued her active career as poet, essayist, and speaker. Her earliest work is a notable contribution to modern poetry. Her later work has broken new ground as she redefines and reimagines women's lives to create a female myth of self-discovery.

Analysis

Adrienne Rich's successive volumes of poetry chronicle a contemporary woman artist's odyssey. In her life and work she has been struggling to break out of patriarchal social and literary conventions, to redefine herself and to create new traditions. W. H. Auden praised her first volume for its stylistic control, its skillful use of traditional themes such as isolation, and its assimilation of influences such as the work of Robert Frost and William Butler Yeats. He wrote: "The poems . . . in this book are neatly and modestly dressed, speak quietly but do not mumble, respect their elders but are not cowed by them, and do not tell fibs." Since then, however, Rich has been reshaping poetic conventions to develop her own themes and to create her own voice, often a radical (and sometimes a jarring) one. Reviewer Helen Vendler termed *Diving into the Wreck* "dispatches from the battlefield." Central concerns of Rich's poetry include the uses of history and language, the relationship of the individual to society, and the individual's quest for identity and meaning. The home is often a site for the working out of these themes.

Auden chose Rich's first volume of poetry, *A Change of World*, for the Yale Younger Poets Award. Despite the title, the poems have to do with resisting change. Rich's early training at her father's hands reinforced her allegiance to a literary tradition of meticulous craft, of "beauty" and "perfection." Accordingly, these poems are objective, carefully crafted, and rhymed, with echoes of W. H. Auden, T. S. Eliot, and Robert Frost. A recurring image is that of the home as a refuge that is threatened by social instability ("The Uncle Speaks in the Drawing Room") or natural forces ("Storm Warnings"). The women in these poems remain at home, occupied with women's tasks such as embroidering ("Aunt Jennifer's Tigers"), weaving ("Mathilde in Normandy"), and caring for their families ("Eastport to Block Island"). A central theme of these poems is the use of art as a technique for ordering experience ("Aunt Jennifer's Tigers" and "At a Bach Concert"). "At a Bach Concert" is written in a musically complex form, a variant of the intricate *terza rima* stanza that Dante used in *The Divine Comedy* (c. 1320). Rich's poem weaves together many strands of poetic technique (assonance, consonance, internal rhyme, off-rhyme, alliteration) and rhetorical devices (oxymoron and parallelism) into a rich textural harmony to develop the theme that formal structure is the poet's gift of love: "Form is the ultimate gift that love can offer—/ The vital union of necessity/ With all that we desire, all that we suffer."

The theme of artistic control and craft is repeated in Rich's second book, *The Diamond Cutters.* Written when Rich was traveling in Europe as the recipient of a Guggenheim Traveling Fellowship, this volume is a tourist's poetic diary. Landscape and scenery are prominent. The book blends two moods, nostalgia for a more beautiful past and ironic disillusionment with a present that falls short of perfection (as in "The Ideal Landscape," "Lucifer in the Train," or "The Strayed Village"). In a profound way, all the characters in this book are exiles, aliens, uneasy in the places they inhabit. The heroines of poems such as "Autumn Equinox," "The Prospect," and "The Perennial Answer" are dissatisfied with their lives, but unable to change. They hold on to history and to the social structures it has produced, refusing to question present conditions. Suppressed anger and unacknowledged tensions lie just beneath the surface of all the poems; the book's tone is passive, flat. Eight years passed before Rich's next book appeared. Its stylistic and thematic changes reflect changes in her outlook.

In her next two books, *Snapshots of a Daughter-in-Law* and *Necessities of Life*, Rich begins to move away from conventional poetic forms, to develop her own style, and to deal more directly with personal experience. Her attitudes toward literary tradition, history, and the home have changed markedly. She questions traditional attitudes toward home and family. As she found the patriarchal definitions of human relationships inadequate, her work became more personal and more urgent.

Snapshots of a Daughter-in-Law is written in a looser form than Rich's previous work. Language is simpler, texture less dense. The title poem is a series of vignettes of women's experiences. It fairly bristles with quotations drawn from Rich's wide-ranging reading. According to the poem, male authorities have always defined women in myths and literature. Thus, women lacked a literature of their own in which to define themselves. Rich wrote that she composed the poem "in fragments during children's naps, brief hours in a library, or at 3 A.M. after rising with a wakeful child." Because of these interruptions, she wrote the poem over a two-year period. In this poem, she wrote, "for the first time, directly about experiencing myself as a woman" rather than striving to be "universal." As the title indicates, these are static, fixed vignettes: the women are trapped, denied scope for action and choice.

Another poem in this volume, "The Roofwalker," speaks again of entrapment. The poem's speaker is a builder or architect who is no longer satisfied with the enclosure he has built. The role of the artist is here redefined. Whereas "At a Bach Concert" celebrated the need for objectivity, distance, and form, the speaker of "The Roofwalker" feels constrained by forms: "Was it worth while to lay—/ with infinite exertion—/ a roof I can't live under?" The poet begins to wonder whether her tools—rhyme, alliteration, meter, poetic conventions—are stifling her imagination.

The well-planned house that Rich rejects in "The Roofwalker" is the house of formalist poetry as well. She finds the measured stanzas, rhymed couplets, and blank verse rhythms of her earlier books too rigid for her present purposes. Writing a poem no longer means finding a form for a preconceived idea. Instead, each experience informs its own expression; the poem is not product, but process. The poet, like "The Roofwalker," must break out of the stultifying traditional structure. Like most of her contemporaries, she now writes in freer forms. Yet Rich never abandons rational structure or rootedness in social context as do some experimental writers.

Rich's next book, *Necessities of Life*, continues her movement toward a freer poetic line and toward subjectivity. Where she formerly spoke of history in terms of objects, products of tradition, she now identifies with historical persons (Antinous, Emily Dickinson, and others). A struggle between death and life, between winter and spring, is in process. Indoor-outdoor imagery carries the weight of these tensions. Poems of death and disappearance take place indoors; the expansive, life-enhancing experiences occur outdoors.

These poems are a retreat from the angry stance of "Snapshots of a Daughter-in-Law" and the daring escape of "The Roofwalker." Because at the time of *Necessities of Life* Rich feels oppressed by the human world, she turns to nature for sustenance. *Necessities of Life* establishes a deep relationship with the world of nature; it is one of the "bare essentials" that preserve the heroine in her difficulties. Through a bond with the vegetable and animal world, the world of warmth and light, the book is able to bring life to bear against death and darkness. Nature's cyclical pattern provides clues for survival. Plants move from winter's icy grip into spring's renewal by learning to exist on little. In order to achieve similar rebirth, humans must consciously will change and force themselves into action. This is the pattern of death and rebirth that structures the book.

Rich's first four books are built on linear oppositions. Balanced groups of stanzas articulate dichotomies between art and emotion, control and chaos, passivity and action, indoors and outdoors. Often characters must choose between alternatives. Tension between polarities becomes a controlling force, focusing the poems' energies. In her next books of poetry, Rich would modify the dualistic structure of the earlier books. At the end of *Leaflets* (1969), she introduces the ghazal, a series of two-line units that conflate many ideas. These poems are collagelike, offering multiple perspectives.

Prompted by her increasing social concern and the leftist political critique evolving in the middle and later 1960's, Rich turned from personal malaise to political struggle, from private meditation to public discourse. Her jarring tone reflects her anger and impatience with language. Rhythms are broken, speech is fragmented. The poems suggest hurried diary entries. Images of violence, guerrilla warfare, and global human suffering suggest an embattled society. Yet anger is close kin to hope: it asserts the wish to effect change. Therefore, alongside the destruction, symbols of fertility and rebirth appear. Rich writes of an old tradition dying and a new one struggling to be born. Fear of change dominated her earlier books, but the "will to change" is paramount here. The poems of this period describe Rich's heroines casting off traditional roles and preparing for journeys. The titles of the next three books represent steps in this process. *Leaflets* is a manifesto for public involvement, *The Will to Change* is the determination to move forward, and *Diving into the Wreck*, the first title to contain a verb, is the act itself.

The evolution of *Leaflets* epitomizes Rich's movement from the personal to the political. The first poem, "Orion," is written in regular six-line stanzas and built on a typical pattern of balanced contrast. Indoors and outdoors, feminine and masculine, stagnation and adventure are the poles. The poem is a monologue in which the speaker blames herself for her failures as a woman. In contrast, the last poem in the book, "Ghazals," is a series of unrhymed couplets arranged in a seemingly random conflation of ideas and images. "Ghazals" is a multivoiced political critique of contemporary America. The heroes and heroines of the book are revolutionaries, protesters, challengers of an old order: Frantz Fanon, Walt Whitman, Galileo, LeRoi Jones (Amiri Baraka), Eldridge Cleaver, Dian Fossey. Turning her back on a political tradition that she now equates with death and destruction, Rich is saddened and estranged. Yet she not only wants to last until the new tradition begins but also will attempt to create that new tradition. To do so, she must substitute new ideas and modes of expression for the old, wishing "to choose words that even you/ would have to be changed by" ("Implosions"). Because the values and attitudes she wants to modify are so deeply entrenched in people's most fundamental assumptions, language itself must be reshaped to provide a vocabulary equal to her task of reconstruction. Consequently, language becomes a crucial issue.

Rich believes that "only where there is language is there world" ("The Demon Lover"). She fears, however, that the English language is "spoiled." If the poet-leafletter is using the "oppressor's language," how may her words avoid contamination?

Her powerful meditation on language and power "The Burning of Paper Instead of Children" (in *The Will to Change*) draws upon her classroom experience with disadvantaged students. Unlike the poet, whose privileged childhood opened the possibilities of language to her, the children of the ghetto find the worlds of literacy and power closed to them. Rich quotes a student whose grammatical awkwardness lends his description of poverty a pointed eloquence: "a child steal because he did not have money to buy it: to hear a mother say she do not have money to buy food for her children . . . it will make tears in your eyes." Because she mistrusts rhetoric, the poet closes her meditation with a prose passage of bald statement.

> I am in danger. You are in danger. The burning of a book arouses no sensation in me. I know it hurts to burn. There are flames of napalm in Catonsville, Maryland. I know it hurts to burn. The typewriter is overheated, my mouth is burning, I cannot touch you and this is the oppressor's language.

Her simple syntax affirms her identification with the disadvantaged student, the oppressed. In her refusal to use complex diction or traditional metrics she argues by implication for a rhetoric of honesty and simplicity.

Rich's poetry revises the heroic myth to reflect women's experiences. *Diving into the Wreck* presents questing female heroes for the first time in her work. On their quests, they reconnect with lost parts of themselves, discover their own power, and build commonality with other women. Women's lives are the central focus as Rich's project becomes that of giving voice to women's experience, developing a "common language" that will bring the "dark country" of women's lives into the common light of day. Yet Rich also claims another task for women: they must struggle to redeem an endangered society. She argues that patriarchy's exaggerated aggressiveness, competition, and repression of feeling have led Western civilization to the brink of extinction. The task of reconstruction must be taken up by women. Working for change, the women in this book seek to turn civilization from its destructive paths by persuasion, creation of new myths, or redirection of anger.

In order to understand and overcome patriarchy's suicidal impulses, Rich attempts to open a dialogue. Almost all the poems in *Diving into the Wreck* are cast as dialogue. Conversation is the book's central metaphor for poetry. The book begins with "Trying to Talk with a Man," a poem that deals with the dangers of an accelerating arms race but also has a deeper subject: the creation of a dialogue between men and women. Perceiving gender as a political issue, Rich calls upon men to join her in rethinking gender questions.

Yet the book comes to question the possibility of real communication. "Translations" examines the gulf between the languages spoken by women and men. In "Meditations for a Savage Child," the concluding poem, scientists cannot teach the child to speak.

Poems: Selected and New, 1950-1974 includes early unpublished poems and several new ones. In the final poem of this book, "From an Old House in America," Rich uses the home image as a starting point for a reconsideration of American history from a woman's point of view. She reimagines the lives of women, from immigrants to pioneers to the new generation of feminist activists. All are journeying. Simple and direct in language, written in stanzas of open couplets, the poem is a stream-of-consciousness meditation that builds in force as it imagines the unwritten history of American women and reaches a profound celebration of sisterhood.

Thus, by the end of Rich's ninth book, the woman at home is transformed from the cautious door-closer of "Storm Warnings" (*A Change of World*) into the active participant in history and the questing adventurer eager to define herself by exploration and new experience.

Transformation is the cornerstone of *The Dream of a Common Language* and *A Wild Patience Has Taken Me This Far*. The poet wishes to effect fundamental changes in social arrangements, in concepts of selfhood, in governmental politics, in the meanings of sexuality, and in language. To that end, transformation supplants her earlier idea of revolution.

The title *The Dream of a Common Language* suggests vision, community, and above all a language in which visions and shared experience may be conceived and expressed. Dream is the voice of the nocturnal, unconscious self breaking into daytime existence. The terrain Rich explores here is the unknown country of the self, discovered in dream, myth, vision, ritual. Like dreams, the poems telescope time and space to make new connections among past, present, and future, between home and world. "Common" signifies that which is communal, habitual, shared, widely used, ordinary. Rich sets great value on the common, choosing it over the extraordinary.

In *The Dream of a Common Language*, the poet affirms that poetry stems from "the drive/ to connect. The dream of a common language." The book's central section, "Twenty-One Love Poems," orchestrates the controlling themes of women's love, power, language, world. Images of light and dark, dream and reality, speech and silence, home and wanderer structure the sequence. There are in fact twenty-two poems, for Rich has included an unnumbered "Floating Poem." Drawing from the sonnet tradition, Rich breaks formal conventions by varying the poems' lengths and departing from strict rhyme and meter. The sequence records a particular lesbian relationship, its joyous beginnings, the difficulties encountered, and the termination of the affair.

The poems ask questions about the meanings of self, language, and love between women, and about the possibilities of sustaining love in a hostile world.
Rich insists upon grounding her explorations in the quotidian as well as the
oneiric world. To be "at home" in the world requires coming to terms with
the ugliness and brutality of the city, the pain and wounds, as well as the
beauty of love and poetry. Deliberately, Rich situates the first sonnet of her
sequence "in this city," with its "rainsoaked garbage."

Because she wishes to escape false romanticism, she seeks to connect the
poems firmly to the world of daily life, to avoid sentimentality, and to speak
honestly of her feelings. Because she wishes to transform the self-effacing
behavior that has typically characterized women in love, she stresses self-
awareness and deliberate choice. Caves and circles—images of roundness,
completeness, wholeness—are dominant. Like the homes of Rich's earlier
work, they are enclosures; however, the meaning of encirclement has been
transformed, for in her new vision the poet no longer escapes from the world
in her narrow room but reaches out to include the world, to bring it within
her protected circle.

Poem XXI, the final poem of the sequence, is a complex network of dreamlike associations, of ritual and archetypal memory. In the sonnet, Rich moves
from dark into light, from the prehistoric into the present, from inanimate
nature ("the color of stone") into purposeful consciousness ("more than
stone"). She becomes by choice "a figure in the light." The clarity of intelligence—"a cleft of light"—shapes her purpose. In drawing the circle she deliberately chooses her place.

Particularly in the last three poems of the book there is a sacramental
quality, as Rich affirms her fusion with a world of women working together
throughout time. Weaving, cooking, caring for children, they are crafting beautiful and utilitarian objects such as ceramic vessels, quilts, and clothing.
Through these tasks, they create mementos of their lives and carry out the
work of making a world.

"Transcendental Etude" is a long meditative poem of great richness and
power. It traces the course of birth, death, and rebirth through a creativity
that heals splits in the natural world and within the self. The poem begins in
the pastoral imagery of an August evening and ranges over the realms of nature and of human life. Rich's vision here transforms the poet's craft. As a
poet, she need not be, as she had once feared, an egocentric artist seeking
undying fame at the expense of those she loves. Instead, through participation in the life of the physical universe, she articulates the patterns of her
own being, of life itself. Thus, Rich's new metaphor of the poet is at once
the most daring and the most simple: the poet is a common woman.

Achieving a selfhood that encompasses both creative work and human relationships, egotism and altruism, Rich and her women heal their psychic
split in the symbolic return to home, to the full self represented by the cir-

cle. The voyage into history, the unconsciousness, the mind is completed in the return.

The next group of books, *A Wild Patience Has Taken Me This Far*, *Sources*, *The Fact of a Doorframe*, *Your Native Land, Your Life*, and *Time's Power*, continue to develop the themes broached in *The Dream of a Common Language*: exploration of women's shared past, the struggle to be "at home" in a strife-torn world, the vision of transforming the self and the world. Here again the imagery is that of simple, ordinary objects important to women's lives: books, kettles, beets. Yet these books speak in a more muted voice, the voice of resolution, acceptance, accomplishment, with less anger.

A Wild Patience Has Taken Me This Far is to a large extent a dialogue with nineteenth century women writers and thinkers: the Brontës, Susan B. Anthony, Elizabeth Barrett Browning. "Culture and Anarchy" takes its title from Matthew Arnold's essay on nineteenth century culture. Arnold longed for a literate, elite, verbal culture; Rich, on the other hand, celebrates a world of women's work, both verbal and nonverbal. Here, growing and cooking vegetables, responding to nature's seasonal rhythms, the simple tasks of women's lives, form a valuable cultural matrix out of which arise the heroic actions of individual women.

Rich's poem is a quilting together of the words of historical women (derived from the diaries and letters of Emily Dickinson, Susan B. Anthony, Elizabeth Barrett Browning, and Jane Addams) and meditation on her own life and work. The women's voices here replace the quotations of male words in "Snapshots of a Daughter-in-Law." Again Rich telescopes time, bringing the earlier women into the circle of her life, joining them in their acts and visions.

In *Sources* Rich returns to her past and engages in a dialogue with her dead father and husband. She is trying to come to terms with her own life and to put the lives of the others into perspective. *Your Native Land, Your Life* and *Time's Power* continue to develop the persona of the poet as representative woman facing the issues of her country and time. Language and poetry and their relation to history remain foci of concern: in "North American Time" she writes

> Poetry never stood a chance
> of standing outside history.
> ....
> We move   but our words stand
> become responsible
> for more than we intended

In the ruefully ironic "Blue Rock" she writes

> Once when I wrote poems they did not change
> left overnight on the page

. . . .
But now I know what happens while I sleep
and when I wake the poem has changed:
the facts have dilated it, or cancelled it.

Time's Power is a book of dialogue, with the poet's mother, her lover, and a
cast of historical figures. "Letters in the Family" is a series of imagined letters written by fictionalized historical persons, such as a friend of the Hungarian partisan Chana Senesh or a South African mother writing to her child.
The book ends with "Turning," a poem of quest for knowledge. It articulates
a question the poet-speaker asks as she tries to understand her ongoing quest:
"So why am I out here, trying/ to read your name in the illegible air?"

Rich's successive volumes of poetry reveal her development as poet and as
woman. As she breaks out from restrictive traditions her voice is achieving
power and authenticity. From a poet of isolation and withdrawal, of constraint and despair, she has become a seer of wide-ranging communal sympathy and great imaginative possibility. She is redefining in her life and poetry the meanings of language, poetry, love, power, and home. In her earlier
life and work, she accepted patriarchal definitions. Consequently, she felt
trapped in personal and poetic conventions: a marriage that curbed her creativity, an aesthetic that split form and feeling, a language that ignored her
experience, a position of powerlessness.

At first she spoke in a derivative voice, the language of the "universal";
reluctant to speak as a woman, she echoed the tone of her male poetic ancestors. Because she hesitated to voice her own experience, her early poems
are highly polished but avoid emotional depth. She grew to mistrust a language that seemed alien. The fragmented, provisional, stark poems of *Leaflets*, *The Will to Change*, and *Diving into the Wreck* record her groping toward a new language in which to voice her deepest concerns. In subsequent
books, she wrote in a freer form, viewing poems as "speaking to their moment."

The transformations of Rich's home imagery parallel her growth of poetic
force and political awareness. In early poems the home was entrapping, because patriarchal voices defined women's roles. As Rich's women became
more self-defining, the old relationships were abandoned or modified to fit
the real needs of the persons involved. Achieving selfhood, Rich's female
heroes came to seize control of their homes, their lives. Through metaphorical journeys exploring the world, women's history, and their own psychic
heights and depths, they struggle for knowledge and self-mastery. Healing
their tormenting self-division, they grow more "at home" in the world. They
recognize and cherish their links to a women's tradition of great power and
beauty and to the natural world. In this process the idea of home has acquired new significance: from frail shelter or painful trap it has grown to a

gateway, the starting point for journeys of self-exploration, and the magic circle to which women return so that they may participate in the work of "making and remaking" the world.

Karen F. Stein

Other major works

NONFICTION: *Of Woman Born: Motherhood as Experience and Institution*, 1976; *On Lies, Secrets, and Silence: Selected Prose 1966-1978*, 1979; *Blood, Bread, and Poetry: Selected Prose 1979-1985*, 1986.

Bibliography

Altieri, Charles. "Self-Reflection as Action: The Recent Work of Adrienne Rich." In *Self and Sensibility in Contemporary American Poetry*. Cambridge, England: Cambridge University Press, 1984. This essay treats *The Dream of a Common Language* and *A Wild Patience Has Taken Me This Far*. Altieri examines the way in which Rich's poetry emphasizes "the connection between composition and constructing a responsible self."

Cooper, Jane Roberta, ed. *Reading Adrienne Rich: Review and Re-Visions, 1951-1981*. Ann Arbor: University of Michigan Press, 1984. This volume is a useful collection of reviews and critical studies of Rich's poetry and prose. It includes Auden's foreword to *A Change of World* and other significant essays. The aim is for breadth and balance.

Gelpi, Barbara Charlesworth, and Albert Gelpi. *Adreinne Rich's Poetry*. New York: W. W. Norton, 1975. This book, the first general introduction to the poet, includes a useful chronology of Rich's life and works. It includes her essay "When We Dead Awaken: Writing as Re-vision" as well as a good selection of the earlier poetry.

Juhasz, Suzanne. *Naked and Fiery Forms: Modern American Poetry by Women, a New Tradition*. New York: Harper & Row, 1976. An early study of the developing tradition of American poetry by women, which sets Rich's work into the context of an evolving feminist tradition. The book examines themes and imagery.

Keyes, Claire. *The Aesthetics of Power: The Poetry of Adrienne Rich*. Athens: University of Georgia Press, 1986. Keyes discusses Rich's poetry as feminist poetry. The introduction provides a biographical and historical overview. Each of the ten chapters discusses one of Rich's books, from *A Change of World* through *A Wild Patience Has Taken Me This Far*.

JAMES WHITCOMB RILEY

Born: Greenfield, Indiana; October 7, 1849
Died: Indianapolis, Indiana; July 22, 1916

Principal poetry

The Old Swimmin'-Hole, and 'Leven More Poems, 1883; *Afterwhiles*, 1887; *Old-Fashioned Roses*, 1888; *Pipes o' Pan at Zekesbury*, 1888; *Rhymes of Childhood*, 1890; *Neighborly Poems*, 1891; *Green Fields and Running Brooks*, 1892; *Poems Here at Home*, 1893; *The Days Gone By and Other Poems*, 1895; *A Tinkle of Bells and Other Poems*, 1895; *A Child-World*, 1896; *Riley Love-Lyrics*, 1899; *Home-Folks*, 1900; *Riley Songs o' Cheer*, 1905; *Early Poems*, 1914; *The Complete Poetical Works of James Whitcomb Riley*, 1937.

Other literary forms

Above all, James Whitcomb Riley was a poet; he did, however, try his hand (apparently with little success) at other literary forms. His second book, *The Boss Girl, a Christmas Story, and Other Sketches*, published in 1886, was a collection of prose pieces which went largely unnoticed. Reprinted in 1891 under the title of *Sketches in Prose and Occasional Verses*, it still attracted no appreciable attention. Other prose sketches were included in his *Pipes o' Pan at Zekesbury*. As Riley's commentator, Peter Revell, points out, these "abortive" efforts at prose show Riley experimenting in an amateurish fashion with various forms of social and psychological realism (*James Whitcomb Riley*, 1970). Riley also wrote one verse drama in three acts, *The Flying Islands of the Night* (1891), which his publisher, Bobbs-Merrill, advertised as "a weird and grotesque drama in verse." Apparently begun in the 1870's, *The Flying Islands of the Night* is a fantastic amalgam of fairy tales, Maurice Maeterlinck, and William Shakespeare. Although Riley was already an established, enormously popular writer by the time *The Flying Islands of the Night* was published, the drama was quite ignored. Finally, with humorist Bill Nye, Riley coauthored *Nye and Riley's Railway Guide* (1888).

Achievements

Although his nickname, "The Hoosier Poet," would suggest that he was writing for and about only Indianans, Riley was probably the most popular poet in the United States during the late 1880's, the 1890's, and throughout the early years of the twentieth century. His more than one thousand poems were eagerly purchased, read, and treasured not only by the rural Midwesterners for whom he ostensibly wrote, but also by the increasingly large numbers of Americans living in urban centers on the east and west coast. Many of his poems were memorized by several generations of schoolchildren, and Riley so perfectly captured and expressed the pastoral myth of the American Eden that a number of his poems have become a permanent part of the collective American psyche. Indeed, it would probably come as a surprise to many Americans that the now largely forgotten Riley was responsible for such familiar phrases and images as "When the frost is on the punkin," "Little Orphan Annie," and "the old swimming-hole." Although these fragments of Riley's work have endured and probably will continue to do so, it is nevertheless also true that, less than a century after his death, Riley is, for all intents and purposes, no longer read. Part of the problem is that the very qualities of his verse which made him so beloved by the readers of several generations ago make him unappealing to contemporary readers. Horace Gregory and Marya Zaturenska are essentially correct in maintaining that Riley wrote poems "that would not depress his audiences, nor strike too deeply into the darkness of their fears and doubts. He had a great dread of the darker places of the soul, and of the sinister or complicated recesses of the mind" (*A History of American Poetry, 1900-1940*, 1946). Riley's brand of sanguine, superficial verse was ideally suited to a nation self-conscious about its new status as a world power and sufficiently prosperous, settled, and urbanized that it could afford to indulge in nostalgia about its "simple" rural origins. In fact, in the poems of "Sunny Jim," Riley tapped that same portion of the American mind which so enjoyed the best-selling novels of Riley's era: *Little Lord Fauntleroy* (1886), *Mrs. Wiggs of the Cabbage Patch* (1901), and *Rebecca of Sunnybrook Farm* (1903). Riley's poems, be they of the "Hoosier" type (written in Midwestern dialect) or of the "Lockerbie" type (in standard English), are of even less interest to critics than they are to modern readers. As Peter Revell has noted in the Preface of his excellent study of Riley, the meanings of Riley's poems are readily apparent (although occasionally the dialect makes them a little difficult to decipher); he chose not to be "literary," studiously avoiding references to classical and contemporary writers and their works; he is not, except perhaps for the dialect, of any technical interest; and his work—so limited in subject, treatment, and style as to be virtually formulaic—shows little apparent development. Even so, whereas readers and critics tend to ignore Riley, the literary historian cannot afford to do so, for his very popularity—not only among rural Midwesterners but also with such well-established literary figures as Mark Twain, James Russell Lowell, Hamlin Garland, and Rudyard Kipling—would suggest that one cannot fully appreciate the American literary and social scene at the turn of the nineteenth century without having some understanding of Riley's life and work.

Biography

James Whitcomb Riley was born on October 7, 1849 (some sources erroneously list the year as 1853), in the village of Greenfield in Hancock County, Indiana. Although is was small (it had a population of three hundred in 1844), Greenfield had some cultural pretensions, and in Riley's youth it saw the establishment of several schools, a library, and a dramatic society. This is important to bear in mind, for although Riley cultivated a public image as a sort of folksy cracker-barrel sage, he would scarcely qualify as one of the rural types whom he depicted so frequently in his verse and for whom he ostensibly wrote. Similarly, his father Reuben (or Reubin) Alexander Riley, far from being a farmer, was a prosperous attorney who had hoped that James (the third child of six, and the second son) would pursue a career in the law.

Reuben Riley, a Pennsylvanian of Dutch ancestry, had established himself as a leading citizen of Greenfield virtually from the town's founding. He edited Greenfield's local newspaper in 1847, and even became its first mayor in 1852. Politically astute and evidently ambitious, he named his second son for Governor James Whitcomb, under whom he served as a member of the Indiana State Legislature beginning in 1844. Not surprisingly, he had little patience with James, a frail, sensitive boy who did rather poorly in school and who evinced no inclination toward any sort of professional or business career. The boy apparently was temperamentally much closer to his mother, Elizabeth Marine Riley, who enjoyed music and published her poems in local newspapers, and to Captain Lee O. Harris, a teacher who reportedly abandoned all efforts to teach arithmetic to young Riley and instead encouraged his interests in reading and acting—two skills which in the nineteenth century were frequently combined in the form of "declaiming": the memorization and dramatic recitation of passages of literature.

Captain Harris' encouragement proved fruitful in more ways than he could foresee, for through his reading Riley came to emulate such writers as Robert Burns and Charles Dickens, who shared with him an awareness of the literary potentialities of "humble" people; he apparently was especially impressed with *The Biglow Papers* (1848) of James Russell Lowell, a work which may well have inspired those attempts at the recording of Hoosier dialect which ultimately became his poetic trademark; and his talents in declaiming eventually led to his remarkably successful career as a poet/entertainer on the lecture circuit throughout the United States. Captain Harris, however, who was to become his lifelong friend, was unable to nurture in young Riley an appreciation for formal education, and at sixteen, he left school to engage in such inauspicious pursuits as clerking in a shoe store and selling Bibles.

In 1870, Riley's mother died, and in September of that year he published in the *Greenfield Commercial* "The Same Old Story Told Again," the first of several poems to be printed in local newspapers during this period of uncertainty about his future. At this time, his concerned father apprenticed him to a house and sign painter, an experience which provided a temporary outlet for young Riley's creativity, and which led to his forming a partnership with two other youths who, collectively known as "The Graphics," traveled throughout Indiana, Illinois, and Ohio painting signs. The experience was an ideal one for the future "Hoosier Poet," for it exposed him to the rural types and dialect which he would incorporate into his verse. So, too, with his experience as an assistant to a traveling vendor of patent medicines, for whom he painted signs and enlivened the "medical lectures" by playing his banjo and reciting dialect poems of his own composition.

It was during this period (approximately 1872 to 1875) that Riley seemed to be actively embarking on a career as a professional actor, and, in fact, he did perform solo as a "humorist" throughout central Indiana, as well as with the Adelphian Society, the local dramatic club of Greenfield. In 1875, Riley's alarmed father managed to pressure him into studying law, but the son, now well into his late twenties, could tolerate the law for only one year. By 1876 he was on the road again, this time with the Wizard Oil Company, another patent medicine business, and the peripatetic Riley came to realize that, with his success as a "recitationist," actor, and packager and seller of products (be they patent medicines or his own poems), he could conceivably make a career out of publishing and reciting poetry.

Back in Greenfield early in 1877, he became associated with the local paper as well as with the Anderson *Democrat*, the circulation of which Riley is credited with increasing six-fold by virtue of his commercial jingles, comic renderings of local news, and such regular features as the column he dubbed "The Rhyme-Wagon." Feeling more confident about his abilities as a writer, Riley began to make serious efforts to publish his poems in local newspapers, but his verses were not always well received. In a rather spiteful response to this cool reception, he decided in the summer of 1877 to prove his point that any poem would become successful and popular if the author were assumed to be "a genius known to fame" by perpetrating a literary hoax: he wrote a poem which he entitled "Leonainie," signed it with the initials "E.A.P.," concocted the story that this was a long-lost poem by Poe newly discovered on the fly-leaf of a dictionary owned by a local gentleman, and arranged for it to be printed in the *Kokomo Dispatch*.

The hoax, which he apparently had envisioned as causing only a local flurry of excitement, generated a nationwide controversy, and Riley was exposed as a fraud within the month. Riley's discomfited editor dismissed him from his job on the Greenfield newspaper, and the incident would be a source of embarrassment for Riley for the rest of his life; it did, however, earn him some local fame and it led to a job with the *Indianapolis Journal*, under the editorship of Judge E. B. Martindale. The move proved to be a fortunate one, for his association with the *Indianapolis Journal* from 1877 to 1888 coincided with the period of his greatest creativity, and pleasant Indianapolis would be his home for the rest of his life.

By 1881, Riley's local reputation as a poet had grown to the point where he signed on with Redpath Lyceum Bureau Circuit, an association which led to his appearances as a poet/entertainer throughout the Midwest, and occasionally in Boston. In June of 1882, Riley published in the *Indianapolis Journal* the first of his poems ostensibly written by a local farmer, "Benj. F. Johnson, of Boone, the Hoosier Poet," a series which proved to be so successful that he felt ready to collect and publish them in book form in 1883. The first edition of *The Old Swimmin'-Hole, and 'Leven More Poems* was financed by George C. Hitt, the business manager of the *Indianapolis Journal*; but the second edition was brought out by Merrill, Meigs, & Co., and so began the mutually beneficial business relationship between Riley and the Indianapolis publishing house which has come to be known as Bobbs-Merrill. According to Revell, Bobbs-Merrill published some ninety titles by Riley; as of 1949, the number of Riley books sold by Bobbs-Merrill was well over three million, although the exact number can never be determined since the sales records prior to 1893 evidently were destroyed. That phrase "ninety titles" is, however, rather misleading, for Riley tended simply to rearrange and reprint his old, tried-and-true poems, many of them having appeared originally in Indiana newspapers. He also would take a single, especially popular poem, have it lavishly illustrated, and sell it as a hardcover book. Indeed, part of Riley's enormous popularity may be attributed to his two illustrators, Will Vawter and Howard Chandler Christy. Christy in particular was adept at evoking the genteel atmosphere of the twilight of the Victorian era, his illustrations being attractively tinted. The bindings featured lettering in gold (see, for example, the lavish *When She Was About Sixteen*, published in 1911).

At the same time that Riley was consolidating his highly lucrative publishing arrangement with Bobbs-Merrill, he was also furthering the remarkably successful career as a poet/entertainer which he had begun in the 1870's and which had received such impetus from his association with Redpath beginning in 1881. His career on the lecture circuit should not be dismissed lightly, for it is clear that it not only made him wealthy, was a form of self-advertisement, and appealed to his strong innate sense of histrionics, but it also helps to explain his great popularity and, moreover, was a major factor in the crystallization of the distinctive Riley poetic style. Evidently Riley, like Ralph Waldo Emerson, was a charismatic speaker: having developed a striking stage presence, Riley could slip in and out of Hoosier dialect at will, and he had so perfectly rehearsed his comic commentaries on his own poems that they seemed to be the spontaneous remarks of an unusually witty, genial man of the soil. The Riley-the-poet whom thousands flocked to see and hear was in actual fact a character or persona created by Riley-the-actor, with every gesture, aside, and intonation meticulously prepared in advance. As Riley himself noted with surprising candor,

> In my readings I had an opportunity to study and find out for myself what the public
> wants, and afterward I would endeavor to use the knowledge gained in my writing. . . .
> While on the lecture platform I watched the effect that my readings had on the audience
> very closely and whenever anybody left the hall I knew that my recitation was at fault and

tried to find out why. . . . Thus, I learned to judge and value my verses by their effect on the public.

The subject matter, the treatment, even the dialect in his poems had been established and polished by years of experience on the lecture circuit, and Louis Untermeyer is probably correct in maintaining that Riley is "patently the most artificial of those poets who claim to give us the stuff of the soil" (*A Critical Anthology: Modern American Poetry* [*and*] *Modern British Poetry*, 1936).

Artificial or not, Riley was so notoriously successful on the lecture circuit throughout the Midwest that in 1887 it was arranged for him to appear at a literary gala at New York City's Chickering Hall on behalf of the International Copyright League. Sharing the spotlight with such luminaries as Mark Twain, James Russell Lowell, George Washington Cable, William Dean Howells, Charles Dudley Warner, Frank Stockton, and Edward Eggleston, Riley was the least-known writer in attendance, and yet so overwhelming was the impression he made during his recitation on the first day of the two-day affair that he was asked to speak again. In Riley's official biographical sketch is the familiar comment by Lowell, reportedly made in the course of reintroducing Riley to the sophisticated New York audience on the triumphant second day of the conference, that in Riley's verse he had found "so much of high worth and tender quality that I deeply regret I had not long before made acquaintance with his work." Lowell went on to call him a "true poet," and such an enthusiastic response from one of the most noted literary figures of the day served only to enhance Riley's career as a lecturer, and he began to appear throughout the United States, often accompanied by fellow-poet Eugene Field or the humorist Edgar W. ("Bill") Nye.

Riley continued to publish volumes of poetry with singular regularity, and in 1891, he paid a triumphant visit to the British Isles, where he was honored with a dinner at the Savoy in London. In 1893, he began his residence on Lockerbie Street in Indianapolis, where he was a boarder in the pleasant brick home of Major Charles L. Holstein. He also acquired the "Old Homestead" in Greenfield, which became his summer residence (in his old age he wintered in Miami). Riley also received numerous honorary degrees, including an M.A. from Yale University (1902) and doctorates from the University of Philadelphia (1904) and Indiana University (1907). He was elected to membership in the National Institute of Arts and Letters in 1908 and to the American Academy of Arts and Letters in 1911. Probably the honors he most valued, however, were the public celebrations of his birthday. In 1911, the schools of Indiana and New York City held commemorative programs in his honor on his birthday, and in 1915 the National Committee of Education directed that his birthday be observed by all public, private, and parochial schools in the United States. Upon his death from heat prostration in 1916 (he already had become a semi-invalid because of a series of paralytic strokes), Riley was so well known as a public figure in Indiana that thirty-five thousand people filed past his body lying in state at the capitol building in Indianapolis. His name had become a household word throughout the United States. His reputation as a poet declined dramatically after his death, perhaps because his poems needed the commanding presence of the genial Riley himself to compensate for their obvious deficiencies; but despite the fact that Riley is now virtually forgotten by the reading public, it is probably true that he will always hold a place in American literary history by virtue of his truly extraordinary popularity at the turn of the nineteenth century.

Analysis

Ordinarily one would be ill-advised to attempt to offer a broad statement concerning 1,044 poems. In James Whitcomb Riley's case, however, his poetic undertakings were so limited in subject, treatment, and style that it is indeed possible to make generalizations about them. Most of his poems fall into one or more of the following categories: pastoralized treatments of life in rural America, sentimentalized renderings of the relationships between family members or friends, and equally sentimentalized evocations of childhood. As illustrations of these three categories, one might consider "When the Frost Is on the Punkin," "Knee-Deep in June," "Nothin' to Say," "The Old Man and Jim," "The Raggedy Man," "Little Orphant Annie," and "The Old Swimmin'-Hole."

In an age when many Americans have never seen frost on a pumpkin—or, for that matter, pumpkin not in a pie—it is rather remarkable that the title of Riley's "When the Frost Is on the Punkin" is still in circulation, even if the poem itself is largely forgotten. Clearly working within the venerable tradition of the harvest poem (John Keats's "To Autumn" is a sterling example), Riley has so generalized and so de-emotionalized the potentially rich subject of the country autumn that the poem is strikingly charmless. Predictably, the air is "appetizin'" and the morning is "crisp and sunny"; the obligatory rooster crows his obligatory "hallylooyer"; and the requisite apples are "poured around the celler-floor in red and yeller heaps," dutifully ready to be made into cider and applesauce. Vague catalogs of stock autumnal delights, however, together with the overdone repetition of "When the frost is on the punkin and the fodder's in the shock," and the patently sentimental conclusion that any "Angels wantin' boardin'" would be more than happy to live in the country at harvest-time, simply cannot salvage the poem. To a nation which was still essentially rural—or, more important, which perceived itself as such—the bland catalogs probably struck deep emotional chords; but to modern readers all that remains of one of Riley's most famous poems is the fundamentally meaningless title.

Not all Riley's poems feature the flurry of farm activity depicted in "When the Frost Is on the Punkin." The other side of Riley's brand of rural American life—the "mild Bohemianism" and "fatuousness" which Donald Pizer has cited as characteristic of Riley's verse (*American Thought and Writing: The 1890's*, 1972)—are perhaps nowhere more apparent than in "Knee-Deep in June," originally published in the *Indianapolis Journal* in 1885. Overlong at eight stanzas, it enjoins one to find an orchard and "Lay out there and try to see/ Jes' how lazy you kin be!—" Although the persona explains in the first stanza that he engages in this sort of activity (or lack thereof) only on "some afternoon[s]," it is nevertheless apparent that he could do this "stiddy fer a year er two," if not for eternity; and the overall impression that one receives from "Knee-Deep in June" is that the Puritan work ethic has been rejected wholesale. Quite typical of Riley's verse are the poem's vague renderings of the details of a country landscape ("Hear the old hen squawk, and squat/ Over ever' chick she's got"), the domestic metaphors (the shadows are "thick and soft/ As the kivvers on the bed/ Mother fixes in the loft/ Allus, when they's company!"), and the strained attempts at quaint humor ("Mr. Bluejay, full o' sass,/ In them base-ball clothes o' his"). Even the reference to death is carefully sentimentalized to contribute to the aura of lassitude:

> Thinkin' of old chums 'at's dead,
> Maybe, smilin' back at you
> In betwixt the beautiful
> Clouds o' gold and white and blue!

In keeping with the theme of the poem, "Knee-Deep in June" is spread out in leisurely fashion over seven pages of the volume *Songs of Summer* and features three illustrations by Will Vawter, including a full-page picture of a man "Sprawl[ed] out len'thways on the grass."

The sentimentality so characteristic of "When the Frost Is on the Punkin" and "Knee-Deep in June" is also evident in the Riley poems which focus on interpersonal relationships rather than on farm life as such. "Nothin' to Say," which was accepted for publication by the *Century Illustrated Monthly Magazine* in 1883 but which did not appear until August of 1887, was an immensely popular poem in its day. It is a dramatic monologue in which a father speaks to his daughter, who has declared her intention of getting married on her next birthday. The girl's mother is dead, having left her baby daughter a "little Bible" with "yer name acrost the page" and some earrings; and, as might well be anticipated, the daughter, in looks and size, is much like the mother. To complete the mother/daughter analogy, the father notes that "It'll 'most seem like you was dead like her!"; but, faced with the inevitability of his child marrying and moving away, the helpless father "hain't got nothin' to say!" A poem equally predictable and sentimental is "The Old Man and Jim," one of Riley's most successful platform pieces. The unidentified narrator records the relationship between an old farmer and his favorite son Jim, "the wildest boy he had." Constitutionally ill-suited to farming, Jim enlists in the army for three months at the outbreak of the Civil War and his father, who is "jes' wrapped up in him," sends him off to the service with the words "'Well, good-by, Jim:/ Take keer of yourse'f!'" Those parting words become the refrain of the poem, as Jim distinguishes himself in battle, reenlists, and dies of his wounds. A woeful tale, "The Old Man and Jim" must have had quite an impact when dramatically recited by Riley.

Considerably less depressing is the sentimentalized rendering of the relationship between a hired man and children in "The Raggedy Man," one of the best-known of the poems Riley wrote depicting child life. Published in the *Century Illustrated Monthly Magazine* in December, 1890, the poem obviously stirred much interest, for Riley felt compelled to explain that "The Raggedy Man was not a tramp, nor was he so ragged as people usually seem to think. He was just a farmer boy from some neighboring family." Perhaps this was literally so, but the poem is told from the point of view of a child, and as a result that farmer boy emerges as a sort of combination hired man and oversized playmate. In the first two stanzas, the Raggedy Man embodies the world of adult labor which is so alien to the child-persona, and in that respect he serves to represent the parental figures who are most prominent in any child's formative years. In the third stanza, the poem begins to slip into the more imaginative aspects of child life, as the Raggedy Man tells how he picked roasted apples from a tree. This playful motif continues in subsequent stanzas, as the child recounts how the Raggedy Man plays "horsey" with him, tells him about giants and elves, pretends to shoot escaped pigs with his hoe (the "Old Bear-shooter"), reveals that the child is actually a prince whose real father has "gone/ To git more money," and "steals" the child and hides him in a "cave" (actually the haymow).

This heavily folkloric rendering of child life in rural America comes to an abrupt end in the final stanza, wherein the Raggedy Man asks whether the child wishes to become "a rich merchunt" like his father. The child predictably responds "'I'm ist go' to be a nice Raggedy Man!'"; but however appropriately "cute" that answer may be, the fact remains that there is an undercurrent in "The Raggedy Man" which is at odds with the folksy, childlike atmosphere it superficially creates. There is a world of difference between the hired man in his insistently "raggedy" attire (that adjective appears some forty-seven times in the eighty-three-line poem) and the persona's father in his "fine clothes"—a difference which is most apparent in the simple fact that the father, although he owns a farm, must hire the Raggedy Man to handle the decidedly nonpastoral, physically demanding chores associated with farm life. In the America which had once proudly proclaimed itself to be a nation of farmer-citizens, there had arisen by Riley's era a dichotomy between the rural poor and those prosperous urbanites who were quite willing to pastoralize their country roots as long as others would (literally) handle the dirty work.

It is difficult to believe that Riley, himself a wealthy urbanite who had enjoyed a comfortable early life, was unaware of the tension generated in the poem by the child's double emotional allegiance to his wealthy, oddly remote father and to the poor, hard-working, fun-loving hired man whom the father employs; but Riley, true to form, does not develop the social consciousness which glimmers so faintly in "The Raggedy Man," and the poem remains essentially an evocation of childhood.

An equally well-known rendering of child life is "Little Orphant Annie." Originally entitled "The Elf Child" and published in the *Indianapolis Journal* in 1885, it proved to be so popular that Riley was able to sell the little poem (four eight-line stanzas) as the lavishly illustrated *Orphant Annie Book*. Annie (or "Allie," as she was originally named) was based on a real person, an orphan who had lived briefly with the Riley children (she apparently has nothing in common with the saucer-eyed comic strip heroine of the same name). In Riley's poem, she was to "earn her board-an'-keep" by doing housework for the persona's family, but she was of special interest to the children because of her knowledge of witches, "Gobble-uns," and "Black Things." She entertains the family's children with her stories of little boys and girls being carried off by these supernatural creatures as punishment for being ill-behaved:

> You better mind yer parunts an' yer teachers fond an' dear,
> An' churish them 'at loves you, an' dry the orphant's tear,
> An' he'p the pore an' needy ones 'at clusters all about,
> Er the Gobble-uns'll git you
> Ef you Don't
> Watch
> Out!

Peter Revell is correct in maintaining that the overt didacticism of "Little Orphant Annie" is atypical of Riley's verse, but he probably underestimates Riley's inclination to introduce such dark elements into "the usually sunny world of Hoosierdom." This element of darkness in Riley's poetry is especially apparent in one of his earliest efforts, "The Old Swimmin'-Hole."

Originally published in the *Indianapolis Journal* on June 17, 1882, and reprinted as the title poem in Riley's first book, "The Old Swimmin'-Hole" proved to be one of the best-loved poems of the 1880's and 1890's, and it is easy to see why. It draws upon that universal tendency to long for a happier, simpler, and ostensibly problem-free past, whether that past be personal or national. In Riley's poem, the highly sentimentalized past is embodied in the controlling image of the swimming-hole, something which would be alien to the experience of most modern readers, but which in Riley's day would be readily acceptable as the vivid symbol of a carefree, self-indulgent youth. Riley's persona—an "old man" from whom "old Time's tuck his toll"—seems to strike a precarious mental balance between smiling nostalgia and acute depression, something which is quite uncharacteristic of Riley's work. The persona recalls that the "gurgle" of the "baby-river" of his boyhood sounded "like the laugh of something we onc't ust to know/ Before we could remember anything but the eyes/ Of the angels lookin' out as we left Paradise." This is an atypically profound way for a Riley poem to begin, and it takes an even more atypical turn as the potentially rich Wordsworthian concept of a prenatal existence is dropped in favor of a Narcissistic interpretation of the attractions of the swimming-hole.

Perhaps sensing that he was moving rather too close to the psychological implications of the swimming-hole, Riley does not pursue the poetic possibilities of the water imagery and instead has the persona recall playing hooky to go swimming. Immediately, however, the element of depression which so striates this poem becomes overt. After a typically Rileyan catalog of vague country delights, the final stanza makes explicit the connection between the mind of the persona and the swimming-hole: "When I last saw the place,/ The scenes was all changed, like a change in my face," and his response to those twin facts is not at all what one would expect in a poem by Riley. "I wish in my sorrow I could strip to the soul,/ And dive off in my grave like the old swimmin'-hole." A Riley persona with suicidal tendencies? Incredible as this may sound, the words on the page, taken at face value, would certainly suggest that the persona is reacting to his aging and the changes in his environment less with cheery nostalgia than with desires for oblivion, even self-destruction.

Riley's contemporary readers evidently chose not to acknowledge the blatant darker aspects of "The Old Swimmin'-Hole," aspects which may reflect the carefully nonpublicized side of the poet (offstage, "Sunny Jim" Riley drank heavily and suffered from exhaustion and depression), or which may reflect the angst-ridden modern man living in a world of isolation and extraordinary change. Much as the speaker in Riley's "Griggsby's Station" yearns to return to "where we ust to be so happy and so pore," far from "the city! city! city!" where there is "none that neighbors with us, or we want to go and see," so too the persona in "The Old Swimmin'-Hole" longs to escape from the miseries of his adult life but realizes that there can be no turning back. Unquestionably there was a dark side to sunny Hoosierdom, but it was a side which neither Riley nor his millions of readers cared to probe. For better or for worse, he will go down in literary history as "Sunny Jim" Riley.

Alice Hall Petry

Other major works
> SHORT FICTION: *The Boss Girl, a Christmas Story, and Other Sketches*, 1886.
> PLAY: *The Flying Islands of the Night*, 1891.

NONFICTION: *Love Letters of the Bachelor Poet, James Whitcomb Riley to Miss Elizabeth Kahle,* 1922; *Letters of James Whitcomb Riley,* 1930.

MISCELLANEOUS: *Nye and Riley's Railway Guide,* 1888; *The Poems and Prose Sketches of James Whitcomb Riley,* 1897-1914 (Homestead Edition, 16 volumes); *The Poems and Prose Sketches of James Whitcomb Riley,* 1900-1916 (Greenfield Edition, 14 volumes); *The Complete Works of James Whitcomb Riley,* 1913 (6 volumes).

Bibliography

Brooks, Van Wyck. *The Confident Years: 1885-1915.* New York: E. P. Dutton, 1952. Riley played an important role in the time covered here. In the Middle West, where later writers would describe darker visions, Riley and Lewis Wallace expressed "smiling aspects." More important writers than Riley himself had a great liking for Riley's writing, including Eugene Field and Theodore Dreiser. Supplemented by footnotes and an index.

Crowder, Richard. *Those Innocent Years: The Legacy and Inheritance of a Hero of the Victorian Era, James Whitcomb Riley.* Indianapolis: Bobbs-Merrill, 1957. Crowder asserts that the significance of Riley transcends his Indiana reputation. The author narrates the poet's career in eleven chapters. From the "westward movement" beginning in 1819, through recognition by 1885, to the "apotheosis" of his death at the age of sixty-seven, Riley is described not only as heroic but also godlike. "Authorities" are given, as is an index.

Kindilien, Carlin T. *American Poetry In the Eighteen Nineties.* Providence, R.I.: Brown University Press, 1956. This study is based on a special collection of verse in the Brown University library, but it is a complete and generous assessment of the works of the period. Riley's contributions are closely analyzed, particularly as they are made to the development of what Kindilien calls "sentimental humor." Contains notes and an index.

Nolan, Jeannette Covert, Horace Gregory, and James T. Farrell. *Poet of the People: An Evaluation of James Whitcomb Riley.* Bloomington: Indiana University Press, 1951. In three brief, appreciative essays, Riley's work is examined as a contribution to children's poetry, as an expression of Victorian values, and as a product of frontier culture in the Midwest. His work therefore compares, sometimes favorably, with the achievements of William Dean Howells and Mark Twain.

Revell, Peter. *James Whitcomb Riley.* New York: Twayne, 1970. The first three chapters examine Riley as a popular poet then review his background and early writing. Three chapters present Riley as a Victorian poet, children's poet, and Hoosier poet. The last three chapters focus on his pastorals, his humor, and the significance of his popularity. Complemented by a chronology, notes, a select bibliography, and an index.

Ziff, Larzer. *The American 1890's: Life and Times of a Lost Generation.* New

York: Viking Press, 1966. Riley plays a part in this book's story, although he is not considered very important in a decade that included William Dean Howells, Henry James, Mark Twain, and Stephen Crane, for example. Still, Riley did contribute to what Ziff calls "the midwestern imagination," which is examined closely in chapter 4 of the book. Includes notes and an index.

EDWIN ARLINGTON ROBINSON

Born: Head Tide, Maine; December 22, 1869
Died: New York, New York; April 6, 1935

Principal poetry

The Torrent and the Night Before, 1896; *The Children of the Night*, 1897; *Captain Craig*, 1902, 1915; *The Town Down the River*, 1910; *The Man Against the Sky*, 1916; *Merlin*, 1917; *Lancelot*, 1920; *The Three Taverns*, 1920; *Avon's Harvest*, 1921; *Collected Poems*, 1921; *Roman Bartholow*, 1923; *The Man Who Died Twice*, 1924; *Dionysus in Doubt*, 1925; *Tristram*, 1927; *Collected Poems*, 1927; *Sonnets: 1889-1927*, 1928; *Cavender's House*, 1929; *Collected Poems*, 1929; *The Glory of the Nightingales*, 1930; *Matthias at the Door*, 1931; *Nicodemus*, 1932; *Talifer*, 1933; *Amaranth*, 1934; *King Jasper*, 1935; *Collected Poems*, 1937.

Other literary forms

Early in his literary career, well before he gained prominence as a poet, Edwin Arlington Robinson wrote a number of short stories that he planned to incorporate in a volume entitled *Scattered Lives*. The stories do not survive, nor does the novel he tried his hand at writing some years later, but the twenty-six pieces of extant prose were collected by Richard Cary in *Uncollected Poems and Prose of Edwin Arlington Robinson* (1975). Of interest primarily for what they reveal of the life of this most private man, these undistinguished prose pieces include essays, autobiographical sketches, introductions to books, and like matter.

It was in drama, particularly in the years 1906 to 1913, that Robinson hoped to make an impression as some of his New York friends had in their attempts to revitalize the theater. Robinson did not relinquish the hope that he could achieve moderate success with his plays until 1917, when he finally recognized that his very considerable skills as a poet were not compatible with those required for the theater. His two published plays—*Van Zorn* (1914) and *The Porcupine* (1915)—were ineffective. The former was produced, however, in February, 1917, by an amateur group that used the facilities of a Brooklyn YMCA. It had a run of seven days.

Robinson was a prolific letter writer. Some of his letters have been collected in three major editions: *Selected Letters of Edwin Arlington Robinson* (1940), compiled by Ridgely Torrence with the assistance of several of the poet's friends; *Untriangulated Stars: Letters of Edwin Arlington Robinson to Harry de Forest Smith, 1890-1905* (1947), edited by Denham Sutcliffe; and *Edwin Arlington Robinson's Letters to Edith Brower* (1968), edited by Richard Cary. The letters that interest the student of Robinson the most are those to Harry de Forest Smith, a close friend from Gardiner, Maine, to whom the poet, during a very difficult time in his life, expressed in an uncharacteristically open fashion his thoughts and feelings on a number of subjects, including his literary likes and dislikes, his own struggles as a writer, his years at Harvard, and his cultural growth.

Achievements

For some twenty years before he gained acknowledgment as a poet of major proportions, Robinson had been publishing some excellent poems, particularly in the form of lyrics with a dramatic base. Indeed, his special genius has always been ascribed to the shorter poem, even though he has thirteen book-length narrative poems to his credit, eleven of which were published individually as books between 1917 and 1935 and two of which—*The Man Who Died Twice* and *Tristram*—were awarded Pulitzer Prizes in the 1920's. In 1921, the first edition of his *Collected Poems* had earned Robinson his first Pulitzer Prize.

In the 1920's, when T. S. Eliot and Robert Frost were acknowledged literary masters, Robinson was hailed by some discerning critics as America's foremost poet. In addition to the three Pulitzer Prizes, he was given honorary degrees by Yale University in 1922 and Bowdoin College in 1925. At the close of the decade, the National Institute of Arts and Letters presented Robinson with a gold medal in recognition of his outstanding accomplishments. Chosen by the Literary Guild of America as a monthly selection, *Tristram* sold over 50,000 copies. Not without good reason, *Tristram* and most of the long blank verse narratives are not read much today; they are dull and wordy. Some, however, contain passages of exceptional power, notably *Lancelot* and *The Man Who Died Twice*—the latter being the most impressive of the long poems.

In many of his shorter poems and in a few of his middle-length narratives, such as "Ben Jonson Entertains a Man from Stratford" and "Rembrandt to Rembrandt," Robinson's use of language is consistently superior and often brilliant. For example, he infuses his infrequently used but nonetheless striking images drawn from the natural world with metaphorical or symbolic meanings that contribute greatly to an understanding of his themes. Whether in the shorter or the longer pieces, Robinson is, above all, a poet of rational content, one who believes that what the poem says is of the utmost importance. His themes are both serious and significant.

Robinson may properly be classified as a traditional poet since he wrote regularly in blank verse, used meter, rhyme, and patterned stanzas, and was attracted to the English sonnet, a form in which his triumphs are many and which he expanded to include nontraditional subject matter, such as prostitution, suicide, and euthanasia. His most accomplished poems, among the best of their kind in English, are relatively brief yet intense and penetrating studies of the residents of Tilbury Town, the imaginary community that Robinson created based on Gardiner, Maine. His themes reflect a full awareness of the painful lives that many must endure. In these superior shorter poems, these compelling character studies, Robinson addresses the need to try to understand one's fellow man and to have compassion for him.

Biography

By the standards of the biographer's world, the life of Edwin Arlington Robinson provides little that is exciting. Born on December 22, 1869, in Head Tide, Maine, the third son of Edward and Mary Palmer Robinson, he led a life characterized by a very low profile, even after he was acknowledged by a number of critics and scholars in the 1920's as America's most distinguished poet. He shunned the public attention that was his for the asking, preferring instead to write in relative seclusion and to associate with only a very few close friends. Occasionally, he consented to an interview, but he never gave lectures or public readings of his poetry, or engaged in any activity in which he would have been the center of attention.

Ten months after his birth, the Robinson family moved to Gardiner, Maine, where his father, who had made his fortune in the timber business, became a civic figure and was elected to the state legislature. Although his father saw little need for his sons to receive college educations, he consented to sending Dean, his first born, to Bowdoin to begin the study of medicine. After Robinson took an extra year of high school and did odd jobs around Gardiner for a period, expressing all the while his disinclination for the world of business (the route taken by Herman, the second born), he was finally permitted to enroll in Harvard in 1891 as a "special student," where he remained for two years. Robinson treasured these years, and although he was never fully accepted by the student literati, he did publish five poems in *The Harvard Advocate*.

The decade following his years at Harvard was beset by family tragedies and discouragement; his resolve to be a writer elicited but few rewards. He paid for the publication of his first book of poetry, *The Torrent and the Night Before*; a friend paid the cost of printing *The Children of the Night*, the second; and *Captain Craig*, the third, was first rejected by five publishers and accepted only on the condition that its expense would be underwritten by friends. Although these volumes contain a number of excellent poems, they received little critical attention. Robinson's fortunes changed in 1905, when Theodore Roosevelt was sent a copy of *The Children of the Night* by his son Kermit. Roosevelt found a sinecure for the poet—who was living in New York in an impoverished state, discouraged, and given to drinking—with the United States Customs Service, a position he was to hold until the Taft administration. It gave him the opportunity to write free from financial worry, a condition which had plagued him since the Panic of 1893 took the family fortune.

He spent the summer of 1911 at the MacDowell Colony in Peterborough, New Hampshire, a retreat for artists to which the poet would return each summer for the rest of his life for three months of uninterrupted writing. The rest of the year he spent in New York, with occasional trips, mostly to Boston, to see friends. Then in 1916, *The Man Against the Sky*, his fifth volume of poetry, was favorably received, and Robinson was recognized as a significant American poet. Toward the end of his life, Robinson devoted nearly all his creative efforts to the long narrative poem, publishing eight book-length poems between 1927 and his death in 1935.

Analysis

In response to a 1931 letter from Bess Dworsky, who was preparing a thesis on Edwin Arlington Robinson's "philosophy," the poet wrote: "I am rather sorry to learn that you are writing about my 'philosophy'—which is mostly a statement of my inability to accept a mechanistic interpretation of the universe and of life." Critics have called Robinson an idealist, a Platonist, a transcendentalist, a pantheist, and many combinations thereof. While it is indeed possible to identify in his poetry some elements of all the above, he was not an advocate of any philosophical system. He was most assuredly aware of the scientific and philosophical concepts that pressed toward a "mechanistic interpretation of the universe and of life," which he rejected in favor of a personal idealism that nonetheless accepted the reality of matter. As Chard Powers Smith argues in *Where the Light Falls: A Portrait of Edwin Arlington Robinson* (1965), "He never denied the material world. What he did was to face it, defy it, and deny its capacity to destroy him." Against the forces of materialism he posited a life of the mind, and, as Smith suggests, "He respected the unique inner integrity of all individuals and he never judged anyone, in life or in fiction [poetry], for he did not know what pressures they had been under."

Several comments that Robinson made serve to illustrate his purpose in writing poetry and provide us with external evidence that, coupled with the internal evidence of the poems themselves, identifies his major thematic concerns. In a letter to Harry de Forest Smith, dated May 13, 1896, Robinson said what he hoped his poems would do:

> If printed lines are good for anything, they are bound to be picked up some time; and then, if some poor devil of a man or woman feels any better or any stronger for anything that I have said, I shall have no fault to find with the scheme or anything in it.

Writing to Smith again in February 3, 1897, Robinson reaffirmed his position: "I also make free to say that many of my verses [were] written with a conscious hope that they might make some despairing devil a little stronger and a little better satisfied with things—not as they are, but as they are to be." Sixteen years later, in reply to William Stanley Braithwaite's inquiry about his central "message," Robinson is reputed to have answered in terms remarkably consistent with his statements made years earlier:

> I suppose that a part of it might be described as a faint hope of making a few of us understand our fellow creatures a little better, and to realize what a small difference there is, after all, between ourselves, as we are, and ourselves, not only as we might have been but would have been if our physical and temperamental make-up and our environment had been a little different.

While this response may sound as if Robinson had embraced the philosophical determinism of the naturalistic writers, Robinson was quick to correct that impression: "If a reader doesn't get from my books an impression that life is very much worth while, even though it may not seem always to be profitable or desirable, I can only say that he doesn't see what I am driving at."

From *The Torrent and the Night Before* to *Dionysus in Doubt*, the last volume to contain significant shorter poems, the dual concept of understanding and compassion, Robinson's major thematic concern, is strongly evident in such outstanding poems as "Luke Havergal," "The Clerks," "The Growth of 'Lorraine,'" "The Whip," "How Annandale Went Out," "Flammonde," "The Gift of God," "Veteran Sirens," "The Poor Relation," "En Passant," and "Eros Turannos." Very closely aligned to the motif of understanding and compassion is the belief exemplified in many of his poems, and most convincingly so in "Eros Turannos," that no one person is ever able to fully understand another person. Although this may seem incompatible with Robinson's preoccupation with understanding and compassion, it is not, for the poet believed that the very act of trying to understand is of extreme value in itself.

In terms of technique—other than the conventions of rhyme and meter—Robinson works consistently in three areas worth noting: image patterns, irony, and the deliberate withholding of information. Robinson is not the New England poet who celebrates or even writes about snow, lilacs, or the like. In fact, he is lean in his use of imagery from the natural world; however, when he does draw upon the natural world, his images are functional, not decorative, and they are often framed in a metaphorical or symbolic context. Wherever his images come from—colors, a visionary light, water, leaves, to name a few sources—they often serve in patterns as ordering devices to provide unity and to enhance meaning. They contribute to the complex texture of some of his best poems, such as "Luke Havergal," "For a Dead Lady," and "Eros Turannos."

Irony is one of Robinson's most consistently employed tools, and he uses it variously to achieve various ends. In "How Annandale Went Out," for example, irony is situational and understated; the doctor-speaker feels that it is absurd in the first place that he is on trial for a justified mercy killing, and he pleads his case almost casually. In "The House on the Hill" and "Eros

Turannos," Robinson is overtly caustic in his attitude toward people who feel compelled to speculate on the circumstances and personalities of others without much in the way of verification. In "The Man Against the Sky," the concept of a mechanistic universe is soundly indicted, while in "Cassandra," sarcasm is leveled, not very subtly, at American materialism. In "New England" the irony is so complex that readers first thought the sonnet was an attack on the rigidity of the Puritan afterglow in New England, when the poem actually denounces those who have wrongly interpreted this region.

While poets such as T. S. Eliot, Ezra Pound, and Wallace Stevens provide what amount to acceptable puzzles in their poetry, Robinson was, for a period, the object of some scorn for his obscurity. Since he was not given to the esoteric, readers perhaps came to him expecting to find neat, rational answers in technically sound poems. Because his language is relatively uncomplicated, descending probably from the Puritan "plain style," readers were confounded and even angered at not being able to determine what some of his poems meant. These interpretive problems derive from Robinson's technique of deliberately withholding information in the poem in order to make the reader think, to reward him when he arrives at his own understanding.

The most accomplished of Robinson's shorter poems, "Eros Turannos" is the favorite of anthologists and the poem most representative of Robinson's major thematic concerns and techniques. Set in a village on the coast of Maine, it recounts the courtship of a man and woman, and then tries to explain what happened to the woman once the man died. The speaker of the poem takes deliberate pains to inform the reader that he is really failing to understand her situation because he actually does not know what, in fact, she is experiencing.

The poem consists of six stanzas of eight lines each, with an ababcccb rhyme scheme and a metrical pattern of iambic tetrameter for all lines except those ending with the b rhyme. These are indented in the text and are in iambic trimeter with one extra unaccented syllable at the end of the line. The title is Greek for "Love, the Tyrant."

At the outset of this poem, which is narrated in the present tense to give its dramatic situation a sense of immediacy, the reader learns that the woman is afraid of the man despite his "engaging mask," that she has just cause for discounting him as a potential husband, but that she is willing to disregard her fears and uncertainties about him because she is more afraid of the "downward years," of growing old alone. Her insecurity is not merely a product of her relationship with the man; rather, it is a component of her personality: she is simply afraid of life.

As "Eros Turannos" progresses to the close of the third stanza, which marks the end of the first part of this little drama, the woman is depicted as being once capable of penetrating with her "blurred sagacity" beneath his mask to the "Judas that she found him"; however, she finally relinquishes all objections, at whatever cost to her, and agrees to the union. So far, the reader may feel that the woman deserves pity, and the man, scorn; but in typical Robinson fashion, the situation is not that simple, for just as the woman has deliberately deceived herself into believing that marrying a man she fears and cannot trust is a lesser evil than growing old alone, so too has he been deceived into marriage by the prospect of living rather comfortably with her in a setting replete with tradition that "Beguiles and reassures him." Robinson adopts the stance that there are inevitably two sides to every story, and he is most reluctant to pass judgments. There are some exceptions, of course, such as the despicable Aaron Stark in the sonnet of that name. By and large, however, if judgment is to be passed, the reader must do so from whatever understanding he comes to in the poems. Almost always, the reader learns to have compassion once he understands the situations confronting the characters, their personal inadequacies or hells—or understands at least to the best of his ability.

The first three stanzas thus establish and resolve, for a time, the problems facing the man and the woman by having them marry. The husband is absent in the second part of the poem, the last three stanzas, and the wife is living alone. From the way she is described in the first four lines of the fourth stanza, it is evident that a considerable time has passed and that she is either in or rapidly approaching old age. In addition, she is suffering from a collapse of her mental faculties. The "pounding wave" repeats the same song: her husband's dirge. The word "illusion" refers to the speaker's conception of the manner in which the wife had viewed her husband who now is dead. Her fears of living alone in the "downward years" have materialized. Hiding from the world, she has become an object of curiosity and idle speculation among the Tilbury Town folk.

At the beginning of the fifth stanza, the speaker, who, in Robinson's characteristic manner, identifies himself as a townsman by the use of "we," comments ironically on the inability of people to know other people and on the penchant "we" have for gossiping. Yet, just as the use of the words "veil" and "visions" reinforces the illusory nature of the wife's assessment of her husband, so do the townspeople fall prey to illusions; they are mistaken in their conception of the "home, where passion lived and died," in their conjectures about the man and woman who enacted the drama. The point that Robinson insists on making is a familiar one in his poetry.

The opening lines of the final stanza state that whatever the townspeople are saying can do the wife no harm, for she has striven with a "god" and is oblivious to everything else. She made a lifelong commitment, not only to her husband, but to "Love, the Tyrant," as well, and she is living with—suffering—the consequences. Exactly "what the God has given" to her is unknown, but in his effort to approximate what he thinks it might be, the speaker formulates three similes. Since he is uncertain, he uses the words "though" and "or" to qualify his perceptions. Although critics uniformly admire the striking images that close the poem, they avoid commentary on what the images mean, preferring instead vaguely to call attention to their symbolic significance. Confusing as these images may be, they represent to the speaker his conception of the woman's mental death, which is what she finally received from the "god," "Love, the Tyrant," once her husband died. When waves break (the first image), they are finished, through, dead; the "changed familiar tree" (the second image) is a tree in autumn, its leaves going or gone, and a symbolic representation of death or impending death; and, lastly, the blind who are driven down "the stairway to the sea" suggest the "downward years" of the first stanza and serve as the concluding representation of death. Blindly driven by "Love, the Tyrant," the wife is being driven to death, just as the blind would drown were they forced into the sea. Words referring to vision and sight form a basic image pattern that unifies the poem and underscores the thematic concern: stanza (1) *mask*; (2) *blurred*, *sees*, *looks*; (3) *sees*, *dimmed*; (4) *illusion*; (5) *veil*, *vision*, *seen*; (6) *blind*. While not explicitly related to the motif, a second pattern of imagery also helps to unify the poem. Since the physical setting is a harbor community, water and nautical imagery is found in the infinitives "to sound" and "to secure," and in the mention of "foamless weirs," "sense of ocean," "pounding wave," "waves breaking," and "like a stairway to the sea." Finally, in keeping with the time of year in the second part of the poem, Robinson refers to the autumnal images of a "falling leaf" and "a changed familiar tree." Robinson is at his best in "Eros Turannos," a moving lyric unified through patterns of imagery, through the consistent use of the present tense, and through a logically balanced structure dividing the poem into cause and effect. It is through the speaker's struggles to understand the wife that the reader comes to an understanding of and compassion for her.

In both "The Whip" and "How Annandale Went Out," as in "Eros Turannos," Robinson withholds from the reader an easy understanding of the central issues of the poems, thus forcing the reader to a scrupulous reading. When the reader does become aware of the circumstances behind the actions of the characters, he understands and feels compassion for them. Both poems, but especially "The Whip," have been the subject of considerable critical attention.

"The Whip," a forty-line poem in five stanzas of eight iambic trimeter lines with an ababbcbc rhyme scheme, is narrated by a Tilbury Townsman who has no obvious connection with the characters whose recent drama, which led to a suicide, he is trying to fathom. The setting is apparently a funeral home. The victim is in an open coffin and the speaker quizzically addresses him.

In the first stanza the speaker reveals that the suicide victim had been married to a woman who treated him tyranically and ruined him. During their marriage he constantly doubted her fidelity and became a cynic. As the poem progresses through the second and third stanzas, the speaker comments that the wife indeed had taken a lover and left. As a result, the husband chose death by drowning. Yet the speaker, recognizing that "the gall we drink/ Is not the mead we cry for," feels that the husband's plight did not justify his suicide. It was not "a thing to die for."

The specifics surrounding the suicide begin to take shape in the fourth stanza as the speaker, still bewildered by the situation, notices a blue mark "like a welt" on the husband's face; and in the final stanza the speaker and the reader come to understanding at the same time. The "chase" referred to in the fifth stanza involved the husband on a horse pursuing the wife and her lover, who were either on one horse or on separate ones. As they were crossing a river, the wife struck her husband in the face with her riding crop; hence the title, "The Whip." He fell off his horse and chose to drown. Earlier in the poem, knowing only that the husband committed suicide, the speaker asks, "Then, shall I call you blind?" He ends the poem with "Still, shall I call you blind?"—a question rhetorically posed, for the speaker has come to the realization that the husband's suicide came at a moment of emotional and physical frenzy. This knowledge finally becoming clear to him, his attitude undergoes a change.

"The Whip" is a little masterpiece of mystery and subsequent revelation. It is a testimony to Robinson's skill that he manages to have both the speaker and the reader simultaneously come to the realization of what actually happened. One of many in his repertoire of shorter poems devoted to the subject of suicide (others include "Luke Havergal," "Richard Cory," "The Growth of 'Lorraine,'" and "The Mill"), its thematic concerns are typically Robinson's: the interdependence of understanding and compassion, and the difficulty of knowing another person. Robinson wants us to understand the factors that lead to suicide and to have compassion for the victims. It should be remembered that, in Robinson's time, suicide was looked upon much more harshly and with much less understanding of the causal factors than it is today.

"How Annandale Went Out" is an English sonnet in which Robinson once again deliberately withholds information in order to make the impact of the poem more powerfully felt. It is also one of his sonnets that expands the range of the form by dealing with euthanasia, hardly the stuff of which sonnets were made prior to the twentieth century.

The doctor-speaker of the sonnet, which is entirely enclosed in quotation marks, is presenting the court with his reasons, however obliquely stated, for committing euthanasia in the case of Annandale, a man whose illness or injury, never identified, had reduced him from a man to a thing. The doctor refers to him in the octet as "it," "apparatus," and "wreck," terms which initially misdirect the reader but which establish the doctor's frame of mind. The doctor calls himself "Liar, physician, hypocrite, and friend," and, in the sestet, asks the court to bear in mind that he knew Annandale before misfortune reduced him to a "ruin." In addition, he asks the court to remember the "worst you know of me" and to consider his position with "a slight kind of engine," which probably refers to a hypodermic needle, the instrument with which he committed the mercy killing. He closes by saying, "You wouldn't hang me? I thought not."

This poem works so well because of the doctor's view that the entire situation of the trial is nothing less than ironic. "It is absurd," he seems to be saying, "that, given the circumstances, I should do anything other than put an end to the terrible suffering of my friend. This trial mocks the very humanitarian impulse in man." The power of the poem resides in the doctor's method of presentation. His ironic indictments, coupled with the very serious nature of the situation, generate tension; and by not identifying the source of Annandale's suffering, Robinson places the focus clearly on the doctor.

It is possible that Robinson's frustrations in not being able to write successful plays or fiction led him to expend the effort that he did on his long blank verse narrative poems. They may have satisfied his need to tell a story, to dramatize at length what he so nicely accomplished in his shorter poems. The longer works, like the shorter poems, are full of troubled characters from all walks of life. In detailed observation that often is tedious and conversations that are often lifeless, Robinson presents characters on the verge of or just after a trauma. Wallace L. Anderson observes in *Edwin Arlington Robinson: A Critical Introduction* (1967) that "most of the poem[s] [are] concerned with . . . efforts to find out why. . . . It is necessary, in other words, for the characters to understand each other and themselves. Robinson's concern in the long poems is essentially the same as in the short ones."

Since they are based, however loosely at times, on the myths that constitute the Arthurian legends, *Merlin*, *Lancelot*, and *Tristram* must necessarily deal with formed characters, events, and eventualities; yet the characters are troubled, they court and reach disaster, and they must gain understanding. Yvor Winters, in *Edwin Arlington Robinson* (1946), remarks of Lancelot in the poem of that name: "[He] is not free, because of the Light; that is, because he has acquired understanding which he before had lacked, and of understanding one cannot divest oneself." With some exceptions understandably made for the Arthurian poems, Robinson's characters, whether in the longer poems or in the superior shorter ones, are often the maimed, the outcast, and the forgotten of society. While many are able to endure their situations stoically, others cannot and, as a result, choose antisocial behavior. For all, the poet has compassion, and he asks that of his readers, too.

Ronald Moran

Other major works
 PLAYS: *Van Zorn*, 1914; *The Porcupine*, 1915.
 NONFICTION: *Selected Letters of Edwin Arlington Robinson*, 1940; *Untrian-*

gulated Stars: Letters of Edwin Arlington Robinson to Harry de Forest Smith, 1890-1905, 1947; *Edwin Arlington Robinson's Letters to Edith Brower,* 1968. MISCELLANEOUS: *Uncollected Poems and Prose of Edwin Arlington Robinson,* 1975.

Bibliography

Barnard, Ellsworth. *Edwin Arlington Robinson: A Critical Study.* New York: Macmillan, 1952. This study is a labor of love. It is thorough and meticulous, provides a perceptive and helpful analysis of Robinson's poetic style, and is especially valuable on the long poems. Searching chapters on the development of Robinson's thought are included.

Boswell, Jeanetta. *Edwin Arlington Robinson and the Critics: A Bibliography of Secondary Sources with Selective Annotations.* Metuchen, N.J.: Scarecrow Press, 1988. This bibliography updates Nancy Joyner's *E. A. Robinson: A Reference Guide* (1978) but does not add much more. Lists only materials published before 1983. The 1,383 items are arranged alphabetically by author. Includes ample annotations, a useful subject index, and a short introduction on Robinson's scholarship.

Fussell, Edwin Sill. *Edwin Arlington Robinson: The Literary Background of a Traditional Poet.* Berkeley: University of California Press, 1954. This study examines closely the influences under which Robinson produced his lyric and narrative poetry (Edgar Allan Poe, Henry Wadsworth Longfellow, Ralph Waldo Emerson, Henry David Thoreau, Nathaniel Hawthorne, William Shakespeare, William Cowper, William Wordsworth, John Keats, Thomas Hardy, Robert Browning, and Alfred, Lord Tennyson). Helpful on the sonnets, and in its analysis of Robinson's diction. Shows Robinson to be a traditional poet, "content with the old-fashioned way to be new."

Hagedorn, Hermann. *Edwin Arlington Robinson: A Biography.* New York: Macmillan, 1938. This early account of the poet's life remains the best. Written by a close friend out of vivid recollections, it is extremely readable, tender, and affectionate. Especially useful on the poet's boyhood, on his friendship with Robert Frost, and on *Tristram.* Includes several anecdotes.

Kaplan, Estelle. *Philosophy in the Poetry of Edwin Arlington Robinson.* New York: Columbia University Press, 1940. This extended analysis of Robinson's thought is a must for any serious student of the poet. Includes a bibliography and an index.

Neff, Emery E. *Edwin Arlington Robinson.* New York: W. Sloane, 1948. This critical study accords Robinson, together with Robert Frost, the foremost place in poetry in the first half of the century. Provides a close analysis of Robinson's American themes, and is thorough on the Arthurian poems. One of the values of this study is in the portraits of the poet's friends. More biographical than critical.

Smith, Chard Powers. *Where the Light Falls: A Portrait of Edwin Arlington*

Robinson. New York: Macmillan, 1965. The best of a number of personal
reminiscences. Provides an affectionate and vivid picture of the poet's character and personality. Seventeen of the 420 pages are composed of notes
and bibliographical references.

Winters, Yvor. *Edwin Arlington Robinson.* Norfolk, Conn.: New Directions,
1946. One of Robinson's best critics and the most persistent of the poet's
admirers, Winters sorts out the essential in Robinson. Cites eleven poems
that "can be equaled . . . in the work of only four or five English and
American poets of the past century and a half." Helpful on the shorter
poems; Winters does not like the long poems. This volume is a stimulating work of biography and criticism. Contains four pages of bibliography.

JOHN WILMOT, EARL OF ROCHESTER

Born: Ditchley, England; April 10, 1647
Died: Woodstock, England; July 26, 1680

Principal poetry

During John Wilmot, Earl of Rochester's lifetime, his lyrics, songs, lampoons, and satires were circulated in manuscript copies among the court of Charles II. A few of his writings were printed as broadsides or in miscellanies; his great "A Satire Against Mankind" was printed as a folio broadside in 1675.

The textual issue of whether a reliable contemporary edition of his poetry exists is a complicated one. In the late summer of 1680, a book professing to be the *Poems on Several Occasions by the Right Honourable the E. of R.* was published under the ostensible imprint of a nonexistent Antwerp printer. In an effort to capitalize on his name and popular reputation as a wild courtier, sixty-one poems were offered, of which many were pornographic and more than a third were not even written by Rochester. Nevertheless, the book was extremely popular and numerous editions were produced to satisfy public demand. In his book *Attribution in Restoration Poetry: A Study of Rochester's "Poems" of 1680* (1963), David Vieth explains that the earliest of these editions was based on a responsible manuscript miscellany copytext, and that despite the shortcomings of *Poems on Several Occasions*, it is the most important edition of Rochester published prior to the twentieth century. Since 1926, many editors have struggled with the Rochester text. The difficulties arose over an unusually problematical canon, the varying authority of texts from which the poems came down to readers, and the obscene nature of some of the genuine poems. In 1968, the definitive critical edition was published: David Vieth's *The Complete Poems of John Wilmot, Earl of Rochester*. In solving the aforementioned difficulties, Vieth found seventy-five authentic poems, eight other poems possibly written by Rochester, and nearly two hundred spurious poems.

Other literary forms

The first complete, unexpurgated edition of Rochester's letters appeared in 1980 as *The Letters of John Wilmot, Earl of Rochester*, edited by Jeremy Treglown. It includes more than one hundred very readable letters to his wife, to his mistress, and to his close friend, the courtier Henry Savile. Rochester's most sustained prose work is the broadside "Alexander Bendo's Bill," which satirized mountebanks and compared them to politicians, the quacks of state affairs. One version of this piece appears in Vivian de Sola Pinto's *Enthusiast in Wit: A Portrait of John Wilmot Earl of Rochester 1647-1680* (1962). There is also proof of Rochester's interest in drama—a scene for Sir Robert Howard's unfinished play *The Conquest of China*, and in 1678 a lengthy adaptation of John Fletcher's tragedy *Valentinian*, called in manuscript *Lucina's Rape*. Rochester did not live to complete the alteration, but in February, 1684, his play was given a magnificent production at the King's Theatre in London.

Achievements

Rochester is the one major poet among the literary courtiers of the Restoration. His standing as a poet still suffers from his reputation as a heartless rake. This view can no longer be taken seriously, since even in those of his love songs which express intense passion and cheerful irresponsibility there is also a powerful current of fidelity. Rochester's devotion to his friends was only exceeded by the sincere intensity of thought and sentiment of the lyrics that he addressed to his wife. He embodied the Restoration definition of wit, not only having the capacity for a clever turn of phrase but also possessing a fierce intelligence. In his satires, he becomes a poet of skepticism, morally indignant, drawn to heterodoxy and paradox, but continually searching for the eternal truths promised by religion and for the assurances of love, friendship, and power.

Although his importance must be decided on the basis of a rather small canon (about seventy-five poems, a hundred letters, and an adaptation of a play), he has maintained a vocal group of admirers. The poet Andrew Marvell thought him the "best English satyrist," Voltaire called him a "Man of Genius with a shining imagination," and Alfred, Lord Tennyson respected the "almost terrible force" of his "A Satire Against Mankind." In the twentieth century Rochester has been described as a traditional Augustan more akin to Jonathan Swift and Alexander Pope than to John Dryden, a destructive nihilist, and a Christian pilgrim journeying not toward a goal but in search of one. The diversity of these viewpoints is exceeded only by their relative narrowness or exaggeration.

The most plausible contemporary view finds Rochester a mature product of the Restoration; his work illuminates the cultural, literary, and intellectual climate of that period. Since the 1968 publication of Vieth's new critical edition of the complete poems, a Rochester revival has been in progress. Numerous books and articles and a concordance to the poems have followed, and in 1980, a major part of *Tennessee Studies in Literature* was dedicated to the poet. Rochester remains the finest lyrical poet of the Restoration, the last important Metaphysical poet, and an influential satiric poet who helped make possible the achievements of the Augustan satirists.

Biography

John Wilmot was born in Ditchley, Oxfordshire, England, on April 10, 1647. He was the son of Henry, Viscount Wilmot, a distinguished Cavalier general, who had fought for Charles I and was made Earl of Rochester by him. Later his father would effect the escape of Charles II from England to exile in France. Anne St. John, his mother, was the daughter of Sir John St. John, a Wiltshire knight and prominent Puritan.

John Wilmot inherited the earldom of Rochester and Adderbury Manor at the age of eleven. A handsome and precocious youth, he entered Wadham College, Oxford, at thirteen, where he was exposed to the most advanced scientific and philosophical thinking of the time: "the real centre of the English Enlightenment." His earliest poetry was written there in celebration of Charles II on his return in May, 1660; these few lines reminded the King of his debt to Wilmot's father. He richly rewarded the son, conferring a master's degree on the boy, granting him a pension of five hundred pounds a year, and arranging for his Grand Tour complete with a learned Scottish physician and virtuoso as his tutor.

After touring France and Italy, he returned to England in the winter of 1664 and joined the court of Charles II, immediately gaining notoriety for wit, profanity, and debauchery. Soon Rochester became the informal leader of a fashionable group of literary wits known as "the merry gang," which included the playwright Sir George Etherege; John Sheffield, Earl of Mulgrave; Charles Sackville, Earl of Dorset; the poet Sir Charles Sedley; and Rochester's closest friend, Henry Savile.

Influenced by the writings of Thomas Hobbes, Rochester interpreted his materialist philosophy as a defense of sensuality and began an active revolt against both Cavalier romanticism and Puritan idealism. Although critics now agree that his reputation as a frantic rake and libertine was largely undeserved, the early lyrics and songs of this period display a determined hedonism and thorough enjoyment of the high-spirited frolic of the Whitehall Palace. In *Royal Charles: Charles II and the Restoration* (1979), Antonia Fraser describes the famous Cornelis Huysmans portrait of Rochester as "a young man of almost insolent sensuality, wide lips curling with devilment, but with 'something of the Angel yet undefaced in him.'" This indiscriminate life of pleasure soon proved unsatisfactory, and thereafter Rochester pursued a less insecure style of living.

In 1665 he met the beautiful young heiress Elizabeth Malet, and with the encouragement of the King he asked her to marry him. When she refused, he abducted her; he was subsequently caught and imprisoned in the Tower. Soon released, he joined the Navy and fought in the Dutch war of 1665 and 1666. His valorous conduct in battle helped to restore him to the favor of the King, and, in 1667, he continued his success by marrying Malet. More honors descended on the twenty-one-year-old Rochester: the King appointed him a Gentleman of the Bedchamber with a salary of one thousand pounds, commissioned him captain in the horseguards, and arranged his summons to a seat in the House of Lords.

By all accounts, Rochester and his wife enjoyed a happy marriage, and four children resulted. Monogamy, however, suffered numerous assaults; the custom of keeping a mistress was followed by most Restoration aristocrats, and Rochester was no different in this regard. Elizabeth Barry, who became the greatest actress of the age, bore a daughter in 1677 and regarded Rochester as the father both of her child and of her career.

The decade of the 1670's marks the real development of Rochester as a poet. Always an impressive conversationalist, he began writing realistic and energetic satires of court life. The outspoken quality of his criticism alienated many of its victims—especially the King, who had him banished from court more than once. This reaction did not deter him from writing more fierce lampoons and from actively supporting the theater. Dryden thanked Rochester for his help with the Epistle Dedicatory to *Marriage à la Mode* (1673). Within two years, however, Rochester attacked Dryden in his satire "An Allusion to Horace" (1675). This work served as a dividing line between the factions of Whig and Tory writers.

The last four years of Rochester's life were characteristically dramatic; the evidence delineates the final stages of his long syphilitic illness and a remarkable spiritual conversion only a few weeks before his death. In the winter of 1679 to 1680, he shocked friends by his sincere interest in meeting Gilbert Burnet, a Scottish clergyman, to discuss the principles of Christianity. Although Rochester had maintained a rigid skepticism throughout his life, these conversations, with the knowledge of imminent death, triggered a sensational repentance. Declaring that religion had brought him the sense of "felicity and glory" that he had missed pursuing worldly pleasures, Rochester died on July 26, 1680, at Woodstock. He was thirty-three, and his death would release a mass of contradictory comment from biographers proclaiming him either an edifying example of conversion or a debauched pornographer with, in Pope's phrase, "a very bad turn of mind." The one truth that can be acknowledged by the evidence is that he possessed "the greatest poetic gift of all the noble Wits."

Analysis

John Wilmot, Earl of Rochester's reputation as a poet has suffered from the overly dramatic legends about his life. Whatever past judgments have been made of his work seem unfairly colored by a considerable amount of untruthful scandal. Although modern biographers tend to rehabilitate such men completely and to give less perfidious definitions to the term "libertine," there is little to be gained here by denying the truth of his professed hedonism and his actual debauchery. Unwilling to allow his biography to overwhelm his work, two contemporary critics, David Vieth and Dustin Griffin, have affirmed the undeniable wit and power of his verses. Appreciation of the value of the early satires, the songs, and "A Satire Against Mankind" develops from first agreeing that Rochester is a product of his own time. Although this work, particularly the late satires, was influential for the Augustans and even shared some of their values, one should view Rochester's poems as mirroring the Restoration milieu socially, intellectually, and stylistically.

The major themes of Rochester's poetry derive from his evaluation of love, friendship, and courtly life. In each of these areas, he weighs man's promise for achieving the ideal against his predilection for evil and folly. As a skeptic, he is not under the mystical spell of religion; his poems reveal a man in search of certainties in the face of an awareness that such serenity is, for him, remote and unrealizable.

As literature of the Restoration, the poems reveal aristocratic attitudes of the past under severe stress from the philosophies of the Enlightenment. Rochester's knowledge of René Descartes, Thomas Hobbes, and John Locke allows him to suspend an automatic acceptance of traditional value systems and instead to question, analyze, and debate issues concerning the human condition.

Griffin, in *Satires Against Man: The Poems of Rochester* (1973), finds that one constant motif of his work was a rational humanist morality. Rather than trusting society or religion to establish laws for the restraint of man, Rochester depends on pleasure and pain and on following "nature" as the way to govern conduct. His tendency toward skepticism causes him to doubt whether morals can guide man to right conduct; in typical Restoration fashion, Rochester insists upon the immediacy of experience both with regard to sensual desires and in more abstract concerns: belief, conduct, and literary convention. Immediacy suggests security, a safe haven from the "ugly cheat" of life. If traditional moral and religious restraints are held in contempt, as they were at court, Rochester has only to rely on sensual contentment. Inevitably, his poems reflect his dissatisfaction with such experience; in fact, his constant theme is the disproportion between our desires and the means for satisfying them. While remaining a sensualist, he never reflects satisfaction in the poetry, because he never loses sight of the ultimate futility of the human condition. His poetry describes the suffering, anger, frustration, and failure of man, and does so with energy and clarity. In failing to achieve security, Rochester's analysis also reveals the zest of man's restless, acquisitive, and competitive nature, while affirming his admiration of personal goodness, of freedom from pretension and greed.

Rochester's poems fall into four chronological categories: Prentice Work (1665-1671), Early Maturity (1672-1673), Tragic Maturity (1674-1675), and Disillusionment and Death (1676-1680). Representative of Rochester's "Prentice Work" is the early poem "A Song: My dear Mistress has a heart" (exact date unknown), a self-consciously conventional poem incorporating characteristics of the courtly love tradition. As in many of his other songs, Rochester explores the complexities of man's sexual nature while entertaining rather than instructing the reader. In two eight-line stanzas of ballad measures, the poet employs the familiar figures and concepts of Restoration lyrics—the enslaving mistress whose "resistless Art" has captured the poet's heart. While recognizing "her Constancy's weak," he is powerless to escape her "Killing pleasures and Wounding Blisses" and must only trust that this poem will convince her of his deepest regard. Without varying from the sophisticated pattern, Rochester writes a tender, graceful love lyric. What seems missing is the poet's individual voice, which would bring this artificial form to life with the sheer intensity of his wit.

Another early poem, "Fair Chloris in a pigsty lay" (exact date unknown), marks him as an authentic poetic voice with its sudden, often brutal, wit that shocks the reader, demanding his notice. Rochester's Chloris is not the conventional dreaming shepherdess of the pastoral; she is a swineherdess of the most lustful and crude sort. Surrounded by her murmuring pigs while she sleeps, Chloris dreams of a "love-convicted swain" who calls her to a cave to rescue a trapped pig, only to throw himself lustfully upon her. Instead of a self-abasing lover pleading with his mistress, Rochester reverses the persona as Chloris finds herself the object of a crude rape. The poem's final stanza undercuts the brutality yet retains the indecency, as Chloris wakes, realizing that it was only a dream. Her innocence is preserved, although she has enjoyed the secret pleasure of a fantasy lover. While maintaining a humorous and playful tone, Rochester adds a final unexpected twist of eroticism which lifts this song above the conventionality of the earlier one. Such a mocking tone foreshadows the poems of his mature period; the "innocent" Chloris becomes the voracious Corinna of "A Ramble in St. James's Park."

The poems of 1672-1673, the period of Rochester's "Early Maturity," reveal his accomplishment as a lyricist and his virtuosity as a satirist. Vieth believes that the satires of 1674 display the zenith of Rochester's achievement, but "A Ramble in St. James's Park" is a triumph. The poem is a comprehensive Juvenalian satire on sexual relations in the *beau monde*, displaying the rake-speaker as one who ridicules the corruption in himself and in his fellow revelers. The speaker describes an after-dinner walk in the Park in search of love. In the Park, once a place of elegance and now a scene of dissipation, he unexpectedly "beheld Corinna pass," who is his mistress and should acknowledge him, but instead "proud disdain she cast on me." Watching further, he sees her leave in a coach with three "confounded asses." Bitterly disillusioned, not by her lust but by her passive and treacherous submission to fools, he curses her for a "fall to so much infamy." The speaker, who had considered himself morally superior to his companions, now concludes with an ironic self-satire, an attack on the pastoral for idealizing such settings, and a lampoon against indiscriminate lust.

The villain is not the libertine speaker but Corinna, who offends all humanity by engaging in sex unfeelingly. Honest lustful passion remains a justifiable principle, while unfeeling sex with affected fools is a far worse sin than mere lust. Rochester shows his displeasure with Restoration men and women who respond to unnatural longings and reject those desires born of natural reason. The material is vigorous and often violent in tone, impatient with the sham of Cavalier and Restoration conventions in love poetry. The best of Rochester's bawdy satires, it is motivated not by its profane qualities but in part by a prejudice against the debasement of sex.

In the period of his "Tragic Maturity," Rochester found his vehicle as a poetic stylist by controlling the heroic couplet for formal verse satire. The influence of the Roman satirists Horace and Juvenal provided some impetus for Rochester; his best model, however, was Horace's disciple, Nicolas Boileau Despréaux, the first major seventeenth century satirist to attempt a re-creation of classical forms. "Timon" and "A Satire Against Mankind" transcend Boileau-Despréaux with their economy of phrase, skillful use of narrative and descriptive styles from one victim's portrait to another, and the command displayed between the realization of the speaker and the various dramatic scenes. John Harold Wilson, in *The Court Wits of the Restoration* (1948), argues that Rochester was roused in the 1670's "to a true misanthropy by the contrast between man's promise and his performance . . . he made war on mankind at large." In these poems, the complacency of mankind provokes an outrage unmatched at any other point in his career.

"Timon" has as its principal speaker a man named Timon, who resembles Rochester in character, interests, and social status. The reference to William Shakespeare's misanthropic Timon of Athens is obvious, although the name may also allude to his honesty in the face of a corrupted humanity. The account begins with an unwilling visit to a dinner party where an insistent host—a total stranger "who just my name had got"—promises that the other guests will be his friends Sedley, Savile, and Buckhurst. Not surprisingly, these assurances remain unfulfilled. Timon's company consists of four fools, "Halfwit and Huff, Kickum and Dingboy." The hostess appears, an ancient flirt, and presides over a tedious banquet complete with displays of corrupted taste in food and poetry. Inevitably, rough verbal antics culminate in bouts of plate-hurling and Timon's own relieved escape into the night.

Rochester establishes the thematic unity of the poem by implying that Timon's social and intellectual standards have been violated by the attitudes and actions of the host, his wife, and the four "hectors." In the earlier model for the poem, the Horatian speaker was a paragon of good sense and propriety. Rochester's Timon flaunts a delighted malice before the rest of the human race and does so in the bawdiest terms. Detailing the physical characteristics of the hostess, Timon develops a vicious portrait; the entire description, however, includes the most damning evidence—the victim's conversation, which displays her foolishness, affectation, and crudity. The speaker's character also comes under scrutiny; his curious interest in the dinner conversation and his obsession with sex create a disturbing uncertainty in the poem. Rochester may have meant to mock Timon for having agreed to attend the dinner party; his skeptical nature should have warned him against finding true companions. Also, the speaker's sexual crudity, although strikingly overt, is at least without affectation. As in the earlier "A Ramble in St. James's Park," the rake admits his belief in sexual freedom, his appreciation for honest, generous lust. Ultimately he finds frustration and humiliation. The same theme which appeared in the earlier work is alluded to in "Timon"; sensual experience is ultimately a failure. Timon realizes the accuracy of this attitude in his comments on the host's wife: "Fit to give love . . . But age, beauty's incurable disease, had left her more desire than power to please." Timon's faults cannot be ignored, but in contrast to the affected hosts and boorish guests he gains the reader's trust.

Rochester's most impressive poem is his "A Satire Against Mankind." It is a discourse in which the speaker offers the paradoxical thesis that it is better to be an animal than a man; however, Rochester is more concerned with emphasizing the loathsomeness of being human than the virtues of being an animal. He attacks Reason itself, the pure rationality that he had formerly worshiped.

The poem reflects the skepticism of the age, and the recurrent motif in Rochester's work of a division between the actual and the ideal. The philosophy of cynicism goes back to classical sources, to Epicurus and the Skeptics. It seems that Rochester adopted their arguments in order to counter particular schools of rationalistic thought such as the vain and strident Christian rationalism of the Cambridge Platonists, the godlike reasoning eminence of the university Schoolmen, and the anti-Aristotelian rationalism of the Anglicans. The exaltation of man, the thesis that God is pure reason, the continual optimism about man's capacities for perceiving the meaning of the cosmos and God's laws through reason—all of these notions were ridiculed by him.

Rochester's immediate, most influential source was Thomas Hobbes, whose materialist-sensationalist philosophy was the basis for his view of human motivation. Every man is an enemy to every other man in his desire for gain, for safety, and for glory. This continual desire for security, for certainty, is characteristic of the libertine, who disdains convention and orthodoxy as paths to power. The rake instead exploits other people's weaknesses, thus gaining mastery over their lives. Those conventional figures of the community who might censure him are hypocrites who have disavowed their true desires for gain and glory. All those virtues that man professes to follow in the name of social order are merely rationalizations of his fear and desire for security, and Rochester improves on Hobbes, believing that man only converts this fear into more "respectable" passions. Rochester exhibits a bitter, relentless cynicism about human possibility; even the rake's mastery proves to be a painful failure.

The poem is a formal verse satire in which the satirist contemplates a particular topic and anticipates the imaginary response of someone else to his thoughts. This structure of the satire has caused much debate among critics who believe that the poem is a philosophical discourse on epistemology and ethics. Other scholars make a good case for the view that the poem is a unified polemic against human pride: pride in reason, learning, and "accomplishment." Griffin accepts both viewpoints while offering his analysis of the work as primarily a four-part discourse, with a speaker presenting and defending the paradox that it is better to be an animal than a man.

The first part of the poem states the thesis, suggesting that all men are equally ridiculous, and proposes a distinction between wits and fools. This difference proves a false one. The second part raises the imagined objections of the satirist's opponent, who offers a distinction between wit and reason which only reveals the ambiguous, confused nature of the opponent's argument. The third part develops the satirist's response to these objections, analyzing first reason and then mankind's "wisdom" and "nature." He seems willing to accept the middle ground between pure instinct and pure reason "which distinguishes by sense." The paradoxical quality of the poem is again asserted as the satirist turns from this compromise to attack all mankind once more. Instinct, although preferable to right reason, remains unattainable since all men are "knaves." The fourth part functions as the epilogue in which the satirist recapitulates his argument and in so doing reformulates his paradox. Significantly, Rochester adds here that all men are slaves, as well as knaves, only some are worse in these respects than others. The final line— "Man differs more from man, than man from beast"—sharpens the total satiric effect of the poem. Animals, after this exacting analysis, still remain closer to the ideal of godlike man ("meek humble man of honest sense") than the rabble (wits, fools, cowards, knaves, and the poet). The beasts are a better reflection of man's moral ideals than is man himself.

"A Satire Against Mankind" remains an impressive effort and an example of the best Rochester was capable of during his mature period. Its effects are beautifully judged, as is its destructive critique of human pretension; however, Rochester's own predicament as a man and as an artist persists with no real hope or secure possibility for a better world.

The sixteen poems of Rochester's final period, the period of "Disillusionment and Death," reflect a decline in the quantity and quality of his work. The most effective poem of this group is "An Epistolary Essay from M. G. to O. B. upon their Mutual Poems" (1679). Serving as a companion piece to "A Very Heroical Epistle in Answer to Ephelia" (1675), this informal critical essay expresses the views on love and poetry of a bold libertine persona, M. G. (John Sheffield, Earl of Mulgrave). The speaker writes to a friend, O. B. (John Dryden), in praise of the latter's poems and in defense of his own violations of the traditional canons of good writing. Furthermore, after having lampooned in "A Satire Against Mankind" the idea that rational man partakes of the divine, Rochester here attacks the idea that poetry has a divine source. By employing this approach, he criticizes conventional wisdom, putting the burden of writing well on the poet's egotism instead of on divine will. The argument concludes with the notion that a poet is his own best critic and must rely on his own self-judgment. The arrogance of the piece marks Rochester's strength as a poet but his weakness as a man.

Confident about his own artistic strengths, he had nothing but contempt for the rabble of hacks and critics. His work possesses the poetic virtues of vigor and force; although often unconventional and strikingly obscene, his poems grow out of a literary tradition both Classical and English. Although the spectacle of mankind provoked in him a Juvenalian outrage and profound disgust, he also revealed his admiration for personal goodness, for a man of Christlike humility and piety. The doubt that such a person existed would plague him his entire life; yet he continued the quest without abject despair. His complex emotional response to the literary, intellectual, and social milieu of the Restoration found an outlet in his poetry. Whether he projects rejection and nihilism or envisions an ideal which proves unreachable, Rochester remains one of the most original and notable poets of the age.

Paul J. deGrategno

Other major works
PLAY: *Lucina's Rape*, 1684 (adaptation of John Fletcher's tragedy *Valentinian*).

NONFICTION: *The Letters of John Wilmot, Earl of Rochester*, 1980 (Jeremy Treglown, editor).

Bibliography
Farley-Hills, David. *Rochester: The Critical Heritage*. London: Routledge & Kegan Paul, 1972. This collection of critical essays on Rochester's work includes comments by his contemporaries and by writers such as John Dryden, Alexander Pope, and Jonathan Swift. Only essays as recent as the early part of the twentieth century are included, and modern reassessments of Rochester are lacking. Even so, this volume offers valuable background material and fascinating insights into Rochester's position in literary history, as he has gone in and out of acceptability.

Griffin, Dustin H. *Satires Against Man: The Poems of Rochester*. Berkeley: University of California Press, 1973. This work offers a discussion primarily of Rochester's satires, with an interesting chapter on "The Pains of Sex" in Rochester's works. A good part of the book focuses on Rochester's "A Satire Against Mankind," offering extensive background on the poem as well as an in-depth examination of the poem itself. Includes a discussion of Rochester's relation to other satirists such as Alexander Pope and Jonathan Swift.

Pinto, Vivian de Sola. *Enthusiast in Wit: A Portrait of John Wilmot, Earl of*

Rochester. London: Routledge & Kegan Paul, 1962. This biography is an updated, expanded version of Pinto's *Rochester, Portrait of a Restoration Poet* which was first published in 1935. Pinto offers the fullest biography of Rochester currently available, with abundant detail on the poet's youth, riotous and colorful life in and out of exile at the court of Charles II, and dramatic deathbed conversion. The social, intellectual, and literary currents of Rochester's day are also treated in depth.

Rochester, John Wilmot, Earl of. *The Letters of John Wilmot, Earl of Rochester.* Edited by Jeremy Treglown. Oxford: Basil Blackwell, 1980. This well-annotated, thorough edition of Rochester's letters affords unique insight into Rochester's life and work. Both sides of the correspondence are included in many cases, and a concise biographical introduction provides a brief but sound overview of Rochester's life.

Treglown, Jeremy, ed. *The Spirit of Wit: Reconsiderations of Rochester.* Oxford: Basil Blackwell, 1982. This collection of modern essays offers various new views of the poet and his work. The essays examine topics such as Rochester's link with the Metaphysical poets, Rochester as a poet of "lyrical realism," and Rochester's attitude toward women. His life and poetry are discussed in the light of the intellectual, social, and political currents of his day.

THEODORE ROETHKE

Born: Saginaw, Michigan; May 25, 1908
Died: Seattle, Washington; August 1, 1963

Principal poetry

Open House, 1941; *The Lost Son and Other Poems*, 1948; *Praise to the End!*, 1951; *The Waking: Poems 1933-1953*, 1953; *Words for the Wind*, 1958; *I Am! Says the Lamb*, 1961; *Sequence, Sometimes Metaphysical*, 1963; *The Far Field*, 1964; *The Collected Poems of Theodore Roethke*, 1966.

Other literary forms

Theodore Roethke devoted most of his energy to his poetry. Ralph J. Mills, however, has filled one small volume, *On the Poet and His Craft: Selected Prose of Theodore Roethke* (1965), with Roethke's essays and reviews. He has also edited *The Selected Letters of Theodore Roethke* (1968). In *Straw for the Fire: From the Notebooks of Theodore Roethke, 1943-1963* (1972), David Wagoner has selected and edited revealing passages from Roethke's 277 working notebooks and 8,306 loose sheets. All three of these books are very useful in understanding Roethke's difficult poetry, for the poet speaks about his own work as well as about poetry in general.

Achievements

Critics often consider Roethke and Robert Lowell to be the most important poets of the postwar generation. Although Roethke's achievement with traditional forms, such as the difficult villanelle, is impressive, he will be remembered primarily for his longer poems, the series of "sequences" in which he broke new ground by forging a unique poetic voice that conveys the intensity and complexity of his emotional, psychological, and spiritual struggles. Roethke created a new style in which one finds a kind of "psychic short hand," to borrow the poet's phrase. With the telescoping and distortion of images, the striking juxtaposition of the commonplace and the bizarre, he evokes a variety of states of consciousness under great stress, including those of the child, the mentally ill, and the mystic. Influenced by William Wordsworth, Walt Whitman, and William Butler Yeats, he explores the depths of the psyche and captures the associative movement of the mind.

Roethke received many honors and awards throughout his career, including two Guggenheims (1945, 1950), the Tietjens Prize (1947), the *Poetry* Magazine Award (1951), the Levinson Prize (1951), and the American Academy of Arts and Letters Award (1952). Yet he did not receive widespread recognition until the publication of *The Waking: Poems 1933-1953*, which won the Pulitzer Prize for poetry in 1953. The last decade of the poet's life was a period in which he received his most prestigious awards and attracted the attention that he so much desired. *Words for the Wind*, new poems, together with a selection of poems from previous volumes, won the National Book Award and the Bollingen Prize in *Poetry* as well as five other awards. *The Far Field* brought him a second National Book Award. Roethke's reputation has been steadily increasing since 1953. His poems have been translated into many foreign languages and there have been a number of critical books and many articles published on his work.

Biography

Theodore Huebner Roethke was born in Saginaw, Michigan, on May 25, 1908, to Otto Roethke and Helen Huebner Roethke. With his brother Charles, Otto Roethke owned an enormous greenhouse consisting of several buildings enclosing 250 thousand square feet under glass. The young Roethke was fascinated by his father's gigantic plant kingdom, and the greenhouse world would later become a literary storehouse of poetic images for the adult poet. In his fifteenth year, however, his ordered life was shattered. After his father and Charles quarreled, the greenhouse was sold. Charles committed suicide several months later, and shortly after that, Otto died of cancer, suffering greatly before his death. Otto's strong influence on his son can be seen in the poetry.

The first member of his family to attend college, Roethke was graduated from the University of Michigan at Ann Arbor in 1929. He spent one term at the University of Michigan Law School and then in 1930 transferred to the graduate school, where he studied English for two terms. Then he did graduate work at Harvard and decided to abandon career possibilities in law and advertising in order to become a poet.

In 1931, *The New Republic* and *The Sewanne Review* published Roethke's poems. After teaching English at Lafayette College, Pennsylvania, from 1931 to 1935, he accepted a position at Michigan State College in East Lansing. During the 1935 fall term, he suffered his first attack of a manic-depressive disorder that was to haunt him for the rest of his life. These mental breakdowns typically lasted from one to six months.

When Michigan State College failed to renew his contract, he accepted a position at Pennsylvania State College from 1936 to 1943 and again for one year in 1948. In 1941, his first volume of poetry, *Open House*, received praise from the critics. Because of his mental illness, he was not drafted during World War II but taught from 1943 to 1946 at Bennington College, Vermont. In 1947 he accepted an associate professorship at the University of Washington in Seattle and was promoted to professor the next year. The University of Washington was to be his academic affiliation for the remainder of his life; here he wrote his best poetry, taught courses on "The Writing of Verse" and "Types of Contemporary Poetry," and attracted many fine students, a number of whom became poets themselves.

In 1953 Roethke married a former student, Beatrice Heath O'Connell, and published *The Waking: Poems 1933-1953*, which brought him the critical attention that he had been eagerly awaiting. During the next decade, he published several more volumes and his reputation grew. He died of a heart attack in 1963.

Analysis

Theodore Roethke can be best understood as a poet in the tradition of nineteenth century English and American Romanticism. His early poetry of the 1940's and 1950's has some significant similarities to that of the English Romantic poets, especially William Wordsworth and John Keats, while his later poetry, especially "North American Sequence," owes a large debt to Walt Whitman. In general, one can see a number of essential Romantic characteristics in his poetry. Although he often objectifies his feelings in concrete images, he also directly expresses emotion. Feeling over analytical reason, spontaneity over logic, exuberance over calculated thinking can be seen throughout his verse; dancing, singing, and jubilant exclaiming are ubiquitous.

Roethke's subject is that of the Romantics—the exploration of the mind or "imagination." While his voyage into the depths of his own mind is, at times, terrifying, it has positive consequences. The imagination's repeated attempts to affirm itself in the face of threatening reality is a constant ritual and a source of tension in Roethke's work. Often the imagination can transform the external world, at least momentarily, and the poet feels redeemed.

Nature functions in Roethke's poetry in a particularly Romantic fashion. He writes of nature not to achieve an objective perception of it or a lyrical description of its beauty, but as a way to attain a more profound awareness, a "vernal wisdom." Nature takes a variety of forms in his poetry; it mirrors the emotional vicissitudes of the poet. It may be vindictive or affirmative to the point that the poet merges momentarily with it. He does make clear, however, that dissolving one's identity and merging with nature is an uncommon experience, for man has a keen wareness of his separateness that is very difficult to ignore. In "Moss Gathering," the poet as a young boy sorrowfully realizes his separateness from the primordial order of nature when he digs up a loose carpet of green moss.

While Roethke is an affirmative poet who sees the process of becoming as ultimately joyful, there is a Keatsian ambivalence in his work. The beautiful and the grotesque, the joyful and the painful are inextricably related. Even "Dinky," one of his "Poems for Children," has a macabre quality fused with its lightheartedness.

Finally, not only Roethke's sensibility but also his style is Romantic. While his style displays a number of Romantic characteristics, such as spontaneity, direct expression of emotion, and intuitive perceptions, the most important characteristic is its meditative quality. As in the important works of Wordsworth and Keats, Roethke's poetry progresses associatively, according to the discursive movement of the mind, not according to the dictates of logic. In short, his best work mirrors the meanderings of the imagination, or to paraphrase him, the goal is to capture the movement of the mind itself.

Roethke has many attributes in common with Wordsworth, who wrote meditative poetry in which the interaction between the mind and the natural world is the central preoccupation. Both poets reveal an aspiring quality in their work; both use simple language; both rely on recollections of childhood as a source of their poetry and a key to their perception of the mystery of the human condition. In *The Prelude* (1850) Wordsworth similarly explains his strange experiences—"that calm delight/ Which, if I err not, surely must belong/ To those first born affinities that fit/ Our new existence to existing things" (see Book I, 11, lines 543-557). Sometimes both poets seem to be expressing animism: "Every flower/ Enjoys the air it breathes" (Wordsworth's "Lines Written in Early Spring," 11, lines 10-11). This Wordsworthian image of natural phenomenon "breathing" appears often in Roethke's poetry. In fact, he takes the idea to its logical conclusion—stones breathing. Yet it is unlikely that either poet really believed that nature and inanimate objects were endowed with sentient life. Both were realistic poets who depended heavily on precise observation. Significantly, Roethke seems to have borrowed Wordsworth's notion of the importance of the "eye close on the object," or as Wordsworth wrote in the Preface to *Lyrical Ballads* (1800), "I have at all times endeavored to look steadily at my subjects."

The mind enmeshed in nature can be seen in the poetry of Keats and Roethke, and both poets describe the mind in similar metaphoric fashion. Roethke writes of "The leafy mind, that long was tightly furled,/ Will turn its private substance into green,/ And young shoots spread upon our inner world" (*Collected Poems*, p. 11); Keats of "some untrodden region of my mind/ Where branchèd thoughts, new grown with pleasant pain . . ." ("Ode to Psyche," 11, lines 51-52). Keats's oxymoronic last phrase suggests the contraries of existence that both Roethke and Keats wrestle with throughout their work. Mutability is a painful reality that is finally accepted and affirmed. Life is viewed as process.

"The Visitant" (*Collected Poems*, p. 100) is Roethke's "La Belle Dame sans Merci," although here the awakened speaker is not so "alone and palely loitering" as Keats's knight; he is also more easily reconciled to his situation than Keats's knight, and the evanescent tone and the delicate evocation of the landscape is in direct contrast to the stark images of Keats's poem. Nevertheless, despite the difference in style in these two poems, there are significant stylistic affinities between the authors. Both use sensuous, suggestive imagery that conveys the complex vicissitudes of the emotions. In their works one sees subtle shifts of feeling and emotionally charged language that works toward a strong identification with external reality.

In Roethke's later poetry Whitman is a strong influence, and he acknowledges this fact in both his poetry and his letters. He borrows Whitman's techniques, especially his cataloging and his free-verse style, his "loose line," in Roethke's phrase. In his long poems, such as "North American Sequence," one finds Whitman's playfulness, irony, and comic relief; like Whitman, Roethke realized that these qualities are necessary in a long work in which it is impossible to maintain a single tone.

Roethke was also influenced by Whitman's mysticism. In "North American Sequence" there is the Whitmanesque desire to achieve a becoming that is not self-conscious—in which the poet tries to dissolve his self, to merge with the landscape. Both poets try to absorb and absolve the self and provide the necessary harmony that the world can never provide. There is the need in both poets to be free from the body by extending it throughout the landscape.

One must be careful, however, not to overstate Whitman's influence. While Whitman's catalogs are often mundane lists, Roethke's are not; rather, he seems to be borrowing nature's rhythm and applying it to the human realm. In general, Roethke does not have that tone of massive innocence that dominates Whitman's poetry. Roethke harmonizes the landscape, makes it part of him, but there is the feeling that it can be done for him alone.

Roethke's poetry developed from his early conventional verse with its regular meter and rhyme to the later innovative poetry with its associative, free-verse style. In his first collection, *Open House*, there are abstract, rhetorical poems as well as sensuous, pictorial ones. The poems of this volume are traditional in form and content, and Roethke does not speak with a unique voice, as he does in his subsequent work. "The Prayer" is a typical early poem with its closed couplets, regular rhythm, and slightly ribald humor. "The Premonition" has lucid images that take on symbolic power: "Hair on a narrow wrist bone" suggests a father's mortality. Minute observation of detail in "Interlude" also takes on symbolic significance. "Mid-Country Blow" shows the power of the imagination that can so dominate the senses that the poet still hears the "sound of the sea" even after his eye has proved his vision false. The poem is reminiscent of many of William Carlos Williams' poems, in which a banal scene is transformed into a vivid experience of near revelation. "The Bat" portrays a deliberate correspondence between the man and the animal realms; "When mice with wings can wear a human face" suggests a mysterious horror in which man participates. In contrast, D. H. Lawrence's poem by the same name emphasizes man's separateness from the demonic bat's universe.

"Idyll" can be taken as the representative poem of the first volume. The gulf between complacency and minatory reality is evoked by the contrast of the sleeping town and the encroaching unnamed "terror." The poem is divided into three stanzas with a rhyme scheme that creates a sense of regularity broken only in the final line. The "we" of the poem is meant to draw the reader into the work, while the present tense emphasizes the immediacy of the poem's situation. The slow rhythm conveys the sense of the inexorable encroaching darkness.

The first stanza depicts a scene in which something is "amiss." A child's tricycle inexplicably "runs crazily," evoking a mood of innocence being menaced. The second line describes the representative man of the sleeping town. He is completely self-absorbed, a stumbling drunk who talks to himself. In stanza two the darkness envelops the "well-groomed suburban town." "Creeps" suggests a bestial presence that the town, "indifferent to dog howls" and "the nestling's last peep," refuses to acknowledge. Like a drunk of the first stanza, the people of the town exist in a self-satisfied state. The final stanza evokes a surrealistic scene—the world is dissolving in "the black revolving shadow" as a far-off train "blows its echoing whistle once." The "unmindful" people go to sleep in their houses precariously located at the "edge of a meadow." The failure of rhyme and the monosyllabic finality of "guns" in the last line emphasize the disconcerting contrast between the complacent town and threatening external reality.

The Lost Son and Other Poems breaks new ground with the "greenhouse poems" and the longer associative poems that form the last section of the volume. These longer associative poems become part of a sequence in the next volume, *Praise to the End!* The title of this later volume is taken from an obscure passage of Wordsworth's *The Prelude* (1, lines 340-350) and provides an important clue to Roethke's basic intention in his volumes of poetry of 1948 and 1951. Wordsworth suggests in this passage of *The Prelude* that the mind can order into a meaningful whole disparate, painful experiences of the past. Like Wordsworth, Roethke believes that the individual can create his identity only after he has plumbed the depths of his psyche, even though this interior journey might be terrifying and could at times lead one perilously close to madness. In this sequence, which focuses upon the psychological development of the child and the spiritual regeneration of the adult, Roethke uses a unique style similar to that of the shorter "greenhouse poems."

"Root Cellar" is a representative greenhouse poem and clearly reveals Roethke's method. The "poem" evokes the paradoxical situation in which the remarkable vitality of natural life seems threatening to the self. The fecund realm of this strange plant life is not a human one; no human could exist in this thriving subterranean world. The cellar represents both womb and tomb, fecundity and destruction. The alliteration in the first three lines stresses the contrary pulls of the life force (evoked by the vitality of the bulbs breaking out of their boxes) and the death wish (evoked by the darkness). The ambivalent nature of the scene is further emphasized by the description of the growing plants in sexual imagery that has negative connotations: "Hunting for chinks in the dark" and "lolling obscenely." As the poet closely observes the procreative forces of nature, he becomes keenly aware of the noxious odor that accompanies vital growth. The sixth line—"And what a congress of stinks!—" divides the poem. Next follows an accumulation of details, stressing the richness and rankness of the plants. Life is seen as an irreversible bursting forth; even the dirt appears to be breathing at the end.

In short, the self feels attracted to and threatened by this subterranean world. The "greenhouse poems" remind one of some of D. H. Lawrence's poems in which he is seeking his primeval self, his deepest being that remains submerged in the primitive regions of nature. The problem for both Roethke and Lawrence is that while man wants to recapture the primal mystery, he feels alienated from his spiritual and physical origins.

The Waking contains a selection from Roethke's previous volumes as well as new poems, some of which owe a large debt to Yeats, as Roethke himself admits. The title poem, however, does not reveal Yeats's influence; with its series of paradoxes and its Wordsworthian exuberance, it might be considered a metaphysical-romantic hybrid. This much-anthologized poem is not only one of the most difficult in Roethke's canon but also one of his best.

The Waking is a villanelle and thus is divided into five tercets and a concluding quatrain; it systematically repeats lines one and three of the first tercet throughout the work. The lines are end-stopped, and the intricate rhyme scheme links the stanzas together. The rhyme scheme and the steady, lofty rhythm creates a sense of inexorable movement.

The structure and rhythm of the poem perfectly fit the content. The first four stanzas alternate two paradoxical truths that the work expresses: "I learn by going where I have to go" and "I wake to sleep, and take my waking slow." In the final stanza these two paradoxes are repeated in the last two lines. Though seemingly the opposites of each other, both suggest an acceptance of the inevitable—more specifically, they suggest an acceptance of mortality amid the flux of everyday existence.

Roethke suggests that underlying the chaos of existence is a fundamental unity. The series of oppositions, paradoxes, and seemingly unrelated statements in the poem are deliberately utilized by the poet to demonstrate an underlying unity. The interwoven rhythm and the repetition link the dissimilar elements together. The intricate form of the poem itself, with its wide-ranging content, suggests that there is coherence in the flux of existence—if one would only allow oneself to become aware of it.

In this poem the self has come to terms with the human condition. In addition to conveying the tone of jubilant resignation, the repetition in the work emphasizes the poet's intense awareness and acceptance of identity. "I wake," "I feel," "I learn," "I hear" are the beginnings of lines. In the middle line of each of the first five stanzas, the poet unfailingly expresses acceptance. Although he feels the presence of death, he can affirm his situation.

Stanza four, the most obscure section of the poem, takes this feeling of affirmation to a mystical point. "Light takes the Tree; but who can tell us how?" The evocation of transcendence is followed by doubts about whether a human can attain it, and the answer to the question is as enigmatic as the original question that prompted it: "The lowly worm climbs up the winding stair." This response is ambiguous, suggesting the procreative power as well as mutability, affirmation as well as negation. While the lowest creature ascends to the heights (a spiral tree is a common image of the transcendent in Roethke), man paradoxically becomes aware of his transitory nature.

At the end of the work, the poet exhorts his reader to "take the lively air." The concluding rhyme (slow/go) breaks the rhythm and creates a sense of finality. The poet has accepted the fact that he will die, yet he realizes that his awareness of his imminent death has made him alive to the possibilities of existence and allowed him a glimpse of the eternal. The final note is one of celebration.

Words for the Wind is Roethke's best single volume. The best parts of the work are the largest section entitled "Love Poems" and the final section, the sequence of five poems entitled "Meditations of an Old Woman." These two sections reveal a new development in Roethke's poetry. "Meditations of an Old Woman" represents the poet's most impressive achievement in capturing the labyrinthine movement of the mind, but the length and complexity of the sequence allows only a few brief comments here on Roethke's remarkable innovations in this mode. The powerful, tormented sensibility evident in the sequence is expressed in a vivid and complex style characterized by subtle tonal changes, comparisons of past and present, recurring symbols, patterns of imagery, and repetition of key words, to name only the most important. The compression of imagery and the intense lyrical quality of the work resemble Keats's odes, while the meditative sequence as a whole has the expansiveness of Wallace Stevens' "variations on a motif."

There are a number of different kinds of love poems in *Words for the Wind,* and they represent an achievement in style of nearly the magnitude of "Meditations of an Old Woman." "The Dream" presents an odd mixture of the sensual and the ethereal. In "Words for the Wind" the poet sings of his communion with his lover. In fact, this title poem evokes an evanescent sensual love similar to that in Denise Levertov's "Our Bodies," although Roethke is much more ethereal than Levertov. In "The Sententious Man" the attitude toward the self and the world is ambivalent. Spiritual emptiness is a formidable threat in these poems, and much of the time there is no separation of the "kiss" and the "abyss." Feeling alienated, the self strives for communion and love.

Roethke vividly expresses the awareness of existential nothingness in "The Renewal": "I paw the dark, the shifting midnight air." Yet the lost self may be found again, for there is the possibility of rebirth in the morning when the poet experiences a mystical identification with the inanimate world: "I touched the stones, and they had my own skin." The constriction of the self is being overcome. "The whole motion of the soul lay bare," the poet says, after he sees the "rubblestones begin to stretch."

In Roethke's final volume, *The Far Field*, he becomes very mystical. Total dissolution of the self is often the goal; it can be seen in the abstract poems of *Sequence, Sometimes Metaphysical,* in the love poems, in the "Mixed Sequence" poems, and in the "North American Sequence." In this latter volume Whitman's influence is particularly evident. Whitman sees death as rejuvenating, and sometimes he describes it erotically or maternally. Like Whitman, Roethke continually, almost ritualistically, discovers death and the beneficent quality inherent in nature. One loses his identity to the point that he is consumed—death is the final culmination of all growth.

Despite its power, the "North American Sequence" does not break new ground, for it is very similar in technique to "Meditations of an Old Woman." *Sequence, Sometimes Metaphysical* is a more original work. First published in 1963 in a limited edition of 330 copies by the Stone Wall Press (Iowa City, Iowa), it came to form the concluding section of *The Far Field*, Roethke's final work. It is an appropriate culmination of the poet's career, examining in an innovative style the recurring themes in his canon—the relationship of the imagination to reality; the possibility of transcendence and the mystical annihilation of consciousness; and the search for identity. "In a Dark Time," the most difficult and probably the best poem of the sequence, focuses upon these themes.

The poem bluntly asks Roethke's obsessive question: "Which I is *I*?" There is no simple answer. Stanza one suggests that the inner "eye" of the imagination paradoxically begins to see "in a dark time," as the despairing poet probes the primordial depths of the psyche. A series of metaphors of the poet's spiritual journey follows. He meets his "shadow," his other self, in the "deepening shade," the ever-darkening journey into the night regions of the soul. The poet exists in an in-between time—he exists between the extremes of the heron, a bird associated with the earth and the sea, and the wren, a bird of the air, as well as between the beasts of the hill and the serpents of the den.

Stanza two suggests that "madness" can be regarded as the spirit's visionary perception as well as the ultimate fragmentation of the psyche. The illogical events of an intrinsically meaningless world are at odds with the spirit's quest, and consequently the poet has known "the purity of pure despair." Here "pure" suggests completeness as well as visionary intensity. "Pinned against a sweating wall" stresses the acuteness of the poet's spiritual torment. Yet this torment, which is both visionary perception and disintegration of the imaginative mind, leaves the poet in confusion: Is he ascending to the ethereal heights or descending to the ignorant depths? He cannot be certain whether he is heading toward constriction in the depths or freedom on the heights, and thus he is left on the threshold.

In stanza three, Roethke states the method by which he works—"A steady storm of correspondences!" Connections between inner and outer worlds occur. "Storm," "A night flowing with birds, a ragged moon" suggest the difficult obstacles that the poet must overcome on his spiritual journey in which he hopes to create a new identity—it is a hope that can become a reality only by the eradication of the conscious ego. After the painful "Death of the self in a long tearless night," the supernatural emerges out of the everyday. The imagination has transformed mundane reality; in the light of the common day, midnight has come "again." Midnight is a magical time for Roethke, the brink of visionary transcendence; "again" suggests that this visionary state has occurred before—perhaps it refers to that time of spiritual unity in childhood when one does not feel estranged from nature.

In stanza four Roethke suggests that it is necessary to descend into the darkness to attain inner illumination. On the brink of transcendence as well as insanity, he cannot reach a transcendent realm and thus remains pondering his identity on the threshold, looking upward. Finally, the soul does complete its journey. Although the poet has fallen to the depths of despair, he now "climbs" out. The poet eradicates his excessively self-conscious ego and attains a heightened awareness in which his sense of estrangement from the external world is overcome.

In the poetry of Roethke, the Romantic problem of the relationship of the self to external reality becomes an obsessive concern. The attempt to over-come the age-old romantic dichotomy between the self and the world can be seen throughout his work, from the earliest poetry to the posthumous volume, *The Far Field*. Roethke searches for his true identity amid the chaos of modern life. The supposition behind this quest is that the mundane world is intrins-ically meaningless, and therefore the poet must affirm reality by his imagi-nation. The mind must endow the external world with meaning or the poet walks a never-ending tightrope over the abyss, always a step away from despair and madness.

For Roethke, the mind is the most efficacious defense against the cold multiplicity of the modern world because it can create order and because it fuses inner and outer worlds. When the mind achieves a complete identifi-cation with the external world, the tension between the self and the world dissipates. To achieve this identification is extremely difficult; but the heroic task of the modern poet, Roethke believed, is to make the attempt.

Allan Chavkin

Other major works
NONFICTION: *On the Poet and His Craft: Selected Prose of Theodore Roethke,*

1965 (Ralph J. Mills, Jr., editor); *The Selected Letters of Theodore Roethke*, 1968 (Ralph J. Mills, Jr., editor); *Straw for the Fire: From the Notebooks of Theodore Roethke, 1943-1963*, 1972 (David Wagoner, editor).

Bibliography

Bloom, Harold, ed. *Modern Critical Views: Theodore Roethke*. New York: Chelsea House, 1988. A collection of critical essays on Roethke ranging from the early trailblazing work of Kenneth Burke to the more recent views of Thomas Gardner and James Applewhite. Contains an index and a bibliography.

Bowers, Neal. *Theodore Roethke: the Journey from I to Otherwise*. Columbia: University of Missouri Press, 1982. Emphasizes Roethke's use of his episodes of mental illness and other states of nonordinary reality as the source and subject of much of his best poetry. Augmented by an index and a bibliography.

Kalaidjian, Walter B. *Understanding Theodore Roethke*. Columbia: University of South Carolina Press, 1987. An introductory reading of Roethke's work with emphasis on the poet's concern with uniting humankind with nature and using unusual psychological states as gateways to new knowledge of the self and the world. Supplemented by an index and a thoroughly annotated bibliography of other criticism.

Malkoff, Karl. *Theodore Roethke: An Introduction to the Poetry*. New York: Columbia University Press, 1966. This early study of Roethke presents a psychoanalytic reading of the poet's work. As a result, many later critics often begin by agreeing or disagreeing with Malkoff, using his work as a benchmark from which to begin their own studies. Contains an index and a bibliography of works by and about Roethke.

Seager, Allan. *The Glass House: The Life of Theodore Roethke*. New York: McGraw-Hill, 1968. This is the only full-length biography of Roethke, written by a scholar and novelist who was also a close friend of the poet.

Stiffler, Randall. *Theodore Roethke: The Poet and His Critics*. Chicago: American Library Association, 1986. Stiffler reviews and evaluates the critical reception of Roethke's works. Contains an index and a bibliography.

Wolff, George. *Theodore Roethke*. Boston: Twayne, 1981. One of the Twayne series of introductory guides to American authors, this book offers a good brief review of the poet's life and work. Contains an index and an extensive annotated bibliography.

CHRISTINA ROSSETTI

Born: London, England; December 5, 1830
Died: London, England; December 29, 1894

Principal poetry

Verses, 1847; *Goblin Market and Other Poems*, 1862; *The Prince's Progress and Other Poems*, 1866; *Sing-Song*, 1872, 1893; *A Pageant and Other Poems*, 1881; *Verses*, 1893; *New Poems*, 1896.

Other literary forms

Commonplace and Other Short Stories (1870) suggests that Christina Rossetti may have once had the notion of becoming a novelist. Unlike other female poets of the period, she wrote a great deal in prose, both secular and religious. "Commonplace," the title story, is not usually considered to be the best of these prose pieces. That honor is reserved for "The Lost Titian," the plot of which revolves around two friends' competitive praise for another friend's painting. In the end, all three discover one another's vanities. "Vanna's Twins" is a touching story of childhood and demonstrates Rossetti's power in delineating character among lower-middle-class Italians. *Speaking Likenesses* (1874), a series of stories told to some girls by their aunt as they pass the time sewing, stands in the shadows of Lewis Carroll's and Jean Ingelow's works of the same period.

Annus Domini (1874) is a devotional prose work, the first of several, which includes a prayer for each day of the year. These pieces were influenced by *The Book of Common Prayer.* Other devotional works include *Seek and Find*, 1879; *Called to Be Saints*, 1881; *Letter and Spirit*, 1882; *Time Flies*, 1885; *The Face of the Deep*, 1892; and *Maude*, 1897.

Achievements

Soon after the publication of *Goblin Market and Other Poems*, *The British Quarterly Review*, a highly respected literary journal of the day, commented that "All [the poems] . . . are marked by beauty and tenderness. They are frequently quaint, and sometimes a little capricious." Rossetti was praised in her time for the clarity and sweetness of her diction, for her realistic imagery, and for the purity of her faith. She was widely read in the nineteenth century, but not often imitated. The latter is true perhaps because she did not introduce innovative techniques or subject matter. She is not read widely today, either, and is usually treated as a minor poet of the Victorian period, being eclipsed by her brother Dante Gabriel Rossetti and his fellow pre-Raphaelite writers. Perhaps the simplicity of Christina Rossetti's faith seems remote and unrealistic to many contemporary readers, but this fact should not diminish her artistic contributions. Andrew Lang, in *The Cosmopolitan Magazine*, June,

1895, left this judgment: "For the quality of conscious art and for music and colour of words in regular composition, Miss Rossetti is unmatched."

Biography

Christina Georgina Rossetti was born on December 5, 1830, the youngest of four children. Her father, Gabriele, an Italian political refugee, was himself a poet and musician. Her mother, of half-Italian parentage, wrote a popular book on Dante, and her older brother, Dante Gabriel, became a noted poet and a leader of the Pre-Raphaelite Brotherhood.

Because of financial problems, the Rossettis moved from Portland Place to Mornington Crescent in 1851 in order for Mrs. Rossetti and Christina to open a small day school for children, thus providing a financial base for the family. By 1854, William Rossetti, Christina's brother, then a clerk in a revenue office, rented a house on Albany Street, where the family lived together. After Mr. Rossetti died in that year, Mrs. Rossetti and the children lived on there until 1867, and it was only because of William's marriage to Lucy Brown in 1874 that Mrs. Rossetti and Christina moved to Torrington Square.

Christina was not a world traveler, but her few experiences abroad did affect her poetry. She went abroad but twice, once in 1861 and again in 1865, and it was the Italian journey that is reflected in so much of her writing. She wrote some poetry in Italian, but her love for Italy can be seen in much of her English work. One excellent example is "Vanna's Twins," the story of an Italian family living in England.

Her first book, published in 1847 when she was seventeen, was a collection of poems privately printed by her grandfather Gaetena Polidori, himself a writer. The volume entitled *Verses* contained sixty-six pages of poems written by Rossetti between the ages of twelve and sixteen. The longest piece in the volume was "The Dead City," a poem which exhibits both immature technique and masterful poetic potential. Immersed in a Poe-like atmosphere, the motif is that of a traveler in a dark wood, having passed from a stage of light. She finds herself in a deserted city resplendent with an ornate palace. A sumptuous banquet is ready, but the guests have turned to stone. The poem anticipates Robert Browning, Matthew Arnold, and T. S. Eliot in its wasteland motif and echoes Keats's sensualism.

By 1850, Christina had become a tangential member of the Pre-Raphaelite Brotherhood, of which her brother Dante was the center, and she published various poems in the Brotherhood's magazine *The Germ*. Although Christina loved her brother dearly and respected the other members of the group, she felt that they were too concerned with morally questionable subjects to engage herself directly in the work. It was, ironically, through the Pre-Raphaelites that she met a young man named James Collison, to whom she was greatly attracted and whom, had it not been for his Catholicism, she might well have married.

In 1862, after having gained much attention through the poems in *The Germ*, Rossetti published a volume entitled *Goblin Market and Other Poems*. The work was greeted with general acclaim, her only critics being metric purists such as John Ruskin. She brought out another volume in 1866, *The Prince's Progress and Other Poems*, which established her as England's greatest living woman poet, since Elizabeth Barrett Browning had died in 1861.

Although Christina was sickly in her youth, it was in 1871 that she became seriously ill with Dr. Graves' disease, which brought many periods of depression. Now she adopted the role of recluse. During these years of severe illness, she experienced several unpleasant events: her sister Maria died of cancer in 1876; in 1877 she and her mother began the miserable nursing of Dante Gabriel through five years of psychotic depression; and in 1886 her mother died. In the midst of all this suffering, Rossetti continued to write. Her third volume of poetry, *A Pageant and Other Poems*, was published in 1881 and praised highly by Algernon Swinburne, the only remaining member of the old pre-Raphaelite coterie. She continued to enjoy the admiration of younger writers such as Theodore Watts-Dunton and Edmund Gosse. Between 1879 and 1892 she published five volumes of spiritual meditations.

In May, 1892, Christina submitted to an operation for cancer, another Rossetti to be the victim of that disease. The operation was not successful; the cancer reappeared in a few months. After considerable suffering she died on December 29, 1894.

Analysis

Christina Rossetti, often thought of as a religious poet, actually became the major woman poet of mid-Victorian England. Her only true competitor, Elizabeth Barrett Browning, died a few months before Rossetti's *Goblin Market and Other Poems* appeared in 1862. "Goblin Market," the introductory poem of the volume, has remained her most famous work, and illustrates her mastery of the lyric. Because much of her lyric poetry is oriented toward children, "Goblin Market" is often classified as a child's poem. Even though the characters in the poem are young girls and goblins with fairy-tale associations, the poem is actually an allegory of temptation and redemption meant for adult reading. Rossetti's common theme of the need for renunciation is prevalent, though in the disguise of whimsical child's play. The poem produces a grotesque comic effect, supported by irregular meter and cumulative cataloging. The tempting fruit of the goblins, described in Rossetti's typical sensual manner as "sweet to tongue and sound to eye," causes Laura to succumb, desiring more, only to discover that her pleasure is terminated.

Lizzie acts as the savior. Like Christ, she goes into the grove of the men selling their wares and offers to buy some, only to discover that they really want her, not her penny. Although she suffers much physical abuse, the evil people are "worn out by her resistance," and she returns home jubilant with her penny in hand, able to comfort Laura with the assurance that one can find happiness without the temptations of pleasure. Later, when both girls have married, they are able to relate to their daughters in didactic fashion how one can avoid the pitfalls of the evil world.

Rossetti's strong visual imagination aligns her with the Pre-Raphaelites' interest in painting. Although she did not paint, Christina had a painter's eye: the love of colors, particularly gold, rose, violet, blue, and green, and the delight in decorative detail inform all her lyrics. Her eye often sees unexpected analogies. In "Goblin Market," for example, she compares Laura's arched neck to a swan and a lily, both natural phenomena, but also to a vessel being launched, a rather startling comparison somewhat in the vein of the seventeenth century metaphysical conceits. In fact, several critics have alluded to her love for seventeenth century poets, especially George Herbert and Henry Vaughan.

In addition to her lyrics, Rossetti wrote a great deal of narrative verse, characteristically on the theme of lost or frustrated love. Most of these love-narratives are romantic and otherworldly; when Rossetti does attempt realism, especially in describing marital love, her images are pale and flat. One of the longer narratives, "The Prince's Progress," developed out of a lyric of 1861; Rossetti expanded it at her brother's suggestion to provide a title poem for her next volume of poetry. Much like the tale of Edmund Spenser's Red Cross Knight, this poem is the story of a princess waiting to be rescued by a prince.

The prince waits in his palace for a full month before leaving to meet his bride. When he finally hears the call, prompted by allegorical voices which represent fleeting time, he discovers that the journey will not be easy. It will be another Pilgrim's Progress. His first delay is the typical temptation of a beautiful maiden who keeps him as Dido detained Aeneas. Following his release, the prince finds himself in a nineteenth century wasteland with a blight lurking in the darkening air, "a land of neither life nor death." Here he discovers a cave with an old hermit who gives him the "Elixir of Life," but the elixir is insufficient. When he eventually leaves the cave, he is again diverted by self-indulgence, and when he finally arrives at his bride's door, he finds that she is dead, her body being prepared for burial. The poem is an interesting narrative in the vein of medieval romances, but it is obviously allegorical. The prince is admonished by the narrator, "You waited on the road too long, you trifled at the gate." The poem is permeated with ironies and allegorical symbolism proclaiming the vices of procrastination.

"From House to Home" is another long narrative, allegorical in character, with lost love at the center. It tells of a variety of states of being. In the first of these states, the narrator is living in an earthly paradise: a castle of transparent glass set against a background of stately trees and pastures full of swift squirrels, singing birds, and leaping lambs. The young lady is called away by a male "angel." Day and night she seeks for him to no avail—he has vanished. Eventually she has a vision of a marvelously beautiful woman who is suffering the usual tribulations of a pilgrim on an allegorical journey. The martyred woman stands on ground with budding flowers, but every flower has a thorn and galls her feet. Cruel laughter and clapping hands remind the reader of the ways of danger and rebuke in life. The martyred one can be read here as both the archetypal man or woman in search of love and the Christian Church attempting to extend its love to others.

Two of the narratives reveal sides of Rossetti's personality that most of her poetry does not demonstrate. One of these, "A Royal Princess," suggests political interests. The poem is about an imagined political situation. A highborn heroine is sympathetic toward the suffering masses who threaten a revolt against the kingdom, and she determines to descend from her secluded, protected palace to help them.

In "The Lowest Room," a poem that Dante Gabriel Rossetti did not like, there is an evident implication that, bound by society's rules, women *must* be passive and *must* play given roles in life. Again, there are two sisters in the poem, but unlike those in other works, only the ideal sister is here rewarded with husband and child. The ideal one is described in feminine language; the other one, less attractive, dreams of Homer's soldiers. Masculine voluptuousness affects her. In projecting such a contrast, Rossetti implies that women in her society are told how to dress, how to act, and how to be successful. There is little room for individuality. The final acceptance of this less attractive female, the speaker of the poem, places her in the role of the typical passive woman waiting for her turn without being able to help in creating it.

Another narrative which takes a critical view of social conventions is "The Iniquity of the Fathers, upon the Children," in which a lady who has a child out of wedlock is tormented by the commmunity. The only justice, the narrator concludes, is that all is "equal in the grave." On the other hand, Rossetti's narrative style can show a fairy-tale naïveté, as in "Maiden Song," a tale of three sisters, Meggan, May, and Margaret, all of whom desire husbands. The first two take the first man who comes along, afraid they will be like Margaret sitting at home singing and spinning. Margaret's patience, however, is amply rewarded; she wins the king of the entire country for her husband.

Rossetti's strong religious faith supported her during continuing illnesses and she began to give most of her attention to writing devotional material. Her first poetry had shown her strong family affection and her religious feelings, particularly the sentiment of renunciation. The later poems (such as "A Novice," "A Martyr," and "I Have Fought a Good Fight") continue to focus on renunciation. The first is a flight from the world into the calm of the cloister; the latter two praise the eager laying down of life for the glory of God. Actually, religious ardour colors most of Rossetti's thoughts and results in much oversimplified verse echoing common platitudes about devotion. A poem such as "Whitsun Eve," however, illustrates poetic maturity, blending the love of God and the love of the beauty of creation. All that is pure in nature is pressed into the service of the one shining lamb.

An interesting aspect of Rossetti's style is her use of the Victorian motif of two voices, so prominently associated with Alfred, Lord Tennyson's poetry. The Victorian world attempted to synthesize the Romantic values of the early nineteenth century with the classical theories of order and restraint more prominently displayed in the eighteenth century. From this attempt came a strong clash of values and great personal frustration. Adding to this problem was the growth of the industrial world and the increase in scientific knowledge. Rossetti's dualism establishes the concept of a universe based on a conflict of opposites, as in "Life and Death," "Twice," "Today and Tomorrow," and "Two Parted."

"Two Parted" deals with one true lover and one betrayer. Ironically, the betrayer in this case is the woman. "Today and Tomorrow" creates a dichotomy of living life to the fullest on the one hand and wishing to die on the other. "Life and Death" begins with a negative statement about life's bitterness, juxtaposing the good things of life with the unpleasant. "Twice" uses the counterpoint of the narrator's offering her heart while the male suggests that her heart is not ripe. In the narrative poems this technique is carried out through the use of two opposing characters. Lizzie and Laura of "Goblin Market" illustrate the dualistic motif; in "Maiden Song" the conflict is between two plain sisters and the beautiful Margaret. This dualism is also apparent in Rossetti's religious poems, where there appears to be a confrontation between different views of salvation or different moral attitudes. A great number of traditional opposites are used here—time and eternity, earthly misery and heavenly bliss—demonstrating the torment of a trapped soul longing for escape. One such poem, "This near-at-hand," stresses the antithesis of heaven and earth.

The religious poems often describe a destructive end which results from the speaker's being torn between duty and desire. Sometimes the choice appears to have been made in error, and when it is, it seems to have arisen from weakness or beguilement. So choice itself becomes destructive; there is no solution; life is an absurdity. Even when the speaker is not caught in a personal dilemma, the poem repeats the impression that the world, as Matthew Arnold suggests in "Dover Beach," is a place of uncertainty, a virtual wasteland, a "darkling plain" where ignorant armies fight by night.

In the midst of all this dualism, the reader is left with the impression that Rossetti is earnestly searching for unity but cannot find it. In the secular love poems she goes so far as to suggest that perhaps as ghosts, removed from the flesh, lovers could achieve such a unity. In the religious poems her solution is, of course, union with God through Christ in death. Needless to say, much of her poetry reflects the struggle in her own life to find some solution to the paradox, irony, and bifurcation that life in general repeatedly offers. Rossetti's poetry reveals a dual personality; one side reflecting Pre-Raphaelite traits of fictional effects and sensual imagery, often set in a dream world; the other reflecting the assurances of her orthodox faith.

John W. Crawford

Other major works

SHORT FICTION: *Commonplace and Other Short Stories*, 1870; *Speaking Likenesses*, 1874.

RELIGIOUS WRITINGS: *Annus Domini*, 1874; *Seek and Find*, 1879; *Called to Be Saints*, 1881; *Letter and Spirit*, 1882; *Time Flies*, 1885; *The Face of the Deep*, 1892; *Maude*, 1897.

Bibliography

Charles, Edna Kotin. *Christina Rossetti: Critical Perspectives, 1862-1982.* Selinsgrove, Pa.: Susquehanna University Press, 1985. Charles shows how literary criticism has changed in the last 120 years, and how these changing attitudes have affected the way in which Rossetti's poems were perceived. Many nineteenth century reviewers concentrated on her religious poems, whereas modern critics focus on her works of fantasy. Suitable for graduate students and advanced undergraduates.

Harrison, Antony H. *Christina Rossetti in Context.* Chapel Hill: University of North Carolina Press, 1988. This is a skillful, well-informed study that links Rossetti's religious beliefs to her Pre-Raphaelite writing techniques and themes. Harrison name-drops the faddish terms used in current literary criticism, yet, his study is useful for any student of Rossetti. Includes a bibliography.

Kent, David A., ed. *The Achievement of Christina Rossetti: England, Scotland, and the Union.* New York: Cornell University Press, 1988. This anthology contains fifteen essays that contribute to Rossetti's growing reputation as an important Victorian religious poet, and as an artist separate from the rest of her famous family. This book would be valuable to any academic library, although it is suitable primarily for advanced students of Rossetti.

Mayberry, Katherine J. *Christina Rossetti and the Poetry of Discovery.* Baton Rouge: Louisiana State University Press, 1989. Mayberry maintains that Rossetti was a meticulous professional writer, and not merely a talented amateur. She argues that Rossetti wrote about her role as a woman, and therefore was an early feminist. This study can be used with Anthony H. Harrison's, above. Supplemented by an index and a bibliography.

Rosenblum, Dolores. *Christina Rossetti: The Poetry of Endurance.* Carbondale: Southern Illinois University Press, 1987. Rosenblum is the first to analyze thoroughly the text of Rossetti's poetry in the light of the new feminist criticism. She especially examines the significance of "Goblin Market," the themes of which are central to all Rossetti's works. This book is dense and technical and is appropriate only for advanced students of Rossetti.

DANTE GABRIEL ROSSETTI

Born: London, England; May 12, 1828
Died: Birchington, England; April 9, 1882

Principal poetry

The Early Italian Poets, 1861 (translation, retitled *Dante and His Circle* with 1874 edition); *Poems*, 1870, 1881; *Ballads and Sonnets*, 1881; *Collected Works*, 1886; *The Works of Dante Gabriel Rossetti*, 1911 (William Michael Rossetti, editor).

Other literary forms

Dante Gabriel Rossetti published the prose sketch "Hand and Soul" in *The Germ* (1850). In 1863, he completed the biography of William Blake left unfinished at the death of Alexander Gilchrist. Four volumes of Rossetti's letters have been edited by J. R. Wahl and Oswald Doughty (1965-1967); his correspondence with Jane Morris has been edited by John Bryson and Janet Camp Troxell (1976).

Achievements

Significant both as a poet and as a painter, Rossetti offers an opportunity to study the relationship between poetry and art.

Among Victorian poets, Rossetti was excelled only by Alfred, Lord Tennyson and Robert Browning, although, unlike other major poets of the period, he published relatively few poems. His work is chiefly concerned with the exploration of individual moments of experience. As a consequence, he worked best at the level of the short lyric or compressed narrative, in which his highly crafted style often achieves remarkable intensity.

Biography

Rossetti, christened Gabriel Charles Dante Rossetti, was born in London, May 12, 1828. His father, Gabriele Rossetti, was an Italian political exile with pretensions as a poet who had published an eccentric commentary on Dante's *The Divine Comedy* (c. 1320) and supported himself teaching his native language. Rossetti's mother, Frances Polidori, although of Anglo-Italian background, was staunchly English in her severe moral standards and religious beliefs. The opposing views of life represented by his father and mother determined a conflict from which Rossetti was never able to free himself. Like his amiable, self-indulgent father in many ways, he was never able to exorcise the accusing voice of his mother's puritanism. He led the bohemian life of an artist, but felt guilty for doing so.

In 1845, Rossetti entered the Academy Schools of the Royal Academy of Art. There he associated himself with a group of young artists—notably, John

Everett Millais and Holman Hunt—who were dissatisfied with the style and subject matter of Establishment painting, but eager to make names for themselves with the Establishment. Because the effects of light and naturalistic detail they sought were also to be found in late medieval art (prior to the painter Raphael), they called themselves the "Pre-Raphaelite Brotherhood" and began initialing their more daring paintings "P.R.B." In 1849-1850, the Brotherhood published a journal, *The Germ*, which included several poems by Rossetti, including "The Blessed Damozel" and the prose piece "Hand and Soul." Also in 1850, Rossetti publicly exhibited a painting for the first time, "*Ecce Ancilla Domine!*" Reviews of the painting—as well as of works exhibited simultaneously by Hunt and Millais—were hostile. Stunned, Rossetti determined never to exhibit his work again (a determination which, on the whole, he maintained). The art critic John Ruskin, however, defended the Pre-Raphaelites, first in a series of letters to *The Times*, then in a pamphlet "Pre-Raphaelitism," and subsequently became Rossetti's patron, although Rossetti's contempt for what he perceived as Ruskin's bourgeois dilettantism prevented them from ever becoming close friends.

In 1850, Rossetti also met Elizabeth Siddal, a sixteen-year-old shopgirl who began serving as a model for members of the P.R.B. By 1852, Rossetti and Elizabeth Siddal were informally engaged. Despite her beauty and the limited artistic ability she developed under his influence, they were poorly matched. It is characteristic of Rossetti that he nevertheless married her in 1860. Their child was stillborn in 1861, and the next year Elizabeth committed suicide.

During the 1850's, while the Brotherhood itself was dwindling away, the reputation of its individual members had begun to grow. Rossetti never became a popular artist (as did Millais), but he began to receive commissions for his work and to attract a circle of younger admirers—two of whom, Edward Burne-Jones and William Morris, joined him in painting "frescoes" on the interior walls of the Oxford Union Society in 1857. There, Rossetti met Jane Burden, the woman he loved off and on for the rest of his life. Burden married William Morris in 1859 but seems to have become Rossetti's mistress in the late 1860's.

Fanny Cornforth was the third woman in Rossetti's life. They met sometime in the late 1850's, and after the death of Elizabeth Siddal, she became Rossetti's "housekeeper." Fanny was illiterate and lowborn, but with a striking voluptuous beauty very different from that of Elizabeth or Jane. Generally detested by Rossetti's friends, she was probably Rossetti's most loving companion.

Remorseful at the death of his wife, Rossetti had buried the manuscript of his poems with her and given up verse until at least 1866, when his relationship with Jane Morris prompted him to return to writing love poetry. In 1869, the manuscript of his earlier work was exhumed and these poems, together with his more recent work, were published as *Poems* (1870). By that time, Rossetti had a fairly steady income from his paintings. In 1862, he had leased "Tudor House," 16 Cheyne Walk, the London home that was to become notorious for his eccentric hospitality and collection of exotic animals. Yet his life during these years was not happy. He had become morbidly sensitive to criticism, and with the unfavorable reviews of his poetry (notably, Robert Buchanan's essay "The Fleshly School of Poetry" in 1871), he began to suspect a conspiracy against him. In 1872, he attempted suicide, and the last decade of his life was characterized by poor health, desultory work, and indulgence in the mixture of whiskey and chloral that became his favorite narcotic. A year after the publication of his second collection of poems, *Ballads and Sonnets* (1881), he died at the seaside town of Birchington, where he had gone hoping to recover his health.

Analysis

Dante Gabriel Rossetti's poetry is conventionally divided into three periods. The first ends in 1850, with the publication of some of his best early poems in *The Germ* and the beginning of his relationship with Elizabeth Siddal. The second ends with her death in 1862; most of the poems from this period, however, were written between 1850 and 1854. The third and last group of poems date from 1868, when Rossetti began writing again after several years of relative inactivity, until his death in 1882. Again, however, most of the poems from this period were written during its first five years.

While these three periods can be differentiated, the actual placement of individual poems is often problematic. Since Rossetti did not publish a book of original verse until 1870 and since he habitually revised his poetry over the years, a particular work might in fact belong to more than one period. "The Blessed Damozel," for example, was written in 1847 and published, first in *The Germ* in 1850; then, in revised form, in *The Oxford and Cambridge Magazine* (edited by William Morris) in 1856; next, with further revision, in the 1870 *Poems*; and, finally, revised yet again, in the 1881 *Poems*.

This habit of lifetime reworking and revision, which extended to certain paintings as well, evidences two characteristics of Rossetti's work—a meticulous craftsmanship that defines the poem as a labored artifact rather than the spontaneous expression of feeling; and an intense personal identification with his own writing, that explains both his reluctance to publish and his extreme vulnerability to criticism. These two characteristics are contradictory if one assumes that personal identification with a text is a function of its truth to prior experience. Rossetti's case, however, argues that identification is not a function of mimesis, but of the act of writing. He identified with his poetry because he himself had written it. To acknowledge a poem "complete" was for him equivalent to acknowledging the end of one of his own life-processes. To bury the manuscript of his poems with the body of Elizabeth Siddal was not simply to bury his own past or sacrifice its achievement; it was, in a real sense, to bury a part of himself alive with her.

This is not to say that personal experience is not the subject matter of Rossetti's poetry—it often is—but that readers should expect to reach that experience only through the mediation of highly wrought style, the presence of which becomes, in his best poems, an index to the intensity of feeling it conceals. His concern with style makes Rossetti a difficult poet. It is difficult to naturalize his poetry—to reduce it to day-to-day familiarity. He offers no personality for the reader to admire—or hate. Indeed, this absence of self is a central concern of his creative effort. Rossetti's poems do not merely hide the self behind the artifice of verse-making; they explore a fundamental opposition between language and feeling—the teasing ability of language almost to control reality and the disillusionment that necessarily follows from recognizing its failure to do so; the apparent communication embedded in a work of art turns out to be a denial of communication.

"The Blessed Damozel," the most familiar of Rossetti's early poems, illustrates this pattern of imaginative effort and disillusionment. The "Damozel" leans out "From the gold bar of Heaven," looking down through space for her earthly lover. Space, however, is vast. The moon itself is no more than "a little feather/ Fluttering far down the gulf." Because she cannot see him, she speaks, imagining the reunion that will come "When round his head the aureole clings." Then "will I ask of Christ the Lord . . . Only to live as once on earth/ With Love." Yet imagination is an unsatisfactory substitute for real love; despite a Dantesque vision of angels in flight, she "laid her face between her hands./ And wept."

The poem turns on the old notion that lovers separated by death can take comfort in the hope of meeting again in the world to come. Rossetti, however, reverses the perspective. It is the lover in heaven who longs for earth; it is the spiritual world that is tormented by desire for the physical—and remains, for all its beatitude, "warm." Moreover, the consolation of hope is, it turns out, no consolation. It merely leads to an intense awareness of loss—not only on the part of the "Damozel" but for the speaker of the poem as well. For the "Damozel" is a fiction, and the parenthetical first-person interjections ground the poem in the fantasy of the earthly lover himself. He claims to "see" "her smile" and "hear" "her tears," but the protestation emphasizes the wishfulness of his dream. If her imagined reunion leads her to "tears," his imagined "Damozel" leads him to a heightened sense of separation from her. The "Damozel" is, as his attempt to visualize her suggests, unknowable. Her death is a barrier he cannot overcome by the language of the poem. The sensuousness of his conception—the "fleshliness" of which Rossetti was later accused—is not a radical characterization of the afterlife, but an implicit mar' of the inadequacy of the earthly imagination.

"The Blessed Damozel" specifies the opposition between language and feeling as an opposition between poetry and eros. The poet's vision attempts to overcome the separation of lovers. His text is an act of desire that confronts him with the fact of desire—hence, of an unfulfilled and perhaps unfulfillable need. The world of Rossetti's poetry is thus one in which desire—generally sexual—defines itself by coming up against its own furthest limit—the verge of satisfaction. It asks the reader to experience the pain of near but never complete realization. It offers a nightmare world, in which all apparent realities are disclosed as expressions of the poet's desire.

The theme of frustrated eros is directly related to the tension between his father's bohemianism and his mother's puritanical morality. It enabled Rossetti to express his erotic sensibility while at the same time punishing himself for its existence. The inadequacy of poetic language is thus a function of the guilt that, in his own life, blocked Rossetti's personal happiness.

"The Bride's Prelude," which was begun in 1848 and returned to later in the 1850's but never completed, illustrates the link between eros, guilt, and the failure of language. The poem, even in its fragmentary form, is Rossetti's longest narrative. It records the conversation between two sisters in an unspecified medieval setting; Aloÿse, the elder, whose wedding day it is, and Amelotte, the younger, who is helping her dress. Aloÿse is strangely silent; then, having knelt in prayer with her sister, she reveals the story of her past life. She had, years before, while her sister was being educated in a convent, fallen in love with a young man, a distant cousin who had yet to make a name for himself in the world, then staying with her powerful family. When her family lost a political struggle and was forced temporarily to flee its ancestral seat, the cousin had deserted them, leaving her with child. Discovering the situation, her father and brothers had reluctantly spared her life but, it would seem—the poem is deliberately vague—killed her illegitimate child. Now, circumstances have changed again; the family is back in power, the cousin has returned, and it is he—Urscelyn—whom she is about to marry. With this revelation, the poem ends. Rossetti wrote a prose summary of a missing conclusion, which his brother later published. Urscelyn, he explains, having become a skilled soldier of fortune and therefore of use to her family, wanting to ally himself with them once more, has offered to marry Aloÿse. Aloÿse, meanwhile, had fallen in love with and secretly betrothed herself to another man, whom Urscelyn, knowingly and treacherously, killed in a tournament. Thus, the enormity of marrying a man who had both betrayed her and murdered her lover is the message she wishes to convey to her sister. In conclusion, Rossetti states that "as the bridal procession appears, perhaps it might become apparent that the brothers mean to kill Urscelyn when he has married her."

The "perhaps" tells all. "The Bride's Prelude" is incomplete because Rossetti was unable to imagine an appropriate ending, and his prose summary is merely an evasion. The poem is also Aloÿse's story, and she, too, cannot bring her narrative to completion. Significantly, the text as it stands makes no mention of the second lover. Urscelyn's flight labels him a betrayer—but

Aloÿse suggests that his motives were political and does not indicate that he knew she was pregnant. In other words, without Rossetti's prose summary, what seems to block Aloÿse's happiness is less the character of Urscelyn than her own sense of guilt. The conclusion that Rossetti claims he intended but could not bring himself to write would have radically altered the moral perspective of the poem. With it, Urscelyn is a clear-cut villain; Aloÿse, despite her youthful indiscretion, is a victim. Without the conclusion, "The Bride's Prelude" is a poem about Aloÿse's own reluctance to accept a happy ending to her years of suffering—to marry the man she had loved and from whom she has been separated by war and family pride. By telling her story to her sister, she confesses and thus overcomes the guilt that is the only obstacle to her happiness. Indeed, when in the closing line of the poem Aloÿse admits that her prayer has been to be able to "Show her what I hide," it appears that confession of the past, not complaint about the present, has been her leading motive. This purgation, however, is precisely what Rossetti does not grant her. She tells her story, but the poem breaks off before the consequences of the telling can be felt.

The ballad form of "The Bride's Prelude" is typical of Rossetti's narrative poetry. He was particularly fond of stanzaic patterns that include a slightly varying refrain. The mode was both satisfyingly medieval (and therefore Pre-Raphaelite) and conveniently disjunctive. Breaking narrative into a series of discrete, artificially defined units obviated the need for a coherent narrative personality. In poems such as "Sister Helen" and "Eden Bower," the repetition of the verse form replaces development of the speaker's point of view as a unifying device. Even in "The Burden of Ninevah," an uncharacteristically ironic "modern" poem of social comment, patterns of repetition qualify the immediacy of the first-person speaker.

In Rossetti's two "modern" narratives, "A Last Confession," and "Jenny," he uses the more typically Victorian mode of dramatic monologue to achieve comparable distancing. Both are poems about erotic failure; in both, erotic failure is related to the failure of language to communicate.

"A Last Confession," which is given the setting "Regno Lombardo-Veneto, 1848," is unique in its treatment of the political issue—the Austrian occupation of Italy—with which Rossetti's father was identified. Its confessional mode is comparable to that of "The Bride's Prelude"; what it confesses, however, is not illicit passion but murder by a rejected lover. The speaker had adopted a little girl deserted by her parents, who, under the rigors of the Austrian regime, no longer had the bread with which to feed her. In time this foster-fatherly love becomes sexual, but whether she responds in kind is uncertain. At length, they are separated and she appears to have taken up flirting with Austrians. On the way to meet with her for the last time, the speaker buys her the parting gift of a knife, such as "Our Lombard country-girls . . . Wear" to defend themselves against each other and the possibility of "a German lover." When she laughs at the gesture—another example of failed communication—he is enraged and plunges the knife into her heart. It is not certain that she is the "harlot" he believes she has become; the act of confession is a strategy aimed at exonerating the speaker, but since we have only his unreliable point of view, his words can never fully realize their intention. The priest who listens to him is allowed no response. The reader is left with an uneasy feeling that the speaker's words, instead of unburdening his conscience, merely reiterate the crime.

The speaker of "Jenny" is a man who has gone home with a prostitute, who, instead of making love, falls asleep on his knee while he meditates on the meaning of her condition and consequently his own. Among the ironies of the poem is the fact that his audience is sleeping. His words, whatever their merit, go unheard. Moreover, Jenny, who might well have added a significant point of view to the discussion, is necessarily mute, so the speaker remains trapped in his own consciousness.

What the speaker thinks he has learned is easily summarized. He begins with an ironic assessment of "Lazy laughing languid Jenny,/ Fond of a kiss and fond of a guinea," and moves on to a more sympathetic recognition of the plight of a prostitute. She is, after all, not essentially different from other women; like them, she is a victim "of man's changeless sum/ Of lust": "Like a toad within a stone/ Seated while Time crumbles on;/ Which sits there since the earth was curs'd/ For Man's transgression at the first." Finally, he sees that even her love of money is merely a reflection of the economic forces at work throughout English society. Then, leaving a few gold coins in her hair, he kisses her sleeping form and departs in the morning light.

Yet even in acknowledging that his own irony is a sign of being "Ashamed of my own shame," the speaker fails to achieve enlightenment. He remains ignorant of his own role in the situation and never gives credit to Jenny for being more than an attractive automaton. He does not blame himself for creating prostitution (although this is not his first such visit); he blames an abstract male "lust," and thus alienates himself from his own desire. The subject of the poem may be somewhat daring, but its inability to come to terms with female sexuality not only betrays Rossetti's participation in a Victorian stereotype, but also, and more significantly, betrays his tendency to treat women as counters in a process of masculine self-discovery. To acknowledge the full humanity of Jenny would legitimatize sexual relations with her: she would no longer be a victim, but a willing partner. She remains asleep, and the speaker's meditation has no practical consequences. The language of the poem, instead of effecting, across social and economic barriers, a relationship with Jenny, further insulates the speaker from significant behavior. He will return to his book-lined room—the books are emphasized in the poem—confident in decent feeling, incapable of decent action.

Rossetti's love poetry, in which the speaker is closely identified with or indistinguishable from the poet himself, contains his most painful accounts of the inadequacy of language. "The Stream's Secret," written in 1869, has been called at once his most revealing and his most concealing poem. Certainly it is a quintessential statement of the dilemma at the heart of his poetry. The speaker, who addresses the stream, exemplifies noncommunication. The stream's "secret" is, finally, that it can neither hear nor speak; that to confide in nature is to confide in a vacuum, not only denying oneself the possibility of a response, but also deluding oneself in the false hope that language is a medium of communication.

"The Stream's Secret" is also one of the most deliberately artful of Rossetti's poems, and its complex play with figures of speech makes it one of his most difficult. Rhetorical trope circles back on rhetorical trope, as in this typical stanza:

> Dark as thy blinded wave
> When brimming midnight floods the glen,—
> Bright as the laughter of thy runnels when
> The dawn yields all the light they crave;
> Even so these hours to wound and that to save
> Are sisters in Love's ken.

Midnight, compared metaphorically to the stream, is itself a means of characterizing the stream; with dawn, it provides a figurative characterization of the personified hours that are "sisters" to allegorized "Love." The reader is encompassed in a world defined by poetic devices. The speaker, in addressing the unanswering flow of water, attempts to anchor this continuum of language in concrete reality, but reality continues to elude him. The poet, who begins by asking when he and his love will be reunited and moves into an imaginary depiction of their reunion, is led, in the poem's final stanzas, to the recognition that Love, whom he first saw as a figure of passionate life, is synonymous with death, and that hope itself, as in "The Blessed Damozel," is a source of tears.

The lesson of "The Stream's Secret" is borne out in Rossetti's major work, the collection of sonnets he called *The House of Life*. Originally published as a group of sixteen sonnets in 1869, extended into a group of fifty "Sonnets and Songs, toward a work to be called 'The House of Life'" in *Poems* (1870); and finally published as a collection of 102 sonnets entitled "The House of Life: A Sonnet-Sequence" in *Ballads and Sonnets* (1881), the precise status of the work remains a problem. As ordered, the collection follows a general pattern of youth to age, love to loss, hope to disillusionment. Whether this ordering represents an organic sequence or is merely an adequate solution to the problem of arranging a large group of related but independent poems written over many years remains the object of critical debate.

The very existence of this critical debate argues that, if there is an organic sequence, it is not self-evident. Moreover, if there is no easy way to put the poems together, that difficulty may be an essential feature of Rossetti's conception. The untitled 1880 sonnet that introduces the collection suggests that the sonnets were written with deliberate reference to the limitations of their medium. "A Sonnet," Rossetti proclaims, "is a moment's monument,—Memorial . . . To one dead deathless hour." Such a poem is not a gesture of communication, but one of memoralization or arbitrary symbolism. Its message, explicit in the poem's leading similes, is akin to the carving on a tomb or the engraving on a coin. Verbal meaning is thus subservient to a role for which verbal meaning may in fact be irrelevant. The workmanship of the artifact increases its value, but one may appreciate the form of an inscription without in fact "reading" its message.

The introductory sonnet does not suggest that readers should look only at the form and not consider the expressive content of the sonnets that follow. Rather, it defines the limited role of the poet's art in the reader's experience of his poetry. Like the figures on John Keats's Grecian urn, the sonnets of *The House of Life* come into passionate being only insofar as the reader invests them with sympathy or understanding. The passion he can expect to experience in responding to the work of art will not be that of the poet-artificer who has provided its material cause, but his or her own. For, like a monument "in ivory or in ebony," the sonnet is not a recapturing of the past but an acknowledgement of its loss, not the living voice of its maker but an obstacle between its maker and the reader of the poem; the poem is like a coin, not of real value, but the sign of goods and services in a potential act of human exchange.

The notion of "a moment's monument" also offers a rationale for the atomistic structure of the collection. Limited to the depiction of discrete events, the poet's format cannot link individual experiences into a total rendering of human life. The whole is inevitably less than the sum of its parts; the work in its entirety cannot overcome the poet's fragmented experience of love and love's loss. (In this respect, the form of *The House of Life* is comparable to the "Short swallow-flights" of Tennyson's *In Memoriam*, which deny the possibility of an integrated response to death, even when the ordering of the poem seems to provide one.)

Sonnet XIX ("Silent Noon") exemplifies the notion of "a moment's monument" and thus typifies the collection. Two lovers pause in a summer landscape, the painterly details of which compose "visible silence, still as the hourglass." Recognizing the special nature of such moments, the poem ends by disrupting the landscape with the imperative cry, "Clasp we to our hearts, for deathless dower,/ This close-companioned inarticulate hour/ When twofold silence was the song of Love." The ultimate experience of love is silence—the postcoital oblivion of "Nuptial Sleep" (the sonnet singled out for its "fleshliness" by Buchanan and so deleted from the 1881 version of the collection). Language itself is therefore necessarily at odds with such states of being. The poet's description of landscape replaces the description of feeling denied here by the nature of feeling. The closing lines of the poem, in which he addresses his feelings, acknowledge their loss. Articulated self-consciousness implies that the "Inarticulate hour" has passed. Time, like the sand in the hour-glass, only passes; it does not develop. Thus, the development of the poem—the formal demand of the sestet—disrupts the special experience of the time it seeks to "clasp."

To memorialize love as verse is thus to admit the loss of love—not only because there is no need to memorialize the living present, but also because language itself is a sign of loss. The laurel, as Rossetti admits, in a trope borrowed from Petrarch, is "Love's Last Gift" (Sonnet LIX), not the sign of continuing favor. If poetic language celebrates not the absent loved one but the poet's isolated self, why then write poetry? This question, which Rossetti poses implicitly in "The Stream's Secret," is central to *The House of Life*.

The four sonnets grouped under the heading "Willowwood" (XLIX-LII) suggest an answer when they identify erotic desire as a longing for submergence in self. The poet who leans over a well to kiss the image of Love which has become the image of his lover is a version of Narcissus, unable to resist the reflection of his own image. Fittingly, the imagery of the four sonnets is derived from the Wood of the Suicides in Dante's *Inferno* (Canto 13). To dwell in the "Willowwood" of unfulfillable desire is to deny wholeness of self and cultivate in its place a self-destructive illusion of personal emptiness. Art, which once confronted man with spiritual truths, has turned, as Rossetti argues in "St. Luke the Painter" (Sonnet LXXIV), "To soulless self-reflections of man's skill."

Thus, the earlier sonnets of sexual fulfillment and momentary happiness give way to poems of loss. Through memory, the poet attempts to idealize and thus recapture lost passion, but memory, as the introductory sonnet suggests, is itself a confirmation of hopelessness. At the same time, even this overreaching logic is impotent in the face of individual experiences. Moreover, the love poems of *The House of Life*, written with at least three very different women in mind, reflect a range of diverse experiences. No summary of the collection is adequate even as a summary.

Like Rossetti's poetic achievement as a whole, *The House of Life* is elusive and, largely for that reason, difficult. It offers a solipsistic world defined totally by the self, a world in which no external reality functions as a measure of the speaker's perceptions. Yet, for this very reason, it blocks the consciousness of the poet from the reader. The dreamer turns out to be the most elusive element in the dream.

In its awareness of the limits of communication, Rossetti's poetry is contemporary. In its basic distrust of—and therefore fascination with—sexuality, it remains solidly Victorian. In its fondness for allegory and contrivance, it exemplifies the Pre-Raphaelite commitment to the Middle Ages. In its concern for the intense experience of the moment, it anticipates the poetics of the last years of the nineteenth century. Rossetti's numerous sonnets on paintings—a genre particularly successful in distancing the reader from the poet—echo similar poems by the French symbolists. His ballad narratives link him to William Wordsworth and Samuel Taylor Coleridge; his concern for the self-sufficient consciousness, with Percy Bysshe Shelley. Rossetti can be said, therefore, to exemplify aspects of many periods but to be typical of none. He is typical only, perhaps, of himself, but it is a self carefully concealed behind, not expressed in, his writing. The study of Rossetti leads to an understanding, not of his own personality or philosophy of life or of the age in which he lived, but of poetry itself—an understanding both of its strengths and of its liabilities. For this reason, his work remains a spur to the imagination.

Frederick Kirchhoff

Other major works

NONFICTION: *Letters of Dante Gabriel Rossetti*, 1965-1967 (Oswald Doughty and J. R. Wahl, editors, 4 volumes); *Dante Gabriel Rossetti and Jane Morris: Their Correspondence*, 1976 (John Bryson and Janet Camp Troxell, editors).

Bibliography

Boos, Florence Saunders. *The Poetry of Dante G. Rossetti: A Critical Reading and Source Study.* The Hague: Mouton, 1976. The laborious research behind this dissertation makes it valuable for the "sources and resemblances" in particular works Rossetti may have drawn upon directly, as well as for information it contains on traditional genres and styles influencing Rossetti more indirectly. The equally laborious prose, however, makes it almost unreadable. Contains an extensive bibliography.

Howard, Ronnalie Roper. *The Dark Glass: Vision and Technique in the Poetry of Dante Gabriel Rossetti.* Athens: Ohio University Press, 1972. A somewhat pedestrian stroll through a selection of Rossetti's poems, examined in detail for their technique and in chronological sequence for their developing vision. The discovery of certain thematic strains of isolation, medievalism, modernity, and doom are not striking. The technical discussions are repetitious, overmeticulous, and crowded with quotation.

Johnston, Robert D. *Dante Gabriel Rossetti.* New York: Twayne, 1969. Tracing the theme of love through various mythical incarnations of women in Rossetti's work, Johnston organizes his chapters according to genre: translations and prose, *The House of Life*, narrative poems, and last academic pieces. Includes a chronology and a bibliography.

Rees, Joan. *The Poetry of Dante Gabriel Rossetti: Modes of Self-Expression.* Cambridge, England: Cambridge University Press, 1981. Largely a study in influence and context, this book examines Rossetti's originality in relation to his Italian predecessors Dante and Petrarch for their treatment of love in sonnet form, and to his Victorian contemporaries William Morris, Alfred, Lord Tennyson, and Robert Browning for their uses of medievalism and the dramatic monologue.

Rossetti, Dante Gabriel. *The House of Life: A Sonnet-Sequence.* Edited by Paul Franklin Baum. Cambridge, Mass.: Harvard University Press, 1928. The lengthy introduction and exhaustive notes are indispensable to the serious study of Rossetti's masterpiece. (The same can be said, to a lesser extent, of Baum's edition of "The Blessed Damozel.") Discusses the structure and composition of *The House of Life.* The appendices discuss the dating of the sonnets and their prosody.

Sonstroem, David. *Rossetti and the Fair Lady.* Middletown, Conn.: Wesleyan University Press, 1970. A brilliant discussion of the roles played by women in Rossetti's life, poetry, and painting. The women who were his mistresses and models in real life become the mythicized muses of his art, including the heavenly lady, the sinful woman, the victimized woman, and the femme fatale. Illustrated.

Vogel, Joseph F. *Dante Gabriel Rossetti's Versecraft.* Gainesville: University Presses of Florida, 1971. As the title suggests, this monograph's narrow focus is upon the strictly technical aspects of Rossetti's verse, with chapters on meter, stanzaic forms, rhyme, and other sound echoing. Offers little or no attempt at interpretation. A final chapter is devoted to "The Blessed Damozel," its prosody and revisions.

MURIEL RUKEYSER

Born: New York, New York; December 15, 1913
Died: New York, New York; February 12, 1980

Principal poetry

Theory of Flight, 1935; *U.S. 1*, 1938; *A Turning Wind: Poems*, 1939; *Beast in View*, 1944; *The Green Wave*, 1948; *Elegies*, 1949; *Selected Poems*, 1951; *Body of Waking*, 1958; *Waterlily Fire: Poems 1935-1962*, 1962; *The Speed of Darkness*, 1968; *Twenty-nine Poems*, 1972; *Breaking Open*, 1973; *The Gates: Poems*, 1976; *The Collected Poems of Muriel Rukeyser*, 1978.

Other literary forms

In addition to her own poetry, Muriel Rukeyser published several volumes of translations (including work by the poets Octavio Paz and Gunnar Ekelöf), three biographies, two volumes of literary criticism, a number of book reviews, a novel, five juvenile books, and a play. She also worked on several documentary film scripts. The translations were exercises in writing during dry spells; the biographies, like her poetic sequence "Lives," combine her interests in the arts and sciences. The two volumes of literary criticism (along with her uncollected book reviews) are central for understanding her views concerning poetry and life.

Achievements

With the publication of *Theory of Flight* in the Yale Series of Younger Poets in 1935, Rukeyser began a long and productive career as a poet and author. Her work also earned for her the first Harriet Monroe Poetry Award (1941), a Guggenheim Fellowship (1943), the Copernicus Award and Shelley Memorial Award (1977), an honorary D.Litt. from Rutgers, and membership in the National Institute of Arts and Letters. She also won the Swedish Academy Translation Award (1967) and the Anglo-Swedish Literary Foundation Award (1978) for her translations.

While Rukeyser has been linked to W. H. Auden, Stephen Spender, and other political poets, her work more clearly evolves from that of Ralph Waldo Emerson, Herman Melville, and Walt Whitman. From Emerson and the Transcendental tradition, she developed her organic theory of poetry, from Melville, her poetry of outrage. From Whitman, however, she obtained perhaps her most distinguishing characteristics: her belief in possibility, her long, rhythmic lines, her need to embrace humanity, and her expression of the power and beauty of sexuality. Her feminist views link her also with Denise Levertov and Adrienne Rich, while her experimentation with the poetic line and the visual appearance of the poem on the page remind one at times of May Swenson.

Although Rukeyser's work has been relatively well regarded, she has received little critical attention. Yet the quality and quantity of her work and the integrity of her feminist and mythic vision suggest that she will come to be seen as a significant figure in modern American poetry.

Biography

Muriel Rukeyser was born on December 15, 1913, in New York City, the daughter of Lawrence B. Rukeyser, a cofounder of Colonial Sand and Stone, and Myra Lyons, a former bookkeeper. Her childhood was a quiet one, her protected, affluent life a source of her insistence on experience and communication in her poetry. In *The Life of Poetry* (1949), she tells of recognizing the sheltered nature of her life: "A teacher asks: 'How many of you know any other road in the city except the road between home and school?' I do not put up my hand. These are moments at which one begins to see."

Rukeyser's adult life was as eventful as her childhood was sheltered. In 1933, at age nineteen, she was arrested and caught typhoid fever while attending the Scottsboro trials in Alabama; three years later, she investigated at firsthand the mining tragedy at Gauley Bridge, West Virginia; and in 1936, she was sent by *Life and Letters Today* to cover the Anti-Fascist Olympics in Barcelona as the Spanish Civil War broke out around her. These crusades dramatize her intense conviction in the sanctity of human life and her desire to experience life actively, and they all served as inspiration for her poetry, fulfilling her declaration in "Poem out of Childhood" to "Breathe-in experience, breathe-out poetry."

Throughout the remainder of a life filled with traveling and speaking for causes in which she intensely believed, Rukeyser never stopped learning, teaching, and writing; she declared that she would never protest without making something in the process. The wide range of knowledge in her poetry and criticism and the large volume of poetry and prose she published testify to this fact. She attended the Ethical Culture School and Fieldston School, Vassar College, Columbia University, and the Roosevelt School of Aviation in New York City, and she learned film editing with Helen Van Dongen. Besides conducting poetry workshops at a number of different institutions, she taught at the California Labor School and Sarah Lawrence College and later served as a member of the board of directors of the Teachers-Writers Collaborative in New York.

Rukeyser made her home in New York City, except for the nine years she spent in California and the time she was traveling. She moved to California in 1945 and shortly afterward married painter Glynn Collins (although the marriage was soon annulled). Three years later, she had an illegitimate son and was disowned by her family, experiences which figure prominently in her poetry after this date. She moved back to New York in 1954 to teach at Sarah Lawrence College.

Rukeyser left Sarah Lawrence College in 1967. Although in failing health, she continued to write and protest. For the Committee for Solidarity, she flew to Hanoi in 1972 to demonstrate for peace, and later that year she was jailed in Washington, D.C., for protesting the Vietnam War on the steps of the Capitol. In 1974, as president of the American center for PEN, a society that supports the rights of writers throughout the world, she flew to Korea to plead for the life of imprisoned poet Kim Chi-Ha. Rukeyser died in New York City on February 12, 1980.

Analysis

"Look! Be : leap," Muriel Rukeyser writes in the preamble to the title poem of her first collection, *Theory of Flight.* These imperatives identify her emphasis on vision, her insistence on primary experience, and her belief in human potential. Focusing on this dictum, Rukeyser presents to her readers "the truths of outrage and the truths of possibility" in the world. To Rukeyser, poetry is a way to learn more about oneself and one's relations with others and to live more fully in an imperfect world.

The publication of *Theory of Flight* immediately marked Rukeyser as, in Stephen Vincent Benét's words, "a Left Winger and a revolutionary," an epithet she could never quite shake although the Marxists never fully accepted her for not becoming a Communist and for writing poems that tried to do more than simply support their cause. Indeed, Rukeyser did much more than write Marxist poems. She was a poet of liberty, recording "the truths of outrage" she saw around her, and a poet of love, writing "the truths of possibility" in intimate human relationships. With the conviction of Akiba (a Jewish teacher and martyr who fought to include the Song of Songs in the Bible and from whom, according to family tradition, Rukeyser's mother was descended), Rukeyser wrote with equal fervor about social and humane issues such as miners dying of silicosis, the rights of minorities, the lives of women and imprisoned poets, and about universals such as the need for love and communication among people and the sheer physical and emotional joy of loving.

Unlike many political poets, Rukeyser tried to do more than simply espouse: to protect, but also to build, to create. For Rukeyser, poetry's purpose is to sustain and heal, and the poet's responsibility is to recognize life as it is and encourage all people to their greatest potential through poetry.

Refusing to accept the negation of T. S. Eliot's *The Waste Land* (1922), Rukeyser uses images of technology and energy extensively in her early volumes to find, in a positive way, a place for the self in modern technological society, thus identifying herself with Hart Crane and with the poets of the Dynamo school. "Theory of Flight" centers on the airplane and the gyroscope. The dam and the power plant become the predominant symbols in "The Book of the Dead," in *U.S. 1,* her next collection.

U.S. 1 also contains a series of shorter, more lyrical poems entitled "Night-Music." While these poems are still strongly social in content, they are more personal and are based on what Rukeyser refers to as "unverifiable fact" (as opposed to the documentary evidence in "Theory of Flight" and "The Book of the Dead"). This change foreshadows the shifting emphasis throughout her career on the sources of power about which she writes—from machinery to poetry to the self. It is this change in conception that allowed Rukeyser to grow poetically, to use fewer of the abstractions for which many critics have faulted her, and to use instead more personal and concrete images on which to anchor her message.

This movement is evident in *A Turning Wind*. She begins to see the power and the accompanying fear of poetry, and her poetic voice becomes increasingly personal, increasingly founded in personal experience. Poetry becomes the means, the language, and the result of looking for connections or, in Jungian terms, a kind of collective unconscious. Rukeyser notices, however, that poetry is feared precisely because of its power: "They fear it. They turn away, hand up palm out/ fending off moment of proof, the straight look, poem." The fear of poetry is a fear of disclosure to oneself of what is inside, and this fear is "an indication that we are cut off from our own reality." Therefore, Rukeyser continually urges her readers to use poetry to look within themselves for a common ground on which they can stand as human beings.

The poetic sequence "Lives" (which extends through subsequent volumes as well) identifies another of Rukeyser's growing interests—"ways of getting past impossibilities by changing phase." Poetry thus becomes a meeting place of different ideas and disciplines. It is a place where the self meets the self, diving to confront unchallenged emotions in the search for truth, and a place where the self can face the world with newly discovered self-knowledge. Using the resources they discover both inside and outside themselves, people can grow to understand themselves and the world better. The subjects of the "Lives" exemplify values and traditions Rukeyser believes are important to the search.

Rukeyser's growth as a person and as a poet, then, has been a growth of the self, realizing her capabilities and her potential and, in turn, the capabilities and potential of those around her. She becomes increasingly open in her later poems, discussing her failed marriage, her illegitimate son and subsequent disinheritance, her son's exile in Canada during the Vietnam War, and her feelings about age and death. Yet while these poems may seem confessional, she is not a confessional poet such as Robert Lowell or W. D. Snodgrass. The details of her life, she tells the reader, are events she must consider from various angles as she dives within herself as Adrienne Rich goes "Diving into the Wreck," looking for the essence of being. "The universe of poetry is the universe of emotional truth." Rukeyser writes in her critical work *The Life of Poetry*, and it is the "breaking open" of her preconceived emotions to discover emotional truth that allows her to become closer to the humanity around her. "One writes in order to feel," she continues. "That is the fundamental mover."

In "Ajanta," Rukeyser makes perhaps her first statement of inner emotional truth according to poet-critic Virginia R. Terris. In this mythic journey within the self, Rukeyser realizes that self-knowledge is the prerequisite for all other kinds of knowledge.

Yet behind her search for self-knowledge and expansion of the self into the world is her belief in the necessity of communication. The silence she experienced at home as a child had a profound effect on her, and in many early poems, such as "Effort at Speech Between Two People," communication is ultimately impossible. This same silence appears to be at the root of many of the world's problems, and Rukeyser's open outrage and inner searching are attempts to right the problem, to achieve communication. By the time she wrote "Ajanta," silence had become a positive force, allowing her the opportunity to concentrate on her journey within.

Rukeyser has at times been criticized for combining disparate images within the same poem, as in "Waterlily Fire," from her collection by the same name, but this seems unjust. Far from being unrelated elements, her images grow, change, and develop throughout a poem and throughout her poetic canon. She puts the responsibility of making connections on the reader; she gives clues but does not take all the work out of the poem: "Both artist and audience create, and both do work on themselves in creating." Rukeyser is not an easy poet, and one cannot read her poetry passively. Yet she is a rewarding poet for those who take the time to look at and listen to what she is doing.

Another distinguishing mark of Rukeyser's poetry is the numerous poetic sequences (such as "Lives") which are connected by a common situation, theme, or character. "Waterlily Fire," for example, is a group of five poems about the burning of Claude Monet's *Waterlilies* at the Museum of Modern Art in New York City. "Elegies" is a collection of ten poems extending over three volumes. "Poem out of Childhood" is a cluster of fifteen poems, of which one is also a cluster of three, centered on Rukeyser's childhood— what she learns from it and how she uses it poetically.

Rukeyser's interest in poetic sequences grew from her training as a film editor:

> The work with film is a terribly good exercise for poetry . . . the concept of sequences, the cutting of sequences of varying length, the frame by frame composition, the use of a traveling image, traveling by the way the film is cut, shot, projected at a set speed, a sound track or a silent track, in conjunction with the visual track but can be brought into bad descriptive verbal things and brought into marvelous juxtapositions.

The sequence makes more apparent to readers the necessity of looking for connections among poems—recurring images, phrases, and sounds—than could separate poems.

In *The Speed of Darkness*, Rukeyser returns to her preoccupation with silence, expressing it both structurally in and as a subject. From her earliest poems, she used space within lines (often combined with a proliferation of colons) to act as a new type of punctuation—a metric rest—but in *The Speed of Darkness*, she places greater emphasis on the placement of the poem on the page to achieve this metric rest, for space on the page "can provide roughly for a relationship in emphasis through the eye's discernment of pattern."

Rukeyser's verse has often been characterized as half-poetry half-prose because of the long, sweeping, encompassing, Whitmanesque free-verse lines especially noticeable in her early poems. In *The Speed of Darkness* and later poems, however, she moves toward shorter lines and works with smaller units of meaning in order to compensate for breathing. At times, her arrangement of these poems ("The War Comes into My Room," "Mountain: One from Bryant," and "Rune," for example) approaches Swenson's iconographs in their experimentation with the visual and physical movement of the line.

Perhaps another reason for the new, shorter lines is that they are more suited for the introspective journeys of Rukeyser's later work than are the long, flowing, altruistic lines she used earlier. They also help her to control more effectively her penchant for verbosity and maintain the development of her images. Yet the length and conclusion of the later lines are not without precedent. Many of the most powerful passages in the early poems were journalistic or cinematic passages, not yet matured but still effective in their performance. "The Book of the Dead" is especially noteworthy in this respect, for it contains the seeds of the concrete image and colloquial diction fully realized later.

Rukeyser's diction also gives ample reason for labeling her poetry half-prose. Yet as startling as it may be to encounter words such as "eugenically," "silicosis," and "cantillations" in her poems, these words make the reader pay attention. She also employs words and even sounds as physical, musical, and thematic ties within and among poems in the same way other poets use rhyme and in the same way she uses image sequences.

With the variety of line length and placement evident in Rukeyser's work, it is not surprising that her canon is characterized by a rich variety of styles. Her experiments with language, line length, and rhythm easily lend themselves to experiments with different verse styles, including but extending beyond elegies, sonnets, odes, rounds, and rondels.

While she uses traditional as well as nontraditional verse patterns, she often treats even her most traditional subjects untraditionally. Because of her belief in the community of humankind, she has written many love poems, yet she approaches even the most personal subjects in an unexpected way. A notable example is "Letter, Unposted" from *Theory of Flight,* which is centered on the traditional theme of waiting for a lover. Yet it is distinguished from other such poems by the speaker's refusal to languish in love and to see nature languishing along with her. The letter remains unposted because the speaker cannot write all the traditional sentimental foolishness expected of her. Instead, as in even the bleakest situations about which Rukeyser writes, she sees the positive side: "But summer lives,/ and minds grow, and nerves are sensitized to power . . . and I receive them joyfully and live : but wait for you." The speaker rejoices in life rather than feeling sorry for herself.

Although a feminine consciousness is evident in every volume of Rukeyser's poetry, *The Speed of Darkness* also begins a new and more imperative feminist outlook. In the same way that she refused to be simply a Marxist poet, she is not simply a feminist poet. Rukeyser sees with a feminist point of view, but rather than rejecting the masculine, she retains valuable past information and revisualizes history and myth with female vitality. For example, in "Myth," one learns that Oedipus was not as smart as he thought he was; he did not answer the Sphinx's riddle correctly after all: " 'You didn't say anything about woman.'/ 'When you say Man,' said Oedipus, 'you include women/ too. Everyone knows that.' She said, 'That's what/ you think.' " "Ms. Lot" adds another perspective to the Biblical story of Lot and his wife, and in "Painters" (from *The Gates*) she envisions a woman among the primitive cave painters.

Other poems written throughout her career on more contemporary issues reveal the strength of women while upholding their nurturing role. The mother in "Absalom" (from "The Book of the Dead") will "give a mouth to my son" who died of silicosis, and Kim Chi-Ha's mother in "The Gates" is portrayed as a pitchfork, one of Rukeyser's few uses of simile or metaphor. She also refuses to let women take the easy way out as some have been trained to do: "More of a Corpse than a Woman" and "Gradus Ad Parnassum," for example, display the vapidity of the stereotypical passive rich woman.

Yet while women are strong in Rukeyser's verse, they are still human. Sex is one of the driving forces in her work, and she frequently expresses the joys of love and sex, especially in *Breaking Open.* Significant examples are the powerful eroticism of "Looking at Each Other," the honesty of "In Her Burning" and "Rondel," and the power of sexual renewal in "Welcome from War." Giving birth is also a powerful image in many of the poems.

"The Gates," a fifteen-poem sequence organized around Rukeyser's trip to Korea to plead for the release of imprisoned poet Kim Chi-Ha, synthesizes her recurring images and messages in a final, powerful poetic statement. Like "Night-Music," this sequence is at once social commentary and personal discovery, but it takes a much stronger stance in demanding freedom of speech and assessing Rukeyser's own development as a poet in the light of Kim Chi-Ha's life.

"Breathe-in experience, breathe-out poetry" begins "Poem out of Childhood," the first poem in Rukeyser's first collection. Muriel Rukeyser wrote a poetry developing organically from personal experience and self-discovery, a poetry bringing the anguishes, miseries, and misfortunes of human beings around the world to her readers' attention, a poetry demonstrating her exhilaration with life and love. Readers cannot hide from reality in her poetry, nor can they hide from themselves. There is always the journey, but possibility always lies at its end: "the green tree perishes and green trees grow." Rukeyser's challenge to the world she left behind is found near the end of "Then" (in "The Gates"): "When I am dead, even then,/ I will still love you, I will wait in these poems . . . I will still be making poems for you/ out of silence." The silence and passivity against which she fought throughout her life will not triumph if her readers are alive to her words and to the world around them.

Kenneth E. Gadomski

Other major works
LONG FICTION: *The Orgy*, 1965.
PLAY: *The Color of the Day: A Celebration for the Vassar Centennial, June 10, 1961*, 1961.
NONFICTION: *Willard Gibbs*, 1942; *The Life of Poetry*, 1949; *One Life*, 1957; *Poetry and the Unverifiable Fact: The Clark Lectures*, 1968; *The Traces of Thomas Hariot*, 1971.
CHILDREN'S LITERATURE: *Come Back, Paul*, 1955; *I Go Out*, 1961; *Bubbles*, 1967; *Mayes*, 1970; *More Night*, 1981.
TRANSLATIONS: *Selected Poems of Octavio Paz*, 1963; *Sun Stone*, 1963 (of Paz's poems); *Selected Poems of Gunnar Ekelöf*, 1967; *Three Poems by Gunnar Ekelöf*, 1967; *Early Poems, 1935-1955*, 1973 (of Paz's poems); *Brecht's Uncle Eddie's Moustache*, 1974; *A Mölna Elegy*, 1984 (of Ekelöf's poem).

Bibliography
Bridgford, Kim Suzanne. "Discoverers of the Not-Known: Louise Bogan, Muriel Rukeyser, Sylvia Plath, May Swenson, and Adrianne Rich." *Dissertation Abstracts International* 50 (August, 1989): 558A. Bridgford describes the ways in which these woman poets transcended the societal roles prescribed by their gender. They broke through to create new forms to express their womanhood in their poetry.
Ciardi, John. *Mid-Century American Poets*. New York: Twayne, 1950. Ciardi profiles fourteen American poets who were active at the midpoint of the twentieth century. His article on Rukeyser is short but comprehensive and offers a short biography and an analysis of her major work. A good overview that illustrates Rukeyser in the context of her contemporaries.

Curtis, Jane Elizabeth. "Muriel Rukeyser: The Woman Writer Confronts Traditional Mythology and Psychology." *Dissertation Abstracts International* 42 (March, 1982): 3994A. Curtis contends that Rukeyser deconstructs the male hero quest pattern in order to allow room for an active female character in her writing. Rukeyser wants to rewrite existing myths so that female characters can be more than passive muses or monstrous mothers to men.

Kertesz, Louise. *The Poetic Vision of Muriel Rukeyser.* Baton Rouge: Louisiana State University Press, 1980. Kertesz provides the first book-length critical evaluation of Rukeyser's work. This book is flawed in that much of Kertesz' analysis is often abandoned in favor of an angry defense of Rukeyser's work against critics who misunderstood it. However, Kertesz puts Rukeyser in context of her time and place, and so provides a valuable study for all Rukeyser students.

Moss, Howard. *The Poet's Story.* New York: Macmillan, 1973. Moss collects the short stories of twenty writers who are much better known for their poetry. In this collection, Moss includes Rukeyser's short story "The Club." Interesting, for it demonstrates Rukeyser's versatility as a writer.

THOMAS SACKVILLE

Born: Buckhurst, England; 1536
Died: London, England; April 19, 1608

Principal poetry

"Induction" and "Complaynt of Henrye, Duke of Buckingham," in *A Myrrour for Magistrates*, 1563 (second edition).

Other literary forms

Thomas Sackville's other contribution to English literature was the play *The Tragedie of Gorboduc*, performed first before a select audience at the Inner Temple (where Sackville was a young student of the law) on January 6, 1561, and then before Queen Elizabeth on January 18, "with grett tryumphe" according to one observer. The title pages of two of the three editions printed in the sixteenth century describe the drama as the joint work of two fellow students, Sackville and Thomas Norton, yet the extent of Norton's contribution is disputed. Because the play was the first in England to use the elements of dramatic blank verse, the regular form of tragedy, and a subject from English chronicle history, its importance in literary history is assured. Moreover, the play is characteristic of the concerns of Sackville's two poems and of his long public life: in language, structure, and theme it focuses on the political evils caused by an insecure succession. Both Norton and Sackville were involved in parliamentary debate on the issue of Queen Elizabeth's reluctance to marry, which was for the majority of the years of her reign a topic of deep national concern.

One other work of Sackville is known, a prefatory sonnet commending Thomas Hoby's 1561 translation of Baldassare Castiglione's *Il Cortegiano* (1528, *The Courtier*). A recent survey of the evidence (by Allan H. Orrick in *Notes and Queries*, January, 1956) has concluded that there is no substance to the tradition that Sackville wrote a number of sonnets and other short poems now lost. Sackville had completed his few writings in belles lettres by early 1561, when he was twenty-five or twenty-six years old and had already embarked upon his entirely absorbing, important career. In addition to his literary writings there have survived interesting letters and documents concerning public affairs.

Achievements

Sackville's literary contemporaries, among them Joshua Sylvester, Thomas Campion, and George Turberville, praised his poetry highly. (Turberville would not himself try, he claimed, to compete with Sackville in the high style of epic.) In a dedicatory sonnet to *The Faerie Queene* (1590-1596), Edmund Spenser acknowledged that Sackville was "much more fit (were leasure to the same)" than he to write Elizabeth's praises. Again, among the portraits of the courtiers of his day in Spenser's *Colin Clouts Come Home Againe* (1595), that of Aetion was probably meant to represent Sackville: "A gentler shepherd may no where be found:/ Whose *Muse* full of high thoughts invention,/ Doth like himselfe heroically sound." Certainly Sackville's high birth and important career encouraged such commendations. As Spenser's lines suggest, Sackville's contemporaries also recognized that his literary achievement mirrored that of his life.

A Myrrour for Magistrates, a composite work which records the fall from power of figures in English history, made an important statement on matters of national import, first bringing into prominence the great Tudor investigation of issues of responsible government seen against a background of problems of recent history, familiar to today's readers in the history plays of William Shakespeare. Sackville's contribution has been recognized as outstanding by readers from his day to the present. Indeed, a false tradition soon developed making Sackville responsible for the planning and inception of the whole project. Sackville's "Complaynt of Henrye, Duke of Buckingham" and especially the artful "Induction" were recognized as first achieving a poetic style appropriate for a national epic. Indeed, Sackville was an important influence upon Spenser in *The Faerie Queene*.

Sackville has thus held an honored if minor position in literary history. His reputation was enhanced by the view (until recently the common one) that between Geoffrey Chaucer and Spenser, English poetry experienced an uninspired, dull period—lightened only by Sackville himself. This judgment is now seen as exaggerated. Still, it points to Sackville's early, transitional achievement in approaching the "golden" style of the New Poetry of the high Elizabethan era.

Biography

Thomas Sackville, Baron Buckhurst and the first Earl of Dorset, was born in 1536 into a noble family. One ancestor had come to England with William the Conqueror, and a more recent ancestor was also a forebear of Queen Elizabeth. Sackville received, in all probability, a thorough and progressive education— for his father was a friend of the humanist educational reformer Roger Ascham, tutor to Queen Elizabeth and author of *The Scholemaster* (1570, which Ascham in fact wrote at Sackville's father's request for the poet's son). He attended Oxford University and then the Inner Temple, one of the Inns of Court, where, as a law student, he produced *The Tragedie of Gorboduc* in 1561. Sometime between 1554 and 1559, when the first edition of *A Myrrour for Magistrates* came out, Sackville had completed his two pieces for that work, although they were not included until the second edition, 1563. The poet's writings were encouraged by his humanistic studies in letters, complemented by an exposure at one of the Inns of Court to affairs and important personages.

His travels to Rome and France (1563-1566), during which Sackville was given the first of many diplomatic assignments by the Queen, then filled out the traditional education of an Elizabethan gentleman.

In his formal education and travels, as in his writings, Sackville always aimed at a public career. In 1558 he first sat as a member of parliament, at twenty-two years of age. On his father's death in 1566, he undertook the management of a vast estate, had already begun a family, and was well embarked on his long career as an ambassador, statesman, and government official. A member of the Privy Council, he sat as Commissioner in a number of trials of national importance. He was perhaps Queen Elizabeth's ambassador to Mary, Queen of Scots, bearing to her the news of her sentence of death; tradition reports that his diplomatic skill and gentle character served him well in this assignment. In 1589 he became a member of the Order of the Garter, and two years later was appointed Chancellor of the University of Oxford. He succeeded Burleigh in 1599 as Lord High Treasurer of England, sat as Lord High Steward at the trial for treason of the Earl of Essex, and was appointed Lord High Treasurer for life upon the accession of James I in 1603. Aging and in progressively worsening health, Sackville remained in active service, dying suddenly at seventy-one or seventy-two years of age while sitting in session at the council table.

His life is not that of the prodigal Elizabethan courtier so much as of the dedicated and active man of public affairs. As the most recent commentator on the poet, Normand Berlin, points out, in Sackville "we have an interesting example of a man's life that imitated art." It is of great interest to the poet's youthful writings on the fall of princes that Sackville's subsequent career so often touched upon the fall of the great from politicial favor (and from life). He himself suffered an undeserved brief period of disfavor after failing to resolve an impossible political tangle associated with the Earl of Leicester's governorship of The Netherlands in 1587. In all these affairs Sackville showed depth of moral wisdom, devotion to his country, and an amiable but upright character. He fulfills to perfection the Renaissance humanistic dictum—indeed, it is the underlying thesis of Ascham's *The Scholemaster*—that practical training in letters and oratory would prepare a young "governor" for wise services to the realm.

Analysis

Thomas Sackville's contributions to *A Myrrour for Magistrates* shows a typical Elizabethan compound of classical, medieval, and "native" elements: Renaissance English literature owes its characteristic variety and vigor to a mixing of sources and styles. Deriving from medieval traditions are the complaint form of tragedy (in which the ghost of a fallen "prince" tells his life story), an interest in the vicissitudes of Fortune, imitations from Dante, and use of dream-vision conventions. At the same time, Sackville turns to the classics, notably to Vergil, for the descent into hell as well as for much imagery and many details, and he evokes an atmosphere of classical myth and ancient history through allusion and example. He also employs artful figures of rhetoric in a manner newly stylish in contemporary Tudor letters and uses such "native" elements as archaic diction and syntax to further the effect of synthesis among diverse literary elements. The result is a dignified and serious mixing of richly traditional elements.

In the sentiments and atmosphere of his two pieces, Sackville evokes the brooding, melancholic air of Elizabethan tragedy, anticipating later Elizabethan achievements in drama. (In his exaggerated expression of extreme emotionality he works, however, quite in the earlier, mid-Tudor literary style.) He includes themes and images which become popular in Elizabethan drama and lyric, praising sleep, likening life to a play, and stressing that murder will not long remain hidden. Although such conceptions have roots in medieval and classical traditions, Sackville has gathered them into one poem where they work together with cumulative effect. Finally, Sackville's evocation of an atmosphere of woe and lamentation goes beyond the mere presenting of misery to anticipate the great Elizabethan treatments of mutability, which culminated in the mature works of Spenser.

A Myrrour for Magistrates was planned as a continuation of John Lydgate's *The Falle of Princis* (1494, which itself followed the model of Giovanni Boccaccio's *De casibus virorum illustrium, 1355-1374*). Sometime after 1550 a group of collaborators headed by William Baldwin undertook to write a series of tragic episodes, selecting from the English historical chronicles those figures and episodes which would fit their design. A running prose commentary discusses each verse tragedy and links them together. Mentioning the authors of many of the pieces and here and there revealing the intentions of the compilers, this commentary evokes a real as well as literary world. The authors included well-known men respected as writers in their time, public figures who had survived the many political shifts of sixteenth century England—in a word, these were men who knew by experience the political reality of the tales they told. A first version was partly printed in 1555 but was suppressed by Queen Mary's Chancellor Stephen Gardiner on suspicion of containing seditious references to contemporary conditions. Publication was made possible upon the accession of Elizabeth, in a first edition, 1559, covering the period from Richard II to Edward IV and a second edition, 1563, presenting new tragedies primarily concerning Richard III.

Today's readers find *A Myrrour for Magistrates* dull, didactic, and emotionally exaggerated. It was very popular in its time, however, going through a good number of editions and receiving successive versions and later imitations. Its analysis of recent political history brought to contemporary readers the latest thoughts on public issues; in addition, it provided some opportunity for the grim sport of seeking allusions to public controversies. The collection played a significant role in furthering the Tudor interpretation of history which has come to be called the Tudor Myth: a long period of destruction and disorder in the Wars of the Roses was England's punishment for violating the divinely sanctioned order when Henry IV deposed the rightful King, Richard II; a happy resolution was recently allowed in the accession of the great Tudor rulers.

Two central convictions underlie this reading of English history. First, the ruler of "magistrate" was believed to be the vice-regent of God, governing by divine right yet still accountable to God. Second, history was seen as a means of teaching political wisdom, presenting a "mirror" which shows (in Lily B. Campbell's words) "the pattern of conduct which had brought happiness or unhappiness to nations and to men in the past." In adopting these views, the authors of *A Myrrour for Magistrates* played down the medieval vision of the capricious falseness of this world's glories, seeking instead to reveal the workings of divine justice in the affairs of men. Sackville thus presents his Duke of Buckingham as vulnerable to the uncertain charms of Fortune *because* of his own moral blindness and as being justly punished for his unscrupulous ambition.

The story of Sackville's contribution to *A Myrrour for Magistrates* is obscure in many details, which were not entirely clarified with the discovery, by Marguerite Hearsey in 1929, of an early manuscript in the author's holograph. Generally, however, the introductory statements by Baldwin give a clear picture. When the first version was suppressed, Sackville proposed a more acceptable selection to which some new tragedies would be added which he would write himself, the whole to be prefaced by his "Induction" (introduction). This plan was not carried through, yet in the second edition (where it belonged chronologically) his "Complaynt of Henrye, Duke of Buckingham," was accompanied by the "Induction" because its literary excellence demanded inclusion.

Sackville chose the rhyme royal stanza of pentameter lines rhyming ababbcc, common in the late Middle Ages for serious verse, for both "Induction" and "Complaynt of Henrye, Duke of Buckingham." Although his strong iambics tend toward a thumping monotony, the effect is no more intrusive than in other mid-Tudor poets. Sackville also uses much alliteration; in Berlin's estimate, nine of ten lines use this device of repetition. Although such old-fashioned poetic techniques have been criticized, they actually benefit Sackville's overall intentions in both poems by helping to create a verbal texture of strong, heavy strokes in which opposition or contrast predominate. His is not a poetry of subtle effects. When the narrator of "Induction" sorrows to see "The sturdy trees so shattered with the showers,/ The fieldes so fade that floorisht so beforne," a stark and fundamental contrast is asserted. The language and imagery highlight significant polarities—summer and winter, day and night, joy and sorrow. The meters, figures, and diction preferred by mid-

Tudor writers here work together to evoke bold, contrastive meanings.

"Induction" sets an appropriate mood for tragedy in the opening description of a harsh winter scene. This seasonal description and the hellish personifications which follow are picturesque, in the sense of using detail and image to evoke a mood rather than to suggest a full allegory or to state meanings directly. The harsh setting and images present a pervasive context for tragedy. By the tenth stanza the external details of winter are reflected in the narrator's inner thoughts about human failings; immediately such thoughts find externalization in trenchant personifications. First the figure of Sorrow conducts the narrator to the porch of hell, where, one by one, are met figures such as Remorse of Conscience, Dread, Misery, Revenge, Age, and Death. Again, the detailed descriptions of each figure contribute to the poem's melancholic atmosphere, but in their cumulative import the visions suggest that unhappiness, deserved or undeserved, is inescapable in the human condition. Sackville keeps his narrator posed between revulsion and sympathy: he fears and yet feels pity for Famine, "how she her armes would tearc/ And with her teeth gnashe on the bones in vayne." In such ways the tragic visions impel emotional participation by the reader.

The portraits of Sleep and Old Age from this section of "Induction" have been much praised. Sackville's description of Old Age (lines 295-336) takes a detail or two from the mysterious old man of Chaucer's Pardoner's Tale; but it also borrows directly or indirectly from many classical and medieval sources. Typically, Sackville adapts and combines traditional materials, forming his own mixture and emphasis. In fact, the entire procession of figures in the middle section of the poem derives from a much briefer listing of personifications in Vergil's *Aeneid* (c. 29-19 B.C., Book VI). Sackville has expanded Vergil's suggestive, brief jottings into full portraits by calling upon many traditional literary images and concepts.

Increasingly, the poem dwells on the presence of change and loss in human affairs. At the end of the procession of figures, the narrator and Sorrow meet Death and then War. The latter presents his shield, in which may be seen historical instances of the destruction of cities and realms, culminating in a vision of vanquished Troy (lines 435-476). The poem has progressed from a view of individual sorrows to the universal principle of mutability seen on the scale of the destruction of civilizations. Moving across Acheron into deepest hell, Sorrow and the narrator enter a realm of intensified gloom and lamentation where the shades of the tragic dead, ghosts of "Prynces of renowne," tell their tales. In this way "Induction" leads up to the tragic narrative told by the Duke of Buckingham.

Sackville's "Induction" is, in Berlin's words, "essentially a mood piece that is brilliant in its evocation of atmosphere, vivid in its imagery, concrete in its description, effective in its fusion of sense and sound, and unified in concept and performance." Generally, the personifications as well as the historical figures are presented as tragic victims of misfortune or of unresistible forces of change. In "Complaynt of Henrye, Duke of Buckingham," however, there occurs a significant shift to a focus on the individual's responsibility for his own sufferings.

As "Complaynt of Henrye, Duke of Buckingham" opens, the speaker Buckingham admits that his own choices led to his destruction, resulting from his opportunistic association with the villainous Richard of Gloucester. From the beginning the poem establishes a didactic manner which seeks to analyze errors of judgment and excesses of ambition. Buckingham's story centers on the gigantic figure of Richard III, according to the Tudor interpretation an arch-villain whose fierce reign constituted the final purgation of a sick England before God permitted the happy rule of the present Tudors. (Modern historians have shown that Richard III was much less evil and his opponents much less wholesome than in the Tudor Myth.)

In supporting Richard, the ambitious Buckingham takes advantage of "the state unstedfast howe it stood." He shares in murders, little thinking that blood will ask for "blud agayne." At this point Sackville interrupts the narrative with the first of five interludes, each an interpolated didactic meditation on a theme befitting the stage reached in the narrative. These interludes help to slow the pace of the narrative, lending a dignity which Elizabethans thought proper to epic subjects; in addition, they help Sackville to generalize from Buckingham's experiences to universal patterns. The first interlude discussed the folly of political murder, which is shown by many examples to lead to a chain of successive murders such as Shakespeare dramatizes in *Macbeth* (1606).

Buckingham resumes his narrative (line 169) to tell of a second wave of murders leading to Richard's coronation and of Buckingham becoming Richard's "chyefest Pyer." Hoping to insure their final security, they kill Richard's two nephews (the notorious murder of the princes in the tower). With this act the chain of murders takes on destructive force, both psychological and social. First the conspirators experience the torments of inner fears, expounded upon in a brief second inteilude (lines 211-238). When the narrative resumes, it reveals destructive external effects as well. Richard rules by fear, not love, violating the great Elizabethan commonplace that the people will lend assent to a benign rule: in the hearts of Richard's lieges there "lurkes aye/ A secrete hate that hopeth for a uaye." The Tudor political theory of the divine right of kings stressed that kings are bound by morality and law. God allows rebellion against tyrants, and brings them war, guilty fear, and untimely death. A third interlude expounds this theme with gruesome historical instances (lines 267-329).

Thus far, Buckingham has described his immorality and errors of judgment objectively, allowing Sackville to survey Tudor political ideas relating to power, ambition, and tyranny. This objective tone weakens as Buckingham now turns from Richard, who has become too cruel even for him and who, moreover, has clearly revealed that Buckingham is next in line for destruction. Although Richard III remains the exaggerated villain of Tudor tradition, Buckingham takes on a certain depth of interest and evokes increasing sympathy. From this point in the narrative, Sackville allows a gradual return to the rhetoric of lamentation so prevalent in "Induction." Buckingham now blames not his moral flaws but fatal errors of overconfidence. He trusts, first, in the strength of his assembled soldiers, who desert him. (In lines 421-494 a fourth interlude expounds upon the folly of trusting the "fyckle fayth" of the mob.) Then, Buckingham places his final confidence in a disloyal friend, Humfrey Banastair, who betrays him to Richard and to death.

Buckingham now breaks off his narration to fall into a faint from grief. His distress over the falsity of a trusted friend will seem less excessive if it is remembered that treason is the arch crime in Dante's *La divina commedia* (c. 1320, *The Divine Comedy*), punished in deepest hell. Although today's readers will find the concluding sections of the poem which elaborate upon this theme exaggerated in their emotional extremes, it is suggestive to note to what degree Sackville has transformed Buckingham into a mistreated and sympathetic figure for the reader's contemplation. The last of the interludes is spoken by Sackville's narrator, for Buckingham remains in a distressed faint, with one brief awakening, from lines 540 to 617. This interlude picks up again the descriptive imagery and lyric movement of "Induction," painting an often-praised picture of the calm of deepest midnight, where the "golden stars" whirl in correct cosmic order and each creature is "nestled in his restyng place." Against this orderly security is shown the despairing unrest of Buckingham, who becomes a figure of genuine terror, emphatically teaching the lesson of the end to which lives such as his will lead, as well as an object for pity. Capping off this impression of desperation, Buckingham concludes with his notorious curse against the progeny of Banastair.

Finally, shaking off his episode of crazed cursing, Buckingham returns to his former objective tone in the poem's concluding six stanzas. He offers himself as a direct mirror to kings, showing that he "who reckles rules, right soone may hap to rue."

In "Induction" and "Complaynt of Henrye, Duke of Buckingham," Sackville achieves two very different ends. The introductory poem evokes a poetic atmosphere for tragic narrative, creating myth through imagery and description. The story of Buckingham is, in contrast, historical and dramatic, presenting and then analyzing Buckingham's actions in a context of serious thought on political themes. The poems together show both the range and the potential of poetry in the mid-Tudor period of English literature. Although Sackville's techniques and themes are seldom subtle, they make up for this lack with a consistency of effect and a concentration on bold contrasts and strong moral certainties. Recent studies of Sackville have found him to be as much a poet of his own time as an innovator anticipating the coming triumphs of later Elizabethan verse. It remains true, however, that he realized as did few of his contemporaries what his medium could accomplish, treating important themes with dignity, consistency, and poetic interest.

Richard J. Panofsky

Other major works
PLAY: *The Tragedie of Gorboduc*, 1561 (with Thomas Norton).

Bibliography
Berlin, Normand. *Thomas Sackville.* New York: Twayne, 1974. This book closely examines Sackville's poems, the play *The Tragedie of Gorboduc*, and assesses his place in literary history. Includes a chronology, a biographical chapter, a discussion of Sackville's part in *A Myrrour for Magistrates*, critical commentaries, sources, and an evaluation of Sackville's work and his historical significance. An annotated bibliography contains many references.

Campbell, Lily B., ed. *Mirrour for Magistrates.* Cambridge, England: Cambridge University Press, 1946. This is the definitive edition of this important compendium of tragical narratives from the sixteenth century. Includes Sackville's "Induction" and "Complaynt of Henrye, Duke of Buckingham." A sixty-page introduction discusses the content and background of the book and comments on Sackville's contribution.

Davie, Donald. "Sixteenth Century Poetry and the Common Reader: The Case of Thomas Sackville." *Essays in Criticism* 4 (April, 1954): 117-127. Primarily a discussion of Sackville's syntax and an exploration of his rhetorical style, this article also discusses other Sackville criticism. An interesting perspective on the poet's rhetoric in relation to the Elizabethan popular tradition.

Sackville, Thomas. *The Complaint of Henry, Duke of Buckingham.* Edited by Marguerite Hearsey. New Haven, Conn.: Yale University Press, 1936. A fine edition that includes the "Induction" and the unfinished "Epilogue." An informative introduction is included.

Swart, John B. *Thomas Sackville: A Study in Sixteenth-Century Poetry.* Groningen, The Netherlands: J. B. Wolters, 1948. Primarily a literary history rather than a critical study, this book gives a good appraisal of Sackville. A biographical chapter is followed by chapters on sixteenth century poetry in general and how to approach it, Sackville's technique, and an assessment of his work. A bibliography is appended.

CARL SANDBURG

Born: Galesburg, Illinois; January 6, 1878
Died: Flat Rock, North Carolina; July 22, 1967

Principal poetry

Chicago Poems, 1916; *Cornhuskers*, 1918; *Smoke and Steel*, 1920; *Slabs of the Sunburnt West*, 1922; *Selected Poems of Carl Sandburg*, 1926; *Good Morning, America*, 1928; *Early Moon*, 1930; *The People, Yes*, 1936; *Chicago Poems: Poems of the Midwest*, 1946; *Complete Poems*, 1950; *Wind Song*, 1960; *Harvest Poems: 1910-1960*, 1960; *Honey and Salt*, 1963; *Breathing Tokens*, 1978 (Margaret Sandburg, editor); *Ever the Winds of Chance*, 1983 (Margaret Sandburg and George Hendrick, editors).

Other literary forms

Besides his poetry, Carl Sandburg wrote a multivolume biography of Abraham Lincoln, composed children's stories, collected American folk songs, and worked for many years as a journalist.

Achievements

In "Notes for a Preface" to his *Complete Poems*, Carl Sandburg remarked,

> At fifty I had published a two-volume biography and *The American Songbag*, and there was puzzlement as to whether I was a poet, a biographer, a wandering troubadour with a guitar, a midwest Hans Christian Andersen, or a historian of current events whose newspaper reporting was gathered into a book *The Chicago Race Riots*.

That puzzlement has persisted since Sandburg's death in the critical reevaluations of his career. Sandburg was by turns journalist, poet, biographer, folklorist, and children's writer, and this is what makes it so difficult to assess his reputation. Was he a great poet, as Gay Wilson Allen has asked, or was he primarily a journalist and biographer? Somehow Sandburg's stature seems greater than the quality of his individual works. Certainly he was a great communicator—as writer, poet, folk singer, and entertainer—whose poetry reached out to millions of Americans, and certainly he was, like his hero, Lincoln, a great spokesman for the common man. Sandburg had a particular genius for reaching out to ordinary people and touching their lives through his poetry and song. In his public performances, one felt the power of a dynamic personality, which helped to establish the popularity of his poems.

During his lifetime, Sandburg published seven major volumes of poetry, and at his death he left enough uncollected verse for an additional posthumous volume, *Breathing Tokens*, which was edited by his daughter Margaret. Contained in these volumes are more than a thousand free verse poems. In *The People, Yes*, he compiled a record of American folk wisdom, humor, and truisms which Willard Thorpe called "one of the great American books."

Besides his six-volume Lincoln biography, he completed biographies of his brother-in-law, the photographer Edward Steichen, and of Mary Todd Lincoln. His delightful children's books, the most popular of which remains *Rootabaga Stories* (1922), were read and admired by many adults, including the architect Frank Lloyd Wright. For many years Sandburg was a regular columnist for the *Chicago Daily News*. In 1928, he was named Harvard Phi Beta Kappa poet, and twice he won the Pulitzer Prize: in 1940, in history, for his *Abraham Lincoln: The War Years* (1939) and, in 1950, in poetry, for his *Complete Poems*. Yet for many Americans he is best recalled as the genial, white-haired folk singer and poet, the embodiment of folksy Americana.

Even though Sandburg was perhaps justly called "America's best loved poet" during his lifetime, his reputation has steadily declined since his death in 1967. Most of all he has suffered from critical neglect, and his poetry has been largely dismissed for its sameness and lack of development, its lack of poetic structure, and Sandburg's lack of control over his material. At least one critic has found merit in Sandburg's last volume, *Honey and Salt*, but the consensus now seems to be that his poetry has been overvalued. It may well be that he will be remembered most for his Lincoln biography, but that judgment waits upon a full assessment of Sandburg's poetic career.

Chronologically, Sandburg belongs with Vachel Lindsay and Edgar Lee Masters as one of the poets of the "Chicago Renaissance." Like these other writers, he was one of the "sons of Walt Whitman." Early in his career, he adopted a style of loose, rhapsodic free verse, massive detail, a line pattern of parallelism and coordination, and the idiom and cadences of ordinary American speech. At his best, he is a verse reporter—a lyrical poet of the marketplace and the factory. His *Chicago Poems* are *vers libre* sketches of the city and its inhabitants in their various moods, but his poetry is often little more than sociological description in the service of liberal ideology. More than the others of his generation, Sandburg was the poet of labor and the common man. Along with Whitman and Lincoln he held a mystical faith in "the American people." He shares Whitman's principle of inclusiveness and his "cosmic affirmations" but lacks Whitman's innate sense of organic form that gave shape to his effusions. Sandburg's Imagist techniques were noted by Amy Lowell, and some of his poems, notably "Fog," may owe something to haiku, but Sandburg never developed a consistent critical theory, and his occasional pronouncements about his work or about the nature of poetry (as in *Good Morning, America*) are for the most part unenlightening.

Sandburg was thirty-six before he enjoyed any prominence as a poet, and much of the credit for discovering and promoting his work must go to Harriet Monroe, the editor of *Poetry: A Magazine of Verse*, which she published out of Chicago beginning in 1912. Through her magazine, she promoted the poetic innovations of the Imagists and the free verse experimentations of Ezra Pound, William Carlos Williams, Marianne Moore, and others. She recognized and encouraged the new American poetic talent of her generation, but she was especially partial to the poets of the "Chicago School." Sandburg must certainly be counted as her protégé, even though he soon found a wider audience.

Although he began as a poet, Sandburg lacked the discipline and control to master fully the art of verse. The prose poem was his natural medium, and the biography of Lincoln was a natural subject for a prairie poet reared in Illinois. Through his biography, Sandburg wished "to restore Lincoln to the common people to whom he belongs." In *Abraham Lincoln: The War Years*, his epic portrait of Lincoln virtually becomes a history of the entire Civil War era, a vast accretion of factual material which presents Lincoln the man in the context of his times. Sensitive to criticism that *Abraham Lincoln: The Prairie Years* (1926) had been too "mythic" and free in its interpretations, Sandburg was determined in *The War Years* to stick close to the historical record. Even Lincoln's major contemporaries—Ulysses S. Grant, Robert E. Lee, Jefferson Davis, and others—receive full biographical treatment. Allen Nevins praised Sandburg's historical biography for its "pictorial vividness" and "cumulative force."

Perhaps Sandburg's greatest poetry appears in the final chapters of volume four of *The War Years*, in which he describes the impact of Lincoln's death on the nation in passages of lyrical free verse that rival in their power and eloquence Whitman's great elegy, "When Lilacs Last in the Dooryard Bloom'd." With characteristic humor, Sandburg observed of his work, "Among the biographers I am a first-rate poet, and among poets a good biographer; among singers I'm a good collector of songs and among song-collectors a nice judge of pipes."

Biography

Carl Sandburg was born on January 6, 1878, in Galesburg, Illinois, the second of five children in the family of August and Clara Sandburg, Swedish immigrants of peasant stock. August Sandburg was a blacksmith's helper with the Chicago, Burlington and Quincy Railroad, and his wife kept house with the children and later took in boarders. The two had met in Illinois while Clara was working as a hotel chambermaid, and August had come to town as a section hand with the railroad. Carl had an older sister, Mary, a younger brother, Martin, and two younger sisters, Esther and Martha. Two other younger brothers died of diphtheria.

The Sandburgs were a thrifty, hardworking family, regular in their Lutheran Church attendance and conservative in politics. The elder Sandburg worked sixty hours a week at the railroad shops and spent his remaining time at home with his family. He had a reputation as a sober, dependable worker. Although both Carl's parents could read, they were not bookish and did not encourage their children's education. August Sandburg was scornful of books other than his Swedish Bible, and he never learned to read or speak English very well. His wife Clara had a better command of English and could sympathize with her son's interest in reading.

Sandburg's memories of Galesburg were of the closeknit, immigrant, working-class neighborhoods, the commemoration of the Lincoln-Douglas debate at Knox College, the pageant of General Grant's funeral procession, the excitement of the Blaine-Cleveland Presidential campaign, and the tension during the railroad strike of 1888. In his childhood autobiography, *Always the Young Strangers* (1953), Sandburg recalls playing baseball in cow pastures, walking along dusty roads to the county fair, carrying water for the elephants at the circus, and swimming in the forbidden brickyard pond. He enjoyed a typical if not always carefree Midwestern boyhood.

With seven children to be fed on his father's fourteen-cent hourly wage, Sandburg knew the pinch of childhood poverty, although his parents managed to provide the family with basic necessities. His elder sister Mary graduated from high school, but his family could not afford the same for Carl, so he left school at thirteen, after completing the eighth grade. From then on, his education came through practical experience. He would have continued in school but the extra income was needed at home. Sandburg wanted to learn a trade, but there were no openings for apprentices; as a teenager, he worked variously as a porter, newspaper boy, bootblack, bottlewasher, delivery boy, milkman, ice cutter, housepainter, and at other odd jobs. From these early job experiences came much of Sandburg's sympathy for labor and his identification with the common man. When he was nineteen, Sandburg spent a summer hoboing his way across the Midwest in boxcars, stopping in small farm towns to work for a meal or a place to sleep. He reached Denver before returning to Galesburg in the fall of 1897.

When the news of the sinking of the battleship *Maine* arrived on February 15, 1898, Sandburg enlisted as an infantryman in Company C of the Sixth Illinois Regiment of the State Militia. The men trained in Virginia and were on their way to Cuba when yellow fever broke out, and they were diverted to Puerto Rico. Along the way, Sandburg carried two books in his knapsack— an infantry drill regulation manual and a dictionary. From the army he sent back dispatches to the *Galesburg Evening Mail*. After his company had spent a month in Puerto Rico with intense heat, poor rations, and mosquitoes, Spain surrendered and the troops were mustered out in New York. By September, Sandburg was back in Galesburg with $122 in discharge pay. He decided to enroll in Lombard College as a special student.

Lombard was a small Universalist liberal arts college with a curriculum flexible enough that Sandburg could concentrate on humanities courses and avoid those he disliked, such as mathematics. Word came to him after his first year that he had been chosen for an appointment to West Point. Although Sandburg readily passed the physical examination, he failed in mathematics and grammar, so he continued at Lombard and became active in basketball, debating, drama, the college newspaper, and the yearbook. A professor there, Philip Green Wright, encouraged Sandburg's writing interests and later arranged privately to publish several of his early poetry volumes. Although he apparently enjoyed college life, Sandburg was never graduated from Lombard; in the spring of his senior year the call of the road proved irresistible, and he left school to wander again as a hobo. This time he worked his way across the country selling stereoscopic slides and absorbing the language and folklore of the people. The next four years found him restless and unwilling to settle down to any steady employment. Once, he was arrested for vagrancy in Pennsylvania and spent ten days in jail. After his release he continued west to Chicago, where he lectured and helped edit a lyceum paper.

In 1908, Sandburg met an organizer for the Social-Democratic Party in Wisconsin, who offered him a job in Milwaukee. At a party rally there, he met a young high school teacher, Lillian ("Paula") Steichen, who was home for the holidays. A shared ardent idealism and belief in socialism attracted them to each other, and by the spring of 1908, they were engaged. They married on June 15, 1908, and settled near Milwaukee. Sandburg continued to work as a party organizer and met Emil Seidel, Socialist candidate for mayor of Milwaukee. After his election, Seidel asked Sandburg to serve as his private secretary. This Sandburg did for two years before returning to newspaper work on the *Milwaukee Leader*. Meanwhile, his first daughter, Margaret, had been born in 1911, and his modest salary at the *Milwaukee Leader* no longer sufficed.

A Chicago newspaper strike in 1913 shut down the major dailies and temporarily expanded the readership of the small socialist tabloid, the *Chicago Daily World*. Sandburg was offered a job with a raise in salary and moved his family to Chicago, but when the strike ended, he lost his position. Several newspaper jobs later, he found a secure place with the *Chicago Daily News*, where he served as a special correspondent and columnist for the next fifteen years.

Meanwhile, Sandburg was writing verses at night and assembling notes for what was to become his monumental Lincoln biography. On a hunch, he submitted some of his "Chicago Poems" to *Poetry* magazine, where they were published in the March, 1914, issue and won the Levinson Poetry Prize that same year. *Poetry* editor Harriet Monroe was at first disconcerted by the boldness of the opening lines of "Chicago," but she recognized their strength and championed their free verse. At the age of thirty-six, recognition had finally come to Sandburg for his poetry. The money from the Levinson prize went to pay the hospital bills for the birth of Sandburg's second daughter, Janet, but he was still not earning enough from his poetry to support his family without his newspaper work. He remained active in the socialist movement and, along with Jack London, contributed much of the copy for the

International Socialist Review in 1915; he became dissillusioned with the socialist position on World War I, however, and eventually left the party, even though he remained liberal in his politics.

A publisher's representative for Holt, Alfred Harcourt, was so impressed with Sandburg's verse in *Poetry* that he asked to examine additional poems and persuaded his firm to publish them as the *Chicago Poems* in 1916. This began a long and cordial relationship between Sandburg and Harcourt, who later founded his own publishing firm. In 1918, Sandburg was sent to New York to cover a labor convention and while there discovered he had been chosen to travel to Sweden as a special war correspondent. His knowledge of Swedish served him well there, and he was glad of the opportunity to learn more about his cultural roots. He spent the remainder of the war in Stockholm, and while he was abroad, Holt brought out his second volume of poetry, *Cornhuskers*.

Sandburg returned to the United States a seasoned reporter and a poet with a growing reputation. In 1920, Cornell College in Iowa invited him to read from his poetry, and Sandburg made his first of many visits there, entertaining the audience with a public reading and then taking out his guitar to sing folk songs for the rest of the evening. This combination of poetry recitation and folk song fest came to be the standard Sandburg repertory on his tours and won for him many admirers. Also in 1920, his third daughter, Helga, was born, and a third poetry volume, *Smoke and Steel*, was published. *Slabs of the Sunburnt West*, another collection of verse, followed in 1922, along with *Rootabaga Stories*, a collection of children's stories that Sandburg had originally written for his daughters.

By 1923, Sandburg was deeply involved in a project that would occupy much of his time for almost the next twenty years—his multivolume Lincoln biography. The plans for the book originally grew from a conversation with Alfred Harcourt about a proposed children's biography of Lincoln, although Sandburg had been interested in Lincoln since childhood and had for some years been storing up anecdotes, stories, books, articles, and clippings about him. As the manuscript progressed, it rapidly outgrew its juvenile format and Sandburg continued it as a full-scale adult biography, written in clear, concise language. The two-volume *Abraham Lincoln: The Prairie Years* met with such immediate success that Sandburg was inspired to continue his biographical portrait in the four-volume *Abraham Lincoln: The War Years*, which won for him the Pulitzer Prize for history in 1940. These same years had seen him publish a fifth volume of poetry, *Good Morning, America*, and *The People, Yes*, a compilation of American folk sayings, proverbs, clichés, and commonplaces.

More than anything else, Sandburg earned critical acclaim for his Lincoln biography, hailed as the "greatest biography by one American of another." Literary awards and honorary degrees were bestowed upon him, including

Litt. D.'s from Yale and Harvard. In 1945, the Sandburgs moved from Michigan to "Connemara," a picturesque mountain farm in Flat Rock, North Carolina, where Mrs. Sandburg continued to raise her prize-winning goats. The 1950's saw Sandburg reap the harvest of his long and successful career. He was honored by the states of Illinois and North Carolina and asked to give a joint address before both houses of Congress on February 12, 1959, the 150th anniversary of Lincoln's birth. During the last few years of his life, Sandburg spent more and more of his time at "Connemara," surrounded by his family and his grandchildren, who called him "Buppong." He died at the age of eighty-nine on July 22, 1967, after a brief illness. After his death, tributes came from throughout the country, including a message from President Lyndon Johnson, who spoke for all Americans when he said that Sandburg ". . . gave us the truest and most enduring vision of our own greatness."

Analysis

In "The American Scholar," Ralph Waldo Emerson foresaw the conditions from which American poetry would emerge when he remarked that "I embrace the common, I explore and sit at the feet of the familiar, the low." The American poet would have to sing of "the shop, the plough, and the ledger." His subject matter would come from the world of trade and commerce and his language would be that of the common man. The democratic muse would be prosaic; there would be no sublime flights of poesy. Still, it would take a vigorous poetic imagination and a clear sense of poetic form to refine this ore to the pure metal of poetry. Otherwise the poet might well be overwhelmed by his material and slip imperceptibly from poetry to prose, from singing to talking. This is the problem with much of Carl Sandburg's verse, and it is intensified by his indifference to poetic craftsmanship and form.

Sandburg makes clear his distaste for formal poetry in his "Notes for a Preface" to his *Complete Poems*. Instead, he is interested in the raw material for poetry, in the unpolished utterances and colloquial speech of Midwest American life. In this same Preface, he lists eight poetic precursors—chants, psalms, gnomics, contemplations, proverbs, epitaphs, litanies, and incidents of intensely concentrated action or utterance which form a vital tradition in the history of poetry. This list closely resembles the folk material he selected and edited for *The People, Yes*, and it suggests in many ways the limitations of Sandburg's poetics. He is the poet of names and places, of trades and occupations—of unreflected experience and undifferentiated fact. Without the discipline of poetic form, however, Sandburg's material proves refractory even by the loose standards of *vers libre*. Robert Frost, a poetic rival, once remarked apropos of Sandburg that "writing free verse is like playing tennis with the net down." The amorphous character and mechanical reiterations in so much of Sandburg's verse point to precisely this lack of the shaping imagination that Frost believed to be essential to the poetic vision.

In *Chicago Poems*, for example, which many critics believe to be the best of his early volumes, the vigorous lines of the opening apostrophe to the city itself are followed by a casual assemblage of character sketches, place descriptions, fleeting impressions, and renderings of urban life. Occasionally the sheer emotional power of a poem will register, as with the grief of "Mag," the frustration of "Mamie," or the anger of "To a Contemporary Bunkshooter," but most of the verses never transcend their prosiness. "Poetry," Sandburg once said, "is the achievement of the synthesis of hyacinths and biscuits," but too often he presents only the latter—the prosaic and commonplace—rather than lyrical compression or poetic eloquence. Notable exceptions can be found in the sustained metaphor of "Fog" or the lyrical delicacy of "Nocturne in a Deserted Brickyard," but for the most part, Sandburg rejects the overrefinement of the genteel tradition by employing the coarse, vigorous language of the common people to present a frank, honest portrayal of his city in all its various moods. Poems such as "They Will Say" express a compassionate regard for the conditions of the working class, though other selections such as "Dynamiter" can be polemically one-sided. As Gay Wilson Allen, the most perceptive Sandburg critic, has observed, "A prominent theme in *Chicago Poems* is the longing of ordinary people for the beauty and happiness they have never known." The poem "Style" shows Sandburg aware of the stylistic deficiencies of his verse, but he insists that, for better or for worse, they are his own.

In *Cornhuskers* and *Smoke and Steel*, Sandburg continued to explore the poetry of the Midwest, rural and urban. *Cornhuskers* includes a wider range of material than his first volume, and many of the poems reveal a new lyricism. Some of the most memorable titles evoke seasonal moods of the prairie landscape—"Prairie," "Prairie Water by Night," "Laughing Corn," "Falltime," and "Autumn Movement." Perhaps the most accomplished poem, "Prairie," shows Sandburg experimenting with variable lines and sprung rhythm. "Fire-Logs" offers a romantic treatment of a Lincoln legend and "Southern Pacific" comments ironically on the fate of a railroad baron.

Smoke and Steel extends the material of the previous volume, but on a less optimistic note. The title poem celebrates America's industrial prowess, but other selections reveal Sandburg's awareness of the darker side of American life in the 1920's—in the cynicism of "The Lawyers Know Too Much" and "Liars" and the gangland violence of "Killers" and "Hoodlums." Even with the inclusion of poems to his wife and daughters, *Smoke and Steel* is a less affirmative volume than Sandburg's earlier work.

By the time *Slabs of the Sunburnt West* was published, Sandburg had reworked the same material too often. Too many of the poems in this short volume are frankly repetitive of his earlier efforts, or else derivative of Walt Whitman in their vague inclusiveness and generalized evocations of "the people."

With *Good Morning, America* and *The People, Yes*, Sandburg introduced a new direction in his work by reverting to the raw material of poetry in the slang and lingo of the people. Henceforth, as a poet of the people, he would take his material directly from them. In *Good Morning, America*, he offers something of an *ars poetica* in "Tentative (First Model) Definitions of Poetry," a collection of thirty-eight whimsical definitions of poetry. The problem with these definitions is that they seem to deny the role of poetic artistry by implying that poetry can be "found" virtually anywhere and that it consists of virtually anything that strikes the poet's fancy. At this point perhaps more folklorist than poet, Sandburg seems satisfied merely to collect and compile the words of the people rather than to exert artistic selection and control over his material. *The People, Yes* may have value as a collection of verbal portraits of the American people, but whether it is poetry in any traditional sense is debatable.

Two subsequent collections, *Complete Poems* and *Harvest Poems: 1910-1960*, each included new material and evinced a deepening of Sandburg's poetic talents. During the 1940's, he experimented with a new form of dramatized poetry or recitation—designed to be read publicly with musical accompaniment. Several of these occasional poems—"Mr. Longfellow and his Boy" and "The Long Shadow of Lincoln: A Litany"—are notable for the new note of somber dignity in his free verse. Sandburg read his Lincoln litany as the Phi Beta Kappa poem at the College of William and Mary in 1944 and used the occasion to draw an implicit parallel between Lincoln's struggle during the Civil War and the nation's efforts during World War II. This same patriotic note was struck in his moving elegy on Franklin Delano Roosevelt, "When Death Came April Twelve 1945."

Sandburg published one additional volume of poems during his lifetime, *Honey and Salt*, which appeared when he was eighty-five. This volume demonstrates the steady mastery and control of his craft that critics had sought for in his earlier work. The verses are less strident and ideological, more quiet and reflective in their wisdom. Several notable poems, including "Honey and Salt," "Foxgloves," and "Timesweep," indicate the range of his achievement in what may be his finest volume. Additional poems of merit appeared in the posthumous volume *Breathing Tokens*, which suggests that William Carlos Williams and others may have been too quick to dismiss Sandburg's poetic achievement on the basis of the *Complete Poems*. Perhaps that achievement must now be reassessed. His two fine collections of children's poems, *Early Moon* and *Wind Song*, also deserve critical attention.

A major objection among Sandburg's critics has been his lack of development. Detractors point to the formulaic nature of his poems and their lack of intellectual content or complexity. They comment on his neglect of prosody and his disdain for the traditional poetic devices that make poetry a "heightened and intensified use of language." They also comment that Sandburg did not master the major poetic forms—the elegy, the ballad, the sonnet, or the lyric. The neglect of form in favor of expression is certainly a trait common to much of modern poetry, and one must ask, finally, whether Sandburg is any more deficient in this respect than his contemporaries, or whether his neglect since his death has been more a matter of present standards of critical taste.

Andrew J. Angyal

Other major works

LONG FICTION: *Remembrance Rock*, 1948.

NONFICTION: *The Chicago Race Riots*, 1919; *Abraham Lincoln: The Prairie Years*, 1926 (2 volumes); *Steichen the Photographer*, 1929; *Mary Lincoln: Wife and Widow*, 1932 (with Paul M. Angle); *A Lincoln and Whitman Miscellany*, 1938; *Abraham Lincoln: The War Years*, 1939 (4 volumes); *Storm over the Land: A Profile of the Civil War*, 1942; *The Photographs of Abraham Lincoln*, 1944; *Lincoln Collector: The Story of Oliver R. Barrett's Great Private Collection*, 1949; *Always the Young Strangers*, 1953; *Abraham Lincoln: The Prairie Years and the War Years*, 1954; *The Sandburg Range*, 1957; "Address Before a Joint Session of Congress, February 12, 1959," 1959; *The Letters of Carl Sandburg*, 1968 (Herbert Mitgang, editor).

CHILDREN'S LITERATURE: *Rootabaga Stories*, 1922; *Rootabaga Pigeons*, 1923; *Abe Lincoln Grows Up*, 1928; *Potato Face*, 1930; *Prairie-Town Boy*, 1955; *The Wedding Procession of the Rag Doll and the Broom Handle and Who Was In It*, 1967.

ANTHOLOGIES: *The American Songbag*, 1927; *The New American Songbag*, 1950.

MISCELLANEOUS: *Home Front Memo*, 1943.

Bibliography

Allen, Gay Wilson. *Carl Sandburg*. Minneapolis: University of Minnesota Press, 1972. In this brief but informative pamphlet, Allen explains how Sandburg changed the course of American literature, despite the critical controversies about his work. Sandburg's major success, according to Allen, was his role as the voice and conscience of his generation. Allen justifies his critical study of Sandburg's life and career based on this role. Contains a bibliography.

Crowder, Richard. *Carl Sandburg*. New York: Twayne, 1964. This insightful work aims to give details of Sandburg's life that are relevant to his writing. Summarizes the prose and verse content of his major works, reviews the critics' reception of each major work, analyzes the themes and craftsmanship in each volume, and appraises Sandburg's achievement in American letters. Includes a bibliography.

Durnell, Hazel. *The America of Carl Sandburg.* Washington, D.C.: University Press of Washington, D.C., 1965. Durnell gives a chronological survey of Sandburg's life and achievement, discusses aspects of American life in his writing, examines Sandburg's place in American literature, and ends with a section on Sandburg and his critics. Includes a bibliography and photographs.

Golden, Harry Lewis. *Carl Sandburg.* Cleveland: World Publishing, 1961. Golden claims not to have written the definitive biography of Sandburg, but merely a brief sketch of the first half of the twentieth century using Sandburg as a reference point. Focuses on the five aspects of Sandburg's career that distinguished him: poetry, history, biography, fiction, and music.

Hallwas, John E., and Dennis J. Reader, eds. *The Vision of This Land: Studies of Vachel Lindsay, Edgar Lee Masters, and Carl Sandburg.* Macomb: Western Illinois University Press, 1976. The editors of this work view all the three authors discussed as having stood outside the main currents of twentieth century poetry. The section on Sandburg examines the poet's motives and methods, asserting the priority of populist traditions rather than intellectual values in his work. Sandburg is depicted as the preserver of traditions and ideals, rather than the breaker of new literary ground. Includes photographs and a bibliography.

MAY SARTON

Born: Wondelgem, Belgium; May 3, 1912

Principal poetry

Encounter in April, 1937; *Inner Landscape*, 1939; *The Lion and the Rose*, 1948; *The Land of Silence*, 1953; *In Time Like Air*, 1958; *Cloud, Stone, Sun, Vine*, 1961; *A Private Mythology*, 1966; *As Does New Hampshire*, 1967; *A Grain of Mustard Seed*, 1971; *A Durable Fire*, 1972; *Collected Poems (1930-1973)*, 1974; *Selected Poems of May Sarton*, 1978 (Serena Sue Hilsinger and Lois Byrnes, editors); *Halfway to Silence*, 1980; *Letters from Maine*, 1984; *The Silence Now: New and Uncollected Earlier Poems*, 1988.

Other literary forms

Although May Sarton considers herself to be first of all a poet, she is also well-known for her fiction and her autobiographical writings. Her first novel, *The Single Hound* (1938), received critical acclaim for its sensitive portrayal of the relationship between a troubled young writer and the elderly woman who serves as his mentor. Alluding to Emily Dickinson's image of the soul attended by "a single hound—/ Its own identity," this novel's title suggests a central theme of Sarton's fiction: the struggle of a vulnerable individual, often an artist, for creative autonomy and self-knowledge. Important subsequent novels include *Faithful Are the Wounds* (1955), a work based loosely on the events surrounding the suicide of the Harvard English professor and author F. O. Matthiessen; *The Small Room* (1961), an exploration of teacher-student relationships in a New England women's college; and *Mrs. Stevens Hears the Mermaids Singing* (1965), a fictional rendering of Sarton's poetic theory through the reminiscences of the poet-protagonist Hilary Stevens. Three later novels treat with sensitivity the problems of aging: *Kinds of Love* (1970), *As We Are Now* (1973), and *A Reckoning* (1978).

Sarton has also contributed significantly to the genre of women's autobiography. In *I Knew a Phoenix* (1959) she focuses on her relationship with her parents, her early education, and her theatrical endeavors and travels during the 1930's. A sequel, *Plant Dreaming Deep* (1968), tells of Sarton's later life, specifically her purchase of the country house in New Hampshire that for years provided a "life-restoring silence" that nourished her art. *Journal of a Solitude* (1973), probably Sarton's best-known work, explores further the importance of solitude for the writer who would "break through . . . to the matrix itself," thus coming to terms with her art and herself. Subsequent journals, *The House by the Sea* (1977) and *Recovering* (1980), deal with the poet's move to the coastal home in Maine, and with her struggle toward "valuing myself again" after professional disillusionment and a bout with breast cancer. *At Seventy* (1984) and *After the Stroke* (1988) chronicle her determination to continue writing daily and living fully despite the exigencies of aging and ill health.

In addition to her novels and journals, Sarton has published *A World of Light: Portraits and Celebrations* (1976), vignettes which profile, among others, the writers Louise Bogan and Elizabeth Bowen. Sarton's articles on writing and on rural life have appeared in *The Writer*, *The Christian Science Monitor*, and *Family Circle*. A documentary, *World of Light: A Portrait of May Sarton*, was produced by Ishtar Films in 1979.

Achievements

Sarton is among the most prolific and versatile of modern American writers. During a career that spanned more than five decades, she has published seventeen novels, almost as many volumes of poetry, a dozen works of nonfiction, and several children's books. With the exception of the period during World War II, she has produced virtually a book a year. Much of Sarton's popular acclaim has come through her novels and journals, which have inspired hundreds of letters from readers moved by her painstaking accounts of her solitary existence or by her frank treatment of aging—of friendship, sexuality, and anger among the elderly; of dying with dignity. She received a Guggenheim Fellowship in poetry (1954), a Phi Beta Kappa Visiting Scholarship (1959-1960), a Danforth Visiting Lectureship (1960-1961), and a National Foundation of the Arts and Humanities grant (1967). She also received numerous honorary degrees from American colleges.

Although Sarton has been labeled—sometimes pejoratively—an "old-fashioned" poet, a "sentimental" novelist, a "lesbian writer," her work is far richer and more varied than such categorizations would suggest. Universal themes pervade her writing: the power of friendship and passionate love, the unique bond between parent and child, the quest for identity and inner order, the responsibility of art and the artist in modern society, the conflicts of the elderly. Sarton is also concerned with the unique dilemma of the female artist, who struggles to be both woman and writer in a male-oriented society. Her exploration of the woman poet's relationship to her creativity, found primarily in *Mrs. Stevens Hears the Mermaids Singing* and in her poems and journals, is perhaps Sarton's most significant literary contribution.

Biography

May Sarton's parents, Eleanor Mabel Elwes and George Sarton, met in Ghent, Belgium, during the early 1900's, while she was an art student and he a promising young scientist-scholar. In 1910 they married, and in 1912 their only daughter, May, was born, during the same spring that George Sarton founded the scientific journal *Isis*. That her father connected his daughter's birth with that of his publication is evident from her account in *I Knew a*

Phoenix of the dedication of one of George Sarton's scientific works to his wife: "Eleanor Mabel, mother of those strange twins, May and Isis." At the outbreak of World War I, Sarton's father decided that he could no longer work in Belgium; thus the family emigrated first to England and in 1916 to Cambridge, Massachusetts, where George Sarton was aided financially by the Carnegie Institute and hired to teach half a course at Harvard University. In Cambridge he wrote his best-known work, the monumental *Introduction to the History of Science* (1928), and Mabel Sarton gained a modest reputation as a designer of furniture and clothing. In *Plant Dreaming Deep*, May Sarton has acknowledged her appreciation for "the rich gifts I was given by a scholar father and an artist mother, each strong in his own right."

From 1917 to 1926 Sarton attended Shady Hill School in Cambridge, an unorthodox institution whose founder, Agnes Hocking, contributed greatly to her love of learning and books. A year at the Institut Belge de Culture Française in Belgium provided Sarton with another important teacher and role model, Marie Closset, who encouraged her students to pay "enlightened homage" to the great literary masters. After graduating from the Cambridge High and Latin School in 1929, Sarton was apprenticed to Eva Le Gallienne's Civic Repertory Theatre in New York, where she remained from 1930 to 1936. During that time she founded and directed the Apprentice Theatre in the New School for Social Research and headed the Associated Actors Theater in Hartford, Connecticut. When her interest in the theater waned, Sarton traveled to England, where she met Virginia Woolf, Elizabeth Bowen, Julian Huxley, and S. S. Koteliansky, who became a lifelong friend. She also returned to a volume of poetry she had begun years earlier, and in 1937 *Encounter in April* was published.

Since the early 1940's Sarton has been a teacher as well as a writer. In 1945 she served as Poet-in-Residence at Southern Illinois University; from 1950 to 1953 she was Briggs-Copeland Instructor in Composition at Harvard; and from 1960 to 1964 she taught writing at Wellesley College. In the early 1960's Sarton bought the country home in New Hampshire whose serenity inspired *Plant Dreaming Deep*, *Journal of a Solitude*, and numerous volumes of poetry—in particular, *As Does New Hampshire*, a collection of poems on nature and solitude dedicated to her neighbors in the village of Nelson. In 1974 the bulk of Sarton's poetry was published in one volume, the *Collected Poems (1930-1973)*. She now lives in York, Maine, and lectures frequently at colleges and universities throughout the United States.

Analysis

"We have to make myths of our lives," May Sarton says in *Plant Dreaming Deep*. "It is the only way to live them without despair." Of the many modern American women poets who are also mythmakers, Sarton speaks often and most urgently about what it means to be a woman and a writer and about the female muse as a primary source of poetic inspiration. In the fourth "Autumn Sonnet" from *A Durable Fire*, she describes the crucial relationship between the woman poet and her muse, that elusive force whose function is "to help me tame the wildness in my blood,/ To bring the struggling poet safely home." As "sister of the mirage and echo," Sarton's muse parallels in some respects the quasierotic, mystical woman invoked by Robert Graves in *The White Goddess* (1948), "she whom I desired above all things to know." For Sarton as for Graves, the muse is also a demonic "shadow," a crucial Medusa-self against whom the poet must struggle and yet through whom she is able ultimately to transform her "wildness" into vital creative energy. For Sarton as for Hilary Stevens, the central character in *Mrs. Stevens Hears the Mermaids Singing*, the muse "destroys as well as gives life, does not nourish, pierces, forces one to discard, renew, be born again. Joy and agony are pivoted in her presence."

To understand Sarton's theory of the muse and its importance to her poetry, one must first examine her view of female creativity, a view that centers on the antithesis between being an artist and being a woman. "I was broken in two/ by sheer definition," she exclaims in "Birthday on the Acropolis," and though she is reacting here to the "pitiless clarity" of the stark Greek light and landscape, the statement describes as well the conflict she experiences in attempting to reconcile her femininity with her art. Like other women writers from Emily Dickinson to Virginia Woolf to Adrienne Rich, Sarton struggles to overcome what Suzanne Juhasz in *Naked and Fiery Forms* (1976) has called the woman poet's "double bind": how to survive as both woman and poet in a culture that considers the two contradictory. As Juhasz and other critics have noted, the result of such a struggle is often psychic fragmentation, a feeling of self versus self. For Sarton, this quest to name and claim an autonomous creative identity is further complicated by her acceptance of the patriarchal definition of woman as "other"—as beloved rather than lover, object rather than subject; in short, as inherently "other than" an active creator. She thus aligns herself with a perspective both Jungian and ahistorical in assuming an archetypal "feminine" that must be innately separate from the active "masculine" principle.

This assumption has enormous implications for her poetics, which posits an inevitable dichotomy between the "feminine" and the "artistic" sensibilities. The creative woman, Sarton suggests in *Mrs. Stevens Hears the Mermaids Singing*, is plagued by a "psychic tension" that compels her to strive for balance and wholeness. Although every person experiences such tension to a degree, it is manifested most intensely in the artist, who goes mad if he is unable to fulfill the need for balance. If the artist is a woman, however, she writes "at the expense of herself as a woman." The woman writer, Sarton concludes, is by definition "aberrant." Yet Sarton views such aberrance not as a liability but as an asset, a source of the woman writer's unique creative power. In this respect she takes issue with Sandra M. Gilbert and Susan Gubar, who argue in *The Madwoman in the Attic* (1979) that the woman who writes typically considers her gender a "painful obstacle" to be overcome and thus experiences an "anxiety of authorship." According to Sarton's schema, in contrast, the woman writer's aberrance serves as a source of wholeness rather than schizophrenia, a constructive rather than a destructive force, for it catapults her not toward neurosis but toward health. Anxiety is especially acute in the creative woman, Sarton acknowledges, as are frustration, fragmentation, and rage; but these feelings of being "rent in two" are precisely the raw material from which female art is sculpted, the female self validated.

Once her aberrance is accepted as a given, Sarton believes, the woman writer can set about the process of self-discovery that lies at the root of meaningful art, especially of poetry. For Sarton, the inspiration for such discovery comes from the muse, that crucial force that "throws the artist back upon herself," thereby facilitating an essential psychic exchange. In some respects, Sarton's muse resembles the classic, passive inspirational source of the male poet, the traditional female lover: she is mysterious, she cannot be pinned down, she "goes her way." As an alternate self to the woman poet, however, she also represents a vital, active aspect of the poetic process, a potent and often demonic force against which the poet is constantly pitted. Like Plato, Sarton believes that creative energy is often a product of irrationality, "frenzy," and that the primary source of this tumult is the "Honeyed muse."

Paralleling and complementing Sarton's theory of female creativity is her poetry itself—more than half a century's worth, written from the 1930's to the present. In several poems about the act of writing, she explores the ambivalence and power that inform the woman poet's struggle for creative identity. Other poems refine and elaborate her view of the muse: as lover, "sister of the mirage and echo"; as demon, she of the "cold Medusa eyes"; and as mother, the core of life and art, "the never-ending/ the perfect tree." The scope and nature of the female poetic process, for example, provide the theme of "My Sisters, O My Sisters," an early poem in four parts. In Section One, the poet discusses the difficulties the woman artist faces in her movement from silence to speech. As "strange monsters," a breed apart, Sarton alleges, women writers must set aside traditional female passivity, "the treasures of our silence," in order to uncover the "curious devouring pleasure" of creativity. Such sacrifices are often problematical, the poet admits, and she offers a catalog of "aberrant" women writers to support her argument: George Sand, who "loved too much"; Madame de Stael, "too powerful for men"; Madame de Sevigny, "too sensitive." Yet only through the self-imposed renunciation of traditional roles, she suggests, have authentic and autonomous female voices emerged: Emily Dickinson, who renounced society so that her art might flourish; Sappho, whose writing fed on "the extremity of spirit and flesh." The contemporary woman writer, Sarton continues, has much to learn from her forebears' attempts to break out of the prison of silence.

In the second stanza Sarton defines "that great sanity, that sun, the feminine power" as a revaluation of qualities typically associated with woman: fecundity, nurture, love. These "riches," which have heretofore sustained men and children, the poet continues, "these great powers/ which are ours alone," must now be used by women to fertilize their own creativity. As a model of the precarious balance for which women must strive, Sarton offers two biblical foremothers: Eve, the purveyor of female speech and knowledge; and Mary, giver of love and maternal nurture. The poet's complex task is to assimilate and affirm both branches of this full-bodied tree.

In the final section, Sarton submits female creativity, woman's solitary art, as a means of "re-joining the source" and thus attaining balance and clarity of vision. Taking to task herself and other women who have "asked so little of ourselves and men/ And let the Furies have their way," the poet calls upon her fellow women writers to claim as their own the "holy fountain" of creative imagination, transforming it into a wellspring of feminine song. Only by appropriating the "masculine" power of creation, the poet suggests, can women "come home to this earth," giving birth from its inner recesses to themselves as artists and as women, "fully human." "That great sanity . . . feminine power" will become a reality, Sarton concludes, when women "match men's greatness" with their own great works of art.

Although "My Sisters, O My Sisters" is Sarton's most overtly feminist poem, other works also describe the woman poet's efforts to assert a vital, autonomous voice. This struggle provides the underlying dialectic of "Poets and the Rain," which addresses the problem of poetic stasis and subsequent rejuvenation. In the first stanza the poet-persona is debilitated by the rain, which reflects her own inertia and despair; she speaks not as an active creator but as a passive receptacle for the words of others. "I will lie here alone and live your griefs," she declares. "I will receive you, passive and devout." Yet as she offers such disclaimers, the poet hears her own creative instincts stirring, faint but intelligible. Plagued by the "strange tides" running through her head, she distinguishes three voices, each of which presents her with a different vision of life and art. The first "singer" is an old man who "looks out and taunts the world, sick of mankind," in a voice "shriller than all the rest." In an interesting reversal of a stereotype, Sarton associates shrillness not with a hysterical "feminine" voice but with a "masculine" cry of pessimism and derision. Although part of her sympathizes with this doomsday prophet, she ultimately rejects the model that he offers. She will "dream a hunting song to make the old hawk scream," but she is not sufficiently moved by the old man's "bird-scream" to adopt such a voice herself.

Contrasted to this male voice are two female speakers whose visions, when combined, posit a more balanced and optimistic stance. The first woman represents the traditional female voice, that of nurturer, comforter, inspirer. Touched by the love that this woman's song exudes, the poet is inspired to "weave" her own "simple song"—to become, that is, herself a voice of feminine wisdom and maternal love. Despite the strong appeal of this choice, however, it is not enough for the creative woman: the singer is "frustrate"; her purity and nestbuilding are essentially passive postures. Despite her connection with the traditional female arts, or perhaps because of it, this woman's song is too simple and static a model for the poet.

The speaker is most moved by the "blurred" yet potent voice of a "great girl, the violent and strong," who asks "deep questions in her difficult song." This description recalls Denise Levertov's celebration in "In Mind" of a "turbulent moon-ridden girl . . . who knows strange songs"; or Louise Bogan's "The Dream," in which a "strong creature . . . another woman" leaps and shouts until her passive counterpart is prodded into life-saving speech and action. In Sarton's poem, the girl's "deep questions" and "difficult song," her fierce commitment to her art and her beliefs, offer the questing poet her most inspirational model. Although she realizes the difficulties inherent in such a vision, the persona determines that her voice, like the great girl's, will emerge from an emotional and intellectual complex, a "labyrinth of mind." At last, "rapt with delight," the poet recites her poem, "leaves of a tree/ Whose roots are hidden deep in mystery."

The special danger inherent in the woman poet's effort to "speak aloud" is also the subject of "Journey Toward Poetry." The poet's ordering of her imaginative experience, Sarton suggests, is analogous to a dangerous journey across foreign yet somehow familiar terrain, a haunting interior journey which produces ultimately for the chary traveler the ideal word or image or perspective. For Sarton, such a poetic voyage usually begins in anger, chaos, and concentrated violence. An array of intense and disturbingly surrealistic images accompanies the "beautiful mad exploration" that is poetry: hills winding and unwinding on a spool, rivers running away from their beds, geraniums bursting open to reveal "huge blood-red cathedrals," "marble graveyards" falling into the sea. One is reminded of William Butler Yeats's "blood-dimmed tide": "the center cannot hold," Sarton implies, when the imagination runs unchecked.

Yet the center does hold. Once the poet's errant imagination is stayed, her inner landscapes soften, become more pastoral. From disorder, to paraphrase Wallace Stevens, emerges a violent order, a silent stillness "where time not motion changes light to shadow." "Journey Toward Poetry" thus serves as Sarton's metaphoric depiction of the poetic process, fraught with danger for any poet, but intensely so for the woman. Beginning in rage or anxiety, at "white heat," the poet's mad racing ultimately gives way to that fruitful ripening of image and idea that inform the "birth of creation." Out of the stillness and solitude that inevitably follow the poet-terrorist's "mad exploration," the "composed imagination" transfigures the ordinary into the extraordinary.

For Sarton, such transfigurations are inspired by a female muse who appears in one of three manifestations: the erotic, the demonic, or the maternal. In her maternal guise, the muse is sometimes a human lover-visitant, sometimes a goddess or mythological figure. One recurring muse-figure is Aphrodite, Greek goddess of love and sexuality who is also linked to ancient Eastern mother-goddesses, such as Ishtar, Isis, and Astarte. Because her powers are both matriarchal and sexual, Sarton often envisages Aphrodite as a primordial goddess of fecundity, "one who holds the earth between her knees." Such a goddess informs "These Images Remain," an early sonnet sequence in which the poet confronts the sexual tension at the heart of the poet-muse relationship. As the epitome of female beauty and eroticism, Aphrodite inspires Sarton to acknowledge her own creative capacity; thus she acts as both muse and mirror for the poet. Yet the "silent consummation" between poet and muse is as precarious as quicksand, Sarton suggests in the fifth sonnet; any union with Aphrodite must be transitory. The poet imagines herself as a sculptor whose creation grows "out of deprivation . . . a self-denying rage," evoked by the longing which accompanies any interaction with the muse. Never will the muse be possessed, the poet realizes, but it is the effort to possess that results in the "masculine and violent joy of pure creation," in the sculptor's lasting images, "great and severe."

In "The Return of Aphrodite," Sarton describes another encounter with the erotic muse, here a "guiltless" goddess who advances "tranquil and transparent,/ To lay on mortal flesh her sacred mantle." The notion of transparency is central to Sarton's view of the muse as an extension of the self, a Medusa through whose eyes one can gaze upon one's mirror image. Unlike the poet's confrontations with Medusa, however, her exchange with Aphrodite is depicted in images of joy and tranquillity. The imagery also is richly erotic: as the mortal poet receives the goddess' "sacred mantle," the "green waves part," only to recede at once after the consummation, leaving in their wake a faint "stain" of light.

The muse for Sarton also appears as a demonic force with which the poet must reckon. Especially in poems about the demise of a relationship and the subsequent loss of creative energy, the muse appears as a fury who must be acknowledged and conquered. In the fourth sonnet of "A Divorce of Lovers," for example, Sarton accuses her lover of "chasing out the furies and the plagues of passion" rather than confronting them. In awe of these demons, the poet is nevertheless aware of the need for such "ghosts." When angels and furies "fly so near," she continues, "they come to force Fate at a crucial pass." This forcing of Fate, in turn, opens up an essential dialogue with the self that ultimately allows the poet to transform her violence and rage into creative energy.

In some poems, Sarton replaces angels and furies with animals, powerful forces that must be accepted and assimilated rather than denied or tamed. In "The Godhead as Lynx," for example, the poet gleans nourishment from the power of the beautiful yet cold mother-lynx, "Kyrie Eleison." The poet images herself as a child transfixed and transfigured by the "absolute attention" that informs the lynx's "golden gaze." Sarton often uses the metaphor of face-to-face confrontation to dramatize the dialogue between poet and muse; here the speaker, though only a child, challenges the lynx by meeting her "obsidian eyes." Rather than fearing confrontation and dreading its aftermath, the speaker undertakes such an experience on her own terms. She abandons her pride and rage before the lynx, a necessary gesture, Sarton implies, if the child is to rejoin the mother, the human to encounter the divine.

Sarton goes on to envision the lynx as a "prehuman" maternal goddess into whose womb the poet-daughter is tempted to crawl. Like ancient goddesses, however, the lynx is linked with both creation and destruction. Despite the strong appeal of her "essential fur," her maternal comfort, she lacks compassion; she is cruel, "lightning to cut down the lamb,/ A beauty that devours without qualm." In her dual guise as beneficent and demonic, therefore, the lynx evokes in the poet an ambivalent response: she is both appealing and frightening, and thus the tension with which the speaker approaches the powerful creature can be used for good or for ill. Through her encounter with the godhead as lynx, the poet's own strength is unleashed. She is forced to grow, at times to groan, but always to think in ways heretofore unknown.

The demonic muse whom Sarton most often invokes is Medusa, the mythological "monster" whose hair writhed with serpents, whose glance turned men to stone. Because Medusa could be viewed only indirectly and because of the mystery and danger associated with her powers, she symbolizes the woman poet's struggle *with* herself *for* herself, thus serving as both a source and a manifestation of female creativity. In "The Muse as Medusa" Sarton describes an encounter with this fury, meeting Medusa as she has met the lynx: one-on-one, "straight in the cold eye, cold." Despite her "nakedness" and vulnerability, the poet challenges the Medusa myth by transforming the legendary monster from a debilitating force to a source of creative rejuvenation. Medusa's stony gaze does not destroy; it transfigures, by "clothing" the naked speaker in the warm, protective garment of thought. "Forget the image," Sarton exults, for this Medusa renews through the paradoxical vitality of her silent presence. "Your silence is my ocean," the poet tells Medusa, "and even now it teems with life."

Yet Medusa herself is not the power responsible for such teeming life; this motion continues in spite of rather than because of her presence. Medusa, after all, "chose/ To abdicate by total lack of motion," and abdicating is something the speaker refuses to do. Instead, Sarton creates a fluid seascape of which Medusa is merely a part, her destructive fury put to use. In remaking Medusa in her own image, the poet acknowledges a vital female creativity and affirms the demonic part of herself. Medusa's face is *her* face, Sarton realizes; the monster's rage emerges from the poet's own "secret, self-enclosed, and ravaged place." As the poem ends, the poet thanks Medusa for her powerful "gift."

In one of her most provocative poems about female inspiration, "An Invocation to Kali," Sarton depicts the muse as both demon and mother, affirming the close connections that she perceives among demonic rage, maternal love, and female creativity. The poem opens with an epigraph from Joseph Campbell's *The Masks of God* (1959), a description of "the Black Goddess Kali, the terrible one of so many names." As an aspect of the woman's creative self, Kali is both inspiring and threatening. Her dual powers intrigue the poet, arousing her envy and admiration; yet an identification with Kali also evokes shame, anger, and fear—that peculiar blend of self-love and self-loathing of one who is both trapped and freed by her art. In Section One, Sarton sets forth this poem's central issue: how best to cope with the demands of the "Black Goddess." A "voracious animal," the Kali within is a violent force whose "brute power" arouses in the poet both apprehension and guilt. Ambivalent toward this potent but demonic force, the poet recognizes and fears its potential for debilitation and entrapment: "I am the cage where/ Poetry paces and roars." What then to do with Kali? the poet wonders. Is she to be murdered or lived with?

Part Two suggests the futility of any effort to kill the goddess; the anguish and rage which this "terrible one" promulgates is too awesome to be negated easily. Instead, the poet asserts, Kali "must have her hour." If the demon is denied, Sarton suggests, she will continue to inflict her bloody reign, but if she is faced "open-eyed," her explosive rage will be revealed for what it is: an emotion essential if creativity is to flourish. For every act of creation, Sarton insists, is preceded by destruction; "every creation is born out of the dark." Unless Kali does her "sovereign work," the poet continues, "the living child will be stillborn."

In the third and fourth sections, Sarton expands the image of Kali as a metaphor for the extreme social violence that has plagued Western culture, especially during the twentieth century. "The Concentration Camps" is packed with gruesome images depicting the tragic results of humanity's efforts to deny its furies, to pretend that violence and existential "dis-ease" do not exist. "Have we managed to fade them out like God?" the poet asks of Hitler's most poignant victims, children. In "turning away" from the "stench of bones," people have "tried to smother" fires that need desperately to burn, as vital reminders of what happens when violence is repressed and then unleashed. All are guilty, Sarton's indictment implies; refusing to meet demons is both a cultural and an individual sickness.

In Sarton's view, the solution to this widespread ailment is "to reckon with

Kali for better or worse," to accept her violence as an essential purging force. Thus the poet turns to the goddess' sacred altar, offering her final invocation to this "terrible one." "Help us to bring darkness into the light," she begs, to see anger and pain in a new way, as "the balance-wheel for our vulnerable, aching love." Only by confronting the Kali within, she believes, can the poet become a "gardener of the spirit," thereby claiming the goddess' "awesome power" as her own.

Whether she appears as an erotic, a demonic, or a maternal force, the female muse serves for Sarton as a key image by which to depict the woman poet's struggle for voice and autonomy. The intense encounter with the muse forces the poet to come to terms with her own power of creativity. This confrontation, in turn, leads the poet closer to the balanced, integrated state which Sarton posits as an ideal. In "Of the Muse," the final poem of *Halfway to Silence*, Sarton offers a powerful and moving assessment of her creative philosophy. Poetry comes not from lies, she insists, but from a "crude honesty" which makes the poet "a great, cracked,/ Wide-open door/ Into nowhere." When young, she continues, the muse was beyond her comprehension, but now she is grateful for her as one is grateful for light. This poem suggests a new direction for Sarton in its emphasis on the link between poetry and honesty, an area of particular concern to many contemporary feminist theorists and women poets. Women and writers have often been praised for lying, Adrienne Rich declares in *On Lies, Secrets, and Silence* (1979). Yet the unconscious, like the body, struggles for truth, Rich continues, and "the complexity and fecundity of poetry comes from the same struggle." Rich's statement might well be Sarton's, so accurately does it describe the theory implicit in "Of the Muse." Fighting to fulfill its desire for truth, Sarton suggests, along with Rich, the woman's poet's "fecund and complex" unconscious is awakened to vital insights and potent speech through her dialogue with that self who is also the muse. Once "misunderstood" as something to be subdued and conquered, the muse is now recognized by the aging poet as a force most closely analogous to light. "We do not thank the light," Sarton explains, "but rejoice in what we see/ Because of it." What she sees is the "crude" but honest power of poetry, its transformative potential. Through the muse, the poet concludes "all things are made new."

Letters from Maine continues this emphasis on the female muse by celebrating love and creative inspiration in old age. In the title work, a sequence of ten sonnetlike poems, Sarton pays homage to a "November muse" who brings her wisdom, clarity, and laughter. Although the poet and her lover-muse eventually separate, the force of her inspiration remains despite the poet's sense of loss: "everything stops but the poem." To encounter the muse as an aging woman poet seems to Sarton a special but difficult gift. In Poem Six she recalls a Nootka Indian legend about a "Primal Spirit," an old woman whom she greets, "deep inside myself," whenever she feels bereft: "Under the words you are my silence." The last poem in the sequence reveals Sarton's struggle to write against all odds, even when the muse appears as Medusa, playing "cruel games." Despite frequent obstacles, the poet expresses confidence in the reliability of her art.

The interwoven themes of creativity and aging recur in two poignant poems near the end of *Letters from Maine*, "Letters to Myself." In the first, Sarton acknowledges a "terrible fear, the fear of feeling" which besets her as she strives to write. Although the poet recognizes her capacity for self-healing, she relies as well on "the dark angel and the silent charm," her muse, to lead her from despair to hope. Through poetry, Sarton asserts in the second poem, one encounters one's deepest self and thereby is changed. Such transformations anticipate the final transformation caused by death itself. The poem ends with a statement of the poet's complex goal: "to sustain tension, yet discover poise,/ For this Magnificat of severe joys."

The Silence Now contains new and uncollected earlier poems, several of which reveal an ongoing concern with the perils and pleasures of silence, a theme central to Sarton's work and that of many other modern women poets. The title poem claims that silence is immense, a realization that motivates the poet to question what it signifies: "At the bottom of the silence what lies in wait?" Sarton responds to her own question by evoking images of transcience from the natural world—dying daffodils, irises almost open, clouds moving rapidly as the sky clears. Such visionary, silent encounters with the world of nature, "moments of pure joy," move the poet as deeply as does the practice of her art.

Two poems about her mother suggest the powerful influence this inspirational figure had on her poet-daughter. In "Dream" Sarton finds herself "inside my mother's death," unable to breathe and struggling to break out of the imprisoning tomb. Despite her horror, she realizes that she could never emerge from the tomb without her mother, for their lives are entangled, "twice-born mystery/ where the roots intertwine." Sarton recognizes the complexity of mother-daughter symbiosis and, finally, experiences it as liberating; when the speaker awakens, she is free.

"August Third" commemorates Sarton's mother on her birthday, as the aging poet recalls her elderly parent's "inexhaustible flame." Mabel Sarton certainly experienced fatigue, her daughter declares, but she knew how to push it aside in order to tend lilies in the early morning. In this poem's moving final stanzas Sarton calls upon her mother for life energy and sustenance: "Mother, be with me." Sarton realizes that she is now older than her mother was when she died, an awareness that somehow gives her strength to greet a new day. From her maternal muse the poet has learned a vital lesson, "never to fail life."

May Sarton is indeed a poet who has never failed life. Her fierce and complex explorations of the creative process, her stunning homages to various female muses, and her rich encounters with both her darkest and most joyful selves inspire those who read her work. Engaged fully with the paradoxes of writing and aging, living and dying, she offers through her work "a house of gathering," a poetic legacy of determined voice and powerful vision. Its rules are deceptively simple: "Work, love, be silent./ Speak."

Mary de Shazer

Other major works

LONG FICTION: *The Single Hound*, 1938; *The Bridge of Years*, 1946; *Shadow of a Man*, 1950; *A Shower of Summer Days*, 1952; *Faithful Are the Wounds*, 1955; *The Fur Person*, 1957; *The Birth of a Grandfather*, 1957; *The Small Room*, 1961; *Mrs. Stevens Hears the Mermaids Singing*, 1965; *Miss Pickthorn and Mr. Hare*, 1966; *Kinds of Love*, 1970; *As We Are Now*, 1973; *Crucial Conversations*, 1975; *A Reckoning*, 1978; *Anger*, 1982; *The Magnificent Spinster*, 1985; *The Education of Harriet Hatfield*, 1989.

SHORT FICTION: *Joanna and Ulysses*, 1963.

PLAY: *The Underground River*, 1947.

NONFICTION: *I Knew a Phoenix*, 1959; *Plant Dreaming Deep*, 1968; *Journal of a Solitude*, 1973; *A World of Light: Portraits and Celebrations*, 1976; *The House by the Sea*, 1977; *Recovering*, 1980; *Writings on Writing*, 1980; *May Sarton: A Self-Portrait*, 1982; *At Seventy: A Journal*, 1984; *Honey in the Hive: Judith Matlack, 1898-1982*, 1988; *After the Stroke: A Journal*, 1988.

CHILDREN'S LITERATURE: *Punch's Secret*, 1974; *A Walk Through the Woods*, 1976.

Bibliography

De Shazer, Mary K. *Inspiring Women: Reimagining the Muse*. Elmsford, N.Y.: Pergamon Press, 1986. This book analyzes contemporary American women poets' sources of creative inspiration, their female muses, a subject much discussed by May Sarton. It includes a substantial chapter on Sarton's poetry and poetic muses, a close reading of *Mrs. Stevens Hears the Mermaids Singing*, and an assessment of Sarton's working relationship with poet Louise Bogan.

Drake, William. *The First Wave: Women and Poets in America, 1915-1945*. New York: Macmillan, 1987. Drake considers the lives and accomplishments of more than twenty-five modernist poets. Sarton is examined in the last chapter as a member of this generation yet as a poet who speaks to and with a new generation as well. Useful as background material.

Evans, Elizabeth. *May Sarton, Revisited*. Boston: Twayne, 1989. This "timely retrospective" updates the 1973 Twayne series volume on Sarton by Agnes Sibley, *May Sarton*. A revaluation of Sarton's lifetime achievement, it offers a useful biographical chapter followed by careful analytical chapters on her work in four genres. Evans focuses on Sarton as a writer who speaks for and about women and as one who considers poetry her primary genre, despite the popular appeal of her novels and journals. Includes a chronology of Sarton's life and accomplishments.

Hunting, Constance, ed. *May Sarton: Woman and Poet.* Orono, Maine: National Poetry Foundation, 1982. Twenty-four strong articles on Sarton's novels, journals, and poetry comprise this collection. It includes an important essay by Carolyn Heilbrun on Sarton's journals and memoirs, as well as Mary Lydon's analysis of French influences on Sarton's writing style. It also contains a useful bibliography by Lenora P. Blouin of Sarton criticism through 1981.

Swartzlander, Susan, and Marilyn R. Mumford, eds. *Critical Essays on May Sarton.* Ann Arbor: University of Michigan Press, 1992. This excellent book contains sixteen essays that analyze both the texts and contexts of Sarton's writing. Informed by feminist literary criticism, these essays link Sarton to an explicitly female tradition and address such topics as issues of female identity in her aesthetic philosophy, her "lesbian consciousness," and patterns of reader response to her work. Nancy Weyant's survey of Sarton criticism since 1981 updates Lenora P. Blouin's earlier bibliography. The volume also includes Elizabeth Evans' critical edition of fifteen unpublished letters from Sarton to Louise Bogan. An essential source.

SIEGFRIED SASSOON

Born: Brenchley, Kent, England; September 8, 1886
Died: Heytesbury, England; September 1, 1967

Principal poetry

The Daffodil Murderer, 1913; *The Old Huntsman and Other Poems*, 1917; *Counter-Attack and Other Poems*, 1918; *War Poems*, 1919; *Picture Show*, 1920; *Recreations*, 1923; *Selected Poems*, 1925; *Satirical Poems*, 1926; *The Heart's Journey*, 1927; *Poems of Pinchbeck Lyre*, 1931; *The Road to Ruin*, 1933; *Vigils*, 1935; *Rhymed Ruminations*, 1940; *Poems Newly Selected 1916-1935*, 1940; *Collected Poems*, 1947; *Common Chords*, 1950; *Emblems of Experience*, 1951; *The Tasking*, 1954; *Sequences*, 1956; *Lenten Illuminations and Sight Sufficient*, 1958; *The Path to Peace*, 1960; *Collected Poems 1908-1956*, 1961; *An Octave*, 1966.

Other literary forms

Siegfried Sassoon is nearly as well known for his prose works as for his poetry. During the twenty years from 1926 to 1945, he spent most of his time working on the two trilogies that form the bulk of his work in prose. The first of these was the three-volume fictionalized autobiography published in 1937 as *The Memoirs of George Sherston*. It begins in *Memoirs of a Fox-Hunting Man* (1928), by recounting the life of a well-to-do young country squire in Georgian England up to his first experiences as an officer in World War I. The second volume, *Memoirs of an Infantry Officer* (1930), and the third, *Sherston's Progress* (1936), describe the young man's war experiences. In the later trilogy, Sassoon discarded the thinly disguised fiction of the Sherston novels and wrote direct autobiography, with a nostalgic look back at his pleasant pastoral life in prewar England in *The Old Century and Seven More Years* (1938) and *The Weald of Youth* (1942). In *Siegfried's Journey 1916-1920* (1945), Sassoon looks again at his own experiences during and immediately following the war. These autobiographical works are invaluable to the student of Sassoon's poetry because of the context they provide, particularly for the war poems.

Two other significant prose works should be mentioned. The first is Sassoon's *Lecture on Poetry*, delivered at the University of Bristol on March 16, 1939, in which Sassoon delineated what he considered to be the elements of good poetry. The second work is Sassoon's critical biography of the poet George Meredith, entitled simply *Meredith* (1948), which also suggests some of Sassoon's views on poetry.

Achievements

According to Bernard Bergonzi, Sassoon was the only soldier-poet to be widely read during the war itself. This gave Sassoon a unique opportunity to influence other war poets, which he did. Though his war poetry has been criticized for being mere description, for appealing to the senses only and not the imagination, for being uncontrolled emotion without artistic restraint, there can be no doubt that Sassoon's poetry represented a complete break with the war poetry of the past in tone, technique, and subject matter. With uncompromising realism and scathing satire Sassoon portrayed the sufferings of the front-line soldier and the incompetency of the staff for the express purposes of convincing his readers to protest continuation of the war. His *Counter-Attack and Other Poems* volume was nearly suppressed because of poems such as "The General," which broke the prohibition against criticizing those in charge of the war effort.

Unquestionably, Sassoon's realistic subject matter and diction influenced other poets, most notably his friend Wilfred Owen, whose poetry was post-humously published by Sassoon in 1920; but Sassoon failed to influence later poetry because, as John Johnston notes, his war poetry was all negative—he provided no constructive replacement for the myths he had destroyed. Nor did Sassoon influence the 1930's because, according to Michael Thorpe, he was still a prisoner of war, and through his autobiographies he retreated from the political struggle of W. H. Auden and Stephen Spender and others into his own earlier years.

When in the 1950's Sassoon finally did have something positive to offer, no one was willing to listen. He was no longer well known or critically acknowl-edged. Certainly his future reputation will rest on the war poems; but in his religious poems of the 1950's, Sassoon did achieve a style of simple expression, compact brevity, and concrete imagery with a universally appealing theme, and this should be noted as a remarkable though largely unrecognized achievement.

Biography

Siegfried Lorraine Sassoon was born in the Kentish weald in 1886, the second of three sons of Alfred Ezra Sassoon and Theresa Georgina Thor-nycroft. His father was descended from a long line of wealthy Jewish mer-chants and bankers who, after wandering through Spain, Persia, and India, had come to settle in England. The family was proud of its orthodoxy, and Siegfried's father was the first to marry outside the faith. Siegfried's mother, in contrast, was an artist, the close relative of three well-known sculptors, and a member of the landed gentry. The marriage was a failure, and Alfred Sas-soon left when Siegfried was five, leaving the younger Sassoon to be reared by his mother as an Anglican.

Siegfried had no formal schooling as a child, though from the age of nine to fourteen he learned from private tutors and a German governess. In 1902 he attended Marlborough, and in 1905 he entered Clare College, Cambridge.

Sassoon's temperament was not disciplined enough for scholarly pursuits; he began by reading law, switched to history, and ultimately left Cambridge without a degree. He returned to Kent where, on an inherited income of five hundred pounds a year, he was able to devote his energies to fox-hunting, racing, and writing poetry. Sassoon loved the pastoral beauty of the Kentish downs and attempted to portray it in a number of dreamy, sentimental lyrics. Between the ages of nineteen and twenty-six, Sassoon had nine volumes of poetry privately published, before he enjoyed a mild success with *The Daffodil Murderer* in 1913. The poem was chiefly intended as a parody of John Masefield's *The Everlasting Mercy*, but Sassoon's poem had a strong human appeal of its own. By this time Sassoon had been befriended by Edward Marsh, the editor of *Georgian Poetry*. Marsh encouraged Sassoon's literary endeavors and persuaded him to come to London in May, 1914, where Sassoon began to move in the literary world and to meet such notable authors as Rupert Brooke. Sassoon, however, felt unhappy and without a sense of purpose, and when he enlisted in the army on August 3, 1914 (two days before England entered the war), it was to escape a sterile existence.

Sassoon's early life had been extremely sheltered, even pampered, and it was a very immature twenty-eight-year-old who went to war, totally unprepared for what he would find. After convalescence from injuries received in a fall during cavalry training, he accepted a commission and went through training as an infantry officer. Thus he did not arrive in France until November, 1915, where he became transport officer for the First Battalion of the Royal Welch Fusiliers. Here he met and befriended the poet Robert Graves. In *Goodbye to All That* (1929), Graves describes his first meeting with Sassoon, and relates how, when he showed Sassoon his first book of poems, *Over the Brazier* (1916), Sassoon, whose early war poems were idealistic, had frowned and said that war should not be written about in such a realistic way. Graves, who had been in France six months, remarked that Sassoon had not yet been in the trenches.

Graves already knew what Sassoon would soon discover, indeed what all the British troops in France were coming to feel: growing disillusionment at the frustration and the staggering casualties of trench warfare. There were 420,000 British casualties in the Somme offensive beginning on July 1, 1916—an offensive that gained virtually nothing. The Somme was Sassoon's most bitter experience in the trenches; after it, he would never write the old kind of poetry again.

In spite of his pacifist leanings, Sassoon distinguished himself in the war. Called "Mad Jack" by his troops, Sassoon was awarded the Military Cross and recommended for the Distinguished Service Order for his exploits in battle: after a raid at Mametz, he took it upon himself to bring back the wounded; in the Somme in early July he single-handedly occupied a whole section of an enemy trench, after which he was found in the trench, alone, reading a book of poetry. Ill with gastric fever in late July, he was sent home for three months, where he worked on poems to be included in *The Old Huntsman and Other Poems*.

While in England, Sassoon met Lady Ottoline Morrell and her liberal husband Philip, at whose home he spoke with such pacifists as Bertrand Russell, listened to open criticism of the war, and heard of Germany's peace overtures and the impure motives of members of parliament who wanted the war to continue.

Sassoon returned to active service in France in February, 1917, but in April he was wounded in the battle of Arras and sent home again. Haunted by nightmares of violence and by what the pacifists were saying, Sassoon resolved to protest the war on a grand scale. In July, in a remarkable move, risking public disgrace and military court-martial, Sassoon refused to return to active duty, and wrote a formal declaration of protest to his commanding officer, which was reproduced in the press and which Russell arranged to have mentioned in the House of Commons. In his letter, Sassoon charged that the war was being deliberately prolonged by the politicians for ignoble purposes, even though there was a chance for a negotiated settlement with Germany, thus leading the men at the front line to be slaughtered needlessly. Sassoon hoped to be court-martialed, so that his protest would have propaganda value. To his dismay, however, the official reaction was largely to minimize the letter. In a moment of despair, Sassoon flung his Military Cross into the Mersey River and vowed to continue his protest.

At that point, Graves stepped in. Graves agreed with Sassoon's letter, but considered the gesture futile and feared for Sassoon's personal welfare. Graves arranged to have Sassoon appear before a medical board and, chiefly on Graves's testimony, Sassoon was found to be suffering from shell shock. The incident was closed, and Sassoon was sent to Craiglockhart hospital in Edinburgh, where Dr. W. H. R. Rivers became his counselor and friend, and where in August he met the brilliant young poet Wilfred Owen. Owen knew and idolized Sassoon as the author of *The Old Huntsman and Other Poems* (which had appeared in May), and Sassoon's encouragement and insistence upon realism had greatly influenced him. At Craiglockhart, during the autumn of 1917, Sassoon composed many of the poems of *Counter-Attack and Other Poems*, which was published the following year.

Owen returned to active duty in November, and Sassoon, feeling that he was betraying his troops at the front by staying away in comfort, returned to duty a few weeks later. He went first to Ireland, then to Egypt, where he became a Captain, then back to France in May. On July 15, Sassoon, returning from an attack on a German machine gun, was wounded in the head by one of his own sentries. He was sent to a London hospital, where he spent the rest of the war.

After the war, Sassoon retreated from the active life, becoming more and more contemplative (he had always been introspective and solitary) until he acquired a reputation as a virtual hermit. Immediately after the war, he joined the Labor Party, and became editor of the literary pages of the *Daily Herald*, where he published satirical pieces with a socialist point of view. His satire of the 1920's, however, was uneasy and awkward, stemming from the fact that the issues of the day were not as clear-cut as the right and wrong about the war had been. Besides, he was not really sure of himself, feeling a need to explore his past life and find some meaning in it. Still, as the 1930's grew darker, Sassoon wrote poems warning of the horror of chemical and biological warfare. No one seemed to want to listen, however, and Sassoon, disillusioned, forsook "political" poetry completely. In part, the autobiographies that he worked on in those years were a rejection of the modern world and an idealization of the past. In part, too, they were an effort to look inside himself, and that same urge characterizes most of his later poetry, which is concerned with his personal spiritual struggle and development.

Thus the incidents of Sassoon's later life were nearly all spiritual. Only a few isolated events are of interest: in 1933, he finally married; he had a son, George, but Sassoon kept his personal relationships private, never mentioning them in his poetry. During World War II, Sassoon's home was requisitioned for evacuees, and, later, fifteen hundred American troops were quartered on his large estate. After the war, Sassoon remained very solitary, and appears to have cultivated his image as the "hermit of Heytesbury." When his volumes of poetry in the 1950's appeared, they were largely ignored by critics and public alike. The fiery war poet had outlived his reputation, but he had reached a great personal plateau: on August 14, 1957, Sassoon was received into the Catholic Church at Downside Abbey. His last poems, appearing in a privately published collection, *An Octave*, on his eightieth birthday (a year before his death), display a serene and quiet faith.

Analysis

In 1939, Siegfried Sassoon delineated his views on poetry in a lecture given at Bristol college. While what he said was not profound or revolutionary, it did indicate the kind of poetry Sassoon liked and tried to write, at least at that time. First, Sassoon said, poetry should stem from inspiration, but that inspiration needed to be tempered by control and discipline—by art. Second, the best poetry is simple and direct—Sassoon disliked the tendency toward complexity initiated by T. S. Eliot and Ezra Pound. Third, Sassoon held the Romantic view that poetry should express true feeling, should speak the language of the heart. Fourth, poetry should contain strong *visual* imagery, the best of which was drawn from nature. Finally, the subject matter of the best poetry was not political (again, he was reacting against the avowedly political poetry of Auden and his associates), but was rather personal, and this examination of self led Sassoon to write spiritual poetry.

A review of Sassoon's poetry will reveal, however, that even in his best poems he did not always follow all of these precepts, and that in his worst poems he seldom followed any. Sassoon's worst poems are most certainly his earliest ones. Sassoon's prewar lyric verses are lush and wordy, in weak imitation of A. C. Swinburne and the Pre-Raphaelites, but full of anachronisms and redundancies. Some, such as "Haunted" and "Goblin Revel," are purely escapist; Lewis Thorpe suggests that Sassoon was looking for escape from his own too-comfortable world. The best thing about these early poems is their interest in nature—an interest that Sassoon never lost and that provided him with concrete images in later pieces. The best poems that Sassoon wrote before the war, *The Daffodil Murderer* and "The Old Huntsman," abandon the poetic diction for a colloquial style, and "The Old Huntsman" reveals a strong kinship with nature.

Sassoon's early, idealistic war poetry is characterized by an abstract diction and generalized imagery. He was writing in the "happy warrior" style after the manner of Rupert Brooke's famous sonnet sequence, and was even able to write of his brother's death early in the war as a "victory" and his ghost's head as "laureled." Perhaps the best example of these early poems is "Absolution," written before Sassoon had actually experienced the war. Sassoon romanticizes war, speaking of the glorious sacrifice of young comrades in arms who go off to battle as "the happy legion," asserting that "fighting for our freedom, we are free." The poem is full of such abstractions, but no concrete images. Its language is often stilted and archaic ("Time's but a golden wind"), and it is the sort of thing that Sassoon soon put behind him.

Edward Marsh, after reading some of Sassoon's earlier poetry, had told him to write with his eye directly on the object. As Sassoon began to experience the horrors of trench warfare, he did exactly that. His poems became increasingly concrete, visual, and realistic, his language became increasingly more colloquial, and his tone became more and more bitter as the war went on. Early in 1916, he wrote "Golgotha," "The Redeemer," and "A Working Party," in which he tried to present realistically the sufferings of the common soldier. Such realistic depiction of the front lines characterized one of two main types of war poetry that Sassoon was to write in the next few years. The best example of sheer naturalistic description is "Counter-Attack," the title poem of Sassoon's most popular and most scathing volume of poetry. "Counter-Attack" begins with a description of the troops who, having taken an enemy trench, begin to deepen it with shovels. They uncover a pile of dead bodies and rotting body parts—"naked sodden buttocks, mats of hair,/ Bulged, clotted heads."

The horror of this description is without parallel, but where Sassoon really excels is in his realistic portrayal of the *psychological* effects of the war. Perhaps his best poem in this vein is "Repression of War Experience" (from *Counter-Attack and Other Poems*). The poem, in the form of an interior monologue, explores a mind verging on hysteria, trying to distract itself and maintain control while even the simplest, most serene events—a moth fluttering too close to a candle flame—bring nightmarish thoughts of violence into the persona's mind. In the garden he hears ghosts, and as he sits in the silence he can hear only the guns. In the end, his control breaks down; he wants to rush out "and screech at them to stop—I'm going crazy;/ I'm going stark, staring mad because of the guns."

Sassoon was not merely presenting realistic details; he was being deliberately didactic, trying to use his poetry to incite a public outcry against the war. When home on leave he had been appalled by the jingoistic ignorance and complacency on the home front. Sassoon's second main type of war poetry made a satirical attack on these civilians, on those who conducted the war, and on the irresponsible press that spread the lying propaganda. Justly the most famous of these poems is "They" (*The Old Huntsman and Other Poems*), in which Sassoon demolishes the cherished civilian notion that the war was divinely ordained and that the British were fighting on God's side. Sassoon presents a pompous Bishop declaring that, since the "boys" will have fought "Anti-Christ," none will return "the same" as he was. The irony of this statement is made clear when the "boys" return quite changed: blind, legless, syphilitic. The Bishop can only remark, "The ways of God are strange." "They" caused a great outcry in England by ruthlessly attacking the Church for forsaking the moral leadership it should have provided.

"They" also illustrates Sassoon's favorite technique in satire: concentration of his ironic force in the last line of the poem. This kind of "knock-out punch" may be seen most vividly in the poem "The One-Legged Man" (from *The Old Huntsman and Other Poems*), which describes a soldier, discharged from the war, watching the natural beauty of the world in autumn and considering the bright, comfortable years ahead. The poem ends with the man's crushingly ironic thought, "Thank God they had to amputate!"

Certainly there are flaws in Sassoon's war poetry. Some of the verses are nothing more than bitter invectives designed merely to attack a part of his audience, such as "Glory of Women," "Blighters," and "Fight to the Finish." Even the best poems often lack the discipline and order that Sassoon himself later advanced as one main criterion of poetry. Further, Sassoon almost never got beyond his feelings about immediate experiences to form theoretical or profound notions about the broader aspects of the war. Sassoon himself realized this lack when in 1920 he brought out his slain friend Wilfred Owen's war poetry, which converted war experiences into something having universal meaning.

The war poetry, however, has a number of virtues as well. It uses simple, direct, and clear expression that comes, as Sassoon advocated, from the heart. Further, it uses vivid pictures to express the inexpressible horror of the trenches. "The Dug Out" (*Picture Show*) is an example of Sassoon's war poetry at its best. In its eight lines, Sassoon draws a clear picture of a youth sleeping in an awkward and unnatural position. The simple, colloquial language focuses on the emotional state of the speaker, and much is suggested by what is left unsaid. The speaker's nerves are such that he can no longer bear the sight of the young sleeper because, as he cries in the final lines, "You are too young to fall asleep for ever;/ And when you sleep you remind me of the dead." Arthur Lane compares such poems, in which the ironic effect is achieved through the dramatic situation more than through imagery, to those in the *Satires of Circumstance* (1914) of Sassoon's idol, Thomas Hardy, suggesting an influence at work.

Perhaps the culmination of Sassoon's attempt to transcend his war experience is the much-admired lyric "Everyone Sang" (from *Picture Show*). It is a joyous lyric expressing a mood of relief and exultation, through the imagery of song and of singing birds. Sassoon seems to have been expressing his own relief at having survived: "horror/ Drifted away." Lane calls these lines "pure poetry" of "visionary power," comparing them to William Wordsworth and William Blake. He might have also mentioned Henry Vaughan, Sassoon's other idol, whose path toward poetry of a very personal spirituality Sassoon was soon to follow.

Unquestionably, it is for his war poetry that Sassoon is chiefly admired. Still, he lived for nearly fifty years after the armistice, and what he wrote in that time cannot be disregarded. He first flirted with socialism after the war; "Everyone Sang" may be intended to laud the coming utopian society. Then he attempted satiric poetry during the 1920's, which must be regarded as a failure. His targets varied from the upper classes to political corruption and newspapers, but the poetry is not from the heart; the satire is too loud and not really convincing. Michael Thorpe points out the wordiness of Sassoon's style in these satires, together with the length of his sentences. One blatant example is "Lines Written in Anticipation of a London Paper Attaining a Guaranteed Circulation of Ten Million Daily." Even the title is verbose, but note the wordy redundancy of the lines:

> Were it not wiser, were it not more candid,
> More courteous, more consistent with good sense,
> If I were to include all, all who are banded
> Together in achievement so immense?

Though he soon abandoned the satiric mode, Sassoon did maintain what Joseph Cohen calls the role of prophet that he had assumed in the war years, by continually warning, through *The Road to Ruin* and *Rhymed Ruminations*, of the coming disaster of World War II; but his total despair for the modern world is expressed in "Litany of the Lost" (1945), wherein, with the ominous line "Deliver us from ourselves," Sassoon bid farewell to poetry of social commentary.

By now he was more interested in his spiritual quest. Next to his war poems, Sassoon's poems of religious searching are his most effective. The quest begins with "The Traveller to His Soul" (1933), in which Sassoon asks, as the "problem which concerns me most," the question "Have I got a soul?" He spends over twenty years trying to answer the question. His work, beginning with *The Heart's Journey* and *Vigils*, is concerned with exploration of self and uncertainty about the self's place in the universe, with increasing questioning about what lies behind creation. With *Rhymed Ruminations*, Sassoon ends the 1930's on a note of uneasiness and uncertainty.

The questions are answered in the three volumes—*Common Chords*, *Emblems of Experience*, and *The Tasking*—which were combined to make the book *Sequences*. In the poem "Redemption" —(from *Common Chords*) Sassoon yearns for a vision of the eternal, which he recognizes as existing beyond his senses. Sassoon's lines recall Vaughan's mystical visions when he asks for "O but one ray/ from that all-hallowing and eternal day." In *The Tasking*, Sassoon reached what Thorpe calls a spiritual certainty, and his best poems in that volume succeed more clearly than the war poems in satisfying Sassoon's own poetic criteria as expressed in 1939. In "Another Spring," Sassoon speaks in simple, direct, and compact language about feelings of the heart—an old man's emotions upon witnessing what may be his last spring. The natural imagery is concrete and visual as well as auditory, concentrating upon "some crinkled primrose leaves" and "a noise of nesting rooks." Though the final three lines of the poem add a hint of didacticism, the poem succeeds by leaving much unsaid about the eternal rebirth of nature and its implications for the old man and the force behind the regenerative cycle of nature. It is a fine poem, like many in *The Tasking*, with a simple, packed style that makes these poems better as art, though doomed to be less familiar than the war poems.

Jay Ruud

Other major works

LONG FICTION: *The Memoirs of George Sherston*, 1937 (comprising *Memoirs of a Fox-Hunting Man*, 1928; *Memoirs of an Infantry Officer*, 1930; and *Sherston's Progress*, 1936).

NONFICTION: *The Old Century and Seven More Years*, 1938; *Lecture on Poetry*, 1939; *The Weald of Youth*, 1942; *Siegfried's Journey 1916-1920*, 1945; *Meredith*, 1948; *Siegfried Sassoon Diaries, 1920-1922*, 1981; *Siegfried Sassoon Diaries, 1915-1918*, 1983; *Siegfried Sassoon Diaries, 1923-1925*, 1985.

Bibliography

Hart-Davis, Rupert, ed. *Siegfried Sassoon Diaries: 1915-1918*. London: Faber & Faber, 1983. This compilation of Sassoon's diaries offers a rare insight into his mind as he went through the terrors of World War I, reporting on it through his poetry. Contains good background information and is supplemented by an adequate index.

Lane, Arthur E. *An Adequate Response: The War Poetry of Wilfred Owen and Siegfried Sassoon.* Detroit: Wayne State University Press, 1972. Lane highlights the use of satire and parody as he analyzes Sassoon's war verse. Contends that Sassoon and others, when faced with the horrors of trench warfare, were charged with creating a new mode of expression since the traditional modes proved inadequate.

Mallon, Thomas. "The Great War and Sassoon's Memory." In *Modernism Revisited*, edited by Robert Kiely. Cambridge, Mass.: Harvard University Press, 1983. Attempts to isolate the effect that World War I had on Sassoon's mind and memory, thus distancing him from life. Mallon's studies concentrate on Sassoon's "twice" written memoirs of his early life.

Spear, Hilda D. "An Unrecognized War Poem by Siegfried Sassoon." *Four Decades of Poetry: 1890-1930* 1 (1976): 141-142. In this brief article, Spear takes a detailed look at two poems by Sassoon, "Haunted" and "The Death Bed." She plots similarities throughout, showing that even though normally separated, they were in fact both taken from Sassoon's war experiences.

Thorpe, Michael. *Siegfried Sassoon: A Critical Study.* London: Oxford University Press, 1967. Thorpe's book follows the life and works of Sassoon, concentrating on his overall work, not merely his "war poetry," with particular attention being paid to his basic underlying framework of ideas. An index and a bibliography augment the text.

JAMES SCHUYLER

Born: Chicago, Illinois; November 9, 1923
Died: New York, New York; April 12, 1991

Principal poetry

Salute, 1960; *May 24th or So*, 1966; *Freely Espousing*, 1969; *A Sun Cab*, 1972; *The Crystal Lithium*, 1972; *Hymn to Life*, 1974; *Song*, 1976; *The Fireproof Floors of Witley Court: English Songs and Dances*, 1976; *The Home Book: Prose and Poems 1951-1970*, 1977 (Trevor Winkfield, editor); *The Morning of the Poem*, 1980; *A Few Days*, 1985; *Selected Poems*, 1988.

Other literary forms

James Schuyler wrote (or cowrote) three novels. Beginning with *Alfred and Guinevere* (1958), the novels deal with the upper middle class and show a good ear for the comic trivialities of ordinary conversation, whether of children and adolescents, sophisticated young adults, or middle-aged couples. They also demonstrate, with their precision in naming, Schuyler's connoisseur's eye for furniture, design, and objects used or displayed in the household. The satiric *A Nest of Ninnies* (1969), cowritten with John Ashbery, lacks the plot and fully developed characters of *What's for Dinner?* (1978), his most substantial novel, giving rich evidence of true command of the form as it traces an alcoholic's recovery in a mental hospital, her husband's simultaneous affair with a widowed friend, and the progress of several other patients on short-term stays in the hospital.

Three of Schuyler's plays have been produced: the one-act pieces *Presenting Jane* (1952) and *Shopping and Waiting* (1953), and *Unpacking the Black Trunk*, another collaboration with a fellow poet (Kenward Elmslie), produced off-Broadway in 1965. He wrote the libretto ("mostly collage from newspapers," he says) for *A Picnic Cantata* (1954), for which the writer Paul Bowles composed the music (for two pianos, percussion, and four women's voices); it was recorded by Columbia Records.

Like fellow New York poets Ashbery and Frank O'Hara, he also wrote art criticism—particularly for *Art News*, where he served for a time as associate editor.

Achievements

Schuyler was a keen observer of the most intimate details of the world around him and of the sensations they evoked in him. His poetry captures those detailed impressions and sensations, however ephemeral they may be. This very ephemerality is the singular distinction of his world, particularly in his presentation of nature. The individual poem lives not so much as a perfected piece of art, frozen under glass; rather, it shimmers with movement

and conveys a sense of being nearly as ephemeral as the impressions it records. Sometimes, of course, the impressions and mood are so fleeting as to
leave the reader with virtually nothing but random actions and details—or
even only words. This is the danger of Schuyler's method—one which its
great propounder, Frank O'Hara, did not always steer clear of himself. Thus,
some poems read as little more than notebook jottings.

Yet the method is also responsible for the brilliance of his two long poems, "Hymn to Life" and "The Morning of the Poem" (the title poem of
the volume for which he was awarded the Pulitzer Prize in 1981). These poems ramble, it is true, down the streams of Schuyler's consciousness, across
several weeks' time, from place to place, subject to subject, mood to mood.
Yet each attains a remarkable unity through the skill and exactness with which
Schuyler has captured his own voice, developed over the course of a rather
short career (barely two decades of serious publishing), in order to penetrate
and reveal his own mental and emotional states. His highly individual, warmly
personal, frankly intimate voice is characterized by unforced humor, gentle
self-deprecation, eagerness, equivocation, wonder, doubt, fascination. This is
the voice, as well, of a series of simple and tender love poems, joyful and
physical without being actually erotic, addressing another man with the greatest ease and naturalness imaginable. Schuyler's achievements in evoking the
processes of nature, love, and mind are praiseworthy, not only for producing
such thought-provoking and appealing major works as the two long poems but
also for many shorter ones that are sure to enchant readers over the years.
Schuyler won several awards other than the Pulitzer Prize, including the Frank
O'Hara Prize from *Poetry* in 1969; he received grants including a National
Endowment for the Arts grant and an Academy of American Poets fellowship.

Biography

Born in Chicago to a family with extensive roots in America, James Schuyler grew up in Washington, D.C., Buffalo, and East Aurora, New York, the
family seat to which he returned. He attended Bethany College in West Virginia, served in the Navy in World War II, and worked for Voice of America
in New York City before traveling to Italy, where he attended the University
of Florence and lived in W. H. Auden's house in Ischia, typing some of the
elder poet's manuscripts (as he notes in his obituary poem, "Wystan Auden"). After he returned to New York in the early 1950's, he became involved in art and poetry circles and took a curatorial position in the Department of Circulating Exhibitions at the Museum of Modern Art, organizing a
number of shows. He also served as associate editor of *Art News*, for which
Frank O'Hara and John Ashbery also worked; together, and with a number
of other young poets, they changed the poetry scene in New York and became a major force in contemporary American poetry. Close friends as well

as colleagues, they often have referred to one another in their books and poems and sometimes collaborated. Painters and musicians are included in this group; various artist friends of Schuyler are not only mentioned in his poems but have contributed cover illustrations for several of his books. Schuyler suffered personal traumas in the 1970's, and his recovery from a nervous breakdown is recorded in poems in *The Morning of the Poem*; he also sustained severe burns after falling asleep while smoking in bed. Nevertheless, in the late 1970's he began reading publicly for the first time. Schuyler died in New York City in 1991 after suffering a stroke.

Analysis

James Schuyler was a master of subtle changes—in growing things, in weather, in time of day or year, in moods and thoughts. These he conveyed appropriately, without big effects, sudden bursts of insight, or harsh contrasts. Rather, his poems have the shimmering magical quality of familiar scenes and objects rendered in watercolor landscapes or still lifes, but they are anything but still: even his most quiet and peaceful scenes contain movement, however nearly imperceptible. Such constant, inevitable movement is the manifestation of life for Schuyler, and through his poetry the reader too gains a more intense appreciation for the many wonders and delights of even the smallest details in this life, once a moment is taken to observe them.

In an interview, Schuyler once said that to him, "much of my poetry is as concerned with looking at things and trying to transcribe them as painting is. This is not generally true of poetry." Evidence of Schuyler's affinities to painting (which doubtless stem largely from his friendship with many painters as well as his own work in the art world) are abundant throughout his work, in his attention to color, light, texture, and other visual effects.

Besides being "very visual," his work also "seems to be especially musical," he goes on to say. Indeed, he counted important composers such as Virgil Thomson and Ned Rorem among his friends and wrote about music from Johannes Brahms and Sergei Rachmaninoff to Janis Joplin and Carly Simon. His is not the music of the conventional sonneteer, however, although he made an obligatory gesture or two in that direction. Rather, his poetry, almost without exception, ignores regular rhyme and meter in favor of free verse, appropriate for his emphasis on endless change. His styles of free verse change radically too, from lines of only two or three syllables in his self-styled "skinny poems," providing a slow, even, almost hesitant, occasionally fragmented pace appropriate for the meditative stance of some of these poems, to lines as long as each individual sentence unit requires (in "The Cenotaph"), to lines a page wide or more in the long poems. Line breaks are often capricious, but this very unpredictability allows him some splendid effects. For example, the minimally punctuated "Buttered Greens" has lines which make sense in one way, until the next line indicates that the last part of the preceding line is meant not as a completion of the preceding thought but as the beginning of a new statement: "inside all/ is not con-/ tent, yet/ the chance/ of it is/ there, free." A reader automatically assumes that "free" modifies "chance," but the next line suggests that it modifies the botanical noun: "there, free/ leaves fall." Often he abandons punctuation altogether, and a whole series of sensory impressions flows down or across the page as unmediated sensory input ("A Sun Cab"). Sentence fragments, composed of nouns, adjectives, and prepositional phrases, are frequent in many of these shorter poems, reminiscent of William Carlos Williams, whom Schuyler acknowledged as an early influence.

Yet musical aspects are present in occasional devices of structure and sound. Words or images are repeated, like leitmotifs; recurring themes and images are particularly important in the long poems, where depiction of rain or of sites in Washington, D.C. acts both as a cohesive device and as a counterpoint to other concerns in the poem. His free-verse lines often emulate the startling and open structures of much modern music. Finally, Schuyler does not neglect the traditional musical devices of sound; pleasing patterns of alliteration, assonance, consonance, and even exact rhyme (though usually internal and never long-sustained) appear casually in occasional poems such as "Song" and "Just before fall."

Most of his poems purport to do no more than map the stream of his consciousness, whether it consists chiefly of external impressions which engage his full attention or of thoughts and feelings and whatever sensory recollections they invoke. Sometimes it is a combination of the two—external impressions giving rise to memories, which are in turn interrupted by more sensory input from the present moment. Schuyler's is very much a poetry of the present. Nearly every poem begins directly in the present tense, often indicating the setting of place, time, weather; recollections of the past may intrude, described in the past tense as appropriate, but their appearance is strongly grounded in the immediacy of the present moment, rather than being a meditation on "remembrance of things past" or "emotion recollected in tranquillity" undertaken as an end in itself.

Time is certainly a central theme for Schuyler, but with an emphasis quite unlike that of most other poets. It passes as quickly (or slowly) for him as for another, but he does not bemoan its passing. He is not without regrets, but these are for friends who have died, lovers who have left: he accepts his move ahead into age, not with resignation but as merely another stage of life, for "Life will change and/ I am part of it and/ will change too."

Such an attitude informs his two longest poems, "Hymn to Life" and "The Morning of the Poem." Each embraces and celebrates change, the prevailing force in his work, the dominant characteristic of all life itself. In the earlier poem, Schuyler takes the reader with him along the paths of his mind and experiences, recording his various thoughts and sensory impressions as time moves on. It begins the day before spring (that is, in March), then moves imperceptibly into April and May. These shifts occur not with an abrupt, secretarial ripping-off of the old month's calendar page but with the gradualism of nature itself: this seventeen-page poem is not broken into sections as the time passes but reveals each new month's presence only in mid-line, appropriately for the subtle recognition of something new in the air, a change that has occurred while one was watching but was perhaps momentarily distracted, watching the many wonderful details all around, so exquisitely conveyed in this poem.

Such unremarked changes, so lovingly dwelt on, are Schuyler's stock-in-trade, for the times *between* (parts of the year or the day) are his favorite poetic subjects. "Song," for example, concentrates on the hour of sunset. It begins: "The light lies layered in the trees" (with melodious alliteration and use of long vowel sounds). Then the sun sets, "not sharply or at once," but in "a stately progress down the sky." Other details around him, however, attract his attention: "Traffic sounds and/ bells resound . . . the grass is violent green." Several color sensations then yield to the sound of a car starting up, as the visual sense surrenders to darkness. Two short lines ("A horsefly vanishes./ A smoking cigarette.") capture the sense of increasing darkness: the normally quite visible insect is lost to sight while the glowing of the cigarette, normally not noticeable in daylight, appears, contrasting with the lack of light around it. Finally, the leaves merge, "discriminated barely/ in light no longer layered," because of the departure of the sun's light.

This poem, like so many others by Schuyler, simply presents a sequence of sensory images, vividly capturing the various components of a particular moment as it is experienced. Schuyler does not pretend to deal with the earth-shattering problems of humanity: that becomes editorial writing, he has said. Consequently, his poetry has often been regarded as trivial. Indeed, many of his poems do fail to register any significant impression. The comic criticism of himself that he quotes in "The Morning of the Poem"—"All he cares about are leaves and/ flowers and weather"—has validity, but not at all as a criticism. These subjects serve as indicators of his own understanding of life—its beauty, its transience, its variability, qualities that every human being must understand and accept to come fully to terms with existence as well as with such major human concerns as love and death.

These important concerns are not in the least absent from Schuyler's work. He often confronts death as he recalls or writes elegies for friend and fellow poet Frank O'Hara, other friends and lovers (Bill Aalto, his first lover, who died of leukemia after they had broken up), and musicians as diverse as Libby Holman, Janis Joplin, and Bruno Walter. Their deaths may be violent or gentle, but Schuyler accepts them with deepest serenity. He portrays love as "quiet/ ecstasy and sweet content." A lovely series in *Hymn to Life* records with utmost simplicity such joys as lying on the beach beside his lover or eagerly awaiting his return from a trip; later poems reveal with welcome understatement the pain of being without him, once the relationship has ended.

Love (and sex) and death, in addition to time and change (indeed, in conjunction with them, for the latter are ineluctably implicated with the former) form the major strands of the intricate but not at all impenetrable tapestry of Schuyler's longest poem, "The Morning of the Poem," which reads almost like a run-on, candid, and charmingly intimate conversational journal. Because it proceeds through sixty-one pages with no break other than a dot in the exact middle of the poem (separating an elegy from a grocery list), it would seem to be all of one piece. Schuyler maintains unity of place—that is, the East Aurora room where he sits at his typewriter—although his thoughts may range to New York City, New Brunswick, England, and Paris, and among similarly diverse subjects. Yet the reader discovers, moving through the poem, that these meditations occur not on a single morning or afternoon but over a nearly two-month span.

"The Morning of the Poem" takes Schuyler from the beginning of July to late August, when he leaves his rural family home in western New York to return to Manhattan. As he sits at his typewriter, thinking of his friend painting in New York (and addressing him, as if in a letter, throughout much of the poem), the weather, assorted deliveries, his aged mother's nagging, and many memories from various stages of the past (last night's dream, cruising another middle-aged man in the grocery store, boyhood and adolescent incidents, lovers and friends and a beloved dog now gone) impinge on his consciousness and accordingly enter the poem. Amid the many surrenders to thought and recollection, the recurring descriptions of the rainy weather, several lawn mowings, and a few passing references to the time of month give readers their bearings as to the progression of time—always to their surprise at its speed.

Schuyler has a vested interest in moving time rapidly—he is looking forward to rejoining his painter friend in New York. His recollections of the past enable time to pass more quickly for him, while the present-tense descriptions of the weather and activities around the house slow it down, reminding him only of the stretch of time still facing him. Yet this does not deny his ability to find pleasure even in the moments that drag on.

Schuyler keeps imagining his friend painting on his rooftop in New York and praises "the dedication of the artist" which characterizes him. Schuyler's question, "Whoever knows what a painter is thinking?," is echoed near the end of the poem, upon receipt of a postcard from composer Ned Rorem: "I wonder what it's like, being a composer?" He finds these other arts mysterious: painting involves colors whose names he can't remember; music demands "so much time" to write down "the little notes," whereas his own writing "goes by so fast:/ a couple of hours of concentration, then you're/ spent." Presented in counterpoint to these other artists, one introduced at the very beginning of the poem, the other at the end, James Schuyler as poet, seated at his typewriter, is seen by the reader to be every bit as dedicated, even when drinking limeade, or just lost in reverie—dedicated to the pursuit of self-knowledge, of an empathy with the life around him, natural and human. It has certainly demanded great effort to make this poem, composed presumably in countless sittings over two months, flow so smoothly and achieve a unity among the many subjects of its meanderings.

A poetry of sheer stream of consciousness, of simple recording of sensory and mental experiences, would seem to be an easy achievement; many lesser poets have attempted it, but without the aura of mystery, celebration, wonder, and joy that Schuyler brings to such moments. He has no poetic program, no ambition to make his poems "more open," as "a clunkhead" suggests: rather, he wants "merely to say, to see and say, things/ as they are." It thus seems important to name things exactly, and he displays a splendidly precise vocabulary of nouns and verbs when describing his environment (climate, plant life, sea life, forest life, furnishings, art works). It is understandably frustrating, therefore, when he fails to remember certain names for things, as throughout "The Morning of the Poem." Yet specific names may not be so important when considered against appreciation for the things themselves and the experiences they create, as he tells his "dead best friend" in "The Morning of the Poem":

> this is not
> your poem, your poem I may
> Never write, too much, though it is there and
> needs only to be written down
> And one day will and if it isn't it doesn't matter:
> the truth, the absolute
> Of feeling, of knowing what you know, that is
> the poem . . .

To capture such "truth," such an "absolute of feeling" in words is, of course, far from easy. In "Hudson Ferry," Schuyler writes, with a kind of comic disgust, "You can't talk about the weather"—it's so easily susceptible to clichés. Yet Schuyler has paradoxically persisted, as "The Morning of the Poem" makes clear. How? He continues to remark that "You can't get at a sunset naming colors," so he uses other means: for example, noting the effects of the sunset in "Song," he is not afraid to use metaphors and similes—but characteristically with freshness and aptness: "An almost autumn sky, a swimming pool awash/ with cinnamon and gentian." Yet he also often mocks the poet's metaphorical and personifying tendencies and can undercut such poeticisms with a deft phrase, like the parenthesis that immediately follows the lines just quoted: "(The sky's the swimming pool, that is)," or the deflation of the grandiose apostrophe "O Day!" with the no less and possibly more appreciative "literal/ and unsymbolic/ day." As he writes in "The Cenotaph":

"The hawkweed flowers are an idea about the color of fire./ The hawkweed are one thing and the fire is another." Thus he reminds the reader that the objects compared retain their own identities; it is the human mind that draws such parallels. For that very reason—that the human mind perceives things by making such comparisons—these poetic figures which indicate similarities must not be omitted from the writing of poetry; they are indispensable to the mind's process of perception. What he does seek to avoid poetically are the familiar standard associations: "fall/ equals melancholy, spring,/ get laid." "An Almanac" succeeds in this splendidly, tracing the passage of the seasons in an utterly fresh way—through nothing but discrete details of action, predominantly human, which indicate clearly the particular changes accompanying each new season, from fall to spring: "Shops take down their awnings . . . In cedar chests sheers and seersuckers displace flannels and wools."

Schuyler's poetry revels in the experience of any sort of weather, season, time of day, environment. He seems equally at home in city and country (though favoring the latter) and can paint a Manhattan street scene as luminously as a Long Island beach or a woodland walk in Vermont. The variety of the scenes he can enjoy and his ability to capture accurately the feel of such a range of experience richly display his appreciation for the fact of change— even in the breakup of love affairs, even in the losses of death. Toward the end of "The Morning of the Poem" he realizes "how this poem seems mostly about what I've lost," yet none of these losses has broken him. He does not elegize them with the typical "life must go on" resolution, for he knows very well that, *sub specie temporis*, there is nothing else life can do: "Life will change and/ I am part of it and/ will change too. So/ will you, and you. . . ." Death is merely another form of this change. The process of life contains "in repetition, change:/ a continuity, the what/ of which you are a part." There is no stability, as each season fades into the next, yet in each season is the promise of the future ones; as Schuyler writes in "Buttered Greens," our life means "leavings and/ the permanence/ of return."

When Schuyler in "The Morning of the Poem" receives a letter from a friend telling of her brother's dying while "the grandchildren and the dogs ran in and out as usual," Schuyler responds quoting the familiar litany, which is no less true: "'In the midst of life we are in death, in the/ Midst of death we are in life.'" This is the essence of Schuyler's attitude toward both life and death, including a healthy recognition of the passage of time and the inevitability of change ("This beauty that I see . . . it goes, it goes."). After he hears about a hurricane on Long Island, Schuyler asks himself in "The Morning of the Poem," "Why so much pleasure in wrack and/ ruin?" It may be the proof it gives of the ephemeral nature of all security and permanence. After all, "the scattered wrack" contains "(always) some cut-up surprise." Change gives no cause for fear or regret, Schuyler suggests through his wonderfully serene poetry; change in nature creates endless sequences of beauty, like the changing days in "Hymn to Life": "each so unique, each so alike." The seasons are predictable, yet full of unexpected variations: a cold, rainy July, a balmy November.

During the course of the marvelous abundance of "The Morning of the Poem," Schuyler, indulging in a favorite pastime, eating ("grapes, oysters/ And champagne"), remarks that "bliss is such a simple thing." So is most of Schuyler's poetry, yet it conveys a rich sense of the world around him and a healthy, joyous approach to existence.

Scott Giantvalley

Other major works
LONG FICTION: *Alfred and Guinevere*, 1958; *A Nest of Ninnies*, 1969 (with John Ashbery); *What's for Dinner?*, 1978.
PLAYS: *Presenting Jane*, 1952; *Shopping and Waiting*, 1953; *Unpacking the Black Trunk*, 1965 (with Kenward Elmslie).

Bibliography
Auslander, Philip. *The New York School Poets as Playwrights.* New York: Peter Lang, 1989. Although the focus of this volume is on plays, the chapter on Schuyler also examines his poetry, including his link to the New York School. An appreciative piece on Schuyler, discussing the imagery in his work, his numerous references to old things, and his thematic treatment of the past.
Greiner, Donald J., ed. American Poets Since World War II. In *Dictionary of Literary Biography.* Vol. 5. Detroit: Gale Research, 1980. Greiner discusses *Freely Espousing*, which he says demonstrates Schuyler's range in form, style, and subject. Notes that he is the observer in his poems, not the participant. Cites his best poems as those that use the landscape to establish feelings, such as "Buried at Spring," an elegy for Frank O'Hara.
Kalstone, David. Review of *The Crystal Lithium. The New York Times Book Review*, November 5, 1972, p. 6. Review says that this volume contains the best poems Schuyler has ever written. Describes his work as having "the coveted directness, the openness to experience his plainest declarations." Praises Schuyler for being attuned to the way the awakened mind functions.
Malkoff, Karl. *Crowell's Handbook of Contemporary American Poetry.* New York: Thomas Y. Crowell, 1973. In the introduction, Malkoff discusses Schuyler's thoughts on the New York poets, of which he was one, and the influence of cubism and Surrealism on their work. Contains further discussion of Schuyler's "projective verse."
Vinson, James, ed. *Contemporary Poets.* 3d ed. New York: St. Martin's Press,

1980. The entry on Schuyler, by Michael Andre, identifies his artistic leanings and his prolific writings. Calls *Salute* representative of his poems, which are "sensitive and perceptive." Notes that much of Schuyler's poetry describes what he sees and what he loves—and that is not New York.

DELMORE SCHWARTZ

Born: Brooklyn, New York; December 8, 1913
Died: New York, New York; July 11, 1966

Principal poetry

In Dreams Begin Responsibilities, 1938; *Genesis, Book I*, 1943; *Vaudeville for a Princess, and Other Poems*, 1950; *Summer Knowledge*, 1959.

Other literary forms

Although Delmore Schwartz thought of himself primarily as a poet, he wrote short stories, plays, and literary and film criticism as well. His masterful 1937 story, "In Dreams Begin Responsibilities," prefigures the major concerns of his later work and provides the title for his first collection of poetry in the following year. *The World Is a Wedding* (1948) contains this and most of the remainder of Schwartz's best stories. The later stories collected in *Successful Love, and Other Stories* (1961) are generally less noteworthy. Schwartz's retooling of William Shakespeare in *Coriolanus and His Mother*, which occupies a large part of *In Dreams Begin Responsibilities*, and the autobiographical *Shenandoah* (1941) are interesting, if not particularly stageworthy, contributions to verse drama. A good sampling of his essays on modern literature and its critics—T. S. Eliot, Ezra Pound, Edmund Wilson, Lionel Trilling—as well as occasional pieces on films such as *The Seven Year Itch* and *The Blackboard Jungle* reveals the characteristic interplay of his mind between high and popular culture, and may be found in the posthumous *Selected Essays of Delmore Schwartz* (1970). Schwartz's papers, recovered and presented to Yale University by his literary executor, Dwight Macdonald, mainly record the abandoned projects that littered Schwartz's career.

Achievements

Schwartz burst onto the New York literary scene when his best-known story, "In Dreams Begin Responsibilities," was published in the front of the first issue of the revised *Partisan Review* in Autumn, 1937. Not yet twenty-four, Schwartz had passionately dramatized the adolescent trauma of the Jewish urban intellectual edging nervously into manhood in the 1930's. Vladimir Nabokov ranked "In Dreams Begin Responsibilities" among his half-dozen favorite modern stories. With the appearance of his first collection of poetry in 1938, Schwartz's reputation was firmly established. This volume, again entitled *In Dreams Begin Responsibilities*, was praised by such luminaries as Allen Tate, John Crowe Ransom, W. H. Auden, and Wallace Stevens as the work of the ablest of the younger American poets. Schwartz's passionate rhetoric and unrelieved pessimism seemed perfectly to evoke the bleakness of the 1930's in poems that explored the tragic gap between human aspiration and fulfillment. Before the age of twenty-five Schwartz was bemoaning lost innocence and passing time and had fastened on his obsessive theme: the failure of life's hopes. Schwartz would embody his own poignant illustration of the life of shattered dreams; only rarely would his poetry approach the brilliance of his first collection.

Schwartz pinned his hopes for enduring fame on *Genesis*, an epic poem that expressed the "Spirit of America" through the life of Hershey Green, the poet's surrogate. Schwartz believed that the poem would confirm him as heir apparent to the modernist mantle of T. S. Eliot, one of his literary heroes. Despite some isolated passages of great brilliance, *Genesis*, too long, too diffuse, too remorselessly narcissistic, failed to embody its grandiose design. For some time, Schwartz continued the saga of Hershey Green, but with a mounting sense of futility; the proposed Books II and III of *Genesis* never appeared.

Vaudeville for a Princess, and Other Poems, a grab bag of poems, comic prose, and literary burlesque, represents a further decline from Schwartz's earlier work. Often his own harshest critic, Schwartz admitted the collection's failure by including only three of its poems in *Summer Knowledge*. The first half of this volume consists of poems, many in revised versions, that appeared originally in 1938; the remainder is made up of new poems, the three from *Vaudeville for a Princess*, and a selection from *Genesis*. Nearly all Schwartz's enduring poetry is contained in this collection, for which he bacame the youngest poet ever to win the prestigious Bollingen Prize. Ironically, it marked the end of his poetic career. The remaining seven years of his life completed the paradigm of the tragic fate of the sensitive artist whose precipitous decline parallels his meteoric rise. Once the most precocious voice of his generation, Schwartz ended as the symbol of dazzling promise only sporadically fulfilled.

Biography

Delmore David Schwartz, who once confessed that his only subject was himself, owed his birth to a fluke, a fact which he never tired of recounting. In order to conceive, Rose Schwartz needed an operation which she financed by selling a French war bond, the gift of an overseas uncle. Since Harry Schwartz was unaware of Rose's ploy, Delmore's birth was the result of a deception which fascinated and repelled the poet for the rest of his life. Life with argumentative and histrionic parents is translated into the art of "In Dreams Begin Responsibilities," where the boy-narrator watches his parents' courtship unfold on the screen of an imaginary theater. When they decide, despite lingering doubts, to marry, the boy leaps from his seat screaming at them to reconsider. Perhaps the most traumatic episode of Schwartz's childhood occurred one summer day in 1921 when Rose dragged him into a roadside café and found her husband with another woman, whom she denounced as a whore. Young Hershey Green in *Genesis* learns that this incident will critically influence his later life. Schwartz's father left home permanently in 1923 when Delmore was nine. Like his parents, Schwartz was to doubt the wisdom of marriage; both of his own marriages were conceived in uncertainty and terminated in divorce.

Brilliant but erratic, Schwartz decided early to become a poet, although he majored in philosophy, earning a B.A. degree from New York University in 1935. He started graduate study at Harvard but left in March, 1937, without taking a degree, returning to New York, where his criticism, poetry, and fiction soon began appearing in magazines. By the early 1940's, Schwartz's life had assumed the sort of pattern it would maintain thereafter, eddying between Cambridge, where he taught composition and advanced writing from 1940 to 1947, and New York, where he served as poetry editor of the *Partisan Review* from 1943 to 1955.

During his adolescence, Schwartz, the child of Jewish immigrants from Eastern Europe who could barely speak English, had lived simultaneously in Irving Howe's "world of our fathers" and the gleaming promised land of the aspiring New York literati. In one of Schwartz's finest stories, "America! America!," a promising young writer, Shenandoah Fish, listens to his mother's poignant tale of immigrant neighbors and gains a new appreciation of their lives that belies his initial contempt. Indeed the first and last names of Schwartz's hero reflect the odd mixture of the grandiose and mundane in his own. The tragedy of Schwartz's life was that the dialectical opposites so beautifully resolved in the fiction of "America! America!" and another fine story, "The Child Is the Meaning of This Life," could not be mediated in the real world. His inherent nobility and high purpose gave way to suspicions about wives, friends, and colleagues, resulting finally in paranoia. At Harvard, he envisioned a faculty cabal convened for the sole purpose of denying him tenure; his jealousy and insults finally alienated his most supportive colleague, Harry Levin. Back in New York, he reviled ancient enemies and steadfast friends alike, and the gloom of his last days was lightened only by friends such as Dwight Macdonald, Meyer Schapiro, and Saul Bellow, whose loyalty he could not destroy.

By then, however, Schwartz no longer cared. A boy wonder in 1938, he never surpassed and only rarely equaled his early achievements. By 1945, the failure of his first marriage, the lukewarm reception of *Genesis*, on which he had staked everything, and his heavy drinking had made him a "changed man" in the opinion of William Barrett, an old friend who renewed acquaintance with Schwartz upon returning from the war. Ironically, the onset of Schwartz's long decline coincided with his solidifying reputation as an American man of letters; by 1947 he was the most widely anthologized poet of his generation (which included Robert Lowell and John Berryman), one of the ablest critics of modern poetry and writing, and an editor of *Partisan Review*, the most respected intellectual journal of its day. Yet the only poetry he published during the remainder of his life was the slight *Vaudeville for a Princess*, 1950, and *Summer Knowledge*, 1959, the bulk of which was selected from his work prior to 1938.

By the 1950's, heavy drinking, sleeping pills, and massive doses of Dexedrine had, according to James Atlas, Schwartz's biographer, exacerbated his chronic insomnia, confirmed his manic-depressive mood cycles, and led to the "notorious paranoia that dominated his last years." After a painful three-year stint at Syracuse University in the mid-1960's, arranged by Meyer Schapiro with the help of recommendations from Robert Lowell and Saul Bellow, whose novel *Humboldt's Gift* (1975) brilliantly evokes Schwartz's last days, the poet returned to New York to die. Sporadically incarcerated in Bellevue, Schwartz finally succumbed to a heart attack in the seedy Manhattan hotel that was his last home, on July 11, 1966.

Analysis

Coming of age in the intellectual climate of New York in the 1930's, Delmore Schwartz could hardly have avoided the twin influences of Sigmund Freud and Karl Marx, whose ghosts meet to analyze the hero's motives in *Coriolanus and His Mother* (1938). Freud argues for Volumnia's primacy in the formation of Coriolanus' psyche, Marx for Rome's. Finally, mother and city merge into a symbol of the past which neither Coriolanus nor the poet can escape. The model is elaborated in one of his best essays, "The Two Audens," which appeared in the first issue of *The Kenyon Review* in 1939. In the essay, Schwartz defined the Marxist Auden, the poet of contemporary social concerns, and the Freudian Auden, who reported the "intuitions of psychic life." While Schwartz preferred Auden's latter persona, it is clearly the interplay between public (ego) and private (id) selves that fascinated him.

Yet it was Eliot who was Schwartz's "culture hero," the seer who discovered new forms and a new idiom for the modern world. Schwartz's ambition was to provide for the 1930's and 1940's the image of the times that Eliot had etched for an earlier generation. So long as Schwartz maintained a degree of Eliot's intellectual objectivity, his poetry, especially that of *In Dreams Begin Responsibilities*, brilliantly fulfilled his program, but he was compelled to treat the history of his times as inseparable from the history of himself. Thus *Genesis* is largely vitiated by Schwartz's obsession with the minutiae of Hershey Green's life, which is still bogged down in adolescence after two hundred pages of verse. James Atlas argues that Schwartz's background militated against the adoption of Eliot's poetic manner—authoritarian, aloof, detached—and that Arthur Rimbaud (whose *Une Saison en enfer*, 1873, he quirkily translated) and especially Charles Baudelaire provoked his rhetorical flights of grief and rage.

Baudelaire, Eliot, and another of his literary heroes, James Joyce, embody Schwartz's obsession with the social alienation of the poet, although Eliot was firmly ensconced in the literary establishment by the 1930's. The titles of such essays as "The Isolation of Modern Poetry," "The Vocation of the Poet in the Modern World," and "The Present State of Poetry" hint at the poet's marginality. Schwartz's alienation as a poet, deepened by his Jewishness, often took the form of a paranoia which he found increasingly difficult to suppress in his poetry.

Most of Schwartz's poetry is based on a varied but traditional iambic pentameter line which tends to lengthen and loosen in his later work. Images of snow—pacifying, concealing, obliterating—and light—dazzling, clarifying, transcending—permeate his poetry. No matter how they are structured and whatever imagery they employ, Schwartz's poems relentlessly explore his intertwined themes: the nature of the self, the alienation of the poet and Jew, the burden of the past, and the defeat of human aspirations. A discussion of his best poems most conveniently follows the order of their appearance in *Summer Knowledge*.

"The Ballad of the Children of the Czar" imagines two events occurring simultaneously in 1916: the Czar's children play with an erratically bouncing ball in their father's garden; six thousand miles away the two-year-old Schwartz eats a baked potato in his high chair. Simultaneity is reinforced by the mention of the poet's grandfather, who, after suffering in the Czar's army, hid in a "wine-stinking barrel" for three days in Bucharest, and escaped to America where he "became a king himself." Yet the poem is no parable of freedom—quite the opposite. The Czar's children cannot control the ball which rolls beyond the garden's iron gate; their frustrated howls are echoed by the infant Schwartz whose buttered potato slips from his hands. Next year the Russian Revolution will seal the fate of the Czar's children, prefigured in the loss of their ball. A lost ball, a dropped potato: man can neither arbitrate his happiness nor control his fate. Children of Czars and immigrants alike are victims of inherited history which is at once irrecoverable and inescapable. Ironically, the very ubiquity of the past underlines man's fatal inability to change it. The poem recalls Aeneas bearing old Anchises on his back as they flee burning Troy; so must all children bear their fathers' weight, the burden of which they can never unload.

"In the Naked Bed, in Plato's Cave" expands Schwartz's discussion of the limits of human knowledge. Underlying the poem is Plato's parable of the cave where chained prisoners face a wall upon which they can see only shadows cast by firelight. So are all men chained, argues Plato, by their limited knowledge; they are doomed to take shadows for the reality that lies in the sunlight outside their cave. Schwartz, lying awake in bed, sees reflected headlights sliding along his wall, and hears the hammering of carpenters, the grinding of truck traffic, and finally the milkman striving up the stairs, his bottles chinking. Perplexed, still woozy from sleep, he greets the morning which heralds the mystery of beginning again and again.

Schwartz takes over Plato's distinction between appearance and reality, but reverses the conclusions of the parable. An actual bedroom replaces the symbolic cave, and the intensity and immediacy of the narrator's impressions contrast with the shadowy and fragmentary perceptions of Plato's chained prisoners. Moreover, the narrator sidles between bed and window, between sleep and wakefulness; Plato's men are perpetual sleepers, condemned to watch an eternal shadow play. Yet the poem's conclusion points equally to human limitations, although in a different manner. The world in time—that is, the world apprehended by the speaker—*is* the real world. Schwartz has met Plato's dilemma, not by resolving its dualism but by denying its existence. "In the Naked Bed, in Plato's Cave" thus confirms the validity of human perception even as it fixes its boundaries.

"Far Rockaway" takes its title from the public beach where New Yorkers cast aside the "rigor of the weekday" with their shoes. The radiant seashore, the swaying light, the "passionate sun," and the glittering sea are positive images which, in the poem's first four stanzas, propose freedom not only from weekday care but perhaps from time itself. The fifth stanza, however, introduces "the novelist," a detached observer, an introspective man whose concern is "the cure of souls" first cited in the epigraph of the poem, where it is attributed to Henry James. In a series of rhetorical questions, the intruder reduces weekend joy to trivial escapism: a "cure" for the body but no surcease for the soul. Day's radiance yields to a "haunting, haunted moon." The lesson of the master, suitably opaque, may be that sensual abandonment, the summum bonum of the masses, is a delusion and is, in any case, impossible for the detached artist, forever on the boardwalk, never on the beach.

A variation on this theme occurs in "Tired and Unhappy, You Think of Houses," wherein another outsider imagines a cozy family scene which, for him, must remain a "banal dream." Turning away to the anonymity of the subway rush, he is "Caught in an anger exact as a machine!" Still another instance of the artist's social alienation is expressed dramatically in "Parlez-Vous Francais?" This time the scene is a barbershop, which, like the beach of "Far Rockaway" and the home of "Tired and Unhappy, You Think of Houses," embodies the communal values of everyday life. On the radio the voice of a demagogue Caesar, probably Hitler, seduces the recumbent men with extravagant promises calculated to appeal to their basest instincts. Enter the writer, "shy, pale, and quite abstracted," whose three-day beard and lack of tie define his separateness. He cries out—in French—that Caesar knows that most men lead lives of quiet desperation and can be deceived by dreams and lies which will inevitably lead them to war and death. Naturally the writer's rage is incomprehensible to the men, none of whom understands this "foreigner"; just as naturally his use of French deliberately underscores his estrangement. Whether the unheeded seer of "Parlez-Vous Francais?," the unnoticed observer of "Far Rockaway," or the wistful dreamer of "Tired and

Unhappy, You Think of Houses," the artist remains divorced from quotidian life.

"Prothalamion" announces Schwartz's forthcoming marriage. Its opening sections treat the subject with Spenserian reverence and dignity: "The feast of bondage and unity" is approached with "great piety"; the poet affirms his need for love and remembrance; the bride's beauty will engender the self-forgetfulness necessary to married life. There follows a catalog of events best forgotten: his mother's rage before her seven-year-old son when she trapped her husband "At dinner with his whore"; his terror at thirteen when "a little girl died," and he first confronted death.

Freud and Marx are invited to the wedding to "mark out the masks that face us there," since "No form is cruel as self-deception." Mozart shows up to reveal the "irreducible incorruptible good," presumably that arising from a life dedicated to high art. Then come jewelers, acrobats, florists, and finally Robinson Crusoe and Charlie Chaplin, as the poem explodes into joyous celebration.

These last two names, however, invoke the loneliness intrinsic to the human condition. The sublime vision of the wedding feast dissolves into something "fantastic and pitiful," as hopes and wishes yield to the "fear" that closes four of the stanza's eight lines. Even as he pledges to live with and care for his bride, the poet alludes to the heavy burden of his own mortality and of hers, which he must henceforth bear on his back. Moreover, the poet's unstable personality poses a threat to the marriage "because my circus self/ Divides its love a million times." Only a God conceived in the gathering darkness of the poet's fears can give the bride the understanding of the husband he wishes to be. The ending is ambiguous. Is the poet making a last desperate plea for the human understanding which will make life with another possible? Or, is he eschewing the lesson of Freud and Marx in embracing a final self-deception, one not so cruel as necessary for the survival of his marriage? The magic of the Spenserian moment is, in either case, long gone.

Burdened with his past in "The Ballad of the Children of the Czar," with his affections in "Prothalamion," Schwartz is finally burdened with his very body in "The Heavy Bear Who Goes with Me." One of his finest and most anthologized pieces, this poem employs a beast fable to examine traditional philosophical dichotomies. Concerning the relationship between mind and body, "The Heavy Bear Who Goes with Me" immediately establishes its context by its epigraph—"The withness of the body"—originally attributed to the distinguished philosopher, Alfred North Whitehead, one of Schwartz's favorite Harvard professors. The bear—"clumsy," "lumbering," "brutish"—represents the grossness of the human body above which the aspiring spirit cannot ascend. "That inescapable animal" has accompanied the speaker from birth, distorting his gestures, thwarting his better impulses, and reducing his existence to a "scrimmage of appetite." The poem's brilliance results from

Schwartz's manipulation of the bear metaphor: its honey-smeared face, its frenzied howling in the night, and its clownish showing-off evoke a primordial force as terrifying as it is grotesque.

An equally brilliant companion piece immediately follows "The Heavy Bear Who Goes with Me" in *Summer Knowledge*. "A Dog Named Ego, the Snow-flakes as Kisses" again explores the gulf between body and soul by means of an animal metaphor. This time the duality is expressed in Freudian rather than Platonic terms; the dog, unlike the bear, is inseparable from the self. Perhaps it is best to consider the dog as an aspect of the self, as its name suggests. Yet the narrator, the central ego of the poem, is the dog's master, at least in the sense that his walking the dog constitutes the poem's dramatic movement. Still another complication in the man-dog relationship is intro-duced by the speaker's description of the dog's actions. By observing the dog, he observes himself, and thereby dramatizes the human ego in the act of self-scrutiny.

Accompanying his master one chilly December evening, the dog Ego is distracted by falling snowflakes. While the man placidly accepts "the snow-flakes as kisses," the dog, growing more and more excited, tries to swallow the snow which continues "falling from some place half believed and unknown." The snow's kisses recall Schwartz's most haunting scene: waking to "the bleak winter morning of my 21st birthday, the windowsill shining with its lip of snow," which concludes "In Dreams Begin Responsibilities." In both contexts the snow—pure, beautiful, evanescent—promises a momentary vision of transcendence in its fleeting life between falling and melting.

Accompanied by such a dog, however, the hungering self destroys the object of its quest. Prey to his appetites embodied in the barking dog franti-cally devouring the snowflakes, the narrator helplessly witnesses the reversal of the master-dog relationship and his consequent enslavement by Ego. The drama of the lost self is played out in the dog's pursuit of the snowflakes, which now signify only illusion and obliteration. As night collapses around him, the speaker's double isolation—from self and heart's desire—is expressed in the repeated ending, "And left me no recourse, far from home."

"A Dog Named Ego, the Snowflakes as Kisses" contains Schwartz's most profound treatment of the self-alienation that results from thwarted aspira-tion. The poem implies, additionally, that this alienation lies at the root of the social estrangement portrayed in so many of his other poems. Whereas "The Heavy Bear Who Goes with Me" dramatizes Schwartz's dualism no less forcefully, "A Dog Named Ego, the Snowflakes as Kisses" is a subtler evoca-tion of the interplay between the physical and spiritual. Taken together, the poems constitute Schwartz's most powerful essay on the endlessly fascinating topic of the divided self.

The new poems in *Summer Knowledge* reveal a mellower Schwartz. On the surface they represent an acceptance of the here and now heralded by an intensified use of light imagery and a new reliance on images drawn from nature. Schwartz describes his newly acquired "summer knowledge" as "supple recognition of the fullness and the fatness and the roundness of ripeness"; it might as easily be recognized as a surrender of the possibility of knowing. This shift from retrospective analysis to intuitive acceptance undermines the dialectical tension that rippled through Schwartz's youthful poems. More and more often his late poetry collapses into prosaic statement as its lines lengthen, its syntax relaxes, and its imagery diffuses. The quintessential poet of urban life and its discontents, Schwartz seems vaguely uncomfortable in his new role as celebrant of nature and its satisfactions. While the later work is more positive in its reconciliation of the self and the world and in its insistence on the primacy of the love equated with "summer knowledge," its forced earnestness and flaccid execution indicate the decline of Schwartz's power.

Among the few later poems that bear comparison with Schwartz's early work, none is finer than "Seurat's Sunday Afternoon Along the Seine." This long poem, consisting of a meticulous description of *Un Dimanche d'été à la Grande Jatte*, interspersed with narrative commentary, employs dazzling visual imagery to re-create the luminosity of George Seurat's greatest painting. Perhaps Schwartz was drawn to the painting (properly called *A Sunday Afternoon on the Island of La Grand Jatte* in English) by the intensity of its light; or, he may have identified with Seurat, whose finest achievement came at twenty-five, when he hardly suspected—in the words of Schwartz's poem— "that in six years he will no longer be alive!" In any event, the poem's depiction of the communal enjoyment of the crowd recalls the weekend revelry of "Far Rockaway" but with a crucial difference. The radiant images of "Far Rockaway" were ironically conceived to expose carefree enjoyment as illusory escapism; reality was the province of the critically observant "novelist" strolling the boardwalk above the beach. In "Seurat's Sunday Afternoon Along the Seine," the shining sun fixes the Sunday people, "In glowing solidity, changeless, a gift, lifted to immortality." The warm leisure of their holiday has been transmuted by Seurat into the transcendent reality that eluded the narrators of Schwartz's earlier poems. Invoking John Keats—"O happy, happy throng,/ It is forever Sunday, summer, free"—whose urn depicted figures immortalized by the painter's art, Schwartz affirms the primacy of immediate sensory experience. The world evoked on Seurat's canvas is ultimate reality; but does reality consist of life's everyday actions, or the formal expression of those actions in works of enduring art?

"Seurat's Sunday Afternoon Along the Seine" may owe something to Wallace Stevens' idea, most poignantly expressed in the similarly entitled "Sunday Morning," that the poet must rediscover the earth. He does so by creating a "supreme fiction" which endows life with the value once conferred by religion. Stevens, who ranked with William Butler Yeats and Eliot among Schwartz's heroes of modern poetry, treated reality as an extension of the artist's imagination and thereby bridged the gulf between the self and the world. In the penultimate stanza of his poem, Schwartz seems in like manner to have resolved the dualism that provided the imaginative framework for so much of his previous poetry. It only remains for the last stanza of "Seurat's Sunday Afternoon Along the Seine" to reestablish the unity of Schwartz's best work and, in the haunting tragedy of its conclusion, provide a fitting coda to his achievement.

The last stanza begins with a final affirmation of the immutability of art, which defies time and change. Although the nineteenth century has yielded to the twentieth and Seurat's painting has been transplanted to Chicago, his art endures: "All of his flowers shine in monumental stillness fulfilled." Abruptly, Gustave Flaubert's voice cries, "Ils sont dans le vrai," referring to people such as those in Seurat's painting, who have apparently discovered the truth—"The kingdom of heaven on earth on Sunday summer day"—and incidentally confirming the ultimate reality of the visible world. Franz Kafka repeats Flaubert's phrase, but in a voice "forever sad, in despair's sickness," fatally poisoning the poem's context. The everyday pleasures of forebears, marriages, and heirs, he suggests, are unavailable to the likes of Flaubert, Kafka, and, of course, Schwartz. As in "Prothalamion," when the invocation of Crusoe and Chaplin shattered the Spenserian moment, the voices of Flaubert and Kafka confirm Schwartz's eternal alienation. The closing lines of "Seurat's Sunday Afternoon Along the Seine" ironically redefine "summer knowledge" as a devastating epiphany of human defeat.

Lawrence S. Friedman

Other major works

SHORT FICTION: *The World Is a Wedding*, 1948; *Successful Love, and Other Stories*, 1961.

PLAY: *Shenandoah*, 1941.

NONFICTION: *Selected Essays of Delmore Schwartz*, 1970; *Letters of Delmore Schwartz*, 1984; *Portrait of Delmore: Journals and Notes of Delmore Schwartz, 1939-1959*, 1986.

CHILDREN'S LITERATURE: *"I Am Cherry Alive," the Little Girl Sang*, 1958.

Bibliography

Atlas, James. *Delmore Schwartz: The Life of an American Poet*. New York: Farrar, Straus & Giroux, 1977. A full-length, comprehensive biography that attempts to cut through the poses and personae of Schwartz. Contains enriching details of Schwartz's life and extracts of his poems illustrating his development as a poet.

Carruth, Hayden. "Comment." *Poetry* 112 (September, 1968): 417-427. Reviews *Summer Knowledge* and notes that while Schwartz is capable of very good poetry, his work is uneven. Likens the good poetry to "wild roses in a bank of weeds."

McDougall, Richard. *Delmore Schwartz*. New York: Twayne, 1974. A straightforward account of Schwartz's work, commenting on his theme of alienation—that is, his self-concept as a Jew and the Jewish influence on his work. Attends to his later more successful poems. A useful introduction to Schwartz.

Phillips, Robert. *Letters of Delmore Schwartz*. Princeton: N.J.: Ontario Review Press, 1984. A collection of important letters by Schwartz that not only reflects his thinking but also the issues of the times. The introduction is sympathetic to Schwartz, noting that he is a man who "put his talent into his work and his genius into conversation." A must for Schwartz scholars.

Pollet, Elizabeth, ed. *Portrait of Delmore: Journals and Notes of Delmore Schwartz, 1939-1959*. New York: Farrar, Straus & Giroux, 1986. Edited by Delmore's second wife, this important collection of journals, notes, and poems will enlighten scholars and readers of Schwartz. In the introduction, Pollet offers some insights into her life with Schwartz and her perceptions of this poet.

SIR WALTER SCOTT

Born: Edinburgh, Scotland; August 15, 1771
Died: Abbotsford, Scotland; September 21, 1832

Principal poetry

The Chase, and William and Helen: Two Ballads from the German of Gott-fried Augustus Bürger, 1796 (translation); *The Eve of Saint John: A Border Ballad*, 1800; *The Lay of the Last Minstrel*, 1805; *Ballads and Lyrical Pieces*, 1806; *Marmion: A Tale of Flodden Field*, 1808; *The Lady of the Lake*, 1810; *The Vision of Don Roderick*, 1811; *Rokeby*, 1813; *The Bridal of Triermain: Or, The Vale of St. John, in Three Cantos*, 1813; *The Lord of the Isles*, 1815; *The Field of Waterloo*, 1815; *The Ettrick Garland. Being Two Excellent New Songs*, 1815 (with James Hogg); *Harold the Dauntless*, 1817.

Other literary forms

Sir Walter Scott's literary reputation rests firmly on his monumental collection of Waverley novels, the final revision of which was issued, in forty-eight volumes, between 1829 and 1833. The novelist produced those classics on a regular basis during the last eighteen years of his life—beginning with the three-volume *Waverley: Or, 'Tis Sixty Years Since* in 1814 and concluding, shortly before his death, with *Count Robert of Paris* and *Castle Dangerous* (under the collective title *Tales of My Landlord*, fourth series), both in 1831. In addition to the novels, Scott also produced (or adapted) eight plays between 1799 and 1830: *Goetz of Berlichingen*, 1799 (translation); *The Iron Hand*, 1799 (translation); *Guy Mannering*, 1816; *Halidon Hill*, 1822; *Macduff's Cross*, 1823; *The House of Aspen*, 1829; *Auchindrane: Or, The Ayrshire Tragedy*, 1830; and *The Doom of Devorgoil*, 1830.

Scott's nonfiction prose includes *Provincial Antiquities of Scotland*, 1826; *Religious Discourses by a Layman*, 1828; *The History of Scotland*, 1829-1830; and *Letters on Demonology and Witchcraft*, 1830. He also produced three biographies of note: *The Life and Works of John Dryden*, first published in 1808 as part of his eighteen-volume edition of that poet's works; *The Memoirs of Jonathan Swift*, 1826 (originally included in the nineteen-volume *The Life of Jonathan Swift*, 1814); and *The Life of Napoleon Buonaparte: Emperor of the French, with a Preliminary View of the French Revolution*, 1827 (9 volumes). In addition, as editor of *Ballantyne's Novelist's Library* 1821-1824 (10 volumes) Scott wrote biographical essays on each writer in the series (including Henry Fielding, Tobias Smollett, Samuel Richardson, Ann Radcliffe, Charlotte Smith, and Fanny Burney); he published those sketches separately in 1825 (2 volumes).

Finally, Scott expended considerable energy on a long list of editorial projects carried out between 1799 and 1831: in addition to the works of John

Dryden and Jonathan Swift and the *Novelist's Library*, one may note *Minstrelsy of the Scottish Border*, 1802 (2 volumes); *A Collection of Scarce and Valuable Tracts*, 1809-1815 (13 volumes); *Chronological Notes of Scottish Affairs from the Diary of Lord Fountainhall*, 1822; and *Lays of the Lindsays*, 1824.

Various editions of *The Journal of Sir Walter Scott* have appeared, beginning in 1890.

Achievements

Sir Walter Scott's literary reputation still rests on thirty novels. Few twentieth century readers and scholars have been interested in his poetry or have taken the time to examine the distinct stages of his literary career. With the publication of *Waverley* in 1814, Scott's literary life as a novelist began and his period of intense poetic production terminated. At the outset, then, one is tempted to view the poetry only in the context of its effect on the fiction— or, from another perspective, the effect of Scott the poet on Scott the novelist.

Ample reason exists, however, for studying the poetry on its own merits, for the imaginative power to be found in Scott's metrical romances, lyrics, and ballads. Some contemporary scholars support the claims of their Victorian predecessors, who argued that Scott, among all of his "British" contemporaries, emerged as the first writer of the Romantic movement. Indeed, although literary historians correctly offer William Wordsworth's *Lyrical Ballads* (1798)—and its significant "Preface"—as the key to understanding British Romanticism, Scott's *The Lay of the Last Minstrel*, published seven years later, reached a far wider audience (in both England and Scotland) than Wordsworth's collection and achieved a more noticeable impact among the poet's contemporaries than did the earlier work. In fact, no previous English poet had managed to produce a work that reaped such large financial rewards and achieved so much popular acclaim.

Interestingly enough, Scott's poetic achievements came in a form radically different from those qualities that marked the traditional "giants" of his age— Wordsworth, Samuel Taylor Coleridge, John Keats, Percy Bysshe Shelley, and Lord Byron. True, Scott considered, at a variety of levels, the prevalent Romantic themes: the rejection of scientific dogmatism, a return to the glamour of past ages, the discovery of happiness in primitivism rather than in modernity, the enjoyment of emotion, a basic belief in humanitarianism. He rejected, however, the radical sentiments of the Romantic movement. By nature and upbringing a conservative, Scott clung to Tory politics and to the established Church of England rather than rising up in actual or intellectual rebellion against such institutions. He had little or no interest in mysticism, overzealous passion, or the dark unconscious. Scott's poetry is distinguished by its considerable clarity and directness; it is the product of a gentlemanly and reasonably satisfied attitude toward promoting the values of his own social class. He did rush back into an imaginary past to seek out heroes and adventurers whom he found lacking in his own early nineteenth century cultural and artistic environment. Such escapes, however, never really detracted from his belief in the challenge of the present intellectual life and the present world, where, if everything else failed, courage would support the intellectually honest competitor.

Chronologically, Scott belongs with the early Romantics; culturally and intellectually, he occupies a middle ground between Scotland and England, and therein, perhaps, lies his ultimate contribution to poetry in English. He captured, first in the poems and later in his prose fiction, the essence of Scottish national pride; that pride he filtered through the physical image of Scotland, through its varied and conflicting scenery and its traditional romantic lore. The entire area—joined politically to Great Britain in 1707, but still culturally free and theologically independent during Scott's day (as it remains even to this day)—stimulated and intensified his creative genius and supplied the substance first for his poetry, then for his prose fiction. Nevertheless, Scott remained distinctly aware of England and receptive to the demands of the English public—his largest reading audience. For them he translated the picturesqueness of the Highlands and the Lowlands, the islands and the borders. While photographing (or "painting," as his contemporaries maintained), through his imagination, the language and the sentiment of Scotland, Scott gave to his English readers scenes and characters that could be observed as partly English. His poetry has a freshness, a frankness, a geniality, and a shrewdness peculiar to his own Scottish Lowlands. Still, as observers of that part of the world quickly appreciate, there is little difference between a southern Scotsman and a northern Englishman—which, in the end, may also be an apt commentary on Scott's poetry.

Biography

The fourth surviving son of Walter Scott and Anne Rutherford, Walter Scott was born on August 15, 1771, in a house in the College Wynd, Edinburgh. At the age of eighteen months, the infant contracted a fever while teething and, in the end, lost the use of his right leg. The circumstance became noteworthy not only for its effect on Scott's personality and his writing, but also as the first fully authenticated case of infantile paralysis in medical history. After the failure of various attempts to remedy the malady, Scott's father sent him to Sandy Knowe, near Kelso (Roxburgh), to live with his grandfather (Robert Scott) and his uncle (Thomas). Although the five years spent there contributed little or nothing toward curing the boy's lameness, they provided some experiences with lasting influence: subjection to republican and Jacobite prejudices; songs and legends taught to him by his grandmother (Barbara Haliburton); a trip to the spas at Bath, with a stopover at London on the way; sea-bathing at Prestonpans, near Edinburgh (and site of one of the key engagements of the Jacobite uprising of 1745), where he learned of the German wars from an old veteran of Invernahyle, one Captain Dalgetty.

In 1778, the boy returned to his father's house in George's Square, Edinburgh, and later that year entered the high school at Edinburgh. From his principal tutor, a strict Presbyterian named James Mitchell, Scott gained a knowledge of Scottish church history, while his mother encouraged him to read William Shakespeare. His health, however, continued to be a problem, so again the elder Scott sent his son off, this time to Kelso to live with an aunt, Jenny Scott. During his half-year's stay there, he met James Ballantyne and the blind poet Thomas Blacklock; there, also, he read James Macpherson's Ossianic poems, Edmund Spenser's *The Faerie Queene* (1590-1596), and Thomas Percy's *Reliques of Ancient English Poetry* (1765). Most important, however, he began to collect ballads, a form and a tradition that would remain with him and influence his own literary and cultural directions. By November, 1783, Scott had prepared himself sufficiently to begin studies at Edinburgh University; he pursued only those disciplines, however, that aroused his interest (law, history, romantic legends, and literature). Further illness reduced his stamina, and his education was interrupted once more when he apprenticed himself to his father, copying legal documents. Eventually he did manage to earn a degree in law (1792) and gain admission to the Scottish bar.

Although Scott did indeed practice law and, after a reasonable period as a novice, did manage to earn a fair income from his labors, his interest focused more sharply than ever on literature, ballads, and Scottish folklore. Thus, between 1792 and 1799—first merely as a companion to the sheriff-substitute of Roxburghshire, then as sheriff-deputy of Selkirkshire—he engaged in his "border raids," exploring the country, collecting ballads and tales, and generally enjoying the hospitality of many and various true and traditional Scottish characters. To that activity he added a deep interest in German literature; he learned the language (but not the formal grammar) well enough to read and to translate, publishing in 1799 an edition of Johann Wolfgang von Goethe's *Goetz von Berlichingen* (1774), one of that writer's earliest heroic creations in which an old knight bows to the forces of decay about him. Scott did not emerge as a public figure, however, until about six years later, when he published *The Lay of the Last Minstrel*. In rather quick succession he became a partner in and large contributor to James Ballantyne's publishing house, gained a permanent appointment (1806) as Clerk of Session at Edinburgh, and was a principal founder (along with John Murray the younger) of *The Quarterly Review*, the Tory rival to *The Edinburgh Review*. In 1813, he declined the honor of being named Poet Laureate of England in favor of Robert Southey. A year later his first novel, *Waverley*, was published.

As Sheriff of Selkirkshire, Scott went, in 1804, to live at Ashestiel, on the banks of the River Tweed (dividing England and Scotland); there he wrote, between 1805 and 1813, *The Lay of the Last Minstrel*, *Marmion*, *The Lady* of the Lake, *The Vision of Don Roderick*, *The Bridal of Triermain*, and *Rokeby*. In 1812 he had begun the construction of a baronial mansion at Abbotsford (near Melrose in Roxburghshire)—once known as the little farm of Cartleyhole belonging to the monks of Melrose. After taking up residence there he could, indeed, lay claim to the title of "Gentleman." He continued to reap financial benefits from his writing, and in 1820 he received a baronetcy. He would, however, be denied the luxury of lasting contentment. Economic depression swept the British Isles in 1825; a year later, the firm of John Ballantyne and Company collapsed, and Scott found himself being left responsible (morally and actually) for most of the publishing house's debts. Rather than declaring bankruptcy, the poet-novelist pressed forward on a number of literary projects in order to pay his creditors. To compound the emotional strain and the problems of failing health, Scott's wife, Charlotte Carpentier, died in the same year.

Thus, the last several years of Scott's life were marked by struggle and overwork; he was kept afloat, so to speak, on the strength of his pride and personal integrity. By 1831, his health had declined seriously; an Admiralty frigate carried him on a sea voyage through the Mediterranean; he had been sent off from Abbotsford with a fresh sonnet by Wordsworth. While on board, he suffered a stroke of apoplexy resulting in paralysis and was forced to return to Abbotsford. There he lingered, from mid-July, 1832, until September 21, when he died quietly in the presence of all of his children.

Analysis

Sir Walter Scott's poetry, unlike that of his Romantic contemporaries, is vigorous, high-spirited, and unreflective. Scott delighted in war and pageantry, in the rich traditions of antiquity. As a Scottish poet born among a people who sought action, he was drawn to his heritage, to his connections with the border chieftains and the House of Buccleuch. Thus, his narrative poems and ballads reflect the character of a strong and proud man who, though he was lame, dreamed of the ultimate masculine activities: of chivalry, adventure, the qualities of feudalism, and the military picturesqueness of another age.

Any survey of Scott the poet must consider his interest in the popular ballad, an interest that came naturally because of the love for the old, harsh times. Scott saw in the popular Scottish ballad a contrast to the relative serenity of his own early nineteenth century. He relished the clannish loyalties, the bravery, the cruelty, the revenge, and the superstitions of the old ballads. Thus, he began with "The Chase" and "William and Helen" (1796)—two translations from the German lyric poet (and, coincidentally, lawyer) Gottfried August Burger (1747-1794); next came three strange, almost mystical ballads contributed to Matthew Gregory ("Monk") Lewis' *Tales of Wonder* in 1801: "Glenfinlas," "The Eve of St. John," and "The Gray Brother." His interest in the ballad reached its height—a scholarly as well as a poetic pinnacle—with *The Minstrelsy of the Scottish Border*, wherein Scott the editor and poet gathered and polished the best examples of what will always be considered the true literature of Scotland.

The ballad, however, was not to be the end-all for Scott the poet, but rather a springboard to other forms and variations of ballad themes. He turned his poetic attention to a series of complex and ornamental romances wherein, instead of the harshness and rusticity of the border, lords, ladies, and even clerics came forth to expound lofty themes in elevated language. Still, the stuff from which the popular ballads sprang is there. In *The Lay of the Last Minstrel*, for example, romantic love blends easily with magic, dwarfs, and goblins, while in *Marmion*, the early sixteenth century battle at Flodden Field in Northumberland, where the English, in 1513, defeated the Scots under James IV, allowed Scott to develop elaborate descriptions of conflict and chivalry, of the detailed instruments of warfare and the awesomeness of border castles. More important in terms of the ballad influence, *Marmion* draws considerable poetic life from its thoroughly romantic narrative—from intrigue, disguise, and unfaithfulness (both clerical and secular). *The Lady of the Lake* intensifies those actions, featuring Highland clans rushing to battle after being summoned by a fiery cross. Scott carried his readers on a tour of chieftain's lodge and king's court, setting the stage for James Fitz-James to reveal himself as King James and to restore the noble Ellen to her true love, Malcolm Graeme. Although the later poems—*The Vision of Don Roderick, Rokeby*, and *Harold the Dauntless*—reveal Scott as more than ready to abandon verse for prose fiction, the worlds of knighthood, sorcery, and the ancient bards and minstrels continued to fascinate him—no matter that the locales and circumstances seemed far removed from that wild terrain north of the River Tweed.

One must not too quickly assume that Scott's poetry contains little beyond historical or romantic re-creations. Although he, himself, readily admitted that his work did not rise to the levels of Wordsworth or Coleridge, he nevertheless remained a legitimate poet, not simply a compiler and reviser of historical verse tales. Scott fully realized the depth and complexity of human emotions; he chose, however, to portray the manifestations of those emotions within the context of his own historical knowledge and his own historical imagination. Thus, he could set forth value judgments and insights into history rather than simply displaying the past as mere background scenery. Scott knew only too well that he was living in the present—in a world marked by political and social revolution to which the romantic past must, for the sake of reason and order, subordinate itself. Nevertheless, history could continue to instruct the present; it could also amuse and it could momentarily ease the confusion within the minds of the poet's readers. History could help a restless and degenerate age to imagine the heroics of an older time.

With only a few exceptions, the poetry of Scott conveys action and excitement, for the poet had learned at an early age to master the conventions of narrative. But narration alone could not carry the essence of the poem. In *The Lady of the Lake*, he demonstrated the quality of painting lovely scenery, giving it dimension, and fusing it skillfully with the poetry of clan life. Scott opened the gates to the Scottish Highlands for his cultivated readers to the south. For the height of action and excitement, however, those same readers had to turn to *Marmion*, to the strong horse striding over green terrain in the fresh air, its shrill neighing and the sun's rays reverberating and reflecting from the shield and the lance of its rider. In fact, the poet stacked his details one upon the other in almost breathless fashion: "Green, sanguine, purple, red, and blue,/ Broad, narrow, swallow-tailed, and square,/ Scroll, pennon, pensil, brandrol."

The major weakness of Scott as a poet is his inability to create believable characters. Margaret of Branksome Hall (in *The Lay of the Last Minstrel*) exudes considerable charm, but she does little beyond fulfilling her function as the typical "fair maid," even amid a fast-paced series of armed encounters and magical spells. Roderick Dhu, Malcolm Graeme, and Lord James Douglas (*The Lady of the Lake*) appear active enough, but they have little else to do aside from their obvious responsibilities as fierce Highland chieftains, outlawed lords, and young knights. Also acting according to form (and little else) are Roland de Vaux (*The Bridal of Triermain*), Philip of Montham (*Rokeby*), and Edith of Lorn and Lord Ronald (both from *The Lord of the Isles*)—although Edith's disguise as a mute page, as well as the dangers she encounters, allows her some room for depth and variety. There is little doubt that Scott's best poetic characters assume the forms not of romantic heroes but of heroic scoundrels, such as the stately forger Marmion and the pirate Bertram Risingham (*Rokeby*), whose evil nature contains some elements of good. Scott addressed this problem himself, stating that no matter how hard he had tried to do otherwise, his rogues emerged as heroes. More accurately, the rogues had more life and depth than did the heroes.

Scott's ballads and verse tales are not, however, anchored to the issues of characterization, to the conflicts between good and evil, or even to the differences between heroes and villains. Virtually obliterating the shallowness of those characters, the poet's almost passionate love for the beauties of nature infuses practically every poem. In that sense, and within the context of his abilities to communicate that love to a relatively large and varied reading audience, Scott may indeed be identified with the early Romantic poets. Traditionally, his sophisticated English readership perceived Scotland—especially the Highlands—as a physical and intellectual wilderness; at best, readers of that day recalled only the Gothic descriptions of James Macpherson's Ossianic poems or the Addisonian sketches of the essayist Henry Mackenzie. Then, with *The Lay of the Last Minstrel*, *Marmion*, and *The Lady of the Lake*, Scott revealed the culture of his native land, and "Cold diffidence, and age's frost,/ In the full tide of my song were lost." He carried his readers on his poetic back "Across the furzy hills of Braid," through "all the hill with yellow grain," and over "To eastern Lodon's fertile plain"; through Scott's lines, his readers far to the south undertook a vicarious trek into a land that had been virtually shut off from their imaginations.

In addition to satisfying the imaginative needs of his Romantic readers, Scott conscientiously guided them through an almost microscopic study of physical nature, as if he were conducting a tour: going over each scene, textbook in hand, noting the various species of plants and shrubs, stones and rocks, surveying "each naked precipice,/ Sable ravine, and dark abyss" to uncover "Some touch of Nature's genial glow." For example, in the description of Lake Coriskin (in *The Lord of the Isles*), the landscape portrait captures the warmth of nature and the poet's feeling for color: in addition to the genial glow of Nature, "green mosses grow" atop Benmore, while "heath-bells bud in deep Glencoe"—all of which serves up a sharp contrast to the "Black waves, bare crags, and banks of stone" that constitute the "bleakest" side of the mountain. Again, in depicting Edinburgh and the camp in *Marmion*, the poet directs his audience to the "rose on breezes thin" that clash headlong with "Saint Giles's mingling din" as he strives to document the specifics of the distance (topographical and imaginative) "from the summit to the plain."

Critical response to Scott's poetry has ranged from kindness to indifference. Perhaps the fairest assessment of his poetry is Scott's own. He never aspired to equal Wordsworth or Coleridge or Byron; he wanted only to enjoy life and literature (indeed, even in that order), disclaiming everything beyond the love of Scotland and its traditions. That love obviously led him to poetry, as it did to prose fiction, to biography, to history, and to scholarly editing and collecting. When he finished with one of those aspects of the good, intellectual life, he simply went on to something else. Literary history must be prepared to accept Sir Walter Scott on his own terms and on that middle ground.

Samuel J. Rogal

Other major works
LONG FICTION: *Waverley: Or, 'Tis Sixty Years Since*, 1814; *Guy Mannering*, 1815; *The Antiquary*, 1816; *The Black Dwarf*, 1816; *Old Mortality*, 1816; *Rob Roy*, 1817; *The Heart of Midlothian*, 1818; *The Bride of Lammermoor*, 1819; *A Legend of Montrose*, 1819; *Ivanhoe*, 1819; *The Monastery*, 1820; *The Abbot*, 1820; *Kenilworth*, 1821; *The Pirate*, 1821; *The Fortunes of Nigel*, 1822; *Peveril of the Peak*, 1823; *Quentin Durward*, 1823; *St. Ronan's Well*, 1823; *Redgauntlet*, 1824; *The Betrothed*, 1825; *The Talisman*, 1825; *Woodstock*, 1826; *The Highland Widow*, 1827; *The Two Drovers*, 1827; *The Surgeon's Daughter*, 1827; *The Fair Maid of Perth*, 1828; *Anne of Geierstein*, 1829; *Count Robert of*

Paris, 1831; *Castle Dangerous*, 1831; *The Siege of Malta*, 1976.

PLAYS: *Halidon Hill*, 1822; *Macduff's Cross*, 1823; *The House of Aspen*, 1829; *The Doom of Devorgoil*, 1830; *Auchindrane: Or, The Ayrshire Tragedy*, 1830.

NONFICTION: *The Life and Works of John Dryden*, 1808; *The Life of Jonathan Swift*, 1814; *Lives of the Novelists*, 1825; *Provincial Antiquities of Scotland*, 1826; *The Life of Napoleon Buonaparte: Emperor of the French, with a Preliminary View of the French Revolution*, 1827; *Religious Discourses by a Layman*, 1828; *The History of Scotland*, 1829-1830; *Letters on Demonology and Witchcraft*, 1830.

TRANSLATION: *Goetz of Berlichingen*, 1799.

Bibliography

Bold, Alan, ed. *Sir Walter Scott: The Long-Forgotten Melody*. London: Vision Press, 1983. Nine essays cover such subjects as the image of Scotland, politics, and folk tradition, and draw upon Scott's poetry for illustration; the essay by Iain Crichton Smith, "Poetry in Scott's Narrative Verse," shows appreciation for the art of the poetry. Includes end notes and an index.

Chandler, Alice. "Origins of Medievalism: Scott." In *A Dream of Order: The Medieval Ideal in Nineteenth-Century English Literature*. Lincoln: University of Nebraska Press, 1970. This important essay examines the role of Scott's poems in preparing the way for popularity of medievalism in the writing of the era. His poetry derived from his scholarly research in medieval literature, and his novels would derive from his success as a poet. Supplemented by footnotes, a bibliography, and an index.

Goslee, Nancy Moore. *Scott the Rhymer*. Lexington: University Press of Kentucky, 1988. Aiming to restore Scott as a poet, this book analyzes in detail his major poems. A discussion of *The Lay of the Last Minstrel* is followed by examinations of the long poems from *Marmion* to *Harold the Dauntless*. These poems are affirmations of romance within self-reflexive frames of irony. Contains ample notes and an index.

Lauber, John. *Sir Walter Scott*. Rev. ed. Boston: Twayne, 1989. Following a survey of Scott's poetry and his turn to fiction, seven chapters analyze major narratives: *Waverly, Guy Mannering, The Antiquary, Old Mortality, Rob Roy, The Heart of Midlothian, the Bride of Lammermoor*, and *Ivanhoe*. The final chapter assesses the reputation of the Waverly novels. Complemented by a chronology, notes, an annotated bibliography, and an index.

Mitchell, Jerome. *Scott, Chaucer, and Medieval Romance: A Study in Sir Walter Scott's Indebtedness to the Literature of the Middle Ages*. Lexington: University Press of Kentucky, 1987. Describes the influences of Geoffrey Chaucer and medieval romances at work in Scott's narrative poetry, early novels, middle novels written during his financial collapse, and novels of the darkly declining years. The style and structure of the novels are analyzed before a conclusion is drawn. Augmented by preface, notes, and an index.

Tulloch, Graham. *The Language of Walter Scott: A Study of His Scottish and Period Language*. London: Andre Deutsch, 1980. In eight chapters and two appendices, Tulloch examines Scott's use of Scots-English in his poetry and fiction. The special features of the language are analyzed in terms of vocabulary, grammar, and spelling. Scott's reading is also examined as a source of his language materials. Includes a bibliography and an index.

SIR CHARLES SEDLEY

Born: Aylesford, England; March, 1639
Died: Hampstead, London, England; August 20, 1701

Principal poetry

"Song: Not *Celia*, that I juster am," 1672; "To Cloris: *Cloris*, I cannot say your Eyes," 1672; "Song: Love still has something of the Sea," 1672; "The Indifference: Thanks, fair *Vrania*, to your Scorn," 1672; prologue to *Epsom Wells*, 1673 (play by Thomas Shadwell); "Advice to the Old Beaux: Scrape no more your harmless Chins," 1693; prologue to *The Wary Widow or Sir Noisy Parrat*, 1693 (play by Henry Higden); "The Knotting Song: Hears not my *Phillis*, how the Birds," 1694; "Song: Smooth was the Water, calm the Air," 1702; "Song: *Phillis* is my only Joy," 1702; *The Miscellaneous Works of the Honourable Sir Charles Sedley, Bart.*, 1702; *The Happy Pair*, 1702.

Other literary forms

Sir Charles Sedley was also known for his plays during his lifetime. His first theatrical venture was translating an act of Pierre Corneille's *La Mort de Pompée*, as a joint project with Edmund Waller, Robert Filmer, Baron Buckhurst, and Sidney Godolphin, performed in 1664, as *Pompey the Great*. Later plays include *The Mulberry Garden* (1668), *Antony and Cleopatra* (1677), and *Bellamira: Or, The Mistress* (1687). Sedley's plays were treated with respect during the Restoration and proved moderately successful at the box office, but they have not survived their era in performance. They are available in Vivian de Sola Pinto's 1928 edition of Sedley's works.

Achievements

Sedley is remembered today as an important figure in a minor literary group: the Restoration court poets, sometimes known as the court wits or "the merry gang" of Charles II. The Earl of Rochester is the most prominent poet in this group; Sedley ranks immediately after him. In his own time, Sedley was known as a man of taste and was as famous for his wit and conversation as for his writings. His judgment on a new play or poem could help to establish or destroy a literary reputation. Today, Sedley is best known for his lyric love poetry. The most immediately apparent elements in his songs are a clever use of persuasion and an underlying Epicurean philosophy. In his biography of Sedley (1927), Vivian de Sola Pinto has noted that as a group the Restoration court poets represent "the triumph of the intellectual and logical side of the Renaissance over the imaginative and emotional elements." This generalization surely applies to Sedley, who was a poet of direct statement and controlled feeling rather than of elaborate conceits and grand passion.

Biography

Sir Charles Sedley was born into a Cavalier family and grew up during Cromwell's Protectorate. In 1656 he inherited his title on the death of his brother, and in February, 1657, he married Katherine Savage. In December, 1657, she bore him a daughter, Katherine, who would become the mistress of James II. Sometime during the decade of the 1660's, Lady Sedley, suffering from the delusion that she was a queen, went permanently insane. In 1672 Sedley arranged for her to be removed to a convent in France, where she died in 1705, outliving her husband by four years. After her departure, Sedley formed a permanent relationship with Ann Ayscough, who bore him a son, Charles, in 1672.

Sedley was among the group of young gentlemen who became the court favorites of Charles II upon his restoration to the throne in 1660. He quickly established himself in the vanguard of the King's merry gang, a group known for its riotous living and dangerous atheistic views. His most scandalous behavior occurred at the Cock Tavern in 1663. Sedley had been drinking with several gentlemen when he appeared nude on the balcony of the tavern before a crowd and proceeded to deliver a mock sermon, which was offensive in both its content and mode of delivery. A trial followed, and Sedley was fined two thousand marks for his indiscreet behavior, half of which is believed to have been remitted by the King. Sedley's behavior during the 1660's was by all accounts fairly wild, but by the early 1670's he had reformed, quite possibly the result of the good influence of Ann Ayscough.

Despite his reputation for debauchery in the first decade of the Restoration, Sedley was not given solely to the pursuit of pleasure. Early in his life, he involved himself in public affairs. He was elected to parliament in 1668 and was apparently sent to France in 1670 on an important diplomatic mission with the Earl of Buckingham, Buckhurst, and Sir George Savile. He retained his seat in parliament for most of his life, performing his most distinguished service during the reign of William III.

Sedley also pursued a second career in letters. He was not a prolific poet, but there is a consistent production of poems and plays from each decade of his life beginning with the 1660's. He may well have written more poems than have actually survived, for most of his verse was not written for publication. When his poems did appear in print, they were frequently anonymous. Since Sedley made no effort to collect his writings during his lifetime, undoubtedly many were lost. The extant poems were intended to entertain a small group who belonged to the same class and knew one another personally. Poetry was a necessary accomplishment for a courtier, and poems were passed in manuscript within the court society.

Sedley's poems were remarkably consistent throughout his life, the poems dating from the 1690's appearing to be cut from the same cloth as those written in the 1660's. Even though Sedley's world changed radically during his lifetime and most of his contemporaries had either died or stopped writing by the 1690's, these changes are not reflected in the substance or style of Sedley's poetry. In like manner, the changes in Sedley's personal life are not reflected in his poetry. At first glance the poems appear to be graceful exercises on a variety of familiar literary themes, as noteworthy for the well-turned phrase as for any probing insights into the human experience, but they do reflect the spirit of an age. In *Restoration Carnival* (1954), Pinto notes that Sedley's poems "grew directly out of his life and are a natural product of the society in which he lived." Nowhere in his life or writings is there any indication that Sedley seriously challenged the values or customs of Restoration society. He lived his life in accordance with the rational skepticism of his class and era and is reported to have "died like a philosopher without fear or superstition." Thus, the consistency of his poetry may well be a reflection of the consistency of his life.

Analysis

Most of Sir Charles Sedley's songs deal with familiar love themes. There are a number of ladies who are alternately encouraging or discouraging, and whose beauty is so striking that it has turned the poet's fancy. The poet is concerned not so much to praise the lady's charms as to persuade her to yield to the pressing demands of time and nature. Sedley was known in his day for the love invitation. Rochester in "An Allusion to Horace: The 10th Satyr of the 1st Book" praises Sedley as a master of persuasion: "*Sidley,* has that prevailing, gentle Art,/ That can with a resistless Charm impart,/ The loosest wishes, to the chastest Heart." A number of Sedley's poems are obviously intended to encourage a lady to yield her virtue. Here, for example, is a short untitled piece on the way the poet passes lonely nights:

> Awake, my Eyes, at Night my Thought[s] pursue
> Your charming Shape; and find it ever new;
> If I my weary Eyes to Sleep resign,
> In gaudy Dreams your Love and Beauty shine;
> Dreams with such Extasies and Pleasures fill'd,
> As to those Joys they seem can only yield;
> Nor do they yield perhaps, wou'd you allow,
> Fair *Amidea*, that I once might know.

Rochester might have been thinking of this poem when he wrote his tribute to Sedley's art. The poem could be part of the sophisticated love games which were played in the comedies of the day, including Sedley's *The Mulberry Garden* and *Bellamira*. To create a feeling of longing within Amidea's heart, the poet employs an argument involving the lover's thwarted expectations of "Extasies," "Pleasures," and "joys," which are only realized in dreams. If one were to extend the argument beyond the poem, one would say that it goes against nature to thwart the fulfillment of such pleasures.

This argument is one more version of an important theme in most of Sedley's love lyrics: the pursuit and realization of pleasure. In a Sedley lyric there are no metaphysical flights which take the reader into another country; the poet is concerned with securing his ease and pleasure in this world. In "An Essay on Satyr," John Sheffield, Earl of Mulgrave, later Duke of Buckinghamshire, notes that "little *Sid*" "Pleasure has always sought, but seldom found:/ Tho' Wine and Women are his only Care,/ Of both he takes a lamentable Share." Most of Mulgrave's portrait, which dates from 1679, involves a nasty attack on the reforms in Sedley's personal life. Nevertheless, for all its venom, it contains a basic truth about Sedley the poet: he always sought pleasure. This statement applies to the late as well as the early works.

This strain of Epicureanism is more than only a ploy in the love game; it is a philosophical principle that was widely held in the Restoration. Sedley presents an Epicurean philosophy most explicitly in two translations from the ancients: "Out of Lycophron" and "To Liber." Sedley's translation of Lycophron, an Alexandrian dramatist who lived in the third century, B.C., stresses the limits of human understanding. Man does not know

> Whither he goes to Heaven or Hell;
> Or after a few moments dear,
> He disappear,
> And at last,
> Perish entirely like a Beast.

He should therefore, not waste his time pondering what is unknowable; rather, he should give himself over to "Women, Wine and Mirth." The tone of this poem is complacent and urbane. There is none of the questioning and rage that one finds in Rochester when he confronts the possibilities of "Nothing." For Lycophron, life is reduced to "a few Moments dear." Even though man in death may be reduced to the status of a beast, Sedley's smooth verse takes the rough edges off this grim knowledge. He uses the possibility of nothing only as an argument to encourage man to secure his pleasure in this life. This Epicurean philosophy is even more emphatically stated in "To Liber," a translation of a Martial epigram. The speaker could be one Restoration gentleman giving another gentleman advice on how to spend his time most profitably. Thus, Liber should think "on charming Objects" and let "easie Beauty warm" his heart. The pursuit of pleasure and the easy satisfaction of appetite are sufficient as guiding principles.

The love lyrics fall into two main categories: those in which the speaker self-consciously considers his own pleasure and ease and how well they are served, and those in which the speaker is an active participant in a flirtation, using his art and cleverness to secure the interest of a particular lady. Part of the charm of the poems in this second category is Sedley's obvious delight in the progress of a flirtation.

Two songs addressed to Phillis—"Phillis, let's shun the common Fate" and "*Phillis* is my only Joy"—fall into the first category. The speaker is as concerned with his own pleasure and ease as with the feelings or needs of Phillis. In the first song, the speaker states his theme in the opening lines: "*Phillis*, let's shun the common Fate,/ And let our Love ne'r turn to Hate." The speaker defines the limits of love, the point at which love ceases to be a pleasure and becomes a burden. The only way to avoid love turning to hate is to leave off loving at the first signs of boredom or disinterest. Thus, the speaker will "dote no longer" than he can, and the couple will part when they begin "to want Discourse,/ And Kindness seems to taste of Force." The speaker envisions love in terms of mild, if delectable, pleasures: "A Smile of thine shall make my Bliss,/ I will enjoy thee in a Kiss." If Phillis should stop loving first, the speaker will "the Blame on Nature lay" and accept his fate without rancor but rather with pride "in Parting well." Love, then, is a kind of bargain. If one does not invest too much of himself in a love relationship, he will experience a fine pleasure and avoid needless pain and suffering.

In "*Phillis* is my only Joy," Sedley celebrates the pleasures that are secured at the price of self-deception. In the second line, the speaker announces that Phillis is as "Faithless as the Winds or Seas," but the rest of the first stanza is about the pleasure he receives from Phillis: She "never fails to please," and she makes him "Happier than before." In the second stanza, the speaker deals with the problems of Phillis' faithlessness, but he reduces it to a game, perhaps best suggested by the telling couplet, "She deceiving,/ I believing." The sense of balance in these two lines and elsewhere suggests that the speaker's self-deception is simply the price he knowingly and willingly pays to secure his own pleasure. When he asks in the final line, "What need Lovers wish for more?" the obvious answer is "Nothing."

In the second main category of Sedley love lyrics, the speaker is an active participant in a flirtation. In such poems, he does not analyze how well his ease and pleasure are served. Rather, his pleasure is revealed by his obvious delight in the business at hand. A number of these verses appear to be designed for real occasions. The most obvious example is "To Amaranta Whom He Fell in Love with at a Play-House." Pinto suggests that the occasion for this poem may have been an encounter between Sedley and a masked lady at the King's House in Drury Lane, which was reported by Samuel Pepys in his diary. The conversation between the two was so sparkling and entertaining that it proved more interesting to Pepys than the performance of *The Maid's Tragedy* (1619). The situation in the poem is dramatic. The speaker encounters a beauty at a playhouse; he soon finds himself experiencing the emotions of the "feigned Love" on the stage: "The Hopes and Fears, in every Scene exprest,/ Grew soon th' uneasie Motions of my Breast." The poet first engages in some idle banter; "And if I ventur'd on some slight Discourse,/

It should be such as could no Passion nurse." Soon he finds himself ensnared ("At last I play'd too near the Precipice"), and then love breaks through like a force—a cultivated force—of nature:

> Your Words fell on my Passion, like those Showers,
> Which paint and multiply the rising Flowers;
> Like *Cupid's* self, a God, and yet a Child,
> Your Looks at once were awful, and yet mild.

Not all Sedley's poems deal with such casual flirtations. Many pay direct compliments to a lady of virtue; some even declare an undying fidelity. Yet even in these poems there is frequently an underlying Epicureanism marking them as the work of Sedley. In one of Sedley's most famous songs, "Not *Celia*, that I juster am," the speaker declares his devotion to Celia. He "would change each Hour" like the rest of mankind, but such are the charms of Celia that he has no choice but to stay where his heart is "at rest." When he concludes that "'Tis easie to be true," it is clear that ease is the condition which permits him to be true.

The presence in the Sedley canon of this poem and several others declaring the speaker's faithfulness creates a minor problem. It is possible to read most of the poems simply as graceful exercises on a variety of common literary themes with no biographical relevance. After all, Sedley wrote lyrics into the 1690's which celebrate the pleasures of flirtation and inconstancy. Nevertheless, there are some poems which invite a more personal interpretation. For example, in *Restoration Carnival*, Pinto calls "Not *Celia*, that I juster am" Sedley's "one great love song" in which he sings of his "real ideal . . . the tranquility of a happy marriage of true minds." Such an assertion is not warranted by the poem itself. Why should the speaker in the Celia poem be closer to Sedley's own feelings than the speaker in one of the Phillis poems?

There are at least two ways to explain this phenomenon. First, all Sedley's poems may have a degree of personal relevance, the seeming contradiction between the speaker of different poems being more apparent than real. The courtiers of the Restoration considered libertinism and marriage as two separate areas of their lives. Rochester, famous for his many sexual escapades, was by all accounts a devoted and affectionate husband and father. Heroes in Restoration comedies such as Dorimant in *The Man of Mode* (1676) also display the same balance between the life of the libertine and the life of a husband. At the end of George Etherege's play, Dorimant is not so much reforming as adding to his life by taking on a wife and engaging in a richer, fuller love relationship than he had experienced before. Second, the sentiments expressed in the Celia poem do appear to have a relevance to certain events in Sedley's life. He may have led the life of a libertine in the early years of his marriage, but when he found the right woman, he publicly declared his devotion to her and committed himself to her for life by going through a form of marriage in 1672 and treating her as his wife for the next thirty years. For Sedley, the concept of marriage was far more important than its legal definition.

Some of Sedley's poems, such as "Constancy," deal with a "marriage of true minds" in which physical attraction is simply the beginning of a long-lasting relationship. This understanding of marriage is at the heart of "To Cloris: *Cloris*, I justly am betray'd," which Pinto sees as being addressed to Ann Ayscough. The poet begins by frankly admitting that he had laid a trap for Cloris, thinking "at first with a small Sum/ Of Love, thy Heap to over-come." The reverse happens, and the poet makes a full declaration of his love, even though he is prevented from marrying Cloris:

> My Hand, alas, is no more mine,
> Else it had long ago been thine;
> My Heart I give thee, and we call
> No Man unjust that parts with all.

So ends the poem in the 1702 edition. In the original 1672 publication of the poem there was an additional couplet: "What a priest says moves not the mind,/ Souls are by love, not words, combin'd." In this couplet, Sedley presents his basic view of marriage, which remained consistent throughout his life: love, rather than social custom, determines a marriage. In *The Happy Pair*, a late poem written in the ratiocinative style of John Dryden's *Religio Laici* (1682), the poet dwells on the horrors of the marriage bed when love is not present:

> With feign'd Embrace they seem Love's Joys to crave,
> But with their Bed, converted to a Grave;
> And whilst their backward Hearts like Load-stones meet,
> They wish their Linnen were the Windingsheet.

The imagery is surprisingly vivid. Sedley is rarely as explicit about the joys of love as he is about the miseries of a mercenary marriage in these lines. His poem ends with a paean to the joys of a lowly marriage where both partners are poor but truly in love. Such a union may belong to a pastoral ideal, but in *The Happy Pair*, it is set against the distorted emotions and values of upper class life, which destroy the chances for true love.

Sedley's views on marriage are consistent with his Epicureanism. If pleasure is the be-all and end-all of existence, love in marriage is the most satisfying pleasure. When love is missing, the marriage is a mockery. Presumably Sedley's unfortunate experience in marrying at a young age for the wrong reasons had taught him this lesson. In *The Restoration Court Poets* (1965), Pinto notes that the conclusion of *The Happy Pair* "with its praise of quiet domesticity shows that the wild gallant of the sixteen-sixties had by the end of the century developed into an Augustan 'man of feeling.'"

Sedley, however, is not remembered today as a forerunner of eighteenth century sentimentalism. He was a poet of his times. To a certain extent, he lived the life that is portrayed so vividly in the world of Restoration comedies, where style, wit, and pleasure are important ends in themselves. This world may not have been quite as amoral as is sometimes thought. The pursuit of pleasure does not rule out the cultivation of sentiment and deep, lifelong attachments, but in the Restoration, it did rule out pomposity and sentimentality. Sedley's poetry exemplifies the grace and wit of an age which too often is remembered only as a time of license and immortality.

Edward V. Geist

Other major works

PLAYS: *Pompey the Great*, 1664 (translation of an act with Edmund Waller, Robert Filmer, Baron Buckhurst, and Sidney Godolphin); *The Mulberry Garden*, 1668; *Antony and Cleopatra*, 1677; *Bellamira: Or, The Mistress*, 1687.

Bibliography
Pinto, Vivian de sola. *Restoration Carnivals, Five courtier Poets: Rochester, Dorset, Sedley, Etherege, and Sheffield*. London: Folio Society, 1954. A thoroughly interesting and illuminating analysis that reveals much about the poets and their works. Offers a worthy overview of Sedley and his poetic achievements. Complemented by a bibliography.
_____. *The Restoration Court Poets: John Wilmot, Earl of Rochester; Charles Sackville, Earl of Dorset; Sir Charles Sedley; Sir George Etherege*. London; Longmans, Green, 1965. This volume compares and examines the critical and theorical views of these four Restoration Court literary figures. The section on Sedley provides criticism helpful to an appreciation and understanding of Sedley's works.
Vinson, James. ed. *Great Writers of the English Language: Poets*. Vol. 1. New York: St. Martin's Press, 1979. The entry by John H. Perry notes that Sedley, one of the chief poets of Charles II's reign, was primarily known for his love poems and songs. He claims that it was Sedley's satires, which betrayed the cynicism of the court, that made him less popular. Praises Sedley for his "perceptive eye and cutting pen."
Wilson, John Harold. *The Court Wits of the Restoration: An Introduction*. Princeton, N.J.: Princeton University Press, 1948. Wilson provides a worthy overview and analysis of early modern English literature from 1500 to 1700 and offers a history and criticism of English wit and humor. Supplemented by a bibliography.

ROBERT W. SERVICE

Born: Preston, England; January 16, 1874
Died: Lancieux, France; September 11, 1958

Principal poetry

Songs of a Sourdough, 1907; *Ballads of a Cheechako*, 1909; *Rhymes of a Rolling Stone*, 1912; *The Rhymes of a Red Cross Man*, 1916; *The Shooting of Dan McGrew and Other Verses*, 1920; *Ballads of a Bohemian*, 1921; *Twenty Bath-Tub Ballads*, 1939; *Bar-Room Ballads*, 1940; *Songs of a Sun-Lover*, 1949; *Rhymes of a Roughneck*, 1950; *Lyrics of a Lowbrow*, 1951; *Rhymes of a Rebel*, 1952; *Songs for My Supper*, 1953; *Carols of an Old Codger*, 1954; *Rhymes for My Rags*, 1956; *Songs of the High North*, 1958.

Other literary forms

Robert W. Service's novels never achieved any degree of literary significance or even popular acceptance; perhaps fiction simply allowed him some diversion from writing verse. The following titles, however, suggest the relationship between Service's poetry and his fiction: *The Trail of '98*, 1910; *The Pretender*, 1914; *The Poisoned Paradise*, 1922; *The Roughneck*, 1923; *The Master of the Microbe*, 1926; *The House of Fear*, 1927. Of greater value to the student are the three major autobiographical pieces, since each helps to cast some light upon both the poet and his work: *Why Not Grow Young?: Or, Living for Longevity*, 1928; *Ploughman of the Moon: An Adventure into Memory*, 1945; and *Harper of Heaven: A Record of Radiant Living*, 1948.

Achievements

Perhaps the simplest way to come to grips with the poetry of Service is to avoid the issue entirely and dismiss the man as little more than a terribly prolific balladeer, the writer of popular frontier verses that rhymed well enough to be memorized by schoolboys and sentimental adults, but which generally lacked poetic merit. A more reasonable approach would be to read the poetry in the light of Service's own intentions. Service saw himself as a grand combination of journalist and teller of tales (a twentieth century Scottish bard, if you will), whose medium was verse rather than the newspaper article or the short story. He preferred to roam certain parts of the world in search of characters whose stories had never really been told—or, at least, whose experiences had never reached a wide audience. In a sense, he listened to people who were themselves glad to come upon an eager listener; he transformed the details of those stories into rhythmic ballads for the benefit of still other listeners—his readers.

Apart from his poetry, he desired nothing more from life than to dream, to live as a recluse and a lover of liberty, to gaze in wonder at the beauty of the world, to observe the complexities and the varieties of the human condition. At the same time, he was a practical man who realized early in life that freedom had to be bought with hard cash; thus, he wrote and worked for that freedom, and in the end he achieved it. His verse remained the natural outlet for his dreams, visions, and observations, the means by which he could share, with ordinary people, the mysteries and joys of human life. As a poet, Service wanted to record, as quickly as possible, the actions and atmospheres of the moment; he did not waste time thinking—he simply saw and then he wrote. Thus, his readers were not required to approach his verse with any complex intellectual, cultural, or historical prerequisites; they needed only to read, to listen, and to imagine.

The achievement of Robert W. Service may well be the triumph of a paradox, of a writer who wanted, essentially, to be left alone with himself and with his thoughts. Nevertheless, he knew that somehow he had to communicate with those around him, to convey to people the essence of myriad experiences (real and imagined) that otherwise they would never see or imagine. He would serve as the surrogate romantic for thousands of people inclined toward romanticism and independence yet rooted to practicality and convention. Service wrote easily, quickly, rhythmically—almost too simply. The boys whooping it up at the Malamute saloon, Sam McGee from Tennessee, the water where the silver salmon play, the great white silence of the wild, the absinthe drinkers of the Café de la Paix, the three grim and gory British Tommies, the grimy men with picks and shovels—all came from the real world of his experience, but all belonged to the private world of his imagination as well.

Bret Harte and Eugene Field were Service's principal models. His poetry was strongly influenced by journalism; like the newspapermen who reported from Africa and the Far East, he sent poetic dispatches from the streets of Paris, the rough terrains of the Yukon, the Mackenzie basin, and the Arctic. Service's achievement was the triumph of *verse* as opposed to poetry; his poems appealed to the romantic young man in the tavern and to the equally romantic old spinster in the parlor. He thrust his heavily rhythmic songs into the hands of the schoolboy, who would recite them, and into the mind of the laborer, who would remember them. By his own admission, however, although he wrote for these people, he intended to please no one but himself.

Biography

The eldest in a family of seven boys and three girls, Robert William Service was born in Preston, Lancashire, England, on January 16, 1874. His father, also Robert Service, worked in a Scottish bank; his mother, Emily Parker, was the daughter of the English owner of a Lancashire cotton mill. From 1880 until 1895, young Service lived in Glasgow, where he received an education of some substance at the Hillhead High School; he also attended some classes at the University and engaged in a self-prescribed reading program at the public library and by way of Miss Bell's Circulating Library. The latter contributed significantly to his taste for literature and to his urge to travel abroad. Early realizing man's dependence upon money, Service worked at the Commercial Bank of Scotland. The drudgery of Glasgow, the bank, and schoolboy athletics, however, quickly gave way to romantic visions of Canada—of cowboys, gold prospectors, and beachcombers. The young man read pamphlets about Canada and set his sights on becoming a sturdy settler in a hard land— on raising grain, riding broncos, and roping steers. In 1895, he crossed the Atlantic aboard a tramp steamer, proceeded to British Columbia, and partook of the freedom of a backwoods ranch in the rough "wild west." From there he made his way up and down the West Coast of the United States, enjoying still more freedom and learning about life on the road.

Despite his love for the vagabond life, Service had a strong practical streak, and in 1903 he determined that a steady job would allow him to save some money, which in turn would provide the necessary independence for writing, travel, and general leisure. After securing a position with the Canadian Bank of Commerce, he moved through its various branches: Victoria and Kamloops in British Columbia, and Dawson in the Yukon. This job was to provide him with more than a solid bank account. Between 1904 and 1912, Service witnessed as a bank clerk and recorded as a writer the decline of the Klondike gold rush that had begun three years after his arrival in Canada. Ironically, his own fortunes ran directly against the tide of the times; such poems as "The Shooting of Dan McGrew" and "The Cremation of Sam McGee" signaled the beginning of his own literary and financial strike.

"The Shooting of Dan McGrew" and "The Cremation of Sam McGee" were published in 1907, in Toronto, as parts of a larger collection entitled *Songs of a Sourdough* (or, in New York, *The Spell of the Yukon and Other Verses*). An insignificant novel followed in 1910, *The Trail of '98*, and then a successful collection, *Rhymes of a Rolling Stone*, two years later. No longer in need of a banking career, Service left Canada in 1912 to cover, for the Toronto *Star*, the brief scuffle involving Turkey, Montenegro, Bulgaria, and Serbia, known as the Balkan War. That experience introduced him to France and Paris; in 1913, he married Germaine Bourgoin, whose father owned a distillery outside Paris, and from that year he maintained residences in France without renouncing his British citizenship. When World War I erupted, Service served first with an American ambulance unit and then with Canadian army intelligence, experiences recorded in *The Rhymes of a Red Cross Man*. After the war, he returned to the highways of the world: the circle began and ended at Paris, with intermediate stops in Hollywood and Tahiti.

Although his Hollywood experience encouraged him to write, between 1922 and 1927, four additional pieces of pure melodrama, those efforts did little to win Service a reputation as a writer of serious fiction. Nevertheless, he continued to reap financial harvests from new verse collections and from complete editions of his poems. He determined to spend the remainder of his days in relative leisure, becoming a quiet and contented gentleman far different from the rough-and-tumble characters who roamed the lines of his ballads and autobiographical verse.

Between the wars, Service found time for two Russian journeys. Returning from the second one, he found himself cut off from his beloved France by World War II; he and his family spent the war years in Hollywood. In 1945, he returned once again to Brittany and Nice, purchased a villa at Monte Carlo, and published, between 1949 and 1956, seven separate volumes of verse and two volumes of his collected poetry. Service died of a heart attack on September 11, 1958—at the age of eighty-four—at his home (appropriately named "Dream Haven") in Lancieux, Brittany.

Analysis

The real difficulty in analyzing the poetic output of Robert W. Service is trying to separate the man from his work—if, indeed, such separation is possible or even necessary. No matter what the poem (for so many of them read as carbon copies of one another), there remains, at the end, the vision of the poet. The reader invariably sees the man of adventure and courage, the headstrong seeker of fame and fortune who, as a relatively young man, left Scotland and sailed for the American continent, there to see and to live with the last generation of pioneers, explorers, and true adventurers. Service detested any reference to himself as a "poet"; the word meant something higher than that to which he aspired or believed he could manage intellectually. To the last, he preferred to be known only as a verse writer, as one who had, since childhood, been talking and thinking in rhyme. In fact, he seemed more inclined toward the talking and the thinking than to expressing his observations and experiences on paper.

In many ways, Service's attitude and actions typified the wandering minstrel of another age, the vagabond strumming on the guitar, singing his own songs, talking about the old times, and telling of countless adventures (actual or imagined). Thus, from the pages of his collected works echo the vigor and the harshness, the tragedy and the ribaldry of the fascinating northern wilderness of Canada. Service virtually immortalized a hundred treks of men and animals through snow and blizzard, privation and suffering, injury and death; yet he also captured in rhyme the sheer glamour and romance of a time when his distant readers equated money with gold dust, love and beauty with a heavily bespangled saloon girl, and art with a whiskey-reeking prospector banging away at an old barroom piano in the corner of a smoke-filled, noisy room. For Service, these were real people in the midst of real experiences—"comrades," he called them, persons with whom he had "tramped God's land together." The triteness and the clichés would come later, from the minds and pens of those who had never seen that about which they were to write and speak.

Yet, the "land God forgot" proved merely a single stop on Service's personal poetic trek. France captured his heart and his rhythmic imagination, first during his bohemian days on the Left Bank, then while he served as a Red Cross ambulance driver during World War I. The songs written in the spring of 1914 reflect his bouts with poverty, when he had to write not for his living, but for his life. Nevertheless, the lines of those pieces are quick and happy attempts to shape the mood of one all too willing to spend his last sous not prudently on bread, but prodigally on beer. In "L'Escargot D'or," Service strolls down the Boul' Mich' in a lingering light that has all the exquisite tenderness of violet. The trees bow to him in their first translucent green; beneath, he sees lamps lit with the purest gold, while from the Little Luxembourg emanates a silver tingle of tiny voices. Boldly, he heads for the gay side of the street and enters the café, a place frequented at one time by Oscar Wilde and John Millington Synge, a place where one may "dream and drain,/ And drown despair." The strength of such poems lies in the reader's awareness that Service has no illusions about his mind or his art. Throughout the first part of *Ballads of a Bohemian* he admits to not being fool enough to think of himself as a poet in the classical sense. Instead, he comes forth as one with a knack for rhyme and an intense love for making verse—or, from another point of view, for "tootling, tin-whistle music." He asks only that his muse bring him bread and butter; if rhyme has been his ruin, he wants only to rhyme until the bitter end—to go down with what he wants to do, rather than be tied to what he has to do.

In August, 1914, however, the happy-go-lucky Bohemian from Glasgow saw the beginning of a world war. At forty, Service felt obliged to pack his happiness away in storage and apply his rhyme to a far different strain. Until that time, he later confessed, his verse had come from a land of his own making—a composite ground of hope, faith, and enthusiasm, of struggle, failure, and eventual triumph. With the coming of war, he believed he saw the end of what he termed "the exultant sunshine [of] our spirits" and the approach of "a deepening shadow of horror and calamity." While the poems of the Yukon carry a noisy, devil-may-care attitude ("there's 'hootch' in the bottle still"), the noise from France on the eve of World War I rings of frustration and fear and uneasiness, emanating from "nightmares of the past." In France, Service saw the shaping of minds in preparation for the battle; he comprehended the heredity and the discipline that sent village men out of their homes to seek barracks and battlefields and, eventually, death. His poems thus bemoan the docility with which farmers and tradesmen don baggy red trousers so as to let "some muddle-headed General" hurl them to destruction for some unknown cause or gain. To be shot in a saloon brawl in Dawson—"pitched on his head, and pumped full of lead"—is one thing; to be a father, a provider, and "fodder for cannon" is quite another matter.

Rudyard Kipling's influence on Robert W. Service (who at times seems to have committed the former's *Barrack-Room Ballads*, 1892, to memory) is quite apparent. Generally, Service favored vigorous description and narrative in long, swinging lines. In his first collection, *Songs of a Sourdough*, he illustrated fully the landscape of northern Canada, while at the same time capturing the fresh atmosphere of an almost unknown land. He wrote of lonely sunsets flaring forlornly down dreary and desolate valleys; of lordly mountains soaring scornfully, as still as death and as stern as fate; of the flames of lonely sunsets and giant valleys that consumed the night (except that his verb is "gulp"); of monster mountains scraping the sky; of an outcast, leper land that only the cry of the wolf can express, the lonely, "fell arch-spirit of the Wild." The poems of that place and of that period almost mirror one another ("Great White Silence," "The Call of the Wild," "The Spell of the Yukon," "The Law of the Yukon"), and the reader should notice particularly the violence of Service's adjectives, the crude satire in reference to men of a more normal and formal mode of existence, and the strong visual images of the naked grandeur of the land that the poet loved—even though God had forgotten it.

This land to which Service committed the early part of his adulthood made him a popular poet—and thus made him a wealthy man. However, he was able to extend his verse beyond the obvious level of "local color." Such poems as "The Shooting of Dan McGrew," "The Cremation of Sam McGee," and "The Ballad of the Black Fox Skin" became popular not only for the entertainment of their stories, but because the poet captured them in sound and rhythm. No doubt Service's yarns would have made first-rate short stories *à la* Bret Harte, Ambrose Bierce, or even Mark Twain. He chose, however, to condense and to versify those tales, giving them the force of brevity and rhyme, and wrapping them in neat packages of his own grim humor and quick command of alliterative phrasing.

Service is sometimes criticized for his failure to provide an accurate reflection of Canadian life. The error rests not with the poet, but with his audience. Service never sought to represent all aspects of Canadian existence. Instead, he chose to depict isolated conditions that prevailed at certain moments in the history of a remote section of the world; he captured with splendid specificity and rhyme the popular conception of the Canadian north.

Service the incurable romantic, the agent of free spirits everywhere, transported his fairly staid audience to the places where they could exercise their suppressed passions, their subconscious enthusiasm for the dangerous and the exciting. He carried to tens of thousands, in clear language and quick meter, the extreme Canadian north, the streets of Paris, the trenches of Flanders. Service possessed a limited but very practical poetic vision. Theories concerning poetry did not interest him. He sought only verse, and seemed quite content to follow the likes of Thomas Hood and Bret Harte, the real fashions of his day. He wanted, simply, to spend his days in the relative calm of his own privacy, testifying to "the rhapsody of existence," where youth and age might affirm, "the ecstasy of being."

Samuel J. Rogal

Other major works

FICTION: *The Trail of '98*, 1910; *The Pretender*, 1914; *The Poisoned Paradise*, 1922; *The Roughneck*, 1923; *The Master of the Microbe*, 1926; *The House of Fear*, 1927.

NONFICTION *Why Not Grow Young?: Or, Living for Longevity*, 1928; *Ploughman of the Moon: An Adventure into Memory*, 1945; *Harper of Heaven: A Record of Radiant Living*, 1948.

Bibliography

Athern, Stanley S. "The Klondike Muse." *Canadian Literature A Quarterly of Criticism and Review* 47 (Winter, 1971); 67-72. Athern encourages critics to examine the Klondike works of Service as a pioneering attempt to mythologize the Canadian gold rush as early environmental history. While not speaking highly of Service's talents, Athern gives valuable insight into Service's initial publications.

Bucco, Martin. "Folk Poetry of Robert W. Service." *Alaska Review* 2 (Fall, 1965): 16-26. Bucco analyzes Service's Yukon poetry from the viewpoint that it used the search for gold as a metaphor for the quest for self. With this as his overriding theme, Bucco shows how Service created a vivid sense of tradition for the men who sought out the elusive riches buried in the forbidding North.

Burness, Edwina. "The Influence of Burns and Fergusson of the War Poetry of Robert Service." *Studies in Scottish Literature* 12 (1986): 135-146. Concentrates only on Service's war poetry and explores the influences that Robert Burns and Robert Fergusson had on Service. Burness draws interesting parallels between the men as she details the effects of realism, humor, and symbolism on the "universal" Scottish mind.

Hirsch, Edward. "A Structural Analysis of Robert Service's Yukon Ballads." *Southern Folklore Quarterly* 40 (March-June, 1976): 125-140. Hirsch suggests that Service's poetry should be judged by the aesthetics of oral traditions and not as literary artifacts. He analyzes some of Service's Yukon ballads as monologue compositions and finds them very acceptable in accomplishing that intent.

Klinck, Carl F. *Robert Service: A Biography*. New York: Dodd, Mead, 1976. The only biography of Service published in modern times, this book is invaluable in studying the life of this amazing poet. Drawing heavily on Service's two-volume autobiography, Klinck follows the poet's career, commenting on the influences that led to such a variance in the subject matter of Service's works.

Klinck, Carl F., and William H. New. "Robert Service." In *Dictionary of Literary Biography*, edited by William H. New. Vol. 92. Detroit: Gale Research, 1990. For those who want a brief history of Service, this article has immense value. Short and to the point, it highlights Service's life and career, while mentioning his more famous works and integrating them into a time frame. A short list of references augments this selection.

Whatley, W. A. "Kipling's Influence in the Verse of Robert W. Service." *Texas Review* 6 (July, 1921): 299-308. Whatley, while recognizing and commenting on Kipling's influence on Service, expresses admiration for the native talents of Service. Through analyzing several ballads, Whatley presents Service's war poetry as nonpropaganda ballads written in the true "carry-on" spirit of Britain.

ANNE SEXTON

Born: Newton, Massachusetts; November 9, 1928
Died: Weston, Massachusetts; October 4, 1974

Principal poetry

To Bedlam and Part Way Back, 1960; *All My Pretty Ones*, 1962; *Selected Poems*, 1964; *Live or Die*, 1966; *Poems*, 1968 (with Thomas Kinsella and Douglas Livingston); *Love Poems*, 1969, *Transformations*, 1971; *The Book of Folly*, 1972; *The Death Notebooks*, 1974; *The Awful Rowing Toward God*, 1975; *Words for Dr. Y: Uncollected Poems with Three Stories*, 1978; *The Complete Poems*, 1981.

Other literary forms

In addition to several articles on the craft and teaching of poetry, Anne Sexton authored a play that ran successfully at the American Place Theatre of New York and several children's books written in collaboration with Maxine Kumin. The play, *45 Mercy Street* (1969), presents the struggle of a woman named Daisy to find meaning in a past and present dominated by religious and sexual conflicts objectified as demons and disembodied voices. Its success suggests that the poet also had talent as a playwright, and critics find the thematic material important biographically and artistically in an analysis of Sexton's career. An important collection of her prose is *Anne Sexton: A Self-Portrait in Letters* (1977); also, a recording of twenty-four poems read by the poet is available as *Anne Sexton Reads Her Poetry*, recorded June 1, 1974.

Achievements

With little formal training in literature, Sexton emerged as a major modern voice, transforming verse begun as therapy into poetic art of the first order. Important for refining the confessional mode, experimenting with new lyrical forms, and presenting themes from the female consciousness, Sexton's work has the controversial impact of any pioneering artist. Despite periodic hospitalization for depression ultimately culminating in her suicide at age forty-six, Sexton contributed richly to her craft, receiving much critical recognition and traveling widely. Awarded fellowships to most of the major writing conferences, she worked closely with John Holmes, W. D. Snodgrass, Robert Lowell, Maxine Kumin, and others. She taught creative writing at Harvard, Radcliffe, and Boston University, and she served as editorial consultant to the *New York Poetry Quarterly* and as a member of the board of directors of *Audience* magazine. In 1963, her second collection of poetry, *All My Pretty Ones*, was nominated for a National Book Award; and in 1967, her fourth collection, *Live or Die*, received a Pulitzer Prize. Sexton also received a Guggenheim Fellowship in 1969 and many honorary degrees from major universities.

Although most critics believe the quality of her work deteriorated toward the end of her life, she had achieved by that time success with a new, highly personal voice in poetry and expanded the range of acceptable subjects to include the intimate concerns of women. In presenting the theme of female identity, Sexton began with a careful lyric formalism and then progressed throughout her career to experiment with open, dramatic forms, moving from the confessional to the surreal. She explored the limits of sanity and the nature of womanhood more fully than any poet of her generation.

Biography

The daughter of upper-middle-class parents, Anne Gray Harvey attended the public schools of Wellesley, Massachusetts, spent two years at Rogers Preparatory School, and one year at Garland Junior College, before marrying Alfred Muller Sexton, whose nickname "Kayo" provides the dedication for her first volume of poems. Although a strictly biographical approach to Anne Sexton's work is dangerously limiting, the significant events of her life serve as major subjects and impetus for her art.

After her marriage, she worked briefly as a model at the Hart Agency of Boston. Then, when she was twenty-five, her first daughter, Linda Gray Sexton, was born. The next year, Anne Sexton was hospitalized for emotional disturbance and several months later suffered the loss of her beloved great-aunt, Anna Ladd Dingley, nicknamed "Nana," in various poems and remembrances. The next year, Joyce Ladd Sexton was born, but within months her mother was again hospitalized for depression culminating in a suicide attempt on her twenty-eighth birthday.

Following her first suicide attempt, Sexton began writing poetry on the advice of her psychiatrist, Dr. Martin, whose name appears in her first collection of poems. On the strength of her first work, she received a scholarship to the Antioch Writer's Conference where she worked with W. D. Snodgrass. Then she was accepted into Robert Lowell's graduate writing seminar at Boston University, soon developing friendships with Sylvia Plath, Maxine Kumin, and George Starbuck. The next year, both of Sexton's parents died in rapid succession. She continued her work, attending the Bread Loaf Writer's Conference and delivering the Morris Gray Poetry Lecture at Harvard, although she was hospitalized at intervals for pneumonia, an appendectomy, and an ovarectomy. In 1960, Sexton studied with Philip Rahv and Irving Howe at Brandeis University and developed a friendship with James Wright. She was appointed, with Maxine Kumin, to be the first scholars in poetry at the Radcliffe Institute for Independent Study. In 1962, she was again hospitalized for depression, but by the end of the year, she recovered and toured Europe on the first traveling fellowship of the American Academy of Arts and Letters. She also received a Ford Foundation grant for residence with the Charles Playhouse in Boston.

In 1966, Sexton began a novel that was never completed. She again attempted suicide in July, 1966. In August, she took an African safari with her husband, but in November, she was hospitalized again when she broke her hip on her thirty-eighth birthday. In May of that year, she received the Pulitzer Prize for *Live or Die* and the Shelley Award from the Poetry Society of America. She taught poetry as a visiting professor in many schools and received many honorary degrees before again attempting suicide in 1970. In 1973, she divorced her husband during another period of hospitalization for depression. Although she continued to write and teach despite frequent intervals of hospitalization, in 1974, she committed suicide by carbon monoxide poisoning in the garage of her home.

Analysis

Anne Sexton's poetry presents a search for self and meaning beyond the limits of conventional expression and form. Although viewing her work autobiographically limits critical understanding of it, readers discover in her work a chronicle of experience that is intensely personal and genuine. Her poems are confessional in that they present statements about impulses formerly unknown or forbidden. Begun for self-revelation in therapy and initially sustained for the possible benefit of other troubled patients, Sexton's poems speak with penetrating honesty about the experience of mental illness, the temptation of suicide, and the dynamics of womanhood. Although less strident in tone than the work of Sylvia Plath, Sexton's work occasionally alienates readers who, like James Dickey, find her work too personal for literary evaluation. At its best, however, Sexton's poetry develops the confessional lyric into an effective modern form.

In her first collection, *To Bedlam and Part Way Back*, scenes from an asylum are set against those of life before and after the speaker's hospitalization. The perspective of these early poems is a daring interior one, underscored by the book's epigraph taken from a letter of Arthur Schopenhauer to Johann Wolfgang von Goethe, including the phrase "But most of us carry in our heart the Jocasta who begs Oedipus for God's sake not to inquire further." Sexton's poems pursue the inquiry into the mental hospital and the mind of the patient as well. In the chantlike poem "Ringing the Bells," for example, Sexton projects the senseless rhythm of institutional life through the consciousness of a patient in the bell choir of a mental ward. The troubled women who "mind by instinct" assemble, smile, ring their bells when pointed to, and disperse, no better for their weekly music lesson. Another well-known portrayal of institutional life, "Lullaby," shows the figure of the night nurse arriving with the sleeping pills that, like splendid pearls, provide a momentary escape for the patients who receive them. Observing the moths which cling to window screen, the patient of "Lullaby" imagines that he will become like them after taking the sedative. "You, Doctor Martin" presents other figures in the mental hospital, including the large children who wait in lines to be counted at dinner before returning to the labor of making moccasins all day long. Although the portrayal of the mental hospital from an insider's perspective provides a fresh subject for experimental lyrics, Sexton's poems of the journey and return (suggested by the volumes title) are among her most complex and effective.

"The Double Image," for example, is a composite of experiences parallel to Sexton's own biography. In the poem, the speaker's hospitalization brings about a separation from her young daughter; the speaker's return to live in the home of her childhood coincides with the final illness of her own mother. Weaving together the present moment of her return home for a reunion with her daughter and events of the past, the speaker reflects on the guilt bounded by past and present sorrow. The three autumns explain her trouble better than any medical theories, and she finds that despair and guilt transform attempts at ordinary life into artifice. Portrait painting becomes a metaphor for control of time and emotions through the rest of the poem. Unable to adjust to the awkward period spent as a grown child in her parents' home, the speaker states repeatedly "I had my portrait done instead." The same response belongs to her mother, who cannot forgive the speaker's attempt at suicide and so chooses to have the daughter painted as a measure of control. A double image forms when the mother learns of her own incurable illness and has her portrait done "instead." The portraits, facing each other in the parental home, serve as a mirror reflection with the figure of the speaker's child moving between them. As the speaker had been "an awkward guest" returning to her mother's home, so the young daughter arrives "an awkward guest" for the reunion with her recovering mother. The child provides both a measure of final identity and guilt.

In "The Division of Parts," the bitterness of inheritance replaces grief as a response to the death of the speaker's mother. As in "The Double Image," the coincidence of the speaker's recovery with her mother's suffering suggests an apparent exchange of death for life. Equipped with the lost one's "garments" but not with grief, the speaker recalls the suffering of her mother, overshadowed now by the ceremonies of the Lenten season. Division of property replaces the concerns of the Christ who waits on the crucifix for the speaker. Her dreams recall only the division of ways: the separation of death and inevitable division of property.

Other poems in the first volume experiment with the voices of experience different from the poet's. "The Farmer's Wife," for example, reveals the isolation and loneliness of a young wife on an Illinois farm. The poem presents the ambivalence of the woman toward her husband, whose work and bed are her lifelong habit. "Unknown Girl in the Maternity Ward" attempts to voice the feelings of an unmarried girl who has just given birth. The emotions and imagery are generalized and undefined in presenting the setting of an urban hospital and the typical unmarried girl in trouble. According to Sexton, the poem marks a pivotal moment in her career, for after reading it, Robert Lowell advised her to develop the more personal voice that gives her finest poetry its power. A poem reflecting conflicting advice is "For John, Who Begs Me Not to Enquire Further." John Holmes, Sexton's teacher for a Boston University poetry workshop, recommended that she avoid the self-revelation becoming characteristic of her work. The directly personal voice won out, not only in this poem of apology to Holmes but also throughout her career. Another early poem, "Kind Sir: These Woods," indicates an awareness that readers in general may disapprove her probing of the psyche, "this inward look that society scorns." The speaker finds in her inward search, however, nothing worse than herself, "caught between the grapes and the thorns," and the search for herself continued to the end of her life.

An epigraph for Sexton's second collection, *All My Pretty Ones*, suggests a reason for the poet's insistence on inner exploration. According to a letter of Franz Kafka, "a book should serve as the ax for the frozen sea within us." Sexton similarly asserted in a later interview that "poems of the inner life can reach the inner lives of readers in a way that anti-war poems can never stop a war." The inner life revealed in *All My Pretty Ones* is primarily the experience of grief, the response to loss of the most precious others expressed in the lines from *Macbeth* (1606) that form the title. "The Truth the Dead Know" and the title poem deal with the death of Sexton's parents during the same year. The first poem eliminates personal references except for a dedication to the parents and simply contrasts the intensity of life and grief with the emptiness and stoniness of the dead. "All My Pretty Ones" addresses the lost father with memories of his belongings, his habits, and his hopes. Disposition of scrapbook photographs provides a way to accept and forgive the disappointments of the past, including the secret alcoholism his daughter can never forget.

The strongest poems of the second volume arise from Sexton's own experience. In "The Operation," the speaker's confrontation with death parallels the illness of her mother, and the speaker considers the uncertainty of life as much as the reality of death. Knowing that cancer, the disease of her mother, the "historic thief" that plundered her mother's home is now invading her own domain, the speaker proceeds helplessly through the preparations for surgery, the experience of losing consciousness, and the recovery phase in doubt of her survival. Then, pronounced better, perhaps cured, by the doctors, she is sent home like a child, the stitches in her abdomen reminding her of the lacing on a football ready for the game. A similar sense of vulnerability appears in "The Fortress," wherein the speaker admits to her sleeping child that a mother has no ability to control life and that eventually it will overtake the child through the suffering of "bombs or glands" ending in death. Beyond

the sense of relationships, especially those connected with motherhood, controlling many of Sexton's poems, there looms a sense of dark knowledge
gained through poetry as a secret or forbidden art. In "The Black Art," for
example, the speaker asserts that a woman who writes will not fit into society,
for she "feels too much, these trances and portents." Home, family, social
life are inadequate expressions for the one who wishes to know and control
the mysterious forces of existence. The poem recalls an earlier statement of
identity, "Her Kind," in which the speaker presents herself as a witch who
is lonely, misunderstood, insane, and unashamed to die in the course of her
journey. The comparison of Sexton's poetry with the black arts places her
work on the level of myth, particularly in her pursuit of death itself.

Live or Die, Sexton's third collection, marks a high point in her career for
handling intimate or despairing material with sure control and an element of
self-irony. The epigraph for this book, taken from Saul Bellow's *Herzog*
(1964), records the admonition to "Live or die, but don't poison everything."
Certainly, the poems of this group reflect the impulse toward love and life
as well as the impulse toward despair and death. The institutional setting
appears in the volume but so does the home and family relationships of
Sexton. "Flee on Your Donkey," one of her best-known poems, develops the
tension between the worlds of private and institutional life. In the poem, a
flood of scenes from the hospital culminates in a desire to escape back to the
normal world that patients enter the hospital to avoid. Similarly, in "For the
Year of the Insane," structured as a prayer to Mary, the speaker struggles to
escape her mental as well as physical confinement. No longer at peace in the
refuge of therapy, a mind that believes itself "locked in the wrong house"
struggles in vain for expression and release. Poems of similar desperation,
"The Addict" and "Wanting to Die," develop other means of escape. The
speaker of the former poem yearns for the hallucinatory realm where drugs
parcel out moments of deathlike experience. "Wanting to Die," one of
Sexton's best-known poems, strives to explain for the uninitiated the hunger
for death haunting the potential suicide. The obsession with methods of dying
replaces the desire for experience of life. Love itself becomes "an infection"
to those seeking the secret pleasure of that final escape from the body will
bring.

Poems of the third collection that deal with survival include those concerned
with children and birth. In "Little Girl, My String Bean, My Lovely Woman,"
the speaker identifies with the approaching womanhood of her daughter
Linda, beautiful even in the uncertain changes adolescence creates. The poem
celebrates the body in its growth and capacity for becoming; the figure of
mother and daughter share the mystery of reproduction that is spiritual, "a
white stone," as well as physical, "laughter," and joy. In "Pain for a
Daughter," the mother discovers in her injured child's suffering a universal
misery that transcends their relationship. The child's foot torn by the hoof

of a horse, she cries out to God, not her mother, and the isolation of the cry suggests not childhood misery but the future pangs of childbirth and death itself. The decision to survive, for the moment at least, appears in "Live," the final statement of the volume. The speaker recounts a shift from life as a dark pretense or game to a moment when the sun rose within her, illuminating the figures of her husband and daughters. The speaker determines herself no longer the murderer she thought, allowing the newborn Dalmatian puppies to live and deciding to survive herself.

Love Poems, Sexton's fourth collection, examines the cycle of roles women play in life and love. Poems of separation and return, for example, include "Touch" and "Eighteen Days Without You," lyrics in which love between a woman and her lover controls survival and existence beyond their union. Throughout the volume, individual body parts achieve significance beyond their function in the physical realm. "Touch" begins, "For months my hand had been sealed off/ in a tin box." Following the arrival of her lover, life rushes into the fingers, spreading across the continent in its intensity. Other celebrations of physical contact include "The Kiss," "The Breast," and "In Celebration of My Uterus." In this last poem, Sexton develops a great song which a whole catalog of women sing as they go about their daily work carrying the "sweet weight" of the womb. The negative side of experience returns in poems such as "The Break," which recounts the depression preceding a fall down the stairs which broke Sexton's hip and forced another lengthy hospitalization. Although the bones are sure to heal, the speaker's heart begins another building process to create a "death crèche," ready for the zeal of destruction when it returns.

The theme of self-destruction is hidden in *Transformations*, Sexton's collection of rewritten fairy tales narrated by a "middle-aged witch," the poet's name for her persona in the tales. For some critics, this collection provides a more objective scheme for Sexton's mythic quest; for others, the subject matter is quaint and unoriginal. Certainly the retold tales are entertaining and effective in the dark, modern twists Sexton creates. "Snow White," for example, tortures the wicked queen without mercy before returning to gaze triumphantly in her mirror "as women do." "Rumpelstiltskin" develops the figure of the dark one within, the doppelgänger trying to escape every man. Failing to gain the queen's child, he splits in two, "one part papa/ one part Doppelganger," completing the division of the psyche. "Briar Rose (Sleeping Beauty)" becomes a tortured insomniac after being awakened by her prince and never knows the sleep of death.

Sexton's last collections, *The Book of Folly*, *The Death Notebooks*, and *The Awful Rowing Toward God* contain many of her previous themes developed in experimental forms, including dramatic changes in style. Critics note a looser structure in the poems written late in Sexton's career; some believe it reflects a deterioration of her creative powers, while others find the experimentalism valuable for its innovation. One of the well-known late poems, "Hurry Up Please It's Time," reflects both the variety of thematic material, the variable stanza lengths, and the intrusion of dialogue, such as those between "Anne" and "The Interrogator." The poem reworks the approach of death and the obsessive derision of life on the part of the dying one. "Ms. Dog," one of Sexton's nicknames for herself and God spelled backward, figures in the poem as the troubled one facing guilt and rejection, the mystery and futility of death. In "Frenzy," another of the last poems, the speaker describes herself "typing out the God/ my typewriter believes in." Through the last years of Sexton's life, her writing sustained her even as her quest darkened. At the end of her life, she sought God when doctors, friends, and family were unable to help her; and her work reflected an outwardly religious search that had formerly been hidden. Although she never revealed that she found God within or without the lines of her poetry, she left behind a brilliant record of her heroic search.

Chapel Louise Petty

Other major works
PLAY: *45 Mercy Street*, 1969.
NONFICTION: *Anne Sexton: A Self-Portrait in Letters*, 1977; *No Evil Star: Selected Essays, Interviews, and Prose*, 1985.

Bibliography
Hall, Caroline King Barnard. *Anne Sexton*. Boston: Twayne, 1989. This useful introduction to Sexton examines her poetry and its chronological development. Describes the arc of her journey through the labyrinth of "madness, love, alienation, guilt and hope toward her answer." Worth noting is the chapter "*Transformations*: Fairy Tales Revisited."
McClatchy, J. D. *Anne Sexton: The Artist and Her Critics*. Bloomington: Indiana University Press, 1978. A collection of documentary and interpretative material—overviews, reviews, and reflections—on Sexton, including what are thought to be three of her best interviews. The volume sets out to establish a balanced critical perspective on this poet's work and includes reprints of journals.
Markey, Janice. *A New Tradition? The Poetry of Sylvia Plath, Anne Sexton, and Adrienne Rich*. Frankfurt am Main, Germany: Peter Lang, 1985. Discusses Sexton's label as a "confessional poet" and notes the criticism of repetition in her poems. In spite of this, cites Sexton's real wish to communicate something meaningful to her audience. This essay offers strong criticism, exploring Sexton's feminist roots and her perception of marriage as a failed institution.
Middlebrook, Diane Wood, and Diana Hume George, eds. *Selected Poems of*

Anne Sexton. Boston: Houghton Mifflin, 1988. The introduction to this volume is clear and concise, noting that Sexton herself disliked the label reductionist and described herself as a storyteller. Discusses the imagery in her works and provides an excellent overview for beginning readers of Sexton.

Schurr, William H. "Anne Sexton's Love Poems: The Genre and the Differences." *Modern Poetry Studies* 10, no. 1 (1980): 58-68. Analyzes her love poems and discusses "That Day" at length, which Schurr describes as "intensely erotic." Argues that Sexton wished to convey the "*impression* of raw emotion in these poems."

Sexton, Linda Gray, and Lois Amcs, eds. *Anne Sexton: A Self-Portrait in Letters.* Boston: Houghton Mifflin, 1977. A compilation of the best and most representative letters written by Sexton, who was an exceptional correspondent. Contains a wonderful collection of letters, arranged chronologically and interspersed with biographical details, and providing much insight about this poet's imagination.

Wagner-Martin, Linda, ed. *Critical Essays on Anne Sexton.* Boston: G. K. Hall, 1989. An important volume of selected critical essays, gathering early reviews and modern scholarship, including essays on Sexton's poems and her life. All the essays offer significant secondary material on Sexton; The introduction by Wagner-Martin is particularly helpful in giving an overview of Sexton's poems. Includes a reminiscence by poet Maxine Kumin, a former teacher and friend.

WILLIAM SHAKESPEARE

Born: Stratford-upon-Avon, England; April 23, 1564
Died: Stratford-upon-Avon, England, April 23, 1616

Principal poetry

Venus and Adonis, 1593; *The Rape of Lucrece,* 1594; *The Passionate Pilgrim,* 1599 (miscellany with poems by Shakespeare and others); *The Phoenix and the Turtle,* 1601; *A Lover's Complaint,* 1609; *Sonnets,* 1609.

Other literary forms

William Shakespeare is perhaps the world's greatest dramatist—certainly, at the very least, the greatest to write in English. Of his thirty-seven plays, written over a career in the theater that spanned, roughly, the years 1588 to 1613, the most important are *Romeo and Juliet* (c. 1595-1596); *Henry IV, Parts I* and *II* (c. 1597-1598); *Hamlet, Prince of Denmark* (c. 1600-1601); *Othello, The Moor of Venice* (1604); *Measure for Measure* (1604); *King Lear* (c. 1605-1606); *Macbeth* (1606); *Antony and Cleopatra* (c. 1606-1607); *The Winter's Tale* (c. 1610-1611); and *The Tempest* (1611).

Achievements

Shakespeare also wrote some of the greatest love poems in English. His short erotic narratives, *Venus and Adonis* and *The Rape of Lucrece,* were typical examples of fashionable literary genres. Other minor poems include contributions to the miscellany *The Passionate Pilgrim* and *The Phoenix and the Turtle,* written for a collection of poems appended to *Love's Martyr* (1601), an allegorical treatment of love by Robert Chester. All of these pale alongside the sonnets, which, in an age of outstanding love poetry, attain a depth, suggestiveness, and power rarely duplicated in the history of mankind's passionate struggle to match desire with words.

Biography

William Shakespeare was born in the provincial town of Stratford-upon-Avon in 1564 and died there in 1616. He spent most of his adult life in the London theaters and quickly attained a reputation as a dramatist, actor, and poet. Shakespeare's company prospered under the reign of James I, and by the time of his retirement from playwrighting about 1612, Shakespeare had acquired a respectable fortune. His career as a poet, distinct from his more public career as a dramatist, was probably confined to perhaps a decade, between 1591 and 1601, although the sonnets were later collected and published (perhaps without his permission) in 1609. Because of the absurd controversies that grew, mainly in the nineteenth century, about whether Shakespeare actually existed, it is worthwhile pointing out that there are many official records (christening record, marriage license, legal documents, correspondence, and so on) which may be consulted by the skeptical.

Analysis

One of William Shakespeare's great advantages as a writer was that, as a dramatist working in the public theater, he was afforded a degree of autonomy from the cultural dominance of the court, his age's most powerful institution. All over Europe, even if belatedly in England, the courts of the Renaissance nation-states conducted an intense campaign to use the arts to further their power. The theater, despite its partial dependency on court favor, achieved through its material products (the script and the performance) a relative autonomy in comparison with the central court arts of poetry, prose fiction, and the propagandistic masque. When Shakespeare briefly turned to Ovidian romance in the 1590's and, belatedly, probably also in the 1590's, to the fashion for sonnets, he moved closer to the cultural and literary dominance of the court's taste—to the fashionable modes of Ovid, Petrarch, and Neoplatonism—and to the need for patronage. Although the power of the sonnets goes far beyond their sociocultural roots, Shakespeare nevertheless adopts the culturally inferior role of the petitioner for favor, and there is an undercurrent of social and economic powerlessness in the sonnets, especially when a rival poet seems likely to supplant the poet. In short, Shakespeare's nondramatic poems grow out of and articulate the strains of the 1590's, when, like many ambitious writers and intellectuals on the fringe of the court, Shakespeare clearly needed to find a language in which to speak—and that was, necessarily, given to him by the court. What he achieved within this shared framework, however, goes far beyond any other collection of poems in the age. Shakespeare's occasional poems are unquestionably minor, interesting primarily because he wrote them; his sonnets, on the other hand, constitute perhaps the language's greatest collection of lyrics. They are love lyrics, and clearly grow from the social, erotic, and literary contexts of his age. Part of their greatness, however, lies in their power to be read again and again in later ages, and to raise compellingly, even unanswerably, more than merely literary questions.

In his first venture into public poetry, Shakespeare chose to work within the generic constraints of the fashionable Ovidian verse romance. *Venus and Adonis* appealed to the taste of young aristocrats such as the Earl of Southampton to whom it was dedicated. It is a narrative poem in six-line stanzas, mixing classical mythology with surprisingly (and incongruously) detailed descriptions of country life, designed to illustrate the story of the seduction of the beautiful youth Adonis by the comically desperate aging goddess, Venus. It is relatively static, with too much argument to make it inherently pleasurable reading. Its treatment of love relies on Neoplatonic and Ovidian commonplaces, and it verges (unlike Christopher Marlowe's *Hero and Leander*, 1598, to which Shakespeare's poem is a fair but decidedly inferior fellow) on moralizing allegory, with Venus as flesh, Adonis as spiritual longing. The poem's articulation of the nature of the love that separates them is abstract and often unintentionally comic—although Shakespeare's characterization of Venus as a garrulous plump matron brings something of his theatrical power to enliven the poem. The poem was certainly popular at the time, going through ten editions in as many years, possibly because its early readers thought it fashionably sensual.

The Rape of Lucrece is the "graver labor" which Shakespeare promised to Southampton in the Preface to Venus and Adonis. Again, he combines a current poetical fashion—the complaint— with a number of moral common-places, and writes a novelette in verse: a melodrama celebrating the prototype of matronly chastity, the Roman lady Lucrece, and her suicide after she was raped. The central moral issue—that of honor—at times almost becomes a serious treatment of the psychology of self-revulsion; but the decorative and moralistic conventions of the complaint certainly do not afford Shakespeare the scope of a stage play. There are some fine local atmospheric effects which, in their declamatory power, occasionally bring the directness and power of the stage into the verse.

The Phoenix and the Turtle is an allegorical, highly technical celebration of an ideal love union: it consists of a funeral procession of mourners, a funeral anthem, and a final lament for the dead. It is strangely evocative, dignified, abstract, and solemn. Readers have fretted, without success, over the exact identifications of its characters. Its power lies in its mysterious, eerie evocation of the mystery of unity in love.

Probably more human ingenuity has been spent on Shakespeare's sonnets than on any other work of English literature. In his outstanding edition entitled Shakespeare's Sonnets (1978), Stephen Booth briefly summarizes the few facts that have led to a plethora of speculation on such matters as text, authenticity, date, arrangement, and, especially, biographical implications. The sonnets were first published in 1609, although numbers 138 and 144 had appeared in The Passionate Pilgrim a decade before. Attempts to reorder the sonnets have been both varied and creative, but none represents the "correct" order. Such attempts simply fulfill an understandable anxiety on the part of some readers to see narrative continuity rather than variations and repetition in the sonnets. The so-called "story" "behind" the sonnets has, as Booth puts it, "evoked some notoriously creative scholarship": speculation on the identity of the young man mentioned in many of the first 126 sonnets, of Mr. W. H., to whom the sequence is dedicated by the printer, of the so-called "Dark Lady" of sonnets 127-152, and of the rival poet of some of the earlier sonnets— all of these matters have filled many library shelves.

Such speculations—which reached their peak in critics and readers wedded to the sentimental Romantic insistence on an intimate tie between literary and historical "events"—are in one sense a tribute to the power of the sonnets.

They are arguably the greatest collection of love poems in the language, and they provide a crucial test for the adequacy of both the love of poetry and the sense of the fascinating confusion which makes up human love. In a sense, the sonnets are as "dramatic" as any of Shakespeare's plays inasmuch as their art is that of meditations on love, beauty, time, betrayal, insecurity, and joy. Each sonnet is like a little script, with (often powerful) directions for reading and enactment, with textual meanings that are not given but made anew in every performance, by different readers within their individual and social lives. What Sonnet 87 terms "misprision" may stand as the necessary process by which each sonnet is produced by each reader.

It is conventional to divide the sonnets into two groups—1-126, purportedly addressed or related to a young man, and 127-152, to the so-called "dark lady." Such a division is arbitrary at best—within each group there are detachable subgroups, and without the weight of the conventional arrangement many sonnets would not seem to have a natural place in either group. Sonnets 1-17 (and perhaps 18) are ostensibly concerned with a plea for a young man to marry; but even in this group, which many readers have seen to be the most conventional and unified, there are disruptive suggestions that go far beyond the commonplace context.

What may strike contemporary readers, and not merely after an initial acquaintance with the sonnets, is the apparently unjustified level of idealization voiced by many of the sonnets—an adulatory treatment of noble love which, to a post-Freudian world, might seem archaic, no matter how comforting. The continual self-effacement of the anguished lover, the worship of the "God in love, to whom I am confined" (110), the poet's claim to immortalizing "his beautie . . . in these blacke lines" (63), idealizations are all born out of a world of serene affirmation. Some of the most celebrated sonnets, such as "Shall I compare thee to a summer's day" (18) or "Let me not to the marriage of true minds" (116), may even seem cloyingly affirmative, their texts seemingly replete, rejecting any subtextual challenges to their idealism.

In the two hundred years since Petrarch, the sonnet had developed into an instrument of logic and rhetoric. The Shakespearian sonnet, on the other hand, with its three quatrains and a concluding couplet, allows especially for the concentration on a single mood; it is held together less by the apparent logic of many of the sonnets (for example, the "when . . . then" pattern) than by the invitation to enter into the dramatization of a brooding, sensitive mind. The focus is on emotional richness, on evoking the immediacy of felt experience. Shakespeare uses many deliberately generalized epithets, indeterminate signifiers and floating referents which provoke meaning from their readers rather than providing it. Each line contains contradictions, echoes, and suggestions which require an extraordinary degree of emotional activity on the part of the reader. The couplets frequently offer a reader indeterminate statements, inevitably breaking down any attempt at a limited formalist reading. The greatest of the sonnets—60, 64, 129, as well as many others—have such an extraordinary combination of general, even abstract, words and unspecified emotional power that the reader may take it as the major rhetorical characteristic of the collection.

In particular lines, too, these poems achieve amazing power by their lack of logical specificity and emotional open-endedness. As Booth points out, many lines show "a constructive vagueness" by which a word or phrase is made to do multiple duty—by placing it "in a context to which it pertains but which it does not quite fit idiomatically" or by using phrases which are simultaneously illogical and amazingly charged with meaning. He instances "separable spite" in Sonnet 36 as a phrase rich with suggestion; another example is the way in which the bewilderingly ordinary yet suggestive epithets sit uneasily in the opening lines of Sonnet 64. Often a reader is swept on through the poem by a syntactical movement which is modified or contradicted by associations set up by words and phrases. There is usually a syntactical or logical framework in the sonnet, but so powerful are the contradictory, random, and disruptive effects occurring incidentally as the syntax unfolds that to reduce the sonnet to its seemingly replete logical framework is to miss the most amazing effects of these extraordinary poems.

Shakespeare is writing at the end of a very long tradition of using lyric poems to examine the nature of human love, and there is a weight of insight as well as of rhetorical power behind his collection. Nowhere in the Petrarchan tradition are the extremes of erotic revelation offered in such rawness and complexity. Northrop Frye once characterized the sonnets as a kind of "creative yoga," an imaginative discipline meant to articulate the feelings that swirl around sexuality. Most of the conventional *topoi* of traditional poetry are the starting points for the sonnets—the unity of lovers (36-40), the power of poetry to immortalize the beloved (18, 19, 55), contests between eye and heart, beauty and virtue (46, 141), and shadow and substance (53, 98, 101). As with Petrarch's *Rime* (after 1327) or Sir Philip Sidney's *Astrophel and Stella* (1591), it would be possible to create a schematic account of commonplace Renaissance thinking about love from the sonnets. To do so, however, would be to nullify their extraordinary power of creation, the way they force ejaculations of recognition, horror, or joy from their readers.

After half a century of existentialism, readers in the late twentieth century understood that one of the most urgent subjects of the sonnets is not the commonplaces of Renaissance thinking about love, nor even the powerful concern with the power of art, but what Sonnet 16 calls our "war upon this bloody tyrant Time." It is no accident that the "discovery" of the sonnets' concern with time and mutability dates from the 1930's, when the impact of Søren Kierkegaard, Friedrich Nietzsche, and the existentialists, including Martin Heidegger, was starting to be widely felt in England and America. The sonnets' invitation to see man's temporality not merely as an abstract problem but as part of his inherent nature—what Heidegger terms man's "thrownness," his sense of being thrown into the world—seems central to a perception of the sonnets' power. Unpredictability and change are at the heart of the sonnets—but it is a continually shifting heart, and one that conceives of human love as definable only in terms of such change and finitude. The sonnets avoid the transcendentalism of Geoffrey Chaucer beseeching his young lovers to turn from the world, or of Edmund Spenser rejecting change for the reassurance of God's Eternity and His providential guidance of time to a foreknown, if mysterious, end. Shakespeare's sonnets rather overwhelm readers with questions and contradictions. In Sonnet 60, for example, time is not an impartial or abstract background. Even where it is glanced at as a pattern observable in nature or man, it is evoked as a disruptive, disturbing experience which cannot be dealt with as a philosophical problem. Some sonnets portray time as a sinister impersonal determinant; some thrust time at the reader as an equally unmanageable force of unforeseeable chances and changes, what Sonnet 115 calls man's "million'd accidents."

In Sonnet 15, it may be possible to enter into an understandable protest against time destroying its own creations (a commonplace enough Renaissance sentiment), and to accede to a sense of helplessness before a malignant force greater than the individual human being. When the sonnet tries, however, by virtue of its formally structured argument, to create a consciousness that seeks to understand and so to control this awareness, the reader encounters lines or individual words that may undermine even the temporary satisfaction of the aesthetic form. Such, for example is the force of the appalling awareness that "everything that grows/ Holds in perfection but a little moment." What is the application of "everything" or the emotional effect of the way the second line builds to a seemingly replete climax in "perfection" and then tumbles into oblivion in "but a little moment"? The sonnet does not and need not answer such questions. In a very real sense it cannot answer them, for readers can only acknowledge time's power in their own contingent lives. What is shocking is not merely the commonplace that "never-resting time leads summer on/ To hideous winter, and confounds him there" (5) but that each reading fights against and so disrupts the logical and aesthetic coherence of the reader's own sense of change and betrayal.

To attempt criticism of the sonnets is, to an unusual extent, to be challenged to make oneself vulnerable, to undergo a kind of creative therapy, as one goes back and forth from such textual gaps and indeterminancies to the shifting, vulnerable self, making the reader aware of the inadequacy and betrayal of words, as well as of their amazing seductiveness. Consider, for example, Sonnet 138. When one falls in love with a much younger person, does one inevitably feel the insecurity of a generation gap? What is more important in such a reading of the sonnets is the insistence that age or youthfulness are not important in themselves: it is the insistence itself that is important, not the mere fact of age—just as it is the anxiety with which a man or woman watches the wrinkles beneath the eyes that is important, not the wrinkles themselves. The note of insistence, in other words, is not attached merely to the speaker's age: it stands for an invitation to participate in some wider psychological revelation, to confess the vulnerability which people encounter in themselves in any relationship that is real and growing, and therefore necessarily unpredictable and risky.

Without vulnerability and contingency, without the sense of being thrown into the world, there can be no growth. Hence the poet invites the reader to accept ruefully what the fact of his age evokes—an openness to ridicule or rejection. The sonnet's insistence on being open to the insecurity represented by the narrator's age points not merely to a contrast between the speaker and his two lovers but rather to a radical self-division. This is especially so in the Dark Lady sonnets, where there is a savage laceration of self, particularly in the fearful exhaustion of Sonnet 129, in which vulnerability is evoked as paralysis. At once logically relentless and emotionally centrifugal, Sonnet 129 generates fears or vulnerability and self-disgust. Nothing is specified: the strategies of the poem work to make the reader reveal or recognize his own compulsions and revulsions. The poem's physical, psychological, and cultural basis forces the reader to become aware of his awful drive to repress words because they are potentially so destructive.

Even in the seemingly most serene sonnets there are inevitably dark shadows of insecurity and anxiety. In Sonnet 116, for example, the argument is that a love that alters with time and circumstance is not a true, but a self-regarding love.

The poem purports to define true love by negatives, but if those negatives are deliberately negated, the poem that emerges may be seen as the dark, repressed underside of the apparently unassailable affirmation of a mature, self-giving, other-directed love. If lovers admit impediments, and play with the idea that love is indeed love which "alters when it alteration finds," that it is an "ever-fixed mark" and, most especially, that love is indeed "time's fool," then the poem connects strikingly and powerfully with the strain of insecurity about the nature of change in human love that echoes throughout the whole collection. Such apparent affirmations may be acts of repression, an attempt to regiment the unrelenting unexpectedness and challenge of love. There are poems in the collection which, although less assertive, show a willingness to be vulnerable, to reevaluate constantly, to swear permanence within, not despite, transience—to be, in the words of St. Paul, deceivers yet true. Elsewhere, part of the torture of the Dark Lady sonnets is that such a consolation does not emerge through the pain.

In short, what Sonnet 116 represses is the acknowledgment that the only fulfillment worth having is one that is struggled for and which is independent of law or compulsion. The kind of creative fragility that it tries to marginalize is that evoked in the conclusion to Sonnet 49 when the poet admits his vulnerability: "To leave poor me thou hast the strength of laws,/ Since, why to love, I can allege no cause." This is an affirmation of a different order— or rather an acknowledgment that love must not be defined by repression and exclusion. Lovers can affirm the authenticity of the erotic only by admitting the possibility that it is not absolute. Love has no absolute legal, moral, or causal claims; nor, in the final analysis, can love acknowledge the bonds of law, family, or state—or if finally they are acknowledged, it is because they grow from love itself. Love moves by its own internal dynamic; it is not motivated by a series of external compulsions. Ultimately it asks from the lover the *nolo contendere* of commitment: do with me what you will. A real, that is to say, an altering, bending, *never* fixed and unpredictable love is always surrounded by, and at times seems to live by, battles, plots, subterfuges, quarrels, and irony. At the root is the acknowledgment that any affirmation is made because of, not despite, time and human mortality. As Sonnet 12 puts it, having surveyed the fearful unpredictability of all life, lovers must realize that it is even "thy beauty" that must be questioned. At times this thought "is as a death" (64), a "fearful meditation" (65)—that even the most precious of all human creations, will age, wrinkle, fade, and die. Just how can one affirm in the face of that degree of reality?

Under the pressure of such questioning, the affirmation of Sonnet 116 can therefore be seen as a kind of bad faith, a false dread—false, because it freezes lovers in inactivity when they should, on the contrary, accept their finitude as possibility. Frozen in the fear of contingency, which Sonnet 116 so ruthlessly represses in its insistent negatives, readers may miss Shakespeare's essential insight that it is in fact the very fragility of beauty, love, poetry, fair youth, and dark lady alike, that enhances their desirability. Paradoxically, it is precisely because they are indeed among the wastes of time that they are beautiful; they are not desirable because they are immortal but because they are irrevocably timebound. One of the most profound truths is expressed in Sonnet 64: "Ruin hath taught me thus to ruminate/ That Time will come and take my love away./ This thought is as a death, which cannot choose/ But weep to have that which it fears to lose." The power of such lines goes far beyond the serene platitudes of Sonnet 116. At his most courageous, man does not merely affirm, *despite* the forces of change and unpredictability which provide the ever-shifting centers of his life; on the contrary, he discovers his greatest strengths *because* of and within his own contingency. To accept rather than to deny time is to prove that man's deepest life ultimately does not recognize stasis but always craves growth, and that fulfillment is built not upon the need for finality, for being "ever fixed," but on the need to violate apparent limits, to push forward or die.

Against a sonnet such as 116, some sonnets depict love not as a serene continuation of life but rather as a radical reorientation. Readers are asked not to dismiss fears of limitation, but to affirm them. It is in the midst of contingency, when meditations are overwhelmed by the betrayals of the past, while "I sigh the lack of many a thing I sought,/ And with old woes new wail my dear Time's waste" (Sonnet 30), that love may open up the future as possibility, not as completion—so long as one accepts that it is time itself that offers such possibility, not any attempt to escape from it.

The typical Renaissance attitude to time and mutability was one of fear or resignation unless, as in Spenser, the traditional Christian context could be evoked as compensation; but for Shakespeare the enormous energies released by the Renaissance are wasted in trying to escape the burden of temporality. The drive to stasis, to repress experiences and meanings, is a desire to escape the burden of realizing that there are some transformations which love cannot effect. Ultimately, it is impossible to get inside a lover's soul no matter how much the flesh is seized and penetrated. The drive to possess and so to annihilate is a desire derived from the old Platonic ideal of original oneness, which only Shakespeare among the Renaissance poets seems to have seen as a clear and fearful perversion—it certainly haunts the lover of the Dark Lady sonnets and we are invited to stand and shudder at the speaker's Augustinian self-lacerations. In Sonnet 144 the two loves "of comfort and despair,/ Which like two spirits do suggest me still" are not just a "man right fair" and a "woman, colour'd ill": they are also aspects of each lover's self, the two loves that a dualistic mind cannot affirm and by which people may be paralyzed.

Throughout this discussion of the sonnets, what has been stressed is that their power rests on the seemingly fragile basis not of Shakespeare's but of their readers' shifting and unpredictable experiences. They are offered not in certainty, but in hope. They invite affirmation while insisting that pain is the dark visceral element in which man must live and struggle. Many of the Dark Lady sonnets are grim precisely because the lover can see no way to break through such pain. What they lack, fundamentally, is hope. By accepting that, for a time, "my grief lies onward and my joy behind" (Sonnet 50), the lover may be able, however temporarily, to make some commitment. Sonnet 124 is particularly suggestive, categorizing love as "dear," costly, not only because it is "fond," beloved, but also because it is affirmed in the knowledge of the world. Moreover, while it "fears not Policy" it is nevertheless "hugely politic." It is as if love must be adaptable, cunning, even deceptive, aware of the untrustworthiness of the world from which it can never be abstracted: "it nor grows with heat, nor drowns with showers." Finally, the poet affirms with a strong and yet strangely ironic twist: "To this I witness call the fools of Time,/ Which die for goodness, who have liv'd for crime." As Stephen Booth notes, Sonnet 124 "is the most extreme example of Shakespeare's constructive vagueness," its key the word "it," which, "like all pronouns, is specific, hard, concrete, and yet imprecise and general—able to include anything or nothing." "It" occurs five times, each time becoming more indeterminate, surrounded by subjectives and negatives: in this sonnet "composed of precisely evocative words in apparently communicative syntaxes which come to nothing and give a sense of summing up everything, the word *it* stands sure, constant, forthright, simple and blank." The blankness to which Booth points has been filled very specifically by generations of readers to force the poem into a repressive argument like that of Sonnet 116. For example, the key phrase "the fools of time" is usually glossed as local, historical examples of political or religious timeservers—but the phrase contains mysterious reverberations back upon the lovers themselves. There is a sense in which men are *all* fools of time. When Sonnet 116 affirms that "Love's not Time's fool," it betrays a deliberate and fearful repression; an unwillingness to acknowledge that Love is not able to overcome Time; time is something that can be fulfilled only as it presents opportunity and possibility to us. People rightly become fools—jesters, dancers in attendance on Time, holy fools before the creative challenge of man's finitude—and men die, are fulfilled sexually, existentially, only if they submit themselves, "hugely politic," to the inevitable compromises, violence, and disruption which is life. Men "die for goodness" because in a sense they have all "lived for crime." People are deceivers yet true; the truest acts, like the truest poetry, are the most feigning.

The twelve-line Sonnet 126 is conventionally regarded as the culmination of the first part of the sequence. Its serenity is very unlike that of 116. It acknowledges that, even if the fair youth is indeed Nature's "minion," even he must eventually be "rendered." Such realism does not detract from the Youth's beauty or desirability; it in fact constitutes its power.

Whether one considers the Fair Youth or the Dark Lady sonnets, then; whether one attempts to see a "hidden" order in the sonnets, or even if one wishes to see a story or some kind of biographical origin "within" them, perhaps their greatness rests on their refusal to offer even the possibility of "solutions" to the "problems" they raise. They disturb, provoke, and ask more than merely "aesthetic" questions; read singly or together, they make readers face (or hide from) and question the most fundamental elements of poetry, love, time, and death.

Gary F. Waller

Other major works

PLAYS: *Henry VI, Parts I, II,* and *III,* 1589-1591; *Richard III,* c. 1592-1593; *The Comedy of Errors,* c. 1592-1594; *Titus Andronicus,* 1593-1594; *The Taming of the Shrew,* c. 1593-1594; *The Two Gentlemen of Verona,* c. 1594-1595; *Love's Labour's Lost,* 1594-1595; *Romeo and Juliet,* c. 1595-1596; *Richard II,* c. 1595-1596; *A Midsummer Night's Dream,* c. 1595-1596; *King John,* c. 1596-1597; *The Merchant of Venice,* c. 1596-1597; *Henry IV, Parts I* and *II,* c. 1597-1598; *The Merry Wives of Windsor,* 1597 (revised 1600-1601); *Much Ado About*

Nothing, c. 1598-1599; *Henry V*, c. 1598-1599; *Julius Caesar*, c. 1599-1600; *As You Like It*, 1599-1600; *Twelfth Night: Or, What You Will* c. 1600-1602; *Hamlet, Prince of Denmark*, c. 1600-1601; *Troilus and Cressida*, c. 1601-1602; *All's Well That Ends Well*, c. 1602-1604; *Othello, The Moor of Venice*, 1604; *Measure for Measure*, 1604; *King Lear*, c. 1605-1606; *Macbeth*, 1606; *Antony and Cleopatra*, c. 1606-1607; *Timon of Athens*, c. 1607-1608; *Coriolanus*, c. 1607-1608; *Pericles, Prince of Tyre*, c. 1607-1608; *Cymbeline*, c. 1609-1610; *The Winter's Tale*, c. 1610-1611; *The Tempest*, 1611; *Henry VIII*, 1613 (with John Fletcher).

Bibliography
Burgess, Anthony. *Shakespeare*. London: Jonathan Cape, 1970. A prolific novelist, linguist, and literary analyst, Burgess here presents an attractive, copiously illustrated, and immensely readable volume. Although many of his insights are conjectural, he is tremendously persuasive. A highly recommended first reference, though the bibliography is limited. The index is useful.

Campbell, Oscar James, and Edward G. Quinn. *The Reader's Encyclopedia of Shakespeare*. New York: Thomas Y. Crowell, 1966. The most comprehensive single-volume reference, this illustrated work remains unsurpassed. Not only does it arrange an immense array of Shakespeare topics in alphabetic order, but it also includes excerpts of the full range of literary criticism and surveys of stage history. The most widely used reference by both experts and amateurs.

Donno, Elizabeth Story. "The Epyllion." In *English Poetry and Prose, 1540-1674*, edited by Christopher Ricks. New York: Peter Bedrick Books, 1987. This brief introductory survey provides the best basic approach to Shakespeare's mythological poems, placing them securely in their contemporary literary context. Includes basic documentary notes and a complete bibliography of all relevant materials. The volume is fully indexed.

Hulse, Clark. *Metamorphic Verse: The Elizabethan Minor Epic*. Princeton, N.J.: Princeton University Press, 1981. Hulse surveys with great learning and enlightening insights the entire range of the Elizabethan mythological poem. Shakespeare's narrative poems are examined in detail and integrated with their literary and cultural backgrounds. Contains sound notes, a complete bibliography, and a thorough index.

Reese, M. M. *Shakespeare: His World and His Work*. Rev. ed. London: Edward Arnold, 1980. Reese's essays on various aspects of Shakespeare, his life, his background, and his writings, constitute one of the best introductions to these topics available in one volume. Although they are best for intellectual and cultural backgrounds, they offer illuminating comments on the poetry. The directions for further reading are helpful.

Roche, Thomas P., Jr. *Petrarch and the English Sonnet Sequences*. New York:

AMS Press, 1986. This is a comprehensive study of the phenomenon of the Elizabethan sonnet sequence, considered primarily from the point of view of its source in Petrarch. It covers the subject completely, and its consideration of Shakespeare's sonnets is unrivaled. The bibliographical apparatus is complete.

_____. "Shakespeare and the Sonnet Sequence." In *English Poetry and Prose, 1540-1674,* edited by Christopher Ricks. New York: Peter Bedrick Books, 1987. The title of this excellent intorductory essay is misleading. In fact it is almost entirely about Shakespeare's sonnets, and the material is concisely presented and rewarding. The bibliographical material is excellent for beginners.

Wilson, John Dover, ed. *The Sonnets.* 2d ed. New York: Cambridge University Press, 1967. The introductory essay of twenty-four pages and the notes and commentary are simply the best ever done on this poetry. The bibliographical material is dated but sound.

KARL SHAPIRO

Born: Baltimore, Maryland; November 10, 1913

Principal poetry

Poems, 1935; *Person, Place and Thing*, 1942; *The Place of Love*, 1942; *V-Letter and Other Poems*, 1944; *Trial of a Poet and Other Poems*, 1947; *Poems 1942-1953*, 1953; *Poems of a Jew*, 1958; *The Bourgeois Poet*, 1964; *The White-Haired Lover*, 1968; *Selected Poems*, 1968; *Adult Bookstore*, 1976; *Collected Poems 1940-1978*, 1978; *Love and War, Art and God*, 1984; *New and Selected Poems 1940-1986*, 1987.

Other literary forms

Karl Shapiro has written one novel, *Edsel* (1971); four books of literary criticism, *Essay on Rime* (1945), *Beyond Criticism* (1953), *In Defense of Ignorance* (1960), and *To Abolish Children and Other Essays* (1968); and several works on prosody. He has also coedited three books on the activity of writers, one with W. H. Auden, *Poets at Work* (1948); a second one with James E. Miller, Jr., and Bernice Slote, *Start with the Sun: Studies in Cosmic Poetry* (1960); and a third volume, *The Writer's Experience* (1964), with Ralph Ellison. *The Poetry Wreck: Selected Essays 1950-1970* (1975) is an anthology of his criticism.

Achievements

Shapiro's literary career has been marked by both success and controversy. He has been labeled polemical, ambiguous, vulgar, inconsistent, uncommitted, and schizoid, yet most critics are agreed upon the vibrant, precise, no-nonsense deployment of language and style in his writings, securing for him a place of eminence in contemporary American letters. Shapiro became famous *in absentia* while serving in the United States Army during World War II, receiving the Pulitzer Prize for Poetry in 1945 even before he was discharged. Before being inducted in March, 1941, Shapiro had published, besides the little-circulated *Poems*, only a handful of poems, including "Necropolis," "University," and "Death of Emma Goldman" in the *Partisan Review* and *Poetry*. By the end of 1941, he had several more poems accepted by those magazines, and the following year he won the Jeanette Sewell Davis Prize, awarded by *Poetry*. In 1942 he wrote, from "somewhere in the Pacific," *The Place of Love* and *Person, Place and Thing*, which brought him to the attention of the public. In 1943 he was included in the anthology *Five Young American Poets*, put out by New Directions, won the Contemporary American Poetry Prize, and was awarded the Levinson Prize by *Poetry*; his poems were circulated many times over in America's leading literary publications. In 1944, he published *V-letter and Other Poems* and obtained a grant from the American Academy of Arts and Letters. With the Pulitzer Prize for Poetry in 1945, he became a Guggenheim Fellow and a Fellow in American Letters, Library of Congress. The same year, he published the highly controversial *Essay on Rime*, which the critic Dudley Fitts called his *ars poetica*. Shapiro distanced himself from the modernist poetics of William Butler Yeats, T. S. Eliot and Ezra Pound, and criticized both mainstream and university-backed poetry. Nevertheless, in 1946 he was honored with the Shelley Memorial Award, and became Consultant in Poetry at the Library of Congress. Shapiro's reputation was on solid ground, and with the publication of *Trial of a Poet and Other Poems* in 1947, he was offered an associate professorship of English at The Johns Hopkins University, the school from which he had dropped out as a sophomore in 1939. He precipitated a controversy by voting against the awarding of the first Library of Congress Bollingen Prize to Ezra Pound in 1948 and defended his position in an article in the *Partisan Review*. His conviction that poetry is the "enemy" of literature and is not meant to be analyzed coldly for ulterior motives by academics and cultural critics was argued most convincingly during the Montgomery Lectures on Contemporary Civilization, published later under the title *Beyond Criticism*. In 1950, Shapiro moved to Chicago to edit *Poetry* magazine, a position he held until 1956, when he moved to Nebraska and began a ten-year editorship of *Prairie Schooner*. He was awarded a second Guggenheim Fellowship in 1953, and taught at various universities, including the University of California, Berkeley, the University of Indiana, and the University of Nebraska. He also lectured overseas under the auspices of the State Department. In 1959, he delivered the Ellison Lectures at the University of Cincinnati. His collection of prizes was augmented by the Eunice Tietjens Memorial Prize in 1960 and the Oscar Blumenthal Prize in 1963; in 1969, Shapiro shared the Bollingen Prize for Poetry with John Berryman. He was Professor of English at the University of Illinois, Chicago Circle, from 1966 to 1968, when he took a position at the University of California, Davis.

Biography

Karl Jay Shapiro was born in Baltimore, Maryland, on November 10, 1913. His father, of Eastern European ancestry, was a customhouse broker and subsequently the owner of a moving and storage company. After his first two years of school, his family moved to Chicago for another two years, and then returned to the South, to Norfolk, Virginia, where Shapiro received most of his secondary education. In 1929, like many other small businessmen, Shapiro's father had to sell out, and the family moved back to Baltimore. Shapiro, a senior, enrolled at Forest Park High School and completed his credits for graduation at Baltimore City College. Apparently he was a poor student, and when he entered the University of Virginia he had to resign after one semester. His performance and attitude were inexplicable to his family, who counted on Shapiro to follow in the footsteps of his older brother, who was dedicated and successful and the winner of many literary awards. It was during this period that Shapiro became aware of such realities as social class, religious animosity, and ethnic differences: as a Russian Jew he was not allowed to mingle with German Jews, and as a middle-class student he was snubbed by the predominantly WASP faculty and classmates. He turned inward, began to write ever more assiduously, studied French for a while, and was privately tutored in Latin. He also studied piano for about two years but had to give it up for lack of money. He was employed in all sorts of odd jobs, in drug and hardware stores, in bars, and eventually as a filing clerk in his father's firm.

During this time, Shapiro saved enough money for a trip to Tahiti, and wrote the *Tahiti Poems*, now lost. Upon his return, he managed to obtain a scholarship to The Johns Hopkins University on the merit of *Poems*. There he went through a religious crisis, and approached Catholicism. At the same time, he gave some thought to changing his name to Karl Camden, in order to appear more Anglo-American and thus more acceptable.

In 1939, Shapiro was asked to leave the University for lack of academic achievement. Ironically, this was also the beginning of a literary success story. His poems were published in *The New Anvil* and *Poetry World*. One in particular, "Self History," appeared in five different newspapers on the East Coast, from Florida to Rhode Island. At a party in 1940, he met his future wife, Evelyn Katz, who became a staunch supporter of his work and acted as his agent while he was in the service. At this time he took up an intensive, salaried training course at the Enoch Pratt Library School in Baltimore, which helped him to secure his first postwar job and exposed him to all kinds of publications.

While in the service, the poet held a desk job, but he saw enough of the incongruities and cruelties of war to mark his sensibility forever. It was here that he developed the tone of the impotent, tragically detached observer, typical of one who "has seen too much." He returned from the war to find himself a literary celebrity, and soon was embroiled in the polemics which have marked his career.

Shapiro's life since 1945 can be viewed from two perspectives. The first would follow his activities on the college and university lecture circuit and as the editor of two important literary magazines. The second would take the unabashed exposés of *The Bourgeois Poet* and of *Edsel* as literal transcriptions of how he lived his life: nonchalantly denouncing the contradictions of the establishment, playing ambiguous games with poorly defined sociological stances, and almost sadomasochistically returning time and again to his own most private problems and encounters. When, in 1967, Shapiro left Evelyn for Teri Kovach, whom he married the same year, the "white-haired" poet appeared to have mellowed somewhat. It turned out, however, that in the

1960's and early 1970's Shapiro, more than a poet, was a true cultural critic "despite himself"; his views on the changing mores and the built-in nihilistic obsessions of American society were brutally expressed in the essay "To Abolish Children," whereas a less harsh but satirized vision of those turbulent years, 1967 to 1969, can be found in *Edsel*.

Analysis

"Everything I've ever known I've *felt*. Maybe my brain is in my fingertips," says the autobiographical protagonist in *Edsel*. Karl Shapiro's poetry can in fact be characterized as a poetry of feeling, of pure, spontaneous, unadulterated sensation. The poet is constantly preoccupied with saying exactly what he perceives at a given moment, and the nature and structure of the poetic text will be of primary importance. In poetry, says Shapiro, all statements concerning morality, politics, the greater social good, religion, and any other function which makes the poem *for* something or somebody are to be avoided as unimportant to the essence of the poem itself. From this perspective, all his books can be read as a series of impressionistic sketches and reveries, deeply grounded in his personal experiences, concerned only with saying what is being felt, concisely and with immediacy.

The early poems, "Washington Cathedral," "Auto Wreck," "Hospital," and "University," are representative of this "gut" response to the world. The themes range from social injustice, decay, and the passing of life to man's alienation from his world. The stanzas of these poems are self-sustaining paragraphs proceeding from an external, almost naturalistic description of what has entered the poet's mind to a reflection on what seems to be happening, often spoken in the first-person plural, and concluding with a comment about the human condition. In other poems, he speaks in the first person, evidencing a tendency to set himself apart from the world, often taking a metaphysical view, as in the emblematic "The Dome of Sunday." Shapiro's concern with the right word, the only word that crystallizes his feelings and renders them real, is clear from his earliest exercises. Concerning the language suited to poetry, Shapiro explains that, since current speakers have inherited the English language quite by chance—downplaying history, as it were—there is no need to express oneself in "high" or "literary" English; rather, the poet should employ the current idiom of everyday life, a "low" and "common" American English that in the poem turns out to be more true and precise than any other mediated and contrived pattern.

The documented yet inexplicable realities of everyday life confirm a recurrent conclusion in Shapiro: everything is arbitrary. The notion slowly emerges that he is an alienated observer, a passerby whose life proceeds with a will all its own, and whose relationship to events and specific situations is casual, chancy, irrelevant, the ultimate causes being infinite and not given to man— to the poet—to fathom. This is apparent, for example, in a poem such as

"Lord, I've seen too much," where Shapiro, referring to his own duty while in the service, spells out his feeling:

> Lord, I have seen too much for one who sat
> In quiet at his window's luminous eye
> And puzzled over house and street and sky,
> Safe only in the narrowest habitat.

The sincerity of the soldier becomes the purity of a child, who wonders in amazement about the mysteries of the cosmos, and finds that he only knows, and feels comfortable and safe in, his immediate surroundings. The poet has in fact "studied peace as if the world were flat," and "faltered at each brilliant entity/ Drawn like a prize from some magician's hat." The second and last stanza of the poem brings the poet's astonishment to universal levels, suggesting an analogy between the poet's experience and Adam's expulsion from Paradise.

Shapiro generally attempts to render his moods and perceptions honestly and dispassionately in a language that becomes increasingly plain, approaching conversation, and richer in emotional intensity. There is no pity or pathos to be encountered, just the crystallization of a moment's feeling, a fleeting moment from life forever framed. Shapiro does not philosophize in his poetry, for poetry, as he frequently insists, is not a tool or servile guinea pig for academicians. Poetry, in his view, is the materialization of the world, the exact opposite of philosophy, which abstracts reality. He believes that poetry is an antilanguage, a counter-language, constituting the only mode in which he can be himself, independent and unique. When, in 1964, he published *The Bourgeois Poet*, the metamorphosis was complete. Shapiro was finally close to the art of children, the untrained, the hallucinated: he assembled the book by picking up at random all the autobiographical passages he had been writing.

In *Adult Bookstore*, Shapiro registers events and impressions with a crystal-clear vision, very sardonic and emotionally detached from the sharp contours of reality; the titles themselves suggest a casual glance at what is going on in the world: "Girls Working in Banks," "Flying First Class," "The Humanities Building," and the "Adult Bookstore." The poems usually end with a casual remark, almost as if to seal the frame of the picture just given. Despite his drive to plunge into the intensity of language, Shapiro here conveys a sense of the playful and the gratuitous, the uncaring attitude of one who has long decided that the work of art is totally independent of both writer and society: he can say, with the protagonist of "The Piano Tuner's Wife," that "He plays his comprehensive keyboard song,/ The loud proud paradigm,/ The one work of art without content."

Peter Carravetta

Other major works

LONG FICTION: *Edsel,* 1971.

PLAYS: *The Tenor,* 1952 (libretto); *The Soldier's Tale,* 1968 (libretto).

NONFICTION: *Essay on Rime,* 1945; *English Prosody and Modern Poetry,* 1947; *A Bibliography of Modern Prosody,* 1948; *Poets at Work,* 1948 (edited with W. H. Auden); *Beyond Criticism,* 1953; *In Defense of Ignorance,* 1960; *Start with the Sun: Studies in Cosmic Poetry,* 1960 (with James E. Miller, Jr., and Bernice Slote); *Prose Keys to Modern Poetry,* 1962; *The Writer's Experience,* 1964 (edited with Ralph Ellison); *A Prosody Handbook,* 1965 (with Robert Beum); *To Abolish Children and Other Essays,* 1968; *The Poetry Wreck: Selected Essays 1950-1970,* 1975; *The Younger Son,* 1988.

Bibliography

Bartlett, Lee. *Karl Shapiro: A Descriptive Bibliography, 1933-1937.* New York: Garden Publishing, 1979. A bibliographic record of all Shapiro's work up to 1977. Includes articles and poems in periodicals, translations of his works, contributions to anthologies, and so on. The annotations include quotations and excerpts from an interview with Shapiro on his publishing history. An appendix lists Shapiro's criticism and reviews. Includes a chronology.

Hammer, Andrea Gale. "Poetry and Family: An Interview with Karl Shapiro." *Prairie Schooner* 55 (Fall, 1981): 3-31. This is a long, very personal and intriguing interview with the poet, interesting for the insight it sheds on the man and his thought. An excellent portrait of Karl Shapiro.

Mills, Ralph J., Jr. *Contemporary American Poetry.* New York: Random House, 1965. A chapter on Shapiro presents a broad, sympathetic view of his work with frequent quotations from the poems. This excellent introductory essay explores the interplay of influences and ideas on the poet. Includes an introduction, a reading list, and a good bibliography.

Reino, Joseph. *Karl Shapiro.* Boston: Twayne, 1981. The first full-length study of Karl Shapiro, this volume closely analyzes representative works showing the range of Shapiro's thought and craft. The text is replete with line-by-line explications. Contains an annotated bibliography which includes essays and reviews on Shapiro and his work.

Richman, Robert. "The Trials of a Poet." *The New Centurion* 6 (April, 1988): 74-81. This review of Shapiro's *New and Selected Poems 1940-1986* does more than simply report on the collection. Provides quick observations of a number of poems as well as a commentary on development and theme. The critic also pulls from Shapiro's nonpoetic writing for elaboration. A good, quick review.

Shapiro, Karl, and Ralph Ellison. *The Writer's Experience.* Washington, D.C.: Library of Congress, 1964. An essay by Shapiro, "American Poet?" is included in this pamphlet. It is autobiographical in part and personal in that it is a commentary on the process of writing poetry. Shapiro also shares a retrospective of his career and his personal struggles. He mentions influences and colleagues, and he comments on the state of poetry in America and in the modern world. An excellent and revealing essay.

PERCY BYSSHE SHELLEY

Born: Field Place, Sussex, England; August 4, 1792
Died: Off Viareggio, Italy; July 8, 1822

Principal poetry

Original Poetry by Victor and Cazire, 1810 (with Elizabeth Shelley); *Posthumous Fragments of Margaret Nicholson*, 1810; *Queen Mab: A Philosophical Poem*, 1813 (revised as *The Daemon of the World*, 1816); *Alastor: Or, The Spirit of Solitude, and Other Poems*, 1816; *Mont Blanc*, 1817; *The Revolt of Islam*, 1818; *Rosalind and Helen: A Modern Eclogue, with Other Poems*, 1819; *The Cenci: A Tragedy in Five Acts*, 1819 (dramatic poem); *Letter to Maria Gisborne*, 1820; *Oedipus Tyrannus: Or, Swellfoot the Tyrant*, 1820; *Prometheus Unbound: A Lyrical Drama in Four Acts*, 1820; *Epipsychidion*, 1821; *Adonais: An Elegy on the Death of John Keats*, 1821; *Hellas: A Lyrical Drama*, 1822; *Posthumous Poems of Percy Bysshe Shelley*, 1824 (includes *Prince Athanase, Julian and Maddalo: A Conversation, The Witch of Atlas, The Triumph of Life, The Cyclops, Charles the First*); *The Masque of Anarchy*, 1832; *Peter Bell the Third*, 1839; *The Poetical Works of Percy Bysshe Shelley*, 1839; *The Wandering Jew*, 1887; *The Complete Poetical Works of Shelley*, 1904 (Thomas Hutchinson, editor); *The Esdaile Notebook: A Volume of Early Poems*, 1964 (K. N. Cameron, editor).

Other literary forms

Except for *A Defence of Poetry* (1840), Percy Bysshe Shelley's essays are not classics of English prose, but they have influenced writers as diverse as George Bernard Shaw, H. G. Wells, and Bertrand Russell, and they are very useful as glosses on the poetry. "On Love," for example, introduces Shelley's concept of the "antitype," the perfect mate, uniquely suited to one's intellect, imagination, and sensory needs, a "soul within our soul," but purged of all one finds unsatisfactory within oneself. Love is defined as the attraction to the antitype. Shelley movingly describes this longing for a mirror image of perfection:

> If we reason, we would be understood; if we imagine, we would that the airy children of our brain were born anew within another's; if we feel, we would that another's nerves should vibrate to our own, that the beams of their eyes should kindle at once and mix and melt into our own, that lips of motionless ice should not reply to lips quivering and burning with the heart's best blood. This is Love.

Love, as the attraction toward refined idealism, figures as well in Shelley's theory of the formative power of poetry.

In *A Defence of Poetry*, he argues that "the great secret of morals is Love." Through identification with the "beautiful which exists in thought, action, or person, not our own," one becomes moral through the process of empathizing. Love is thus an act of the sympathetic imagination. Because poetry, and literature in general, enhances and exercises the ability to empathize, it is an agent of tremendous potential for the moral regeneration of mankind. It goes without saying that the poet thus has a high office in the government of morality; he is Shelley's "unacknowledged legislator." By this phrase Shelley did not primarily mean that poets are unacknowledged for the good they do, but rather that they themselves were not and could not be aware of the power of their beauty. Shelley's poet is not in control of his power, for, in the language of his great metaphor of the creative process,

> the mind in creation is as a fading coal which some invisible influence, like an inconstant wind, awakens to transitory brightness: this power arises from within, like the colour of a flower which fades and changes as it is developed, and the conscious portions of our natures are unprophetic either of its approach or its departure.

Hence, poets do not control their inspiration—in fact, when writing begins, the most intense phase of inspiration has already passed; they express more than they understand; they feel less than they inspire; they are "the influence which is moved not, but moves. Poets are the unacknowledged legislators of the World."

Achievements

One of the six greatest English Romantic poets, Shelley is arguably the most versatile stylist among all English poets. His genius for versification enabled him to employ an astonishing variety of stanzaic patterns and poetic forms with equal facility. He has two basic styles, however—the sublime or rhapsodic, heard in such poems as *Alastor*, "Hymn to Intellectual Beauty," *Prometheus Unbound*, and *Adonais*; and the urbane or conversational style, found in poems such as *Julian and Maddalo: A Conversation*, *Letter to Maria Gisborne*, and *Epipsychidion*. In this latter mode, especially in the standard pentameter line with couplets, Shelley grew increasingly conservative prosodically, achieving a control almost neoclassical in balance and poise. Lyrical, unremitting intensity, however, is the defining quality of Shelley's verse.

Biography

In *Great Expectations* (1860-1861), Charles Dickens has the convict Magwitch put his life's story, as he says, into a mouthful of English—in and out of jail, in and out of jail, in and out of jail. Percy Bysshe Shelley's life falls into a similar pattern—in and out of love, in and out of love, in and out of love. Shelley admitted as much in a letter to John Gisborne, written the year he was to drown in a boating accident, and expressive of a truth he discovered too late: "I think one is always in love with something or other; the error, and I confess it is not easy for spirits cased in flesh and blood to avoid it, consists in seeking in a mortal image the likeness of what is perhaps eternal." At the age of twenty-nine, Shelley was still looking for his antitype; he believed he had found her, at last, in a nineteen-year-old Italian girl imprisoned in a nunnery, and had written one of his greatest poems, *Epipsychidion*, in celebration, typically disregarding the impact the poem would have on his wife Mary. Mary, however, had been party to a similar emotional event five years earlier when Shelley had abandoned his first wife, Harriet Westbrook Shelley, then pregnant with his second child, to elope with Mary. Both times Shelley speculated that the women could live with him, together, in harmony—the first combination, wife Harriet as sister, lover Mary as wife; the second combination, as stated metaphorically in *Epipsychidion*, wife Mary as Moon, Teresa Viviani as Sun to Shelley's earth, with a comet, Claire Claremont, Mary's half-sister, zooming into their "azure heaven" as she willed.

One of Shelley's great biographers, Kenneth Neill Cameron, says that Shelley was rather ahead of his time, at least ahead of today's liberal divorce laws, but most readers still find the facts of Shelley's love-life disturbing. His vision of love is wonderful; his idealism that sought to change the world through love and poetry is wonderful; the reality of that vision and idealism translated into life was a disaster. Shelley knew it and this awareness caused him to seek self-destruction.

His intense fits of love aside, Shelley could be the most thoughtful and loving of men. He was selfless, generous to a fault, a brilliant radical devoted to saving the world and just as passionately devoted to the pursuit of Metaphysical truth. Edward John Trelawny provides a description of Shelley in his study, German folio open, dictionary in hand (Shelley always read literature in the original—Greek, Latin, Spanish, Italian, German—so that he could be sensitive to the style and linguistic nuances of the art), at 10 A.M., and the identical picture at 6 P.M., Shelley having hardly moved, forgetting he had not eaten, looking tired and pale. "Well," Trelawny said, "have you found it?," referring to some Truth Shelley sought. "Shutting the book and going to the window," Shelley replied, " 'No, I have lost it': with a deep sigh: 'I have lost a day.' "

Shelley was born into a family of landed gentry. His father Timothy was a Member of Parliament and his grandfather Bysshe Shelley was a very wealthy landowner. Shelley studied at Eton, where he rebelled against the hazing system; fell madly in love with a cousin, Harriet Grove; attended Oxford, briefly, until his expulsion for printing a pamphlet defending atheism; and completed his teenage years by eloping with sixteen-year-old Harriet Westbrook, the daughter of a wealthy merchant. Harriet and Shelley had two children, Ianthe and Charles, the latter born after Shelley had left Harriet to elope with Mary Godwin, the sixteen-year-old child of Mary Wollstonecraft, author of *A Vindication of the Rights of Woman* (1792), and William Godwin, author of *The Inquiry Concerning Political Justice and Its Influence on General Virtue and*

Happiness (1793). After Harriet committed suicide by drowning, probably because of her pregnancy with another man's child, Shelley married Mary. The couple lived in England for a while, but left for Italy to protect Shelley's health and to escape the group of friends, including William Godwin, who had come to depend on Shelley for financial support.

In Italy, they settled near Lord Byron, who had fled England for his own personal reasons—a divorce and a child allegedly by his half-sister. Mary and Shelley had two children, Clara and William. When Clara died from an illness exacerbated by the traveling that Shelley forced upon his family in Italy, the lovelight seemed to wane in the Shelleys' marriage. The following year, 1819, Shelley's son died, and even greater despondency descended on them. Shelley was also disheartened by his ineffectiveness as a poet—no popularity, no audience, no hope of saving the world through his poetry. In *Adonais*, his eulogy for John Keats, Shelley tempts himself to put the things of this world aside, to die. On July 8, 1822, Shelley and Edward Williams set sail from Leghorn, too late in the afternoon considering their destination and with a storm pending. They drowned in the brief tempest. Several weeks later the two bodies were discovered on separate lonely beaches. In Shelley's pockets were a book of Sophocles and Keats's latest volume of poems, opened as if he had been reading. Byron, Trelawny, Leigh Hunt, and some Italian health officials cremated the bodies, Hellenic style, on the beach. Trelawny claims that Shelley's heart would not burn, or at least did not burn, and that he salvaged it from the ashes. Shelley, who likened the poet to fire and who prominently used the image of releasing one's fate to the stream, thus lived and died the myth of his poetry.

Analysis

Percy Bysshe Shelley mutedly noted in his Preface to *Prometheus Unbound* that he had "what a Scotch philosopher terms, 'a passion for reforming the world.'" One might think that this would have endeared his work at least to the reading public left of center and to later readers who value the reforming spirit in mankind. Yet Shelley was almost able to name his readers, they were so few, and today, of the six major poets who dominate the canon of British Romanticism—William Blake, William Wordsworth, Samuel Taylor Coleridge, Byron, Keats, and Shelley—it is still Shelley who remains the least popular. For one reason or another, and though Shelley will always have a cadre of eloquent apologists, dedicated scholars, and brilliant explicators, he is usually out of favor with a significant group of readers. He has been criticized for bad thinking, for bad writing, and for bad living. Devaluations of his thought and poetry have largely been overcome, but this last, especially when made by sensitive feminist readers who find his narcissistic theory of love stupidly, if not heartlessly, destructive to the women in his life, is difficult to refute, if one grants its relevance to his art. Shelley's theme of *self*-destructiveness leads to his poetry's most brilliant moments, but perhaps the weakness in Shelley's use of the antitype motif is that it fails to recognize even the possibility that the mate—the woman—exists in her own right, and that her likeness to the fiction of the poet's imagination might not be the best or safest evidence of her worth. In Lord Byron's *Manfred* (1817), the concept of the antitype is also used, but Byron is critical of the theme from the woman's point of view—Manfred has destroyed his lover, Astarte, with this dangerously egotistical love and madly strives to win her forgiveness. Shelley seems incapable of such a critique of his most important theme; therein may lie the weakness in his work. Except in this respect, Shelley was not in the least simpleminded concerning the problem of reforming the world according to his standards. Shelley desired more than the world could ever offer; he knew it, but he could not stop trying to close the gap between the ideal and the real, the vision and the fact. So powerful is his honesty that tension pervades his poetry, idealism playing against skepticism, irony hedging assertion. He ardently believed that man was perfectible, if man would only will it. At its most optimistic, his poetry seeks to arouse the reader's will to strive for perfection; at its most pessimistic, it is the poet's private struggle with the desire to escape through death.

One might take a poem of balanced opposites as a synecdochic introduction to Shelley's thought and art. *Julian and Maddalo: A Conversation* presents the issues, the imagery that typically embodies them, and the quest to dissolve division in nature, society, and personal life. The conversants in this urbane, sophisticated debate are Julian, a thin disguise for Shelley, and Maddalo, or Lord Byron. Julian, the Preface suggests, is the idealist, "passionately attached to those philosophical notions which assert the power of man over his own mind, and the immense improvements of which, by the extinction of certain moral superstitions, human society may be yet susceptible." Maddalo is the card-carrying cynic, and the tragedy from Julian's point of view is that Maddalo is one of the few who might be capable of changing the world, if he would only will it. It is Maddalo's weakness to be proud; he does not think the world worth the effort. A maniac also enters the poem as a character who was destroyed through unrequited love. Finally, Maddalo's little daughter is the ever-present, romantic image of mankind's potential.

The poem opens with a vision of harmony. Julian and Maddalo have been riding along the Lido of Venice, a waste of a beach, at sundown, and Julian responds to the correspondence he senses between the inner and outer worlds:

> . . . I love all waste
> And solitary places; where we taste
> The pleasure of believing what we see
> Is boundless, as we wish our souls to be:
> And such was this wide ocean, and this shore
> More barren than its billows.

Not much later, Maddalo will offer a constricted image of the soul, but for now, Shelley allows his better half to continue. Disagreeing with earlier Romantic work of Wordsworth and Coleridge, which argued for the suffiency of man's relationship with nature, Julian/Shelley adds a companion to the landscape experience: "and yet more/ Than all, with a remembered friend I love/ To ride as then I rode." The friends are in perfect accord with each other as well as with nature. As they gallop along the beach, the wind brings the "living spray" into their faces, the blue heavens open, "stripped to their depths," and the waves send forth a "sound like delight . . ./ Harmonizing with solitude," carrying into their hearts "aereal merriment." The personal relationship is as perfect: "the swift thought,/ Winging itself with laughter, lingered not,/ But flew from brain to brain." As they turn homeward, however, division slowly enters the poem, beginning with a discussion on "God, freewill and destiny:/ Of all that earth has been or yet may be." Julian takes the brighter side, Maddalo, the darker. Shelley represents the argument metaphorically as two perceptions of landscape. Julian first offers a perception of the dissolution of the landscape's natural boundaries created by the light of the setting sun; Maddalo then counters with a brilliant image of the constricted soul and the madding passions, the bell of the insane asylum.

Julian first calls attention to the division between East and West, earth and sky. The Alps are a "heaven-sustaining bulwark reared/ Between the East and West"; only "half the sky/ Was roofed with clouds of rich emblazonry"; the sun pauses in a "rent" between the clouds; the hills are separate like a "clump of peaked isles." Then quite dramatically light begins to do its work of transformation:

> . . . as if the Earth and Sea had been
> Dissolved into one lake of fire were seen
> Those mountains towering as from waves of flame
> Around the vaporous sun, from where there came
> The inmost purple spirit of light, and made
> Their very peaks transparent.

This diffusion of water with fire, earth with air, air with fire, and water with earth, completed in the fleeting intensity of the sun's pause, becomes a vision of hope for human reconciliation through love. The sun's light is love and just as it can dissolve the perception of landscape boundaries so can the emotion dissolve boundaries in personal life and society. Nature teaches a lesson; even the city becomes a divine illusion, "Its temples and its palaces did seem/ Like fabrics of enchantment piled to Heaven."

Maddalo, however, is not taken by the vision. He insists on observing the sunset from a "better station." Between them and the sun is now imagined the madhouse, "A windowless, deformed and dreary pile," its bell tolling "In strong and black relief" for the maniacs to begin their evening prayers. Looking at his image of the bell and the asylum, Maddalo interprets:

> And such . . . is our mortality
> And this must be the emblem and the sign
> Of what should be eternal and divine—
> And like that black and dreary bell, the soul,
> Hung in a heaven-illumined tower, must toll
> Our thoughts and our desires to meet below
> Round the rent heart and pray—as madmen do
> For what? they know not,—till the night of death
> As sunset that strange vision, severeth
> Our memory from itself, and us from all
> We sought and yet were baffled!

If Byron literally spoke these lines, they are among the best lines of poetry he ever composed. The soul is no beach stretching to the horizon; it is finite, and dreary, and obfuscating. It provokes the heart with its spirituality to strive for the infinite in complete bewilderment, till death closes the quest. There is nothing eternal and divine; it is simply mortality at odds with itself. In the twilight, the "black bell became invisible" and the enchanted city "huddled in gloom," its ships, towers, palaces—emblems of commerce, church, and government—faded into the absurdity of night.

The following day, Julian argues that

> . . . it is our will
> That . . . enchains us to permitted ill—
> We might be otherwise—we might be all
> We dream of . . .
> Where is the love, beauty and truth we seek
> But in our mind? and if we were not weak
> Should we be less in deed than in desire?

Maddalo counters that such human weakness is incurable, that no matter how strong an argument Julian can make to prove the perfectibility of mankind, empirical evidence and experience will undermine it. Maddalo adduces as evidence the case of a maniac, who was like Julian an idealist but has been destroyed by unrequited love. Their visit to the maniac's cell in the asylum whose bell they had heard the preceding night reveals a man of rent heart, musing disjointedly and pathetically on his suffering. Still in love, he refuses to commit suicide because he does not want his former lover to feel responsible for his death. Julian feels that if he had the opportunity to befriend the man, he might save him, but the strength of Maddalo's argument has been felt. After many years, Julian returns to Maddalo's castle and learns from his grown daughter that the maniac's lover returned and he recovered; then, however, they separated once more. At Julian's entreaty, she reveals the whole story, but out of bitterness toward the world he refuses to disclose the resolution (as Shelley refuses to disclose it to his readers): "the cold world shall not know," concludes the poem. The debate has not resolved the issue.

The maniac's recovery, although temporary, indicates that love is in the force that Julian has maintained, *if* one can sustain the will to love. Thus the poem returns to its starting point: clearly one can will to love, or, at least, act as if one loved, but constancy is the problem, as the maniac's lover indicates.

The same tensions which animate *Julian and Maddalo* inform Shelley's first major poem, *Alastor.* The poet-persona of *Alastor* begins as a happy youth. He seeks knowledge and truth from philosophy, nature, history, and travel, and experiences moments of high inspiration, as when, standing amidst the ruins of the cradle of civilization, "meaning on his vacant mind/ Flashed like strong inspiration, and he saw/ The thrilling secrets of the birth of time." On his quest he has been cared for by an Arab maiden, who brings food to him from her own plate and watches him dream innocently throughout the night, till to her father's tent she creeps "Wildered, and wan, and panting," but he does not recognize her love for him. Then, one night after leaving her locale, he has "a dream of hopes that never yet/ Had flushed his cheek." He dreams of his antitype, the perfect female of intellect, imagination, and sense to match his own. She speaks in low solemn tones of knowledge, truth, virtue, liberty; she next breathes the "permeating fire" of her pure mind in a song of passionate poetry; then, in the most erotic passage one will find in the Romantic canon, they join in sexual climax. She arises and the dreamer sees

> . . . by the warm light of their own life
> Her glowing limbs beneath the sinuous veil
> Of woven wind, her outspread arms now bare,
> Her dark locks floating in the breath of night,
> Her beamy bending eyes, her parted lips
> Outstretched, and pale, and quivering eagerly.

He receives her, "yielding to the irresistible joy,/ With frantic gesture and short breathless cry," folding his frame in "her dissolving arms." At the moment of climax, "blackness veiled his dizzy eyes, and night/ Involved and swallowed up the vision; sleep,/ Like a dark flood suspended in its course,/ Rolled back its impulse on his vacant brain."

One would wish to sleep forever to have such dreams, for how can such a dream be fulfilled? The world, which was once so beautiful to the poet, now appears vacant when he awakens. Cryptically, the narrator tells us that "The spirit of sweet human love has sent/ A vision to the sleep of him who spurned/ Her choicest gifts." Was the Arab maiden one of those gifts, or was she merely the catalyst of an awakening sexuality? Regardless, he now "eagerly pursues/ Beyond the realms of dream that fleeting shade," knowing that the realm beyond dream is most likely death. He moves madly through society and nature more to burn out than to seek a likeness of the veiled maid. When he tires or seeks infrequent nourishment, an image of the maid's eyes forces him on. In a passage that underscores the narcissism of his quest, the reflection of his own eyes in a fountain where he drinks provokes her shadowy presence.

He moves on, following a stream to its unknown source, for he has dimly perceived an analogue between "What oozy cavern or what wandering cloud" contain its waters and what mysterious source his own thoughts and visions may have. He finally stops in a virginal nook above the perilous mountain landscape and prepares to die. He is "at peace, and faintly smiling" as the crescent moon sets on his life: "His last sight/ Was the great moon," which as it declines finally shows only the tips of its crescent:

> . . . the alternate gasp
> Of his faint respiration scarce did stir
> The stagnate night:—till the minutest ray
> Was quenched, the pulse yet lingered in his heart.
> It paused—it fluttered.

The moon sets, and he dies. Why does his heart pause and flutter? Is he duped by the moon's tips appearing to be eyes, or does he smile faintly because he is aware of the irony? Or does he move from irony to the excitement of belief at the moment before final truth? The reader cannot know, but the poem's narrator finds little hope for the world when "some surpassing Spirit,/ Whose light adorned the world around it" dies an untimely death not with "sobs or groans,/ The passionate tumult of a clinging hope;/ But pale despair and cold tranquillity."

As he moved like a phantom through the landscape, the poet of *Alastor* recognized that nature provided a condition like love for its animate and inanimate beings—swans floating in pairs, "Ivy clasp[ing]/ The fissured stones with its entwining arms"—but that he belonged outside the circle. Shelley could not maintain the romantic myth that, as Coleridge wrote in "This Lime-tree Bower My Prison," "Nature ne'er deserts the wise and pure," or, as Wordsworth wrote in "Lines Composed a Few Miles Above Tintern Abbey," "In nature and the language of the sense,/ [is] the anchor of my purest thoughts, the nurse,/ The guide, the guardian of my heart, and soul/ Of all my moral being." Shelley did write in his essay "On Love" that one seeks correspondence with nature when one is denied human love; he paraphrased an unknown source to the effect that, if one were in a desert, "he would love some cypress." As is evident in *Julian and Maddalo* and *Alastor*, Shelley preferred human companionship, because there is a force impelling the physical world which is antithetical to love. Shelley called this force Necessity, or physical determinism. *Mont Blanc* provides its principal image.

In what becomes a showdown of sorts between mind and matter, imagination and necessity, Shelley begins *Mont Blanc* by recognizing that mind shares with matter a significant feature. The sense impressions that flow through the mind's stream of thought are impelled by a force as mysterious as that which drives the river from its home in the clouds down the mountain's ravine. Is it the same force? Critics have struggled with this problem, for Shelley did not make the matter very clear, or perhaps it is as clear as possible without being reductive of a difficult metaphysical question. On the one hand, Shelley imagines the Power as residing above the world of mutability, "Remote, serene, and inaccessible," but not without profound effect on the world below. The Power's image is the mountain's summit, which none can see but which all can feel in the form of the forces it releases that destroy and preserve, its glaciers and its rivers. Its position is amoral, perfectly non-anthropomorphic. The glaciers wreak their havoc, "The dwelling-place/ Of insects, beasts, and birds" their spoil. "The race of man," too, "flies far in dread; his work and dwelling/ Vanished, like smoke before the tempest's stream." On the other hand, majestic rivers, such as the Arve of Mont Blanc, derive from the same source and are "The breath and blood of distant lands." Can the mind of man be a manifestation of such a power? This is the question to which the poem leads, but just as Shelley offers the answer in the final stanza, he undermines it.

Addressing the mountain he says, "The secret strength of things/ Which governs thought, and to the infinite dome/ of heaven is as a law, inhabits thee!" While thought may be governed by a psychological determinism, Shelley seems to imply a distinction between causally determined thought and the products of imagination—poetry and value. He stresses that "Mont Blanc yet gleams on high," above the vicissitudes of our world, where "In the calm darkness of the moonless nights,/ In the lone glare of day, the snows descend/ Upon that Mountain, none beholds them there," and without fanfare he begins describing, valuing, and symbolizing what he has just indicated none behold:

> Winds contend
> Silently there, and heap the snow with breath
> Rapid and strong, but silently! Its home
> The voiceless lightning in these solitudes
> Keeps innocently, and like vapour broods
> Over the snow.

The winds pile the snow for the coming glacier with the quality of "breath," because, while the glacier will bring death, its next state of being as river will bring life—"The breath and blood of distant lands." Likewise emphasizing the absent force of mind that now interprets and values the cold causality of the mountain's secret summit is the acknowledgement that all of this is happening "Silently . . ./ . . . but silently!" No ears, no sound; no perceiver, no value. The poem concludes: "And what were thou, and earth, and stars, and sea,/ If to the human mind's imaginings/ Silence and solitude were vacancy?"

Something in the human mind renders value, recognizes or makes meaning for this universe, or decides there is no meaning. These are acts of ultimate power; the rest is a "dull round," as the human mind itself may enact when it refuses to transcend the path of association with its power to create, to vision, and to will. Shelley does not make this case as forcefully as it is presented here, however; he concludes with a question, not the strong declarative the reader might wish. The imagining undermines the assertion of "The secret strength of things"; the surmise of the conclusion undermines the imagining. This ambivalence does not derive from some precious sense of caution, but from Shelley's genuine uncertainty.

Shelley's belief in the power of love was unequivocal, however, and *Prometheus Unbound* reveals on a mythic scale the transformation that will occur when love rather than fear and hatred binds relationships among nations and mankind. *Prometheus Unbound* is a psychological drama that, along with other works of the Romantic period, asserts the power of mind in transforming the world. The French Revolution having failed to rid France of despotism, British writers sought to fulfill by individual transformation the apocalyptic hopes it had aroused. The logic was simple: if the mind and heart of the reader could be changed, the world would be changed. Thus Wordsworth, the major poet of the period, writes at the height of his optimism: "Paradise, and groves/ Elysian, . . ./ . . . why should they be/ A history only of departed things" (Prospectus to *The Recluse*). The hope of the Romantics was not naïve, but rather a variation of an eternal hope to improve the world.

Shelley's promise was that if humanity could just will to love, everything wonderful would follow. Thus, Prometheus, the mythic champion of mankind, chained to a rock in the Indian Caucasus for three thousand sleepless years, finds that he no longer hates the tyrant, Jupiter, and as a consequence the universe swells with the love, the growth, and the energy of springtime.

Ironically, Prometheus' transformation begins, not more than fifty-five lines into the first act, as he dwells on the satisfaction he will feel when Jupiter is dethroned and made to kiss "the blood/ From [Prometheus'] pale feet," which could then trample him, except that he would disdain Jupiter too much to do so. Then he says: "Disdain? Ah no! I pity thee," for the suffering Jupiter will endure at his demise, and his pity leads to grief: "I speak in grief,/ Not exultation, for I hate no more,/ As then, ere misery made me wise." There is a significant relationship between Jupiter's power and Prometheus' hatred, Jupiter's demise and Prometheus' love: though he has been the hero of mankind, Prometheus has been responsible for the tyranny of the universe, because he empowered Jupiter with his hate—in fact, willed the inflictions of Jupiter upon mankind. When he transcends his hatred to love, Jupiter inevitably falls. It is the dialectic of the master and the slave; the slave's willed obeisance gives the master his power. Prometheus recalls his curse, which began the reign of Jupiter, and the reader begins to understand one half of the dialectic.

On a literal level, perhaps it appears foolish that the sufferer could hold power over the oppressor, as Prometheus claims, but, if one considers the action on the psychological level, where Shelley intended the battle to be fought and won, one can understand that a mind indulging in hatred blights the potential joy of life. At some level, Prometheus understands this, and retracts his curse, yet he must still undergo a test from the furies (perhaps representing his historical consciousness) which brings to his sight the truth of mankind's condition. The Reign of Terror of the French Revolution, the rejection and murder of Christ, the general wave of personal violence and horror, are all summoned to reveal this darkest truth: "those who endure/ Deep wrongs for man, and scorn and chains, but heap/ Thousand-fold torment on themselves and him." The plight of mankind is absurdly tragic: "The good want power, but to weep barren tears./ The powerful goodness want: worse need for them./ The wise want love, and those who love want wisdom;/ And all best things are thus confused to ill."

Prometheus' response to this futility is: "Thy words are like a cloud of winged snakes/ And yet, I pity those they torture not." "Thou pitiest them?" the fury cries: "I speak no more," and vanishes defeated. Prometheus' love has endured. From this moment on, the action of the play moves forward, as if on its own pattern of necessity, to overthrow Jupiter and rejuvenate mankind. As love trickles down through the universe and the society of mankind, there are "thrones . . . kingless," men walking together without fawning or trampling, all "Scepterless, free, uncircumscribed." Though still subject to chance, death, and mutability, ruling over them like slaves, man is free, liberated consciousness, "The King/ Over himself." The "mind-forg'd manacles," to quote William Blake's "London," are sundered. The mind of man is now "an Ocean/ Of clear emotion/ A heaven of serene and mighty motion."

Yet, as wildly joyous and supremely optimistic as *Prometheus Unbound* is, the reader is warned at the close that even this mythic bliss cannot remain unguarded. Should the world fall again into its tyranny, the morality that will reincarnate her beauty, freedom, and joy again must be this:

> To suffer woes which Hope thinks infinite;
> To forgive wrongs darker than Death or Night;
> To defy Power which seems Omnipotent;
> To love, and bear; to hope, till Hope creates
> From its own wreck the thing it contemplates;
> Neither to change nor falter nor repent:
> This . . . is to be
> Good, great and joyous, beautiful and free;
> This is alone Life, Joy, Empire and Victory.

Prometheus Unbound is a difficult reading experience, a highly pitched lyric extended over four acts, without tonal relief, but it is essential reading for the student of Shelley and the Romantic period.

Part of Shelley's vision in *Prometheus Unbound* is that man would be passionate, "yet free from guilt or pain/ Which were, for his will made, or suffered them," and that women would be

> . . . gentle, radiant forms
> From custom's evil taint exempt and pure;
> Speaking the wisdom once they could not think,
> Looking emotions once they feared to feel
> And changed to all which once they dared not be.

Many might find Shelley a prophet of modern morality, or immorality, depending on point of view, but it is certain that even the most liberal in the nineteenth century could not quite live this ideal, not even Shelley's handpicked women. In *Epipsychidion*, however, he allows himself a pure fantasy of relational perfection that celebrates his discovery, at last, of his antitype. The chief skepticism of the poem is not that he might be excessive in his rapture, but rather that language is not capable of adequately expressing his rapture, its object being perfection. The poem opens with a rhapsodic invocation without parallel in English literature, and struggles throughout with its diction to aggregate images and symbols that might invoke a rhetoric of infinity. Shelley has found the veiled maid of *Alastor*: "I never thought before my death to see/ Youth's vision thus made perfect. Emily,/ I love thee; . . . Ah me!/ I am not thine: I am a part of *thee.*"

This perfect woman was Teresa Viviani, the teenage daughter of the governor of Pisa, who had confined her in a nunnery. The Shelleys became interested in her plight and this lovely victim of paternal tyranny inflamed Shelley's soul. He imagines how perfect it would be if Emily/Teresa could join him and Mary in a *ménage à trois*, for he has never been one of the "great sect,/ Whose doctrine is, that each one should select/ Out of the crowd a mistress or a friend,/ And all the rest, though fair and wise, commend/ To cold oblivion," though the moral code might demand such behavior. "True Love in this differs from gold and clay,/ That to divide is not to take away." Thus, if Mary would be the Moon—"The cold chaste Moon . . ./ Who makes all beautiful on which she smiles,/ . . ./ And warms not but illumines"—Emily would be the Sun and together they would form those spheres of influence "who rule this passive Earth,/ This world of live, this *me.*" Finally, however, he and Emily both fly out of orbit, leaving the moon behind, to dwell in a paradisal isle.

Language cannot deal with the infinite limits of this vision: "The winged words on which my soul would pierce/ Into the height of love's rare Universe,/ Are chains of lead around its flight of fire.—/ I pant, I sink, I tremble, I expire!" Sympathetic readers of Shelley wince at these moments; his detractors triumph. Even Shelley was a bit embarrassed by the emotion of this poem, because the woman it celebrated finally married a boor. Shelley wrote to John Gisborne: "The 'Epipsychidion' I cannot look at." Mary Shelley also had a difficult time looking at it; *Epipsychidion* is the only poem in her excellent edition of Shelley's poems on which she does not comment.

Shelley often wore his heart on his sleeve for daws to peck at, to paraphrase William Shakespeare's Iago, especially in the great series of poems representing himself as the *poète maudit*, the suffering poet vainly striving to save those who reject him. "Hymn to Intellectual Beauty," "Ode to the West Wind," and *Adonais* constitute the constellation and farthest reaches of this personal myth. Of course there is a great deal of vanity involved. One perceives that the world is not perfect; one attempts to save it and fails, thereby proving that the world really is bad, even worse than one thought. One then strives harder, becoming more assured that one is needed and that one's work is essential, rejection feeding vanity in a wicked, self-defeating cycle. Throughout, one retains one's heroic self-image.

In "Hymn to Intellectual Beauty," Shelley describes the dynamics of his dedication to poetry. While on a youthful search for truth, in much the manner of the poet of *Alastor*, he calls on the "poisonous names with which our youth is fed," God, ghosts and heaven, without success; he sees nothing, he hears nothing that responds to his Metaphysical anxieties in a direct way. He experiences something, however, that profoundly moves him. As he muses deeply "on the lot/ Of life" within the context of nature's springtime regeneration, "Sudden, thy shadow fell on me;/ I shrieked, and clasped my hands in ecstasy." The shadow is that of the spirit of beauty, an inexpressible something that transiently brings value to life—life's only value—by evoking in the receiver, its guest, a pulse of spiritual joy. If it could be a permanent experience, "Man were immortal, and omnipotent." The poet says that his life has been dedicated to creating a medium for evoking this spiritual condition. He vows that he will dedicate his "powers/ To thee and thine— have I not kept the vow?" he asks the spirit. His hope has been that if others could be given the experience of spiritual ecstasy, the world would be reborn. The time he has spent in reading, thinking, writing—those hours know, he says, that joy never

> . . . illumed my brow
> Unlinked with hope that thou wouldst free
> This world from its dark slavery,
> That thou—O awful Loveliness,
> Wouldst give whate'er these words cannot express.

In seeking to suggest this evanescent condition, Shelley creates several of the most alluring similes in English, such as, in the fourth stanza: "Thou— that to human thought art nourishment,/ Like darkness to a dying flame!" As the mind is a fading coal, so the darkness intensified makes thought appear brighter, thereby nourishing its waning condition so that it does not appear to be waning at all. The loveliness of verse makes the mind seem as full of beauty and intensity as the moment of inspiration had promised. The poem's opening lines, however, are the ultimate of Shelleyan perfection: "The awful shadow of some unseen Power/ Floats though unseen amongst us!" It is "Like clouds in starlight widely spread,—/ Like memory of music fled,—/ Like aught that for its grace may be/ Dear, and yet dearer for its mystery." These lines are Shelley in his power, for no other poet has so effectively failed to express the inexpressible and thereby succeeded in his attempt to evoke it. While Shelley was curiously winning the battle of expression, however, he was losing the war.

Unlike the modern age, which conceded, in the words of W. H. Auden, that "poetry makes nothing happen," the Romantic and Victorian periods permitted their artists to believe that they could and ought to be effectual. Several seemed to be: Wordsworth, Charles Dickens, Alfred, Lord Tennyson, and Robert Browning had enormous moral influence. Shelley did not; in fact, Matthew Arnold, the great social and literary critic of Victorian England, likened Shelley to an "ineffectual angel, beating in the void his luminous wings in vain." In 1819, at the age of twenty-seven, Shelley wrote his most perfect poem on his ineffectuality. "Ode to the West Wind" is a prayer for power to further the vision of *Prometheus Unbound* in nineteenth century England and Europe, by a poet who has been battered with failure.

In its five terza rima sonnet stanzas, which describe the autumn of earth, sky, sea, and poet—the elements of earth, air, water, and fire—Shelley's impassioned ode takes the literal cycle of the seasons through metaphorical transformations to approach an answer to the question: "If rebirth happens in nature, can it happen in society, with my verse, like the west wind, as the catalyst of the transition from near death to new life?" The first and last stanzas are illustrative of the metaphorical union the poet seeks with the regenerative wind. Stanza one presents the west wind in its dual function of destroying and preserving, driving dead leaves "like ghosts from an enchanter fleeing," and blowing seeds to "their dark wintry bed" where they will "lie cold and low,/ Each like a corpse within its grave, until/ [the wind of spring] shall blow/ Her clarion o'er the dreaming earth" to awaken the seeds to life. Of course, the dead leaves have the function of preserving the seed beds.

In the final stanza, the poet prays that his "dead thoughts" might be driven "over the universe/ Like withered leaves to quicken a new birth!" His seeds are his words, and because he is the equivalent of fire, his words are likened to ashes and sparks—some merely functional, some inspirational—that are now dormant in the waning hearth that is his life. Thus, if his verse could be sufficiently empowered by spirit, like a wind, he might produce a conflagration through the blowing about of ashes and sparks. As the spring of stanza one had her clarion, his verse will be "to unawakened Earth/ The trumpet of a prophecy." "O Wind," he closes, "If Winter comes, can Spring be far behind?" Clearly, if those leaves of stanza one—"Yellow, and black, and pale, and hectic red,/ Pestilence-stricken multitudes"—which have been accurately interpreted as the suffering races of mankind, and those leaves of stanza five—the poet's "dead thoughts"—can both be set afire by the spark of the poet's verse, both may rise from the ashes to new life. The final question, however, is threatening to the dream, for though it is certain that spring follows winter in nature, it is not at all certain that if total spiritual darkness covers mankind, a springtime of recovery will follow.

In stanza four of "Ode to the West Wind," Shelley represents himself as praying to the wind "in my sore need": "Oh! lift me as a wave, a leaf, a cloud!/ I fall upon the thorns of life! I bleed!/ A heavy weight of hours has chained and bowed/ One too like thee: tameless, and swift, and proud." He finally shed the weight of hours to join, not the wind, for that is to be bound still in the world of process, change, and dying hopes, but a poet of his generation who preceded him into the realm "where the eternal are." His elegy for John Keats, *Adonais*, signaled the final shift of his quest from social and personal visions of resurrected worlds and discovered antitypes to transcendence of human life and care.

Shelley believed that Keats had been mortally wounded by a scurrilous review of his early work, *Endymion* (1818). "The savage criticism," he says in his Preface to *Adonais*, "produced the most violent effect on his susceptible mind; the agitation thus originated ended in the rupture of a blood-vessel in the lungs; a rapid consumption ensued, and the succeeding acknowledgements . . . of the true greatness of his powers, were ineffectual to heal the wound thus wantonly inflicted." This is not casebook medicine, but it does say something about the doctor who provides such an empathic diagnosis. Shelley self-consciously identified with Keats's early rejection and sought as well to identify with his early death.

Through the first thirty-seven stanzas of the poem, Shelley's narrator mourns Adonais' untimely death, culminating with the fancy of Shelley's image visiting the tomb in homage to a dead fellow-poet. The group of mourning poets stands aside to smile "through their tears" at this maudlin creature "Who in another's fate now wept his own." The muse, Urania, among the mourners for one of her most gifted, asks him his name; his response is to make "bare his branded and ensanguined brow,/ Which was like Cain's or Christ's." Then, in a moment of intense self-consciousness, Shelley disrupts this indulgent self-projection to criticize with truth—"Oh! that it should be so!" He is no important, mythical sufferer; though it has been his dream to be one, the comparison will not hold. Shortly, the poem moves to the second phase of its development, the realization that the living must not mourn for Adonais, who has "awakened from the dream of life," but for themselves: "*We* decay/ Like corpses in a charnel; fear and grief/ Convulse us and consume us day by day,/ And cold hopes swarm like worms within our living clay."

The second movement concludes with a pivotal question: "What Adonais is, why fear we to become?" The poem's third movement, stanzas 52-55, becomes darkly suicidal, but triumphant in its grasping of a new direction, a new vision. Life is imaged as a "dome of many-coloured glass" which "Stains the white radiance of Eternity,/ Until Death tramples it to fragments." Beyond Life is the Platonic "One," the blinding light of truth which mankind knows only from its shadows manifested in material form. "Die," the poet challenges, "If thou wouldst be with that which thou dost seek!" The beauties of natural, human, and aesthetic forms are "weak/ The glory they transfuse with fitting truth to speak." The challenge then becomes personalized as the poet addresses his heart, the image of his mortality and emotional life: "Why linger, why turn back, why shrink, my Heart?" Its hopes are gone, its love is gone, "what still is dear/ Attracts to crush, repels to make thee wither." The sky smiles, the wind whispers the invitation of Adonais: "oh, hasten thither,/ No more let Life divide what Death can join together." He feels the source of the fire he has represented as a poet, beaming, "Consuming the last clouds of cold mortality." Finally, the poem's concluding stanza aggregates the principal imagery of Shelley's major poetry to illustrate that throughout his work an undercurrent has been moving to this moment of poetic self-annihilation: the West Wind descends to blow; as in *Alastor*, the "spirit's bark is driven,/ . . . far from the trembling throng/ Whose sails were never to the tempest given"; the earth and skies, in contrast with the vision of *Julian and Maddalo*, are "riven" to accept the poet, rather than fused to involve him with a romantic vision of earth; he is now "borne darkly, fearfully, afar:/ Whilst burning through the inmost veil of Heaven,/ The soul of Adonais, like a star,/ Beacons from the abode where the Eternal are." The vision was shortly to descend to fact with Shelley's death by drowning.

Shelley admitted to a "passion for reforming the world." He sought an aesthetic medium that would inspire the will of man to close the gap between vision and reality. Shelley's art and thought are unique in the extremes that they bring to English literature; indeed, their fragile loveliness represents the hope and despondency possible only in an age that fervently believed in the infinite potential of man. He was a child of his age, and succeeding generations and imaginations will always need to be challenged by his visions.

Richard E. Matlak

Other major works

LONG FICTION: *Zastrozzi: A Romance*, 1810; *St. Irvyne: Or, The Rosicrucian*, 1810.

NONFICTION: *The Necessity of Atheism*, 1811 (with Thomas Jefferson Hogg); *An Address to the Irish People*, 1812; *Declaration of Rights*, 1812; *A Letter to*

Lord Ellenborough, 1812; *Proposals for an Association of . . . Philanthropists*, 1812; *A Refutation of Deism, in a Dialogue*, 1814; *History of a Six Weeks' Tour Through a Part of France, Switzerland, Germany, and Holland*, 1817 (with Mary Shelley); *A Proposal for Putting Reform to the Vote Throughout the Kingdom*, 1817; *An Address to the People on the Death of the Princess Charlotte*, 1817?; *Essays, Letters from Abroad, Translations, and Fragments*, 1840; *A Defence of Poetry*, 1840; *Shelley Memorials*, 1859; *Shelley's Prose in the Bodleian Manuscripts*, 1910; *Note Books of Shelley*, 1911; *A Philosophical View of Reform*, 1920; *The Letters of Percy Bysshe Shelley*, 1964 (2 volumes; Frederick L. Jones, editor).

TRANSLATIONS: *The Cyclops*, 1824 (of Euripides' play); *Ion*, 1840 (of Plato's dialogue); "The Banquet Translated from Plato," 1931 (of Plato's dialogue *Symposium*).

MISCELLANEOUS: *The Complete Works of Percy Bysshe Shelley*, 1926-1930 (10 volumes; Roger Ingpen and Walter E. Peck, editors); *Shelley's Poetry and Prose: Authoritative Texts and Criticism*, 1977 (Donald H. Reiman and Sharon B. Powers, editors).

Bibliography

Bloom, Harold. ed. *Percy Bysshe Shelley*. New York: Chelsea House, 1985. An excellent selection of some of the most important works on Shelley published since 1950. Bloom's introduction, an overview of Shelley's poetry, can be highly recommended. Of the ten other essays, the most useful for the student are probably "Scepticism and Platonism," by C. E. Pulos, the essays on *Prometheus Unbound*, by Frederick A. Pottle, and *Adonais*, by Jean Hall, "Orpheus and the West Wind" (on Shelley's esotericism), by James Rieger, and "Shelley's Last Lyrics" by William Keach. Essays by Leslie Brisman, Paul de Man, and Paul Fry are suitable only for advanced students.

Cameron, Kenneth Neill. *Shelley: The Golden Years*. Cambridge, Mass.: Harvard University Press, 1974. This major, lengthy work of biography and criticism covers the later period of Shelley's life, from 1814 to 1822, when all of his great poetry was written. Cameron examines Shelley's prose works and gives crystal-clear readings of all the major poems. He views Shelley's work in a historical context, and this acts as a necessary counterweight to Wasserman's philosophical readings.

Holmes, Richard. *Shelley: The Pursuit*. London: Weidenfeld & Nicolson, 1974. Reprint. London: Quartet Books, 1976. By far the liveliest and most readable of Shelley's biographies. Holmes's Shelley is not the ethereal, Ariel-like creature of Romantic tradition, but a more human, if not always so likable, figure. Some reviewers objected to what they felt was a too sensational treatment of some of the controversial episodes in Shelley's life, and there was general agreement that Holmes's discussions of the poetry lacked balanced critical judgment.

Pulos, C. E. *The Deep Truth: A Study of Shelley's Scepticism.* Lincoln: University of Nebraska Press, 1954. This brief volume can still be recommended as one of the best introductions to Shelley's philosophical thought. Pulos reads Shelley in the light of the skeptical tradition, and this acts as a corrective to studies which may have overemphasized Shelley's Platonism. Written when it was still necessary to rescue Shelley from charges of incoherence, Pulos shows that apparent inconsistencies in Shelley's thought can be attributed to his refusal to be dogmatic and to his attempt to balance idealism and empiricism.

Rogers, Neville. *Shelley at Work: A Critical Inquiry.* 1956. 2d ed. Oxford, England: Clarendon Press, 1967. Much of this volume is based on an examination of Shelley's notebooks. Rogers traces the evolution from drafts to finished poem, which is particularly useful for the "Ode to the West Wind" and "To a Skylark." Rogers views Shelley as a Platonic thinker, and this is probably the best exposition of this aspect of Shelley's work. This approach is no longer very fashionable (it is not represented in Harold Bloom's anthology), but it needs to be taken seriously.

Sperry, Stuart M. *Shelley's Major Verse: The Narrative and Dramatic Poetry.* Cambridge, Mass.: Harvard University Press, 1988. This excellent study of *Queen Mab, Alastor, The Revolt of Islam, Prometheus Unbound, The Cenci, The Witch of Atlas, Epipsychidion,* and *The Triumph of Life* attempts to synthesize philosophical, psychological, and biographical approaches to Shelley. Traces the source of Shelley's poetic impulses to his emotional experiences as a child—of the power of love, largely—but this psychoanalytic approach is never jargon-ridden and Sperry is too good a scholar not to vary his approach when the poem demands it.

Wasserman, Earl R. *Shelley: A Critical Reading.* Baltimore: The Johns Hopkins University Press, 1971. Wasserman's massive, detailed readings of virtually all Shelley's major poems ("To a Skylark," *The Witch of Atlas,* and *The Triumph of Life* are omitted) have been extremely influential. Wasserman emphasizes Shelley's metaphysical skepticism and discusses his conceptions of existence, selfhood, reality, causation, and their relation to transcendence. Some of the readings are very dense and may be intimidating for the beginning student, but no serious student of Shelley can ignore them.

SIR PHILIP SIDNEY

Born: Penshurst, England; November 30, 1554
Died: Arnhem, The Netherlands; October 7, 1586

Principal poetry

Astrophel and Stella, 1591 (pirated edition printed by Thomas Newman), 1598 (first authorized edition); *Certaine Sonnets*, 1598; *The Psalmes of David, Translated into Divers and Sundry Kindes of Verse*, 1823 (with Mary Sidney Herbert, Countess of Pembroke); *The Complete Poems of Sir Philip Sidney*, 1873 (2 volumes); *The Poems of Sir Philip Sidney*, 1962 (William A. Ringler, Jr., editor); *The Psalms of Sir Philip Sidney and the Countess of Pembroke*, 1963 (J. C. A. Rathmell, editor).

Other literary forms

Although Sir Philip Sidney's best-known work is *Astrophel and Stella*, his major work, the one to which he devoted most of his literary energy and much of his political frustration, was *Arcadia* (originally entitled *The Countess of Pembroke's Arcadia*). This long, much-revised epic prose romance was written and revised between 1578 and 1586; it was first published in an unfinished version in 1590, again in 1593 in a revised and imperfect version, and repeatedly in many editions for more than a century. The equivalent in prose of Edmund Spenser's *The Faerie Queene* (1590-1596), it is an encyclopedic romance of love, politics, and adventure, incorporating many stories and discussions of philosophical, theological, erotic, and psychological issues. Almost as important is Sidney's critical treatise, *Defence of Poesie* (1595; published in another edition as *An Apologie for Poetry*), written about 1580, and setting forth in a seductive, if never quite logically coherent argument, a celebration of the nature and power of poetry, along with some prescriptive (and perceptive) comments on the current malaise of English poetry, drama, and the literary scene generally. Other works Sidney wrote include *The Lady of May* (1578), a pastoral entertainment; the first forty-four poems in a translation of the Psalms, later revised and completed by his sister Mary; a number of other miscellaneous poems, prose treatises, and translations, mainly designed to further the cause of the Protestant faction in Elizabeth's court.

Achievements

"Our English *Petrarke Sir Philip Sidney* . . . often comforteth him selfe in his sonnets of Stella, though dispairing to attaine his desire. . . . " Thus Sir John Harington in 1591, and generations of readers have similarly sighed and sympathized with Astrophel's tragicomic enactment of "poore Petrarch's long deceased woes." In literary history, *Astrophel and Stella* marks a poetical revolution no less than William Wordsworth's *Lyrical Ballads* (1800) or T. S. Eliot's *The Waste Land* (1922); the poem is the product of a young, ambitious poet, acting upon his impatience with the poetry he criticized in his manifesto, *Defence of Poesie.* "Poetry almost have we none," he wrote, "but that lyrical kind of songs and sonets," which "if I were a mistresse would never persuade mee they were in love." Sidney has also had a special place in England's broader cultural history. Part of his fascination has been the ways succeeding ages have appropriated him: as a lost leader of the golden Elizabethan age, Victorian gentleman, anguished Edwardian, committed existentialist, apolitical quietist, even a member of the Moral Majority. Like all great writers, Sidney and his works have been continually reinterpreted by successive ages, his poems and his life alike inscribed into different literary, political, and cultural discourses. As contemporary scholars have become more attuned to both the linguistic and ideological complexity of Renaissance literature generally and to the new possibilities of contemporary critical methods, Sidney's writing has been seen, both in its seemingly replete presence and its symptomatic gaps and absences, as central to an understanding of Elizabethan poetry and culture.

None of Sidney's poetry was published in his lifetime, and yet along with his other writings it circulated among a small coterie of family and court acquaintances during the 1580's. Sidney's vocations were those of courtier, statesman, Protestant aristocrat, and patriot before that of a poet, and his poetry encourages the piecing together of a more problematic Sidney than that afforded by conventional hagiography. Sidney's writings often served, as A. C. Hamilton argues, "as a kind of outlet for political interests, compensating for the frustrations and failures" of his life: "problems that prove insurmountable in his career" were transposed and wrestled with in his fictions.

Sidney's major poetic work, *Astrophel and Stella*, in particular marks the triumphant maturity of Elizabethan court poetry, the belated but spectacular adaption of Petrarchanism to English aristocratic culture. It remains one of the most moving, delightful, and provocative collections of love poems in the language, all the more powerful in its impact because of the variety of needs that strain within it for expression—erotic, poetic, political, religious, cultural. One may read it, as Harington did, as the expression of thwarted, obsessive love, but it opens itself, like its author, to much richer readings, which reinforce Sidney's position as the central literary and cultural figure in the English Renaissance before William Shakespeare.

Biography

Sir Philip Sidney was born into one of England's leading aristocratic families. His father was one of Elizabeth I's most loyal civil servants, serving as Lord President of Wales and Lord Deputy of Ireland. On his mother's side, Sidney was related to the influential Leicester family, one of the major Protestant powers in the country. He was educated under the stern Calvinist Thomas Ashton at Shrewsbury School, along with his lifetime friend and biographer Fulke Greville; in 1568 he went to Oxford, but he left without a degree in 1571 and in 1572 went on a Grand Tour through Europe, where he was introduced to and widely admired by major European scholars and statesmen, especially by leading Huguenot and German Protestants. In 1575 he returned to England and joined Elizabeth's court. He contributed a masque, *The Lady of May*, to one of the royal entertainments in 1578 and was employed by the Queen in a number of minor matters. Unfortunately, he alienated Elizabeth, partly because he was so forthright in his support of European and English Protestant ideals and partly because of his own personal charisma. In a stormy career at court, he alternated between periods of willing service and periods of retirement to his sister's house at Wilton, near Salisbury, where an increasing number of Elizabethan poets, intellectuals, and thinkers were gathering—almost as an alternative to the Queen's court. In 1580 he quarreled with the Earl of Oxford over whether the Queen should consider marrying the French Catholic Duke of Anjou. His advice on the matter was ignored, or played down, and he contemplated going illegally to the New World. Elizabeth's attitude to the man the English court so much admired (almost as much as many Europeans) was an ambivalent one: Sidney was probably too much a man of outspoken principle to be of use to her in her devious political dealings.

Sidney's literary career therefore developed in part out of the frustrations of his political career. Most of his works were written in his periods of chosen, or enforced, retirement to Wilton, and often grew out of discussions with friends such as Fulke Greville and Edward Dyer and his sister, Mary. He looked at the poetry being written in England, contrasted it most unfavorably with that of European courts, and so set out deliberately, by precept and example, to improve it. The result was an outburst of writing that marked a literary revolution: *Defence of Poesie*, probably started by 1579, was a sophisticated, chatty, and persuasive theoretical treatment. *Astrophel and Stella*, written in 1581-1582, is the first major Petrarchan sonnet collection written in English; the continually revised romance, *Arcadia*, dedicated to his sister, was started in 1578, and was still being revised shortly before his tragic death in the Battle of Zutphen in 1586. Sidney was given a hero's funeral in London. Monarchs, statesmen, soldiers, and poets from all over Europe sent condolences, wrote memorials, and for the next sixty years or so Sidney's person, prestige, and power hung over the English court and culture as a reminder of how the Renaissance ideal of the courtier could be combined with Protestant piety.

Analysis

Sir Philip Sidney was educated to embrace an unusual degree of political, religious, and cultural responsibility, yet it is clear from his comments in *Defence of Poesie* that he took his literary role as seriously. Both this critical treatise and his *Astrophel and Stella* are manifestos—not only of poetic but also of broader cultural practice. Both look forward to a long-needed renaissance of poetry and culture generally. For Sidney, poetry and its broader social uses were inseparable. Indeed, it is only with distortion that one can separate a "literary" from a "social" text, even with a Petrarchan love sequence such as *Astrophel and Stella*. Like other Elizabethan court poets, Sidney's poetry was written within a structure of power, and it tries to carve out a discursive space under ideological pressures which attempted to control and direct the languages by which the court operated. The court was more than a visible institution for Sidney and his contemporaries: it was a felt pressure which attempted to fix and determine all that came within its reach. Sidney's life and poetry are especially interesting examples of how the Elizabethan court's power operated upon poetry. The court poets—for example, Sir Walter Raleigh, or the Earl of Oxford—acted as spokesmen for the court's values, and yet inevitably the strains and tensions of their roles show through in their poetry. Poetry was both an expression of the power of the court and a means of participating in that power. Where a poem like Raleigh's "Praised be Diana's Fair and Harmles Light" shows the court contemplating its own idealized image, Sidney's poetry has a more uneasy relation to the court's power. Although on the surface his writing appears to embody, in Terry Eagleton's words, a "moment of ideological buoyancy, an achieved synthesis" of courtly values, Sidney's own position in the court makes his poetry an especially revealing instance of the struggles and tensions beneath the seemingly replete surface of the court and court poetry alike.

More than any of his contemporaries before John Donne and Shakespeare, Sidney's poetry evokes a felt world of bustling activity, psychosocial pressure, cultural demand—in short, the workings of power upon literary and historical discourse. The institutions that shape the poetry—the court, its household arrangements, its religious and political controversies—are evoked in the tournaments (41), the gossip of "curious wits" (23) and "courtly nymphs" (54), and make up an atmosphere of energetic worldliness. What distinguishes Sidney's poetry is the forceful way that something more than the glittering surface of the court energizes it. Despite his posthumous reputation as the perfect Renaissance courtier, Sidney's public career was one of political disappointment and humiliation; he seems to have been increasingly torn between public duty and private desire, much in the way the hero of his sonnet sequence is.

As Richard McCoy has shown, all Sidney's works are permeated with the problem of authority and submission. Like himself, all his heroes (including Astrophel) are young, noble, well-educated and well-intentioned, but as they become aware of the complexities and ambiguities of the world, they become diverted or confused, and Sidney finds himself caught between compassion and condemnation of their activities. In *Arcadia*, Sidney attempted to solve in fiction many of the tensions that beset his life, and *Astrophel and Stella* similarly served as an outlet for political and social frustration. In the prose romance, Sidney's narrative irresolution and (in an early version) premature and repressive closure reveal deep and unsettling doubts; similarly, the ambivalences and hesitations, the shifting distance between poet and character, the divided responses to intellectual and emotional demands in *Astrophel and Stella*, articulate Sidney's ambivalent roles within the court.

One of the fundamental influences which give Sidney's life and poetry their particular cast is Protestantism. Indeed, perhaps the most potent factor disrupting the repleteness of the court poetic was Sidney's piety and his struggle with creating a Protestant poetic. In A. C. Hamilton's phrase, Sidney was "a Protestant English Petrarch." Unlike his close friend Fulke Greville, for whom a radical Augustinian suspicion of metaphor and writing itself consistently undermined poetry's value, Sidney tried to hold together what in *Defence of Poesie* he terms man's "erected wit" and his "infected will." Indeed, what Sidney perhaps uniquely brought to the Petrarchan lyric was a self-conscious anxiety about the tension between courtly celebration and Protestant inwardness, between the persuasiveness and rhetoric and the self-doubt of sinful man, between the insecurity of man's word and the absolute claims of God's.

The tension in Sidney's writing between the courtly and the pious, John Calvin and Baldassare Castiglione, disrupts *Astrophel and Stella* most interestingly. Sidney's own theory sees poetry focusing on the reformation of will and behavior, and it is possible to read his own sequence as an exemplum of the perils of erotic love, or, in Alan Sinfield's words, "the errors of unregulated passion." Sidney displays Astrophel deliberately rejecting virtue, treating Stella as a deity in a "direct challenge to Christianity" and to right reason. His cleverness is displayed in trying to avoid or repel the claims of reason and virtue, and the outcome of the sequence is the inevitable end of self-deception. The inwardness of *Astrophel and Stella*—not necessarily, it should be noted, its supposed autobiographical dimension, but its concern with the persona's self-consciousness, even self-centeredness, as lover, poet, courtier— is thus a fascinating blend of Petrarchan convention and Protestant self-concentration, and one which points to a distinctive late sixteenth century strain within the inherited vocabulary and rhetoric of the poet in his role in the court.

When Sidney returned from his Grand Tour, he looked back across the Channel to the sophisticated academies and court circles which were encouraging writers, scholars, and musicians, and which were united by a synthesis of Christian, usually Protestant, piety and high Neoplatonism. The French academies, in particular, displayed a self-consciousness that distinguished them very strongly from the medieval courts. Shortly after Sidney's return, his sister Mary became the Countess of Pembroke and established at Wilton what one of her followers was to term a "little Court," dedicated, both before and after his death, to continuing the renaissance of English courtly culture. Sidney's whole literary career became a frustrated attempt to realize a new role for the court poet, one based upon the integrity and responsibility of values which he was unable to embody in his public life, and which more and more he poured into his writing. His remark to the Earl of Leicester that he was kept "from the courte since my only service is speeche and that is stopped" has wider application than to its occasion, the French marriage crisis. It articulates a frustration toward the traditional subservience of a poet to the court, a stubborn insistence on forging a distinctive role for the poet.

Part of the fascination Sidney has traditionally evoked is what is often perceived as his ability to balance opposite ideological, rhetorical, or vocational demands upon him. Certainly in *Defence of Poesie*, and *Astrophel and Stella* the elements of such a dialectic can be found. The promise of divinity that Astrophel perceives in Stella's eyes is, in Sidney's sympathetic comedy, wittily undermined by his self-consciousness, bashfulness, physical overeagerness, and human imperfection. In *Defence of Poesie*, Sidney describes poetry as a fervent reaching for the sublime, veiling truth in order to draw its reader toward it, and asserts that the power to move and so to bring about an enactment of poetry's transforming powers certainly lies within man's godlike nature. Yet for Sidney there was the seemingly inseparable problem of man's "infected will," and the reformed emphasis on man's depravity and the untrustworthiness of the mind seems to have posed crucial problems for him and for the possibility of creating a Protestant poetic. While elements of an opposition between rhetoric and truth, humanism and piety, Calvin and Castiglione, can be isolated, despite his most anxious intentions, Sidney does not manage to hold them together satisfactorily. In fact, his very fascination for later ages and his centrality for understanding sixteenth century poetry are grounded in such contradictions. "Unresolved and continuing conflict," in Stephen Greenblatt's phrase, is a distinctive mark of Renaissance culture, and Sidney's is a central place in that culture.

The versification of the Psalms, started by Sidney about 1579 and revised and completed by his sister, the Countess of Pembroke, after his death, comprises the first post-Reformation religious lyrics that combine the rich emotional and spiritual life of Protestantism with the new rhetorical riches of the secular lyric. There are distinctive Protestant notes—a strong stress on election in Psalm 43, echoing Théodore Bèze's and Calvin's glosses rather than the original text, for example—and other Psalms, where a strain of courtly Neoplatonism is highlighted, notably in Psalm 8, which (like Pico della Mirandola rather than Calvin) presents man as a privileged, glorious creation "attended" by God, an "owner" of regal and "crowning honour." Man emerges as a free and wondrous being, like his creator, "freely raunging within the Zodiack of his owne wit," as Sidney put it in *Defence of Poesie*. Here Sidney juxtaposes, without integrating them, the great contraries of his age.

It is now generally believed that the Psalms were originally drafted by Sidney early in his career, perhaps about 1579. Also written in this early period are a number of miscellaneous poems, including the so-called "certain sonnets" and many of the poems inserted into *Arcadia*. These are mainly of interest for showing Sidney's eager experimentation—with quantitative verse, pastoral dialogue, song, metrical and stanzaic patterns, and above all the appeal to the feelings of the reader, notably in "Leave me ô Love, which reachest but to dust" and the magnificent double sestina from *Arcadia*, "Yee Gote-heard Gods."

Sidney's most sustained and most celebrated work is his sonnet sequence *Astrophel and Stella*, probably written in 1582, which dramatizes a frustrated love affair between a courtier and an admired lady. As Germaine Warkentin has shown, Sidney may have been tinkering with his "Certain Sonnets" during 1581-1582, abandoning them the next summer "to compose one of the three most distinguished sonnet sequences of the English Renaissance." Certainly *Astrophel and Stella* conveys an intensity that suggests a short burst of concentrated writing.

This sequence of 108 sonnets and eleven songs anatomizes the love of a young, restless, self-conscious courtier, Astrophel, for a lady, Stella, his star. His purpose is set out in the opening sonnet, in which he claims, "I sought fit words to paint the blackest face of woe/ Studying inventions fine, her wits to entertaine." The reader is taken into the familiar world of Petrarchan convention and cliché: Astrophel the doubting, self-conscious, aggressive lover; Stella, the golden-haired, black-eyed, chaste and (usually) distant and (finally) unobtainable lady. The figures are equally familiar—debates between Hope and Absence, denials of loving at first sight, the frustrated desire alleviated by writing, the beautiful woman with the icy heart who pitilessly resists siege, and the final misery of the lover who ends his plaints in anguish, swearing in the end by all he has left, her "absent presence." Like the best *Petrarchisti*, Sidney makes the traditional motifs intensely dramatic. For the first time in English poetry since Geoffrey Chaucer, C. S. Lewis suggests, "a situation is not merely written about: it is created, presented, so as to compel our imaginations." Earlier Petrarchan poets such as Thomas Wyatt had conveyed urgency and conversational informality, but, read as a whole, English poetry had not, since Chaucer, been distinguished by such continual, even restless, conflict and energy.

Modern critics, reacting against earlier impressionistic, Romantic criticism, have shown how the energy and variety of Sidney's poetry rests on a thorough exploitation of the riches of Renaissance rhetoric—through his use of apostrophe, dialogue, irony, shifts in decorum, and modulations of voice. As Ringler points out, perhaps "the most valuable product of his studies and disputations in Oxford was the thorough training he received in logic and formal classical rhetoric"; to these he added intense study and practice in ways of loosening the rhythmic movement of English line and working within the formal demands of stanzaic and metrical form. By a thorough familiarity with the conventional techniques of Renaissance love verse—which he parodies in 6, 9, and 15, for example—Sidney works within the eloquent courtly poetic, mocking and adapting it where necessary. Sidney uses his poems as workshops, experimenting with a great variety of stanzaic patterns and with devices such as inversion and feminine rhyme. Above all, he tries continually to juxtapose the movement of formal verse with an immediacy of idiom and logical development to involve his reader in the often tortuous movements of his character's broodings, arguments, and self-deceptions. Especially notable is the lightness and wit with which even Astrophel's most tortured self-examination is presented. Parody, the exaggerated use of erotic or literary clichés and puns, are all obvious enough, but the whole sequence is characterized by a sophisticated playfulness—the outrageous puns on "touch" in 9 leading to the self-pity (Astrophel's, not Sidney's) of the last line, the tongue-in-cheek anguish of the sonnets on Cupid, and the uproariousness of some of the erotic sonnets. Above all, the humor of the poet, indulging in his own mastery of language and able to dramatize his character, invites his readers to share his enjoyment at the varied follies and complexities of human love.

If the Petrarchan tradition and the resources of Elizabethan rhetoric afforded Sidney a wonderfully flexible and rich poetic vehicle, there is nevertheless something limiting, even disturbing, about the literary mode in which he is working. Petrarchanism purports to be about love, and specifically about the obsession of a lover for a lady before whom he feels inferior, humble, and yet ennobled. Paradoxically, the sonnets become a weapon in an attempted mastery of the woman and their focus is exclusively upon the anguish and achievements of the male lover. The conventions of Petrarchanism are those of a male-dominated society and its rhetorical strategies serve to elevate the woman only to subjugate her.

As Ann Jones and Peter Stallybrass have argued, "to Stella, Astrophel may speak of love as service," but outside his devotion to friends, "he can suggest a sub-text of masculine domination." Within the struggle for mastery, rhetoric and erotic convention alike becomes means of domination. Stella herself is, like other Petrarchan mistresses, reduced to a disconnected set of characteristics, acknowledged only as they are manipulable or impinge on her lover's consciousness. She is entirely the product of her poet-lover's desires. *Astrophel and Stella* is a theater of desire in which the man has all the active roles, and in which she is silent or merely iconic, most present when she refuses him or is absent. Astrophel does not want—although it is arguable that Sidney might—to call into question the power of his anguish or the centrality of his struggles of conscience, yet it seems legitimate to ask what Stella might reply to Astrophel's earnest self-regarding pleas for favor. Even if her replies are not "in" most of the poems (and where they are, as in Song 8, they are reported through Astrophel), what might she say? Is her silence the repression of the character or of Sidney? Does her silence reflect a whole cultural blindness that fixes women as objects of gaze and analysis within a society they did not invent and could not control? When one considers in these ways how the dynamics of Sidney's text function, once again one finds "literary" and "cultural" texts interacting.

An older criticism faced (or perhaps avoided) these issues by focusing on the biographical "origins" of the sequence. In part an outcome of the Romantic valorization of poetry as the overflow of sincerity or genuine experience, criticism sentimentalized the obvious connections between Sidney's life and the fiction of Astrophel and Stella into a poetic *roman à clef*. Undoubtedly, Sidney plays with his reader's curiosity about some kind of identification between himself and Astrophel and between Stella and Lady Penelope Rich (née Devereux) to whom as a youth Sidney's family nearly arranged a betrothal and in whom he may possibly (though there is no firm evidence either way) have had more than a literary interest. Sidney certainly builds into his sequence references to his career, to his father, to contemporary politics, to his friends, and—of most interest to the curious—to Lady Rich's name in two sonnets (24, 37) which were omitted from the first publication of the collection, perhaps for fear of embarrassing repercussions. Even so, the relationship between Sidney and his characters and between the events of his life and those seemingly within his poems should not be simplified. Just as Sidney manages simultaneously to have much in common with Astrophel, be sympathetic with him, and yet to criticize or laugh at him, so the gap between Stella and the historical Lady Rich is even wider—at best one can regard some of the references to Stella as sly or wistful fantasies. As to whether Sidney and Lady Rich were sexually involved, *Astrophel and Stella* gives no firm evidence.

A more rewarding approach is to try to trace the way the poems are traversed by a variety of overlapping and in many cases contradictory influences, including court politics, the psychology of love, poetry, rhetoric, and Christianity. Within its confusions, tensions, and contradictons, *Astrophel and Stella* highlights the diverse and often contradictory pressures and possibilities which constitute the situation of an Elizabethan poet and lover. One of the distinctive possiblities of Petrarchanism was to set the traditional medieval debate on the nature of love in terms of the lover's psychology and within the demands of the codes of courtly behavior. Part of the fascination Petrarch had for English poets in the late sixteenth century was their puzzlement about how the Petrarchist conventions might fit their experiences. The prestige and suggestiveness of Petrarchanism allowed poets to examine not only the relationship between love and poetry, but also the way its worldview, its rich schematization of human experience, and their own changing social and individual realities intersected.

One of the dominant concerns of the sequence is undoubtedly that of the problems and difficulties of erotic experience—although depicted entirely from the male viewpoint. *Astrophel and Stella* typically focuses on the "thrownness" of love—on the lover finding himself within a preexisting structuring of experience, a "race" that "hath neither stop nor start" (23), but which continually disrupts his sense of a preexistent self. Sexuality becomes an object to be examined, supervised, confessed, and transformed into poetry. It should be noted, however, that the "self" that is put into question in *Astrophel and Stella* is not, or not primarily, that of Sidney. The poet offers his poems to an audience of sympathetic listeners as a mirror less of his experiences than of theirs. The intellectual tensions observable in *Astrophel and Stella* are dramatized as paradigms, the effect of which is to highlight the readers' or hearers' awareness of their own experiences. Sidney's poems work upon their readers, suggesting and manipulating although never compelling into meaning. At times he refers to quite specific members of his audience— to other lover-poets in 6, in which Astrophel distinguishes his own "trembling voice" and the sincerity of his love from those of other lovers and so provokes them to respond by praising their own mistresses or talents. At times his suffering hero will ostensibly address a rather special audience—"I Stella's ears assayl, invade her ears," he says in Sonnet 61; or he (or Sidney) will address a friend (as in Sonnet 14), and even occasionally himself (as in 30). Yet the most important audience is unnamed: the readers who, through the poem's history, will read them, meditate upon and act out their drama.

Surveying the history of Sidney criticism, especially in the past forty years, one discovers a curious anxiety to find a coherent, sequential organization not merely made possible by the poems, but as a required means of reading them. *Astrophel and Stella* is thus often read as if it were a poetic novel. C. S. Lewis cautions against treating the Petrarchan sequence as if it were "a way of telling a story"; *Astrophel and Stella* is, he says, "not a love story but an anatomy of love," while Max Putzel speaks of the poems' "careful disorder." On the other hand, A. C. Hamilton argues that "the sonnets are organized into a sequence with a unifying structure," and other critics have written of what they see as careful structure and sequence. In Hamilton's scheme, sonnets 1-12 form an introduction, 13-30 concentrate on Astrophel's isolation, with 41-68 concerned with his moral rebellion, 71-85 with his attempt at seduction, and the remainder with his failure. Such divisions differ radically among the proponents of a narrative structure; in short, if a reader wishes to find a narrative development and final irresolution rather than an exercise in love's variety, then *Astrophel and Stella* is open to such a reading. Perhaps the most satisfying sequential reading of the collection is that by Ann Rosalind Jones, who stresses that although it is possible (and peculiarly satisfying) to see Astrophel as undergoing a gradual disintegration and loss of control,

Sidney's sequence does not use the linking devices of other poets, such as Dante or Maurice Scève, which might strongly encourage a reading of the sequence as a growth in self-knowledge. Even when one constructs a sequence, it is primarily characterized by an unstable, eddying movement, "dramatically *dis*ordered," as Jones argues. "Even at the end of his experience," Astrophel can "predict the course of his writing no better than the course of his love" and so each sonnet becomes a new starting place. In short, while *Astrophel and Stella* allows for a linear development, it does not force one upon a reader, encouraging one just as readily to view Astrophel's experience as unpredictable, random, and even as an exemplum of failure.

One recurring pattern is a tension between the demands of the public world of politics and responsibility and the private world of erotic desire. In many sonnets, Astrophel presents love in terms of a debate between traditional abstractions such as desire and reason, love and duty. Part of the reader's enjoyment lies in watching him, through Sidney's fond but penetrating perspective, indulging himself in false logic (52) or in seeing his dutifully constructed arguments against love undermined by the simple appearance of his beloved, as in 5, 10, or in the amusing self-contradictions of 47. Astrophel tries in vain to keep his two worlds and their demands separate. He claims that love gives him a private place, a sense of self from which the demands of courtly responsibility are shown to be trivial, but caught between conflicting worlds of self-indulgence and political responsibility, he ends by succeeding in neither. The reader watches him corrupting his avowedly pure love into sensuality by the deviousness of political rhetoric. In Sonnet 23 he appears to reject the world, but in Sonnet 69 he expresses Stella's conditional encouragement of his advances in terms of the court's own language. Since, he argues, she has "of her high heart giv'n" him "the monarchie," as a king, he too can take some advantage from that power.

At the root of Astrophel's self-deception is the structure of Petrarchanism itself, which, as John Stevens and others have pointed out, was at once a literary convention and a very serious courtly game, one "in which three powerful discourses meet and join hands: love, religion, and politics." *Astrophel and Stella* is based on a formula by which the man is subjected to his lady while, at the same time, the situation enables him to pour fourth his eloquence in an attempt to influence her. The relationship is parallel to the relationship between courtier and monarch—built on absolute loyalty and subjection, frustration and rejection—interlaced with devious manipulation for the favors of the capricious, distant beloved. Thus while Astrophel speaks of the "joy" inspired by Stella and of his own "noble fire," he is attempting to manipulate Stella's vulnerability, seeking power over her in the way the devious courtier seeks hidden but real power over the monarch. In terms of sexual politics of the Renaissance court, Astrophel's world is one shared primarily by other male courtiers, using language as a means of domination and treating women as subject to their desire, much in the way courtiers themselves were at the mercy of the monarch.

Thus the reader watches Astrophel indulging himself in small subtle ways— playing on grammar in 63, twisting Stella's words, speaking openly to her in a kind of "manic playfulness," and allowing (or being unable to prevent) the emergence of the underlying physicality of his desires in a series of fantasies of seduction (71, 72, 74, 79, 80, 81). The songs serve especially well to high- light the wish-fulfillment of Astrophel's frustrations—especially the drama- tization in Song 5 of Astrophel's self-involvement, and the graceful fantasy of Song 8, viewed wistfully by the narrator from a distance and culminating in Sidney's clever and moving breaking down of the distance between narra- tor and character in the final line, where he confesses that "my" song is broken.

As the sequence draws to its inevitably inconclusive end, Astrophel's fan- tasies become less and less realizable. He indulges in self-pity and then more realistically accepts the end of the relationship, vacillating between joy and grief, optimism and despair, dedication and unfaithfulness. As Hamilton points out, the mutability of human love which haunts so many Elizabethan sonnet sequences, especially Shakespeare's, enters Sidney's only indirectly, but where he immerses himself in the intensity of the living moment, as the sequence ends, he realizes he is "forever subject to love's tyranny, a victim of *chronos* forever caught in time's endless linear succession."

Readings of *Astrophel and Stella* inevitably point to it as a quintessential ideological and literary struggle, where a variety of impulses struggle for mastery. Like the best love poems, it asks its readers to look at themselves. Stella herself, the guiding metaphor of the sequence, is distinguished by her nature, behavior, influence, and power, always requiring, like a text, inter- pretation. Astrophel, like the reader of his creator's sequence, is an exegete of love. "What blushing notes doest thou in margin see," he asks, and goes on, as all readers do with the whole sequence, to choose his own convenient misunderstanding of Stella. Astrophel may state that all his "deed" is to "copy" what in Stella "Nature writes" (3) or assert that "Stella" is, literally, the principle of love in the cosmos (28), and that the words he utters "do well set forth my mind" (44), but Sidney knows, as his readers do, that love and its significance and its expression in language are far more complex mat- ters.

Astrophel and Stella is what Roland Barthes terms a "playful" text, one that depends strongly on its audience, inviting participation both to repro- duce the process, intellectual and emotional, by which the poem's struggles came to be verbalized and to go beyond them, adding one's own preoc- cupations. *Astrophel and Stella* has a capacity to invade its readers, to di- rect and inform their responses, but as well, to open them to an awareness that it functions only through a process of deliberate reciprocity. It is this joyful welcome to its readers that makes it such a landmark in English poetry.

Gary F. Waller

Other major works
FICTION: *Arcadia*, 1590, 1593, 1598 (originally entitled *The Countess of Pembroke's Arcadia*).
PLAY: *The Lady of May*, 1578 (masque); "Fortress of Perfect Beauty," 1581 (with Fulke Greville, Lord Brooke; Phillip Howard, Earl of Arundel; and Baron Windsor of Stanwell).
NONFICTION: *Defence of Poesie*, 1595 (also published as *An Apologie for Poetry*).
MISCELLANEOUS: *Miscellaneous Prose of Sir Philip Sidney*, 1973.

Bibliography
Connell, Dorothy. *Sir Philip Sidney: The Maker's Mind*. Oxford, England: Clarendon Press, 1977. A thoughtful text that considers Sidney's life and art in a biographical and historical context. Connell discusses in detail important historical influences on Sidney. Supplemented by maps, a bibliography, and an excellent index.
Hamilton, A. C. *Sir Philip Sidney: A Study of His Life and Works*. New York: Cambridge University Press, 1977. A strong study of Sidney's life, poetics, and selected works and an excellent general survey that places his work in a biographical context. Includes an appendix, notes, a bibliography, and an index.
Kay, Dennis, ed. *Sir Philip Sidney: An Anthology of Modern Criticism*. Oxford, England: Clarendon Press, 1987. A frequently insightful collection of scholarly criticism. Kay's comprehensive introduction places Sidney in a cultural heritage and surveys the changes that have occurred in the critical approaches to Sidney's work. Complemented by a chronology, a bibliography, an index, and a list of early editions.
Kinney, Arthur F., ed. *Essential Articles for the Study of Sir Philip Sidney*. Hamden, Conn.: Archon Books, 1986. A collection of twenty-five insightful articles with a wide range of critical approaches. Topics include Sidney's biography, *The Lady of May*, *Defence of Poesie*, *Astrophel and Stella*, *Arcadia*, and *The Psalmes of David, Translated into Divers and Sundry Kindes of Verse*. Supplemented by a bibliography.
Myrick, Kenneth. *Sir Philip Sidney as a Literary Craftsman*. Lincoln: University of Nebraska Press, 1965. A very informative survey of Sidney's work as it reflects a critical project and approach to poetics. Specific attention is given to *Arcadia*, including a summary of plot and a character list. Contains notes and an index, as well as a valuable list of studies on

Sidney from 1935 to 1964.

Sidney, Philip, Sir. *Sir Philip Sidney: Selected Prose and Poetry.* Edited by Robert Kimbrough. Madison: University of Wisconsin Press, 1983. In this lengthy and thorough work, Kimbrough gives detailed attention to *Defence of Poesie, Astrophel and Stella*, and *Arcadia.* Kimbrough also surveys the critical approaches to Sidney. Contains a chronology and a select bibliography.

SIR ROBERT SIDNEY

Born: Penshurst Place, England; November 19, 1563
Died: Penshurst Place, England; July 13, 1626

Principal poetry

Sir Robert Sidney's poetry was unpublished during his lifetime. His poetry remained in manuscript, probably at Penshurst, until the early nineteenth century, when it found its way into the Warwick Castle Library. The manuscript was first positively identified by P. J. Croft in 1973 and purchased by the British Library in 1974. It has subsequently been printed in a modern-spelling version by K. Duncan-Jones and was published as *The Poems of Robert Sidney* in 1984 by the Oxford University Press.

Other literary forms

Unlike his more famous brother Philip and his sister Mary, Robert was not a prolific writer. Indeed, his career as a poet was probably confined to a few years, possibly as few as two. There are many letters by him in the Sidney papers, but he published no literary work in his lifetime.

Achievements

The discovery of the manuscript of Robert's poetry in the 1970's added a distinctive voice to the courtier poets of the late sixteenth century. In his manuscript's ninety pages of nervous, often corrected handwriting are the works of a new Elizabethan poet of outstanding interest. Robert does not quite possess Philip's variety or intimate control of tone and mood within a poem (the emotions of his verse are expressed in broader sweeps) but his ear is highly sensitive, and his poems reverberate with the great commonplaces of Elizabethan life and literature—time, absence, grief, and deprivation. Like his contemporary Sir Walter Raleigh, Robert Sidney turned to poetry only occasionally, yet he found in it a commitment that went beyond emotional solace; and, like Raleigh's, Sidney's verse reveals the ideological power of the Elizabethan court over those who struggled for articulation within its frantic center or (in Robert's case) on its anxious margins.

Biography

During his life and after, Robert Sidney was overshadowed by the brilliance of his elder brother Philip. He was a dutiful son of a family that was ambitious but relatively new to the power-struggles of the Elizabethan aristocracy. In his early life, Robert had none of the prestige or flamboyance of Philip. He dutifully went on his grand tour of Europe, pursued by letters of advice from his brother as to his reading, chivalric bearing, acquaintances, and finances. In 1585, he accompanied Philip, who had been appointed governor of

Flushing, to the Low Countries, and was present at the Battle of Zutphen, where Philip was mortally wounded. Philip's death seemed to represent the death of an entire age. From the late 1580's, Elizabethans became increasingly bewildered and disillusioned, as the Armada victory turned sour, court infighting grew more and more frenetic, and the Queen cultivated the trappings of high Neoplatonism to hold in check the corruption and confusion beneath the surface of the court.

In the shadow of his brother, Robert had undergone the usual initiation of the Elizabethan courtier. In 1584, he married Barbara Gamage, a young Welsh heiress—after some rather sordid negotiations. Their letters later show them to have grown into a most loving couple. He constantly addresses her as "sweet heart" or "dear heart," and the letters are full of sadness at his absence from her. In 1594, he wrote that "there is no desyre in me so dear as the love I bear you and our children . . . you are married, my dear Barbara, to a husband that is now drawn so into the world and the actions of yt as there is no way to retire myself without trying fortune further."

The intense strain of being an honest courtier during the 1590's is evident throughout his letters. Indeed, it might be said that Philip had the good fortune to die in 1586; Robert had to live on. In 1587, he was his brother's chief mourner, and, like his sister Mary, may have turned to poetry at this time partly in order to continue his brother's literary ideals. In 1588, he was appointed to Philip's old position of Governor of Flushing, and, with only a few brief breaks, usually to carry out some unpalatable diplomatic task imposed by Elizabeth, he spent most of the next decade in the Low Countries, his chief interest being to return home. Constantly exhorted to live up to his brother's standard, he seems to have been regarded by the Queen as a convenient workhorse.

After years of frustration, Robert Sidney's fortunes improved under James's reign. Life at Penshurst in the early seventeenth century was celebrated in that most harmonious of poems by Ben Jonson, "To Penshurst," in which he praised what appeared to its aristocratic proprietors to be the rich, cooperative life of an organic and humane community. Incidentally, Jonson does not here explicitly mention Sidney as a poet—although this would not have been entirely unusual, as outside his immediate circle even Philip's reputation as a poet had hardly been mentioned before his death. In 1605, Sidney was created Viscount de Lisle, and in 1618, Earl of Leicester. He died in 1626, age sixty-two, having survived his elder brother by forty years and his elder sister by five.

Analysis

The retrieval of the manuscript poems written by Robert Sidney was arguably the most important such Renaissance discovery of the past hundred years. The Sidney manuscript is the only extant substantial body of verse by an Elizabethan poet in his own handwriting and incorporating the poet's own revisions. In addition to their intrinsic interest, these poems dramatically change the present view of the literary activities of the Sidney circle, that unique, closely connected family group which was inspired by the genius and person of Sir Philip Sidney.

Although references to the literary interests of all the Sidneys, including Robert, are found in many dedications, letters, and prefaces of the period, there are few references to him as a poet. George Chapman wrote of him in 1609 as "the most Learned and Noble Concluder of the Warres Art, and the Muses." There is a tradition that he wrote the lyrics for his godson Robert Dowland's *Musicall Banquet*, and he may have written verses in honor of his daughter's marriage. Certainly, like the rest of his family, Robert was widely praised as a generous patron of literature. It is significant that the distinctive note of the other Sidneys' encouragement of poets was that they were poets themselves. "Gentle *Sir Philip Sidney*," wrote Thomas Nashe, "thou knewest what belonged to a schollar, thou knewest what paines, what toyle, what travel, conduct to perfection."

As with his sister Mary, Robert's poetic career may have started seriously only after his brother's death. It is clear that she did not begin to write seriously until after 1586, when she took upon herself the vocation to continue his work in forwarding the Elizabethan poetic Renaissance. The bulk of her work, an impressive body of poetry and prose, grows directly out of Philip's inspiration: she edited his manuscripts, completed his versifying of the psalms, and wrote or translated a number of works directly influenced by his critical theories or dedicated to his memory. It may be that Robert also wrote his verse as a similar, although less public, attempt to continue his brother's poetic intentions. He may have decided that Mary, more permanently settled at Wilton in the 1580's with the increasing comings and goings of Fulke Greville, Edmund Spenser, Samuel Daniel, and other poets, was better placed to forward the literary revolution of the Sidneys. It was to her that he sent the one extant copy of his manuscript, possibly during one of his much-desired but infrequent visits to England.

The obvious comparisons are, then, between Robert's poetry and that written by Philip and Mary. Like his brother's, Robert's poems are in the form of a Petrarchan miscellany of sonnets and songs, although they show a greater variety of metrical and stanzaic patterns than the normal sonnet sequence of the 1580's and 1590's, a characteristic he may have derived from Mary, whose psalms are the most impressive formal experimentation in English verse before Gerard Manley Hopkins. In the Countess' 165 psalms, there are 164 distinct stanzaic and metrical patterns, some of them being remarkably complex and subtle. Robert's are technically less ambitious, although they certainly reflect a similar interest in working with complex patterns of verse—as evidenced by the three unusual thirteen-line stanzas of

"Upon a wretch that wastes away/ Consumed with wants." Here the complex rhyme scheme (aab cccb ddeeb) and the varying line length (886886-33666 syllables) are reminiscent of the Countess' experiments, as indeed are many of Robert's pastorals and songs. None of the patterns exactly matches those of Mary Sidney and the diction is naturally closer to the typical love poetry of the era (such as in *England's Helicon*, 1600) than to her *Psalms*, but they arise from the same fascination with formal experimentation: just as in Mary's Psalms only once is the stanzaic pattern repeated, so in Robert's twenty-four songs he never repeats a pattern, and within particular poems, too, he displays a technical virtuosity comparable to that of his brother and sister. Song 1, "O eyes, a lights devine," for example, skillfully mixes lines of varied length, with a predominantly iambic beat. Like both Philip and Mary, he uses feminine rhyme very skillfully in the songs (as in Song 10, "You whoe fauor doe enioy"), and his technical skill is seen in such sophisticated mixtures as blending of rhyming anapests with the regular iambics in Song 4 ("My soule is purest fine/ doth not aspyre"). Like Mary, Robert shows an excellent control of movement and balance within single lines, as, for example, in the final lines of Sonnet 21: "Or if on mee from my fayre heauen are seen/ Some scattred beames: Know sutch heate giues theyre light/ as frosty mornings Sun: as Moonshyne night."

If Robert shares something of Mary's technical daring, the most important influence is nevertheless that of his brother. Robert's sequence is clearly modeled on *Astrophel and Stella* (1591): it mingles sonnets with longer, more emotionally diffuse songs, and like Philip's, Robert's sequence contains an interesting transformation of biographical reference into a devious fiction. The whole sequence is characterized by an opaque melancholy, a mood of disturbance and brooding which, while endemic to Petrarchan sonnets in general, nevertheless takes as its subject Robert's reading of his own political and personal career. While the collection is a typical Petrarchan miscellany, it is united even less than *Astrophel and Stella* by narrative or personae and is held together, more explicitly than in any other collection of late Elizabethan lyrics, by that most powerful of institutions and ideological forces, the Elizabethan court.

Robert's poetry was probably written during his long, frustrating tour of duty in the Low Countries, perhaps begun (like Mary's) in the late 1580's but (at least in the one extant copy) copied probably at some time between 1596 and 1598. Perhaps Robert's poetry was a reaction not only to his depressing exile from England but also to the melancholy duty of occupying his brother's old post. Much of Robert's verse could be read as a moving expression of a frustrated politician's world of escape, yearning for his wife and children and home at Penshurst. Sonnet 7, "The hardy Captein vnusde to retyre," speaks directly of his turning from the Low Countries "to the West" where "loue fast holds his hart" (Song 6). The sixth Song of the collection is an especially revealing piece—as well as being the most impressive poetically. Like Raleigh's famous and haunting "As you Came to the Holy Land," it is based on the traditional lost ballad of a pilgrim traveling to Walsingham. Robert's version is a 136-line poem, hauntingly evocative in its use of the ballad with its traditional dialogue, here occurring between a Pilgrim and a Lady who presumably represents Robert's wife. Certainly, "the knight that loves me best," who "greefs liuerie weares," who "to the west . . . turns his eyes," to whom she refers is Robert's wistful projection of his own exiled self held by duty to the Low Countries away from what later in the poem he terms: "the lady that doth rest near Medwayes sandy bed." Penshurst Place, the Sidney home, stands on the Medway River just outside Tonbridge and almost due west of Flushing. Interestingly enough, Robert revised this particular line to read "near ritch Tons sandy bed," which of course refers to Tonbridge.

Song 6 is the most clearly autobiographical poem in the sequence, projecting a partly calculated, partly wistful view of Sidney's frustrated personal and political career. The bulk of the collection, in traditional Petrarchan fashion, is ostensibly concerned with love and is similar to a host of sequences written in the 1590's, such as Daniel's *Delia* or Michael Drayton's *Idea*, although no poem mentions any identifiable or even coherently fictional mistress. The diction is typical of the English *petrarchisti*. The lovers "sowle" exists "in purest fyre" (Song 4); he accepts both the joys and griefs of love, in his "bands of service without end" (Sonnet 13). Readers encounter the familiar world of Petrarchan paradox: on the one hand, there is the high idealism of the lover who affirms the beauty of "those fayre eyes" which "shyne in theyr former light" (Song 12); on the other hand, there are the "paines which I vncessantly susteine" (Sonnet 2). The lady's beauties are "born of the heauens, my sowles delight" (Sonnet 3), while the lover's passions are "purest flames kindled by beauties rare" (Sonnet 4), as he contemplates in pleasurable agony how she takes "pleasure" in his "cruelty" (Sonnet 25), asking her why she "nowrishes" poisonous weeds of cold despair in love's garden instead of the plants and trees of love's true faith and zeal (Song 22).

This basic Petrarchan situation of frustration, contradiction, and paradox is decked out in familiar Neoplatonic garb. The world is a dark cave where love's lights never shine except through the beloved's eyes, the "purest stars, whose neuer diying fyres" (Sonnet 1) constantly burn a path between the heavens and the lover's soul. Sexual desire is rarely explicitly mentioned: the dominant mood is that of melancholy, the recurring emphasis on the lover's self-torturing helplessness, and to an unusual degree, on torture, disease, and violence. The lover is a continually lashed slave, flung from rocks, a leper, racked by gangrene, or in violent wars.

Even with the marked emphasis on violence, this is a world familiar to readers of Renaissance lyrics. Robert's work is less versatile, metrically and metaphorically, than Philip's, with no double sestinas or quantitative verse and little of Philip's sly humor. What distinguishes Robert Sidney's poems from the mass by second-rate poets such as Thomas Watson and Henry Constable and from the anonymous verse of a miscellany like *England's Helicon* is his remarkable control of form and tone, and his frequent use of a cryptic and direct address, not unlike the aphoristic tone of some of Greville's poems. Typical is the brief, pessimistic Song 17, which seems to reflect upon deeply tragic events in the poet's experience.

Robert Sidney's poetry, like the work of Philip and Mary, shows a deep commitment to the craft of poetry as well as to its inspiring or calculated consolations of erotic or political favor. It is more than conventional Petrarchan regret when he asserts that even "the most perfect stile cannot attaine" the expression of the mistress' beauties or the pangs of love. The poems are the work of a poet with a highly sensitive ear, and a range of tone that, while not broad, is deeply resonant, especially receptive to the way emotions may be attached to metaphors of absence and loss. In his *Caelica*, Greville often takes up the conventional assertion that, when apart, true lovers are paradoxically closer because of the spiritual nature of their love; but he places the motif in a grimly realistic context, affirming instead that "absence is pain." Similarly, Robert's brooding over absence, delay, and loneliness have more than a conventional "feel" to them. Over and over again, the poet suffers from "greefs sent from her whom in my sowle I bless" (Song 23); constantly he feels that "delaies are death" (Song 18), as he waits "on unknown shore, with weather hard destrest" (Song 22). Such common Petrarchan motifs are made peculiarly effective especially through the grave, deliberate melancholic movement of the lines, which convey the passion, the hopelessness, and yet the continuing devotion of the lover.

Intellectually, Robert's verse is as rich a revelation of the peculiar strains and repressions of the Elizabethan aristocracy as that of Philip or Mary. His poetry, however, seems more detached from their particular religious interests. One of the most revealing notes of the literature of the Sidney circle is its continual attempt to balance the idealism of high Neoplatonism, and its emphasis on the autonomy of the human will and man's desire for perfection, with the psychological and political demands of a strong Calvinistic piety, emphasizing God's transcendence of humanity and the corruption and worthlessness of human aspirations. It is interesting that Robert seems relatively indifferent to this great intellectual debate; nor is there any sense that he was especially interested in the more extreme varieties of Neoplatonic or magical philosophy associated with John Dee or Giordano Bruno, which were current in the 1580's. Perhaps living isolated from the mainstream of English philosophical developments in the 1580's and 1590's, he was untouched by such speculation; altogether, Robert's character and interests were more pragmatic and less speculative. His poetry had more immediate ends in view. A typically aspiring courtier, directing his poems at particular (never, of course, stated) ends, the intellectual tensions of his verse remain the stock-in-trade of the Petrarchan poet; his sequence is poetically but not intellectually sophisticated.

The particular feature of Robert Sidney's poetry which makes his work important to readers of the ideologically opaque power struggles of the Elizabethan aristocracy is the intense way it articulates the silent power of the dominant institution of the age, the court. The basis of the Petrarchan sonnet collections of the late sixteenth century is not primarily erotic, despite their Petrarchan apparatus. Sexual desire is used—by Robert's brother, as well as by Spenser, Daniel, Raleigh, and others—as a metaphor for political desire and frustration. Most of Robert Sidney's poems do not evoke the frustrated sexual passion of a lover; they use that basic Petrarchan situation as a metaphor for political powerlessness and aspiration. The "lights divine" from which the lover is "exiled," "the only cause for which I care to see," and "these purest flames kindled by beauties rare," may be read as conventional Neoplatonic complements of a beloved only if the realities of Elizabethan politics and the court's control of the discursive structures of both politics and poetry are ignored.

No less than Raleigh's "Cynthia" or "Praised be Diana's Fair and Harmless Light," Robert Sidney's sonnets articulate the ideological dominance of the Elizabethan court; unlike Raleigh's—except in their intense anxiousness and their overly insistent protest of absolute devotion—they do not articulate any opposition to that hegemonic discourse. As his brother Philip's *Astrophel and Stella* so triumphantly shows, one of the distinctive features of the Petrarchan sequence is its encouragement to readers to decode it in a variety of ways— as erotic self-evaluation, philosophical meditation, or moral debate. Robert's poems can be read as intense, extreme Neoplatonic poems of compliment and frustration, but they acquire an urgency and become rooted in the material life of late Elizabethan society when they are read as compensations for political powerlessness.

Not all of Robert Sidney's poems can be read so directly in this way—there are a variety of translations, songs, and other miscellaneous pieces which may be seen as typical "workshop" exercises designed to show or practice his skills—but through the whole collection, one senses the enormous power of the Elizabethan court, creating and controlling its subjects by exerting power over their language, over their metaphors of political as well as poetical expression. The political world in which Robert Sidney had, between 1586 and 1598, a marginal part, can be read from his poetical text: finally the poetical text (the poems extant in his slim notebook) and the social text (the events which constitute the milieu in which he wrote) are indistinguishable, each flowing into the other to articulate the material and metaphorical dominance of the Elizabethan court.

It is fascinating to see the emergence into literary and critical consciousness of such an interesting poet almost four hundred years after he wrote. When it was written, Sidney's poetry aimed to demonstrate his fitness to take part in the power of the court, but it demonstrated as well that he was a Sidney in another way—in his devotion to the craft and the importance of poetry. A decade or more after he wrote these poems, Robert Sidney was praised by Ben Jonson as a man of generosity, responsibility, and piety. Jonson speaks of how his children might "Reade, in their vertuous parents noble parts,/ The mysteries of manners, armes, and arts." Robert Sidney's distinction in "armes and manners" was no mystery; he was a Sidney, a name which, as Jonson put it, was in "the impresse of the great." Until the rediscovery of his manuscript, however, Robert Sidney's "arts" were indeed unknown. Perhaps by the time Jonson wrote "To Penshurst," Robert himself had all but forgotten his youthful poetry. He had, after all, achieved his comfortable if minor place in the Jacobean aristocracy. One can only be glad that the longer span of history sometimes uncovers what the short time of individual men happens to bury.

Gary F. Waller

Bibliography

Croft, Peter J. *The Poems of Robert Sidney: Edited from the Poet's Autograph Notebook.* Oxford, England: Oxford University Press, 1984. This important book-length edition includes an extended introduction which concerns the life and work of Sidney. For this alone, the text is invaluable. This work also, however, contains a chronological table of the life and times of Sidney and his complete works. The poems are supplemented by extended notes and commentaries which aid greatly in their explication. This is a valuable source for the study of Sidney.

Hay, Millicent V. *The Life of Robert Sidney, Earl of Leicester, 1563-1626.* Washington, D.C.: Folger Shakespeare Library, 1984. This rather pedestrian book-length account of Sidney is of value because of its extensive bibliography. Each of its chapters contains notes, and there is a good account given of his poetry. The work also contains a genealogical table and a thorough index.

Sidney, Robert, Sir. "The Poems of Robert Sidney." *English* 136 (1981): 3-72. This unique article, edited by Katherine Duncan-Jones, presents a thorough collation of the poems of Robert Sidney. It is important because it modernizes the spelling in the poems. While it is rather complete and the changes appear accurate, the modernization of the verse is somewhat disappointing.

Waller, Gary F. "Sir Robert Sidney." In *Early Poetry of the Sixteenth Century.* London: Longman, 1986. Waller puts the short literary life of Sidney into perspective in this fine essay. Short, yet thorough, this work centers on the strain of Sidney's life as a courtier, his comparison with his more widely known, flamboyant brother Philip and his sister Mary. The work contains fine notes, a concise chronology, general bibliography, and notes.

CHARLES SIMIC

Born: Belgrade, Yugoslavia; May 9, 1938

Principal poetry

What the Grass Says, 1967; *Somewhere Among Us a Stone Is Taking Notes*, 1969; *Dismantling the Silence*, 1971; *White*, 1972, revised 1980; *Return to a Place Lit by a Glass of Milk*, 1974; *Biography and a Lament*, 1976; *Charon's Cosmology*, 1977; *Classic Ballroom Dances*, 1980; *Austerities*, 1982; *Weather Forecast for Utopia and Vicinity: Poems 1967-1982*, 1983; *Selected Poems 1963-1983*, 1985; *Unending Blues*, 1986; *The World Doesn't End*, 1989; *The Book of Gods and Devils*, 1990.

Other literary forms

In addition to his poetry collections and translations, Charles Simic edited, with Mark Strand, *Another Republic* (1976), an influential anthology that provided many American readers with an introduction to contemporary poetry in Europe and Latin America. Simic also edited *The Essential Campion* (1988), a selection of the lyrics of Thomas Campion. He has published books of essays, *The Uncertain Certainty* (1985) and *Wonderful Words, Silent Truth* (1990).

Achievements

Among Simic's many awards are a Guggenheim Fellowship (1972-1973), grants from the National Endowment for the Arts (1974-1975 and 1979-1980), the Edgar Allan Poe Award (1975), a National Institute of Arts and Letters and American Academy of Arts and Letters Award (1976), and an International Association of Poets, Playwrights, Essayists, and Novelists (PEN) International Award for Translation (in 1970 and 1980). In 1984 he was awarded a MacArthur Foundation Fellowship, and his book of prose poems *The World Doesn't End* received the Pulitzer Prize for Poetry in 1990.

Biography

Charles Simic was born in Belgrade, Yugoslavia, in 1938, and emigrated to the United States in 1954. "My travel agents were Hitler and Stalin," he has said. When Simic was three years old, a house across the street from his family's home was destroyed by a bomb. For young Simic and his friends, the war (so serious and terrible for adults) was often a source of fun. There were guns and air-raid sirens to imitate—and, toward the end, a thriving salvage business in gunpowder. The chaos and menace of that time survive in Simic's poems, along with its variety, wonder, comedy, and sadness. For Simic, the city survives as well. "My mother is calling my name out of a tenement window," he has said. "She keeps calling and calling. My entire psychic life is there."

Simic settled in Chicago, where he attended Oak Park High School and the University of Chicago. After finishing a stint in the army, he lived in New York, working at a variety of jobs (shirt salesman, house painter, payroll clerk) and attending New York University, where he earned his B.A. Another part of his education took place in the New York Library, where he read all the folklore and anthropology he could find, as a way of introducing mythic consciousness into his poetry. He ended up making his own myths of things common and close to home: brooms, ballroom dances, the fingers of a hand.

Simic published his first two books, *What the Grass Says* and *Somewhere Among Us a Stone Is Taking Notes* with Kayak Press; *Dismantling the Silence* (composed of some poems from the first two books, plus new ones) was issued by Braziller in 1971. To his surprise, his increasing reputation brought him invitations to teach. He has taught at the California State University at Hayward and is currently professor of English at the University of New Hampshire. He lives with his wife, Helen Dubin, a dress designer, with whom he has two children.

Analysis

In his autobiographical essay "In the Beginning . . . ," Charles Simic describes one of the first great influences on him, the family radio:

> The nights of my childhood were spent in the company of that radio. . . . Once I heard beeps in Morse code. Spies, I thought. Often I'd catch a distant station so faint I'd have to turn the sound all the way up and press my ear against the rough burlap that covered the speaker. Somewhere dance music was playing or the language was so attractive I'd listen to it for a long time, as if on the verge of understanding.

This solitary attentiveness, this fascination with the barely intelligible, with speech so far away that it seems transmitted from silence, has characterized Simic's poetry from the beginning. In attentive silence, he says, he can come closer to "the way things are."

Simic's poetic sensibility combines a surrealistic fascination with recurring archetypes and an imagist concern for precise observation of things. His first influences were poets with a gift for the primitive and a knack for using language to evoke origins: Vachel Lindsay, Hart Crane, Carl Sandburg, Theodore Roethke (in particular his poem "The Lost Son"), and the Yugoslav Vasko Popa (whose work Simic has translated). He has also been influenced by the blues, with its verbal inventiveness, eroticism, and tragic sense of life.

"Butcher Shop," like many of Simic's poems, ushers the reader into a mysterious world: late night, after hours. Here the implements of butchery take on their own dark lives. The blood on the butcher's apron becomes a map "of the great continents of blood," while glittering knives are reminiscent of altars in some ominously dark church where "the cripple and the imbecile" are brought "to be healed."

Simic's love for ordinary objects enables him again and again to rebuild the universe with them at the center. When he describes a butcher's bloody apron, nothing but it exists. It emerges anew from its mysterious origins, part of a myth of nourishment—a river where the reader, with Simic, can be fed.

Simic's "object poems" are justly among his most celebrated works. In "Bestiary for the Fingers of My Right Hand," the thumb becomes a "fat worm/ They have attached to my flesh"; the middle finger is stiff, a querulous, questing old man; the fourth, with its occasional inexplicable twitches, "is mystery." The hand's transformation is nothing so simple as mere personification. Rather than being made human simulacra, the fingers are animated—that is, they assume their own vibrant lives, the equal of any animal or human.

The imagination animates all Simic sees. Why should people, Simic's poems assert, have a monopoly on lives? His poems turn the pecking order upside down, reserving special reverence for the ugly, the ignominious. "Brooms," from *Return to a Place Lit by a Glass of Milk*, is a lavish celebration of brooms, a compendium beginning with their knowledge (including self-knowledge): they know of the Devil's existence, and they are aware of their own mysterious life, which Simic suggests in images of trees in an orchard. Section 2 moves to broom lore, explaining that in dream analysis they are interpreted as "omens of approaching death." In public they resemble "flat-chested old maids"—a comparison both wildly imaginative and devilishly accurate.

One secret of this poem's liveliness is that while the subject remains constant, the context veers wildly, from dreambooks to jails to tenements. In section 3, the lives of saints and astronomers are shown to contain the origins of brooms. To make "the first ancestral broom," arrows were harvested from Saint Sebastian's back and bound together with the rope that Judas Iscariot used to hang himself. The broom's handle was one of the stilts on which Nicolaus Copernicus mounted to touch the morning star.

Section 4 presents the teachings of brooms, ending with advice on levitation: "I suggest remembering:/ There is only one God/ And his prophet is Mohammed." This reference seems at first a hilarious red herring—but then the reader remembers that Muhammad is said to have levitated. Simic is interested, first and last, in the sense of nonsense, the wedding of the ordinary with the sweepingly important. Here, as so often in his poems, the holy and the silly are intertwined.

Simic loves to create worlds, then dismantle them to silence and invisibility. In the end, the Brooms disappear into their origins in mythic time: "Once, long ago."

Simic's fascination with combining the intricate and the simple has a connection with philosophy. He reads philosophy—particularly Martin Heidegger, for he admires that thinker's determination to reexamine what is simple and taken for granted. Simic sees the poet's task as similar.

In *Charon's Cosmology*, Simic keeps his mythic tone but reveals a growing sense of history. The menace and destruction he witnessed as a boy make their way into his work. "Eyes Fastened with Pins" has Death as its main character—personified, with unsettling humor, as an ordinary working stiff, having to prowl unfamiliar parts of town in the rain while his neighbors relax on the backyard steps drinking beer. In "Charon's Cosmology," Death's boatman gets confused about which side of the river is which—each side has an identical pile of corpses.

Classic Ballroom Dances contains even more history. A poem called "Baby Pictures of Famous Dictators" marvels quietly at history's constant odd juxtapositions, its strange plots and casting: carnival freaks, Thomas Alva Edison inventing the light bulb, a famine that rages in India. The infant dictators pose in their sailor suits, lovable and innocent as any other babies. Yet the photographer's black hood, trembling in the breeze, is silently ominous.

For Simic, history is made of small moments, inconsequential but resonant. "Classic Ballroom Dances" shows grandmothers wringing chickens' necks and nun schoolteachers pulling boys' ears. The poem is, in fact, a dance, a box step of four-line stanzas that lead the reader through a list of ordinary rituals, ancient patterns of habit, from pickpockets' crafty steps as they work a crowd that has gathered at the scene of an accident to "the ancient lovers, cheek to cheek,/ On the dancefloor of the Union Hall." To see all these gestures in the same light changes them, makes the reader reconsider their identities.

Simic calls the list poem "the poetic equivalent of quilt-making. One cuts the patches into signs and symbols of one's own cosmology, then one covers oneself with it on a cold winter night." He remembers his elders as they reverently learned dances from foot patterns traced on the floor with chalk, so they could repeat time-hallowed movements. "The world," Simic says, "is a ballroom full of mirrors and we are the inspired or awkward dancers."

Also in 1980, Simic published the revised version of his long poem *White*, which explores and dramatizes the source of his poetic impulse, personified as White—"his muse," Peter Schmidt has written, "of strangeness and new selfhood." The poem's task is set in its first lines: "Out of Poverty/ To begin again"—the implicit task of every poem. In the first two parts of *White* the poet speaks; the third and last belong to White herself. She is identified with what Simic has called "a state that precedes verbalization," which embraces all possibilities. White will always remain beyond him: "I thought of you long before you thought of me," she reminds the poet. Yet her elusiveness is not to be mourned: "the most beautiful riddle has no answer."

Austerities intensifies an impulse central to Simic's work: the desire to use the fewest possible words to produce the largest possible effect. He exercises once again his gift for combining the archetypal with the everyday, as in "Drawn to Perspective," a painterly poem that renders one hushed moment on a summer evening with pared-down images of a parent calling a child, a boy on skates, and a couple poised to embrace.

In *Unending Blues*, Simic adopts a more personal, relaxed voice than ever before. In "To Helen," he announces in blues style,

> Tomorrow early I'm going to the doctor
> In the blue suit and shirt you ironed.
> Tomorrow I'm having my bones photographed
> With my heart in its spiked branches.

He fashions a setting for the heart—it will resemble an old nest in a bare crabapple tree in autumn—that spins out further and further until a new world is complete. A poetic phenomenologist, Simic writes poems that demonstrate the notion (derived from Edmund Husserl and Martin Heidegger) that the world is made of objects people intend through their attention. That is, the human act of attention reveals and creates their significance. This attention operates in the book's other poem addressed to Helen, this time in praise of a sea cucumber. He has never seen one but likes the "cold and salty" sound of its name, so he proposes diving into a dark, treacherous ocean to harvest some of these "lovely green vegetables" for a salad. Like many Simic poems, this one exhibits a childlike spirit that takes delight in creating a vivid world and then imagining an adventure in it.

The World Doesn't End, a volume of prose poems, received the Pulitzer Prize for Poetry in 1990. Simic found this hybrid form congenial because of its versatility. Whereas the lyric poem is essentially static, focusing on only one moment, the prose poem is mobile. "You write in sentences, and tell a story, but the piece is like a poem because it circles back on itself."

In contrast to the finite, boxlike forms of Simic's lyrics, these poems seem to speak out of an unseen, infinite story, the spaces between them no more than pauses for breath. Titles appear at the tops of pages only for the four tiny lyrics the book includes, which function as resting places amid the striding prose. The table of contents features the first phrase of each poem, followed by an ellipsis, the notation for silence. Indeed, these prose poems create their context directly from silence. "Where ignorance is bliss . . . " creates a world from a proverb:

> Where ignorance is bliss, where one lies at night on the bed of stupidity, where one prays on one's knees to a foolish angel . . . Where one follows a numbskull to war in an army of beatific dunces . . . Where the roosters crow all day. . . .

In *The Book of Gods and Devils*, Simic returns to the lyric, writing poems that hark back to his years as a young man in New York, reading and wandering Fourteenth Street, Hell's Kitchen, the old Fourth Avenue booksellers' row. As he wrote the book, he has said, he was aware of an impulse to follow the custom of pagans: to create gods or demons for places where he had had particularly intense experiences. He marvels at the many "gods" that populate a large city such as New York: objects of worship, objects of fear.

In "Shelley" he remembers reading the poet first on a rainy New York evening, having bought a tattered volume at a secondhand bookstore. Though he still speaks English with an "atrocious Slavic accent," he is captivated by the Romantic poet's flowing language. Flush with Percy Bysshe Shelley's sense of the phantasmagorical, he begins to see the people around him as portentous and archetypal. In a rundown coffee shop, the owner, a retired sailor, gladly refills Simic's cup "with a liquid dark as river Styx"; he has dinner in his accustomed Chinese restaurant, with its silent "three-fingered waiter." The poem captures the deep sense of the world's strangeness experienced by the intense youth who reads Shelley's "Splendors and Glooms" by the light of city storefronts. Even Simic's rented room, to which he contemplates returning, has become strange and fearful, "cold as a tomb of an infant emperor."

With this volume Simic discovers how to use this archetypal method to illuminate lived experience. These poems are anecdotal, but not slack. Their luminous details enrich the world. As always, Simic dwells on the inconsequential detail that means the world: a "pale little girl with glasses" who appears in the door of a Chinese restaurant, a "little white dog" that "ran into the street/ And got entangled with the soldiers' feet," a woman who runs by shrieking, "hugging a blood-stained shirt."

The early impulses are all here, but amplified and extended—made more accessible. Speaking of this volume, Simic has described himself as both a realist and a surrealist, pulled between two ways of seeing. Never before in Simic's work have the real and surreal had such equal voices. The world is here, attended by its mysteries—a strange union of time and timelessness. Increasingly, the poet's attitude is one of astonishment and awe before the world.

As in all Simic's work, there is between and behind the lines the pressure of the unspeakable, that which belongs to silence. Simic's poems do not lift silence, but tantalizingly part its ineffable curtains. "We are always at the beginning," he says, "eternal apprentices, thrown back again and again into that condition."

Angela Ball

Other major works

NONFICTION: *The Uncertain Certainty*, 1985; *Wonderful Words, Silent Truth*, 1990.

TRANSLATIONS: *The Little Box*, by Vasko Popa, 1970; *Four Modern Yugoslav Poets*, 1970; *Homage to the Lame Wolf: Selected Poems 1956-1975*, by Popa, 1979.

EDITED TEXTS: *Another Republic*, 1976 (with Mark Strand); *The Essential Campion*, by Thomas Campion, 1988.

Bibliography

Contoski, Victor. "Charles Simic: Language at the Stone's Heart." *Chicago Review* 48 (Spring, 1977): 145-157. This excellent article outlines Simic's efforts "to interpret the relationship between the animate and inanimate" in his poems. Contoski analyzes Simic's use of language from *What the Grass Says*, his first book, up to *Return to a Place Lit by a Glass of Milk*.

Hart, Kevin. "Writing Things: Literary Property in Heidegger and Simic." *New Literary History: A Journal of Theory and Interpretation* 21 (Autumn, 1989): 199-214. Especially useful for readers wishing to explore the relationship between Simic's poetry and the philosophy of Heidegger. Citing examples from Simic's poems, Hart extensively explores Simic's affinity with Heidegger's phenomenological philosophy.

Jackson, Richard. "Charles Simic and Mark Strand: The Presence of Absence." *Contemporary Literature* 21 (Winter, 1980): 136-145. This article persuasively links the "surrealist moods" of Charles Simic and Mark Strand, exploring (with frequent references to Martin Heidegger and Jacques Lacan) the "absolute priority these two poets give to the ontological function of language."

Schmidt, Peter. "*White*: Charles Simic's Thumbnail Epic." *Contemporary Literature* 23 (Fall, 1982): 528-549. Schmidt analyzes the revised version of Simic's long poem *White*, illuminating its importance to Simic's work as a whole. While centering on *White*, Schmidt's discussion provides a thoroughgoing orientation for readers of Simic's poetry. Walt Whitman and Ralph Waldo Emerson, "those ambiguous foster-parents," are shown to have played a central role in the poet's development.

Simic, Charles. Interview by Molly McQuade. *Publisher's Weekly* 234 (November 2, 1990): 56-57. This lively interview focuses on Simic's origins as a poet and on the autobiographical basis of *The Book of Gods and Devils*.

_____. *The Uncertain Certainty: Interviews, Essays, and Notes on Poetry*. Ann Arbor: University of Michigan Press, 1985. This volume collects much of what Simic has said about poetic theory and practice. Of these interviews and essays, particularly noteworthy are the interview with Sherod Santos, in which Simic discusses the genesis and development of his work, and Simic's essay "Negative Capability and Its Children," in which he explores John Keats's notion of the poet as "capable of being in uncertainties." *The Uncertain Certainty* is an invaluable aid to understanding not only Simic's work but also the nature of poetry itself.

LOUIS SIMPSON

Born: Kingston, Jamaica, British West Indies; March 27, 1923

Principal poetry

The Arrivistes: Poems 1940-1949, 1949; *Good News of Death and Other Poems*, 1955; *A Dream of Governors*, 1959; *At the End of the Open Road*, 1963; *Selected Poems*, 1965; *Adventures of the Letter I*, 1971; *Searching for the Ox*, 1976; *Caviare at the Funeral*, 1980; *The Best Hour of the Night*, 1983; *People Live Here: Selected Poems, 1949-1983*, 1983; *Collected Poems*, 1988; *In the Room We Share*, 1990.

Other literary forms

Louis Simpson's contributions to criticism and literary analysis include *James Hogg: A Critical Study* (1962) and *The New Poets of England and America* (1957), which includes consideration of poets bound by no political creed or literary school. It pointed the direction poetry was to take in subsequent years, especially Simpson's. Simpson's only novel, *Riverside Drive* (1962), won critical respect but convinced him that his talent was better suited to poetry. *North of Jamaica* (1972) is a prose account of his childhood in Jamaica, his wartime experiences, and his career at Columbia University and the University of California at Berkeley. It leads into Simpson's ideas on poetry as he saw it being practiced and as he thought it should go. The book shows how much of Simpson's poetry derives from his own life, how seamlessly the two are joined.

Simpson's study of Ezra Pound, T. S. Eliot, and William Carlos Williams, *Three on the Tower* (1975), was praised for its insight and objectivity, rendered in an informal style. A second critical study, *A Revolution in Taste: Studies of Dylan Thomas, Allen Ginsberg, Sylvia Plath, and Robert Lowell* (1978), argues that in the 1960's poetic sensibility shifted from the formalism of W. H. Auden, returning to the experimental tradition established by Pound, Eliot, and Williams. *A Company of Poets* (1981) collects many of Simpson's critical essays, reviews, and interviews. A later volume, *The Character of the Poet* (1986), provides further clarification of his poetics. These volumes, along with his anthology *An Introduction to Poetry* (1967), provide the student with a rich selection of Simpson's thoughts on the poetry and poets of his times and a helpful guide to Simpson's own life and poetry. The foreword to his *Selected Prose* (1989) points up the importance of this material to anyone who wishes to understand the whole of Simpson's poetic career. The book includes autobiography, fiction, literary criticism, poems, letters, and a journal. Simpson wished "to make this book about life and literature." A life *in* literature emerges.

Simpson has also translated poems by Arthur Rimbaud, Guillaume Apollinaire, Heinrich Heine, the Italian Pier Paolo Pasolini, and the Brazilian João Cabral de Melo Neto. His other work includes a masque and two verse plays.

Achievements

Simpson's literary career has generated enough commentary to rank him among the major poets of the second half of the twentieth century. His war poems have been called the best to come out of World War II, and his criticism has gained him additional respect. His poetic reputation was scarcely established when he was awarded the Prix de Rome (1957). Other awards followed—a Medal for Excellence from Columbia University, honorary degrees, fellowships, and grants, including two Guggenheims. He won the Pulitzer Prize in 1964 for *At the End of the Open Road*. Perhaps much of the respect he has enjoyed as a critic and poet stems from his not aligning himself with any school or movement. At a time when the Academic warred with the Beat, Simpson marched to his own poetic rhythms. He passed through the waters of the "deep image" without being caught in their currents. Wordsworthian influences have been noted, and Simpson gives important attention to Walt Whitman in his poetry, but evidence of influence is slight when it comes to craft, sensibility, precept, or direction. Using the forms and devices that were necessary to express his poetic vision and to speak in a voice that was his own, he has stood apart from, not above, his own subjects and themes and from that vantage point illuminate a common humanity.

Biography

The material of Louis Simpson's life is of particular importance because of its relation to his poetic development. He was born Louis Aston Marantz Simpson in Kingston, Jamaica, on March 27, 1923. His father was a lawyer of Scottish descent, his mother a Jewish immigrant from southern Russia. The parents had met when Rosalind de Marantz went to Kingston from New York City to appear in a film. A brother had been born first, then Louis. Following the breakup of the marriage in 1930, Rosalind went to Toronto. Louis was sent with his brother to Munro College, a private school a hundred miles from Jamaica. Louis was to remain there until he was seventeen. His father remarried, and another child was born. When Louis was near graduation, his father died, leaving most of his estate to his new family. Louis and his brother were made to leave their parental home immediately. On his own, Louis returned to school, where he excelled in literary studies and developed two goals: to be a writer and to leave Jamaica. At sixteen, he was already writing and publishing poetry and prose. In 1940, when he received an invitation from his mother to visit her in New York City, he packed his suitcase and left Jamaica for good.

In New York, Simpson entered Columbia University, where he studied under Mark Van Doren. In 1943, he joined the army and was sent to Texas.

Military life turned him into a dog soldier with little respect for officers. The army also enabled him to see Texas, Louisiana, and Missouri. He took part in the Normandy invasion, fought at Bastogne, and visited London and Paris. By war's end he had gained United States citizenship, won the Bronze Star with cluster, twice earned the Purple Heart, and grown cynical. He wanted to tell the story of the "real war . . . from the viewpoint of the materials— the shovel, the mud, the hole in the mud. . . . physical discomfort may be the ultimate horror." This principle would guide him in telling all "real wars" he was to wage back in the United States.

At Columbia University to continue his studies, he suffered delayed shock and left for Paris, where he briefly studied at the University of Paris before dropping out and frequenting the coffee houses. He published his first book of poems, *The Arrivistes*, at his own expense. It received little notice, and he returned to New York, where he worked for five years in a publishing house, reading manuscripts. Meanwhile, he married, became a father himself, divorced, and remarried. In 1955, he published his second volume of poems and joined the faculty of Columbia, working on his doctorate in comparative literature, which was granted in 1959. Hired to teach at the University of California at Berkeley, Simpson left for the "dream coast" the same year he published his third volume of poems. After winning the Pulitzer Prize, he took a position in 1967 at the State University of New York at Stony Brook, where he continues to write and teach. He has traveled extensively, going to Australia and several times to Europe, visiting his mother who lives near Pisa, Italy.

Analysis

Louis Simpson's development as a poet encompasses virtually the entire second half of the twentieth century. His first volume, *The Arrivistes*, includes poems of mixed forms and subjects. A sestina, a ballad, and a versified dialogue are found among lyrics on war, love, and death. In the book's mixture of classical and modern materials, one finds Simpson's major interests—the city, love, war, and art—all explored with irony and wit. His images have sharpness and emotive force: for example, "the sun was drawn bleeding across the hills" ("Jamaica"). Simpson's interest in the wanderer is evident in "The Warrior's Return" (the warrior being Odysseus) and in "Lazarus Convalescent," in which the biblical Lazarus faintly suggests the poet coming from the "hell" of war to speak to the living. Succinct to the point of aphoristic, many lines cut through literary self-consciousness. "Room and Board" creates a somber city scene; set in France, it expresses genuine feelings through vivid imagery.

In *Good News of Death and Other Poems*, Simpson continues to show interest in romantic love, war, death, the loss of hope, and the ironic contrast between classical and modern values. Here the rhythms are less regular, and the rhymes have loosened. Simpson's characteristic irony and wit are well represented, along with a sensitivity to the seasons, a softening of war's disillusionment, and a corresponding emphasis on lyrical love tinged by a sense of loss or mild sorrow. "The Man Who Married Magdalene" demonstrates the confident handling of voice, tone, and manner that is found increasingly in the poems: "But when he woke and woke alone/ He wept and would deny/ The loose behavior of the bone/ And the immodest thigh." In "Memories of a Lost War," Simpson has discovered a way to shape experience into a form that releases sharp meaning: "The scene jags like a strip of celluloid,/ A mortar fires,/ Cinzano falls, Michelin is destroyed,/ The man of tires." Simpson's gift of juxtaposition has found a way to mix disparate bits into a vivid, felt image, creating a moving collage.

Literary portraiture, another of Simpson's strengths, often combines with his interest in objective reality. In "American Preludes," America's past comes under scrutiny, and "West," in open stanza and irregular line, shows a growing interest in modern America. The social commentary in many of the poems hints at a growing focus on the course the United States is taking and the lives of those who inhabit the land. He finds boredom and features that are false and fragile. "Good News of Death," a pastoral, returns to the bucolic past in rhyme and regular lines to express the idea that the classical past is reborn in the birth of Christ. The "good news" is that Christ offers salvation to humankind.

A Dream of Governors is the first collection to be divided into sections, each titled, reflecting the poet's concern with the arrangement of the poems. In the first group, poems are cast mainly in regular lines and rhymed stanzas, and there is a mixture of classical and modern. The classical lovers in "The Green Shepherd" remain unaffected by the great westward thrust of empire, while the "dragon rises crackling in the air" over the Western Hemisphere. The dragon as symbol of ensuring devastation of the land appears again in the title poem, "A Dream of Governors," the dream being "The City," which the Knight rescues from the dragon, only to become king and grow "old/ and ludicrous and fat." The poem ends as the dragon rises again. Demonic characters and gloomy overtones are to be found in other poems in this collection as well. "To the Western World" concludes grimly: "And grave by grave we civilize the ground." "The country that Columbus thought he found . . . looks unreal," the poet muses in "Landscape with Barns." "Only death looks real." Even America's vaunted freedom "is the basilisk," and the poet's reaction to the Land of Opportunity is to realize that "the melancholy of the possible/ Unmeasures me" ("Orpheus in America").

The idyllic past, only a fantasy, sends the poet to the Old World, where he finds a graveyard. The poetry is becoming more autobiographical as the lines and stanzas continue to open. The poet's voice sounds more like natural speech: "But I am American, and bargain . . . where the junk of culture/

Lies in the dust" ("An American in the Thieves' Market"). In "The Runner," which occupies roughly a third of the entire volume, war is seen through the eyes of a soldier whose journey takes the reader through war as Simpson saw it himself. Following it, "The Bird" injects a fairy-tale quality into the grim aspect of war. Simpson's interest in the surreal may have suggested the vision of a young German soldier who is sent to work in a concentration camp, all the while singing the refrain, "I wish I were a bird." The rhymed quatrains with their three-stress lines create an otherworldly atmosphere. There are Russian tanks, and there is "a little bird . . . flitting"—the transformed soldier. The same stanzaic pattern is used in one of Simpson's most celebrated war poems, "Carentan O Carentan," which reads somewhat like a ballad and focuses on the poignancy of death in war with ironic overtones.

The love poems in the final section continue the mixture of pastoral and classical with modern characters and scenes rendered in regular rhymed stanzas. The volume ends with "Tom Pringle," a poem spoken in the voice of a young man who "will watch the comets' flight . . . And wonder what they mean." Tom Pringle could watch the comets' flight, but Simpson had to return to America.

At the End of the Open Road looks squarely at modern America and its recent past. The voice is often conversational, classical allusions have been dropped, and the lines and stanzas are unrhymed and irregular. Simpson's penchant for focusing on the objects of his world and its people is clearly evident. The mood is serious, and the irony is restrained. "In California" begins with the poet speaking in his own voice—"Here I am"—but by the end, the "I" has become "we." He has joined those who travel the open road and come to the western gate, where they must "turn round the wagons." He discovers that "there's no way out" ("In the Suburbs"). The suburbs trap the body and spirit, and the seeking continues: "I tread the burning pavement. . . . I seek the word. The word is not forthcoming" ("There Is").

Turning to his own past, the poet remembers his grandmother's house, where "there was always chicken soup/ And talk of the old country" ("A Story About Chicken Soup"). He has learned "not to walk in the painted sunshine/ . . . But to live in the tragic world forever." Simpson employs again the narrative form to reveal his vision of the world, blending the open form with a voice closer to his own, as in "Moving the Walls," in which a modern voyager, collecting gewgaws, misses the deeper mystery of the world. The men who sought the golden fleece sought the grand and beautiful mysteries. Looking around, the poet doubts that he sees "any at sea."

Many of the poems reflect the poet's journey from Europe to Japan as if in search of fulfillment, a deeper perception. Searching is thematic and culminates thus: "I am going into the night to find a world of my own" ("Love, My Machine"). Simpson has found that Whitman's open road "goes to the used-car lot"; in "Walt Whitman at Bear Mountain," the angel from "In California" appears again, dancing "like Italy, imagining red," still ambiguous. The search is for a way out of a spiritual cul-de-sac. In the final poem, "Lines Written near San Francisco," the American dream turns out to be "cheap housing in the valleys// Where lives are mean and wretched."

A dozen new pieces in *Selected Poems* revive thoughts of impending disaster, rendered in striking imagery. In "The Union Barge on Staten Island," the poet sees a threat in nature itself: "Under your feet, the wood seems deeply alive./ It's the running sea you feel." The animals "felt the same currents," and ominous clouds drift "over the Wilderness, over the still farms." The poet discovers in "Things" that "machines are the animals of the Americans." Yet he finally feels a kinship with those whom he has been observing from a distance: "Who lives in these dark houses?/ I am suddenly aware/ I might live here myself" ("After Midnight").

The eye turned inward becomes the basis of *Adventures in the Letter I*, in which Simpson looks beyond contemporary America and finds the Russia his mother used to describe. The poems are often autobiographical, freed of rhymed stanzas and regular lines. The lines do not invariably begin with capital letters. Simpson wants his poetic language to look more like the speech it is becoming. "Adam Yankev" creates a portrait of the artist looking at himself, realizing that, though his head is "full of ancient life," he sees "houses,/ streets, bridges, traffic, crowds," people whose "faces are strangely familiar." No longer alienated by what he sees, the poet finds that "things want to be understood."

Though still somewhat disengaged from the world, the poet feels a kinship. In "The Photographer," a still life gives ideas "a connection." Simply to look is to find meaning, a kinship. In a longer poem telling of a man having an affair that ends in the grim reality of paying alimony and child support, the poet's sympathy is evident in the final vision of the man's life: "Maybe/ he talks to his pillow, and it whispers,/ moving red hair" ("Vandergast and the Girl"). Kinship is also evident in the poet's speaking as the ghost of a dead man: "And I, who used to lie with the moon,/ am here in a peat-bog" ("On a Disappearance of the Moon"). In "An American Peasant," the poet shares the peasant's trust in "silence" and distrust of "ideas."

Some of the poems read like letters to the reader: "My whole life coming to this place,/ and understanding it better" ("Port Jefferson"). In the poet's ancestral past lies the meaning he has been seeking. In "A Friend of the Family," the technology that deadens the spirit of America spreads to Asia while the speaker envisions nights in Russia, where a "space-rocket rises" and is called "Progress." The poet realizes that Anton Chekhov "was just a man," that the world is peopled by Vanya and Ivanov, that "people live here . . . you'd be amazed." As the poet says in "Sacred Objects," Whitman's "light" was "to form individuals," those who live in the moment and for the moment find their "sacred objects" in the "life you really have."

Searching for the Ox opens with Simpson reminiscing about his boyhood on the shore of Kingston harbor and tracing his life to the present. The wanderer's life has been poetically circular. To advance is to come back to the starting place, though one continues to change, to discover. In many of the poems, the poet's life unfolds without a sense of kinship or connection with the objects and people that earlier had taught him where the mystery lies and perhaps how to engage with it. "Words are realities," he reminds the reader. "They have the power/ to make us feel and see" ("The Springs of Gadara"), as do people, places, things. Mechanical lives and repetitious rounds continue as though waiting for some meaning to break the cycle; when they are transformed into a poetic vision, their meaning becomes felt, implicit.

The poet's sense of pointless repetition and continued disengagement threads through places, times, and the lives of the people remembered or envisioned. "Cliff Road" ends at "a fence on a cliff,/ looking at the lights on the opposite shore." The way through and beyond this impasse lies in the word. Baruch always wanted to study the Torah ("Baruch"). Like the old man, the poet says, "We have been devoted to words." With this faith in the word and its redemptive power goes a continuing attachment to the real world just beyond the senses. Abstractions lead away from the objects that give meaning. In "Searching for the Ox," the speaker says, "I find my awareness/ of the world . . . has increased." The search ends in the discovery: "There is only earth."

The final section includes more snapshots of the world the poet is journeying through, recording, a journey that shifts to his ancestral past and forward to the present. At the same time, the poet looks outward and inward. Changed by what he sees, he changes it, the part humankind imposes on the world, the "Machine." By recognizing the monotonous, mechanical nature of a shelling machine, for example, he has changed it. Recognition by "a total stranger" of the thing that makes human life mechanical gives character, even life, to both.

In *Caviare at the Funeral*, the poet continues seeing kinship and connection in the world, inner and outer, past and present. The opening poem, "Working Late," weaves memories of the poet's father with images from nature that suggest the poet's mother. The moon "has come all the way from Russia," as the mother had done, a sojourner like her son. Still, the son feels a kinship with his father, whose light shines in the study—it "now shines as late in mine." Shards from the everyday world resonate in his memory as the portraits of individuals unfold around and through them. As the artist's sensibility gives them meaningful shape, a world of meaning is created. Poetry gives the poet what he seeks: meaning from the inert objects that claim his attention.

The poet remains the outsider, observing events and individuals and occasionally commenting on them, though he often lets a description of a scene make the comment. In "Little Colored Flags," the poet envisions the bland typicalness of small-town life; the sea is tucked away "behind the last house at the end of the street," all but unnoticed, suggesting that those who do not see the world around them become prisoners of their own limited vision. The poet paints scenes in which people sense the futility of life, having surrendered to the mechanical motions of a technological world. "Unfinished Life" provides a telling symbol: "A hubcap went rolling in circles, ringing as it settled." The sound is not the music of the spheres, nor the Sirens' call. It is the shrill voice of trapped spirits.

Simpson reiterates his faith in the redemptive power of words in "Profession of Faith" and again in "Why Do You Write About Russia?" The soul of poetry is the "voice." That voice deserves to be heard, for it expresses the poet's "love," his "infinite wonder." Only it, the poet suggests, offers a way out of the "dream" everyone lives. The quest is for "a life in which there are depths/ beyond happiness." A kinship with the past, geographical and ancestral, is nurtured by sound, "such as you hear/ in a sea breaking along a shore." The sounds of nature, of the past, and of people form a universal bond.

In the final section of the volume, Simpson's trip to Australia is presented in poetic snapshots and a prose piece. The theme of the outsider persists in "Out of Season": "when I am away from home/ . . . it is as though there were another self/ . . . waiting to find me alone." Persisting too is the faith that there may be a reason for being "in one place rather than another."

The Best Hour of the Night reflects a continued interest in the scenes and characters in Russia and the Modern United States. The forms remain free, and the dramatic narrative continues to weave commentary and image out of ordinary things and people. "Quiet Desperation" portrays another individual trapped in the monotony of modern life. All his searching can accomplish is a "feeling of pressure" that leads to a vague idea of the depths, the wonder and mystery, beyond the surface world, but they evade him. "The Previous Tenant" offers a similar portrait, of a man in yet another suburb who has had an affair that destroys his marriage. The speaker approves of the affair, for in "such ordinary things" the vigor, if not the beauty, of life can be seen. Modern life still exacts a heavy price: one's spirit is buried "under the linoleum," ingested by the things the culture has disgorged, "brown material/ grained like wood, with imitation knotholes" ("In Otto's Basement").

The poems in *People Live Here* are grouped without attention to chronology, Simpson points out. He ends with a prose reflection on his early life, up to World War II, and his artistic credo: "I don't write for myself. . . . I write poems in order to express feelings I have had since I was a child . . . to express the drama, the terror and beauty of life." The close affinity between Simpson's poetry and prose reflections is evident in the final section of *People Live Here* and *In the Room We Share.* Fully a third of this latter volume is given over to journal entries describing a trip to visit his mother in Italy. In both his poetry and his prose, Simpson continues to record the world. The poetry, because it is more compressed and focused than the prose, becomes a window through which the reader sees what the poet sees. The elements synthesize; poetry is achieved.

Simpson has always been keenly aware of nature's presence—the trees, the sea, the wind. These elements surround many of his experiences, like ministering spirits. The poems in *In the Room We Share* show him returning again and again to his past, to his search beyond happiness, to the drama of life and the scenes and characters that generate it. In "Words," the poet is reading his poems to a group of students, talking to them as through a glass, seen but not heard. Memories of his own youth return to the room he is sharing with the young people, who wonder what he might have to say that might have meaning to them. He tells them how he began to write: when his senses were stirred by an image of "gray eyes, long golden hair," he found the genesis of poetry, "a vision of beauty." Are the youths listening to him? Likely not.

Simpson recapitulates familiar subjects: his war experienc, life in New York City and the suburbs, experiences in Germany, France, Italy, Jamaica, Russia, scenes from the American landscape. The poet is the transcontinental observer, giving life to what he sees, voice to nature and people, meaning to everything, though he is always the outsider, the other person in the room "we" share. Considering the lives of his neighbors (in "Neighbors"), the poet remains attuned to sights and sounds, "as though a world were building/ its likeness through the ear."

Simpson's circular journey has taken him from gloomy predictions of disaster and a sense of alienation to an enfolding vision. In sound, the sea, the word, Simpson sees kinship. The walls of his world form concentric circles from the poet outward, enclosing himself, his neighborhood, city, country, the whole world, but these walls dissolve in the poem. Form both encloses and releases. The poem is a glass that alternates as a mirror and a transparent pane. Simpson's poetic has constructed a room shared by all those who read him, but a room without walls. The past and present are interwoven, and a kinship is achieved in the shared vision. By speaking in his own voice, speaking in the language of the "common man," Simpson has made his poetry an experience that synthesizes thinking and feeling into a common humanity. In the end, he comes back to himself, the end of the open road, and finds a world of things and individuals in a room constructed out of his memory—seeing through the used car lot, beyond the empty dreams, like an angel in the gate.

Bernard E. Morris

Other major works

LONG FICTION: *Riverside Drive*, 1962.

NONFICTION: *James Hogg: A Critical Study*, 1962; *North of Jamaica*, 1972; *Three on the Tower: The Lives and Works of Ezra Pound, T. S. Eliot, and William Carlos Williams*, 1975; *A Revolution in Taste: Studies of Dylan Thomas, Allen Ginsberg, Sylvia Plath, and Robert Lowell*, 1978; *A Company of Poets*, 1981; *The Character of the Poet*, 1986.

ANTHOLOGY: *An Introduction to Poetry*, 1967.

MISCELLANEOUS: *Selected Prose*, 1989.

Bibliography

Cox, C. B. "The Poetry of Louis Simpson." *Critical Quarterly* 8 (Spring, 1966): 72-83. Reprinted in *On Louis Simpson: Depths Beyond Happiness*, edited by Hank Lazer. (See Lazer, below.) One of the best essays on Simpson's early work, Cox's work discusses Simpson's war poems, points out the dream element in his early work, and distinguishes his imagery from that of the Imagists. Cox also notes certain persistent elements in Simpson's work, the sense of alienation and the search motif.

Flint, R. W. "Child of This World." *Parnassus* 11, no. 2 (1983/1984): 302-317. Reprinted in *On Louis Simpson: Depths Beyond Happiness*, edited by Hank Lazer. (See Lazer, below.) Flint discusses the "unmistakable voice" in *People Live Here*, which he sees as establishing a bond of intimacy between the poems and their readers. He gives a close reading to several of the poems, pointing out Simpson's mastery of irony and parody in his treatment of suburban characters. In Simpson's dramatic narrative, Flint sees elements of Anton Chekhov, John Cheever, and other masters of the narrative.

Lazer, Hank, ed. *On Louis Simpson: Depths Beyond Happiness*. Ann Arbor: University of Michigan Press, 1988. Simpson himself says one "should definitely have" this book, which runs to almost 400 pages. Lazer's introduction surveys the criticism of Simpson's work from the beginning. The book itself offers shorter reviews and longer essays that would otherwise remain beyond the reach of most readers, enabling the reader to see how all Simpson's writing and thinking bear on the poetry.

Moran, Ronald. *Louis Simpson*. New York: Twayne, 1972. Chiefly important as the only book-length study of Simpson's literary career, this work opens with a brief biography and then examines the first five collections of poems and Simpson's one novel, *Riverside Drive*. Moran discusses critical response to each of the publications and places many of the poems in the larger context of Simpson's thought, emphasizing the development of the "emotive imagination" in his poetry. A brief annotated bibliography concludes the nearly 200 pages.

Roberson, William H. *Louis Simpson: A Reference Guide*. Boston: G. K. Hall,

1980. This book attests the importance of Simpson's contribution to contemporary poetry. Lazer describes this reference work as "an invaluable book for anyone interested in Louis Simpson's writing and in critical reactions to that body of writing." The 172-page volume begins with a survey of Simpson's poetic career and critical reputation. Part 1 lists the writings by Simpson, and part 2 lists writings about him. Two indexes help the reader through the myriad titles and references.

Stitt, Peter. "Louis Simpson: In Search of the American Self." In *The World's Hieroglyphic Beauty: Five American Poets*. Athens: University of Georgia Press, 1985. Stitt follows Simpson's development through "three distinct phases" and traces the unifying sensibility in the poetry, looking closely at a number of the poems along the way. One of the longer essays on Simpson, this is one of the most illuminating as well.

L. E. SISSMAN

Born: Detroit, Michigan; January 1, 1928
Died: Boston, Massachusetts; March 10, 1976

Principal poetry

Dying: An Introduction, 1968; *Scattered Returns*, 1969; *Pursuit of Honor*, 1971; *Hello, Darkness: The Collected Poems of L. E. Sissman*, 1978 (Peter Davison, editor).

Other literary forms

Little, Brown published *Innocent Bystander: The Scene from the 70's*, in 1975, a collection of L. E. Sissman's "Innocent Bystander" columns from *The Atlantic Monthly*.

Achievements

In a tragically shortened career, Sissman managed to create a substantial, if not major, body of work that illustrates the way in which very traditional forms can be harnessed to intensely autobiographical, often mundane material to produce poetry of a high order. Confronted in his late thirties by death as an immediate, oppressive reality—"Very few people know where they will die,/ but I do: in a brick-faced hospital"—his verses dwell, too excessively at times, upon the clinical details of standard medical procedures, hospital dramas, burnishing them with wit, irony, and a sheen of erudite lyricism: "My awesome, glossy x-rays lay me bare/ In whited spaces: my skull glows like a moon/ Hewn, like a button, out of vivid bone" ("Hello, Darkness").

Sissman was both modest and precise about his aesthetic stance: "I write traditional, scanning, stanzaic verse, with special emphasis on iambic pentameter and the couplet." Yet, this adamantly conservative commitment to conventional techniques, which included a playful tendency to paraphrase admired contemporaries and past masters in his work, was fused with a refreshing willingness to take advantage of the new thematic freedom featured in the confessional lyrics of Robert Lowell, Anne Sexton, and Sylvia Plath, fellow New Englanders who also favored, in the main, a formalist style. Consequently, despite an early, lifelong allegiance to W. H. Auden and Auden's deft merger of private experience and public commentary, Sissman's best poetry, at its peak when contemplating family history or imminent personal dissolution, depends heavily upon a sense of autobiographical exactitude and diarylike fidelity to realistic detail, however fictional or transfigured.

In line with John Donne's and Andrew Marvell's ventures in the same area, seduction was another subject that seemed to elicit Sissman's strongest efforts, as in "In and Out: A Home Away from Home, 1947" and the punning "Pursuit of Honor," but the poems most likely to endure are those keyed to the pressure of a terminal illness, poems such as "Dying: An Introduction," "A Deathplace," and the harrowing "Hello, Darkness" sequence, where all the impressive resources of the poet are thrown into battle against the hovering specter of oblivion. Other poems have their charms and moments of undeniable power, among them "The Big Rock Candy Mountain," an elegy for a half-brother, but these too frequently dissipate their emotive energies at crucial moments, as well as their author's gift for clever metaphors, by retreating into self-indulgent pyrotechnics, piled-up images, literary distractions, and the kind of preciousness that can result when laboring with received modes without firm control.

Neither pioneer nor genius, Sissman's main contribution lay in the production of a series of skillful narrative and lyric poems that chronicle, with wit and grace, a single life's unfolding dimensions, a body of verse which should, as X. J. Kennedy has suggested in his perceptive and touching retrospective for *Parnassus* (Fall/Winter 1979), be read as "one enormous poem: an effort to recapture his past, interpret it, fix it, set it in order." This represents a significant achievement, if only as a reminder that poetry's essential humanity still wells from just such a constant reification of ordinary existence for communal benefit.

Biography

Louis Edward Sissman was born in Detroit, Michigan, on January 1, 1928, the only child of Edward James and Marie (née Anderson) Sissman, though his father apparently had children during a former marriage. Edward Sissman was in advertising, and his wife, according to "Parents in Winter," had run away from Ontario at the age of seventeen to go on the stage, eventually playing the Palace Theater in New York, taking up the piano and winning the Bach prize before settling down to marriage. In his Introduction to *Hello, Darkness*, Peter Davison summarizes Sissman's parents as "peripatetic, homiletic, and remote," the father renting rather than buying the large dilapidated building in downtown Detroit that served as their home and his commercial art studio because of his fear of being restricted by ownership.

Money was not a problem, however, and Sissman attended the Detroit Country Day School between 1937 and 1944. He was one of the Quiz Kids on national radio and won the National Spelling Bee Prize in 1941, but he resented his parents and teachers for pushing him into such exhibitions, as an essay entitled "Confessions of an Ex-Quiz Kid" makes clear. Ambivalent feelings about his father, which contained a fair degree of Oedipal resentment, lasted until his father's death in 1974, a year after his mother had died.

In 1944, not yet seventeen, Sissman entered Harvard, but two years later was expelled, the causes given in "Guided Missiles" as "laziness and insubordination." He remained in the area, however, working as a stack boy at the Boston Public Library, and was readmitted the next year. He also began writing poetry, mostly imitations of English Renaissance poets, and studied under John Ciardi, Andrew Wanning, and Theodore Morrison. When he graduated cum laude in 1949, he did so as Class Poet and winner of the Garrison Poetry Prize. A year earlier, he had also been married, but the union was brief and childless.

After leaving Harvard, Sissman worked for a year as a copy editor at Prentice-Hall, then took a job as production manager with the A. S. Wyn publishing house in New York. He returned to Boston in late 1952 to serve as a campaign aide with the John F. Kennedy staff and, in 1953, became a senior writer with Boston's John C. Dowd advertising firm, where he would remain until 1956. That year he was appointed vice president and creative director for the Kenyon and Eckhardt advertising company, also in Boston. On November 27, 1958, he married Anne Bierman, and they moved to the rural town of Still River, an hour's drive west of the city. Their marriage lasted until his death.

In the 1960's, while still a successful advertising executive, Sissman's poems started appearing with increasing regularity in *The New Yorker* and elsewhere, but it was the frightening diagnosis of Hodgkin's disease in 1965 and subsequent radiation treatments that drove him into verse-writing with renewed vigor, almost desperation. In 1966 he wrote the title poem for *Dying: An Introduction*, his first effort to join autobiographical candor with traditional formulas. The collection itself was published in 1968; the same year he was given a Guggenheim Fellowship, which was followed in 1969 by an award from the National Institute of Arts and Letters. His most treasured honor came in 1971 when he was asked to be Harvard's Phi Beta Kappa Poet.

The period between 1970 and his death was a period of extraordinary achievement: he served as contributing editor at *The Atlantic Monthly*, where his "Innocent Bystander" column was a regular feature for five years; he contributed poems and reviews to *The New Yorker*; and he wrote the potent verses of the "Hello, Darkness" sequence under the gun of progressive physical deterioration. Davison has pointed out that Sissman could no longer write poetry after the end of 1974, although his prose was unaffected. As predicted by "Dying: An Introduction," his death came in a Boston Hospital a few months after his forty-eighth birthday.

Analysis

Aside from the title poem, which has the fear of death behind its fierce drive, the poetry in L. E. Sissman's first collection rarely manages to attain the kind of intensity that generates first-class art. Confessedly obsessed with the challenge of using difficult forms, such as villanelles and canzonis, in a language where there is a relative paucity of rhymes, the poet's devices, many of them clever, draw too much attention to themselves, as in the playful "Just a Whack at Empson," where at least the subject matter suits its light verse jacket: "Each greening apple has its browning spot:/ 'The rank of every poet is well-known.'" The pun on Browning and its shrewd denial of Empson's offensive sentence in the second line demonstrate the delightful talent for apt connections and sly technical tricks that are evident throughout *Dying: An Introduction*.

When dealing with more serious matters, however, the habitual resort to puns and obtrusive rhymes, to endless tag lines from other poets and ceaseless amplification of tropes, can create a humorous detachment that destroys the poem's quest for transcendence, even as it wins the reader's admiration. In "Two Encounters," for example, which is divided into halves, "At the Inn, 1947" and "At the Fair, 1967," stressing Sissman's concentration upon a scrap-book past and his love of William Wordsworth, the opening lines exemplify the strengths and limitations of such a modus operandi:

> Your mink scarf smells as if it smoked cigars,
> And soot clings in the corners of your eyes,
> And cold has cancelled your pale cheeks in red,
> And you stand faintly in a veil of Joy.

The list continues, affirming Sissman's habit of never knowing when enough is enough, and the tenor of the lines, arch images of a cigar-smoking dead mink and cheeks stamped by red ink, establishes a mood of youthful insouciance appropriate to the time and place, the speaker's undergraduate days— aided by the borrowing from Randall Jarrell—but in the "altered circum- stances" of meeting his "Dark lady of a dozen sonnets" twenty years later, the tone is capable of evoking rue, nothing deeper, even though the ending is salvaged by a beautiful closing on a ferris wheel: "To hold your airborne arm/ Twenty years later is to ride the calm/ World's rim against the gravity of time."

"Two Encounters" is a good poem, generally successful in what it attempts and accomplishes, yet the very nature of its professional performance, its studied self-consciousness, appears to preclude leaps into the sublime. It favors, instead, literature over life, in the sense that risks—of self, of com- prehension—are usually avoided, and felt responses are tuned to a distancing knowledge of other poets, other poems, so that poems entitled "Peg Finnan's Wake in Inman Square" and "Sweeney to Mrs. Porter in the Spring" are inescapable presences, inviting possibly fatal separations between experience and artifice. Even in "Parents in Winter," where the portraits of his mother and father might be expected to tap richer feeling, Sissman cannot resist ending "Mother at the Palace, 1914" with coy echoes: "And winning the Bach prize, and having sowed/ Such seeds and oats, at last to marriage./ And so to me? But that's another story."

Only in "Dying: An Introduction" do Sissman's narrative gift and comic reflexes find an appropriate vehicle, the wry perspective of the persona accentuating the tension supplied by the bleak situation, which involves three visits to the doctor, once for an examination, the second time to have a slice of a dangerous lump removed for a biopsy, and the third visit to hear the dreaded results: cancer of the lymph nodes or Hodgkin's disease. Divided into five sections, the poem moves from "Summer still plays across the street" to the last section's November setting, which, ironically, has "a thick smell of spring," heightened by laughing "college girls" parading in "ones and twos" and "twos and threes" down the street. The previous section's humorous details—"One *Punch* and two/ *Times* later comes the call" in the waiting room, culminating in "one *Life* further on"—resolves into a series of lean lines that melds unaccustomed spring awareness with memory (of a young sexual episode) and meditative slowness, the autumn world viewed through a new veil of "finity" as

> . . . oddly, not as sombre
> As December,
> But as green
> As anything:
> As spring.

Death's grip, "mixing memory and desire," to quote from T. S. Eliot, a Sissman favorite, has instilled new life.

In many ways, *Scattered Returns* is a duplicate of *Dying: An Introduction* the same olio of charming, witty, often facile versifications of vagrant experience and recovered "spots of time," perceived, as usual, through a net of literary associations—the third poem in the title sequence is "Three Derivative Poems," inspired by Eliot. To match the starkness of "Dying: An Introduction," there is "A Deathplace," which foretells: "A booted man in black with a peaked cap/ Will call for me and troll me down the hall/ And slot me into his black car. That's all." Assisted by monosyllabic deliberateness, the simple diction and matter-of-fact attitude underlines the fearful banality of death's impact, its routine quality to others, while the terse last sentence simulates its abrupt finality. Unfortunately, the sequence itself climaxes with "Sonatina: Hospital," which represents Sissman at his precious worst, straining after a sardonic conceit that eludes sought-for reverberations.

The sole thematic difference between *Scattered Returns* and *Dying: An Introduction* might be seen in the ambitious sequence, "A War Requiem," that concludes the former. Composed in 1969, a year after the assassinations of Martin Luther King and Robert Kennedy when antiwar feelings were reaching fever pitch, the sequence contains thirty-two sections or individual poems and ranges from "New York, 1929" through four decades to "Twelfth Night, 1969." Not too surprisingly, the whole is less than its parts, since it is a case of a minor talent struggling to encompass an awesome theme: the manner in which American history had conspired to produce the disasters of the late 1960's. When read as narrative, a string of dramatic and lyric moments from the author's past as that past intersected with and humanized crucial national events, "A War Requiem" unwinds like a slowly flipping comic strip, broad and fine strokes blurred at times into caricature.

Most often, the sequence functions efficiently where Sissman is content to isolate his governing metaphor without forcing extra literary or political implications upon it, as in Section 28, "New York, 1967," when reflections in Manhattan's ubiquitous plate glass windows and a lowered glance captures the city's dehumanizing patterns, "an absurd/Theatre without end and without word." Another successful Section, 14, "The '46s, 1945," briefly encapsulates the hungry delight with which crowds, weary of war's deprivations, greet the new car models in Detroit and "sniff the fruit of peace." A portrait of the Kennedys, disguised as the "O'Kanes" in Section 17, "The Candidate, 1952," is also generally on target, especially the final picture of John F. Kennedy, "moody, willful, and mercuric man," as prisoner to ambition, "easy in his bonds, under the dour/ And time-releasing sedative of power."

Other sections are much less felicitous in their convergence of private recollections and historic dramas, once again exposing Sissman's weakness for misplaced witticisms and easy literary allusions—Eliot is echoed several times. In Section 25, "Talking Union, 1964," for example, in trying to convey the new television image pursued by contemporary labor leaders, which entails smoothness and lies or nonsequiturs, he cannot help subsiding into: "So gentlemen/ Are made, not born, with infinite labor pains." Section 30, "New York, 1968," a short, impressionistic sketch of Manhattan's clamor, glibly appeals to "The Love Song of J. Alfred Prufrock" for its climax, small voices connecting, "and we come true/ To one another, till the rising town's/ Unhuman voices wake us, and we drown." Probably the surest indicator of "A War Requiem's" larger failure, which does not detract from the brilliance of many of the sections, can be found in the image chosen to complete the entire poem, that of a snowy owl glimpsed planing "down its glide path to surprise a vole." This is not only familiar, owing a debt to Sylvia Plath and, no doubt, others; it is also trite and inadequate to its complex subject, however well executed.

With the exceptions already noted, the same can be said of the collection as a whole and emphasizes that Sissman, for good or ill, epitomizes *The New Yorker*-type poet in full flight, as roughly defined by the deft verses published in that journal during Howard Moss's long tenure as its poetry editor— *Scattered Returns* is dedicated to Moss, whom Sissman had met at Harvard. The specimen virtues are real and worthy of praise, among them accessibility, formalist intelligence, and an educated predilection for irony, but they do encourage elitist conformity, a poetry of exquisite sensibility (the adjective is instructive) that mandates a voice of muted nuance and wry detachment so persistent as to ensure monotony and, worse, a narrow vision of life's (and poetry's) vigorous variety. For Sissman, being a *New Yorker* poet meant repeated reinforcement of serious defects in style and substance which undermined the bulk of the poetry appearing in the three volumes published during his lifetime.

When putting together *Hello, Darkness: The Collected Poems of L. E. Sissman* a few years after its author's death, Peter Davison, literary executor, decided to group all of the poems written after 1971, except for some occasional verse, at the end of the volume. These appear as "A Posthumous Collection" and are broken down into four divisions: "Descriptive and Satirical," "Nostalgic and Narrative," "Light and Dreamy," and "Hello, Darkness," the latter being probably among the latest. The first group occupies the middle range of Sissman's achievement, although several of the poems are marked by an appealing retreat from mere virtuosity, as in the pleasantly chilling fable of "The Clearing in the Woods" and "Spring Song," a more ragged quest to configure death's approach that overcomes self-indulgence to soar into bitter hatred for the notion of perishing like "a leafless log of body" thrown on a December fire. "The Persistence of Innocence" also strikes a responsive emotional chord, despite lapses into preachy rhetoric.

The verses in the "Nostalgic and Narrative" section are further stories from the past reworked into typical pastiches of astute observation, extended tropes, and time-softened sentiment. "At the Bar, 1948" can serve for the rest, replete with wit and genuine skill and charm, but it reminds the reader that autobiography requires more from poetry, that the specifics of someone else's life can be as dull as home movies, unless transmuted into universal terms. The best of this lot is actually "A Late Good Night," which shuns confession to record a frustrated man's passage into suicidal ends.

The small handful of fragments and whole poems in "Light and Dreamy," true to their Hollywood name, are dominated by characteristic playfulness, urbane resistance to the banal impositions and surreal possibilities inherent in ordinary existence. "To Your Uterus: An Uncompleted Call" is one worth a quick look, and "Dear John," an amusing versified letter, is another. The last two, "Cockaigne: A Dream" and "Three American Dreams: A Suite in Phillips House," are weightier endeavors. The former flows along with customary smoothness; a series of dream perspectives upon city scenes from the dreamer's past manages to vivify the anticipated waking up to middle-of-the-night reality and feelings of loss, the dream's "only evidence being my tears/ Of joy or of the other, I can't tell." More hungry for significance, "Three American Dreams" sees America through biography, the nightmare of success, failure, and death's ever-threatening erasure of both. It is of a piece in the Sissman mode, excessive in its language and metaphors at times, but far from inert.

The central texts of "A Posthumous Collection" surface, however, in the "Hello, Darkness" portion of the book, starting with the first poem, "Negatives," which makes a virtue of Sissman's worst flaw, his sways into dense language and image, as if afraid to prune away potential meaning. The tone is bravely jocular—"Hello, black skull. How privily you shine/ In all my negatives"—and exaggeration is a logical evolution of such a voice as it searches for the right figures of speech to convey the negatives' inner design and purpose:

> The tubular members of my rib cage gleam
> Like tortile billets of aluminum;
> My hand shines, frozen, like a white batwing
> Caught in a strobe.

When the climax comes, it brings the necessary release of irony and insight, diminishing death's menace; future "coroners" are imagined as accepting his mere hunk of dead meat as his "true bills," instead of the fluorographs and X rays which reveal the beauty and plan beneath flesh's frail husk. "December 27, 1966" is less sharp, less impressive, because it is hampered by so many tired comparisons, speaking of the moon as a half-dollar, of death's temptation in terms of high stakes and "the veiled dealer" vending "bad cards." Even so, the slowly building drift into a closing image of the same moon floating past in dead serenity, "tailed by her consort of stars," has the merit of a sudden, fertile disjunction in its clash with the shivering nightwatchman (himself) "pressed against the falling glass."

The third poem, "Homage to Clotho: A Hospital Suite," a set of seven stanzas or sections that follow the speaker from a hospital stay and operation to an uncertain future at home, demonstrates Sissman's easeful mastery of form and language when pressed by consciousness of death into more telling brevity, a use of abundant poetic resources for needed structural variations, not mere display or compulsion. The initial section reifies the threat, airless and tense, enveloping the entire sequence, "a vacuum waiting for a rupture in/ The tegument," while he resides, in life, in the hospital, upon the sufferance of authorities until "my vistas wither, and I die." Governed by contraries, the poem is effective, and the second section introduces a change in tone and tenor, a wish for a woman poet, who sounds like a parody of Marianne Moore, to be singing his song at this brief and fleeting hour. Section three resumes a direct address, thinking how easy it is to be watching a film, how easy to accept its end, which acts as preamble to the persona suffering a long needle injected into his pelvic arch in pursuit of bone-marrow in front of "starched and giggling girls." Roles are reversed, and he is the movie star.

Though still intent upon the idea of passive anguish and spectacle, of helplessness under the care of others, section four returns to the eight-line formula of section two to observe, from a calm distance, a male nurse shaving him for the operation. The nurse's casual reassurances are obviously resented for masking indifference, but the overt response is the language (prose) and common sense of the street: "It is that he must make his living, too." The lack of stress on "living" gives it added sarcasm in a hospital context. Another variation in the "suite" of verses comes with the startling switch into full-blooded protest in the fifth section, which begins: "If Hell abides on earth this must be it." The "it" refers to the recovery room, where he lingers in pain and uncertainty between life and death, a metaphor for the whole experience, where he can finally resort to the gift for analogy he delights in exhibiting without violating formal restraints, as in describing the dryness overwhelming him, "his own/ Throat-filling Gobi, mucous membrane gone/ Dry as Arabia." The images pile up and are explained in a well-deserved climax: "such wet dreams/ Afflict the dessiccate on their interminable way/ Up through the layers of half-light to day"—contraries persist, unifying the sequence, but tonal alterations avoid monotony.

A conversational style prevails in section six, which is constructed around a basic comparison between walking to the bathroom with his "wheeled I.V. pole" and the riddle of Sphinx, which Oedipus solved, that saw man in the last state of his life as a three-legged creature attached to a cane. Unable to urinate, the persona must accept defeat and return to his bed to await the aid of a young man with "his snake-handler's fist of catheters." The ultimate image welds together further contrasts with harrowing precision, his body kept alive by being "tethered" to various "bottles, bags, and tubes," to the point where its importunities dun the mind "in this refined,/ White-sheeted torture, practiced by a kind,/ Withdrawn white face trained in the arts of love." Besides once more using irony to amplify polar reversals and displacements, the arts of love as kindness, survival rituals, not sexual manipulations, the poem has established a schema that incorporates ancient Greece, the antithesis of the arctic modern hospital where the body and rote rule, which patently prepares the reader for the last section.

Clotho, one of the three Fates in Greek mythology charged with determining each person's life span by the length of the thread they sever, is finally granted her homage, after the persona has been released and is met at home by autumn leaves, "fat, sportive maple leaves" that are blown on his shoes, as if including him "in their great fall." A subtle undercurrent might be adduced here in conjunction with the earlier Sphinx reference, since his fall from health is hardly of the stature of Greek tragedy. Unrepentant punster, he must clamber up "enneads of stairs" to the bedroom where he will recompose himself to enduring existence, a "world of voices and surprises," for as long "as Clotho draws my filament," until "her sister widows" cut it off and "send me to befriend the winter leaves." This quiet, seasonally cyclical climax to the poem and to the sequence articulates a thoughtful decline into civilized acceptance of death and its modern lack of drama as the sole sane reaction contemporary art can muster.

In the first five sections treated as film scenes, "Cancer: A Dream," Sissman shapes a more surreal drama. The setting is a movie studio, with the persona envisioned as an actor repairing to his dressing room after a wearying piece of acting, Shakespearean rage "torn to dated tatters" for an audience of "cavefish." All he can do, like a patient after surgery, facing death and constant, humiliating observation, is to "undress shakily and lie me down/ In dust on the vast desert of the bed." What ensues in the next four scenes, skillfully handled to join literal and fantasy elements with a minimum of shock, entails a shift of scene and directions from a script girl, plus an embarrassing inability to respond to the sexual advances of an aged female poet, all of which can be associated with the conditions of a man in the death-throes of a debilitating disease. The climax, a brilliant bit of grotesque maneuvering, has him center stage, performing the dance of death with cancer's crab—perhaps it is another self as well, certifying Sigmund Freud's death instinct and affirming the poem's deeper dimensions.

"Tras Os Montes," the final poem in "A Posthumous Collection," equally well sustained, may be the strongest Sissman ever wrote. After two memorial sections devoted to dead parents, illuminating their dying more than their lives to echo his own disintegration, the mountain allusion is realized in an allegorical assault upon mountains "In Company" with eleven friends, actual people whom the author expected to attend his funeral. This section, first of three in the poem titled for the sequence, concludes with death as a form of military disgrace, a body thrown from a parapet,

> . . . gaining weightlessness
> As its flesh deliquesces, as its bones
> Shiver to ashes—into an air that crawls
> With all the arts of darkness far below.

"A Deux" is the heading for the second section, a farewell to a beloved mate, a "new scenario" in which his death is falling upward, into a "stormcloud from the springing field," where he can spy on her "and rain farewells/ And late apologies on your grey head" before, with a bold, haunting metaphor, the sun lights up his remains as "a tentative rainbow,/ An inverse, weak, and spectral kind of smile."

Dying is a solo act, however, as Sissman knew, and the third section, "Alone," reverts to the dependence upon paradoxes, a series of ironic oppositions, that motored the other death poems. The persona's climb to death is now in the guise of an isolated infiltrator, casting off his human ties in "the same selfish spirit" that had inspired Sissman's "lifelong journey" in the first place.

Thus, death is birth, the primal paradox, the egoistic art that reared "imperial Rome" returning to earth, "its inveterate love/ For the inanimate and its return." If too dense, on occasion, to match the achievement of its predecessors, "Alone" does not disgrace them, and the sequence, like the collection, manifests sufficient emotional and artistic energy to guarantee Sissman's poetic survival.

Edward Butscher

Other major work

NONFICTION: *Innocent Bystander: The Scene from the 70's*, 1975.

Bibliography

Gunton, Sharon R., ed. *Contemporary Literary Criticism*. Vol. 18. Detroit: Gale Research, 1981. The entry on Sissman notes that in an era of experimentation, he "clung to stanzaic verse, the iambic foot, couplets, and sonnets."

Kennedy, X. J. "Innocence in Armor." *Parnassus: Poetry in Review* 8 (Fall/Winter, 1979): 48-63. Reviews *Hello, Darkness: The Collected Poems of L. E. Sissman* and *Innocent Bystander: The Scene from the '70s*. Also discusses Sissman's "other" life as an advertising executive and how this counted against him as a poet. By and large a sympathetic review that sees Sissman's strength in the narrative poem. Calls his poem "Cancer: A Dream" harrowing in its description of hospitals and praises it for its "sustained length, in such cold intensity."

Pritchard, William H. "Innocence Possessed." *The Times Literary Supplement*, No. 3982 (July 28, 1978): 847. Discusses Sissman's poem "Dying: An Introduction" and the impact it has coming from Sissman's own experience of being "introduced" to his death. Says that in many ways Sissman was "possessed by his past." Cites his last poems as his best, especially "Tras Os Montes."

Updike, John. "Witness to His Dying." *The New York Times Book Review*, May 14, 1978, p. 10. In reviewing *Hello, Darkness: The Collected Poems of L. E. Sissman*, Updike defines the "Sissmanesque" mode as being one with "fascinating specificity" and describes it as "dense but dancing blank verse varied by spurts of rhyme." He says Sissman's poetry is less American than British in form and style. The three volumes of Sissman's poetry sum up a world in themselves, a rarity in modern poetry.

Williamson, Alan. "Comment: *Hello, Darkness: The Collected Poems of L. E. Sissman*." *Poetry* 132, no. 1 (November 1, 1978): 100-102. Notes Sissman's "indiscriminate curiosity about how life is lived on the surface," an unusual approach for a poet. Reveals that this poet's strength is his power to suggest the "symbolism of incidentals." On the other hand, notes his struggle to bring his verse to the level of "truly private feeling."

EDITH SITWELL

Born: Scarborough, England; September 7, 1887
Died: London, England; December 9, 1964

Principal poetry

The Mother and Other Poems, 1915; *Twentieth Century Harlequinade and Other Poems*, 1916 (with Osbert Sitwell); *Clown's Houses*, 1918; *The Wooden Pegasus*, 1920; *Façade*, 1922; *Bucolic Comedies*, 1923; *The Sleeping Beauty*, 1924; *Troy Park*, 1925; *Poor Young People*, 1925 (with Osbert Sitwell and Sacheverell Sitwell); *Elegy on Dead Fashion*, 1926; *Rustic Elegies*, 1927; *Popular Song*, 1928; *Five Poems*, 1928; *Gold Coast Customs*, 1929; *Collected Poems*, 1930; *In Spring*, 1931; *Epithalamium*, 1931; *Five Variations on a Theme*, 1933; *Selected Poems*, 1936; *Poems New and Old*, 1940; *Street Songs*, 1942; *Green Song and Other Poems*, 1944; *The Weeping Babe*, 1945; *The Song of the Cold*, 1945; *The Shadow of Cain*, 1947; *The Canticle of the Rose*, 1949; *Façade and Other Poems*, 1950; *Gardeners and Astronomers*, 1953; *Collected Poems*, 1954; *The Outcasts*, 1962; *Music and Ceremonies*, 1963; *Selected Poems*, 1965.

Other literary forms

In addition to her many collections of poetry, Edith Sitwell wrote several volumes of critical essays, biography, autobiography, social history, and fiction. Foremost among her critical studies are *Poetry and Criticism* (1925), *Aspects of Modern Poetry* (1934), and *A Poet's Notebook* (1943). Her critical biography *Alexander Pope* (1930) was meant to serve as a vindication of the man and poet. Having as much of an affinity for Queen Elizabeth as for Pope, she wrote of England's controversial monarch in *Fanfare for Elizabeth* (1946) and *The Queens and the Hive* (1962). *Bath* (1932) is a work of social history. *I Live Under a Black Sun* (1937) is a fictionalized biography of Jonathan Swift. She also edited several anthologies, of which *The Pleasures of Poetry* (1930-1932, 1934), *The American Genius* (1951), and *The Atlantic Book of British and American Poetry* (1958) are the best known. Her rather acerbic autobiography, which was posthumously published, is entitled *Taken Care Of* (1965).

Achievements

The best compliment ever paid Sitwell was Evelyn Waugh's statement that she took the dullness out of poetry. Never boring or tiresome, the worst her adverse critics could say about her was that she was eccentric and exhibitionistic, her poetry too experimental. A few of her literary enemies—and at one time they were almost as numerous as her friends—did go a step further, however, and labeled her early poetry pretentious, rambling, vacuous.

Geoffrey Grigson, Julian Symons, and F. R. Leavis are only a few of the critics who thought her a dreadful poet; but William Butler Yeats, Cyril Connolly, Stephen Spender, Dylan Thomas, and T. S. Eliot believed she was one of the most creative artists of the twentieth century.

Sitwell's early poems produced a series of shocks. To some, her verse was artificial; others could see that she purposefully created an artificial world. Her teeming imagination fashioned a luscious, semimechanical microcosm, one having "furry light" from "a reynard-coloured sun," trees that "hissed like green geese" with leaves as "hoarse as a dog's bark," a domain populated by "poor flaxen foundlings . . . upon a darkened stair." The world she wrote about in her poetry was, as she put it, "like a bare egg laid by the feathered air."

Of her seriousness as an artist, there is no doubt. A childless woman, she actually lay in her bed and labored for as long as six hours a day for more than forty years to bring forth reams of poetry. A few of her creations may be idiot brainchildren afflicted with echolalia; more are precocious offspring of her metaphysical imagination; most are somewhere between these extremes. In short, though she was wildly eccentric in all she did and wrote, she was still a poet of emotional depth and sincere human concerns. What she wrote was hardly for the common man, but she often maintained that the public enjoys poetry, "unless it is lethally boring or they are frightened out of doing so by bad critics." The matter, the form, the method employed by so many of her contemporaries aroused her ire. Like an electric eel in a pond full of catfish, she attacked such poets for their lack of tactile and visual sensibility and their inability to please those sensibilities by means of the written word.

Most admirers of her work rank the poems of her last years higher than the verbal legerdemain of her experimental period. Louise Bogan is one of the few who prefers Sitwell's earlier efforts to her later brooding reflections on the world's evils. In many of her early poems, Sitwell was more concerned with evoking beauty, with producing sonorous effects, than with communicating ideas; but in her later work she manifested a somberness and intensity, an almost grieving understanding of, and compassion for, the sufferings of humanity.

Allen Tate summarized Edith Sitwell best when, shortly after her death, he commented that she was "one of the great poets of the twentieth century . . . a remarkable and independent personality."

Biography

Edith Sitwell, daughter of Sir George and Lady Ida Sitwell and sister of the two writers Osbert and Sacheverell, was born at Scarborough, Yorkshire, in 1887. Though reared in an atmosphere of wealth and culture, her early years, as her brother Osbert wrote in his *Left Hand, Right Hand* (1944), were emotionally trying. An unwanted child, she suffered considerable physical and nervous anguish in being reared by a tyrannical father, who, among other things, made his only daughter wear a painful device to improve the shape of her aquiline nose. At an early age she announced her intention of becoming a genius, and soon after she learned to write, she tried her hand at poetry. Physically, she grew to be a tall, pale, distinguished-looking young woman with heavy-lidded eyes and a Plantagenet presence.

Early in the 1920's, Edith, Osbert, and Sacheverell emerged as a literary cult of three. Their circle was graced by such figures as Yeats, Virginia Woolf, Aldous Huxley, and Eliot. The most prolific of the three Sitwells, Edith produced volume after volume of poetry, and she took to reading her work to literary groups. *Wheels*, an iconoclastic annual publication which she founded and edited, outraged many. Critics and philistines not appreciative of her efforts often felt the sting of her tongue.

Between 1914 and 1929, in what might be called her initial period, she reacted strongly against the "banal bucolics" of the Georgian poets and wrote a great deal of nonrepresentational verse, which to some extent parallels the paintings of Pablo Picasso and the cubists. During her middle period, which extended from 1930 to 1940, she abandoned her dream world of sensuous mood and tonal patterns, her "pure poetry," to write poems that, like Eliot's *The Waste Land* (1922) denounced the barbarism, the hypocrisy, the misdirection of modern society. At the time, she regarded poetry as akin to moral wisdom, and she delighted to play the role of a Sibyl or Cassandra. To accentuate her six-foot frame, she dressed in long flowing gowns, sometimes of startling Chinese red, sometimes of intricate brocade, and she swathed her head with tall turbans. To make herself even more notoriously recognizable, she wore heavy jewelry and gold amulets. She painted her long nails with bright silver polish and adorned her thin fingers with marble-sized rings. All this was done, she said, as a gesture of defiance against her upbringing and as an act of faith in herself. For the sake of variety, however, she would often dress simply and entirely in black. One day, when asked for whom she was mourning, she responded: "For the entire world."

An eccentric but fascinating woman, Sitwell attracted the attention of many major celebrities and moved among them. Her famous friends and foes were legion. She was especially fond of such diverse personalities as Pavel Tchelitchew, Cecil Beaton, Gertrude Stein, Jacob Epstein, Alec Guinness, and Marilyn Monroe. She had little use for D. H. Lawrence, Lytton Strachey, H. G. Wells, George Moore, and John Galsworthy. It took her almost forty years to forgive Noel Coward for a devastating spoof, *London Calling* (1923), of her and her brothers. Friendships, rivalries, and public spats made her life interesting, but the central theme of her life remained poetry. In 1933, she was awarded a medal by the Royal Society of Literature. Honorary degrees from Oxford, Leeds, Durham, and Sheffield universities followed, and she was made an associate of the American National Institute of Arts and Letters.

In 1941, she entered her final period and turned, like Eliot, to traditional values, spiritual matters, and orthodox Christianity. Thirteen years later she was made a Dame Commander of the Order of the British Empire. The following year, Dame Edith Sitwell was received into the Roman Catholic church. Evelyn Waugh, who served as her godfather, cautioned her at the time that all too many Catholics were bores and prigs, crooks and cads, and that he himself was really pretty awful; but he added, mainly for Dame Edith's edification, how much worse he should be without the Faith. She took Waugh's words to heart, and shortly after her reception, when questioned what meant most to her, with the zeal of a convert she replied: "The love of God, the love of mankind, and the future of humanity." With such ideals uppermost in mind, she spent her final years in London, devoting herself even more zealously to literature. She continued to create and to encourage fledgling writers to do likewise, often writing warm introductions to their books. She died on December 9, 1964, after several months of illness.

Analysis

The pattern for much of Edith Sitwell's early verse can be found in her first published work, *The Mother and Other Poems*, wherein she deals with a prissy, dollhouse world full of such exotic objects as tambourines, mandolins, parakeets, nutmeg trees, and chinoiserie. Technically, the third poem in the collection, "Serenade," is one of the best. In its music of evening, the primacy of darkness is established in the opening lines: "The tremulous gold of stars within your hair/ Are yellow bees flown from the hive of night." In attributing the sun's color to the stars, she suggests a causal relationship between darkness and light, night and day. The yellow bees, born from the mothering hive of night to experience the darkness of the evening world, find the blossoms of the eyes of the beloved more fair "Than all the pale flowers folded from the light." Finally, "Serenade" pleads that the loved one open dreaming eyes "Ere those bright bees have flown and darkness dies."

Most of the poems in *Clown's Houses* and *The Wooden Pegasus* are similar to those in *The Mother and Other Poems*, but the poems making up *Bucolic Comedies* deal less with rhythm and exotica and more with what Sitwell labeled "sense transfusions." Though at first glance most of these poems may seem comedic nonsense, a careful reading indicates that even their oddest images have a purpose. In "Aubade," for example, Sitwell depicts the sad stupidity of a servant girl on a country farm coming down to light a morning fire: "Jane, Jane,/ Tall as a crane,/ The morning-light creaks down again." The dawn "creaks" about Jane because early light does not run smoothly. It is raining and Jane imagines each drop of moisture hardening into a "dull blunt wooden stalactite." Facing daily chores of weeding "eternities of kitchen garden," she senses flowers that cluck and mock her. (The flowers "cluck" for they are cockscombs.) The flames of the fire remind her of the carrots and turnips she has continually to clean and cook. Her spirits hang limp as "the milk's weak mind." Like so many of Sitwell's early poems, "Aubade" contains recollections of her own childhood. Thinking of the servant, Jane, brings to the poet's mind "The shivering movement of a certain cold dawn light upon the floor suggestive of high animal whining or whimpering, a half-frightened and subservient urge to something outside our consciousness."

Sitwell's early volumes caught the attention of only a limited number of readers, but on June 12, 1923, after reciting her *Façade* at London's Aeolian Hall, she achieved instant notoriety. Everything about her performance provoked controversy. She sat with her back to the audience, barely visible behind a transparent curtain adorned with a crudely painted moonface. The ostensible purpose of the curtain was to allow the audience to concentrate chiefly on the auditory qualities of the poems. The moon face was in keeping with the dreamlike world of apes, ducks, grotesque lords and ladies, clowns, peasants, and servant girls she had written about. Rumors of the nature of *Façade* had reached the literary world after one or two private recitations, and on opening night a large and curious audience was present.

Sitwell chanted her poems through an instrument called a "Sengerphone" (named after its inventor, George Senger). Out of the Sengerphone, which was made of compressed grasses meant to retain the purity of magnified tonal quality, came such baffling words as "The sound of the onycha/ When the phoca has the pica/ In the palace of the Queen Chinee!" Music may have the power to soothe the savage breast—and there was little adverse reaction to William Walton's orchestration—but the response to Sitwell's poetry bordered on the primitive. After the performance the audience became so threatening that the poet had to remain on stage behind the curtain. Someone whispered to Sitwell that an old lady was waiting to hit her with an umbrella. Disgruntled spectators complained loudly that they were victims of an enormous hoax. They had come to *Façade* expecting to enjoy Walton's music and hear some edifying verse. What they heard sounded like gibberish. Had they listened more attentively they might have found subtle criticisms of modern life, innuendoes of decay, death, nothingness.

Never had more brickbats been hurled at a poet. In her defense, when Sitwell wrote *Façade* she believed a change in the direction, imagery, and rhythms of poetry had become necessary, owing, as she expressed it, "to the rhythmical flaccidity, the verbal deadness, the dull and expected patterns" of modern poetry. The poems in *Façade*, consequently, are in most cases virtuoso exercises in verbalizing, studies in rhythmical techniques. "Fox Trot," "Ass-face," "Sir Beelzebub," "Waltz," and "Hornpipe" are excellent examples of her rhythmical techniques; these poems, in particular, consist of experiments concerning the effect that sound has on meaning.

One trisyllabic word, Sitwell discovered, had greater rapidity than three monosyllabic words. Two rhymes placed immediately together at the end of each of two lines, furthermore, would be like "leaps in the air." In "Fox Trot," for example, she wrote: "'Sally, Mary, Mattie, what's the matter, why cry?'"/ The huntsman and the reynard-coloured sun and I sigh." Other experiments were made to discover the influence of rhythm on the thickening and thinning, sharpening and softening, of consonants, as in certain lines of "Waltz": "The stars in their apiaries,/ Sylphs in their aviaries. . . ." These lines in turn are followed by others which end at times with a dissonance, at other times with a rhyme. To produce a waltz rhythm she used disyllabic rhymes to begin as well as to end lines, "Daisy and Lily,/ Lazy and silly," followed by two long lines with assonance: "Walk by the shore of the wan grassy sea—/ Talking once more 'neath a swan-bosomed tree."

When Sitwell published *Façade* she attempted in a long and complicated preface to rebut the protests and complaints of her critics. Those willing to accept her prosodic theories were still troubled by her startling imagery. Such conceits as "wan grassy sea," "swan-bosomed tree," "foam-bell of ermine," and "asses' milk of the stars," she maintained, were partly the result of condensations where the language of one sense was insufficient to cover meaning or sensation. The use of such imagery, she hoped, would "pierce down to the essence of the thing seen," revealing attributes which at first might appear alien to a tired eye or unresponsive ear. Perhaps the chief reason why *Façade* was so widely misunderstood was that Sitwell experimented with abstract patterns. Then, too, the apparent vacuity of some of the poems caused them to be suspect. They were useless; they were butterflies; but butterflies, she protested, can adorn the world and delight the beholder.

No two poems in *Façade* are alike; indeed, they differ radically from one another. "Hornpipe" is a jaunty piece set to nautical music. "Trio for Two Cats" has more than an amusing title; its fast rhythm creates an eerie mood accentuated with castenets. "I Like to Do Beside the Seaside" is set to a tango rhythm. "Scotch Rhapsody" begins with "Do not take a bath in Jordan, Gordan," and a heavy drumbeat sounds throughout. "By the Lake" has a slow pace and its cold imagery depicts a lonely winter night with two estranged lovers recalling a happy past. "Polka" has such clever running rhymes as "Robinson Crusoe rues so" and the "poxy, doxy dear." "Popular Song" is a joyful and carefree lyric about "Lily O'Grady,/ Silly and Shady,/ Longing to be/ A lazy lady." "Sir Beelzebub," who calls for "his syllabub in the hotel in Hell/ Where Proserpine first fell," is meant to mock the Victorians and their poet laureate, "Alfred Lord Tennyson crossing the bar."

In "The Drum" the verse conveys a sense of menace, of deepening darkness, through the use of subtle dissonances. It opens: "In his tall senatorial,/ Black and manorial/ House where decoy-duck/ Dust doth clack—/ Clatter and quack/ To a shadow black." The words "black," "duck," "clatter," and "quack" with their hard consonants and dead vowels, Sitwell explained, are "dry as dust, and the deadness of dust is conveyed thus, and, as well, by the dulled dissonance of the 'a's,' of the 'u' in 'duck' followed by the crumbling assonance of 'dust.'" A duck's quacking, she obligingly added, was for her one of the driest of sounds: "It has a peculiar deadness." In such Sitwellian fashion she explained other aural qualities of "The Drum." As for its essential meaning, she noted that it sprung from a story about witches and witchcraft told by the seventeenth century neoplatonist Joseph Glanvill:

> Black as Hecate howls a star
> Wolfishly, and whine
> The wind from very far . . .
> Out go the candles one by one,
> Hearing the rolling of a drum . . .
> Where the drum rolls up the stair, nor tarries.

Sitwell's verse was so radical that she often had to supply instructive analyses of individual poems. "Said King Pompey," she was kind enough to explain, is built upon "a scheme of R's . . . to produce a faint fluttering sound, like dust fluttering from the ground, or the beat of a dying heart." There are obvious *r* sounds in the opening lines of the poem, but to what extent, it is reasonable to ask, do the *r*'s suggest "dust fluttering from the ground"? Sitwell would respond by expatiating upon affective language and synaesthetic exchange. A reader willing to consider the poem with an open mind is likely to fathom her technical experimentation with synaesthesia, but whether he will affirm her theories about echo and meaning is another matter.

As soon as a reader is willing to accept her theory of *r* sounds, he is then asked to consider other aural impressions. Certain words ending in *ck*, she goes on, "cast little imperceptible shadows." In "The Bat" she plays upon such words as "black," "quack," "duck," and "clack," in order, she says, to contrast shadows "so small yet so menacing, with . . . flat and shadeless words that end with 't' and with 'd.'" Some of the *a*'s, she contends, have neither depth nor body, are flat and death-rotten, though at times the words in which they occur cast a small menacing shadow because of the *ck* ending, and frequently these shadows are followed almost immediately by flatter, deader, more shadeless words.

A few years after *Façade*, Sitwell turned from phonological hypothesizing to conceptualizations of time. Between 1924 and 1928, she devoted three long poems to finite time—*The Sleeping Beauty*, *Elegy on Dead Fashion*, and *Metamorphosis*. Each of these works has a richness that deserves critical attention; but, more important, she slowly overcame an agonized preoccupation with the destructiveness of time. Of the three poems, *Metamorphosis* is the most important. Time initiates the metamorphosis of the poem's title, and in her verse Sitwell searches for a solution to the infernal behavior of contemporary man. Her hope at the end of the poem lies in the generative power of the sun, and she writes: "To rouse my carrion to life and move/

The polar night, the boulder that rolled this,/ My heart, my Sisyphus, in the abyss." The writing of *Metamorphosis*, however, left Sitwell in an even deeper spiritual abyss.

Sitwell followed *Metamorphosis* with one of the strongest poems of her early period, *Gold Coast Customs*. Admirers of her poetry thought it a sensation. William York Tindall labeled it "her *Waste Land*, footnotes and all." Yeats wrote that it was ennobled by the "intensity . . . endurance . . . wisdom" missing from much of contemporary poetry, the "something absent from . . . literature being back again. . . ." What Yeats especially liked about *Gold Coast Customs* was its concentration on the sterility of modern life. Relying on G. F. W. Hegel's *The Philosophy of History* (1932) and anthropological findings as sources, Sitwell began *Gold Coast Customs* by drawing parallels between an African tribe of cannibals and a Lady Bamburgher, a metaphorical goddess of materialism overly concerned with social rites. Convulsive rhythms suggest a *danse macabre*.

At the close of the poem, there is an intimation of the sacred, a quest for belief, some resolution of the futility of contemporary life. Sitwell's direction, broadly hinted at in the conclusion, was toward Christianity. Her lines allow the inference that she had become fully cognizant of the evil continuously erupting in the hearts of men. Convinced that there must be a greater design for life, that all moves toward a Day of Resurrection, she ends *Gold Coast Customs* with the words:

> Yet the time will come
> To the heart's dark slum
> When the Rich man's gold and the rich man's wheat
> Will grow in the street, that the starved may eat—
> And the sea of the rich will give up its dead—
> And the last blood and fire from my side will be shed.
> For the fires of God go marching on.

During the time that Sitwell wrote *Gold Cost Customs*, she began to reflect upon the sufferings of Christ, "the Starved Man hung upon the Cross, the God . . . who bears in his heart all wounds." Suffering became a dominant theme in several of her poems. In "Still Falls the Rain" she wrote of the bombing of London during World War II. A red flare dripping from the sky to the earth symbolizes blood—blood that stains the sky. On earth, where the bombs find their mark, actual bloodshed takes place, a slaughter comparable to the crucifixion of Christ. The rain of Nazi bombs falls upon guilty and innocent alike, upon Dives and Lazarus. Despite man's horrendous deeds, his shedding of blood, Christ stands willing to forgive: "'Still do I love, still shed my innocent light, my Blood for thee.'"

"The Shadow of Cain," as its title indicates, is about modern fratricide. Its narrative concerns the second Fall of Man, symbolized by the dropping of the first atomic bomb on Hiroshima. The poem had its origin on September 10, 1945, when Edith and her brother Osbert were on a train going to Brighton, where they were to give a reading. Osbert pointed out a paragraph in the London *Times*, a description by an eyewitness of the actual dropping of the bomb. What most impressed the witness was "a totem pole of dust that arose to the sun as testimony to the murder of mankind. . . . A totem pole, the symbol of creation, the symbol of generation." Although most of the poem came into Edith's head as Osbert read the *Times* report, she did not write it down for several months. She continually revised it in her mind, and the poem passed through several stages. When she finally put pen to paper, she wrote how, after "that epoch of the Cold," the victims of the immolation reached an open door. All that was left to them were primal realities:

> The Fate said, "My feet ache."
> The wanderers said, "Our hearts ache."
> There was great lightening
> In flashes coming to us over the floor:
> The Whiteness of Bread
> The Whiteness of the Dead
> The Whiteness of the Claw—
> All this coming to us in flashes through the open door.

The above lines, Sitwell claims, came to her in a dream. The three flashes of lightning she explains as three primal realities of preservation, death, and struggle. Beyond the open door she saw spring returning; for there was still the grandeur of the sun and Christ returning with the life-giving wheat of harvest. Then came the horror, the symbol of which was seen by the eyewitness at Hiroshima. A gulf was torn across the world, stretching its jaws from one end of the earth to the other. Loud were the cries in the hollow from those who once were men, and yet "those ashes that were men/ Will rise again."

The horror of Hiroshima affected Sitwell deeply. Did God in some mysterious way declare Himself through such suffering? She began to incorporate into her work the re-creating energy of divine love. Her interest in prosodic experimentation was over. No longer would she tinker with sound effects, with the mechanics of rhyme. She encapsulated all of her principles of versification into one central dictum: "Poetry should always be running on pleasant feet, sometimes swift, sometimes slow."

As a poet she now wanted to vent the depths of her heart in sonorous, free-flowing lines that would touch the hearts of others. To express truths about human beings and the universe, to point them in the direction of salvation, became her purpose. In her final period, her poems were hymns to the glory of life.

G. A. Cevasco

Other major works

LONG FICTION: *I Live Under a Black Sun*, 1937.

NONFICTION: *Poetry and Criticism*, 1925; *Alexander Pope*, 1930; *Bath*, 1932; *The English Eccentrics*, 1933; *Aspects of Modern Poetry*, 1934; *Victoria of England*, 1936; *Trio*, 1938 (with Osbert Sitwell and Sacheverell Sitwell); *A Poet's Notebook*, 1943; *Fanfare for Elizabeth*, 1946; *A Notebook on William Shakespeare*, 1948; *The Queens and the Hive*, 1962; *Taken Care Of*, 1965.

ANTHOLOGIES: *Wheels*, 1916-1921; *The Pleasures of Poetry*, 1930-1932, 1934; *Planet and Glow Worm*, 1944; *A Book of Winter*, 1950; *The American Genius*, 1951; *A Book of Flowers*, 1952; *The Atlantic Book of British and American Poetry*, 1958.

Bibliography

Brophy, James D. *Edith Sitwell: The Symbolist Order.* Carbondale: Southern Illinois University Press, 1968. Brophy examines the themes and techniques of Sitwell's admittedly difficult poetry. He finds in her work a coherent use of modernist symbolism. The imagery of darkness and shadow connects her with English seventeenth century metaphysical poets. A valuable study for close analysis of her poems and critical views. Supplemented by a select bibliography and an index.

Cevasco, G. A. *The Sitwells: Edith, Osbert, and Sacheverell.* Boston: Twayne, 1987. Edith and her younger brothers, all writers and famous personalities, are brought together in an excellent, compact survey of their writings and family life. Their texts are shown to respond to the major events that shaped the twentieth century: two world wars, a depression, and the opening of the atomic age. Contains a chronology, notes, a select bibliography, and an index.

Elborn, Geoffrey. *Edith Sitwell: A Biography.* London: Sheldon Press, 1981. An intimate portrait of the woman, poet, and publicity seeker, this useful book traces Sitwell's life from her birth as an unwanted female to her solitary death (by her own command). Early travels exposed her to the world and many friendships with famous people brought her into literary and artistic circles in England and the United States. Includes memorable photographs that illustrate her life, twelve half-plates, two plates, notes, a bibliography, and an index.

Glendinning, Victoria. *Edith Sitwell: A Unicorn Among Lions.* London: Weidenfeld & Nicolson, 1981. The major work on Sitwell's life and times, this revisionary appraisal separates the myths from the newer status of her work. Glendinning discusses her poetry, her criticism, and her seriousness and sensational literary relationships. Two groups of photographs, one a series of portraits in color, illustrate the beauty and eccentricity that were hers. Complemented by six plates, seventeen half-plates, notes, and an index.

Pearson, John. *Facades: Edith, Osbert, and Sacheverell Sitwell*. London: Macmillan, 1978. A detailed, year-by-year account of the literary activities, travels, and relationships of the famous sister and her brothers, which places Sitwell in her literary environment. Her conversion to Roman Catholicism and its effects on her proud soul fills a poignant chapter. Photographs are placed throughout the text. Contains seventeen plates, notes, and an index.

Salter, Elizabeth. *The Last Years of a Rebel: A Memoir of Edith Sitwell*. London: Bodley Head, 1967. Salter was secretary to the poet from the time Sitwell was sixty-nine until her death. The author brings out Sitwell's humor, her loyalty, and her creative power. Salter has also published a companion book of extraordinary photographs and drawings. Presents an inside view from a devoted friend. Includes five plates, and six half-plates.

JOHN SKELTON

Born: Northern England, possibly Yorkshire; c. 1460
Died: London, England; June 21, 1529

Principal poetry

The Bowge of Court, 1499; *Phyllyp Sparowe*, c. 1508; *Ware the Hawk*, c. 1508; *The Tunnyng of Elynour Rummyng*, 1508; *Speke, Parrot*, 1521; *Collyn Clout*, 1522; *Why Come Ye Nat to Courte*, 1522; *The Garlande of Laurell*, 1523; *Pithy, Pleasaunt and Profitable Workes of Maister Skelton, Poete Laureate*, 1568; *The Complete Poems of John Skelton, Laureate*, 1931 (Philip Henderson, editor).

Other literary forms

In addition to the poems listed above, John Skelton also wrote a play, or, more properly, an interlude (a short allegorical morality play) called *Magnyfycence* (1516), which counsels monarchs against excessive liberality. Skelton also participated in a popular form of court entertainment called "flyting," in which two courtiers trade insults before an audience of their peers. In particular, Skelton flyted one Christopher Garnish, and some of his "insults" persist in the *Poems Against Garnish* (1513-1514).

Finally, Skelton translated a significant number of works and had a reputation as an excellent Latinist. His translations apparently included the works of Diodorus Siculus, Cicero's *Familiar Letters* and Guillaume Deguilleville's *La Pélerinage de la vie humaine*. The latter two works, mentioned in *The Garlande of Laurell*, do not survive. Skelton also composed a moral guidebook: *Speculum Principis* (1501, *A Mirror for Princes*).

Achievements

Modern readers find Skelton's work hard to understand and appreciate. He lived and wrote just as the literary Renaissance and political Reformation began to reshape England. Skelton reveals in *The Garlande of Laurell* that he perceived himself to be the heir of the medieval poets Geoffrey Chaucer, John Gower, and John Lydgate. His language resembles the Middle English of these three forebears but, like the English of his contemporary Sir Thomas Malory, borders on what is now termed "Modern" English (the conventional boundary date between Middle and Modern English is 1500). The difficulty in reading Skelton, then, comes not from the archaic quality of his language but from its deliberate, often playful, polyglot tendencies and its unusual metrical properties. Skelton intermingles French and Latin words and phrases in many of his poems, often producing the kind of interlingual mix known as "macaronic" verse. He also loads his poems with allusions to the Bible and to contemporary political events. Metrically, Skelton's poetry surprises readers used to the iambic pentameter line that became the norm for English poetry after William Shakespeare. In many poems Skelton uses trimeter (six-syllable) couplets with irregular rhythm. This meter is so characteristic of his poetry that it has become known as Skeltonic.

In his lifetime, Skelton was well rewarded and admired, although perhaps not as completely, or as consistently, as he might have liked. He is thought of today as the first poet laureate of England: that honor, however, was conferred upon him not by the King but by the University of Oxford (1488) and later by the University of Louvain (1493) and the University of Cambridge (1493). The laureateship, which today implies particular patronage of the King or Queen and entails the responsibility of writing public occasional verse, entitled Skelton to be recognized as a graduate with a degree in rhetoric. Although the implications of laureateship were not the same for Skelton as for a poet such as Alfred, Lord Tennyson (laureate to Queen Victoria), the honor was nevertheless great, and Skelton doted on the accomplishment for the rest of his life. Indeed, he named his last major work, which sums up his poetic career, *The Garlande of Laurell*. Skelton did enjoy the special attention of Henry VII, by whose grace he wore a robe of green and white, the Tudor colors, embroidered "Calliope," for the muse of epic poetry.

The first collected poems of Skelton appeared in 1568, were edited by Thomas Marshe, and were reissued in 1736. A new two-volume edition, produced by the Reverend Alexander Dyce (1843), bridged the gap between the Renaissance and the current editions, notably *The Complete Poems of John Skelton, Laureate* (1931), edited by Philip Henderson.

Biography

John Skelton's life and poetry are closely bound up with the world of the Tudor court under Henry VII and Henry VIII. The first sure facts about his life have to do with the laureate degrees discussed above. Two years after the award from Oxford, Skelton received glowing praise in William Caxton's preface to *The Boke of Eneydos* (1490). Caxton made clear his admiration for Skelton's immense knowledge of Latin, his translations, and his ability to write in English. Thus, by about the age of thirty, Skelton was known as a scholar and poet. At about this time he became officially connected with the court of Henry VII, writing occasional state poems and eventually becoming official tutor to Prince Henry, who was intended to become a priest. Skelton himself took holy orders in 1498.

In 1502 Henry's older brother Arthur, the heir to the throne, died. Young Henry, now the next in line for the throne, no longer needed quite the same kind of instruction, and Skelton was sent from the court to be the rector of Diss, an area on the borders of Suffolk and Norfolk, ninety miles from London. It is uncertain how Skelton took this "exile." On the one hand, he clearly enjoyed the prestige of his royal connection. On the other, his first major poem, *The Bowge of Court*, written before his removal to Diss, established his recognition of the traditional problems of a courtier's life, including battles with hypocrisy, deceit, flattery, and despair.

At Diss, Skelton continued to write satirical poems as well as perform his clerical duties with apparent gusto. Skelton's life at Diss has been immortalized in a collection of stories by an anonymous author or authors, *The Merie Tales of Skelton* (1567). It is difficult to say how much truth is contained in this group of stories, which show Skelton teasing his puritanical bishop and flaunting his wife and child before his parish. In general, Skelton emerges in these tales as lusty, witty, and mischievous. If the tales are not true in fact, many biographers have assumed that they are true in spirit.

In 1509, Henry VIII became king, and Skelton initiated a campaign of compliments and requests designed to bring him back to court. In 1512, he returned to London officially titled *Orator Regius*—orator to the king. From that time on, Skelton lived in London and flourished as a satirist, attacking the evils of court life, particularly the abuse of power by figures such as Thomas Wolsey, whose rise to power apparently made Skelton jealous and certainly angered him. In 1521 and 1522, he wrote three satires directed at Wolsey: *Speke, Parrot*, *Collyn Clout*, and *Why Come Ye Nat to Courte*. Despite the bitterness of these poems, Skelton's wrath toward Wolsey seems later to have abated—or, at least, he lost his willingness to embarrass publicly the powerful man. His last known work, a part-prose, part-Skeltonic critique of Lutheranism, includes a dedication praising Wolsey.

Skelton died on June 21, 1529, and was buried at St. Margaret's Church in Westminster.

Analysis

In 1490, William Caxton described John Skelton in glowing terms. He apparently viewed Skelton as a perfect example of a rising court scholar and poet, one worth praising in print. Desiderius Erasmus, who epitomizes the early Renaissance humanist, met Skelton in 1499 and admired him. Yet the poet fell rapidly into obscurity after his death, surfacing in literary surveys only to be described as "beastly" or "scurrilous." These contradictions are easier to explain than might be supposed. First, Skelton's literary career underwent a marked shift beginning with the publication of *The Bowge of Court* in 1499. Until that time, Skelton's work had been what Caxton's remarks suggest: scholarly, patriotic, sagacious. As he began to criticize political and religious changes in England, a new persona emerged. Subtly in *The Bowge of Court*, more fully in *Ware the Hawk*, and full blast in *Speke, Parrot*, Skelton reveals a sensibility by turns bitter, vitriolic, ribald, self-righteous, and intolerant.

Second, Skelton's reputation changed because his fundamental values were misperceived by later generations. Since he wrote in an unusually diffuse, free-spoken, irreverent manner, readers, especially in the nineteenth century, lost sight of the essentially conservative values that underlie his work. Skelton became accustomed, while relatively young, to certain habits of life. He associated himself with the Tudor court, he was devoutly religious, and he was committed to a certain kind of learning and literature which emphasized knowledge of Latin. When his stability was challenged by changes in government, church, and education, his poetry changed drastically. All of his major work treats the theme of personal instability in a shifting world.

Thus, in *The Bowge of Court* the condition of a courtier is revealed as "Dread"; in *Phyllyp Sparowe* language and convention are twisted to reveal new, ironic possibilities of expression; in *Ware the Hawk* the sanctity of the Church is defended with a kind of comic hysteria. *Speke, Parrot* is the culmination of his stylistic experimentation; for many students today, this poem is unreadable, an impenetrable jungle of Latin, French, random allusion and odd statement. Skelton's poems after *Speke, Parrot* retain some of these macaronic devices but are not quite as difficult, and in *The Garlande of Laurell* he returns to the relatively straightforward form of the dream vision.

The Bowge of Court, Skelton's first long poem, is an allegorical dream vision in the tradition of Chaucer's *Hous of Fame* (1372-1380). The title might be translated as "Patronage of Court" since "bouge" means free rations or board, as in the kind of stipend given to courtiers. The pattern of the poem resembles the Chaucerian dream vision as it was imitated in fifteenth century works such as *The King's Quair* and *The Court of Love*.

The poem's prologue introduces the speaker as a poet who is having trouble writing. When he falls asleep, he dreams of a stately ship, the *Bowge of Court*, carrying a cargo of Favor. The dreamer meets a lady-in-waiting to the owner of the ship; he tells her his name is Dread. The allegorical situation becomes apparent. The main character, Dread, represents anxiety: like the poet-narrator, he cannot gain a firm foothold in life, and he seeks aid or reassurance from outside himself. Dread, unfortunately, has come to a very bad place for stability. Not only is the *Bowge of Court* a ship, but its favors are also dispensed only for money and only at the command of the ship's pilot, Fortune.

Dread's very nature—his fearfulness—makes him the target of attack by his fellow passengers on the ship. Almost immediately he is caught up in a network of intrigue involving Favell (Flattery) and Suspect. Similarly, five other characters (ranging from the pickpocket Harvy Hafter to Deceit) increase Dread's anxiety, until he jumps overboard to escape them. At this point the dreamer awakens, and the poem ends.

The Bowge of Court differs significantly from dream visions by earlier writers, which usually provide a "psychopaunt," or dream guide, for the narrator. Dread is alone, and no one helps him draw a moral from his experience. *The Bowge of Court* criticizes court folly in the typical fashion of satire, but it also, perhaps more significantly, provides an analysis of Dread as a state of mind, and throws an emphasis on the speaker's insecurities.

While Skelton was rector of Diss he composed ironic elegies for two of his parishioners. Witty as these are, they are surpassed in whimsicality by the long, unusual poem *Phyllyp Sparowe*, in which Skelton eulogizes the pet bird of Jane Scrope, a young neighbor. The poem, written in Skeltonic trimeter, has been said to imitate the quick jerky movement of a sparrow.

The poem begins with a version of the Catholic burial mass, lamenting the death of the pet bird. Much of the poem is filtered through the mind of Jane, who both laments Philip lavishly and remembers with pleasure his charming habits in life. She imagines all the birds holding a mass in his honor, and she searches her memory for books that might provide him with an epitaph. In this section of the poem Skelton relies on the reader's knowledge that parodies of the mass are traditional; he also assimilates Philip into the tradition in which Ovid and Catullus exploit the sexual implications of a sparrow who hops around in his mistress' lap and tries to get under the covers of her bed.

Furthermore, the poem contains a section headed "Commendations"; here Skelton, abandoning Philip, praises Jane herself. In all sections of the poem Skelton freely adds snippets of Latin or French. *Phyllyp Sparowe* ends with an epilogue, clearly written after the rest of the poem had circulated, defending what had apparently struck many critics as blasphemous or inappropriate. Although Skelton does not offer a detailed defense of his own work, he might well have argued for its essential conservatism in religious matters. Skelton does not burlesque the burial mass or use it for vulgar purposes; he simply includes it among the devices by which he pokes fun at Jane's excessive mourning. Ultimately, the poem encourages a turning away from bathetic grief either to a happy contemplation of the past or to the celebration of Jane herself, who is young, alive, and human. Thus the poem's values and moral lesson are quite conservative; only the poem's exterior form is new and "shocking."

Ware the Hawk shows Skelton, in his role as rector of Diss, calling down God's wrath upon another parson who brought his hawk into Skelton's church and allowed it to defecate on the altar. The poem is simultaneously scathing and funny, although the humor is of a distinctly learned kind; for example, Skelton puns on "hawk" and the Latin word *hoc*. He invokes a catalog of the great tyrants of history in order to convey the enormity of his scorn for the offending parson and his hawk. The incident, whether real or fictional, gave Skelton an excuse to list what he considered various licenses taken by the parish priests. His wrath grows out of all proportion to the comic absurdity of the particular offense. Skelton seems to criticize both the speaker, who rants so futilely, and the man who allows his falcon to defile the sacred altar of God. Skelton puts his understandable sentiments into the mouth of a near-lunatic, again demonstrating the typical split in his work between conservative subject and unorthodox method.

Fourteen years after writing *Ware the Hawk* and *Phyllyp Sparowe*, Skelton produced his series of political poems attacking Cardinal Thomas Wolsey, who symbolized for Skelton the corruption of power in both church and state. In Wolsey, Skelton saw the decline of the old political and religious order he respected. Moreover, Skelton disliked the changing attitude toward education in the 1520's (in particular he lamented the decline of Latin studies in favor of Greek, and Wolsey himself established in 1520 a professorship of Greek at Oxford). Skelton thus had moral, political, and literary grudges against Wolsey, and they all came spilling out in *Speke, Parrot*, a macaronic mélange of history, biblical allusion, and moral reflection.

The speaker is Parrot, a natural mimic, who stands for the poet himself. The parrot is traditionally both poet and pet, and these dual identities suggest the duplicity of living at court while satirizing the court. The flexible pose allows Skelton to shift between scathing critical statements and sycophantic requests for food and treats. Description cannot do justice to the baffling effect of reading this poem, created by the mix of riddle, proverb, lyric, oath, and allusion. Throughout the poem, Parrot praises himself and indirectly criticizes Wolsey without naming him. He veils his criticism by using biblical names to stand for Henry and Wolsey.

Speke, Parrot attacks more than Wolsey alone. It attacks the world at present, the instability of fortune, the vanity of human wishes, and the inadequacy of eloquence. Parrot touches bitterly on all of these pitfalls of the human condition. Insofar as Parrot offers Skelton's views, the poem again shows him using a radically new—nearly opaque—poetic technique to defend the ideas and systems to which he has become accustomed.

After the exuberant chaos of *Speke, Parrot*, *Collyn Clout* appears as a plain-spoken, modest attempt to assert much the same values. Like Dread and Parrot, the heroes of Skelton's earlier poems, Colin Clout knows that the world is in trouble; unlike them, he knows that he is part of the world. Since Colin is himself a minor cleric he is implicated in the current problems he perceives in the Church. He seems to hold two positions at once (much like Parrot as poet and pet), both reporting overheard evil tidings about clerical abuses, and pointing out that these rumors may be false. Although his manner of doing so is new, he resembles Parrot in his tendency to back away from criticism to the safe pose of naïveté.

The poem depicts a world gone awry. The higher-placed clergy are corrupt, and the lower ones (such as Colin), who may themselves be good, are afraid to speak out. The aristocrats, unwilling to assert their power, give themselves over to leisure. The poem focuses criticism on the bishops and on one bishop in particular, who, Colin prophesies, is headed for a fall despite his present power. It becomes certain that this man is Wolsey when Colin describes both his typically elaborate clothing and the tapestries that adorn the walls of his home, Hampton Court.

The specific abuses which Colin laments are predictable: he claims that the clergy are greedy, ignorant, lascivious. The bishops live in luxury while the common people suffer. On the other hand, it is clear that Colin respects the sincere clergy, and he particularly laments that the nuns and monks have been turned out of their cloisters under Wolsey's regime.

After Colin has gone on for more than a thousand lines, the opposition is given a chance to speak for itself. Rather than offering a defense, however, Colin's respondent simply acknowledges the criticism and threatens to punish and condemn the critics. Colin's only possible escape at this point is to commit himself to Christ, stop writing, and disappear from view. As did Dread, he finally gives up and escapes, leaving behind his poem as a record of experience. Not resigned to the world's decay, he is nevertheless powerless to stop it.

The third of Skelton's attacks on Wolsey concentrates on the Cardinal's political abuses. *Why Come Ye Nat to Courte* has neither the plain speaking voice of Colin Clout nor the wise folly of Parrot. Instead, the poem seems to be a pastiche of satirical ballads unified only in their criticism of Wolsey. Among other things, Skelton blames Wolsey for misusing the Star Chamber (Henry's advisory council) and for inciting the war with France that began in 1522 and resulted in unpopular new taxes.

Whereas *Collyn Clout* and *Speke, Parrot* juxtapose the attitudes of a self-righteous speaker against the ill-doings of Wolsey as a symbolic monster, *Why Come Ye Nat to Courte* resembles a flyting, or insult match, in which both parties swing wildly at each other and everything; even Wolsey's physical deformity is fair game for attack. To the reader familiar with the other anti-Wolsey poems, little in this one seems new, and the very length of the poem (some twelve hundred lines) underscores its lack of structure. This lack is, arguably, in itself a key to the poem's meaning: enraged and baffled by Wolsey's complete moral corruption, which seems responsible even for the Cardinal's diseased eye, the speaker has lost the capacity both for objective judgment and calm reportage. Like the cardinal, the poet has developed limited vision, and only by a deliberate widening of perspective is he able to go on to write *The Garlande of Laurell*.

As the title suggests, Skelton here forcefully reminds the reader of his own claim to wear the garland of laurel, symbol of the poetic vocation as handed down by Apollo. Unlike Chaucer and other medieval poets who dismiss their own claims to greatness and affect a modesty about their work, Skelton heralds himself as the new Homer of England. Like Dante in the fourth canto of the *Inferno* (c. 1320) joining the band of great classical poets, Skelton depicts himself as being welcomed into the Court of Fame by his great English predecessors Chaucer, Gower, and Lydgate, none of whom, he carefully points out, officially earned the right to wear the laurel.

Despite Skelton's ultimate inclusion in the Court of Fame, he acknowledges that some might carp at his being so honored. The poem takes the form of a dream vision in which Skelton's candidacy for Fame is assessed at the recommendation of Pallas. The Queen of Fame, however, disapproves of him because of his stylistic experimentation: he has not written in the ornate aureate style of which she approves. He partially assuages her by actually introducing, in this poem, a series of lyrics in honor of the Countess of Surrey and other noble ladies.

Later, Skelton's accomplishments as a poet are reviewed, after which he is so cheered by the crowd (whose fickle favor he scorns) that he ascends to Fame without a formal judgment. *The Garlande of Laurell* also presents a loftier vision of poetry than that which pleases the fickle Queen of Fame and the rabble who crowd about her gates. For part of the poem Skelton walks with Occupation (who represents his calling as a poet) through a paradisiacal landscape where he sees Apollo himself playing the harp. Compared with this serenity, the ironically intoned list of Skelton's works, in which *Speke, Parrot*, for example, is described as a commendation of ladies (which it is not), seems beside the point. In fact, it is surprising that Skelton, whose later poetry was so caught up in the incidental events of his day, saw his vocation as originating in a divinely ruled pastoral grove. Even more surprising, the poem offers itself, at the end, to the correction of Cardinal Wolsey, as if Skelton were pulling back somewhat from his recent harsh criticism.

Skelton's identification with Apollo and the great poetic tradition of England confirms that he is a literary, as well as a political and religious, conservative. In stressing the importance of the poet as visionary seer, he gives even more power to the predictions and complaints made in his earlier works. Unlike Dread in *The Bowge of Court*, Skelton is a dreamer with a guide and mentor—not only Occupation but also Pallas, goddess of wisdom.

Diane M. Ross

Other major works

PLAY: *Magnyfycence*, 1516.
NONFICTION: *Speculum Principis*, 1501 (*A Mirror for Princes*).

Bibliography

Carpenter, Nan Cooke. *John Skelton*. Twayne's English Authors Series 61. New York: Twayne, 1968. This introduction contains a preface, a chronology, and an outline of Skelton's life. Carpenter discusses all of his important poetic works and highlights in a very useful way the poet's intimate technical knowledge of music, dance songs, and popular song tags. Skelton's reputation and influence is also discussed. Includes notes and references.

Fish, Stanley Eugene. *John Skelton's Poetry*. New Haven, Conn.: Yale University Press, 1965. This volume in the Yale Studies in English series is an overview of the work which presents Skelton as a poet interested in invoking reader-response by personally engaging his subjects. Medium-length (268 pages), with an introduction by the author.

Heiserman, Arthur R. *Skelton and Satire*. Chicago: University of Chicago Press, 1961. The first chapter gives some background on Skelton's scholarship and outlines the theory of this book: that satire focuses on an object of attack, using a mixture of devices, personae, and careful diction to control the audience's response. Heiserman applies this definition to the poetry, declaring that *The Bowge of Court* is his most successful poem, *Speke, Parrot* his most interesting failure, and *Collyn Clout* the least challenging artistically.

Kinney, Arthur F. *John Skelton, Priest as Poet: Seasons of Discovery*. Chapel Hill: University of North Carolina Press, 1987. Maintaining that Skelton's primary vocation—the priesthood—was fundamental to his literary work, Kinney attempts to give a comprehensive evaluation of his poetry. The five chapters follow the development of Skelton's poetics chronologically. Kinney reads the poems with enjoyment, simplicity, and elegance. Supplemented by notes and a thorough index.

Lloyd, Leslie John. *John Skelton: A Sketch of His Life and Writings*. 1938. Reprint. New York: Russel & Russel, 1969. This volume is a reprint of a 1938 edition, with a new preface by the author. Lloyd discusses Skelton's early years and the early poems, as well as *Phyllyp Sparowe*, *Magnyfycence*, and the satires. The last chapter, "A Poet's Faith," covers *The Garlande of Laurell* and "A Replycacion." Includes appendices of Skelton's translation and his "Lost Works," as well as a glossary and an index.

Pollet, Maurice. *John Skelton: Poet of Tudor England*. Translated by John Warrington. Lewisburg, Pa.: Bucknell University Press, 1971. (Original title: *John Skelton (c. 1460-1529): Contribution à l'Histoire de la Pre'renaissance Anglaise*. Paris: Didier, 1962.) An introduction to Skelton, his poetry, and his age, which follows his career from cleric-poet in the court of King Henry VII through the satires written against Thomas Wolsey to his last years and his struggle against the Lutherans. Complemented by appendices, a bibliography, and an index.

Walker, Greg. *John Skelton and the Politics of the 1520's*. New York: Cambridge University Press, 1988. Part of the Cambridge Studies in Early Modern British History series. Discusses the political and social views of Skelton and gives a history of English political satire, as well as a view of the politics and government in England during the first half of the sixteenth century.

DAVID SLAVITT

Born: White Plains, New York; March 23, 1935

Principal poetry

Suits for the Dead, 1961; *The Carnivore*, 1965; *Day Sailing*, 1968; *Child's Play*, 1972; *Vital Signs: New and Selected Poems*, 1975; *Rounding the Horn*, 1978; *Dozens*, 1981; *Big Nose*, 1983; *The Walls of Thebes*, 1986; *Equinox and Other Poems*, 1989; *Eight Longer Poems*, 1990.

Other literary forms

David Slavitt has produced translations of Vergil, Ovid, and Seneca. He has written numerous books of fiction under his own name and others under the pseudonyms Henry Sutton, David Benjamin, Henry Lazarus, and Lynn Meyer. He has also written three books of nonfiction. Slavitt served as a writer at *Newsweek* from 1958 to 1965.

Achievements

Slavitt has won several awards, including the Pennsylvania Council on the Arts Individual Artist Fellowship in fiction (1985) and poetry (1987), a National Endowment for the Arts Fellowship in Translation (1988), the National Academy and Institute of Arts and Letters Award (1989), and the Rockefeller Foundation Artist's Residence at Bellagio (1989).

Biography

The son of Samuel Saul and Adele Beatrice Rytman Slavitt, David was born in White Plains, New York. Slavitt attended Phillips Academy in Andover, Massachusetts, during which time he published his first poem, a parody of John Greenleaf Whittier's "Snowbound," in *Providence Journal.* In 1952 he entered Yale University, where he studied with Cleanth Brooks, Robert Penn Warren, Richard Sewall, and Paul Weiss. Slavitt was Scholar of the House at Yale and followed William F. Buckley, Jr., as anchor of the Yale debate team. Slavitt was graduated magna cum laude in 1956. That year he married Lynn Nita Meyer, with whom he has had three children, Evan, Sarah, and Joshua. After divorcing his first wife in 1977, Slavitt was married to Janet Lee Abraham, a physician, in 1978.

In 1957 Slavitt received an M.A. at Columbia University, writing his master's thesis on the poetry of Dudley Fitts, who had taught Slavitt at Phillips Academy. Slavitt taught in the English department of Georgia Technological University in 1957-1958 prior to taking a job at *Newsweek*. Since then, Slavitt has taught, lectured, given poetry readings, and led writing workshops at such institutions as Yale, Harvard University, Bennington College, Hollins

College, the University of Texas, the American University, the Folger Shakespeare Library, and the Library of Congress. In 1977, he was a visiting lecturer at the University of Maryland; from 1978 to 1980, he was a visiting associate professor at Temple University. In the years since he has taught at Columbia University, Rutgers University, and University of Pennsylvania.

Analysis

David Slavitt has written in a range of poetic styles, from tightly crafted poems treating mythical or historical subjects to poems in looser forms better suited to more contemporary concerns such as his family, the nightly news, and visits to F. A. O. Schwarz. Slavitt's wide vision of humankind is enhanced by his formal study in history and classical literature, his translations of Virgil, his work as "*Newsweek*'s witty, offbeat, irreverent movie critic," and his writing of popular novels under the pseudonyms Henry Sutton, David Benjamin, Lynn Meyer, and Henry Lazarus. He has been praised for his ability to find poetry not only in the domestic occasion but also simultaneously in his understanding of current affairs and historical events. As a result, there is a dark side to Slavitt's poetry, a side that seems almost fearful of death, no doubt concerned about the world as it must appear when viewed and analyzed by the historian-classicist. For a poet such as David Slavitt with an impressive intellectual range that renders him uniquely aware of the continuous reenactment of grave mistakes because human beings rarely learn from history, the only certitude ultimately is form, and the only objective validation for behavior is not one's performance itself, but how one's behavior is reported later, most often by others.

Examining Slavitt's first collection of poetry, *Suits for the Dead*, John Hall Wheelock, editor of the Scribner Poets of Today series, notes among other qualities the poet's command of form and point of view, two characteristics that continued to distinguish Slavitt's poems. Wheelock stresses "the brilliance and clarity of [Slavitt's] work, its brisk pace and taut resonance of line, its sardonic counterpoint, and, above all, its dramatic tensions." *Suits for the Dead* is remarkable, as are the first books of many first-rate poets, for the territory it marks off as Slavitt's own, the juxtaposition of the historical and mythological to images of the contemporary world. Such juxtapositions are subtle reminders of the cyclical nature of history, the arbitrariness of what is regarded as significant about events from the past, the contrariness concerning which of these events to celebrate and which to ignore, and, finally, the necessity of questioning authorities to determine why certain events and not others have been judged historically significant and whether they have been accurately portrayed.

While these concerns are brought to light in *Suits for the Dead*, they receive a greater depth of treatment and clarity of articulation in Slavitt's second volume, *The Carnivore*. Here again Slavitt deftly juxtaposes scenes from contemporary life to images of lasting historical import. "Item from Norwich" expresses the predicament a poet who has been strongly influenced by his classical background must confront. The poem depends for its success upon a series of images. For example, "the bit before the baseball scores: the man/ seventy-two, found in a tarpaper shack" sets up in Slavitt's mind a comparison with "the Syrian, Simeon Stylites, [who] raised near Antioch/ a column three feet around and sixty high," upon which he perched for thirty years, until his death. Slavitt then moves in this same poem to "the regimen of the Egyptian monasteries" and then back to "the man by the dump" in Norwich. The images Slavitt rolls before the reader suggest an ongoing motion picture of history and significant events, and he questions whether they are, in fact, the same. The poem concludes by noting how natural, how futilely human it is to record such senses: "The impulse [to make such records] is always with us." What is history? Slavitt seems to ask. What is news? Which events merit reenactment, even celebration? Do the historical events that are remembered rise above the "traditional mortifications" of events found newsworthy today?

Yet there are more than these epistemological concerns in *The Carnivore*, since history is full of reminders of aging and death and the inevitable hardship of endings. Slavitt writes in this volume about aging film heroes in old Westerns, Leonardo da Vinci's last years, wreckers smashing gables, the practice of fishing with grenades, and Eskimos floating away on ice floes. An excellent example of his concerns comes in "The Lemmings," where Slavitt writes that "they begin to swim/ westward in the nobility of despair." Then, however, he adds an overlooked complication: "who can say the conclusion/ is the obvious drowning . . . ?" Slavitt reinforces here and elsewhere in the volume the notion that the writer-recorder and not the actor is the maker of history. In "On Realpolitik and the Death of Galba," he writes, "There are some that say/ the death of Galba was noble, some say not." After all, in reviewing historical occurrences, historians must either record accurately and without the filter of subjectivity, so that later generations can interpret and evaluate such events themselves (which means that they must record all events), or sit among poets in a Platonic celebration of the event, re-creating it with the republic and its hero in mind, with the lone goal of making the event memorable. No doubt history, like the news it immortalizes, depends on who tells the story.

The question of authority permeates *The Carnivore* since it spells some kind of death, not only of the historical figure but also potentially of self-determinacy in interpreting events. In "Planting Crocus," the speaker's son "is certain the flowers will come, because I have said/ they would." Readers are required as they read such poems to ask not only who has authored their past and the history of their species but also who has authored their future, their expectations. For many children, Benjamin Franklin is portrayed in school as a historical figure who provided a model for earnest endeavor; the truth of his past is only whispered behind their backs. Slavitt writes with typical wit in "Financial Statement": "Benjamin Franklin, egomaniac, lecher,/ a penny saved is a penury earned."

Day Sailing is equally concerned with the theme of authority and self-determinacy. Though Slavitt rises to a more hopeful note in many of these poems, he is somewhat concerned that his craft may be, ultimately, no better than other kinds of crafts, including in the title poem, "a skill, a trade, a duplicity,/ a small boat." He admits in this poem, "I am no sailor, but there is no virtue/ wholly irrelevant," as if to suggest a continued search for the causes of this captivity he is beginning now to understand. He describes this captivity in "Another Letter to Lord Byron" as a lack of "something to do." He writes, "It must be dull to be dead. You can't write,/ or, if you do, you can't send it off to the printer/ the way you used to." Slavitt is concerned still with the issue of authority as he perceives it, and the poems in this collection are often concerned with the act of creativity as a kind of breaking free of captivity, the deathlike state that prevents one from finding "something to do." In "Cape Cod House," he writes about "the builder of this room who had a sense/ of grace and gave more than a thought to grandeur." In "Three Ideas of Disorder," he models his behavior after that of his son, "who has learned the tough/ tyranny of blocks" by stooping himself "to make an architectural monster of some kind." For Slavitt these are expressions that break free from the prison-house of self-consciousness and silence. As he says to George Garrett in "Upon Receiving a Book of Poems," comparing Garrett's gift of his book to another friend's gift of a crystal bowl, "I have read your book, and flicked my nail/ against its rim, and having done so, thank you,/ for the air rings, sings with a clear tone." Sometimes one can break free of captivity in that way. Sometimes one cannot.

The problem is a matter of articulation, as it is described for historians in *The Carnivore* and the tales they tell. In "Plymouth Rock," the true story of what happened "is suppressed/ because we prefer to derive from the rock its gray/ certainties than to romp on the sand. Half-dressed/ little sailors and whores in the school's Thanksgiving play/ wouldn't be right." Slavitt, though in a lighter tone, has not progressed substantially from his earlier position in *The Carnivore*: history is the record someone chooses to keep. Without truth, one is a victim, a captive of another's fiction. There seems to be little protection in *Day Sailing*. When some sort of protection is built, the result is ironic, as in "Precautions," where the poet recounts efforts to protect his boat against a promised hurricane. When the hurricane does not appear, he bemoans the fact that the unsecured boats of the "careless weekenders" have survived: "Battered to bits/ they should have been, all wrecked, and only mine/ secure in a just world." In this unjust world, the poet likens the person who takes precautions to a Noah who might have awakened to find that the promised rain never developed, or a Lot who might have left a city "to which nothing at all happens." Fortunately, Slavitt's sense of irony permits him an acceptance of his place among other captives. All humans are somewhat like the seals, in a poem of that title, that, trapped inside a zoo, lose their "natural seal sense,/ and being captive,/ acquire dependence." There is ample recompense for Slavitt, however, in "Pruning," where the reader is reminded that he or she can "read/ with prickered fingers some of the rose's poems." Again, there is a hopeful moment in Slavitt's "The Covenant," which begins, "Let the world be wary of my son,/ be gentle with him, be reverent."

The logical extension of such thinking, however, leads one back to form, to appearance, to the way the intensity of color changes depending on what is held beside it. These concerns seem to have occurred to Slavitt in his next two volumes of poetry, *Child's Play* and *Vital Signs: New and Selected Poems.* Between the publication of *Day Sailing* and *Child's Play*, Slavitt published two books of translations, Vergil's *Eclogues* (1971) and *Georgics* (1972), the product of seven years' hard work. Slavitt approached these translations wholly as a matter of challenge, not simply of technique but of understanding as well. The poet's understanding of the *Eclogues* was to influence his sense of his own time and the place of the writer among daily events as being inescapably exhilarating, almost unbelievable; his notion of the importance of form and juxtaposition was also influenced by Vergil. The central concern of the *Eclogues*, what Slavitt describes as "the lit biz," enabled Slavitt to recognize Vergil's anguish over his own reading public. Slavitt's translations— which involve summary, critical interpretation, and commentary, often through direct address of the present-day audience—made him aware of form as a kind of salvation, a method for overcoming the subjectivities that surround him, as apparent in the heavy reliance on forms in *Child's Play.*

Child's Play articulates an unmistakably darker vision for Slavitt. The poet attempts to fall back upon old and trusted remedies for his increasingly cynical view of the modern world—children and form—but those methods fail. For example, his three "children's stories" and the title poem all look to the innocent and childlike vision as redemptive, but come up instead with the coarse understatement that "kings are always whimsical" and apt to suffer the rebellion of their minions: "It always happens. The leader knows it will,/ next time be worse." Not even Peter Pan, in "Child's Play," is spared. Most viewers respond to the appearance, the form, the certainty their experiences tell them to trust: "They ooh and ah delight, surprise,/ who do not see the piano wire/ or the rigging in the flies." Slavitt seems to suggest that history is a tale of loss, rejection, deception, and uncertainty. The question is, "What/ do you tell your children?"

The answer in *Vital Signs* is that one tells them one's personal history and arranges history to reflect in its very form, in its continuous efforts to clarify, who, exactly, one is. The section of "selected poems" includes all the poems from his previously published books, as is often the case in such collections. Yet though Slavitt said in an interview with John Graham in *The Writer's Voice* that arranging poems in a volume is "about the same sort of thing as determining what order the acts ought to go on, say, an Ed Sullivan show," here he carefully arranges his poems by subject and theme. By viewing his life's production in this way, Slavitt is able to tell his children—and his readers—"This is the way I thought about the cello," for example, "as a young man, but this is the way I think about it now." *Vital Signs* reads like home films, carefully edited not to show the random events of passing years, but to reveal the changing perception, the certainty turned uncertainty in the growth of the poet's mind. Even the new poems are so grouped, in a careful effort to re-create the formal rendering of the changing mind, perhaps offering a truer picture of history than the events others have recorded for posterity and study. As Slavitt writes in "Wishes," "who can be so knowing/ and still believe there is luck in a meteorite?" The arrangement of poems in *Vital Signs* might be seen as exactly this statement aesthetically applied, a commitment to the form as one way of knowing and to the content of knowledge or theme as something more changeable, less dependable.

Rounding the Horn reinforces Slavitt's continuing concern with form. In this collection of fifty-five poems, all of them written in different forms, Slavitt is committed in some epistemological way to rhyme while dealing with some of the old subjects and themes, built around the metaphors of voyaging, escape, and adventure. Many of these poems seem simpler, though darker in their simplicity: "The clown is supposed to be sad," writes an earnest Slavitt, "but what about the xylophone player/ who has more reason . . . ?" Slavitt calls attention to his learning less in this collection, perhaps, than in his earlier books. Still, he is a disciplined craftsman, writing with humor and wit about life and its complexity. He deals with people, including a vandal, an old woman with a cane, the painter Claude Monet, a pitcher. He deals with events, such as college reunions, "Youth, Age, Life, and Art." He takes his reader abroad, to Poland and Italy, to Greece and Charles Dickens' inkwell. There is still an urge to find something permanent, but in the world of this collection, one sees the product and wonders whether one will become a part of it. "Garbage" notes "the tendency of/ things to turn sooner or later into junk,/ scrap, detritus" and clarifies that this tendency exists not only among "objects and ornaments" but also "ideas and people."

Dozens seems to be an effort to eschew as garbage all ideas and people and hold instead to the certainty of form. The collection is exactly what the title suggests, a book-length poem of 144 twelve-line stanzas. What is clearly of greatest importance about *Dozens* is not the subject, which has failed to impress some of Slavitt's critics, but the power of form when put to the use

Slavitt intends in this collection. There is a narrative plan here, and the narrative is spoken in a voice not always reminiscent of the earlier Slavitt, the poet who has served as a resigned observer of the human condition against a background of history and classical literature. Slavitt's invective in this long poem would be incorrectly approached, however, if one were to try to separate it altogether from his earlier work. In "Touring," the opening poem in *Child's Play*, Slavitt wrote, "Architecture, painting, tapisserie . . . / but gore is what we tour. The seriousness/ of a nation comes from the seriousness of its crimes." In stanza 18 of *Dozens*, he describes "a dreadful city, as Whitman's/ Camden is a dreadful city. The worse/ it is, the better it is."

Perhaps the persistence of this view sets critics on edge. The poem seems to take place in Central America (though it might be any number of other places). A revolution is taking place outside a hotel. The point of it all is "not the end of the world but, say, the fun/ of the end of the world." No doubt one can hear irony in this statement, but the argument is unrelenting, forcing the reader to recall "Garbage" from *Rounding the Horn* in an effort to understand this particular assault on the human condition. At the end of "Garbage," the speaker claims that he tries to believe in God, and pictures God as a garbage-picker with gloved hands, who comes across the speaker as he sifts through debris. Perhaps God will pause and remember, says the speaker, "that I/ was once supposed to fit somewhere, that I was/ not always garbage." *Dozens* captures a world-turned-rubble: "Let the grubby truth/ be carted away—with New Haven, a grubby place." If one does not look too long at dismal reality, the poem says cynically, one may be able to imagine that "the broken down world" can "heal/ as the poets have taught us to think it may. It may/ if we say so often enough and loud enough."

Big Nose, Slavitt's next collection of poems, does not "say so often enough and loud enough." In fact, the introductory "To His Reader" is hardly charming. The voice, once again, rings with invective that jolts the relaxed reader into defensiveness. Slavitt concludes, "You and I depend thus on one another, and serve, but you are not my friend. Nor am I yours." Slavitt does not seem to be in the "lit biz" to make friends, but he is clearly able to stimulate readers and tell stories. "Big Nose" is an excellent narrative of a Western criminal, Big Nose George Parrott, who is hanged and then made into a pair of boots to be worn by the sheriff. Soon the sheriff, who wears the boots proudly at first, becomes the object of horror and leaves town— still trapped, however, by his past. This narrative represents something new for Slavitt, though it was foreshadowed by the long narration of *Dozens*. One must wonder why the introductory material was so long in coming, considering Slavitt's long affection for Vergil.

The Walls of Thebes brings Slavitt at perhaps his best. This collection walks a higher ground, passing through personal graveyards, forcing the poet to confront episodes of his past, which he does with clarity and surprising objectivity. As he says in "Reading," in looking through his poems before reading them to an audience, "They're an album of my life." This is a sobering collection of poems, often offering accounts of personal nightmare, but unsentimentalized and earned: "Each of us has suffered losses, each/ has felt the terrible wrench of the earth/ shrinking beneath his feet." In some ways, the old themes return, a search for the appropriate form as well as a search for answers to questions Slavitt has been asking all along: What is of permanent value? What authors one's understanding of history? When does the simple event become historically significant? Perhaps the most affectively moving of Slavitt's poems in this collection is "Bloody Murder," in which he speaks with unquestionable discipline of events that came "after the burglar bludgeoned my mother/ to death with a bathroom scale and a large/ bottle of Listerine." At the recommendation of the police, he hired "Ronny Reliable's/ Cleaning Service" to clean up afterward. "I still wonder/ who would choose that kind of employment," Slavitt says—and, more than that, who of that occupation could leave behind a bloodstain. More than any other of Slavitt's collections, this poem reveals a turning inward, relying on snapshots, vignettes, and a variety of reminiscences that force the poet to reevaluate his personal history, much as he did in a more objective manner in *Vital Signs.*

The later collections seem to flow from a kind of meditation hinted at in *The Walls of Thebes. Equinox* and *Eight Longer Poems* tend to focus somewhat more than Slavitt's earlier works on domestic events as well as on the time-tested subject of historical and classical study. "Monster Dance," in *Eight Longer Poems*, concerns the dance Slavitt's grown son performs each night at bedtime to reassure the poet's younger son that there is nothing to fear. Slavitt takes on subjects such as his own partial deafness as a means of exploring larger questions. Naturally, Slavitt looks back in these collections as well, considering "a whole decade/ of what I thought of as civilization."

Slavitt will continue to be approached carefully by readers. He is uniquely capable of exploring American culture in the context of the past. In his later work he has become slightly more introspective than earlier in his life, as though now that he has a life to reflect upon, and not merely an intellect to play with, the time has come to reevaluate his relationships with those closest to him, including himself.

Patrick Bizzaro

Other major works

LONG FICTION: *Rochelle: Or, Virtue Rewarded*, 1966; *The Exhibitionist*, 1967 (as Henry Sutton); *Feel Free*, 1968; *The Voyeur*, 1969 (as Henry Sutton); *Anagrams*, 1970; *Vector*, 1970 (as Henry Sutton); *A B C D*, 1972; *The Liberated*, 1973 (as Henry Sutton); *The Outer Mongolian*, 1973; *The Killing of the King*, 1974; *King of Hearts*, 1976; *That Golden Woman*, 1976 (as Henry Lazarus);

Jo Stern, 1978; *The Sacrifice*, 1978 (as Henry Sutton); *The Idol*, 1979 (as David Benjamin); *The Proposal*, 1980 (as Henry Sutton); *Cold Comfort*, 1980; *Ringer*, 1982; *Alice at 80*, 1984; *Secrets*, 1985 (with Bill Adler); *The Agent*, 1986; *The Hussar*, 1987; *Salazar Blinks*, 1988; *Lives of the Saints*, 1989.

NONFICTION: *Understanding Social Life*, 1976 (with Paul F. Secord and Carl W. Backman); *Physicians Observed*, 1987; *Virgil*, 1991.

TRANSLATIONS: *The Eclogues of Virgil*, 1971; *The Eclogues and the Georgics of Virgil*, 1972; *The Tristia of Ovid*, 1986; *Ovid's Poetry of Exile*, 1990; *Five Plays of Seneca*, 1991.

EDITED TEXT: *Land of Superior Mirages: New and Selected Poems*, 1986 (by Adrien Stoutenburg).

Bibliography

Booklist. Review of *The Walls of Thebes*, by David Slavitt. *Booklist*, October, 1986. Discusses life and art ("the cruel injustices of the former and the inadequate consolations of the latter") as the themes of Slavitt's book. Praises volume as touching while noting that it is also "often troubling."

Garrett, George. "An Amoebaean Contest Where Nobody Loses: The Eclogues of Virgil Translated by David R. Slavitt." *Hollins Critic* 8 (1971): 2-14. This review-article deals with Slavitt's translations of Vergil's *Eclogues.* In it Garrett comments extensively about Slavitt's approach to the translations.

Kaganoff, Penny. Review of *Eight Longer Poems*, by David Slavitt. *Publishers Weekly* 237 (March 30, 1990): 56. Praises Slavitt's "inventiveness and proficient manipulation of language" while alleging his "excessive" references to "blood" and "wounds." Also discusses Slavitt's effort to transform "personal suffering into universal circumstance."

Slavitt, David. Interview by George Garrett and John Graham. In *The Writer's Voice: Conversations with Contemporary Writers*, edited by George Garrett. New York: Morrow, 1973. This interview is often cited for its reliable insights into Slavitt's broad range of interests as a writer of fiction, poetry, and essays. It highlights many of his adjustments that follow his translations of Vergil.

Wheelock, John Hall. "Introductory Essay: Man's Struggle to Understand." In *Poets of Today VII*, edited by John Hall Wheelock. New York: Scribner, 1960. This is the introduction to Slavitt's first full collection of poems, published in the Scribner's Poets of Today series. Wheelock identifies themes and techniques used by the young Slavitt—an identification remarkable for its continuing applicability.

CHRISTOPHER SMART

Born: Shipbourne, near Tunbridge (England); April 11, 1722
Died: King's Bench Prison, London; May 2, 1771

Principal poetry

On the Eternity of the Supreme Being, 1750; *On the Immensity of the Supreme Being*, 1751; *On the Omniscience of the Supreme Being*, 1752; *Poems on Several Occasions*, 1752; *The Hilliad*, 1753; *On the Power of the Supreme Being*, 1754; *On the Goodness of the Supreme Being*, 1755; *Hymn to the Supreme Being, on Recovery from a Dangerous Fit of Illness*, 1756; *A Song to David*, 1763; *Poems*, 1763; *Ode to the Earl of Northumberland*, 1764; *Hymns for the Amusement of Children*, 1772; *Jubilate Agno*, 1939 (as *Rejoice in the Lamb*, 1954); *Collected Poems*, 1950 (2 vols., edited by Norman Callan).

Other literary forms

In London Christopher Smart did hackwork for booksellers, wrote songs for Vauxhall Gardens entertainment, and edited the magazine *Midwife: Or, Old Woman's Magazine* from 1749 to about 1750. *The Works of Horace, Translated Literally into English* (1756) is a prose translation of the poems from the Latin; *A Translation of the Psalms of David Attempted in the Spirit of Christianity, and Adapted to the Divine Service, with Hymns and Spiritual Songs for the Fasts and Festivals of the Church of England* (1765) was rendered from the Hebrew in poetic form; another translation, *The Works of Horace Translated into Verse*, came out in 1767.

Achievements

Smart became a fellow of Pembroke Hall, the University of Cambridge, in 1745, and attained college office after receiving his master's degree in 1747. He won the Seaton Prize for poetry every year from 1750 to 1755, with the exception of 1754, when he did not enter.

Biography

Christopher Smart was born in Kent, where his father served as steward to William, Viscount Vane. His earliest love was Lord Vane's daughter Anne, but the two were forced apart. A precocious student, he was sponsored by the Duchess of Cleveland for enrollment at Pembroke Hall, Cambridge. Her forty-pound annuity allowed him to concentrate upon both scholarship and social life in college, where he gained a reputation as a hard drinker and incurred heavy debts. He received his bachelor's degree in 1742, followed by a master's in 1747, with election to college office the same year. He also married Anna Marie Carnan; the marriage was kept secret until its discovery forced him to give up his position. Yet Smart was allowed to keep his connection in order to compete for the Seaton Poetry Prize each year. He won the prize in 1750, 1751, and 1753; after skipping a year of the competition in 1754, he came back to win again in 1755. The Seatonian odes are not considered successful, but they show the religious attitudes for which Smart was noted as well as his practice of the cataloging technique as a strategy.

Smart had left Cambridge for London in 1749 to make a living as a writer, taking various hack assignments in a variety of forms. On jobs for booksellers, mostly for his wife's stepfather John Newbery, he wrote humor, fables, lyric verses, and epitaphs. As a periodical writer he remained poor and undistinguished, even as editor of *Midwife: Or, Old Woman's Magazine.*

He was befriended by such noted figures as Samuel Johnson, Oliver Goldsmith, Thomas Gray, and David Garrick, who helped him during his periods of alcoholism and madness. Johnson supposedly did some of Smart's periodical writing, and Garrick performed in 1759 to raise money for him. Even with help from friends, however, Smart's family fell apart; his wife and two daughters moved to Ireland and remained there with his sister.

The study of Smart's life and his works has customarily revolved around his madness, which seems to have begun around 1756. He was confined several times for madness and for debts. Though there is no agreement on the causes or the exact label for his madness, it is generally considered to have been a religious form of monomania. His poem entitled *Hymn to the Supreme Being, on Recovery from a Dangerous Fit of Illness* (1756) is considered evidence of the techniques that would make his later works worthy of note. This poem receives notice as pivotal in his literary development from religious and technical perspectives.

His compulsiveness and his fixation seem to have a shared religious root, resulting in what was considered his most bizarre public behavior: praying aloud whenever and wherever the inclination struck him. He said once, "I blessed God in St. James's Park until I routed all the company." Such behavior was categorized as enthusiasm in the eighteenth century, and the adjective "enthusiastic" was applied to many Dissenters seized by religious fervor.

Although his friends did not agree on the necessity for Smart's confinement, he was kept in St. Luke's Hospital from 1757 through part of 1758. When released that year, he seemed to grow worse, and mental problems caused him to be placed in asylum from 1759 to 1763. Under these circumstances he seemed to behave quietly and occupy himself with religious activities, his writing, and domestic chores. Among his friends who visited, Johnson said, "I did not think he ought to be shut up. . . . His infirmities were not noxious to society. He insisted on people praying with him; and I'd as lief pray with Kit Smart as anyone else." During this second confinement he wrote his major works, *Jubilate Agno* (begun in 1759), which remained unfinished and unpublished during his lifetime, and *A Song to David* (1763), his most important work.

Upon returning to society, having lost all contact with his family, Smart became involved in a series of bitter conflicts with other journalists, in which he revealed an indignation or self-righteousness that has been frowned upon since that time. The literary result of these feuds was *The Hilliad* (1753) a verse satire written in imitation of the *Dunciad* (1728, 1742) of Alexander Pope but by no means equal to it.

Smart continued to deteriorate physically and behaviorally after he returned to London life, but he concentrated more and more on the writing of poetry and focused to an even greater extent on religious subjects. He published *A Translation of the Psalms of David* in 1765 and his verse translation of Horace in 1767, several years before his final incarceration, which began in 1769. A number of biographical questions exist relating to the actual composition of his religious poems, with some critics interested in whether several were written simultaneously. Smart seems to have hoped that some of his works would be adopted by the Church of England for its liturgy, since his psalms and their arrangement not only imitate the Hebrew and the Anglican prayer-book of his day but also follow the sequence of the Christian year.

Because Smart was not only a literary scholar and linguist but also a student of natural phenomena, he drew these interests into his poetry. Much of what he knew about science came from books and reading, but he insisted upon studying God's works in nature so that he could celebrate all of creation.

The year 1769 brought further debt and lack of control, resulting in a final incarceration in King's Bench prison for debtors. During this year Smart wrote *Hymns for the Amusement of Children*, a book of verses sharing his knowledge of nature and his love of God. It was in this prison that he died, remaining outwardy optimistic and happy regardless of his problems. He seems to have been absolutely sure of his salvation; at least he asserted his certainty flamboyantly and repeatedly, often to the discomfort and irritation of others. His masterpiece, *A Song to David*, was the primary reason for his reputation as a writer and the work on which his reputation as a poet rests to this day.

Analysis

A Song to David was first published in 1763, the year Smart was released from his second period of confinement. Such timing must have had more than a little to do with the speculation about the connection between madness and poetry which has remained a constant in criticism of Smart's literary productions. James Boswell, Samuel Johnson's famous biographer, seems to have begun the discussion that occupied Smart's contemporaries even when they were admiring of the work, as Boswell was. The Romantic poets William Wordsworth and Leigh Hunt were among the first to consider *A Song to*

David a great lyric. Generally the Romantics were appreciative of Smart, but the Victorian Robert Browning is credited with reviving interest in his works. There is widespread agreement about the high quality of *A Song to David*, even though critical appreciation of Smart's other work waxes and wanes as tastes change.

Writing a song of praise to the great Hebrew psalmist appears to have been a deliberate act of emulation on the neoclassical poet's part. Although he suggested that good poetry was inspired by God rather than the muse, it is known from his translations of Horace into both poetry and prose that Smart learned how to apply the theory and advice gained from his reading of the Roman poet. Typical of his era, however, he did not hesitate to combine classicism with Old Testament techniques and New Testament concepts. The trend toward imitation of Hebrew poetry seems to have been initiated by Bishop Robert Lowth's *Praelectiones de Sacra Poesi Hebraerorum* (1753, lectures on the sacred poetry of the Hebrews), published ten years earlier than *A Song to David*. This work attracted attention in scholarly and literary circles and even stimulated popular interest with its analysis of Hebrew poetics and the technical devices of Old Testament poetry.

A Song to David does more, however, than follow a trend. It is in some ways unique, and it expresses a personal exhilaration that illustrates the neoclassical concept of the sublime. This sublime, or grand and exalted effect, is never grandiose or bombastic. A look at the formal properties of the poem reveals that Smart was certainly in control, rather than insane, when he wrote this tribute to his hero and model, King David.

The poem is made up of eighty-six stanzas, each of which follows the same basic pattern: two lines of iambic tetrameter followed by an iambic trimeter line and then a repetition of this sequence, making a six-line unit. The rhyme scheme is *aabccb*, with all the end rhymes masculine. An outline of the poem's structure, made by Smart himself and labeled "Contents," is placed between the quotation from 2 Samuel 23:1-2 and the opening stanza.

The quotation introduces David as the subject capsules his life, from his ancestry to his anointing by Samuel and his sacred gift of poetry and song. Traditional interpreters of Hebrew Scripture will find in this passage allusions to the various subtopics addressed within the poem proper: David's ancestry, his monarchy, his sacred gift of poetry and song. David's lineage from the family of Jesse is essential to Smart's establishment of the connection between his Old Testament subject and Jesus Christ. Christian theology teaches that God became man in the form of Jesus of Nazareth, a descendant of the house of David, son of Jesse.

David was anointed King of Israel by Samuel, the same prophet who had anointed the first king, Saul. David, who was close friends with Jonathan, Saul's son, was not only the warrior who slew the Philistine giant Goliath but also served Saul's court as harpist, singer, and poet. The Book of Psalms in the Old Testament is traditionally considered the work of David. David was also the mastermind behind the design of the temple, which was built by his son Solomon (1 Chronicles 28). In the poem proper, Smart goes into more detail, establishing traditional biblical grounds for his treatment of David.

Identifying Smart's concept of David as well as the biblical allusions permeating the stanzas is essential in reading the poem. The David of this poem is not simply the David of the Old Testament and of Jewish history. The David addressed at the beginning of the poem combines the king, the harpist, and the Old Testament type (symbol) of Christ. Evidence from this poem and others, including translations of the Psalms, reveals that Smart incorporates into his David figure the Orpheus of classical mythology, the symbol of the poet as maker, who duplicates on the earthly plane God's act of creation. This creative power provides the thematic basis for the catalog of natural creation that dominates certain prominent sections of the poem. The singerking is developed thus as the model for the way to praise God and the leader of Christendom in the various acts of praise, just as the psalmist or song leader might direct the congregation in communal praise. As a preliminary way of getting into a celebratory posture, Smart also praises David himself.

Stanza 5 begins the section on David's life, with each stanza from 5 through 16 developing details to support an adjective applied to David in the fourth stanza: "Great, valiant, pious, good, and clean,/ Sublime, contemplative, serene,/ Strong, constant, pleasant, wise!" The history and folklore traditionally associated with the hero are deftly introduced in this passage, with references to well-known characters and minor ones who were a part of David's rise to glory. The close friendship with Jonathan and the feats of the young hero are given more attention than the illicit love affair with Bathsheba, which Smart touches upon very briefly. The colorful story of sex, murder, and repentance from 2 Samuel 11 and 12 is mentioned only as "his fall" and is presented as an example of how David "rose [to] his eminence o'er all" by learning from his sin. David's first wife, Michal, and the young girl Abishag, who was supposed to be a comfort to his old age, are mentioned in stanza 17 as means to show the superior importance of his muse, whose influence was greater than that of any of David's women.

The subjects inspired by his muse are then treated generally in a succession of three stanzas: God, angels, man, and the world. Then he begins a catalog of creation, which he turns into his own hymn of praise, making vivid word pictures, especially in the lines describing precious stones. The power of this inspired musicianship to overcome not only human foes but also spiritual and demonic ones is the subject of the next three stanzas.

The next section of the poem, introduced by the thirtieth stanza's focus on seven "pillars of the Lord," refers to another creation of David, an architectural act of praise known as Solomon's temple. Allusions are made to the seven pillars of wisdom from the ninth chaper of Proverbs, the seven days of creation as recounted in the first chapter of Genesis, and the decorative pillars of the temple as described in 1 Kings 5-8. The majority of critics, however, see this passage as built upon the rites and symbolic system of Freemasonry, which is traditionally associated with the builders of the temple. Each stanza begins with the name of a letter of the Greek alphabet, with vowels and consonants alternating.

Two stanzas complimenting David's knowledge introduce what Smart calls "an exercise upon the decalogue," referring to the Ten Commandments received by Moses. Ever intent upon bringing the Hebrew vision of God and the Christian together, Smart reminds his reader to follow the advice of Saint Paul and "turn from old Adam [from the Book of Genesis] to the New [Jesus Christ]." A profusion of images forms the next catalog, which makes a glorious presentation of God's creatures participating in the grand impulse of nature to praise the Creator. This call to celebration and participation is developed under the heading of adoration, with David the singer as its leader. The word "ADORATION" is artfully placed in a different line within each stanza, so that it is given strategic emphasis. Certain of these stanzas reveal Smart's paraphrasing of psalms, including myriad details in the passages he had earlier labeled exercises upon "right use" of the seasons and "how to subdue" the senses. The abundance of creation, with its systematic and plenary chain of being, is suggested, creating a joyous and effervescent tone of love and unity.

Stanza 72 begins the crescendo that develops to the finale, which was described earlier in Smart's outline as "an amplification in five degrees," once again suggesting the Masonic Order. Repetition of a series of adjectives, much like the repetition of "ADORATION," precedes the nature imagery used to define and illustrate the individual words: "sweet," "strong," "beauteous," "precious," and "glorious." Each adjective is taken through its own degrees of comparison, with sentences built around its meaning.

The last stanza of the poem is also the final one in the adjectival series, with its focus upon the meanings of "glorious" as summed up in the person of Christ the King, who took upon himself human form. Having brought together the creation, the incarnation, and the resurrection, which are the foundation of traditional Judeo-Christian belief, Smart ends on a note of triumph that seems as much a personal declaration as a thematic one: "DETERMINED, DARED, and DONE."

Emma Coburn Norris

Other major works

LIBRETTOS: *Hannah: An Oratorio*, 1764; *Abimelech: An Oratorio*, 1768; *Providence: An Oratorio*, 1777.

TRANSLATIONS: *The Works of Horace, Translated Literally into English*, 1756; *A Poetical Translation of the Fables of Phaedrus*, 1765; *A Translation of the Psalms of David Attempted in the Spirit of Christianity*, 1765; *The Works of Horace Translated into Verse*, 1767.

MISCELLANEOUS: *Mother Midnight's Miscellany*, 1751 (as Mary Midnight); *The Nonpareil: Or, The Quintessence of Wit and Humor*, 1757 (as Mary Midnight).

Bibliography

Bond, William H. "Christopher Smart's *Jubilate Agno.*" *Harvard Library Bulletin* 4 (1950): 39-52. This article is a comprehensive attempt to put the poem's fragments together. Examining the holograph manuscript leads Bond to believe that Smart took about four years to write these verses and originally set up an antiphonal structure but eventually lost control over it.

Devlin, Christopher. *Poor Kit Smart.* Carbondale: University of Illinois Press, 1961. This biography includes critical commentary on individual poems as well as an attempt to evaluate Smart's works as a whole. Devlin's emphasis follows his subject's paramount concern: religion.

Dillingham, Thomas F. "'Blest Light': Christopher Smart's Myth of David." In *The David Myth in Western Literature*, edited by Raymond-Jean Frontain and Jan Wojick. West Lafayette, Ind.: Purdue University Press, 1980. The biblical David is central to Smart's highest poetic achievements, says Dillingham, whether used as subject, as in *A Song to David*, or as a model for imitation, as in the translations and biblical paraphrases. Smart combines the Old Testament figure with the Greek Orpheus and Christian theology in seeking a unified vision for his faith.

Havens, Raymond D. "The Structure of Smart's *Song to David.*" *Review of English Studies* 14 (1938): 178-182. This work is old but not outdated, and it is a highly regarded source with which to begin a study of Smart's major work. The poem's structure is analyzed from a mathematical and a mystical point of view. Attention is devoted, for example, to Smart's dependence upon the numbers three and seven and their multiples.

Sherbo, Arthur. *Christopher Smart: Scholar of the University.* East Lansing: Michigan State University Press, 1967. This book-length work concentrates on biographical material interpreted through a detailed look at eighteenth century history. The poems are discussed in their contemporary setting without extensive analysis.

DAVE SMITH

Born: Portsmouth, Virginia; December 19, 1942

Principal poetry

Bull Island, 1970; *Mean Rufus Throw Down*, 1973; *The Fisherman's Whore*, 1974; *Cumberland Station*, 1976; *Goshawk, Antelope*, 1979; *Dream Flights*, 1981; *Homage to Edgar Allan Poe*, 1981; *In the House of the Judge*, 1983; *Gray Soldiers*, 1983; *The Roundhouse Voices: Selected and New Poems*, 1985; *Cuba Night*, 1990.

Other literary forms

Dave Smith's productivity as a poet does not exhaust his pen. He has produced scores of reviews and essays on poetry and poetics, many of them as a columnist for *The American Poetry Review. Local Assays: On Contemporary American Poetry* (1985) collects many of these pieces. Smith's map of the contemporary scene is revealed in *The Morrow Anthology of Younger American Poets* (1985), which he edited. Smith also edited and wrote the introduction for *The Pure Clear Word: Essays on the Poetry of James Wright* (1982). In these activities, Smith has helped to define the critical context for his own work, for the poets of his generation, and for the canon of major influences on that generation. An enthusiastic reviewer, Smith has been faulted by some for excessive generosity. Nevertheless, his stature as a critic is rising to match his standing as a major poet of his era.

Smith's first novel, *Onliness* (1981), won critical acclaim. As Alan Bold wrote for the *Times Literary Supplement* (November 27, 1981), "*Onliness* is no tentative beginning, but an ambitious attempt to write the Great American Novel by bringing myth, archetype, allegory and abstraction to a fluent narrative." The usually sober-minded poet became an adept prose stylist who unveiled a comic wit not often realized in his poetry. At once erudite, folksy, and bizarre, *Onliness* fashions a version of the American South that owes more to Flannery O'Connor than to William Faulkner, yet Smith has made it a region of his own. *Southern Delights* (1984), a collection mixing stories and poems, is a less satisfying display of Smith's narrative skill.

Achievements

Smith is a poet of inclusion. Working during a period characterized by emotional coolness and reductionism, Smith has been one of very few swimming in the opposite direction. His poetry is unashamedly passionate— exuberantly so. He almost never merely outlines a theme; he elaborates it with lavish care. Given these tendencies, it is not surprising that the characteristic Smith poem does not sit neatly on a single page. He has helped to bring back the long poem, both meditative and narrative. Smith is a brooder, a storyteller, and a moralist.

For these poems, Smith has created a rhetoric based on long lines and longer sentences—a rolling terrain of accumulating phrases and clauses. He is not, usually, a metrical poet, but rather a poet of sweeping cadences and accentual rhythms. His style is particularly Southern: affinities with Faulkner, Robert Penn Warren, and James Dickey are evident. Like them, Smith tends toward the baroque. He has built an ornamented and oratorical style that stands somewhere between colloquial idiom and grandiloquent rapture.

Much of Smith's work is a poetry of memory and yearning. The memories are personal, familial, and communal. In the best poems, they are also universal. Some of his work tries to give retrospective testimony to his (and everyone's) inarticulate youth. He is often sneaking up on the young boy, forcing him to explain himself, and encountering some kind of evocative silence or near-silence. To recapture the past is part of that severe yearning in Smith's poems. Passionate desire, however, can carry the poet in other directions: to see something clearly enough; to trust one's perceptions and one's heart; to answer nature's alternately strange and familiar glance. Smith, like the poets of ages past, is simply after the meaning of life. The intellectual life alone, without the felt underpinning of the physical life, is something that Smith distrusts, just as he has little patience for the questions of poetic form until there is the pulse of significant content.

A frequent device in Smith's work is the generative image or symbol. From the early "Medieval Tapestry" through such poems as "The Spinning Wheel in the Attic," "Under the Scrub Oak, a Red Shoe," "Blue Spruce," and "Crab," Smith uses his central image not merely for verbal accuracy or to invoke a single correspondence, but as a center for the intersection of many planes of thought and feeling. In such poems, as in the story poems with their enigmatic, fabulous glow, there is the hope—if not the proof—that all experience is connected in a way that one may ultimately grasp. Smith's vision is clearly in the romantic tradition.

Smith is a poet of full commitment to all that poetry can be. His long reach risks many things, including excess, but he does not choose to hold back. His special gifts and his special ambition are profoundly mated. His craft is in knowing when, and how, to go on. Norman Dubie's claim that Smith is the greatest poet of the American South is hard to dispute. Indeed, Smith may take his place among the foremost writers of any kind that the South has produced.

Biography

David Jeddie Smith spent nearly all of his first thirty years in or near the tidewater region of Virginia. The collection of towns and villages clustered around the fishing and shipbuilding economy of the lower Chesapeake Bay formed the scenes of his childhood. Born in Portsmouth, he began rearing his own family in nearby Poquoson. It was there, after graduating from the University of Virginia in 1965, that Smith began his teaching career at Poquoson High School. Soon after his marriage in 1966 to Deloras Mae Weaver, Smith traveled to Edwardsville, Illinois, to work toward a master's degree at Southern Illinois University (1967-1969). Returning to Poquoson, Smith spent the next three years on active duty in the Air Force. He continued his teaching with night classes at local colleges.

Smith began writing in the late 1960's and ran his own small press, Back Door, for a number of years. The press's colophon, a dilapidated shack, was an emblem not only for a typical shoestring small press operation, but also for the shoestring lives of the characters that Smith would write about so often. The marginal but deeply felt and patterned lives of the Atlantic watermen provide the subject of Smith's first small collection, *Bull Island*, and of individual poems in later volumes. People living on the brink always appeal to Smith.

The geography of Smith's imagination embraces his own immediate region, his ancestors' mid-Atlantic wanderings, and the caldron of United States history: the Chesapeake from Norfolk to Baltimore, and the slow ascent westward to the mountains of Maryland, Virginia, and West Virginia. In much of Smith's work, the song of his time in this place becomes mixed with the lingering, ghostlike voices of landmarks and battlefields.

The traditions of this part of the South and his admiration for the common man and the physical life are aspects of the sensibility that Smith brings to his work. There is also Smith the man of letters: no noble savage at all, but rather the winner of graduate degrees in literature and the university teacher. The boy who had gone hunting year after year with his grandfather would find himself stalking the long commons of the contemporary American poet—academe. In his work, Smith has managed to subdue this bifurcation and, sometimes—as in "The Roundhouse Voices," in which words and deeds are explicitly measured against one another—to exploit it.

In 1972, Smith began a program of study at Ohio University that allowed him to earn a Ph.D. in 1976 with a creative dissertation. He was in residence for only the first and last years, spending 1973 to 1974 teaching at Western Michigan University and 1974 to 1975 at Cottey College in Nevada, Missouri. By the time the degree was completed, Smith had published his first two full-length collections and had won critical acclaim as well as such honors as represented by a Bread Loaf Fellowship (1975) and his first National Endowment for the Arts Fellowship (1976). While *Cumberland Station* was being readied for publication, Smith was offered the directorship of the creative writing program at the University of Utah. He held that position for four years. Life in the American West provided the landscape and inspiration for Smith's next book, *Goshawk, Antelope*, which, in 1980, was a finalist for both the Pulitzer Prize and the National Book Critics Circle Award.

During 1980 and 1981, Smith brought to publication three books—two poetry collections and a novel—while working as a Visiting Professor at the Binghamton campus of the State University of New York. These collections, *Dream Flights* and *Homage to Edgar Allan Poe*, marked Smith's imaginative return to his tidewater roots, although with modifications of style and sensibility.

The imaginative return anticipated the actual one. After spending the academic year 1981-1982 as Director of Creative Writing at the University of Florida in Gainesville, Smith moved with his wife and three children to Richmond. There, as Professor of Creative Writing at Virginia Commonwealth University, Smith continued to write and to build upon the reputation that had risen meteorically in little more than a decade. *In the House of the Judge* contains some of Smith's most demanding work in longer forms. *The Roundhouse Voices*, an interim summary of his career as a poet, assured his permanence in the history of American letters. After what (for a writer as prolific as Smith) seemed like an unusual interval, *Cuba Night* appeared, a collection signaling the continued growth in craft, vision, and stature of the poet at middle age.

Analysis

Generalizations about the memory-laden nature of much of Smith's work have obscured the variety of ways in which his themes are developed, just as generalizations about his style do not reflect the wide range of experimentation in his work. The thorough reader will find many Smith poems that are short, lyric outbursts—and even poems in highly patterned stanzaics. *Mean Rufus Throw Down* contains pieces using full or subdued rhymes in couplets, tercets, and quatrains. In this volume, the variety of techniques may be accounted for as the searching experimentation of the young poet. Each volume, however, has its traditionally patterned efforts. "The Collector of the Sun," in *Goshawk, Antelope*, shows Smith at home with the difficult couplet quatrain. In *Homage to Edgar Allan Poe*, there is a studied return to the manipulation of older conventions (one aspect of the "homage"). For Smith, this kind of discipline is not always rewarding; it often seems that such strictures are at war with his truest poetic impulses. Still, one would not want to do without "The Abused (Hansel and Gretel)," a sonnet, or "Under a White Shawl of Pine," with its delicately flowing alternating rhyme quatrains.

Because Smith is usually expansive, the terse, compact sketches of film stars (such as "Doubling Back with Bogart") in *The Fisherman's Whore* are welcome surprises. Because he is often unrelievedly solemn, the grim whimsy of "The Suicide Eaters" (in *Goshawk, Antelope*) reminds readers that there is range to the emotive notes that Smith can strike. Certainly the ongoing drama of being a husband and father often leads Smith to the backward-looking stance (as his own childhood and his own parents are recalled), but often enough such subjects leave him firmly planted in the present and looking to the future. "In Snow, a Possible Life" is one of Smith's gentlest poems of family feeling, and it is one of a number of pieces that suggest a poetic credo. Here, a dominant image focuses the poem's emotion. In "The Dark Eyes of Daughters," another poem of domestic concern (both are in *Goshawk, Antelope*), focus is achieved by a careful orchestration of images and figures of speech.

"The Dark Eyes of Daughters" recounts a moving instance of "love's division." The speaker, angered at his daughter's cat for attacking a tame quail, finds himself outside kicking the cat, and then, in almost the same instant, realizes that his young daughter is looking on, a witness to his brutality. In this moment of unplanned but decisive action, the father has become implicated in complex losses. Simply enough, the world will never be the same. He knows it and wishes against the change in his daughter's knowledge and heart; but the wish is futile.

The poem provides an experience focused by a series of similes and metaphors and by a careful metamorphosis of images. The heated action and the distance it has created are figured in the noise of "the back door/ still banging like a ripped/ shred of memory." The impulse to wish the truth away is like that of "a man in a car/ that's dropped something/ to howl down a quiet street." The oppressiveness of the truth is a "light/ banging hard overhead" and "this slow gouging/ of sparks that is the world." The "intense unloosening stare" of the cat's eyes gives way to consciousness of "the fixed and heart-dark/ pupils of the child startled/ to see what cruelty is." The revealing, vengeful sun, the cat, the daughter, and the painful truth she is learning are all brought together—in spite of the speaker's contrary wish: the "sun the color of a cat" falls "on her struck face that is/ learning to mouth these words/ without end." Finally, the sun, "like flint, strikes."

This same sun, at the beginning of the poem, was weakly invoked by the phrase "the dew dulls out." The sun as flint reaches back to the "gouging . . . sparks." The "spatter of quail feathers" at the poem's opening looks forward to the penultimate movement, the daughter's words "a beginning already long lost/ like pawprint or feather." The absorption of this tight structure of reverberating images into the illusion of artless, passionate utterance is characteristic of Smith's best work and especially of the more modulated passions of *Goshawk, Antelope*.

More ambitious, and perhaps more central to Smith's developing manner, is "Night Fishing for Blues," in *Cumberland Station*. This poem exemplifes Smith's interest in the physical life, especially the actions of work and sport in the region he knows best. To that level of concern is added another dimension as the region's historical ghosts drift through the poem, helping to universalize its experience and revealing an unexpected theme. The urge to test one's self, to do some single thing well, excites Smith in a way that is reminiscent of Ernest Hemingway, although Smith's language is more emotionally charged. The black woman in "Night Fishing for Blues" is a version of Smith's heroic figure; heroic not in worldly stature, but in the full giving of herself to the task at hand. What she *does* defines her; no explanations are necessary. Yet, in this poem, the woman is something more. She is part of a loose allegory, for the poem is a complex fable.

The scene is Fortress Monroe, Virginia, where the "big-jawed Bluefish" slam "into banked histories of rock/ pile." This place is near "where Jefferson Davis/ hunched in a harrowing cell." Already, before the central event is under way, Smith has built a context that links the present experience with the long shadow of the Civil War. Military metaphors identify the masses of fish as "convoys, a black army, blue/ stained sequins rank after rank." To this place the speaker has "come back"—but how far back?

The fishing begins in the unexpected company of three blacks: two men in "Superfly shirts" and "a grandmotherly obelisk." The speaker becomes involved in a pitched battle with the fish, and the intensity builds with the proliferation of the enemy and the fisherman's success: "I haul two, three at a time, torpedoes, moon-shiners. . . . " The woman watches, transfixed, "canting/ to Africa, a cluck in her throat, a chain/ song from the fisherman's house." The speaker cannot, or will not, take the time to understand this song or its meaning. He has reached a pinnacle of perfect action: "I know I have waited/ a whole life for this minute." The woman is fishing well, too, but the speaker pays no heed to her call for recognition: "*I ain't doing so bad/ for an old queen.*"

In a wild crescendo of hauling and slinging lines, the speaker feels for a moment that he has "caught the goddamndest/ Blue in the Atlantic. She screams: *Oh my God!*" He has hooked the woman's face. In an instant the ignored fellow-fisher has become—or has been mistaken for—prey and enemy. Readers have seen a tragic accident of innocence, ignorance, and selfishness, as well as an act of fate.

When the hook is removed, the woman and the speaker set to fishing once again. Now, their lines tangle; they have "caught each other but we go on for the blue blood of/ ghosts that thrash in the brain's empty room"—a contest of old habit with no real aim. Then the two admit that nothing else has been caught; the fish have ceased to bite; they can untangle themselves at last. Says the woman, "*Sons they done/ let us go.*" In her final action, the woman shows the others how to pack the caught fish. At dawn, as the speaker returns home,

> thousands of Blues fall from my head,
> falling with the gray Atlantic, and a pale veining light
> fills the road with sea-shadows that drift in figure
> eights, knot and snarl and draw me forward.

This vague epiphany is a movement forward in the speaker's moral life. "Night Fishing for Blues" is a compelling poem, a visually rich, taut narrative that suggests the reenactment of old passions and the redeeming power of passions of another order. The images of blue and gray, of weaponry, and of lines tangled and freed work their way through the poem with the hard tug of the inevitable.

Urgency is in every movement and in the hard rivets of sound and rhythm: "to pitch through tideturn and mudslur/ for fish with teeth like snapped sabers." This is torrential Smith in high gear, at the verge of excess, collapse, and presumption, but making a grandly successful world of words that is beyond the reach of craft alone.

A representative poem of return, "The Tire Hangs in the Woods" (*Dream Flights*), may be one of Smith's best. In it the speaker journeys back to a place where he first "went to dream" and where, later, he and his friends "stared, with our girls, into the sky." While in many of his poems Smith's persona returns only in memory, in this piece memory is spurred by the actual return to that "secret place" whose totem is the hanging tire. The stream of memories is clustered around this central image, first introduced in juxtaposition to "somebody's rubber" which is "hung on a berry vine."

Once in focus, the hanging tire becomes the "black holes" of lifted mouths in the Churchland Baptist Church, and thus an evocation of religious mystery and yearning. The generative image is then likened, in turn, to genitals, "Poe's pendulum," "an arc of blackness/ gathering the hung world in its gullet," and the "sexual O" of a girl's mouth. In its cumulative power, the hanging tire is the "Ghost-heart of this place" where the speaker's present and past have intersected and where imagination has given memory a reality of the highest order. This poem is, at bottom, a romantic poem. The unpromising woods behind a friend's house take the place of a Tintern Abbey or a lime-tree bower.

Under the spell of the occasion, the mute but mysteriously charged adolescent is fused with the articulate, worldly-wise adult who returns. It is as if they have each longed for this meeting, each shoved his feet in the circular space and swung out to a point in the woods' darkness where time vanishes. The poem conjures up the touching of a truth—a miraculous truth—as present and past meet. The truth is not reducible, however, to direct utterance: it is pure, vital feeling willed and caught by the transcendant imagination.

These woods are, simultaneously, a place of death and of hope. They hold "thickets of darkness" and are marked by a "dead-end" and by "stillness . . . ticking like throat rattle." Paradoxically, they are also the setting for the trials and triumphs of *rites de passage*: the fistfight over a girl and love's early, earnest promises. In the present, the speaker gives the tire a shove "and sure enough I hear the tick and all that was/ is, and a girl straightening her skirt walks/ smack against you and screams." Transitions like these (note the pronoun shift) keep the poem suspended between now and then, life and death, time and timelessness. The hanging tire—still, spinning, or swinging— mediates the poem's potentially erratic flights. In its haunting shape and motions the movement toward revelation takes place: "me in the tire spinning my childish words" to "swinging like a secret in the dark/ woods" to "I . . . swing in absolute black./ The whine of the rope is like a distant scream./ I think, so this is it. Really it." In Smith's conclusion, colloquial idiom stands in place of the traditional romantic's ecstatic shriek, shrunk down to the simile of the rope's whine.

"The Tire Hangs in the Woods" carries forward and refines many of Smith's stylistic habits. In it, he makes use of the long, complex sentence that sprawls over many lines and gains power by accumulation. The first fourteen lines of the poem comprise only two sentences, and many other sentences roll on for five or six lines. As the poem moves toward its conclusion, however, the sentences become more and more compact until the final movement, in which there are four sentences in three lines. This increased frequency of full stops is an effective device for moving the poem toward closure, toward the silence that is left to speak after the words have done all they can. Syntactical complexity in this poem does not fall into the knotty opacity of some of Smith's earlier work, nor are his rhythms here as clotted with spondaic bursts. Still, Smith is lavish in his use of sound patterns to release and spring strong rhythms. A line such as "gone dull as soap-scum, the husband grunting" is reminiscent of Gerard Manley Hopkins and of the strong-stress lines of Anglo-Saxon poetry.

The yard in which the tire hangs is, until Smith's poetry touches it, a very ordinary place: a place, in fact, to be overlooked, if not avoided. It is to traditional poetic settings just what many of Smith's central characters are to heroes: solitary, obscured, abused, just barely surviving. It is a dying place whose dignity Smith senses and celebrates. Smith's treatment of place, image, and self in this poem links "The Tire Hangs in the Woods" to the great American tradition. Here, the singing and soaring of Walt Whitman blend with the down-to-earth speaking of the birch-swinger, Robert Frost. Yet it is entirely his own, the kind of masterpiece that only Dave Smith could write.

Like many of the poems in *Cuba Night*, Smith's most mature collection, "Southern Crescent" can lay claim to being a new American masterpiece. It is a rich meditation etched out of narrative detail, dialogue, feeling-drenched thoughtfulness, and precise imagery. Riding the return train trip with his wife from her father's funeral, the poet records the desolate America through which only old trackbeds pass. The scene aggravates the sadness he feels for his wife's loss as its debris mixes with his guilt at never having liked his father-in-law. Still, searching for the right words, hovering near them, he manages to be of some use to his wife. They pass a poor shack where a man gives them the finger, his hovel lit up for Christmas, the lights flickering.

Only the speaker sees this, and he is forced to laugh. In explaining what happened to his wife, in their interchange of question and answer, they reach a new intimacy beyond the formalities of the grievous occasion. An unexpected perspective is gained, and an unexpected peace. Like Smith's best work, this is a small story perfectly told—or shown. The reader is left to feel the connection between the woman's father, the man along the tracks, and the ways in which our actions may unexpectedly fulfill another's needs.

Smith's work is so fully of his time (and place, one must add), and yet so fully transcendent. His is a voice that sometimes breaks stride with the patterns of standard written syntax as Smith grasps for the inclusive statement. He frequently sends parts of speech rolling into one another to form a redeemed mother tongue with some of the comfortable scaffolding torn away. Over and over again, however, Smith's magnetic cadences draw us in, focus our attention, lead us to resolve what we have rubbed up against. And then the voice is clear and penetrating. It is a voice that has a proper place in the timeless chorus.

Philip K. Jason

Other major works

LONG FICTION: *Onliness*, 1981.

NONFICTION: *Local Assays: On Contemporary American Poetry*, 1985.

ANTHOLOGY: *The Morrow Anthology of Younger American Poets*, 1985 (edited).

MISCELLANEOUS: *Southern Delights*, 1984.

Bibliography

Balakian, Peter. "Heroes of the Spirit: An Interview with Dave Smith." *Graham House Review* 6 (Spring, 1982): 48-72. Smith responds to questions about the large number of downtrodden characters in his work, his affinity with romantic tradition, his narrative impulse, and the complex issue of Smith's identity as a regional writer. Particularly useful are observations on the strong-stress rhythms of Anglo-Saxon poets and of Gerard Manley Hopkins as they influence Smith's own work.

Christensen, Paul. "Malignant Innocence." *Parnassus: Poetry in Review* 12 (Fall/Winter, 1984): 154-182. Christensen's is one of the most comprehensive examinations of Smith's work, discovering in the poet's voice a version of an American and Southern archetype mediating between youth and age, initiate and elder. Christensen provides a rich understanding of the mythic taproots of Smith's career and of his major themes.

Swiss, Thomas. " 'Unfold the Fullness': Dave Smith's Poetry and Fiction." *The Sewanee Review* 91 (Summer, 1983): 483-490. Swiss examines the architecture of *Dream Flights*, *Homage to Edgar Allan Poe*, and *In the House of the Judge,* collections that mark Smith's imaginative homecoming. In these and in his novel (*Onliness*), "Smith's strong attraction to violence, to stories of southern life marked by tragedy, is tempered by a vision which is fundamentally romantic."

Vendler, Helen. "Dave Smith." *The Music of What Happens: Poems, Poets, Critics.* Cambridge, Mass.: Harvard University Press, 1988. Vendler here modifies her original view that Smith is a regional Southern writer. She now argues, on the basis of *Goshawk, Antelope,* that he is "a distinguished allegorist of human experience." Vendler still admires the "torrential, impatient, exasperated" Smith whose "language is theatrical, even melodramatic." She notes Smith's clouded optimism, how he often "undoes his hopes as he utters them."

_____. "'Oh I Admire and Sorrow.'" In *Part of Nature, Part of Us: Modern American Poets.* Cambridge, Mass.: Harvard University Press, 1980. Originally published in *Parnassus* (Spring/Summer, 1977), this is the first extended statement by a major critic on Smith's work. Vendler enjoys the momentous energy in Smith's style, the range of his subjects, and his ambition. She praises especially his poems about the Civil War and about fishing. The essay examines several representative poems from Smith's earlier books.

Weigl, Bruce. "Forms of History and Self in Dave Smith's *Cuba Night.*" *Poet Lore* 85 (Winter, 1990/1991): 37-48. In examining the long poem "To Isle of Wight," Weigl stresses Smith's mythmaking ability and his ongoing struggle with his Southern heritage. Smith's romantic attachment to the Old South is complicated by his "struggling against those racist tendencies so subtly woven into the fabric of a culture he is at once part of and at odds with." Weigl explores the range of Smith's prosodic virtuosity. He notes Smith's active recognition of the need to "embrace the whole of who and what we are personally and historically."

_____, ed. *The Giver of Morning: On the Poetry of Dave Smith.* Birmingham, Ala.: Thunder City Press, 1982. This first slender collection of comment on Smith's work fittingly assesses the amazing first dozen years of his career. The lead essay by Robert DeMott develops Smith's notion that the poem is a moral act, examining his ambition and success. Other essays are by Weigl, Helen Vendler, and Terry Hummer. Included also is an interview conducted by H. A. Maxson.

STEVIE SMITH

Born: Hull, Yorkshire, England; September 20, 1902
Died: London, England; March 7, 1971

Principal poetry

A Good Time Was Had by All, 1937; *Tender Only to One*, 1938; *Mother, What Is Man?*, 1942; *Harold's Leap*, 1950; *Not Waving but Drowning*, 1957; *Selected Poems*, 1962; *The Frog Prince and Other Poems*, 1966; *The Best Beast*, 1969; *Scorpion and Other Poems*, 1972; *The Collected Poems of Stevie Smith*, 1981.

Other literary forms

Stevie Smith published three autobiographical novels, the best-received of which was her first, *Novel on Yellow Paper* (1936). A book of her drawings (with captions) called *Some Are More Human Than Others: Sketchbook* appeared in 1958. She also wrote short stories, essays, book reviews, and a one-act radio play.

Achievements

Smith's first novel received warm reviews in 1936, and she enjoyed a popularity that was sudden but relatively stable until the 1950's, when she fell out of fashion for a number of years. By the early 1960's, however, she was back in the public eye, and she remained popular, giving readings in which she sometimes sang her poems in an odd, singsong voice, until her death in 1971. She won the Cholmondeley Award for Poetry in 1966 and was awarded the Gold Medal for Poetry by Queen Elizabeth II in 1969.

Biography

Born Florence Margaret Smith, Stevie Smith belonged to a family made up of women from the time she was four, when her father disappeared to make a career for himself as a sailor. That year, 1906, she moved with her mother, sister, and aunt to a house on Avondale Road in the London suburb of Palmers Green. Smith lived there for the rest of her life. By 1924 her mother had died and her sister had moved to Suffolk. From then on, she shared the house with her adored Aunt Margaret, whom Smith affectionately called "the Lion Aunt."

Smith was not university educated and was never married. The nickname "Stevie," acquired when she was eighteen, is a reference to Steve Donaghue, a famous jockey. After her graduation from secretarial training college, she got a job as a private secretary at a publishing firm in 1923. She kept this job for thirty years, until she finally devoted herself to writing full time. She died of an inoperable brain tumor in 1971.

Analysis

Stevie Smith populated the margins of her poems with idiosyncratic drawings of swimmers and potted plants, ghosts and dogs, howling children and flirting couples. She doodled this art herself, when, as she explained, she was "not thinking too much. If I suddenly get caught by the doodle, I put more effort into it and end up calling it a drawing. I've got a whole collection in boxes. Some are on tiny bits of paper and drawn on telephone and memo pads." Smith insisted that the drawings be published with her poems, even though they do not technically "illustrate" the words on the page. Instead, she chose drawings which seemed to her to illustrate "the spirit or the idea in the poem."

In some ways, reading Smith's poetry is like fishing in one of her boxes filled with drawings on loose sheets and tiny bits of paper. As one moves from one drawing to another, one poem to another, the habits of her imagination become familiar. One can identify concerns (death, spinsterhood, sexuality) that appeared early and persisted late, name maneuvers (analysis of myth, parody of family roles) that recur again and again. One learns to recognize the spatialization of her impatience with categories through images of claustrophobia ("Souvenir de Monsieur Poop"), to expect her assumption of the proximity between love and hate ("I HATE THIS GIRL"), to look for the ways in which grief feeds the heart ("So to fatness come"). She moves back and forth among forms—from rapid stanzas with fixed rhyme schemes ("Nourish Me on an Egg," "Do Take Muriel Out") to long poems constructed of rhyming couplets ("The Passing Cloud," "The Hostage"), to looser, more narrative lines ("Dear Karl," "The Abominable Lake"). Yet the procedure from one poem to another—or one collection to another—does not present itself as neat linear development.

It is possible, however, to sketch out a set of preoccupations that Smith found compelling enough to return to throughout her career. One of the most conspicuous of these concerns is her investigation of inherited stories: fairy tales, narratives from the Bible, legends, and myths. Smith takes as her premise that material culture and literary culture constitute overlapping territories and is at pains in many of her poems to demonstrate the ways in which Western culture has organized itself in response to certain famous stories. In a late poem called "How Cruel Is the Story of Eve," for example, she argues the disturbing repercussions that Genesis, with its snake and its apple and its falling woman, set in motion: "What responsibility it has/ In history/ For cruelty." She goes on to address the collective resistance of skeptical readers, who might call her estimation of the effects of Eve's story exaggerated: what is the meaning of this legend, she asks, "if not/ To give blame to women most/ And most punishment?"

Smith is interested in stories and images that have saturated the cultural imagination of her society—stories that have defined and continue to influence the position of women, to shape attitudes about animals and wildness, to teach lessons about romance and relationships. Her poems refer back in literary history to William Blake (in her "Little Boy Sick") and across boundaries of genre when she appropriates fairy stories (in "The Frog Prince") or Arthurian legends (in "The Blue from Heaven"). As Smith points out, these stories color all human thought and are therefore important to anyone interested in disrupting some of those thoughts.

If Smith's exploration of inherited stories uncovers some of the ways in which culture grids according to gender or species, her survey of the roles inherited and negotiated within families reduces the scale of the inquiry while maintaining precise attention to instances of ill fit between individuals and the roles in which they find themselves. Adults are irked at having to give up the colors and excesses of childhood ("To Carry the Child"); children with absent fathers are cynical from babyhood ("Infant"). Women with husbands and children weep over frying pans ("Wretched Woman") or lash out—"You beastly child, I wish you had miscarried,/ You beastly husband, I wish I had never married" ("Lightly Bound")—while women who refuse to compromise themselves by investing in less-than-adequate relationships doubt their own decisions and worry about isolation: "All, all is isolation/ And every lovely limb's a desolation" ("Every Lovely Limb's a Desolation"). Because Smith delights in circling round a situation, sizing it up from all angles, there also are poems that defend solitude—speakers who argue, for example, that the best personal prescription is to "shun compromise/ Forget him and forget her" ("To the Tune of the Coventry Carol"), despite the risks of isolation. The typical attitude of a wife toward her wifehood, a mother toward her motherhood, or a child toward her childhood is discomfort and cynicism. Figures in Smith's poems are perpetually chafed by the discrepancy between their needs and the roles into which they believe they have been, one way or another, stuck.

For all her self-consciousness about cultural slots, Smith feels no obligation to limit her renditions of them to tragic monotones. Her preference for reading Agatha Christie novels in translation, for example, clearly indicates that she relished the humor of a poor fit. "If you read her in French," she once remarked, "you get a most exotic flavor, because there never was anything more English than the stuff she's writing. It's great fun that the translations are rather poor." Smith administered her critical, antic judgment to anything in sight, including her own loyalties—to Anglicanism, for example. While she remained personally loyal to the church her whole life, she cheerfully poked poetic fun at the awkward positions into which God perpetually forces His underlings.

She argues in one early poem, for example, that the human impulse to make dogs into pets has always been prompted by the unbearably cramped space of the will to which people find themselves restricted when they see, on the one hand, "Nature and Free Animals" and on the other hand God Himself. The poem begins with God's irate pronouncement that humans have committed the one moral error He cannot abide: "they have taught [dogs] to be servile . . . To be dependent touching and entertaining." Given human pride in legal systems that articulate and protect human rights, to complain that having "rights to be wronged/ And wrongs to be righted" insults a God-given wild dogginess might strike one as ludicrous. Yet Smith celebrates the possibility of uninhibited if violent life that animals represent while poking merciless fun at the ways in which human laws and orders actually trivialize death. The person God reprimands in this poem shoots back a feisty self-defense: "Nature and Free Animals/ Are all very fine," the speaker grants, but with them "on the one side/ And you on the other,/ I hardly know I'm alive." Squeezed from both directions, humans have no room to exercise either instinct or will, and it is precisely this unpleasant sensation that compels them to make dogs into pets. Having made her irreverent point, Smith undoubtedly chuckled at the anagrammatic joke of resisting God by putting a leash on His name spelled backwards.

Not being one to shy away from the unorthodox destinations toward which her unorthodox theories point her, Smith accepts the fact that her celebration of animals must accommodate violence. Thus, in a poem called "The Zoo," a lion "sits within his cage,/ Weeping tears of ruby rage" because he has been deprived of his natural capacity for violence. "His claws are blunt, his teeth fall out,/ No victim's flesh consoles his snout," the speaker reports sympathetically, concluding that it is no wonder that "his eyes are red/ Considering his talents are misused." Not neglecting the role God plays in this scenario, Smith gives Him due credit for having bestowed upon the lion "lovely teeth and claws/ So that he might eat little boys."

Oddly as such a compliment rings, other of Smith's treatments of animals suggest that it is not an entirely backhanded one. The reader may wince at being made politely to admire the lion's gift for making snacks of little boys, but when one is presented with the alternative of allying oneself with pet owners as depicted in poems such as "Jumbo," the crunching of bones begins to have a certain raw dignity:

> Jumbo, Jumbo, Jumbo darling, Jumbo come to Mother.
> But Jumbo wouldn't, he was a dog who simply wouldn't bother
> An ugly beast he was with drooping guts and filthy skin,
> It was quite wonderful how "mother" loved the ugly thing.

What Smith ridicules here is not the ugliness of Jumbo but rather the human compulsion to assert its will even over such a mangy beast. Jumbo's unwillingness to be bothered with his yodeling "mother" is a caustic enough comment on humans' clumsy interference with naturally occurring systems in which dogs, with wonderful indifference, eat dogs. Smith takes clear delight, however, in pushing the caricature one step further. In linking humans' desire to lord it over the likes of Jumbo with the sacred job of mothering, she insinuates that perhaps people are not as far removed from the harshness of nature as they wish to believe.

Crass as one may find such an intimation, Smith doggedly pursues the possibility that "the love of a mother for her child/ Is not necessarily a beautiful thing" ("A Mother's Hearse"). "Mother, if mother-love enclosure be," one child protests, "It were enough, my dear, not quite to hate me." While another Brontë-like waif trails about tapping at windowpanes and crying that "you have weaned me too soon, you must nurse me again," the speaker corrects the misapprehension of the unhappy ghost. Would she indeed "be happier if she were within?" Smith guesses not: "She is happier far where the night winds fall,/ And there are no doors and no windows at all" ("The Wanderer"). Just as God and beasts are understood to restrict the possibility for human action by having prior claim on both divine instruction and animal instinct, claustrophobia of the will looms over the enterprise of motherhood. What Smith seems, in fact, to be suggesting is the unattractive possibility that domination is one of the primary (and primal) motivations of humankind. The desire to dominate warps even the best-intentioned of projects—warps even love.

If mothers threaten to smother their little darlings, the conspicuous absence of paternal will allows children to rule in worlds of lopsided power. The gigantic quantity of control one presumes that parents wield over their toddlers, for example, dwindles rather rapidly in "Papa Love Baby" when the child administers judgment:

> I sat upright in my baby carriage
> And wished mama hadn't made such a foolish marriage.
> I tried to hide it, but it showed in my eyes unfortunately
> And a fortnight later papa ran away to sea.

Such radical shrinkage of adult presumption would be comic except for the child's disturbing admission that its keen and unforgiving wit carries with it the burden of responsibility: "I could not grieve/ But I think I was somewhat to blame."

Even more disturbing than this image of a preschooler having to shoulder the blame for her own abandonment, the articulate baby of "Papa Love Baby" tells her brief tale in a way that hints darkly at incest:

> What folly it is that daughters are always supposed to be
> In love with papa. It wasn't the case with me
> I couldn't take to him at all
> But he took to me
> What a sad fate to befall
> A child of three.

The shrinking line lengths of this stanza, which ends with an admission of her tender age, remind us of the inevitable physical advantage that even a stupid papa enjoys over his little girl. The sexual suggestiveness of the poem stays, by all means, at the level of nebulous suggestion: the father "took to" the child who did not "take to him." Yet the reader can hardly help wondering why such a turn of events would constitute a "sad fate" and why, despite the fact that the poem concerns itself primarily with the child's disdain for her "unrespected" father, its title should highlight the fact that in spite of that childish contempt, "Papa Love Baby."

The place children occupy in the various structures they find themselves to have inherited from adults constitutes one of Smith's most persistent preoccupations. *A Good Time Was Had by All*, her first published volume of poetry, begins and ends with poems that treat this issue. "The Hound of Ulster" and "Louise" frame the collection, typifying her vision of how the tension between adulthood and childhood shapes most human relationships. Despite what is normally thought of as the distance separating grownups from youngsters, she was at perpetual pains to point out their complicated proximity. "We are," as she once remarked, "as much the child's old age as he is our youth."

In "The Hound of Ulster," a "courteous stranger" urges a little boy to "take a look/ In the puppy shop," with its tantalizing array of dogs: "Could anything be merrier?" This adult script, rendered instantly suspect by the ease with which it fits the pattern parents proverbially warn their children against (never accept rides, candy, or invitations from strangers), does not, however, turn genuinely sinister until the last lines of the poem. Upon the child's polite inquiry regarding what it might be that "lurks in the gray/ Cold shadows at the back of the shop," the stranger warns that Cuchulain, the legendary Irish warrior also known as the Hound of Ulster, "lies tethered there . . . tethered by his golden hair."

As a child, the legend goes, Cuchulain killed a fierce dog that attacked him. The dog belonged to Chulain, who grieved over the death of his pet. Upon seeing the owner's grief, the child took it upon himself to be watchdog for Chulain until a new dog could be found. Thus he earned the name of Cuchulain, which translates to "the hound of Chulain." Cuchulain is also known as "the Hound of Ulster" in reference to the Ulster cycle of Gaelic literature.

If, as "Nature and Free Animals" suggests, humans make pets of dogs as a way of securing for themselves a modicum of space within which their wills—bounded by animals from below and God from above—can operate, the childhood feat of Cuchulain represents a double seizure of power. Having been mortally threatened by the dog, the child first dispenses with the beast that dares to trespass beyond his already-liberal bounds, then appropriates the bestial vigor of the dog—but only temporarily. In Smith's structure of competing territories between people and animals, then, Cuchulain's ability to negotiate his way between those territories ensures a much more spacious scope for the exercise of his strength.

In the poem, however, the hound stands as an image of paralyzed will, "tethered by his golden hair/ His eyes are closed and his lips are pale/ Hurry little boy he is not for sale." Having asked too much, the curious child is sent on his way. Only the poem's speaker, familiar with the puppy inventory and protective of the shop's tethered secret, seems to exercise any genuine control in this poem, and it is a control of exhibition. The reader's or the boy's access to dogs of the will is strictly limited to spectatorship, while the speaker extends the invitation and controls the display, blending the roles of poet and zookeeper.

"Louise," the final poem in *A Good Time Was Had by All*, repeats the eerie childhood experience described in "Papa Love Baby": articulate intellectual power darkened by traces of sexual powerlessness. Louise sits on a suitcase in the "suburban sitting room" of Mr. and Mrs. Tease, having traveled all over Europe with her mother but having "never been long enough in any nation/ Completely to unpack." The only words she speaks in the poem are wistful ones—"Oh if only I could stay/ Just for two weeks in one place." Her thoughts are quickly followed by her mother's advice, "Cheer up girlie," because they will indeed be stopping here for at least two weeks, as it will take Louise's father that long to come up with the money they need to move on. The poem (and the collection) thus ends on a note of bewilderment colored by the reader's response to the idea of hosts called "Mr and Mrs Tease": "The poor child sits in a mazy fit:/ Such a quick answer to a prayer/ Shakes one a bit." That the near-instantaneous answer to her wish should send Louise down the emotional path of something as complicated as a "mazy fit" demonstrates part of what makes Smith's abnormally astute, hyperintuitive children such disturbing combinations of sophistication and vulnerability. While their wishes conform to a formula of Cinderella simplicity, their intuitive gifts expose the problems inherent in reductive answers. A homesick child gets to stay in one house for two weeks, but how reassuring is it when that house is presided over by hosts by the name of "Mr. and Mrs. Tease"? The predicament of Louise, caught between her apparent powers of shaping the adult world and her childish susceptibility to the adults who nevertheless continue to rule it, haunts the body of Smith's work right up to her death.

Sometimes children manage to elude adult authority—exhibiting, as a poem such as " 'Duty Was His Lodestar' " gleefully demonstrates, particular skill in ducking out of verbal structures. As Smith herself has explained, the premise of this poem is a child's having "been told that duty is one's lodestar. But she is rebellious, this child, she will have none of it, so she says lobster instead of lodestar, and so makes a mock of it, and makes a monkey of the kind teacher." What we're presented with is "A song" (the poem's subtitle) in which speaker and lobster damage their relationship but then mend it and celebrate their reunification:

> Duty was my Lobster, my Lobster was she,
> And when I walked with my Lobster
> I was happy.
> But one day my Lobster and I fell out,
> And we did nothing but
> Rave and shout
>
> Rejoice, rejoice, Hallelujah, drink the flowing champagne,
> For my darling Lobster and I
> Are friends again.

The seriousness of duty as presented by adult to child is replaced by the celebration of relationship. Duty, meant to fix the child's respectful attention and serve as a sober guide, gives way to friendship, charged with gospel-choir enthusiasm.

In "Our Bog Is Dood," Smith parodies the limits of the religious imagination in a humorous anecdote about the difficulties of achieving interpretive consensus. In this poem, the children chanting "Our Bog is dood" reveal to the speaker that they know their Bog is dood "because we wish it so/ That is enough." Here, Smith lays out for the reader's amusement (or admiration; the two are neighboring concepts as far as she is concerned) the acts of sheer and reckless will by which both children and children of God collapse the distance between wish and belief, constructing verbal worlds that they inhabit with collective placidity until prodded to articulate the specifics of those worlds. "Then tell me, darling little ones," the speaker inquires, feigning innocence, "What's dood, suppose Bog is?" This flummoxes them, for though they give the irritating speaker an answer quick enough ("Just what we think it is"), they soon began arguing with one another, "for what was dood, and what their Bog/ They never could agree." The speaker proves to be exempt from this hostility not by virtue of having answers to the issues of Bog or dood but rather by a willingness to let the questions lie unanswered, to walk beside rather than into "the encroaching sea,/ The sea that soon should drown them all,/ That never yet drowned me."

Yet it is irrepressibility that Smith celebrates in the children of "To Carry the Child," which suggests that the labor of carrying a child does not end at birth or even when the baby learns to walk but rather at the nebulous juncture separating childhood from adulthood. In this poem she describes the moment of being allowed to stand on one's own two feet not as a moment of independence but of diminishment. Grownups are "frozen," while children are "easy in feeling, easily excessive/ And in excess powerful." Growing in this poem is an act not of growing up but of growing into, a process of entrapment: what can the poor child, then, do, "trapped in a grown-up car-

apace,/ But peer outside of his prison room/ With the eye of an anarchist?"
That Smith visualizes adults as a population of "handicapped" children speaks
to the vigor with which she gripped onto the idea of children as a models
for the independent imagination, gradually able to hold onto their mobility
of vision only from within a claustrophobic space.

If the encroaching rigidity of a carapace threatens to reduce the imaginative scope of a child to the rolling of eyeballs, then the architecture of domesticity constructs somewhat less restrictive but still idiosyncratic frames of
reference. In "Numbers," that such frames of reference limit the bounds of
the imagination becomes a matter of literal concern as well, since the information that fails to make its way into the boundaries of the poem's window
frames is the small fact that the speaker's house sits on a four-hundred-foot
cliff. The poem lists numbers of objects that romp about or spread outside
one house:

> A thousand and fifty-one waves
> Two hundred and thirty-one seagulls
> A cliff of four hundred feet
> Three miles of ploughed fields.

Four windows provide views of the waves and the fields, while one skylight
provides visual access to a square of sky. Thus the occupant of the house is
able to perceive a little bit of most of what lies beyond the walls of the
house: four windows' worth of the thousand and fifty-one waves; four windows' worth of the three miles of fields; one of the two hundred and thirty-
one seagulls. Only the four-hundred-foot cliff upon which the house sits is
invisible, suggesting that while frames of domestic reference may indeed offer access to snippets of the world at large, they ground themselves, obliv-
iously, on the precarious edges of things. What is disturbing about this poem
is not so much the cliff as the apparent unconsciousness with which the inhabitants of the house are perched upon it.

Harold's courage in not only confronting but in leaping such cliffs is what
stirs the admiring eulogy of acrophobic Harold in the title poem of Smith's
1950 collection, *Harold's Leap*. "Harold was always afraid to climb high,/
But something urged him on." Smith lavishes the energy of this poem not
on Harold's failure to accomplish anything beyond his own death-by-leap but
on the dizzying height of the rocks, the sheer will Harold mustered. That she
applauds his leap in spite of its futility suggests that since death is the project looming over all other projects anyway, to take one's death into one's
own legs constitutes the only possible act of frank courage.

This unblinking attitude toward death constitutes, in fact, one of the most
conspicuous stripes by which Smith's work may be recognized. Her stance
toward it veers from the dismissive to the devoted but always takes careful
account of its reliability as a solution. In "Death Bereaves Our Common

Mother, Nature Grieves for My Dead Brother," an early poem from *A Good Time Was Had by All*, death is noted as a shift in verb tense: "He was, I am." The subject is a dead lamb, a drawing of which (lying on its back with its four legs straight up like a dead bug) decorates the poem. This ditty on death is casual to the point of flippancy, despite its professed compassion— "Can I see lamb dead as mutton/ And not care a solitary button?" Lest one suspect that she reserves this easy tone for animals, Smith describes the death of one Major Spruce in another poem in the same volume in nearly identical terms. "It is a Major Spruce/ And he's grown such a bore, such a bore. . . . It was the Major Spruce./ He died. Didn't I tell you?" ("Progression").

In the title poem of *Tender Only to One*, Smith borrows a familiar convention of gooey sentimentality to demonstrate her feelings for death. Here, the petal-plucking speaker performs that hoary ritual of virginhood—loves me, loves me not—in order to discover the name of him to whom she is tender. In the end, the bald flower manages to convey the message: "Tender only to one,/ . . . His name, his name is Death." While it is difficult to tell precisely whether the speaker with such a quantity of tenderness to bestow is surprised by the outcome of her experiment, the ease with which the stanza contains the name of the beloved suggests that the news does not perturb her. The entire display, apparently, is presented for the reader's benefit.

Another poem in the same collection fancies death as stage two of a doctor's prescription. When the solicitous physician observes that "You are not looking at all well, my dear,/ In fact you are looking most awfully queer," my dear replies that yes, indeed, the pain is "more than I can bear, so give me some bromide." She will go away to the seashore, where the tides, naturally, will take care of the situation, carrying the speaker "beyond recovery" ("The Doctor"). "Come Death (I)," meanwhile, reprimands Christianity for teaching people to be brave in facing death, for courage is not even necessary. "Foolish illusion, what has Life to give?" the speaker inquires scornfully. "Why should man more fear Death than fear to live?" "From the Coptic" shapes the relationship between life and death into a narrative, as it describes three angels trying to coax clay into manhood. The first two angels promise the clay happiness, to little effect: "the red clay lay flat in the falling rain,/ Crying, I will stay clay and take no blame." Upon identifying himself as Death, however, the third angel produces immediate results: "I am Death, said the angel, and death is the end,/ I am Man, cries clay rising, and you are my friend."

Given the array of instances in which Smith warmly clasps the hand of death, that her most famous poem draws on the human dread of dying may say more about the kind of poems people wish to anthologize than it does about any alteration of her sensibility. "Not Waving but Drowning" is, however, the title poem of the 1957 collection, suggesting at the very least that

she wished her readers to take a look at this fable of how gestures of despair
and even catastrophe get mistaken for something else:

> Nobody heard him, the dead man,
> But still he lay moaning:
> I was much further out than you thought
> And not waving but drowning.

This poem, with its disturbing pun on panicky signal and casual acknowledgement, suggests that civilized systems of communication fail to accommodate emergencies. Schooled in polite noninterference and having no mecha-
nism for detecting anything outside the bounds of that inarticulate propriety,
one simply assumes that any waves at all are bound to be waves of greeting.
This sorry state of communicative affairs is further complicated by the fact
that the swimmer's ability to articulate difference is overwhelmed by the
very medium through which he swims: how can he be expected to clarify for
others the distinction between waves of greeting and waves of alarm when
all of his waves are immersed in even more and perpetual waves of water?
The enterprise seems doomed from the beginning.

Smith's refusal to desert these individual victims of isolation, her cocking
of the ear to the persistent voice of a dead man, offers a fragile consolation.
Prodded and coached by this plucky mistress of lost voices, her readers learn
at least to recognize the coarseness of their own powers of interpretation. If
one fails to make out the words of the drowned swimmer, one can at least
be assured that it is not for the lack of his having gurgled out a message.

Allyson Booth

Other major works

LONG FICTION: *Novel on Yellow Paper,* 1936; *Over the Frontier,* 1938; *The
Holiday,* 1949.

DRAWINGS: *Some Are More Human Than Others: Sketchbook,* 1958.

ANTHOLOGIES: *The Poet's Garden,* 1970; *The Batsford Book of Children's
Verse,* 1970; *Me Again: Uncollected Writings of Stevie Smith,* 1981 (edited by
Jack Barbera and William McBrien).

Bibliography

Barbera, Jack, and William McBrien. *Stevie: A Biography of Stevie Smith.*
    London: Heinemann, 1985. Barbera and McBrien's literary biography is
    well researched and very readable.
Bedient, Calvin. "Stevie Smith." In *Eight Contemporary Poets.* London: Ox-
    ford University Press, 1974. Bedient's study is useful for its discussion of
    individual poems.
Pumphrey, Martin. "Play, Fantasy, and Strange Laughter: Stevie Smith's Un-

comfortable Poetry." *Critical Quarterly* 28 (Autumn, 1986): 85-96. Pumphrey uses some of the basic assumptions of play theory to approach Smith's poems. He discusses her use of fairy-tale elements and describes her as an "anti-confessional" poet.

Sternlicht, Sanford. *Stevie Smith.* Boston: Twayne, 1990. Sternlicht's book is a good introduction to Smith's work. It includes chapters on her novels and nonfiction as well as chronological descriptions of Smith's development. The book contains a chronology of Smith's life and a selected bibliography.

Storey, Mark. "Why Stevie Smith Matters." *Critical Quarterly* 21 (Summer, 1979): 41-55. Storey analyzes the ways in which Smith makes critics uncomfortable: her apparent lack of development, the drawings, the singing voice, the simplicity.

Williams, Jonathan. "Much Further Out Than You Thought." *Parnassus: Poetry in Review* 2 (Spring/Summer, 1974): 105-127. This article is a meditation by a personal friend of Smith, most interesting for its quotations from a 1963 interview.

W. D. SNODGRASS

Born: Wilkinsburg, Pennsylvania; January 5, 1926

Principal poetry

Heart's Needle, 1959; *Gallows Songs*, 1967 (translation, with Lore Segal); *After Experience: Poems and Translations*, 1968; *Remains: Poems*, 1970 (as S. S. Gardons); *Miorita*, 1975 (translation); *The Führer Bunker*, 1977; *Six Troubadour Songs*, 1977 (translation); *Traditional Hungarian Songs*, 1978 (translation); *If Birds Build with Your Hair*, 1979; *The Boy Made of Meat*, 1983; *Magda Goebbels*, 1983; *D.D. Byrde Callyng Jennie Wrenn*, 1984; *A Locked House*, 1986; *Kinder Capers*, 1986; *Selected Poems, 1957-1987*, 1987; *W. D.'s Midnight Carnival*, 1988 (with paintings by DeLoss McGraw); *The Death of Cock Robin*, 1989 (with paintings by DeLoss McGraw).

Other literary forms

Although W. D. Snodgrass is known primarily as a poet, he has also published criticism and translations. *In Radical Pursuit: Critical Essays and Lectures* (1975) offers original perspectives on the works of Homer, Dante, William Shakespeare, Fyodor Dostoevski, and others, but its greatest interest lies in several essays in which Snodgrass follows Edgar Allan Poe in giving his own "philosophy of composition." His translations are diverse and interesting. *Gallows Songs* (1967) and the translations included in *After Experience* (1968), *Miorita* (1975), and *Six Troubadour Songs* (1977), offer a diverse selection of poetry which includes the Rumanian folk poem "Miorita" and works by Christian Morgenstern, Gérald de Nerval, Arthur Rimbaud, Rainer Maria Rilke, and Victor Hugo. They are effective English poems that remain faithful to the originals. Snodgrass also became interested in autobiographical sketches. Six of these have appeared in magazines and were planned for collection in an autobiographical book to be entitled *After Images*.

Achievements

Snodgrass' first book, *Heart's Needle*, won the Pulitzer Prize in 1960, but since then he has published sparingly. He once remarked that few American poets ever have a true "mature" period, and, perhaps to ensure such maturity, he has not rushed into print until he is thoroughly satisfied with what he has written. The result is that he has written comparatively little, although his work shows continued growth and variety. After the purely "confessional" poems of *Heart's Needle*, he developed distance and objectivity in *After Experience*, but without losing the human voice of the earlier volume. In *The Führer Bunker* he made a radical departure in an ambitious effort to draw believable portraits of Adolf Hitler and his principal associates during their final days. In *Selected Poems, 1957-1987* he collected the best poems from the three earlier volumes and added a number of new poems, which had mostly appeared in hard-to-find, limited editions. For his achievements he has received a number of poetry awards, and his poems are frequently included in anthologies.

Snodgrass' style has been equally innovative. Breaking from his teachers and from the prevailing trends of contemporary poetry, he chose a simple, lyrical style rather than the obscure, intellectual style his models provided. His language is plain, colloquial, and candid, and his images and symbols are drawn from nature or ordinary life and experience. In prosody he is a traditionalist, employing complex stanza forms and intricate rhyme schemes. In most of his poems the form is wedded to the content so that they work together to reveal the meaning. In addition, the poems are dramatic. They are concerned with real problems of this world—problems of identity, marriage, academia, art, war—and the persona is faced with a choice. What he decides is usually either the effect or the cause of the action. Snodgrass' reputation is secure because he speaks so directly about these universal problems.

Biography

William DeWitt Snodgrass was born in Wilkinsburg, Pennsylvania, on January 5, 1926. After a normal boyhood he enrolled at nearby Geneva College in 1944. Two years later, he was drafted into the Navy and sent to the Pacific. For the first time, he was truly on his own, away from home and familiar surroundings. World War II and its aftermath carved itself into his memory, and he would draw material from this experience for his poetry.

Following his discharge, two events occurred that were very important in his development as a poet: his marriage and his transfer to the University of Iowa to join the writers' workshop. At Iowa he found a group of talented students and skilled teachers who encouraged him to perfect his technique. Although he eventually broke with his teachers, who preferred highly intellectual poems following the traditions of the French Symbolists and the English Metaphysical poets, he would later tell an interviewer that he would never have written poetry if he had not gone there. He remained at Iowa for seven years, completing work for an undergraduate degree, an M.A., and an M.F.A. While his years there might have made him into a poet, they had a disastrous effect on his marriage, which ended in a divorce and separation from his young daughter in 1953. Snodgrass tried to adjust to this experience through his writing and through psychoanalysis; the result was the long poem "Heart's Needle," a two-and-a-half-year chronicle written while the events were taking place. The immediacy of the experience and the intensity of his feeling of loss help to give the poem its power.

After leaving the University of Iowa, Snodgrass was a college professor and writer-in-residence at several universities, including Cornell, Wayne State, and Syracuse, as well as a frequent participant in writing conferences. In 1979, he became Distinguished Visiting Professor of English at the University of Delaware in Newark.

Analysis

Henry David Thoreau's words in *Walden* (1854), "I should not talk so much about myself if there were anybody else whom I knew as well," could easily be applied to most of W. D. Snodgrass' early poetry. It has been called "confessional poetry" because of the intense focus on the poet's private life and concerns. Snodgrass, often labeled one of the founders of the confessional movement during the 1950's, used himself as the subject of his first volume of poetry; but while his poems are an examination of his own experience, he does not fall into the role of the moralist, making generalizations about what he has learned and suggesting how others can find happiness through his example. One might think that such poetry would be of little interest to anyone other than the poet. Why should the reader be interested in his problems of adjustment, which are not really extraordinary experiences? Other confessional poets have written about insanity, homosexuality, and suicide, but Snodgrass is concerned with mundane affairs, many having to do with the family—leaving home for the first time, the loss of innocence, illusions, and love. It is this quality of familiarity, however, which accounts for the appeal of Snodgrass' first volume.

The persona developed in the poems is honest, candid, and sincere. Snodgrass says in his essay "Finding a Poem":

> I am left with a very old-fashioned measure of a poem's worth—the depth of its sincerity. . . . Our only hope as artists is to continually ask ourselves, "Am I writing what I *really* think? Not what is acceptable; not what my favorite intellectual would think in this situation; not what I wish I felt. Only what I cannot help thinking."

Most important, the persona is human with a voice that one might expect to hear in the world. At times he is pompous, absurd, and silly, but the poetry reveals that he is aware of this weakness. He speaks in this world, about this world, and the reader is better able to understand his own problems of adjustment by living through them with the poet.

Several of the poems in *Heart's Needle* are concerned with identity, with discovering one's own name. Far from being a mere label or external description, a name expresses the profound reality of the being who carries it. In the Old Testament, creation is not completed until all things brought into existence have a name. Further, a name carries with it the possibility of knowledge. By reason of its nature a name imparts knowledge, and by one's name one can reveal to others who he is.

In "MHTIS . . . OU TIS," which is dedicated to R. M. Powell, Snodgrass' psychotherapist, he uses the story of Odysseus escaping from the Cyclops by a trick, identifying himself as no man (*ou tis*): "I had escaped, by trickery, as no man." This surrender of his identity, he realizes, is a much worse fate, and he implores his psychotherapist to restore him. He calls him his "dead blind guide" because Powell's strategy with him was to remain out of sight at all times, forcing Snodgrass to speak and clarify his problems in his own way and in his own words. The poem closes with these lines: "My dear blind guide, you lead me here to claim/ Still waters that will never wash my hand,/ To kneel by my old face and know my name."

The problem of a name occurs again in "A Cardinal." It is about a poet who goes into the woods for inspiration but finds that he cannot complete his verses because he cannot escape the crass, materialistic world even there. In the underbrush are "beer cans and lover's trash." He hears the squeal of the mill whistles, the whine of the freight cars, the trucks on the super-turnpike, and the chant of the air cadets marching. When he sees a cardinal above him with a green insect in his beak, he recognizes it as a confirmation of the evil that is in all things. Nature is "red in tooth and claw," or, as Snodgrass says it, "celebrate(s) this ordinal/ of the red beak and claw." In the bird-eat-insect, man-eat-man world in which he lives, he is foolish to think that he can write poetry, but then comes the turning point in the poem. He realizes his absurdity in blaming his lack of energy and creativity on something outside himself. When he hears the cardinal sing, he hears it as a song of natural self-assertion: "The world's not done to me;/ it is what I do." In asserting himself, the bird sings his name, confident in his identity, announcing it to the world: "I music out my name/ and what I tell is who/ in all the world I am."

Snodgrass announces his own name in "These Trees Stand. . . ." The line "Snodgrass is walking through the universe" is the natural final step in the process of a very personal poet naming his own name. It is his announcement that he has found his identity and will proclaim it to the whole universe. Snodgrass admits that it is "one of the most absurd and pompous things" he has ever heard, but pomposity has its place in poetry too, as long as one is aware that he is being pompous. He may not be able to reconcile estranged lovers or alter civilization's downward course, but he can wipe his glasses on his shirt to see himself and the world around him more clearly.

Being able to name one's own name is an important concern of a confessional poet such as Snodgrass; acceptance of loss is another. A number of his early poems are about loss. "Ten Days Leave" has a young soldier return to his home to find that his childhood is gone forever. In "Orpheus," he assumes a literary mask in a futile but necessary attempt at rescuing Eurydice, whose only crime was to love, which is impossible in a world ruled "by graft and debt." His most sustained and profound treatment of loss, however, is in the ten-poem sequence, "Heart's Needle."

The title of the poem comes from an old Irish story of a man who, when told of his daughter's death, says, "And an only daughter is the needle of the heart." For Snodgrass, the "Heart's Needle" is the loss of his daughter Cynthia through divorce. The poem in ten parts chronicles a two-and-a-half year period that he spent trying to adjust to this loss. The poem records the two battles that the poet has to wage. The first is external, the fight with his former wife which led to the divorce and which continued afterward: "Our states have stood so long at war." The other is the internal one of love and guilt. He loves his child and does not want to give her up, but in the succeeding years he marries again and has another child. His attempts to maintain a close relationship with Cynthia are only causing her further emotional harm. He is left with the dilemma: "I cannot fight/ or let her go."

Images of war, trapped animals, blasted lives, newly planted seeds, and withered flowers are interspersed with the passing of the seasons, which show the breakup of the marriage and the growing distance between him and his daughter. It is the imagery rather than any overt statement that shows the reader that the poet was able to maintain his identity and establish a workable relationship with his daughter. The poem begins in the winter but ends in the spring. The first poem is set within the context of the "cold war," with soldiers falling and freezing in the snows of Korea, but the final poem is set in the park, where Snodgrass and his daughter roast hot dogs and feed the swans. Earlier, there is an image of a fox with his paw in a trap, but in the final poem the red fox is trotting around bachelor pens. Together, Snodgrass and his daughter look at the bears imprisoned behind bars, but he has found a way to liberate himself through the knowledge that even though they are separated, "You are still my daughter."

Each part of the poem is carefully crafted; the third section is a good example. It is still early in the separation, but the unrest and pain are apparent. The poem begins with the image of two parents holding the hands of a child and together swinging the child over a puddle; but as soon as the hurdle is successfully cleared, they "stiffen and pull apart." He recalls that they were reading in the newspapers about the Korean War, about the cold and pain, about the land that was won and lost, and about the prisoners that were taken. The outcome of the battles, paralleling those of his own marriage, was satisfactory to no one. Then he returns to the child's hands and remembers that once in a playful game he tugged too hard, dislocating her wrist. The resolution of the poem recalls the decision that Solomon once had to make in a dispute over a child between two women, each claiming to be its true mother. Like the real mother in that story, Snodgrass offers to give his daughter up for her own good. The three episodes and the conclusion are closely tied together and reflect the inner struggle of the poet. Even the rhyme scheme (aabccb) reflects it. Each stanza begins with a couplet, but the second rhyme is delayed in each to emphasize the separation and loss recorded in the last line of each stanza. To reinforce this, the sixth line of each stanza is shortened from four feet to three.

The seasons mark the passing of time and the changing relationships of a man and his daughter. It is not a sentimental recital of events but rather an honest treatment of hurt, shared blame, and a growing awareness of their separateness. Snodgrass has said that a poet must write what he really thinks and feels, and in "Heart's Needle" he has apparently been successful.

Much of Snodgrass' life has been in the world of academe, and he has written about it in a number of his poems. "The Campus on the Hill" is based on his life while teaching at Cornell, but it could represent many colleges during the 1950's, marked by the complacency of the students in a world that seemed to be falling apart. "The Men's Room in the College Chapel" suggests an inversion of the traditional view of man's spiritual nature triumphing over his animal nature. Whereas earlier cultures retired to caves to carve totemic drawings to their "dark gods" or to the catacombs to write "pious mottos of resistance," the subversive humans of today go into the four gray walls to "scribble of sex and excrement,/ draw bestial pictures and sign their name."

In "April Inventory" the poet turns to himself as a teacher to list his own weaknesses and strengths. Spring is an appropriate season to watch the catalpa tree and the cherry blossom; but then, so quickly, the blossoms fall. The poet realizes that his own period of productivity will be similarly brief, and so far he has not accomplished much that can be measured. The recognition goes to "the solid scholars" who "get the degrees, the jobs, the dollars," but they also get ulcers. He cannot bring himself to read secondary sources, plot summaries, or memorize dates. He prefers to teach "Whitehead's notions," or a song of Gustav Mahler, or to show a child the colors of a luna moth. He prefers to learn "to name my own name," to give enjoyment to the woman he loves, and to ease an old man's dying. At the end of the poem he seems content that gentleness and loveliness are also important, and that these will survive where other accomplishments will fail.

Snodgrass does not often write satire, but he does in "The Examination." At first reading, the poem appears to be a sinister fantasy of black-robed figures with single eyes and ragged nails performing a lobotomy on a birdman named Garuda. It seems to have happened long ago and far away because they mark on the brain "with a crow's quill dipped into India ink" and use silver saws to cut away the dangerous areas, but they have an anesthetic, which enables them to remove the brain from the skull and stitch up the incision so that there is no seam. It is only in the last few stanzas that one realizes just who these black-robed figures are, who Garuda is, and what are some of the greatest failings in educational institutions. Snodgrass's professors are those who fear any challenge to their own established systems and thus clip Garuda's wings so that he can "fly no higher than his superiors fly." The irony is that even after being stripped of his powers of creative thought, of his reproductive powers, and his sensitivity, their "candidate" will return to thank them and become a black-robed professor himself. Snodgrass' experience has taught him that too often it is the academic conformist who receives the high grades and is encouraged to go on to graduate school, where he is again dutifully rewarded for recalling his professor's opinions and returning them to him in an examination.

A number of poems on specific paintings are also related to Snodgrass' teaching, since the idea for them grew out of his substituting, for one night, in an adult education course on art. He acknowledged that he knew very little about art, but that did not stop him from teaching that night or from writing poems about the paintings that interested him most. Snodgrass' poems on paintings raise questions that the viewer might have when first looking at a painting, and he offers a guide to understanding what the artist intended to say, a short course in art appreciation through the eyes of a novice art critic. Yet, he is writing poetry, not interpretive notes for a catalog of an art exhibition.

The five paintings he selects are carefully chosen and share a common theme. In the essay "Poems About Paintings," Snodgrass says that this theme was "the transformation of matter into energy." In "Matisse: 'The Red Studio,'" the paintings on the walls draw all the energy of the artist so that he disappears completely, leaving only a blank space at the center of the canvas: "His own room drank him." As his art objects become real, he becomes unreal and is transformed or absorbed into them. In "Vuillard: 'The Mother and Sister of the Artist,'" Snodgrass sees a devouring relationship between the mother and her daughter. All things in the room belong to her and even the child is being transformed into one of her mother's objects. The color of the daughter's dress is the same as the wallpaper behind her, and she appears to be vanishing into the wall. "Monet: 'Les Nympheas'" seems to absorb the viewer in the same way that it does the clouds, which appear to be beneath the lilies in the water.

The last two poems in the series are longer and add a wider significance to the theme. In "Manet: 'The Execution of the Emperor Maximilian,'" Snodgrass is concerned with the public's reaction to the work. Based on a historical event that deeply disturbed all of Europe, Édouard Manet's painting treated the execution with cold detachment. It is even comic in comparison to Francisco Goya's "The Executions of May 3, 1808," upon which it is based, and the public almost rioted when Manet's painting was first shown. Snodgrass' poem is a variation of the theme of "transformation of matter into energy" because its focus is on the energy aroused in the viewer.

In order to include the reaction to the painting in his poem, Snodgrass uses two voices. One, interspersed throughout the poem, gives a poetical prose account of the historical events of Maximilian's life and death. The major part of the poem is the voice of a viewer asking questions and making observations concerning the meaning of the painting in a colloquial, prosy sort of verse. He notes the strangeness of the three portrait groups. The dapper Mexican soldiers in the firing squad, "like ballet girls," are dressed in "natty" European uniforms. One of the soldiers, given a prominent place in the painting, looks "less like a penguin" than the others, but he seems totally unconcerned with what is happening as he inspects his gun. The second group, the peasants watching from the wall, are totally unconcerned with what is happening before their eyes. The viewer says, "Surely someone must come/ Declare significance, solve how these things relate/ To freedom, to their life's course, to eternity." The third group, Maximilian and the two men being shot with him, is the most perplexing because of their total insignificance in the painting. One cannot even be sure which one is the emperor: "Which IS the man? No doubt he should stand at the center,/ Yet who gets shot in a frock coat and sombrero?"

Snodgrass' interpretation of the painting emphasizes the complete breakdown of the order in the state as the Mexican soldiers are given European uniforms and the "Emperor of all the Firmament" is clad in a Mexican sombrero. The indifference of all the principals signals the rise of individualism and relativism where technology (the soldier inspecting his gun) is more important than a human life. By implication, Manet shows in his depiction of Maximilian's death the complete insignificance of any individual life. This bleak view of the world, perhaps more than anything else, caused the furor which first greeted the painting, and Snodgrass has captured it in his poem.

The last painting in the group, "Van Gogh: 'The Starry Night,'" is the clearest representation of pure energy engulfing matter, and Snodgrass emphasizes this in his poem with his contrast between the solidly built town and the swirling, rushing, violet sky overhead. The ordered rows of houses enclose the ordered lives within, while the sky is "a spume of ancient/ vacuum shuddering to reclaim/ its child." To capture the energy of the painting and to show its contrast between order and disorder, Snodgrass uses a form with two alternating styles: simple, orderly blocks of words describe the town, and wild, disorganized arrangements of words depict the sky. In addition, he has interspersed throughout the poem quotations from Vincent Van Gogh's letters, as if to remind the reader that behind the colors and shapes there was an energetic mind fervently at work. In this last poem on paintings, Snodgrass effectively combines form and content to create a remarkable poetic equivalent for the charged energy of the painting.

One theme that is pervasive in Snodgrass' poetry is man's inhumanity to man, especially as it is revealed in war. What is human nature when it is sorely tested? "After Experience Taught Me . . . " asks whether the most basic law is that of self-preservation. It is a poem using alternating voices, that of the philosopher Spinoza and that of a military drill officer. Contrasted as they are in language and approach, they nevertheless agree that man's ultimate wish is "to be, to act, to live." In the last stanza the poet's voice speaks for the first time to challenge them both: "What evil, what unspeakable crime/ Have you made your life worth?"

Snodgrass raises a similar question in "A Visitation," in which he allows the ghost of Adolf Eichmann to return and confront the speaker with the charge that had he been living in Eichmann's time and in his place he would have done the same things, for "You've chained men to a steel beam on command." Snodgrass is attempting to say that Eichmann was a human being who went terribly wrong, but he was a human being. One must remember that humans do have this possibility for evil, even great evil. To deny this possibility is to ignore a vital part of human nature, and so Eichmann's ghost returns to issue a warning.

Snodgrass' fullest treatment of the evil brought out by war is in *The Führer Bunker.* The book is an ambitious attempt to portray the last month of Adolf Hitler's life as he and his faithful followers huddle in the bunker preparing for their deaths. In twenty poems, Snodgrass allows them, through soliloquies and dramatic monologues, to reveal their true selves, which they have hidden from others and even from themselves. Moreover, for each speaker the poet selects a different verse form.

Contradictions, character flaws, and irrational acts are vividly portrayed. Magda Goebbels reveals her plan to kill herself and her six children "to preserve them from disloyalty." The contradiction inherent in killing someone to preserve him escapes her, and this is underscored by the modified villanelle form she uses. The complex but artificial verse form suits her character. Four of the poems are spoken by Albert Speer. He appears to be always in control; even his stanzas show the mind of the architect as each line becomes progressively longer to form a one-sided pyramid. Yet he is like his friend the cancer specialist who is unknowingly dying of cancer: "He neglects his knowing." Hermann Fegelein, Eva Braun's brother-in-law, deserves death for many reasons, but he is sentenced to die for the wrong reason, being accused of complicity in Himmler's treason. He says, "I wish/ to sweet shit Id of known." Eva considers her death as the reason for her living.

Adolf Hitler, quite predictably, is the most complex of the nine characters who are allowed to speak. He reveals his childhood fantasies, his sexual perversions, and his misplaced affections. He shows his concern for his dog Blondi, but he is oblivious to the torture and death of his own supporters, cursing them as being "Too gutless/ Even to get killed." On his last day, he is reckoning his place in history by the millions whose death he has caused. Hitler reveals himself as almost pure evil. He reveals almost nothing about himself that would explain the devotion his last followers give to him, unless it is the purity of his evil and his power to accomplish it.

The Führer Bunker is a remarkable work. It was published as "A Cycle of Poems in Progress," and Snodgrass has added fifty new poems to the twenty original ones. One of the later poems is "Magda Goebbels -30 April 1945," in which he creates a different, but nevertheless appropriate, verse form to fit her character. Based on the nursery rhyme the mother speaks to her six children to the tune of "Here we go round the mulberry bush," preparing them for the spoonful of cyanide that she is offering them: "This is the spoon we use to feed/ Men trapped in trouble or in need,/ When weakness or bad luck might lead/ Them to the hands of strangers."

Heinrich Himmler, head of the SS, is a new character added to the cast. Since he based his extermination policies on pseudoscientific experiments and theories, his three poems are written on graph paper in twenty-five-line acrostics. The first line begins with the letter A, and each subsequent line begins with the next letter of the alphabet, omitting only the X. The form shows a methodical but simplistic mind, one interested in logic and order but which fails to see the paradox of slaughtering millions to "benefit humanity." His poems are a defense of "the fully rational mind." Most of the poems, in fact, could be called rational defenses of each character's participation in this inhuman drama.

If Birds Build with Your Hair contains a series of realistic poems on nature in which Snodgrass celebrates elm trees, cheery saplings, owls, barns, and other things. "Old Apple Trees" is about the life and individuality shown in these old trees, which have deep roots and twisted but distinct characters. They are different from the pruned, identical nursery trees of his neighbor. The trees are like the battered lives of workmen "bent too long over desks, engines, benches," but they are still full of life. This life is shown by the poet's visit to the Greek bar with the belly dancers and the blessing by the trees when he returns. The trees stand as white-haired elders of Thebes swaying in a dance ritual to remind readers of the poem that they must cherish life and their own uniqueness.

A Locked House returns to the confessional poetry of *Heart's Needle*, with several poems describing the breakup of a marriage. "Mutability" is a villanelle that demonstrates that in human relationships the only certainty is that of change: "It was all different; that, at least, seemed sure." "One Last Time" reveals one last act of gentleness, when the one he had loved caressed him publicly, but that was three years earlier, and it was not repeated. One of the most beautiful and poignant poems in the series is "Old Jewelry." Bracelets, rings, and pins were bought as "emblems of what lasts." They were precious things with long histories, but now they are "Laid out for buyers in a glass showcase," another symbol of love that dies. The title poem, "A Locked House," shows that one can lock a house to keep it safe, but there is no such security for those who live within it. People care for and protect their possessions, but the love of man and wife is lost or stolen before either realizes it. Now, when he returns, the house still stands locked and untouched, because those who wished to protect it have abandoned it.

Snodgrass' poems on Cock Robin, in collaboration with painter DeLoss McGraw, seem to be a radical departure from his earlier work. The partnership began in 1982, when McGraw wrote to ask permission to use W. D. Snodgrass as a character in some color lithographs he was painting. These then led to a series of poems on Cock Robin in which "W. D." plays a key role. Normally, McGraw would first do the painting and Snodgrass would write a poem to accompany it. Since the project involved two of the poet's primary interests, poems on paintings and children's verse, the result was more a continuation rather than a break from his earlier poems. In college he had written many children's poems, and in 1962, he wrote "The Boy Made of Meat," which answers the question, "Why do they make boys always eat meat?" by listing a number of other foods that are more tasty and just as nutritious.

The Cock Robin poems are difficult to analyze because some are written in nonsense verse, as in "W. D., Don't Fear That Animal": "My hat leaps up when I behold/ A rhino in the sky;/ When crocodiles upon the wing/ Perch on my windowsill to sing." Such verse sounds like William Wordsworth recorded by Lewis Carroll. The more serious problem, however, is access to the paintings that prompted the poems, since they appeared in limited, hard-to-find editions. The book jacket of *Selected Poems, 1957-1987* has a color photograph, *W. D. Creates a Device for Escaping*, which helps to explain the references in the poem to the green foot and the red foot, the blood-red hands, and the arm and leg through the spokes of a wheel. W. D.'s burden in carrying the dead Cock Robin is reinforced by the references to Ixion's wheel and "Sisyface" (in reference to the mythical figure Sisyphus) rolling a stone. The paintings do not present a unified narrative, according to McGraw, but Snodgrass has attempted to give it some coherent structure. He calls Cock Robin a comic version of Orpheus, the god of song, and he is, at times, the alter ego of W. D. Based on the nursery rhyme, Snodgrass universalizes the symbol to represent the poet's life, death, and resurrection.

One poem, "The Charges Against Cock Robin," lists his crimes: the content and range of his songs, his dress, and his nonconformity. In other poems, his friends either desert him or practice character assassination. W. D. warns him of his enemies: "The Brutish are coming; the Brutish;/ The Rude-Coats with snares and bum-drumming!" When Cock Robin is killed, unlike the original poem, no one will accept the blame, not even the sparrow. W. D. does escape, however, disguised as Cock Robin, and near the end of the sequence, phoenixlike, he rises from the ashes.

Despite the fact that the series of poems deals with serious issues, Snodgrass never loses the light touch of nursery rhyme. One of the poems in *Kinder Capers*, "A Darkling Alphabet," appears to be a children's alphabet rhyme, but it helps the reader to understand Snodgrass' poetic credo. For the letter *Y* he writes: "*Y* is for Yes and that's/ the poet's word. He must affirm/

What makes ideacrats/ and joiners itchy. He can't squirm." The common thread in all of Snodgrass' poetry is an affirmation: the celebration of life, wholeness, and humanity. His achievements entitle him to a secure place in the literature of the twentieth century.

Edwin W. Williams

Other major works

NONFICTION: *In Radical Pursuit: Critical Essays and Lectures*, 1975; *Six Minnesinger Songs*, 1983 (translation); *The Four Seasons*, 1984 (translation).

Bibliography

Gatson, Paul L. *W. D. Snodgrass*. Boston: Twayne, 1978. The first book-length study of Snodgrass, this volume is the fullest available introduction to his life and works. It offers insightful studies of the major poems in Snodgrass' first three volumes. The text is supplemented by a chronology, notes, a select bibliography, and an index.

Goldstein, Laurence. *"The Führer Bunker* and the New Discourse About Nazism." *The Southern Review* 24 (Winter, 1988): 100-114. This article raises a concern that poems about Hitler might elevate him to the stature of a charismatic figure because of the absoluteness of his power. A review of the form and content of the most important poems, however, shows how completely Snodgrass has revealed the twisted nature of Hitler and his supporters.

Mazzaro, Jerome. "The Public Intimacy of W. D. Snodgrass." *Salmagundi* 19 (Spring, 1972): 96-111. Mazzaro shows that much of Snodgrass' early poetry has an existential philosophy, and he selects a number of poems to illustrate the themes of being, choice, self-deception, and despair. This existentialism is linked to his confessional mode to show how his poetry takes on a universality by its use of detail.

McClatchy, J. D. *White Paper on Contemporary American Poetry*. New York: Columbia University Press, 1989. A fellow poet writes a long chapter about the lyricism in Snodgrass' poetry. He sees the confessional mode as dominant in his early poems and then modified in the later works, but never abandoned.

Phillips, Robert. *The Confessional Poets*. Carbondale: Southern Illinois University Press, 1973. Phillips defines the confessional mode in modern American poetry and discusses the six major poets in the movement. Snodgrass' central role is shown through a close study of the poems in *Heart's Needle* and *Remains*. His success results from his sincerity and his ability to communicate personal loss while avoiding sentimentality.

Snodgrass, W. D. "W. D. Snodgrass: An Interview." Interview by Elizabeth Spires. *The American Poetry Review* 19 (July/August, 1990): 38-46. The interview covers a wide range of topics, from the origin of Snodgrass' confessional poetry to his intentions in writing *The Death of Cock Robin.* Snodgrass mentions a number of other poets who have influenced him in his development.

GARY SNYDER

Born: San Francisco, California; May 8, 1930

Principal poetry

Riprap, 1959; *Myths and Texts*, 1960; *Hop, Skip, and Jump*, 1964; *Nanao Knows*, 1964; *The Firing*, 1964; *Riprap, and Cold Mountain Poems*, 1965; *Six Sections from Mountains and Rivers Without End*, 1965; *A Range of Poems*, 1966; *Three Worlds, Three Realms, Six Roads*, 1966; *The Back Country*, 1967; *The Blue Sky*, 1969; *Sours of the Hills*, 1969; *Regarding Wave*, 1970; *Manzanita*, 1972; *The Fudo Trilogy: Spel Against Demons, Smokey the Bear Sutra, The California Water Plan*, 1973; *Turtle Island*, 1974; *All in the Family*, 1975; *Axe Handles*, 1983; *Left Out in the Rain: New Poems 1947-1986*, 1986.

Other literary forms

Gary Snyder's pioneering journal of personal environmental discovery, *Earth House Hold* (1969), was subtitled "Technical Notes and Queries To Fellow Dharma Revolutionaries," a descriptive invitation to examine the treasure of the planet and to consider how it might be employed for the benefit of all living species. It represents the culmination of the work Snyder began nearly two decades before when he conceived of a major in literature and anthropology at Reed College, and its somewhat tentative, propositional format expresses the spirit of a movement that recognized the destructive aspects of modern industrial society and sought alternative approaches to the questions of planetary survival. Although Snyder was sometimes referred to disparagingly as "a kind of patron saint of ecology" by critics trapped in more conventional social arrangements, his interest in the environment has proved to be as perceptive and enduring as his best poetry, and the publication of *The Practice of the Wild* (1990) has deepened the context of his interests, offering the wisdom and experience of a lifetime spent living in and thinking about the natural world. The book is a linked series of reflective essays, and its amiable, reasonable tone—similar to Snyder's conversational voice in his interviews, most notably those collected in *The Real Work: Interviews and Talks, 1964-1979* (1980)—permits the power of his intellectual insights, his scholarly investigations, and his political theories to reach an audience beyond the experts he hopes to equal in his argument. Combining energetic conviction and poetic eloquence, Snyder's essays are intended to be a "genuine teaching text" and "a meditation on what it means to be human." They demonstrate his philosophy of composition as it reveals a poetics of existence and have been written to stimulate "a broad range of people and provide them with historical, ecological and personal vision."

Achievements

Before "ecology" had become a password of political correctness, Gary Snyder was devising a program of study designed to create a language of environmental advocacy; after many trendy westerners had long since recoiled from the rigors of Eastern thought, Snyder completed a curriculum of apprenticeship in Japan and went on to develop an American version of Zen applicable to his locality; as Native American life and lore gradually seeped into the area of academic interest, Snyder continued his examinations of the primal tribal communities that lived in harmony with the North American land mass for pre-Columbian millennia and worked to apply their successes to contemporary life; while hippies and dropouts returned to the button-down corporate culture after a brief dalliance with a counterculture, Snyder built his own home at the center of a small community that endures as an example of a philosophical position in action; and most of all, while some of the other voices that arose during the post-"Howl" renaissance of the New American Poetry have become stale or quaint, Snyder's use of a clear, direct, colloquial but literature-responsive language made it possible for his concerns to reach, touch, and move a substantial audience through his poetry.

Snyder's varied interests have given him extensive material for his poems, but the appeal of his work is not dependent on a program calculated to educate or persuade. Much more than argument, the poetry is an outgrowth of the processes of Snyder's life—his work, his family, his intellectual and athletic interests, his cultural convictions, and his rapport with the landscape. He has been able to illustrate effectively how art and life can be intertwined in a reciprocal interchange that does not depend on academic procedures or traditional schools (while not denying their usefulness as well), an interchange that enriches and expands both realms, and in this he joins Herman Melville (the sailor), Henry David Thoreau (the naturalist), Ralph Waldo Emerson (the philosopher and teacher), and Walt Whitman (the celebrator) in a line of American artists whose work was, in a profound sense, the spiritual and aesthetic expression of their life's focus. *Turtle Island* won the Pulitzer Prize in 1975.

Biography

Gary Snyder was born in San Francisco in 1930, the son of Harold Alton and Lois Wilkie Snyder. His parents moved back to their native Pacific Northwest in 1932, where they settled on a dairy farm near Puget Sound in Washington. Snyder's mother moved to Portland, Oregon, to work as a newspaperwoman when Snyder was twelve, and reared Snyder and his younger sister Anthea as a single parent, insisting that Snyder commute downtown to attend Lincoln High, the most intellectually demanding school in the Portland system. In 1947, he received a scholarship to Reed College, where he devised a unique major in anthropology and literature. Early in his college years, he joined the outdoor groups the Mazamas and the Wilderness Society and took up backcountry hiking and skiing and snowpeak mountaineering. His first poems were published in the Reed College literary magazine. He lived in an old house shared by a dozen other students similarly interested in art and politics, including the poets Philip Whalen and Lew Welch, who became his close friends. Snyder wrote for *The Oregonian* newspaper at night and spent the summer of 1950 on an archaeological dig at old Fort Vancouver in Washington. At about that time, he was briefly married to Allison Gass, a fellow student.

Upon graduation from Reed, Snyder completed one semester of graduate studies in linguistics at Indiana University before transferring to the University of California at Berkeley to study Oriental languages. During the summers of the years he pursued graduate work, he took a job first as a fire-watcher in the Cascade mountains and later, after he was fired in the McCarthy-era hysteria of 1954, as a choker-setter for the Warm Springs Lumber Company. Utilizing skills in woodcutting he had learned from his family and neighbors, Snyder "was often supporting himself" in his student years, and his first accomplished poems were related to these experiences as well as to his work on a trail crew in Yosemite in 1955.

That fall, Snyder met Allen Ginsberg and Jack Kerouac and became involved in the exploding art scene in San Francisco, where he took part in the historic Six Gallery reading where Ginsberg read "Howl" in public for the first time. Snyder followed this extraordinary performance with his own poetry in a very different vein and was also successful in capturing the attention of the audience. He and Kerouac shared a cabin in Mill Valley, California, through that winter and spring, and then Snyder traveled to Kyoto, Japan, to take up residence in a Zen temple, beginning a twelve-year sojourn in Japan that was broken by a nine-month hitch as a crewman on the tanker *Sappa Creek* and a brief return to San Francisco in 1958. His translations from the Chinese poet Han-shan, who lived in the seventh century, were published in the *Evergreen Review* in 1958 as "Cold Mountain Poems," and his first collection, *Riprap*, was published by Cid Corman's Origin Press in Japan in 1959.

Working as a part-time translator and researcher of Buddhist texts, Snyder eventually became a student of Rinzai Zen under Oda Sesso, Roshi (master), and established contacts with activist groups concerned with ecology, women's issues, and world peace. His next collection, *Myths and Texts*, was published in 1960, the same year he married the poet Joanne Kyger. In 1962, he traveled to India with Ginsberg, Peter Orlovsky, and Kyger, and his association with the poet Nanao Sakaki drew him into artistic circles in Tokyo in 1964. He returned to the United States to teach at Berkeley in 1965, won a Bollingen grant, and returned to Japan. His marriage with Kyger was over when he met Masa Uehara, a graduate student in English, and they were married in 1967.

With his wife and his son, Kai, who was born in Kyoto, Snyder returned to the Western Hemisphere, settling in the northern Sierra Nevada mountains, where he built a home (called "Kitkitdizze," meaning "mountain misery") in 1970 with a crew of friends. His first book of poems reflecting his commitment to his native country, *Turtle Island* (from an old Native American name for the continent), was published in 1974 and won the Pulitzer Prize. During this time, Snyder was traveling to universities three or four months a year to read poetry, working on the needs of his immediate mountain community, and serving the state of California as the chairman of its Arts Council. At the end of the decade, he published a collection called *The Real Work: Interviews and Talks, 1964-1979* (1980), and in 1983, he published *Axe Handles*, poems written during the previous ten years. In 1985, he joined the English department at the University of California at Davis, where he taught literature and ecological matters, and he began to travel widely, visiting Hawaii, Alaska, China, and parts of Europe to speak "on the specifics of Buddhist meditation, ecological practice, language and poetics, and bioregional politics." The poems he had written but left uncollected were published in *Left Out in the Rain: New Poems 1947-1985*. In 1988, he was divorced from Masa Uehara and married Carole Koda, and in 1990, he completed a book that presented a program for personal renewal and planetary conservation called *The Practice of the Wild*. That same year, a compilation of comments, reminiscences, poems, and assorted other statements was published by the Sierra Club under the title *Gary Snyder: Dimensions of a Life* in celebration of the poet's sixtieth birthday. In his seventh decade, Snyder continues work on his "poem of process," *Mountains and Rivers Without End*, and trains students at Davis to deal with environmental crises. The hero-figure Kerouac patterned after Snyder in *The Dharma Bums* (1958), "Japhy Ryder," has become the source of wisdom, the poet Gary Snyder, now grown into an elder of the tribe.

Analysis

Among many evocative statements about his life and work, a particularly crucial one is Gary Snyder's claim that

> As a poet, I hold the most archaic values on earth. They go back to the late Paleolithic; the fertility of the soil, the magic of animals; the power-vision in solitude, the terrifying initiation and rebirth; the love and ecstasy of the dance, the common work of the tribe.

The social and philosophical principles he has expressed are the fundamental credo of his convictions as a man and an artist. He uses the word "archaic" to suggest "primal" or "original"—the archetype or first pattern from which others may evolve. His citation of the late Paleolithic era as source-ground stems from his belief that essential lessons concerning human consciousness have been learned and then lost. Thus Snyder devotes much time to the study of ancient (and primitive) cultures. The values he holds stand behind and direct his poetry, as it is drawn from his studies and experiences. His values include a respect for land as the source of life and the means of sustaining it; a respect for all sentient creatures and for the animalistic instincts of humans; a recognition of the necessity for the artist to resist social pressure in order to discover and develop power from within; an acknowledgement of the necessity for participation in both communal ritual and individual exploration of the depths of the subconscious to transcend the mundane and risk the extraordinary; an acceptance of the body and the senses—the physical capabilities, pleasures, and demands of the skin; and a feeling for the shared labor of the community, another version of "the real work" that unites the individual with a larger sense and source of meaning. Neither the poet as solitary singer nor as enlightened visionary is sufficient without the complex of relationships that joins the local, the bioregional, and ultimately the planetary in an interdependent chain of reliance, support, and enlightened use of resources. It is with these values in mind that Snyder defines an ethical life as one that "is mindful, mannerly and has style," an attitude that is crucial to the accomplishment of "the real work."

Each of these precepts has an important analogue in the technical execution of the poems themselves. As Jerome Rothenberg has observed, "where I continue to see him best is as he emerges from his poems." Poetically, then, "the fertility of the soil" is worthless without the labor that brings it to fruition, and as Snyder has commented, "the rhythms of my poems follow the rhythms of the physical work I'm doing and life I'm leading at any given time—which makes the music in my head which creates the line." The linkage between the rhythmic movement of the body, the larger rhythmic cycles of the natural world, and the structure of words in a particular poem follows the precepts that Charles Olson prescribed in the landmark "Projective Verse" essay (1950), and Snyder, like Ginsberg, Robert Creeley, and others, has always favored the creation of a particular shape or form to suit the purpose of the poem under attentive development. The rhythms of a particular poem are derived from an "energy-mind-field-dance" that, in turn, often results from labor designed to capitalize on the life of the earth.

Similarly, when Snyder speaks of "the magic of animals," he is identifying one of his central subjects, and the images of many of his poems are based on his observations of animals in the wild. The importance of wilderness and the manner in which animals seem to interact instinctively with their natural surroundings are, for Snyder, keys to his conception of freedom. The magic of their existence is part of a mystery that humans need to penetrate. Thus, as image and subject-animals and their ways are an important part of the "etiquette of freedom" Snyder's work serves.

The concept of the "power vision in solitude" is derived from both the shamanistic practices that Snyder has studied in primitive societies and the varieties of meditation he has explored in his research into and expressions of Buddhist thought. Its immediate consequence in poetry is the necessity for developing a singular, distinct voice, a language with which one is comfortable, and a style that is true to the artist's entire life. For Snyder, this has meant learning to control the mood of a poem through tonal modulation, matching mood to subject and arranging sequences of poems that can sustain visionary power as well as intimate personal reflection. "The terrifying initiation and rebirth" is a corollary of the power vision. It implies that once a singular voice has been established, it must be followed according to the patterns of its impulsive organization—in other words, to its points of origin in the subconscious. Snyder speaks of the unconscious as "our inner wilderness areas," and sees in the "depths of the mind" the ultimate source of the imagination. The exploration of the wilderness within is vital to the image-making function of poetry.

The "love and ecstasy" Snyder speaks of stems from the revolt that Snyder and his colleagues led against the stiff, formal, distant academic poetry favored by critics in the 1950's, and its application has been to influence the colloquial nature of his language, to encourage the use of primitive techniques such as chant to alter perceptive states, to permit the inclusion of casual data from ordinary existence to inform the poem, and, most of all, to confront the most personal of subjects with honesty and self-awareness. There is a discernible narrative consciousness present in Snyder's poetry even when he avoids—as he generally does—personal pronouns and definite articles. Yet his resistance to cultural authority is balanced by his praise for the "common work of the tribe," the artistic accomplishment that he treasures. As he has said, "I feel very strongly that poetry also exists as part of a tradition, and is not simply a matter of only private and personal vision." Explaining his interests in Ezra Pound, William Carlos Williams, Wallace Stevens, John Milton, and others, Snyder says he wants "to know *what* has been done, and to see *how* it has been done. That in a sense is true craft." Almost paradoxically, considering his emphasis on originality, he advocates (and practices) extensive examination of multidisciplinary learning, explaining that knowledge of the past saves one "the trouble of having to repeat things that others have done that need not be done again. And then also he knows when he writes a poem that has never been written before."

Snyder's first two collections, *Riprap* and *Cold Mountain Poems*—which were published together initially in 1965 and reached a "fourth incarnation" in 1990—are evidence of the writing and thinking that Snyder had been doing through the mid-1950's. *Riprap* took shape while Snyder was working on a backcountry trail crew in 1955, and its title is at first a description of "stone laid on steep, slick rock to make a trail for horses in the mountains," then a symbol of the interlinkage of objects in a region and a figure for the placement of words in a poetic structure. It serves to connect language and action, reflective thought and the work that generates it. The poems in the collection are dedicated to the men Snyder worked with, the "community" of cohesion and effort he joined, men who knew the requirements of the land and who transmitted their skills through demonstration. *Riprap* includes elements of the oral tradition Snyder intersected, and the title "celebrates the work of the hands" while some of the poems "run the risk of invisibility" since they tried "for surface simplicity set with unsettling depths." Poems like "Above Pate Valley" and "Piute Creek" begin with direct description of landscape and move toward an almost cosmic perspective concerning the passage of time across the land over geological epochs. The specific and the eternal coalesce:

> Hill beyond hill, folded and twisted
> Tough trees crammed
> In thin stone fractures
> A huge moon on it all, is too much.
> The mind wanders. A million
> Summers, night air still and the rocks
> Warm. Sky over endless mountains.
> All the junk that goes with being human
> Drops away, hard rock wavers.

Poetry, as Snyder put it in "Burning: No. 13" from *Myths and Texts*, is "a riprap on the slick road of metaphysics," helping one find meaning and explaining why one reads "Milton by Firelight" (the title of another poem) and finds new versions of hell and "the wheeling sky" in the Sierras.

The *Cold Mountain Poems* are "translations" (in the Poundian sense) from Han-shan, a hermit and poet of the T'ang dynasty, and they represent Snyder's identification with a kind of nature prophet at home in the wild as well as his inclination to isolate himself from those aspects of American (or Western) society he found abhorrent until he could fashion a program to combat the social ills he identified. As in most effective translations, there is a correspondence in sensibility between the two artists, and Snyder's comfort with the backcountry, as well as his growing sense of a cross-cultural and transepochal perspective, may be seen in lines like

> Thin grass does for a mattress,
> The blue sky makes a good quilt.
> Happy with a stone underhead
> Let heaven and earth go about their changes.

Calling Han-shan a "mountain madman" or "ragged hermit," Snyder expresses through the translations his admiration for a kind of independence, self-possession, and mindful alertness that he saw as a necessity for psychic survival in the Cold War era, a husbanding of strength to prepare for a return to the social struggle. "Mind solid and sharp," he says, he is gaining the vision to "honor this priceless natural treasure"—the world around him ("the whole clear cloudless sky")—and the insight ("sunk deep in the flesh") to understand the complementary wonder within.

Written at about the same time as *Riprap, Myths and Texts* is Snyder's first attempt to organize his ideas into an evolving, complex structural framework. In it, Snyder's wilderness experience is amplified by the use of Pacific Coast Indian texts, which are set as a kind of corrective for the exploitation and destruction of the environment that Snyder sees as the result of misguided American-European approaches to nature. The crux of the matter is the failure of Judeo-Christian culture to recognize the inherent sacredness of the land, and Snyder uses what he feels is a kind of Buddhist compassion and a Native American empathy as a corrective thrust. The three books of the collection are called "Logging"—which uses the lumber industry as an example of "technological drivenness" that destroys resources and shows no respect for the symbolic or ritualistic aspect of the living wilderness; "Hunting"—which explores the intricate relationship between the hunter and the quarry (and between mind and body) in primitive societies; and "Burning"— which is somewhat less accessible in its intriguing attempt to find or chart a symbolic synthesis that integrates the mythic material Snyder has been presenting into a universal vision of timeless cycles of destruction and rebirth.

As Snyder defines the terms, in a preliminary fashion, the myths and texts are the "two sources of human knowledge—symbols and sense-impressions." The larger context at which he aims—the "one whole thing"—is built on the power of individual poems, and among the best are ones like "Logging: No. 8," in which the logged ground is likened to a battlefield after a massacre; "Logging: No. 3," in which the lodgepole pine is treated as an emblem of nature's enduring vitality; "Logging: No. 13," in which a fire-watcher reports a fire ("T36N R16E S25/ Is burning. Far to the west") and seems more interested in the abstract beauty of the landscape than in any specific situation; and among several hunting songs, the exceptional "No. 6," which carries the dedication, "*this poem is for bear.*"

Snyder read the original version of "The Woman who Married a Bear" in an anthropology text in Reed College and was fascinated by the interaction of the human and animal cultures. He devotes a chapter to the story in *The Practice of the Wild* (1990), lamenting that "the bears are being killed, the humans are everywhere, and the green world is being unraveled and shredded and burned by the spreading of a gray world that seems to have no end." His poem is placed at the convergence of several cultures and is structured by the different speaking "voices"—not specifically identified but clear from tone and context. First, in a quote from the anthropological text, the bear speaks: "As for me I am a child of the god of the mountains." Then, a field scientist, observing the data:

> You can see
> Huckleberries in bearshit if you
> Look, this time of year
> If I sneak up on the bear
> It will grunt and run.

This relatively matter-of-fact, outside position is replaced by a tale of the girl who married a bear: "In a house under the mountain/ She gave birth to slick dark children/ With sharp teeth, and lived in the hollow/ Mountain many years." A shift has been made to the Native American culture, and what follows is the burden of the legend, as the girl's tribe goes to reclaim her. The next voice is the hunter addressing the bear:

> honey-eater
> forest apple
> light-foot
> Old man in the fur coat, Bear! come out!
> Die of your own choice!

Now the poet enters, turning the tale (text) into poetry (myth): "Twelve species north of Mexico/ Sucking their paws in the long winter/ Tearing the high-strung caches down/ Whining, crying, jacking off." Then the tale continues, as the girl's brothers "cornered him in the rocks," and finally the "voice" of the bear-spirit speaks, as through a shaman perhaps, in the "Song of the snared bear":

> "Give me my belt.
> "I am near death.
> "I came from the mountain caves
> "At the headwaters,
> "The small streams there
> "Are all dried up.

In a deft conclusion, Snyder reduces the dramatic tension by the interposition of the disarmingly personal. As if inspired by the story, he begins to imagine himself a part of the Paleolithic hunter culture: "I think I'll go hunt bears." Yet he is too solidly grounded in reality to go beyond a reading of the text: "Why shit Snyder,/ You couldn't hit a bear in the ass/ with a handful of rice." Although, of course, in the poem, he has hit the target squarely by assimilating the different voices (as different strands of culture) into his own modern version of the myth.

During the 1950's, Snyder began work on a "poem of process" somewhat akin to Pound's *Cantos* (1970) or Williams' *Paterson* (5 vols., 1946-1958) that he called *Mountains and Rivers without End*. The first division was published in six sections in 1965, and Snyder explained that it was structured by "very close correspondences between the external and internal landscape," and that he was moving back and forth, "breaking down the limit between the psychic and physical," as Tzetvan Todorov puts it in *The Fantastic* (1973). The title was taken from a Chinese scroll that progressed horizontally, apparently into a future "without end." Other sections have appeared through the years in various journals, and Snyder in conversation with David Robertson in 1989 remarked that the finished product would take a new shape and that the poems should be treated individually until the sequence is completed. Snyder has conceded that the separate sections contain a great deal of information, but hopes that eventually "there will be enough reverberations and echoes from the various sections so that it will be self-informing." In discussing his method, he has emphasized the use of a *ku* or key phrase in each section, such as the third line from the last in "Bubbs Creek Haircut," which has the phrase "double mirror waver"—an image of infinite regression and reflection that is at the crux of Buddhist thinking concerning mutual interdependence. This is similar to his technique of raising questions in one section that are answered in a later one, and Snyder has stressed the necessity for creating a sufficient body of the poem before the total framework could be seen, even by the poet.

With *Regarding Wave*, Snyder's work turned from the mythic and philosophical toward the intimate and immediately personal. He had begun a family (his son Kai was born in 1968) and returned to the United States, and the poems recall his last days in the Far East and his sense of how he had to proceed after returning to his native land at a time of strife and turmoil. The family poems are celebratory, written in wonder, open and exuberant in the first flush of parenthood, expressing his delight with his wife Masa and their infant son. There are poems that are like meditations on the sensual: "Song of the View," "Song of the Tangle," or "Song of the Taste," and poems that are drawn from the experience of rearing a child, like "The Bed in the Sky" or "Kai, Today," which is an awestruck reflection on the act of birth, or the supra-mundane "Not Leaving the House," in which Snyder admits "When Kai is born/ I quit going out," and justifies his inward angle of view by concluding "From dawn til late at night/ making a new world of ourselves/ around this life."

Yet since Snyder found in his return to the New World beyond "ourselves" that the political situation in America in 1969 was troubling ("Off the coast of Oregon/ The radio is full of hate and anger"), and even before landing was warned that "beards don't make money," he began to plan the outlines of a life as a poet and activist in the United States. The effects of his action become more clear in his next collection, but the cast of his mind is apparent in the transitional "What You Should Know to Be a Poet," which calls together what he had learned from his life to that point:

all you can about animals as persons
the names of trees and flowers and weeds
names of stars, and the movements of the planets
and the moon.

your own six senses, with a watchful and elegant mind

and then blends it with a kind of resolution to confront the bestial nature of humans in order to prepare to engage the evil at large in the world, as expressed in the crucial central stanza beginning, "kiss the ass of the devil." From that point, the poem alternates positive aspects of existence ("& then love the human: wives   husbands   and friends") with an acceptance of the trials and burdens of life ("long dry hours of dull work swallowed and accepted/ and livd with and finally lovd") until it concludes with an unsettling sense of the future, "real danger.   gambles.   and the edge of death."

Snyder's ambivalent feelings about living in America are again expressed in the hilarious "Smokey the Bear Sutra," in which the familiar symbol of the forest service is depicted as a kind of Asiatic avenging demon protecting the environment and resisting polluters. Published in 1973 as a part of *The Fudo Trilogy*—a pamphlet that included "The California Water Plan" (a section of *Mountains and Rivers*) and "Spel Against Demons"—it combines Snyder's serious concerns about the environment and his continuing pursuit of Asiatic culture with his characteristically engaging high good humor. The chant, "Drown their butts; soak their butts" is presented in mock seriousness as a mantra of righteousness, while Smokey is depicted more as a lovable child's pet than the fierce scourge of evil that the archetype suggests. The comic conception works to keep Snyder's considerable anger under control, so that he does not turn his poetry into polemic. By then fully involved in the bioregional movement and committed to the local community of San Juan Ridge, where he had built a home, Snyder in the early 1970's followed a dual course in his poetry. The overarching theme of his work was to protect and preserve "Turtle Island—the old/new name for the continent, based on many creation myths," and it was expressed in "poems that "speak of place, and the energy-pathways that sustain life" and in poems that decry the forces of destruction unleashed by the stupidity of "demonic killers" who perpetrate "aimless executions and slaughterings."

These poems were published under the title *Turtle Island* (1974), sold more than 100,000 copies, and won the Pulitzer Prize. Among the most memorable poems Snyder has written, the ones that explore the "energy pathways" sustaining life include the unique "The Bath"—a Whitmanesque rapture in appreciation of the body that challenges the latent Puritanism and fear of the skin in American society by describing in loving detail the physical wonder of his son, his wife, and himself in a bath. The sheer glory of the body glowing with health and the radiant reflection of the natural world around them build toward a feeling of immense physical satisfaction and then toward a complementary feeling of metaphysical well-being. The frankness of the language may be difficult for some readers, but Snyder's tasteful, delicate, and comfortable handling of it makes his declaration "this is our body," an echoing chorus, an assertion of religious appreciation. In an even more directly thankful mode, the translation of a Mohawk "Prayer for the Great Family" unites the basic elements of the cosmos in a linked series of gem-like depictions, concluding with one of Snyder's essential ideas: that there is an infinite space "beyond all powers and thoughts/ and yet is within us-/ Grandfather Space/ The Mind is his Wife." Other expressions of "eternal delight" include "By Frazier Creek Falls," "Source," and "The Dazzle," as well as many poems in the book's last section, a kind of basic history primer called "For the Children," that convey considerable emotion without lapsing into obvious emotional tugging.

The more overtly political poems and sketches tend to be somber, frequently employing a litany of statistics to convey grim information that needs little additional comment, but in "The Call of the Wild," Snyder's anger is projected in language purposefully charged with judgmental fervor. Avoiding easy partisanship, Snyder condemns, first, "ex acid-heads" who have opted for "forever blissful sexless highs" and hidden in fear from what is interesting about life. His image of people missing the point of everything by living in trendy "Geodesic domes, that/ Were stuck like warts/ In the woods" is as devastating as his cartoon conception of advanced technology declaring "a war against earth" waged by pilots with "their women beside them/ in bouffant hairdos/ putting nail-polish on the/ gunship cannon-buttons." Snyder did not publish another book of poems until 1983, when *Axe Handles* was issued by North Point Press.

The poems in *Axe Handles* have a reflective tone, moving inward toward the life Snyder has been leading in his local community, to which he dedicated the collection. His concerns do not change, but in a return to the more spare, lyrical poems of *Riprap*, Snyder condenses and focuses his ideas into "firm, clean lines of verse reminiscent of Ezra Pound's *Rock-Drill* cantos," according to critic Andrew Angyal. The title has a typically dual meaning, referring to language as an instrument for shaping meaning and to the entire meaning of tools in human life. The theme of "cultural continuity" is presented in terms of Snyder's passing his knowledge on to his family, friends, and readers and is explicitly explained in the parable of the title poem. The book evokes an ethos of harmony in cycles of renewal and restoration, rebirth and reconsideration. Snyder moves beyond his specific criticism of human social organizations in the late twentieth century and toward, in Angyal's words, his "own alternative set of values in communal cooperation, conservation, and a nonexploitative way of life that shows respect for the land." The compression and density of Snyder's thinking are evident in the poem "Removing the Plate of the Pump on the Hydraulic System of the Backhoe," which reads in entirety

> Through mud, fouled nuts, black grime
> it opens, a gleam of spotless steel
> machined-fit perfect
> swirl of intake and output
> relentless clarity
> at the heart
> of work.

The pursuit of "relentless clarity" in everything characterizes Snyder's life and art, but the pressures of the search are alleviated by his congenial nature and sense of humor. While emphasizing the importance of Zen "mindfulness," Snyder has also stressed that "a big part of life is just being playful." In accordance with this approach, Snyder has kept dogmatic or simplistic solutions out of his work and has cherished the wild and free nature of humankind. In a recent poem, "Off the Trail," which he wrote for his wife Carole Koda, he envisions a life in which "all paths are possible" and maintains that "the trail's not the way" to find wisdom or happiness. "We're off the trail,/ You and I," he declares, "and we chose it!" That choice—the decision to go against the grain "to be in line with the big flow"—has led to a poetry of "deeply human richness," as Charles Molesworth puts it in his perceptive study of Snyder's work, in which "a vision of plenitude" leads to a "liminal utopia, poised between fullness and yet more growth." This utopian conception is, as the poet sees the universe, composed of elements that are "interconnected, interpenetrating, mutually reflecting, and mutually embracing." In making these connections, Snyder's poetry remains firmly grounded on the human values he sees as the fundamentals of existence. As he has said, "In a visionary way, what we would want poetry to do is guide lovers toward ecstasy, give witness to the dignity of old people, intensify human bonds, elevate the community and improve the public spirit."

Leon Lewis

Other major works

NONFICTION: *Earth House Hold: Technical Notes and Queries to Fellow Dharma Revolutionaries*, 1969; *The Old Ways*, 1977; *He Who Hunted Birds in His Father's Village: The Dimensions of a Haida Myth*, 1979; *The Real Work: Interviews and Talks, 1964-1979*, 1980; *Passage Through India*, 1983; *The Practice of the Wild*, 1990.

Bibliography

Almon, Bert. *Gary Snyder.* Boise, Idaho: Boise State University Press, 1979. An analytical examination of Snyder's work in terms of his Buddhist background and interests. Sharply focused, somewhat esoteric, and occasionally narrow in approach. Knowledgeable and reliable on the poet's use of material from Asiatic culture.

Faas, Ekbert, ed. *Towards a New American Poetics.* Santa Barbara, Calif.: Black Sparrow Press, 1978. Contains an informative critical essay and an interview that covers areas not usually touched.

Halper, Jon, ed. *Gary Snyder: Dimensions of a Life.* San Francisco: Sierra Club Books, 1991. A semibiographical tribute in which sixty-five friends, fellow-workers, and members of Snyder's family write about the poet and his work. Varying tremendously in quality and interest, there are many informative and revealing contributions by well-known (Allen Ginsberg, Ursula Le Guin) and unfamiliar individuals.

Molesworth, Charles. *Gary Snyder's Vision: Poetry and the Real Work.* Columbia: University of Missouri Press, 1983. An intellectually adept, stylishly written, and perceptive study of Snyder's writing through the early 1980's. The single best critical study to date.

Murphy, Patrick, ed. *Critical Essays on Gary Snyder.* Boston: G. K. Hall, 1990. A comprehensive, well-chosen collection of critical essays by one of Snyder's most intelligent critics. Ranging from the earliest responses to the poet's work through three decades of criticism, this book is evidence of the variety of perspectives Snyder's work has brought forth. Murphy's forthcoming *Understanding Gary Snyder* (Columbia: University of South Carolina Press, 1992) promises to be a valuable study of Snyder's writing to the present.

Snyder, Gary. *The Real Work: Interviews and Talks 1964-1979.* Edited by William Scott McLean. New York: New Directions, 1980. A crucial collection of interviews and talks that indicate, in detailed and lucid prose, the direction of Snyder's thought and the principles of his poetics.

Steuding, Bob. *Gary Snyder.* Boston: Twayne, 1976. Steuding follows the format of the Twayne critical series, mixing biographical information with a critical examination of each book Snyder wrote through *Turtle Island.* In conversation with Snyder, he worked out his basic thesis, and his remarks are essentially accurate if a bit pedestrian. Biographical sketch of the poet's life through the mid-1970's and an annotated bibliography. For a more current bibliography, see Katherine McNeil's *Gary Snyder: A Bibliography* (New York: Phoenix Books), 1983.

GARY SOTO

Born: Fresno, California; April 12, 1952

Principal poetry

The Elements of San Joaquin, 1977; *The Tale of Sunlight*, 1978; *Where Sparrows Work Hard*, 1981; *Black Hair*, 1985; *Who Will Know Us*, 1990; *Home Course in Religion*, 1991.

Other literary forms

Living up the Street: Narrative Recollections (1985), *Small Faces* (1986), and *Lesser Evils: Ten Quartets* (1988) are collections of autobiographical essays that deal mainly with Gary Soto's memories of growing up in a Chicano community; he addresses issues such as race, class, and religion by relating personal vignettes.

Achievements

Gary Soto has received public and critical praise for his poetry and prose memoirs, which explore the pleasures and difficulties of life for working-class Chicanos. Many readers respond to the direct emotional appeal of his writing and his ability to write clearly and imaginatively about his ethnic background. He received an award from *The Nation* magazine for his poem "The Discovery" in 1975 and the United States Award from the International Poetry Forum in 1976 for his first book, *The Elements of San Joaquin*. His second collection of poems, *The Tale of Sunlight*, was nominated for a Pulitzer Prize. His nonfiction writing has also garnered awards, including the American Book Award in 1985 for *Living up the Street*.

Biography

Gary Soto was born into a Chicano family in 1952 in Fresno, where, according to his essay "Being Mean," his father and grandfather worked in blue-collar jobs at Sun-Maid Raisin and his mother peeled potatoes at Reddi-Spud. Because of the family's poverty, exacerbated by the father's early death in a work-related accident, Soto was forced to earn money as an agricultural laborer in the San Joaquin Valley and at a tire-retread factory in Fresno. Soto's work, especially his early poems, focuses primarily on this personal history. Although he never mentions it in his poems, Soto does have an impressive academic background: he was graduated magna cum laude from California State University at Fresno (1974), received a master of fine arts degree in creative writing from the University of California at Irvine (1976), and has taught at the University of California at Berkeley in the Department of English and Chicano Studies since 1977.

Soto was married to Carolyn Oda, a Japanese American, in 1975, and they have one daughter, Mariko.

Analysis

Although Gary Soto was born into a Catholic family and attended parochial schools in Fresno, California, religious issues are discussed only in his late work; primarily, he is attracted to and obsessed by the issues of race and poverty that dominated his early life and the importance of memory for a poet.

The Elements of San Joaquin, Soto's first book, is divided into three sections that neatly compartmentalize his early experiences: he moves from urban portraits of Fresno to the agricultural landscape of the San Joaquin Valley and closes with memories of his childhood and adolescence.

The opening poem, "San Fernando Road," describes and is dedicated to Leonard Cruz, a Chicano working in a factory, and it sets the mood for the first section and the book as a whole. An allusion to the four natural elements of the title—earth, air, fire, and water—is made in the poem, but there is nothing invigorating or revitalizing here. The air Leonard breathes contains "the dust/ Of rubber" from the factory, the water sits in the "toilets/ No one flushed," the men's "arms/ Were bracelets/ Of burns," and the earth on which he sleeps (he is homeless) only makes him shiver "Like the machinery/ That went on and on." It is no wonder that Leonard's body is weakening as he works; he has lost contact with the earth that gives life. The only hint of life or vibrancy comes in the hideous image of a woman "Opening/ In her first rape." Soto evokes the hopelessness of the environment by suggesting that this is not the last time the woman will be violated.

Section 2 looks at the lives of farm workers in the San Joaquin Valley, where "nothing will heal/ Under the rain's broken fingers." A typical poem, "Harvest," once again carefully details the importance of the four elements, but in this case they do affect the growth cycle. The fire of the sun works on "the vineyard that never failed," the wind moves the dust of the earth and Soto's own voice across the crops, and the "ropes of rain" fall on the "thick harvest." Unfortunately, the worker in the field, Soto himself, does not share in the natural production of wealth: "ropes of rain dropped to pull me/ From the thick harvest that was not mine."

Memories of friends in the neighborhood and family members are the focus of section 3. The oppressive mood of the poems about factory workers and agricultural laborers does not lift here. In fact, the deprivations become engraved in the poet, like the bracelets of burns on the factory workers' arms. In "Moving Away," addressed to Soto's brother, he remembers moments when "the one we hated/ Watched us from under a tree." That gaze is still on him; it belongs to the "white stepfather" who replaced Soto's own father. Although what troubled the stepfather "has been forgotten," Soto, speaking for his brother as well, concludes that "what troubled us has settled/ Like dirt/ In the nests of our knuckles/ And cannot be washed away." There are no purifying waters in this very powerful and depressing first book.

His second book, *The Tale of Sunlight*, is distinctive in that the poet creates two characters, Molina and Manuel Zaragoza, who take the focus off Soto's own life experiences. Molina, a Chicano alter ego of Soto, and Manuel, a cantina owner in Taxco, Mexico, allow him to escape the solipsistic world of poems narrated in the first person. This is the only time in Soto's career when characters other than the poet become the principal focus of the work.

In *Where Sparrows Work Hard*, Soto returns to familiar sights: the neighborhood, the tire factory, the fields, and family. As this book progresses, however, there are some happy, sometimes comic moments that relieve the despair.

"Mission Tire Factory, 1969" is another version of the opening poem of *The Elements of San Joaquin*: in "San Fernando Road," Leonard "swept the dust/ Of rubber . . . into his nostrils" and "Went into ovens/ Squint-eyed," and in the later poem Soto recalls the "the wash of rubber in our lungs" and "the oven we would enter, squinting." Clearly there are problems with returning to familiar sights too often: the language becomes predictable and stale. Soto manages to save the poem, however, by focusing the reader's attention on the particularized humanity of the workers without sentimentalizing them. Manny, injured on the job, is carried to the work shed by his fellow workers (including Peter, who pinches "at his crotch"), and all the bleeding man can say is, "Buy some sandwiches. You guys saved my life." Soto comments with candor and compassion that his ignorance was "outdone only by pain."

The second section contains another tire-factory poem which is both comic and disturbing. In "Mexicans Begin Jogging" (the title itself is flippantly comic), Soto is apparently working with undocumented immigrants; when the border patrol arrives at the factory, he runs from the shop at his boss's orders. Soto, who shouts that he is an American, does not object to the discrimination, because the boss presses "a dollar in my palm." "Since I was on his time, I ran/ And became the wag of a short tail of Mexicans." Soon he breaks into a yuppie jog and "a great silly, grin" because he has outwitted the prejudiced employer; an exploited worker enjoys few things more than getting paid an hourly wage plus a dollar bonus for doing no work at all. Soto treats the same subject matter in a prose piece, "Black Hair," in *Living up the Street*. Except for the metaphor of the wagging tail, the story is very similar to the poem except in one important detail: in "Black Hair" he is able to address the distance he feels from some of his fellow workers, a distance that is lessened somewhat when he runs with the illegals. "Among the Mexicans I had few friends because I was different, a *pocho* who spoke bad Spanish. At lunch they sat in tires and laughed over burritos, looking up at me to laugh even harder." In the poems this honest recognition of the separation among the workers is absent.

The third section contains a poem that suggests the new directions Soto's work will take in subsequent volumes. "Angel" leaves the world of the economically disfranchised and their tales of work woes and arrives in a gentler, more personal area. Here Soto watches his wife as she sleeps, "heavy/ And tilting with child," and he reflects not on his own grim past, but on the child's future. He pictures the tiny fingers, which "bloom like candles," even though it is still weeks before the baby "slides from water/ And blood, his blue hands/ Tightening on air." He does not despair about the child's future, perhaps because Soto has by this time escaped his old working-class life and joined the privileged world of academics; instead, he can only expectantly wait for "that good day/ When this child will kick/ His joints into place." After the arrival of that child, kicking *her* joints into place, Soto wrote a number of buoyantly hopeful poems about Mariko, his daughter.

Black Hair examines familiar themes. There is the sense of resignation and bitterness that Soto feels when he recalls his early farm-worker experiences: "Work in dust, get up in dust. Beer makes it go." There are recollections of childish mischief directed against the "enemy": with a friend he "started/ Kicking a Republican's fence,/ The pickets working loose." In the title poem, "Black Hair," there is pride in having brown skin and being a Chicano: Soto, at age eight, worships a baseball player and fellow Chicano, Hector Moreno, and assumes "his crouch . . . before an altar/ Of worn baseball cards" in his room. There are wonderfully surprising metaphors throughout the poems: garbage is a "raffle of eggshells and orange peels"; a column of ants on the ground is a "loose thread to an old coat"; crying is like "rope/ Going taut."

The changes that do appear in this book derive from Soto's relationship with his daughter. The childlike quality of many of his earlier poems is redoubled here because of the young girl's presence. At times this childlikeness becomes too dull and almost puts the poems to sleep. In France they walk hand in hand, "smiling/ For no reason other than/ Everything is new"; when his daughter asks "What's that? . . . there's no greater/ Pleasure than saying,/ Beats me. Let's go see." This conversational, matter-of-fact diction can disappoint the reader who seeks sparkling or inventive language. Yet the presence of the daughter in these poems allows a new side of Soto's character to shine through. Instead of seeing himself as a victim and the enemy as Republicans, he includes himself in a catalog of human transgressions: while watching and admiring ants with his daughter he waxes philosophical for a moment and admits that "many people, whole countries,/ May go under because we desire TV/ And chilled drinks, clothes/ That hang well on our bodies." Ants are better than humans, and Soto is human. The daughter, however, also permits Soto to write fairly innocent, anger-free poems about simple joys. Instead of concentrating on the exploitation inherent in the economic system, Soto explains to his daughter that "if we buy a goldfish, someone tries on a hat." The exchange of wealth between buyer and seller seems almost like play; gone are the dust from rubber, the hot ovens the factory workers have to enter, and the injustice of substandard wages. Now "If we buy crayons, someone walks home with a broom"; with "a small purchase here and there,/ And things just keep going."

Soto avoids sentimentality in these generally happy poems by admitting the quirks of childhood. When he wants to walk in nature to a special spot with his daughter, she responds in a typically modern, spoiled way, "Daddy please, why/ Don't we get in the car/ And be over there." His amused annoyance is entertaining. The poems generally are admirable for the new range of emotions that Soto permits himself. With this collection, he is no longer solely the angry young man; now he is the proud father as well.

"Who Will Know Us?"—the title poem of Soto's fifth volume—asks the difficult question, "Who will know us when we breathe through the grass?" Despite the gravity of the question, thought up while he is "on a train, rocking toward the cemetery/ To visit the dead," the collection as a whole does not dwell on difficult or macabre questions; instead, it celebrates life in typical Soto fashion—by praising the quotidian and remembering the past.

In "Eve," the poet repeats a story that is similar to one in the prose collection *Lesser Evils: Ten Quartets*. In "Starting Young," the adolescent Soto meets a precocious thirteen-year-old, Sue, in a shed belonging to a neighbor, and they pull down their pants and touch each other. He worries needlessly about impregnating her, and the story of early investigative romance ends sweetly. In the poem "Eve" Soto goes all the way with a girl on her father's workbench in the barn; when she unfastens her skirt, her "kinked hair" is "thick as a child's black scribbling." Again he worries, needlessly, that he has impregnated her; the poem ends with no shotgun solutions to problems, but a melancholy dictum: people said that "it should hurt the first time,/ Then stop . . . how they lied." Pain goes hand in hand with love and sex—first time, every time. The comparison between the versions in prose and poetry reveals little more than the obsessive quality of Soto's work: he returns again and again to subjects that he finds worthy of his attention, not concerned that this is country he has already discovered. He wants to mine the mountain until the ore is gone.

One of the concluding poems in the book, "Evening Walk," is pleasantly self-effacing. Soto, while walking with his daughter, tries to tell her "poor stories" about the old days when he "picked/ Grapes like nobody's business" and "lugged oranges and shared plums with Okies." Mariko will have none of it. Soto concludes that he is "a bore to the end," while Mariko runs and skips ahead, dragging a branch that flutters "like a green fire." Her only eagerness is for an evening without him; the parent-poet-storyteller senses the inevitable hostility of the younger generation. In typical fashion, Soto accepts stoically and with humor the march and skip of time.

Yet when it comes to religion, a subject that Soto largely ignored in his early poems, he nostalgically yearns for old-fashioned sanctity. In *Home Course in Religion*, published in 1991, Soto catalogs the items he misses in post-Vatican II Catholicism: pagan babies, holy water in the cupboard, Mass said in Latin, and meatless Fridays. The modernization of the church has even invaded the most primitive forms of worship: "At the altar of Mary, we have electric bulbs,/ Not candles, sitting in votive cups." The altar "lights up like a pinball machine" when one drops a quarter in the slot for each sin. The early radical Soto has become movingly conservative; he wonders, "How do we kneel and pray at such a place?" Many of these poems also recall his adolescent initiation into the sometimes mysterious, sometimes comic rites of the faith.

This collection also focuses considerable attention on Soto's relationship with his stepfather, Jim, but in this case the poet does not reminisce with pleasure. In contrast to the imaginative re-creations of his father, who died before Soto really knew him, the evocations of his stepfather are hauntingly realistic, almost naturalistic. The father is associated with his La-Z-Boy recliner, his Jack Daniels, his racism, and the "pounding of fists that pounded boxes all day." After Soto records on a cheap tape recorder an argument between his mother and Jim, he replays the vicious piece "until the voices slurred to a crawl/ And the tape recorder died." As the batteries fade, Soto notices that the plastic statue of Jesus, "marble white and hollow," captures the afternoon glow from the window, but it offers no consolation for the fear and anger the young boy is feeling. Soto appreciates the ritual of Catholicism, but he seems to suggest that the value of the faith for relieving anguish is minimal.

In the last few poems of the book, Soto escapes from memories of youth and evaluates his adult life, which seems to be packed with distracting facts and activities. He watches television, reads student papers, studies karate, and examines Japanese and Impressionist Art. A moving line positioned amid all this clutter is "I want very badly to know how to talk about Christ." Yet the faith is absent; instead, Soto finds whatever redemption there is in his daily existence—his daughter's games, his humor, his marriage.

The subjects that Soto addresses in his poems are very similar; in many ways, however, this is not the same poet who began writing in the 1970's. Soto has matured; he has established a very successful career by looking into his past, but his work published in the 1990's suggests that his main concern is trying to find spiritual sustenance in a very middle-class, comfortable life. He says, "We invent misery for our bodies,/ Then our minds, and then, having nothing else to do/ Look for ways to make it stop." Gary Soto's poems are trying to stop the pain through humor, through nostalgia, and through intense living in the present.

Kevin Boyle

Other major works

NONFICTION: *Living up the Street: Narrative Recollections*, 1985; *Small Faces*, 1986; *Lesser Evils: Ten Quartets*, 1988.

EDITED TEXT: *California Childhood: Recollections and Stories of the Golden State*, 1988.

Bibliography

Armour-Hileman, Vicki. Review of *Where Sparrows Work Hard*. *Denver Quarterly* 17 (Summer, 1982): 154-155. Armour-Hileman notes what many critics call attention to: the similarity between Soto and his teacher Philip Levine in subject matter, "a surrealistic bent," and short, enjambed lines. She finds fault with the "inaccuracy of the images" in many of Soto's poems and "their elliptical movement." She does admire the poems in which Soto "becomes not an ethnic poet, but a poet who writes about human suffering." His writing in the last third of this collection she considers a "great success."

Cooley, Peter. "Two Young Poets." *Parnassus* 7 (Fall/Winter, 1979): 299-311. In this extremely laudatory examination of Soto's two earliest collections, Cooley calls Soto "the most important voice among the young Chicano poets." He praises Soto's ability to re-create his lost world of San Joaquin with "an imaginative expansiveness." This is a crucial essay for understanding the initial praise given to Soto and how his work seemed to speak for a generation of Chicano Americans.

Paredes, Raymund A. "Recent Chicano Writing." *Rocky Mountain Review* 41, nos. 1/2 (1987): 124-129. Paredes admires Soto's writing because "ethnic and class consciousness constitute an essential part of his literary sensibility." He faults Soto, however, for his portrayal of women: "As he depicts them, their roles are wholly conventional." He does not find the portrayals of women to be totally offensive, but he chides the poet for "performing unremarkably" on this issue.

Soto, Gary. Interview by Jean W. Ross. In *Contemporary Authors*, vol. 125, edited by Hal May and Susan M. Trosky. Detroit: Gale, 1989. In this excellent interview, Soto reveals his early literary influences (Philip Levine, Theodore Roethke, and Weldon Kees), and he admits that, except for his first two books, his work is not "heavily concerned with Mexican themes." At Berkeley he has taught the same three or four books in his Chicano authors class "because some of the things being published by Chicanos aren't really good."

Wojahn, David. Review of *Black Hair*. *Poetry* 146 (June, 1985): 171-173. In this review of Soto's fourth collection, Wojahn accuses him of displaying the "brooding confusions of the pubescent mind" and thereby creating a book that is a "distinctly minor achievement." Wojahn believes Soto's abandonment of the surrealistic poetics and myth-making of his earlier books for "anecdotes of adolescence" was a mistake. Soto's poetic line is "blasé" and the language too journalistic to appeal to this contemporary poet and critic.

ROBERT SOUTHEY

Born: Bristol, England; August 12, 1774
Died: Greta Hall, Keswick, England; March 21, 1843

Principal poetry

Poems, 1795 (with Robert Lovell); *Joan of Arc: An Epic Poem*, 1796, 1798, 1806, 1812; *Poems*, 1797-1799; *Thalaba the Destroyer*, 1801; *Madoc*, 1805; *Metrical Tales and Other Poems,* 1805; *The Curse of Kehama*, 1810; *Roderick, the Last of the Goths*, 1814; *Odes to His Royal Highness the Prince Regent, His Imperial Majesty the Emperor of Russia, and His Majesty the King of Prussia*, 1814; *Minor Poems*, 1815; *The Poet's Pilgrimage to Waterloo*, 1816; *The Lay of the Laureate: Carmen Nuptiale*, 1816; *Wat Tyler: A Dramatic Poem*, 1817; *A Vision of Judgement*, 1821; *A Tale of Paraguay*, 1825; *All for Love, and the Pilgrim to Compostella*, 1829; *Poetical Works*, 1829; *The Devil's Walk*, 1830 (with Samuel Taylor Coleridge); *Selections from the Poems*, 1831, 1833; *Poetical Works*, 1839; *Oliver Newman: A New-England Tale (Unfinished): With Other Poetical Remains*, 1845; *Robin Hood: A Fragment*, 1847 (with Caroline Southey).

Other literary forms

Robert Southey's collected prose works comprise almost forty volumes, ranging from literary criticism to biography, from fiction to translations. *Letters from England by Don Manuel Espriella* (1807) is a satiric commentary on everyday life in contemporary England, while *Sir Thomas More* (1829) reveals Southey again examining society, this time by way of conversations between the spirit of the departed More and Montesimos (Southey himself). His so-called novel, the seven-volume *The Doctor* (1834-1847), concerns Dr. Daniel Dove of Doncaster and his horse Nobs; as a fantasy and a commentary on life, the excruciatingly lengthy piece reminds one of Laurence Sterne's *Tristram Shandy* (1759-1767)—without the artistic qualities of that remarkable work of fiction. Hidden within Chapter 129 of Southey's effort lies the first-known telling of the nursery classic "The Three Bears."

Life of Nelson (1813) and *Life of Wesley and the Rise and Progress of Methodism* (1820) head the list of Southey's biographical studies. Others of note include *A Summary of the Life of Arthur, Duke of Wellington* (1816); the *Life of John, Duke of Marlborough* (1822); *Lives of the British Admirals* (1833-1840); and *The Life of the Rev. Andrew Bell* (1844, one volume only), the Scottish-born educationist who founded the National Society for the Education of the Poor. Southey's historical writings include the *History of Brazil* (1810-1819), *The History of Europe* (1810-1813), and the *History of the Peninsular War* (1823-1832). In 1812, Southey published *The Origin, Nature, and Object of the New System of Education*. This was followed by *The Book of the Church* (1824), *Vindiciae Ecclesiae Anglicanae* (1826), and *Es-*

says Moral and Political (1832).

Southey was also an editor and translator. Among his edited works are *The Annual Anthology* (1799-1800), *The Works of Chatterton* (1803, with Joseph Cottle), *Palmerin of England* (1807), Isaac Watts's *Horae Lyricae* (1834), and *The Works of William Cowper* (1835-1837). Southey's notable translations include Jacques Necker's *On the French Revolution* (1797), Vasco Lobeira's *Amadis de Gaul* (1805), the *Chronicle of the Cid* (1808), Abbe Don Ignatius Molina's *The Geographical, Natural, and Civil History of Chili* (1808), and *Memoria Sobre a Litteratura Portugueza* (1809).

Achievements

During his lifetime, Southey enjoyed moments of popularity and success; there were even those among his contemporaries who believed that he ranked with the best of his nation's poets. He outlived Samuel Taylor Coleridge, Sir Walter Scott, Charles Lamb, William Hazlitt, Lord Byron, Percy Bysshe Shelley, and John Keats, yet rarely does one find mention of his name in a discussion of the significant figures and forces that shaped British Romanticism in the first part of the nineteenth century. Although Southey is deep in the shadows of William Wordsworth and Coleridge, appearing in literary histories only as their mediocre associate, his poetry deserves a careful reading, especially that written before 1801. This early work reveals an extremely high degree of versatility, not always appreciated by those who study only the first rank of nineteenth century British Romantics. The simplicity and directness of language found in Southey's early ballads and short narratives echo Wordsworth's *Lyrical Ballads* (1798), but the pieces succeed because the poet could rise above pure imitation. He could also write irregular odes and heroic epistles that demonstrated his knowledge of the Augustan Age; he knew how to create sublime imagery with the aid of biblical themes, and he could plunge downward to concoct playful exercises with pigs and gooseberry pies. He was adept in a variety of poetic forms: the elegy, the sonnet, the sapphic, the ballad, the metrical tale.

The content of Southey's poems is as varied as the form. While at Balliol College, Oxford, during the period of his enthusiasm for republicanism, he wrote a dramatic poem on Wat Tyler, the leader of the peasant revolt of 1381, while four years later his piece on the first Duke of Marlborough's victory at Blenheim (August, 1704) during the War of the Spanish Succession graphically underscored the poet's sentiments on the futility of war—"But what good came of it at last?" In what seemed a radical shift of poetical gears, Southey rode hard and fast upon the waves of the Gothic horror narrative in "God's Judgment on a Wicked Bishop" (1799), in which he adapted the legendary story of a tenth century German Bishop who was attacked and then devoured by a pack of rats. At the outset of the nineteenth century, he turned to a series of epic poems—*Thalaba the Destroyer* and *The Curse of Kehama* being two examples—that placed him alongside his contemporaries in the Romantic quest for glamour and the grandeur of distant places and even more distant times.

Southey's greatest weakness may have been his inability to recognize his own limitations as a poet. He remained unaware of what he could do best. He took his role as poet laureate of England far too seriously—especially in the light of the fact that the honor came only because Sir Walter Scott refused to accept it. Not only did he exercise poor political and critical judgment by attacking Byron, but he also wrote, in 1821, the unnecessarily lengthy *A Vision of Judgement*, in which he attempted to transport the recently departed King George III into heaven; Byron, of course, replied in a similarly entitled poem (1822): "If Mr. Southey had not rushed in where he had no business, and where he never was before," wrote Byron in his Preface, paraphrasing Alexander Pope's *An Essay on Criticism* (1711), "the following poem would not have been written." Southey never appreciated his skill as a writer of shorter and less ambitious poems wherein, for example, he could calmly reflect upon his personal love of good books in his own large library, as in "My Days Among the Dead Are Past." Perhaps, also, he never realized the extent to which he could display his talent with language, as in the onomatopoetic and highly animated "The Cataract of Ladore." Interestingly enough, when Southey could isolate himself from the perils and problems of a large, ugly world, he achieved considerable maturity as a poet. Unfortunately, the periods of imaginative seclusion were both irregular and inconsistent.

Biography

Although born at Bristol, the son of Robert Southey and Margaret Hill Southey, Robert Southey spent most of his first fourteen years at Bath, in the company of his mother's half-sister, Miss Elizabeth Tyler. Biographers describe Tyler as a lady endowed with strong personal attractions, ambitious ideas, an imperious temper, and a significantly large library. The last-mentioned asset allowed young Southey early introductions to dramatic literature, classical poetry, and the epics of Edmund Spenser. Thus, his entrance into Westminster School in April, 1788—after shorter terms at small schools in Corston and Bristol—found him well prepared to pursue learning. Nevertheless, he demonstrated little interest in subjects outside the narrow limits of his own idiosyncratic reading tastes: ceremony, ritual, and world mythology and religion. Four years later, the school authorities expelled him for his published essays against Westminster's system of corporal punishment, specifically the flogging of students by their masters for trivial offenses. Through the efforts of his maternal uncle, the Reverend Herbert Hill, Southey gained entrance to Balliol College, Oxford (after first having been refused admission by Christ Church because of the Westminster School incident). The significant events during his undergraduate term proved to be friendships formed with

Samuel Taylor Coleridge and Robert Lovell. The three determined to emigrate to the banks of the Susquehanna River in America, there to embark upon a scheme of an ideal life of unitarianism and pantisocracy (a Utopian community in which all members would rule equally). Interestingly enough, the relationship acquired even stronger ties (which would eventually cost Southey considerable money and labor) when the friends married the three daughters of the widow of Stephen Fricker, an unsuccessful sugar-pan merchant at Westbury. Southey's marriage to Edith Fricker occurred in November, 1795.

When Elizabeth Tyler heard of her nephew's proposal to leave England, she evicted him from her house. By that time, Southey had embarked upon several literary projects, and, fortunately, a young publisher, Joseph Cottle, came to his aid and purchased the first of his epic poems, *Joan of Arc*. Moreover, his uncle, Herbert Hill, invited him to visit Lisbon, resulting in *Letters in Spain and Portugal* (1808) and *Madoc*. Returning to London, he began to study the law, but soon abandoned that exercise (as he had turned from divinity and medicine at Oxford) and once more focused his attention on poetry. Seeking seclusion, Southey moved first to Westbury, then to Burton (in Hampshire), producing additional ballads and eclogues and working hard on his *History of Brazil*. In April, 1800, serious illness forced him to seek the temperate climate of Portugal, where he remained for a year, completing *Thalaba the Destroyer* and continuing to plod along with the Portuguese history. Back in England, he settled first at Keswick, then moved to Dublin as secretary to the chancellor of the Irish exchequer, Isaac Corry. He then moved to Bristol, but the death of his mother and infant daughter drove him away from his birthplace; in 1803, partly to satisfy his wife, Southey and his family took up residence at Greta Hall, Keswick; there, practically under the same roof as his brother-in-law Coleridge, he made his home for the remainder of his life.

Work and activity at Keswick brought Southey into close association with Wordsworth and, more important, provided the motivation to produce his most ambitious poetic works. Financial pressures (particularly the support of Coleridge's family in addition to his own), however, forced him to forsake poetry temporarily for more lucrative prose projects, which he churned out in significant quantity between 1803 and 1832. At Greta Hall, he amassed a library in excess of fourteen thousand volumes, including works that he eventually edited and translated. Between 1808 and 1839, he edited and contributed to the *Quarterly Review*, the result of his association with Sir Walter Scott. That relationship proved to be most advantageous to Southey's literary career, for although Scott could not arrange to secure for his friend the post of historiographer royal, he did, in 1813, transfer the offer to be poet laureate from himself to Southey. To his credit, the latter accepted the honor only on condition that he would not be forced to write birthday odes to the sovereign or to members of the royal family. Unfortunately, however, he did manage to get into trouble with Byron and others of the liberally inclined Romantic poets when he wrote *A Vision of Judgement* and seemingly challenged liberal opinion. Despite squabbles with his contemporaries, his reputation remained high, as witnessed by offers to edit the *Times* of London and to serve as librarian of the Advocates' Library, Edinburgh—both of which he declined.

In November, 1837, Edith Southey passed away—for years she had been failing mentally. The poet-essayist himself, according to contemporary accounts, had by this time become afflicted with softening of the brain, manifested by an obvious indifference to everyone and everything except his beloved books. Suddenly, near the end of his sixty-fourth year, Southey remarried (on June 4, 1839)—one Caroline Ann Bowles, a poet and hymnodist with whom he had maintained a close correspondence for more than twenty years. When the couple returned from their wedding tour, Southey's condition worsened; he passed gradually from insensibility to external matters into a complete trance and died on March 21, 1843. The poet laureate was buried in Crosthwaite churchyard, and friends placed memorials in Westminster Abbey and Bristol Cathedral.

Analysis

Robert Southey's poetical career proved, indeed, to have been a struggle: his desire to create from impulse and inspiration came into conflict with his duty to earn money from his pen. During his early period, he wrote a large number of ballads and metrical tales for the *Morning Post* at the then-going rate of one guinea a week. When he republished those in book form, money again became the principal motive, as it did once more in 1807 when he had to support Coleridge's family as well as his own. At that time he announced that, if necessary, he would take on more reviews and articles for the magazines and would write additional verses for the newspapers. Thus, judgment and analysis of his poetry must balance what Southey wanted to do with what he had to do. Throughout his professional life, he tried desperately to preserve the time for literary labors worthy of his talent; as long as that division existed, he could perform his hack work without fear of humiliation or sacrifice. Unfortunately, time and energy eventually failed him, and his poems—both serious and popular—became less salable; after 1820, he saw himself as more historian than poet.

In 1837, two years prior to the illness that would eventually incapacitate him, Southey prepared the last collected edition of his poems to be published during his lifetime. That task provided an opportunity for the poet to survey his own work, to rank as well as to analyze. Thus, concerning the narrative poems, he thought *Joan of Arc*, written when he was nineteen, to have the least merit, although the piece did constitute the first stage of his poetic development. *Thalaba the Destroyer*, published five years afterward, allowed

Southey to achieve poetic maturity, to set aside the law of nature and permit his poetic fancy to wander freely. For that reason, he chose not to control the rhythmic structure of his blank verse; rather, the lines of that poem follow a spontaneous melody, dividing themselves into varying lengths. In addition, the poet tended to interrupt the ordinary iambic cadence with a sudden trochaic or dactylic movement: for example, "Lo! underneath the broad-leaved sycamore/ With lids half closed he lies,/ Dreaming of days to come."

While a schoolboy at Westminster, Southey had formed the idea of a long poem, epic in form and content, based upon each of the important religions (he considered them to be mythologies) of the world. For Mohammedanism, he eventually wrote *Thalaba the Destroyer*; *The Curse of Kehama*, published in 1810, focused on Hinduism. In the later poem, he again allowed his fancy and his imagery to range freely, seemingly unconcerned with the orthodox notions and sympathies of the vast majority of his readers. For whatever the reasons, however, in *The Curse of Kehama* Southey returned to rhyme; more accurately, he attempted to compromise between the rambling blank verse of *Thalaba the Destroyer* and the symmetry of the traditional English epic form. *Madoc* had been begun before he set to work on *The Curse of Kehama*, but Southey, believing the former to have been his most significant poem, set it aside until he could devote his full attention to it. Finally published in 1805, *Madoc* evidences a pleasing melody and an easy, fluent, and graceful narrative diction. Unfortunately, it met with the least favorable reception of all his long poems.

The failure of *Madoc* did not deter Southey from his grand epic design. In *Roderick, the Last of the Goths*, he produced a long narrative poem that succeeded because the versification and theme managed to complement each other. Relying on the issue of subjugation and underlining it with moral grandeur and tragedy, the poet easily held the interest of his contemporary readers. He began with a single and momentary sin of the passions by an otherwise consistently virtuous monarch and proceeded to unravel the consequences: the slaughter of Christians by Moors in a battle lasting eight days; the king's escape after the battle and his deep remorse and self-inflicted penance of a long and solitary hermitage while others thought that he had been slain; the king's dream, in which his mother appears with instructions to deliver his country from the Moors; and the departure and eventual encounter with the sole survivor of a massacre, who tells the king of the tragedy and inspires him to both personal and patriotic revenge. Southey demonstrated, in *Roderick, the Last of the Goths*, his ability to sustain a narrative while at the same time developing a character, a hero, through a series of meaningful and related adventures: Roderick, in the guise of a priest, passes through the country, meets old friends, and is recognized only by his dog. Finally, the king leads his forces in triumph over the Moors, after which he disappears.

Southey achieved effective rhythm to complement the narrative of Roderick's adventures by taking full advantage of proper names derived from Spanish and from various Moorish and Gothic dialects. He sought diversity of both rhythm and language, knowing well how John Milton, for example, had underscored the substance of his theme in the opening book of *Paradise Lost* (1667) with his roll call of Satan's evil host. Thus, in a single passage of twenty-six lines from Book IV, the poet relies on the effect of a dozen or so proper names to vary his rhythm, as

> Skirting the heights of *Aguiar*, he reached
> That consecrated pile amid the wild
> Which sainted *Fructuoso* in his zeal
> Reared to *St. Felix*. on *Visionia's* banks.

Further, Southey reinforced his narrative with heavy descriptions of natural scenery, furnishing rhetorical respites from the action and the passion of events. He viewed such pauses as essential to the long narrative poem, particularly when they followed long episodes of emotional strain or exaltation. From a positive point of view, the descriptive respites filled the imagination with the sights and the sounds of the beauties of nature, allowing the long narrative poem to serve as a true work of creative art. Southey made such attempts in all of his long poems, but he reached the highest levels of perfection in *Roderick, the Last of the Goths*.

Although Southey's occasional poetry includes his weakest efforts, there are rare moments of eloquence when the poet is able to give free rein to his emotions. Consider, for example, his "Ode, Written during the Negociations with Buonaparte, in January 1814." Southey truly detested the diminutive emperor of the French, and he attacked his subject on moral grounds, as well as on the obvious political and patriotic levels. His passions were further aroused by the sight of those individuals who worshiped what they believed to have been the wonders of Napoleon's political and military successes. The poet saw the emperor only as a mean tyrant: "And ne'er was earth with verier tyrant curst,/ Bold man and bad,/ Remorseless, godless, full of fraud and lies"; for those personal and political crimes, demanded Southey, Napoleon must pay with his life.

Another of Southey's occasional poems should be mentioned—the "Funeral Ode on the Death of the Princess Charlotte"—for its lines are as sensitive and serene as those on Napoleon are harsh and bitter. The poet gazes about the burial grounds at Windsor, where, "in thy sacred shade/ Is the Flower of Brunswick laid!" Then, further surveying the scene, he comments on others lying there—Henry, Edward, Elizabeth, Ann Seymour, Mary Stuart. Nevertheless, the piece serves as more than a roll call of history, for Southey loses sight of neither his subject nor the tragedy of Charlotte's passing: "Never more lamented guest/ Was in Windsor laid to rest."

In the final analysis, Southey must be seen as a nineteenth century child of the Augustan Age who contributed little to the poetry of Romanticism. Confusion arises when literary historians too quickly connect him with Wordsworth and Coleridge, forgetting, perhaps, that the relationship existed on a personal rather than an artistic level. Artistically and intellectually, Southey had almost nothing in common with the major figures among the first generation of British Romantic poets. He waited until practically the end of his literary life—in the Preface to the 1837-1838 edition of his *Poetical Works*—before setting forth what amounted to his poetical and intellectual declaration of independence from the new literature of pre-Victorian England. Southey chose to spend a lifetime with his books, rather than in the company of men; he would retire to a life of literary pursuit, "communing with my own heart, and taking that course which upon mature consideration seemed best to myself."

Southey further maintained that he had no need for the new schools of poetry, for he had learned poetry from the masters, confirmed it in his youth, and exemplified it in his own writing. Indeed, few would deny Professor Renwick's assertion that "No poet since Dryden wrote such pure clean English so consistently." Unfortunately, unlike his contemporaries who set and then followed new trends, Southey seemed more inclined to practice and develop the *craft* of poetry rather than its art. He never really learned (either in or out of school) that poetry had to come from sources other than labor and learning. Nevertheless, he possessed an ardent and genial piety, a moral strength, a poetic power of depth and variety, and an ability to develop a range of literary forms and interests. In those respects, he deserved the name and the honor of poet laureate.

Samuel J. Rogal

Other major works

LONG FICTION: *The Doctor,* 1834-1847.

PLAY: *The Fall of Robespierre,* 1794 (with Samuel Taylor Coleridge).

NONFICTION: *On the French Revolution,* 1797 (translation); *Amadis de Gaul,* 1805 (translation); *Palmerin of England,* 1807 (translation); *Letters from England by Don Manuel Espriella,* 1807; *Chronicle of the Cid,* 1808 (translation); *The Geographical, Natural, and Civil History of Chili,* 1808 (translation); *Letters in Spain and Portugal,* 1808; *Memoria Sobre a Litteratura Portugueza,* 1809 (translation); *The History of Europe,* 1810-1813; *History of Brazil,* 1810-1819; *The Origin, Nature, and Object of the New System of Education,* 1812; *Life of Nelson,* 1813; *A Summary of the Life of Arthur, Duke of Wellington,* 1816; *Life of Wesley and the Rise and Progress of Methodism,* 1820; *History of the Expedition of Orsua and Crimes of Aguirre,* 1821; *Life of John, Duke of Marlborough,* 1822; *History of the Peninsular War,* 1823-1832; *Sir Thomas More,* 1829; *Essays Moral and Political,* 1832; *Lives of the Brit-*

ish Admirals, 1833-1840; *The Life of the Rev. Andrew Bell*, 1844.

RELIGIOUS WRITINGS: *The Book of the Church*, 1824; *Vindiciae Ecclesiae Anglicanae*, 1826.

ANTHOLOGY: *The Annual Anthology*, 1799-1800.

MISCELLANEOUS: *The Works of Chatterton*, 1803 (edited with Joseph Cottle); *Horae Lyricae*, 1834 (edited); *The Works of William Cowper*, 1835-1837 (edited).

Bibliography

Bernhardt-Kabisch, Ernest. *Robert Southey*. Boston: Twayne, 1977. A study of *Joan of Arc* follows a sketch of Southey's early life. Chapter 3 assesses his personality and lyrical poetry. The central chapters analyze his epics and the verse of his laureate years. The last chapter is a survey of Southey's prose. Contains a chronology, notes, a select bibliography, and an index.

Carnall, Geoffrey. *Robert Southey and His Age: The Development of a Conservative Mind*. Oxford, England: Clarendon Press, 1960. Part 1 focuses on Southey as Jacobin, devoted to radical reform and democracy. Part 2 analyzes Southey as Tory, advocating strong government and conservativism. Finally, the question is examined whether Southey should be called an apostate. Supplemented by illustrations, two appendices, and an index.

Chandler, Alice. "Broadening the Vision: The Lake Poets and Some Contemporaries." In *A Dream of Order: The Medieval Ideal in Nineteenth-Century English Literature*. Lincoln: University of Nebraska Press, 1970. This essay sets Southey in the context of his contemporaries. They share a common vision of medievalism as a corrective to threats of chaos from events of the French Revolution. Southey is interesting for having used medievalism for both his radical and his conservative writing. Includes footnotes, a bibliography, and an index.

Curry, Kenneth. *Southey*. London: Routledge & Kegan Paul, 1975. Part 1 reviews Southey's life: the formative years and the productive years. Part 2 surveys the prose: social and political criticism, biographies, autobiographies, histories, and journalism. Part 3 examines the poetry: early poems, long poems, laureate poems, and an estimate of Southey as a poet. Complemented by a bibliography and an index.

Simmons, Jack. *Southey*. London: Collins, 1945. A substantial biography of modest length, this book details Southey's education, his friendship with Samuel Taylor Coleridge, and his sojourn in Portugal. His fame leads to political controversies, and his declining years begin with the death of his daughter Isabel. Contains illustrations, a note on the Southey family, a list of Southey's works, notes, and an index.